C. T. Newton

The Collection of Ancient Greek Inscriptions in the British Museum,

Vol. 3

C. T. Newton

The Collection of Ancient Greek Inscriptions in the British Museum,
Vol. 3

ISBN/EAN: 9783337731366

Printed in Europe, USA, Canada, Australia, Japan

Cover: Foto ©ninafisch / pixelio.de

More available books at **www.hansebooks.com**

THE COLLECTION OF

ANCIENT GREEK INSCRIPTIONS

IN THE BRITISH MUSEUM

EDITED BY

SIR C. T. NEWTON, K.C.B.

PART III

PRIENE, IASOS AND EPHESOS

BY

THE REV. E. L. HICKS, M.A.

LECTURER IN CLASSICAL ARCHÆOLOGY AT THE OWENS COLLEGE, MANCHESTER
SOMETIME FELLOW AND TUTOR OF CORPUS CHRISTI COLLEGE, OXFORD

PRINTED BY ORDER OF THE TRUSTEES

AT

THE CLARENDON PRESS, OXFORD

1890

CONTENTS OF PART III.

ILLUSTRATION IN PART III.

DIAGRAM OF No. CCCCLXXXI .

To FOLLOW PAGE 116

THE FOLLOWING WORKS HAVE BEEN QUOTED IN AN ABBREVIATED FORM.

Bulletin de Correspondance Hellénique. Athens and Paris, from 1877 ; in progress.

(C. I.) Böckh, Corpus Inscriptionum Græcarum. Berlin, 1828–1853.

(C. I. A.) Corpus Inscriptionum Atticarum consilio Academiæ litterarum regiæ Borussicæ editum. Berlin, 1873; i n progress.

(C. I. L.) Corpus Inscriptionum Latinarum consilio et auctoritate Academiæ litterarum regiæ Borussicæ editum. Berlin, 1863 ; in progress.

Dittenberger, Sylloge Inscriptionum Græcarum. Leipzig, 1883.

Ephemeris Epigraphica, Corporis Inscriptionum Latinarum Supplementum, edita jussu Instituti Archæologici Romani. Rome, 1872 ; in progress.

Ephesos, various works on, cited in full on p. 68.

Greek Inscriptions, the Collection of Ancient, in the British Museum. Edited by C. T. Newton. Part I, Attika, edited by E. L. Hicks. Oxford, 1874.

—— Part II, edited by C. T. Newton. Oxford, 1883.

Hermes, Zeitschrift für classische Philologie. Berlin, 1866 ; in progress.

Hicks, E. L., Manual of Greek Historical Inscriptions. Oxford, 1882.

Journal of Hellenic Studies, published by the Council of the Society for promoting Hellenic Studies. London, 1880 ; in progress.

Kaibel, G., Epigrammata Græca ex lapidibus conlecta. Berlin, 1878.

Lightfoot, Dr. J. B., late Bishop of Durham, The Apostolic Fathers, Part ii, S. Ignatius, S. Polycarp. London, 1885.

Marquardt and Mommsen, Handbuch der Römischen Alterthümer. Leipzig, 1873–1887.

Meisterhans, Grammatik der Attischen Inschriften (2nd ed.). Berlin, 1888.

Mittheilungen des deutschen archäologischen Instituts in Athen. Athens, from 1876 ; in progress.

Μουσεῖον καὶ Βιβλιοθήκη τῆς Εὐαγγελικῆς Σχολῆς. Ἐν Σμύρνῃ, 1876 ; in progress.

Numismatic Chronicle and Journal of the Numismatic Society. London ; 1st series, 1836–1860 ; 2nd series, 1861–1880 ; 3rd series, from 1881 ; in progress.

Revue Archéologique. Paris, 1844–1859. Nouvelle Série, from 1860 ; in progress.

Röhl, Inscriptiones Græcæ antiquissimæ præter Atticas in Attica repertas. Berlin, 1882.

Waddington, W. H., Fastes des Provinces Asiatiques de l'Empire Romain depuis leur origine jusqu'au règne de Dioclétien ; première partie. Paris, 1872.

Waddington-Le Bas, Voyage archéologique en Grèce et Asie Mineure. Paris, 1848 ; in progress.

Wilmanns, G., Exempla Inscriptionum Latinarum. Berlin, 1873.

PART III.

CHAPTER I.

INSCRIPTIONS FROM PRIENÈ.

INTRODUCTORY NOTE. THE CONTROVERSY BETWEEN PRIENÈ AND SAMOS.

The most important of the inscriptions from Prienè have reference to a long standing dispute between Prienè and Samos touching the ownership of certain lands on the continent. The circumstances of this dispute have been sketched by Böckh (C. I. 2905, compare 2254) and MM. Waddington-Lebas (Voyage Archéologique, Part v, 186 foll.). But the excavations carried on at Prienè in 1869 by Mr. Pullan, by direction of the Society of Dilettanti, have resulted in the discovery of many documents upon the subject unknown to previous scholars. These marbles, together with most of the Prienè inscriptions published by Waddington-Lebas, were presented to the British Museum in 1870. The inscriptions were engraved on the antæ and on the external face of the walls of the pronaos of the temple of Athenè Polias, the walls being built with large blocks of marble, the joining of which afforded a beautiful specimen of ancient masonry. The inscriptions followed on without regard to the joints of the wall-stones, as will be seen later on to be the case with the πολιτεῖαι inscriptions from the Artemision at Ephesos. It has been therefore no light task to prepare these documents for the reader. For some of the wall-stones never reached the Museum, and many of those which came were broken into fragments. These have had to be pieced together, lacunae allowed for, and the position of one slab in relation to others determined. In many cases the practised eye of the masons at the Museum was able to determine the probable joinings of the stones, where it was impossible to judge from the internal evidence of the inscriptions. The plan on p. 7 will show the reader in what manner the marbles have been re-arranged. The Prienians appear to have regarded this cella as a kind of muniment room, containing the documentary evidence of their title to the disputed lands.

A short survey of the controversy between the two cities will explain the order in which the following documents are grouped, and will supersede the necessity of a detailed commentary on the subject-matter of each inscription.

The Samians appear to have laid claim from time immemorial to a district upon the mainland adjoining the Prienian frontier. In whatever way this district may have come into the possession of the Samians,

whether as the prize of war (as we shall find to be probably the case), or in some other way, certain it is that Prienè viewed the Samian occupation as an encroachment, and the disputes which arose in consequence between the two states formed no insignificant feature in the history of either people.

Plutarch tells us (Quæst. Græc. 20) of an early war (circa B.C. 550) between Prienè and Samos, probably concerning these lands, in which, after varying fortunes, the Samians were defeated with the loss of a thousand men. They accordingly withdrew from the mainland, and Prienè resumed possession of the district, her claim to it being strongly supported by Lygdamis, then tyrant of Naxos, B.C. 540-525 (C. I. 2254, lines 15-19). This settlement lasted only for six years, when the Milesians, espousing the cause of Samos, inflicted upon the Prienians so terrible a defeat at a place called Δρύς, that 'Ο παρὰ Δρυΐ σκότος became a proverb at Prienè. The Samians immediately seized upon the disputed territory (C. I. ibid., lines 20, 21), but through the mediation of Bias, the Prienian sage, who went as ambassador to Samos, the two states were again reconciled, and the Samians appear to have withdrawn from the mainland (C. I. ibid., line 22 foll.).

In the year 440 B.C. war broke out between Miletos and Samos 'concerning Prienè,' says Thucydides (i, 115), an expression from which we may infer that the cause of contention was the same as before, but that the Milesians now sided with the Prienians. The result was that Samos was defeated and reduced to the condition of a tributary by the Athenians under Perikles (Thucyd. i, 116, 117; Plut. Pericl. 28), and the Prienians apparently were established in their possession of the district under dispute. In Greek literature nothing more is heard concerning the question, but inscriptions enable us to trace the controversy through several subsequent stages.

When Alexander crossed over into Asia (B.C. 334), Prienè was one of the towns that opened their gates to him. Whether Alexander made any award concerning the disputed lands is uncertain. No. cccc is an edict of his concerning Prienian territory, but no mention of Samos occurs, nor the names of any of the disputed lands. But a reference to Alexander's expedition in No. ccccIII, line 146, seems to imply that he did make some award in favour of Prienè.

Antigonos, who bore the kingly title from B.C. 306 to B.C. 301, was certainly applied to by one of the contending states, perhaps Samos. This is stated in No. ccccii, lines 141 foll., but no other inscription remains bearing upon that appeal. Antigonos replied apparently that the apportionment of territory should stand as it did at the time of Alexander's expedition (No. ccccii, 145, 146).

The earliest of the extant documents concerning the controversy is the letter of King Lysimachos to the Samians, now at Oxford (C. I. 2254; see a more careful copy in my Greek Historical Inscriptions, No. 152). The latter portion of this curious letter is broken off, so that we cannot certainly say whether the award of Lysimachos was in favour of Samos or Prienè. We learn however that both parties had appealed to him, the question at issue being the right to a district called ἡ Βατινητὶς χώρα; this district, and the appeal to Lysimachos concerning it, are referred to more than once in No. ccccii. The decree of divine honours to Lysimachos (No. ccccı), and his gracious reply (No. ccccıı), will show that he was at one time of his reign on very friendly terms with Prienè, and could hardly then have given a decision against them. I shall endeavour to show (on No. ccccıı) that this correspondence with Lysimachos falls within the last period of his reign, B.C. 287–281; and I incline to the belief that his award concerning Batinetos was not altogether adverse to Prienè. It is even possible that the gratitude of the Prienians towards Lysimachos was partly earned by a favourable decision.

The next document dealing with the dispute is No. cccc111*, which occupied a large surface of the wall of the pronaos; being inscribed on the right-hand return of the anta which contained the dedication and decree of Alexander and the correspondence with Lysimachos (Nos. cccxcix—ccccıı). This lengthy document is an award of the Rhodian people, who had been invited to arbitrate (as ἔκκλητος πόλις) between Samos and Prienè touching the possession of a fort named Κάριον and the land surrounding it, ἡ περὶ τοῦτο χώρα. A Rhodian Commission was appointed, and delegates from Samos and Prienè appeared before them first at Rhodes itself, in the temple of Dionysos: then the arbitrators visited the disputed localities, and listened to the claims of either party on the spot; and lastly, a final hearing took place in the Artemision at Ephesos (No. cccc111, lines 1–24). The position of Rhodes in the third century B.C. was such as to well qualify it to arbitrate in a controversy of this kind. Amid the perpetual wars of the time, the Rhodians aimed at maintaining an attitude of armed neutrality. Their extensive commerce and great wealth made

them anxious for peace. They seldom interfered in the wars around them, but, when they did, it was with decisive effect. Demetrios 'the taker of cities' had besieged them in vain for a year (B.C. 305–4), and they had emerged from the conflict with increased influence. Sixty years later (B.C. 246–239), in the reign of Ptolemy Euergetes, they inflicted a severe defeat at Ephesos upon the Egyptian fleet, though it was commanded by the famous Athenian Chremonides (Droysen, Hellenismus, iii, 1, p. 407; and his citations from Polyænos, v, 18; Stobæos, Floril. xl, 8). We shall have occasion later, in dealing with the decree from Iasos concerning Philip V and the Rhodians, to note the unique position of Rhodes among the other cities of the Levant.

The date of this Rhodian award can be determined within narrow limits. Mention is made in line 132 of Antiochos (Theos) 'son of Antiochos' (Soter), who reigned B.C. 261–246. In line 134 Prienè is spoken of as involved in ὁ Λαοδίκειος πόλεμος †, and this can hardly be anything else than the war waged by Ptolemy Euergetes against Laodikè and her son Seleukos II. During this war (B.C. 247–243) nearly all the Ionic cities sided with Egypt. And if (like Smyrna, see C. I. 3137, and Greek Historical Inscriptions, No. 176) Prienè shut her gates against the generals of Euergetes, it is certain the city must have suffered; especially as its rival, Samos, was now an Egyptian naval station (see Droysen, Hellenismus, iii, 1, p. 320). In No. cccc111, line 153, we are told of a commander of Ptolemy (Philadelphos) being stationed at Samos.

Antiochos Theos is the latest monarch, and ὁ Λαοδίκειος πόλεμος the latest event, mentioned in the award; and if my interpretation of this phrase is correct, the date of the award is about 240 B.C., a little later than the date suggested by Droysen (iii, 1, 331). The character of the writing would agree with this date.

The heading of the Rhodian award is happily preserved, and is very explicit. After giving the names of the five arbitrators, and of the delegates from Samos and Prienè respectively, and having stated the circumstances under which the award was delivered, the Rhodians proceed to affirm in brief that they hold the claim of Prienè to Karion and its environs to be fully proved (lines 1–27). They add that they have made two copies of the award (ἀπόφασις), and have delivered one to the authorities at Samos and the other to the authorities at Prienè (lines 27–44). Then there followed a recital at length of the arguments that had been employed on either side (lines 45–154). Finally the arbitrators sum up and pronounce judgment in favour of Prienè (lines 154–157). Appended was a specification of

* Waddington-Lebas, misled by the twice-repeated decision (No. ccccı, lines 26 foll. and 156 foll.), imagined that there were two awards made by Rhodes recorded in two distinct documents,—an earlier one concerning Κάριον and Δρνοῦσσα, and a later one concerning a certain φρούριον and ἡ περὶ τοῦτο χώρα. It is however sufficiently clear that the φρούριον is identical with τὸ Κάριον, and that the land about it was named Δρνοῦσσα. A careful study of the marbles, together with MS. copies of the lost portions, has convinced me that the whole of No. cccc111 is one continuous document (see Plan); and I have not accepted Waddington-Lebas' restoration of lines 99–100, where I was at first inclined to follow these scholars in finding a reference to a previous award of Rhodes.

† Λαοδίκειος πόλεμος is formed after the analogy of Χρεμωνίδειος πόλεμος (Athen. vi, p. 250 F): Λαοδικηνὶς would be the adjective if the reference had been to a city Laodikeia.

the exact boundaries between the Samian and Prienian lands: of this survey only the beginning is preserved (lines 158–170). Of the recital of the pleadings many lines have been lost. But enough remains for us to see clearly the precise questions at issue, the chief arguments urged by Samos and Prienè, and the final award of Rhodes. Incidentally also this inscription does more. For it recovers from oblivion a curious history of the Prienian people, and its vicissitudes during the struggles of the kings of Asia, Egypt, Thrace, and Macedon.

The question at issue was the ownership of Karion and its neighbourhood, the Samians asserting that the Prienian occupation of them was a modern encroachment. The arguments on either side were based partly on inscriptions, partly on written histories, and also on the circumstances of previous arbitrations. It is probable that the Samian arguments are recited first, inasmuch as it was the Samians who had raised the discussion, and they are mentioned first in lines 8, 10, 11, 14, 29. If so, the Samian delegates must have begun by tracing back their occupation of the disputed lands to early times. Although only a few words here and there can be recovered of *g*, *h*, *i*, *k*, yet we can conjecture the bearing of these fragments upon the argument, by comparing them with the completer parts of the document. Thus, in line 45, the reference to Batinetos is probably made in order to show very early Samos had held possessions on the coast. They had argued in this way in the appeal before Lysimachos (C. I. 2254; Greek Historical Inscriptions, No. 152). For the same purpose they refer to the partition of the land of οἱ Μελιεῖς (lines 47 foll.), —an event quite unknown to us, but evidently familiar to the historians of those districts, and frequently alluded to in this award (compare lines 55, 103, 108, 119). It appears that the Karion and its adjoining land Dryussa originally belonged to Melia, a Karian town mentioned by Hekatæos (as quoted by Stephanus Byzantinus, s. v.). It was probably a native Karian town, with which the Prienian colony at first was glad to unite itself (lines 47, 48); but when the Greek colony grew stronger, Melia was destroyed and its territory divided amongst its Grecian neighbours. Apparently this took place in the sixth century B.C., for in lines 105 foll. it is spoken of as earlier than the defeat at Δρύs. In this partition the Samians affirmed that Karion and Dryussa were allotted to Samos. We may suppose that in *h* the Samian advocates brought down their claims to a later date, but their arguments are lost. In *i* we reach (as it seems) the arguments of the Prienians. They begin their reply with a reference to the 'Histories of Mæandrios* of Miletos,' endeavouring to show that the Samian account of the partition of Melia was incorrect (lines 53 foll.). Their allusion to the Pan-Ionian festival reminds us that the Prienians had been granted the privilege of appointing a priest of Poseidon at that celebration (Strabo, viii,

p. 384; xiv, p. 639; compare No. CCCCXXVI *post*). In lines 58 and 60 two minor towns of this coast, Μαραθήσιον and Ἄναια, are said to have been acquired (by the Samians ?), the one from the Milesians, the other from the Kolophonians. This curious bit of information is confirmed by what we know from other sources. Strabo (xiv, p. 639) says that Marathesion at one time belonged to Samos, but the Samians exchanged it away to the Ephesians for Neapolis which was nearer to them. At a still earlier date Marathesion had, it seems, belonged to Miletos. That Anæa belonged to Samos in historical times we know from Thucydides (iv, 75; iii, 19, 32; viii, 19) who tells us how the exiled oligarchs of Samos established themselves at Anæa, and did serious injury to the Athenian cause therefrom; (compare a similar story of Anæa, in earlier days, recounted by Pausanias, vii, 4, § 3). In *s* we shall find a further reference to Mæandrios, and to the Samian possession of Pygela (or Phygela), a little town close by Marathesion and Anæa. The fragmentary state of this part of the award is the less to be regretted, as it dealt merely with antiquarian arguments like those in *i*, which the Rhodian arbitrators review later on in *r* and *s*.

The Prienians next endeavour to show (*k*, *l*, *m*, *n*, *o*) their uninterrupted occupation of Karion and Dryussa. They make mention of a στάσις which had occurred at Prienè; a 'Tyranny' had been set up, whereupon the δῆμος, flying to the Karion under the command of an irregularly appointed φρούραρχος, took possession of the fort and murdered the garrison as being partisans of the Tyrant (lines 65 foll.). The point of their argument seems to be that this forcible occupation of the Karion was not to wrest it for the first time from the Samians, who never had any claim to it, but was an act of self-defence on the part of the democrats. We may conjecture perhaps that the Tyrant at Prienè and his partisans in the Karion were in correspondence with Samos, and that Samos endeavoured to take advantage of the dissensions of Prienè to strengthen her own footing on the mainland. The Τυραννίς lasted two or three years: then the δῆμος returned, but the possession of the Karion and its environs still remained in their hands. They had even sold thirty-seven allotments of the disputed land, and, later on, five more lots. Documentary evidence was produced for the facts thus stated: and from these the date of this revolution can be pretty closely determined. The flight of the δῆμος to Karion was ἐπὶ στεφανηφόρου Μακαρέως (No. CCCCIII, lines 65, 125). They were restored in the third year from this, ἐπὶ στεφανηφόρου Λύκου (line 82). The appeal to Lysimachos concerning Batinetos was in the fifteenth year from Lykos (lines 123, 126). But among the documentary evidence cited by the Prienians concerning their triennium of exile were decrees sent by them at that time, ποτὶ τοὺς βασιλέας Δη]μήτριον καὶ Λυσίμαχον (lines 76, 77). This could not be earlier than B.C. 306, when Lysimachos assumed the title of

* This writer is named by Strabo, xii, p. 552; Athenaeos x, p. 454 B; Macrobius, Saturn. i, 17. § 21. His date is doubtful, but he is probably not earlier than Alexander.

King; it was moreover some fifteen years earlier than his award concerning Batinetos (lines 125, 126). Now Lysimachos died in 281, and it will be shown on No. cccvi that the Batinetos award cannot have been much earlier than B.C. 287; so that our dates are ascertained within about ten years. It seems natural however to suppose that the communications which passed between the exiled δῆμος and Kings Demetrios and Lysimachos would take place at a time when they were in the neighbourhood of Prienè. Perhaps they applied to Demetrios while he was engaged in besieging Rhodes (B.C. 304), and to Lysimachos while engaged in the campaign which ended at Ipsos (B.C. 301). The chronological table subjoined on p. 5 is based upon these calculations. It is even open to conjecture that the oligarchical revolution at Prienè was due to the same impulse which overturned the democracy in other Asiatic cities, viz. the coalition of Kassander with Lysimachos against Antigonos and Demetrios (B.C. 304–301). We shall have occasion later, in dealing with the Ephesian decrees discovered by Mr. Wood, to say more of this movement. Demetrios and his father were everywhere the idols of the democratic party.

In *r* and *s* the Rhodian arbitrators review the arguments of either side. The Samians had represented the Prienians as having encroached upon the Samjan lands (lines 99 foll.): they also asserted that the Prienians had never claimed Karion until the tyranny mentioned above, when their exiled δῆμος seized the fort and pillaged the neighbourhood, and upon their restoration three years afterwards, still retained forcible possession of the lands (lines 119 foll.). We have already seen (in lines 65 foll.) the Prienian account of this στάσις, and its bearing on their plea. The Samians also cited testimonies from the historians * that Karion and Dryussa were allotted to Samos. As for the testimony of the historians, the arbitrators affirm that it is all in favour of Prienè, with the sole exception of the 'Histories of Mæandrios of Miletos,' a book the authenticity of which they declare to be commonly doubted (line 123). Another strong point in the case for Prienè was the consideration of previous awards. Alexander and Antigonos, the Prienians urged (lines 141 foll.), had both confirmed their

possession of that which Samos declared to be an encroachment. And again from the time of the restoration in the year of Lykos down to the appeal to Lysimachos about Batinetos, a period of fifteen years, not one word had been uttered by Samos against the Prienian possession of Karion and Dryussa. Prienè had sold forty-two lots of this land, and no remonstrance had been received from Samos (lines 124 foll.). Disputes about private encroachments had arisen (ἀμφισβασίας ποθ' αὑτοὺς ἰδιωτικὰς γεγόνειν [π]αρορίας, line 129), but the Prienian title to Karion had not been questioned at all. In the appeal to Lysimachos also Samos recognised the Prienian title to Karion (line 130); they had recognised it later on when they had complained of Prienian encroachments during the reign of Antiochos Theos; they had recognised it when Samos passed under Egyptian control, and when [Anti]ochos the admiral stationed at Samos by Ptolemy Philadelphos was applied to by the Samians to maintain their rights on the mainland against Prienè † (lines 151–154).

An historical explanation has already been suggested of the Λαοδίκειος πόλεμος of line 134. The δυσχερεῖς καιροί, which in line 132 are said to have overtaken Prienè in the reign of Antiochos Theos, can hardly be other than the defenceless position of Prienè before the invading forces of Ptolemy Philadelphos in the Second Syrian war (see Droysen, iii, 1, pp. 319, 320). Ephesos was already held by an Egyptian garrison; and the capture of Magnesia ad Mæandrum by Kallikratidas of Kyrenè (Polyænos, ii, 27; cited by Droysen, ibid.) placed the Prienians at his mercy. The Rhodians finally dismiss the Samian arguments (lines 154 foll.), and declare the Prienian claim to the Fort and its neighbourhood (i. e. Karion and Dryussa) to be fully made out. They made their award accordingly, and the document concluded with a careful specification (z) of the boundaries between the Samian and Prienian frontier, the various landmarks being revisited and restored by the Rhodian commission.‡

The next documents, Nos. ccccIV, ccccV, belong to the time of Roman supremacy in Asia Minor. Upon the defeat of Antiochos by the Scipios, a swarm of envoys hastened to the senate from the various cities of Asia Minor (Polyb. xxii, 1) with all

---

* The historians named (lines 109, 120, 121) are Duris, Theopompos, who are well known; also Mæandrios, whom we have already mentioned; Olympichos, Euagon, Uliades of Samos; Eualkes and Kreophylos of Ephesos. Of these last Eualkes and Kreophylos are both named by Athenæos as writers of 'Ἐφεσιακά (xiii, 573; viii, 361). Olympichos is quoted by Clement of Alexandria (Protrept. p. 41 Potter) as stating the image of Hera at Samos to be the work of Smilis: 'Ολύμπιχος ἐν Σαμιακοῖς ἱστορεῖ (compare Overbeck, Die Antike Schriftquellen, No. 342). Uliades of Samos is named by Plutarch (Aristides, 23) as one of the Greeks who took the chief part in renouncing the leadership of Sparta and of Pausanias, and insisting upon Athens placing herself at the head of a Greek confederation against Persia. Whether this Uliades the Samian admiral is identical with the historian of our inscription is very doubtful. Of Euagon I can find no trace, unless he is the ancient historian of Samos who is classed by Dionysios of Halikarnassos with Hekataeos and others (De Thucydide judicium, 5) and called Εὐγέων. Dobree restores Εὐγαίων as the name of the Samian antiquary cited by Suidas, s. v. Νῆτι: compare Photius' Lexicon (ed. Porson) s. v. Νῆτι. Meineke (Analecta Alexandrina, pp. 60, 61), in dealing with a fragment of Euphorion preserved by Ælian, Hist. Anim. xvii, 28, in which Euphorion has followed this Samian antiquary, approves of the restoration of his name as Εὐγαίων, which Suidas s. v. recognises as an ἀνομα εἰρων; so that it would be rash to suggest that in all these passages we ought to read Εὐάγων. Euagon was more probably a writer of the fourth century, to which belongs Euagon the disciple of Plato, who came to a bad end in his native city of Lampsakos (Athen. xi, 508; Diog. Laert. iii, 46).

† I adopt here the suggestion of Droysen (Hellenismus. iii, 1, 331) that this happened in the 'Second Syrian War,' and that [Anti]ochos was the first Egyptian commander stationed at Samos. From a new régime the Samians might hope for a more favourable consideration of their claims.

‡ For similar specifications of boundaries, see Böckh, C. I. 5594. 5774. 5775.

kinds of petitions and grievances to lay before their new masters. The senate prolonged Manlius' appointment in Asia for another year, and determined to send out to him ten Commissioners (πρισβευτρί, No. ccccv, line 8; compare Polyb. xxii, 7) to settle the apportionment of territory and tribute according to certain general instructions given them, while they were left to their own discretion as to details (Livy, xxxviii, 39). Among other disputed claims which came before Manlius and the Commissioners, was the old dispute between Samos and Prienè (No. ccccv, lines 6, 7), which Manlius seems to have settled in favour of Samos. Upon the departure of Manlius from Asia, the Prienians appear to have remonstrated against this decision. It is possible that the mutilated Senatusconsultum, No. ccccv, is part of a decree revoking Manlius' decision and reaffirming the award of Rhodes (line 8), in reply to an embassy to Rome from Prienè stating their grievance (lines 4–6), and renewing their allegiance to the Senate (line 3). A fragment of another Senatusconsultum, bearing doubtless upon the same subject, is preserved at the upper edge of No. ccccv.

At all events in No. ccccv the Senate very curtly dismissed the claim of Samos by declining to reconsider the award of Rhodes. The bluntness with which (lines 10–12) they ignore the decision of Manlius, may be taken to imply that the Senate had little respect for his opinion. Waddington is probably right in suggesting that the Samians had purchased the favourable award of the Consul. The expressions of his own legate concerning him (Livy, xxxviii, 45), 'tuum privatum latrocinium, . . . stipem a tyrannis castellanisque deviis colligens,' and the phrase of Polybios (xxii, 18), αὐτὸν δὲ νομίσας ἕρμαιον εἶναι τὸ προσπεπτωκὸς κ.τ.λ., quite bear out this view of his character.

Nos. ccccvi, ccccvii, ccccviii. are portions of a specification of boundaries drawn up by a joint commission of Samians and Prienians, appointed to restore the old landmarks in accordance with the award of Rhodes, by order of the Senate: see notes ad loc.

From No. ccccxii, which is perhaps a letter from Ptolemy Euergetes, we learn that not only Samos but Miletos also (compare p. 1) had a controversy with Prienè about the limits of their respective territories. The people of Smyrna, it seems, had been called in to arbitrate in the matter, just as Rhodes had done on a previous occasion.

This controversy between Prienè and Samos receives illustration from similar disputes between other cities. There were certain lands in Krete which were claimed both by Hierapytna and Itanos. The quarrel was referred to the Roman Senate, and an inscription in C. I. No. 2561 b (Addenda, ii. p. 1100), contains the decision given by an ἔκκλητος πόλις, probably Paros, together with a review of the controversy. The date of that document is given by Böckh as 57 or 58 B.C. A similar dispute went on for centuries between the Messenians and Lacedæmonians respecting the Ager Denthcliates, a strip of land lying between the western slope of Taÿgetos and the upper course of the river Nedon. The controversy respecting it lasted from the time of the Messenian Wars (see Grote, ii, chap. vii.) down to the reign of Tiberius, when it engaged the attention of the Senate (Tacit. Ann. iv, 43; compare Pausan. iv, 4. § 2). Among the most interesting of the recent discoveries at Olympia is the actual award of the Milesians in favour of Messenè, referred to in the passage of Tacitus. It was inscribed upon the pedestal supporting the statue of Nikè by Pæonios (Archäol. Zeitung, 1876, p. 128; compare 1878, p. 104).

CHRONOLOGICAL TABLE OF THE SAMOS AND PRIENÈ DISPUTE.

(FROM THE ABOVE-MENTIONED INSCRIPTIONS.)

PROBABLE DATE. B.C.	NAME OF MAGISTRATE, &c.	EVENT REFERRED TO.	INSCRIPTION WHICH GIVES THE EVENT AND DATE.
305	Ἀθηναγόρας στιφανοφόρος.	. . . .	cccciii. 66.
304	ἐπὶ στεφαν. Μακαρίως.	Flight of δῆμος to Κάρμον—τυραννίς.	cccciii. 66, 112, 124, 125.
301	ἐπὶ στεφαν. Λύκου, ὅς ἐστι ἀπὸ Μακαρίως τέταρτος.	End of τυραννίς—return of δῆμοι.	cccciii. 80 foll., 94, 112 foll., 124, 138.
300	ἐπὶ στεφαν. Καλλιστράτου.	. . . .	cccciii. 84, 89.
296	[ἐπὶ στεφαν. . . . . . ὅς ἐσ]τι ἀπὸ Καλλιστράτου πέμπτος.	Five more lots of the disputed land sold by the Prienians.	cccciii. 89, 90.
288	Νίκανδρος στιφανοφόρος.	. . . .	cccciii. 126.
287	ἐπὶ στεφαν. τοῦ θεοῦ τοῦ μετὰ Νίκανδρον, ὅς ἐστι ἀπὸ Λύκου πεντεκαιδέκατος.	Appeal to Lysimachos concerning Batinetos.	cccciii. 125, 126, 130; compare cccci, ccccii, and C. I. 2254.
Between 261–246	διαγεναμένων ἐτῶν πλειόνων καιροὶ δυσχερεῖς at Prienè.	Samian remonstrances under Antiochos Theos.	cccciii. 131 foll.
Between 258–246	. . . . .	Antiochos, a general of Ptolemy Philadelphos, appealed to by the Samians.	cccciii. 133.
About 240	.	Rhodian award.	ccccii. the whole, especially 99 foll.; compare ccccv. 10 foll.
189	Cn. Manlius consul.	Cn. Manlius, after defeat of Antiochos, readjusts the boundaries, with ten Commissioners.	ccccv. 7, 8.
135	Servius Fulvius consul.	Senatusconsultum in favour of Prienè.	ccccv, see date in line 3.

c

In the Plan (p. 7) the portions of inscribed marble, which either were copied by travellers or were brought home to the British Museum, are indicated by firm black outlines to indicate their edges when preserved; broken edges are indicated by wavy thin lines.

Those marbles which are preserved in the Museum, and those only, are marked in the plan by having their measurements given: with the exception of such fragments as were too small in the plan to allow of the insertion of figures. These measurements will be appended below.

The views of this Temple, as given by Mr. Pullan in Part iv. of 'Antiquities of Ionia,' Pll. 14 16, 17, make it plain that the courses of masonry were arranged throughout so that one narrow course came in after two broad courses. The broad courses vary a trifle from 20 in., the narrow course is a little under 1 foot wide. This invariable arrangement of the masonry was a datum of the greatest help in determining the arrangement of the inscriptions. Some blocks again were restored to their relative position by the fact of their inscriptions reading into one another. In other cases, where the return face of the antæ-stones was inscribed, the sequence of the lines of one inscription enabled me to fix the sequence of the other.

Portions of masonry indicated by dotted outlines, are supplied by conjecture; there being no record of them.

It was long ago observed by Chandler ('Antiquities of Ionia,' i, p. 13) in respect of these inscriptions upon the Temple at Priene, that, 'from the degrees of magnitude in the letter, it may be conjectured, a regard was had to perspective, the greater being higher, and more remote, the smaller nearer to the eye; so that at the proper point of view for reading, all might appear nearly of the same proportion.' This variation in size,—which could not well be exhibited in the uncial printed text,—afforded a further key to the position of the blocks. In the block marked cccciii *a* a gradual transition is to be traced line by line from larger to smaller letters. In the lost portions copied by Mr. Murray, though the measures of the blocks are not preserved, his memoranda usually record the exact size of the letters, which was of equal importance. Moreover it was generally possible to infer, from the number of lines in his MSS., whether the block from which he copied belonged to a broad or to a narrow course.

On cccciii *l* the inscription commences at some inches' distance from the upper edge of the block, proving that probably the block above it was not inscribed. I have therefore, from this as well as other indications, placed it at the top of a column of inscription.

Moreover the right-hand portion of the fragment cccciii *c* (2) is 'set back,' i.e. its surface is slightly depressed below the left-hand portion of the surface. The depressed surface is uninscribed. This feature will agree with the ground-plans by Mr. Pullan (ibid. Pt. iv, Pll. 5, 6). Indeed it appears to have been usual in building the antæ of a temple, to make the foremost courses from top to bottom a little wider than the rest, so as to give to the fronts of the antæ something of the appearance of a pilaster.

It is singular that nothing should be inscribed below cccciii *k*. This may be explained by a remark of Mr. Pullan (ibid. p. 29), that 'at the sides (of the pavement) adjoining the walls (of the pronaos) there were ranges of pedestals upon which statues had been placed.' The inscription may possibly have been discontinued at this point because the wall surface beneath was obscured by the erection of a statue or other monument.

Forgetting the arrangement of the masonry, and looking only at the inscriptions, we have before us three entire columns of inscription, and the lower portion of a fourth column (Nos. cccci.–ccccvi). In the courses above these last must have come the royal letter No. ccccxii, and the documents connected with it. If, as seems likely, the Senatus consulta, Nos. ccccıv and ccccv, occupied the bottom of the fourth column, then on the upper courses of a fifth column were inscribed the specifications preserved in Waddington-Le Bas, Part v, Nos. 200-1, 203-4, 206-7, of which only a small portion has been preserved in the British Museum (Nos. ccccvi–ccccviii). One might, with something like certainty, indicate the courses in which these blocks once stood. Thus, No. ccccvii certainly ranged with ccccii *b*.

Some of the fragments now in the British Museum are represented in the plan without measurements, because they are too small in the plan to be marked with legible figures. Their measurements are accordingly given here.

	in.		in.		in.		in.
cccc *a* (1)	7¼	by	8¼	cccciii *e* (1)	4	by	7
cccc *a* (3)	4½	,,	10	cccciii *e* (2)	9¼	,,	18
cccc *b*	8½	,,	16	cccciii *g* (2) ..	4½	,,	15
cccc *c*	6¼		8¼	cccciii *h* (1) ...	[illegible]	,,	1
cccc *d* ...	3½		7	cccciii *h* (2)	1¾	,,	3¾
cccci *b* (2)	3¼		8	cccciii *k*	8¼	,,	9¼
cccci *d*	4¾	,,	3½	ccccv *b* (2)	9	,,	13½
cccci *f*	8½	,,	10½				
ccccii *c*	10	,,	15				
cccciii *b* (1) ...	3¼	,,	10¾				

(This last fragment would come outside of the right-hand margin of the Plan.)

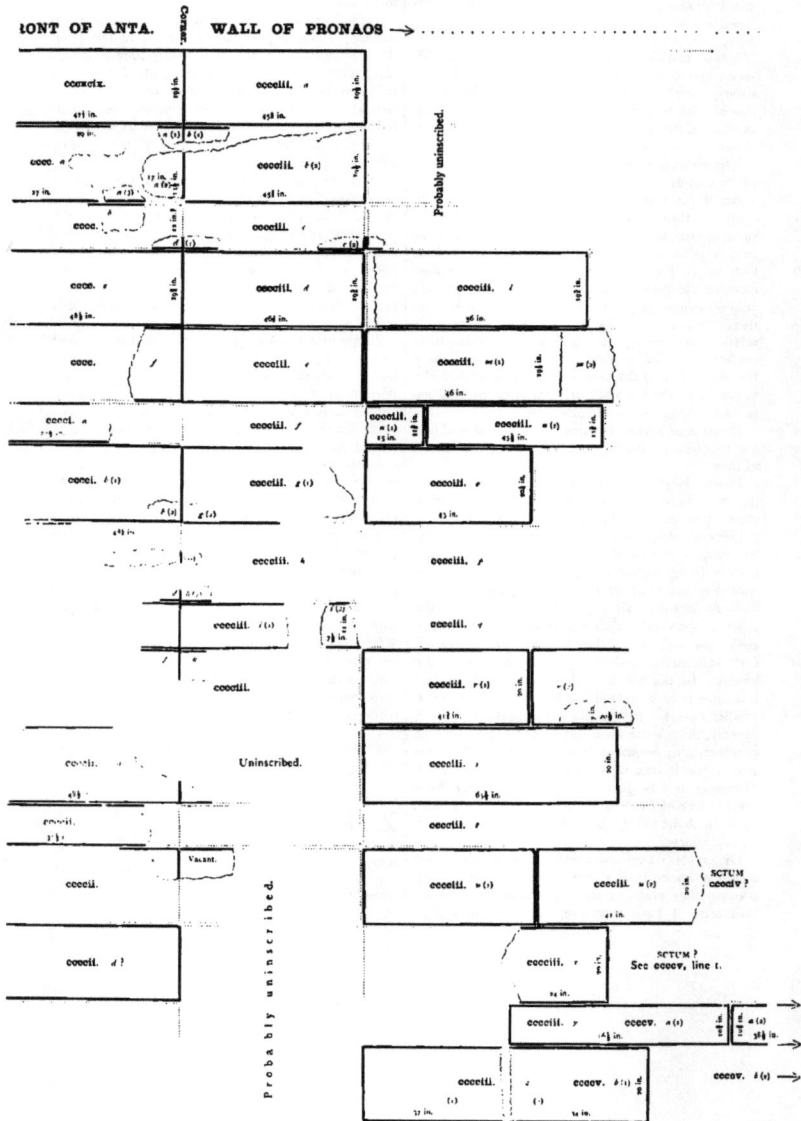

RONT OF ANTA. Corner. **WALL OF PRONAOS →** . . . .

Probably uninscribed.

cccccix. cccciii. *a*

47½ in. 45½ in.

30 in. *a* (2) *b* (2)

cccc. *a* ccccii. *b* (2)

27 in. 17 in. 45½ in.
a (3)

cccc. cccciii. *c*

cccc. *e* ccccii. *d* ccccii. *l*

48½ in. 48½ in. 36 in.

cccc. / cccciii. *e* cccciii. *m* (2) *n* (2)

46 in.

ccccl. *a* cccciii. / cccciii. *o* (2) cccciii. *p* (2)

15 in. 45½ in.

cccci. *b* (2) cccciii. *g* (2) cccciii. *q*

43 in.

b (2) *g* (2)

cccciii. *h* cccciii. *r*

cccciii. *i* (2) cccciii. *s*

ccciii. cccciii. *t* (2) *t* (2)

41¼ in.

Uninscribed. cccciii. *u*

6½ in.

cccciii. *v*

Vacant.

ccccii. ccccii. *w* (2) cccciii. *x* (2) SCTUM ccccv ?

44 in.

cccciii. *d* ? SCTUM ?
See ccccv, line t.

cccciii. *y* ccccv. *a* (2) ccccv. *a* (2)

36½ in.

cccciii. ccccv. *b* (2) ccccv. *b* (2)

Probably uninscribed.

Block of white marble from one of the antæ of the Temple of Athenè Polias, Prienè. For its measurement and position, see the Plan, p. 7. (On the return face of the stone is the inscription, No. ccccIII α.) Presented by the Society of Dilettanti, 1870. C. I. 2904; Waddington-Le Bas, Part v, 187; Antiquities of Ionia, Part i, pp. 12, 13.

ΒΑΣΙΛΕΥΣΑΛΕΞΑΝΔΡΟΣ
ΑΝΕΘΗΚΕΤΟΝΝΑΟΝ
ΑΘΗΝΑΙΗΠΟΛΙΑΔΙ

Βασιλεὺς Ἀλέξανδρος
ἀνέθηκε τὸν ναὸν
Ἀθηναίῃ Πολιάδι

We learn through Strabo (xiv, p. 641) that Alexander offered to the Ephesians to defray the entire cost of the rebuilding of their temple of Artemis ἐφ' ᾧ τε τὴν ἐπιγραφὴν αὐτὸν ἔχειν. The Ephesians declined the offer, adroitly urging ὡς οὐ πρέποι θεῷ θεοῖς ἀναθήματα κατασκευάζειν. Our inscription shows that the Prienians had no such scruple. The worship of Athenè at Prienè is known to us from its coins both of the autonomous and Imperial periods (see Mionnet). The figure of Athenè Nikephoros on the Imperial coins of Prienè is doubtless the Athenè Polias of this inscription, whose colossal statue in her temple is specially mentioned by Pausanias, vii, 5, § 3. Fragments of this statue were found on the floor of the temple, and are now in the British Museum. See Antiquities of Ionia, Part iv, pp. 25–31.

Inscription in large clear characters, 1½ inches in size, on one of the antæ of the Temple of Athenè Polias, Prienè. The first part (a, b, c, d) is pieced together out of a number of fragments. e is published by Waddington-Le Bas, Part v, 188. f is from a copy made by Mr. A. S. Murray at Prienè from a stone which was not brought home; compare Mittheilungen, 1880, p. 339. For the position and measurements of these blocks, see the Plan, p. 7. Presented by the Society of Dilettanti, 1870.

```
 a ΒΑΣΙΛΕΙΙΣΑ. . . . . . ΡΟΥ
   ΤΠΝΕΝΝΑΥΛΟΧΠΙΙ . . . . . . . . .
   ΤΠΝΟΣΟΙΜΕΝΙΕΙΣΙ . . . . . ΛΙΙU
   . . ΜΟΥΣΙ . . . . . . . . ΕΡΟΥΣ
 5 ΕΧ . . . . ΑΓ . . . . . . . ΑΙΤΑΣΟΙΚΙ
   ΑΣΤΑΣΕΝΙ ΟΛΕΙΠΑ . . ΣΚΑΙΤΗΓ
   Λ ΟΠΛΜΟ. . ΠΟΙΕΙΡΙ . . . . . . . .
 b . . . . ΑΙΣΑΝΔΕΠ . . . . . . .
 c ΤΟΔΕ . . ΑΙΜΥΡΣ . . . . . . . .
10 . ΑΙΓ . . . . . . . . . . . . . ΟΡΑΙ  d
 e . ΙΝΙΙΣΚΠΕΜΗΝΕΙΝΑΙΤΟΥΣΔΕΚΑ
   ΤΟΙΚΟΥΝΤΑΣΕΝΤΑΙΣΚΩΜΑΙΣΤΑΥ
   ΤΑΙΣΦΕΡΕΙΝΤΟΥΣΦΟΡΟΥΣΤΗΣ
   ΔΕΣΥΝΤΑΞΕΩΣΑΦΙΗΜΙΤΗΜΠΡΙΗ
15 ΝΕΩΜΠΟΛΙΝΚΑΙΤΗΜΦΡΟΥΙ . ΝΕ
   ΦΗ . . . . . ΑΓΕΙ . . . . . . . .
 f . . . . . . . . . . . . . . ΔΙΑ . . .
   . . . . . . . . ΟΜΜΙΑΠΟΤΑΣΔΙΚΑΣ . .
   . . . . . . . . . . . . . . ΝΕΙΥΜΑΣ
20 . . . . . . . . . . . . ΔΙΚΑΣΤΗΡΙΟΝ
   . . . . . . . . . . . . . . . ΔΗΜΑ . . .
   . . . . . . . . . . . . . . . ΥΜΑΣ . . .
```

```
 a Βασιλέως Ἀ[λεξάνδ]ρου
   Τῶν ἐν Ναυλόχῳ [κατοικούν- ?
   των ὅσοι μέν εἰσι [Πριηνεῖ]ς α[ὐτ]ο-
   νό]μους ε[ἶναι καὶ ἐλευθ]έρους
 5 ἔχ[οντ]ας [τὰ γήπεδα ? κ]αὶ τὰς οἰκί-
   ας τὰς ἐν [π]όλει πᾶ[σα]ς καὶ τὴν
   χώραν, ο[ἱ δὲ] Πριηνε[ῖς . . . . . .
 b . . . . . . αἷς ἂν δίω[νται . . . . .
 c τὸ δὲ . . [κ]αὶ Μυρσ . . . . . . . .
10 κ]αὶ Π . . . . . . . . . . . χώραν d
 e γυνώσκω ἐμὴν εἶναι, τοὺς δὲ κα-
   τοικοῦντας ἐν ταῖς κώμαις ταύ-
   ταις φέρειν τοὺς φόρους· τῆς
   δὲ συντάξεως ἀφίημι τὴμ Πριη-
15 νέαμ πόλιν καὶ τὴμ φρου[ρὰ]ν ἐ-
   φ' ᾗ [ . . . . . . εἰ]σάγει[ν . . .
 f . . . . . . . . . . . . . . . . . . . διὰ . .
   . . . . . . . . . . . . . . τὰς δίκας .
   . . . . . . . . . . . . . . . νει ὑμᾶς
20 . . . . . . . . . . . . . . δικαστήριον
   . . . . . . . . . . . . . . . δημα . .
   . . . . . . . . . . . . . . . . ὑμᾶς . .
```

This seems to be an edict of Alexander issued after the reduction of the Greek cities on the Asiatic coast. Prienè was one of the cities which submitted without a blow; and this inscription appears to relate to the apportionment of lands (lines 2, and 5–7) and the adjustment of tribute. Such readjustment would be natural after the expulsion of the Persian garrisons, and the emancipation of the Greek towns. Naulochum (line 2) is named by Pliny, N. H. v, 29, § 31, as a town near Prienè. It must have been a small port at the mouth of the Mæander, as is noted by Waddington-Le Bas, Part v, No. 186, where an eponymous hero Naulochos is mentioned.

Line 9. Μυρσ . . . must be the name of one of the κῶμαι referred to in line 12.

The end of line 1 is given on a fragment the return of which contains the beginning of lines 7, 8 of No. ccccIII. The endings of lines 3–6 are given on a fragment the return of which contains the commencement of lines 10–14 of No. ccccIII. The fragment d, containing ΧΩΡΑΙ, line 10, has on its return the portions of proper names which form part of lines 16, 17, of No. ccccIII. The fragment e placed at lines 9, 10, is broken at the top, bottom, and right, but is perfect on the left edge; it probably formed part of this narrow course of masonry (see Plan, p. 7). Line 7 is intersected by a joint in the wall-stone: but the stems of the letters tally exactly, and the dowel-holes are traceable by means of which the two blocks were joined together.

Naulochon, it appears from this edict, was regarded by the Prienians as their port, and stood in their territory; its position is conjecturally marked in Rayet, Milet et le Golfe Latmique, Pl. ii. We can believe that many Prienians lived there, and many foreigners also, including Samians, for purposes of trade. When therefore Alexander made Prienè free from tribute (line 14), the question arose whether the inhabitants of Naulochon should enjoy the same exemption. Alexander apparently makes a distinction. The Prienian inhabitants of Naulochon (if my restorations are correct) are to be αὐτόνομοι and ἐλεύθεροι (lines 3, 4), self-governed and independent; moreover they are to retain undisputed right over their land, and over any property they may hold within or outside of Naulochon. The metoiks would pay tribute to Alexander, and perhaps a μετοίκιον to Prienè. The next lines (7-10) are broken; but they evidently referred to other κῶμαι which stood within Prienian territory. We might perhaps restore :—οἱ δὲ Πριηνε[ῖς οἰκούντων ἐν |

κώμαις] αἷς ἂν δέω[νται ἀτελεῖς]. Some of these hamlets and their land Alexander decrees to be his own (γινώσκω ἐμὴν εἶναι, line 11), and the inhabitants of these dependent κῶμαι are to pay tribute to him. The inscription should be studied in connexion with Arrian, Anabasis, i, 17, where we read how Alexander organized the Greek territories on the western shore of Asia Minor which he had just delivered from the yoke of Persia. Arrian, however, makes no mention of Prienè. We must credit Alexander with the desire to develope local self-government wherever possible, although he was really indifferent to the usual division of Greek parties into democrats and oligarchs. On the terms αὐτόνομον and ἐλεύθερος see Droysen, Hellenismus, i, 1, p. 233. It may be assumed that the words γινώσκω ἐμὴν εἶναι are intended to designate this territory as βασιλικὴ χώρα, or royal domain, like the lands described in an inscription found by Dr. Schliemann at Ilion (see Droysen, ibid. ii, 2, pp. 377 foll.). Respecting the citadel of Prienè (line 15) and the jealous care with which its independence was guarded by the citizens, the reader is referred to an interesting inscription published in the Journal of Hellenic Studies, iv, p. 237.

CCCCI.

On several broken blocks from one of the antæ of the Temple of Athenè Polias at Prienè: unpublished. Presented by the Society of Dilettanti, 1870. Copies of *b* (1) and *c* were made at Prienè by Mr. Newton from stones which were not sent to England : see also Mittheilungen, v, p. 340, for lines 10–13. For the measurements and position of these antæ-stones, see the Plan, p. 7.

```
            a B A Σ I Λ E ,

      ΕΔΟΞΕΤΛΙΔΗΜΠΙΓΝΩΜ
      ΛΕΥΣΛΥΣΙΜΑΧΟΣΕΝ⁻ΕΤΣ
      ΕΠΙΜΕΛΕΙΑΝΔΙΕΤΕΛΙ ΙΟΙΟΊ
  5   ΙΕΛΝΚΑΙΝΥΝΑΠΟ⁻   ΛΑΣ ᴜΥΝΑΜ
   b(1) . . . . . . .  (See Cursive Text.) . . . . . . . . . . .
        . . . . . . . . . . . . . . . . . . . . . . . . . . . . . .
        . . . . . . . . . . . . . . . . . . . . . . . . . . . . . .
        . . . . . . . . . . . . . . . . . . . . . . . . . . . . . .
  10    . . . . . . . . . . . . . . . . . . . . . . . . . . . . . .
        . . . . . . . . . . . . . . . . . . . . . . . . . . . . . .
        . . . . . . . . . . . . . . . . . . . . . . . . . . . . . .
        . . . . . . . . . . . . . . . . . . . . . . . . . . . . . .
        . . . . . . . . . . . . . . . . . . . . . . ΔΙ ᴧι        b(2)
  15    . . . . . . . . . . . . . . . . . . . . . ᴜΡΑ⁻ ΤΗ

    c  ΣΙΙΕΙ ΔΙ_ ΙΛΣΑΥ . . . . . . . . . . . . . . . .
       ΠΛΗΣΙΟΝ . . . . . . . . . . . . . . . . . . . .
       . ΑΙΔΕΚΑΙΒΩΜΟΝΑΥ . . . . . . . . . . . . . .
       ΤΟΝΕΝΙΑΥΤΟΝΤΟΥΣ . . . . . . . . . . . . . .
  20   ΤΗΜΠΟΛΙΝΚΑΙΣΤΕΦΑ ΙΗΦΟΡΕΙΝΙ ᴜ  ᴢΙ⁻ᴄ.ᴧιᴧᴢΑΠΑΡ
       ΚΑΙΠΟΜΙⁿΗι , ᴄᴧᴩᴄ   ΥΣΤΕΙΡΦΙΣΚΑΙΤΑΣΣΥΝΑΡΧ
       ΚΑΙΤΟΥΣΡΟΛΙΤΑΣΓΙ . . . . . . . . . . . . . . .
       ΛΥΣΙΜΑΧΟΥΣΥΝΕΙΝ . . . . . . . . . . . . . . .
       ΝΑΙΔΕΤΟᴧΕΓⁿΙΤΗΣΔ . Ο  (these last eight letters are very faint)
  25   ΙΕΡΟΠΟΙΟΙΣΤΟΜΦΥᴧ . . . . . . . . . . . . . ᴧΝΑ  d
       ΘΗΝΑΙΟΙΣΔΙΔΟΤΑΙ . . . . . . . . . . . . . . ᴧΝΔ
```

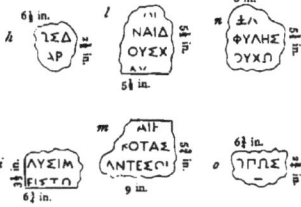

f . . . . ⌣ . . . . TON
. . . . ΙΕΡΟΣΞΞΕ
. . . . ΛΝΜΕ . Δ
. . . . ΑΣΙΛΕ ΑΓΟ
. . . . ΤΕΜ . . Η

a   Βασιλεῖ [Λυσιμάχῳ.]

Ἔδοξε τῷ δήμῳ· γνώμ[η στρατηγῶν ? ·] Ἐπειδὴ ὁ βασιλεὺς Λυσίμαχος ἔν τε το[ῖς πρότερον χρόνοις ἀεὶ
ἐπιμέλειαν διετέλ[ει] ποιού[μενος τοῦ δήμου τοῦ Πριη-
5   νέων, καὶ νῦν ἀποσ[τεί]λας δύναμ[ιν πρὸς τοὺς Μάγν-
b (1)   ητας ?] καὶ τοὺς ἄλλους πεδιεῖς κατὰ γῆ[ν διέσωσε
τὴν] πόλιν· δεδόχθαι τῷ δήμῳ ἑλέσθαι πρεσβ[ευτὰς
ἐκ πά]ντων τῶμ πολιτῶν ἄνδρας δέκα οἵτινες ἀφικόμ-
ενοι] πρὸς αὐτὸν τό τε ψήφισμα ἀποδώσουσι καὶ συνησ-
10   θ]ήσονται τῷ βασιλεῖ ὅτι αὐτός τε ἔρρωται καὶ ἡ δύναμις καὶ τὰ λοιπὰ πράσσει κατὰ γνώμην, καὶ ἐμφανιοῦσι
τὴν εὔ]νοιαν ἣν ἔχων διατελεῖ ὁ δῆμος πρὸς τὸν βασιλέα
Λυσ]ίμαχον καὶ στεφανήσουσιν αὐτὸν στεφά[ν]ῳ [χρυσῷ
ποιησάμενοι] ἀπὸ χρυσῶν χιλίων· στήσει δὲ [ὁ] δῆμο[ς   *b* (2)
15   τοῦ βασιλέως ?] ἄγαλμα χαλκοῦν [ἐν τῇ ἀγορᾷ ? καὶ π]αραστή-
c   σει ἐγ δε[ξ]ιᾶι αὐ[τοῦ . . . . παρα-
πλήσιον . . . . [ἱδρύσασθ-
αι δὲ καὶ βωμὸν αὐ[τοῦ καὶ θύειν . . . . . καθ᾽ ἕκαστον ἐνιαυτὸν τοὺς [ἱεροποιοὺς ?
20   τὴμ πόλιν, καὶ στεφανηφορεῖν το[ὺ]ς πολίτας ἅπαν[τας,
καὶ πομπὴν πέμπε[ιν το]ύς τε ἱερεῖς καὶ τὰς συναρχ[ίας
καὶ τοὺς πολίτας πά[ντας . . . .
Λυσιμάχου συνεῖν[αι . . . . δοῦ- ?
ναι δὲ τὸν ἐπὶ τῆς δ[ι]ο[ικήσεως ? . . . . τοῖς
25   ἱεροποιοῖς τὴμ φύλ[αρχον ? . . . . Π]ανα-
θηναίοις δίδοται [. . . . . Παναθη]να-   *d*
e   ι . . . . πά]ντων τῶν πολιτῶν
. . . . τὰ] ἱερεῖα κατ᾽ ἐνιαυτ[ὸν
. . . . συντελῇ τὴν θυσίαν
30   . . . . ἐν τῇ χώρᾳ κατὰ
. . . . βωμὸν ἱδρύσα]σθαι καὶ θύειμ βα-
f   σιλ . .] . . . . τον
. . . . μ]έρος ἐξε-
λὰν ?] . . . . αν με[τ]ὰ
35   . . . . β]ασιλέα πο-
. . . . τε μ[έρ]η ?

A decree of the people of Prienè, ordaining divine honours to king Lysimachos.

It is pieced together out of a number of fragments. Mr. Pullan had marked *b* (1) as one of the ante stones. The little fragment *b* (2) seems certainly to fit in where I have placed it. This is verified by the change of construction from the plural στεφανήσουσιν in line 13, to στήσει δὲ [ὁ] δῆμο[ς in line 14, compared with 15, 16; in lines 17 foll. the construction reverts to the infinitive. At first it seemed that the five lines of *e* or *f* must be the endings of lines 22-26 of *c*. But they will not read into one another, and therefore *e*, *f* must have come in somewhat later. The stone containing *e* was marked to be sent to England, but was broken up in the transit. The other fragments, given in uncials only, cannot be placed with any certainty, although the character of the writing seems to mark them as parts of this inscription. The conclusion of the decree was inscribed on *f* (see the Plan). In line 2 στρατηγῶν is suggested by Nos. ccccxv, line 20; ccccxx, line 38; ccccxxvii *a*. By *al συναρχίαι* in line 21 is meant the whole body of magistrates: compare Aristotle, Politics, vi, 14. § 4 = 1298 A; and a good note in Foucart-Le Bas, Megara, No. 35 *a*. Observe the Ionic form *ἱρεῖτ* in line 21. The expressions in lines 7 foll. may be compared with the language of Lysimachos' reply (No. ccccii). The value of the crown in line 14 is great; but the people of Mitylenè (C. I. 2167 *d*, ii, Add. p. 1025) vote a crown to Augustus of twice this amount: *πεμφθῆναι δὲ καὶ στέφανον ἀπὸ χρυσῶν διϲχιλίων.* The *[Π]αναθηναίοιϲ* of lines 25, 26 will be the Panathenæa or festival of Athenè Polias at Prienè.

In 1854 an inscription was discovered in Samothrace by Messrs. Blau and Schlottmann (edited by them in the Monatsberichte d. Berlin. Akad., 1855, p. 623; and better restored by Sauppe, in the Jahresbericht über das Gymnasium zu Weimar, 1856, p. 15), in which divine honours are decreed to Lysimachos in return for his public services to that state. The conclusion has some expressions very similar to the present inscription: *Ἀγαθῇ τύχῃ [βασι]λίωϲ Λυσιμάχου καὶ τῆϲ πόλεω[ϲ ἐψ]ηφίσθαι τῷ δήμῳ, ὅπωϲ ἂν ἀξίαϲ [χά]ριταϲ ἀποδιδῷ ἡ πόλιϲ τοῖϲ [εὐ]εργέταιϲ, ἱδρύσασθαι βωμὸν [βα]σιλίωϲ Λυσιμάχου Εὐεργέτου [ὡϲ κ]άλλιστο[ν] καὶ θύειν κατ' ἐνιαυτὸ[ν καὶ ἱερ]εύειν τοὺϲ ἐννέα ἄρχοντα[ϲ κ]αὶ στεφανηφορεῖν τοὺϲ πολίταϲ.* For the historical circumstances which are referred to in this decree, the reader is referred to the notes on the next document (No. ccccii).

CCCCII.

On the front face of several of the lower blocks from one of the antæ of the Temple of Athenè Polias, Prienè. Unpublished. Presented by the Society of Dilettanti, 1870. *d* was copied by Mr. Murray at Prienè from a stone which was not sent to England. For the measurements and arrangement of the stones, see the Plan, p. 7. For *e* see below.

a   . . . .
```
ΤΓ ΔΗΜΩΙΧΑΙΡΕΙ
ΣΕΒΕΥΤΑΙΑΝΤΙΌΙΝΕ
Κ     ΟΤΕΨΗΦΙΣΕΜ,
ΙΜΙΝΚ   ΟΙΣΥΝΗΣΘΕΝΤΕΣΕ
ΕΡΡΩΣΟΑΙΗΜΑΣΤΕΚΑΙΤΟΥΣΦΙΛ
ΔΥΝΑΜΕΙΣΚΑΙΤ.ΓΡΑΓΜΑΤΑΚΑΤΔ
ΧΩΡΑΝΔΙΕΛΕΓΗΣΑΝΓΑΡΑΓΛΥ_ΙΩΣΤΟΙΣΕΝΤΩΙ
ΣΜΑΤΙΓΕΓΡΑΜΜΕΝΟΙΣΕ ΙΦΑΝΙΧΟΝΤΕΣΓΕΡΙ
ΓΕΥΝΟΙ, ΗΣΕΧΕΙΟ, ΜΟΣΕΙΣΗΜΑΣΚΑΙΟΤΙ
```
b
```
ΕΠΙΣΤΕΙΛΔ  ΔΙ  ΙΩΝΓΕΙΘΑΡΧΕΙΝΕΩ
ΣΤΡΑΤΗΓΟΥ  ΗΚΟΥΣΕΝΓΡΟΘΥΜΩΣΚΑΙΟ
ΑΦΙΣΤΑΤΑΙΤΩΝΗΜΙΝΧΡΗΣΙΜΩΝΚΑΙΓ·
ΜΕΝΗΣΤΗΣ ΘΡΑΣΥΓΟΤΕΜΑΓΝΗΤΩ
ΛΙΤΓΝΤΤ  ΤΩΝΤΩΝΣΥΝΕΓΙΓΟΡ
```
c
```
ΘΑΝΤΩΝΚΑΙΙΔΙΙ
ΕΛΕΣΔΕΗΜΙΝ
ΡΚΑΙΓΡΟΤΕΡΟ
ΣΓΕΡΗΞΕΙΝ
```

d 'Large characters on stone from antæ': copied by Mr. Murray at Prienè.
```
ΗΜΙΝ
ΤΗΙΤΕΟ . ΩΡ
ΥΜΑΣΓΟΙΟΥΜ
ΕΥΧΑΡΙΣΤΟΥΣ
ΑΤΡΟΣΚΑΙΥΛ
ΩΓΩΝΒΑΣ
ΑΜΕΝΑ
ΗΜ  Σ
```

e   ΡΚΛ   The lettering of *e* proves it to be part of the same. It is
      ΝΚΑΙΓ   broken on all sides, and its position is uncertain. It measures
                 6 in. by 4½ in.

a [Βασιλεὺϲ Λυσίμαχοϲ Πριηνέων τῇ βουλῇ] καὶ τῷ δήμῳ χαίρει[ν· οἱ παρ' ὑμῶν πρὸϲ ἡμᾶϲ πρ]εσβευταὶ Ἀντισθένη[ϲ καὶ οἱ μετ' αὐτοῦ ἀφι]κ[όμενοι τ]ό τε ψήφισμα [ἀπέδοσαν ἡμῖν, κ[αὶ αὐτ]οὶ συνησθέντεϲ ἐ[πὶ τῷ

ἐρρῶσθαι ἡμᾶϲ τε καὶ τοὺϲ φίλ[ουϲ καὶ τὰϲ δυνάμειϲ καὶ τὰ πράγματα κατὰ [πᾶσαν τὴν χώραν διελέγησαν παραπλησίωϲ τοῖϲ ἐν τῷ ψηφί]σματι γεγραμμένοιϲ ἐμφανίζοντεϲ περί τε τῆ]ϲ εὐνοία[ϲ] ἧϲ ἔχει ὁ δ[ῆ]μοϲ εἰϲ ἡμᾶϲ καὶ ὅτι

b ἐπιστειλά[ντ]ω[ν ἡ]μῶν πειθαρχεῖν Σω . . . . [τοῦ
στρατηγοῦ [ὑπ]ήκουσεν προθύμως καὶ ο[ὐδαμῶς
ἀφίσταται τῶν ἡμῖν χρησίμων καίπ[ερ πορθου- ?
μένης τῆς [χ]ώρας ὑπό τε Μαγνήτω[ν αὐτῶν
13 κ]αὶ τῶν στ[ρατιω]τῶν τῶν συνεπιπορ[ευομένων
c . . . . καὶ κοινῇ] πάντων καὶ ἰδίᾳ
καθ᾽ ἕκαστον ? . . ἐπιμ- or λυσιτ]ελὲς δὲ ἡμῖν
φαίνεται ? . . . . ὥσπε]ρ καὶ πρότερο[ν
. . . . ὥ]σπερ ἠξίω[σαν

20 [οἱ παρ᾽ ὑμῶν πρεσβευταί ? κ.τ.λ.]
d . . . . ἡμῖν . . . .
. . . . τῇ τε θ[ε]ωρ[ίᾳ ? . . . .
. . . . ὑμᾶς ποιουμ . . . .
. . . . εὐχαρίστους . . . .
25 . . . . . . θυγ]ατρὸς καὶ ὑω[ν . . . .
. . . . . . φιλανθρ]ώπων βασ[ιλε . . . .
. . . . αμενα . . . .
. . . . ημ . . . .

This is the letter of Lysimachos in reply to the preceding decree, No. cccci, the language of which it closely follows. The two blocks *a* and *b* read into one another. The fragment *c* doubtless belongs to this document; but the sequence of *b* and *c* is conjectural. The fragment *e* also seems, from the style of the letters, to have belonged to this document. The fragment *d* also probably belongs to this same inscription, although its position is uncertain. As however both *c* and *d* appear to be uninscribed on the return face, they must have belonged to the lowest courses (see Plan, p. 7).

I have attempted in the Introduction (*ante*, p. 4) to indicate the occasions on which Lysimachos interfered in the disputes between Samos and Prienè; and I have there suggested that the honours decreed to him by the Prienians (No. cccci) may have been dictated in part by gratitude for his favourable decision. But the reason assigned by the Prienians in their decree is, that he has interposed with an armed force to prevent the Prienian territory being ravaged by 'the Magnesians and the soldiers campaigning with them' (Nos. cccci, line 5; cccci, lines 13-15). It is obvious that the Magnesia here referred to is Magnesia on the Mæander, and the πεδιεῖς of No. cccci, line 6, are the inhabitants of the valley of the Mæander, which was bounded on the North by Mount Mykalè and on the South by Mount Latmos, and is about six miles wide (τὸ Μαιάνδρου πεδίον, Herod. i, 161; Thucydides, iii, 19; compare Strabo, xii, p. 577; and No. cccx *post*, where these incursions are again mentioned). There is only one period in the reign of Lysimachos, into which these events will naturally fit. Lysimachos reached the zenith of his power about 287-286 B.C. (Droysen, Hellenismus, ii, 2, pp. 312 foll.); and from that time there began between him and Seleukos Nikator a rivalry which deepened into avowed hostility, until Lysimachos met his death in battle against Seleukos at Koroupedion B.C. 281. In 286 B.C. Lysimachos had possession of a large number of the Greek cities of Asia Minor, and it is difficult to determine what was the boundary between his realm and that of Seleukos. Prienè had all along maintained an independent position, perhaps making use of Gaulish mercenaries for that purpose (Droysen, ibid. iii, 1, p. 261). The city was exempt from tribute since the time of Alexander (No. cccc), and mistress of its own citadel (see the decree of the Prienians in honour of a φρούραρχος published by me in the Journal of Hellenic Studies, iv, p. 237). But although so far independent, Prienè was obliged, as we see, to place herself under the protection of Lysimachos. Coins of Lysimachos struck at Magnesia prove that town also to have belonged to his realm (Rayet, Milet et le Golfe Latmique, i. p. 168), and it is of course possible that the incursions mentioned in our documents had no political signification. But we may conjecture that Magnesia up to this time formed part of the Syrian dominions, and that the soldiers who helped the Magnesians in their raid upon Prienè belonged to the army of Seleukos. Nos. cccci and cccci would therefore be assigned to the last five years of Lysimachos' life. We may perhaps identify Σω . . . . , the general of Lysimachos named in No. cccci, line 11, with the Sosthenes who in B.C. 279 saved Macedon from the Gauls. He probably marched inland from Ephesos (κατὰ γῆ[ν], line 6 of No. cccci).

If *d* really formed part of this document, it seems as if in line 25 there is a reference to Arsinoè the daughter of Lysimachos, whom in 285 B.C. he married to Ptolemy Philadelphos. The 'sons' (ὑῶν, ibid.) would be the sons of Lysimachos by his last wife Arsinoè, daughter of Ptolemy Soter, sister (and afterwards wife) of Ptolemy Philadelphos.

CCCCIII.

Inscribed upon the right hand return of one of the antæ of the Temple of Athenè Polias, Prienè. For the measurements and position of the blocks see Plan, p. 7. Presented by the Society of Dilettanti, 1870. Only the following portions are published, viz. :—
a, by Waddington-Le Bas, Part 3, 205; *e*, ibid. 189; C. I. 2905 E; Mittheilungen 1880, p. 339; *t*(1) and *r*(2), by Waddington-Le Bas, ibid. 190, 191; *r*(1), C. I. 2905A; *u*(1) and *u*(2), by Waddington-Le Bas, ibid. 192; *u*(1), C. I. 2905 B; *y*, C. I. 2905 C; Waddington-Le Bas, ibid. 193; *z*, C. I. 2905 D; Waddington-Le Bas, ibid. 194.

a   ΓΡΙΗΝΕ.ι   ΑΜΙΩΝ
ΕΥΦΑΝΙΣΚΟΣΚΑΛ/ΞΕιΝΟΥΚΑΘΥΟΕ
ΣΙΑΝΔΕΝΙΚΑΣΙΔΑΜΟΥΑΓΗΣΑΝΔΡΟ
ΞΥΔΑΜΟΥΤΙΜΑΓΟΡΑΣΠΟΛΓΜΑΚΛΕΥΣ
ΛΟΣΤΡΑΤΟΣΤΕΙΣΥ   ΝΔΡΟΣΓι

ΤΩΝΥΜΟΥΑΙΡΕΘΕΛ   ΥΔΑ

b ΤΟΥΡΟΔιΩ   ∠ѧΩΡι

  ᴀϡΑι   ϋιΓΟΤΙΓΡΙΑΝΓ

      ϡѕѧλιΤϋΥϕϼϋΥΡΙΟΥΟΚΑΛΕιɴⱭιᴀ

10   ϼΙΟΡΥΓΕΡΟιΑΜϕΙΣΒΑΤΟΥΝΤΙΣΑΜΙΟΙΚΑΙΓΡΙΑΝΕιᴢ

    ΑΞΙΩΘΕΝΤϹ ϛΤΟΥΔΑΜΟΥΥΓΟΣΑΜΙΩΝΚΑΙΓΡΙΑΝΕ

    ΩΝΑΝΔΡΑΣΛΓΟΔΕΙΞΑΙΟΙΤΙΝΕΣΚΡΙΝΟΥΝΤΙΚΑΙΟΡΙ

    ΞΟΥΝΤΙΚΑΙΛΓΟΦΑΝΟΥΝΤΑΙΗΣΥΛΑΥΣΟΥΝΤΙΔΙΚΑΙΟΛΟ

    ϛΙΙϛ   ΝΤΩΝΑΙΡΕΘΕΝΤΩΝΥΓΟΜΕΝΣΑΜΙΩΝ

c . . . .

. . . .

15   . . . . ∠ѧѧ   ι   *c* (2)

   (1)   ΩΙΩΙϋ∠   ιΓΟΛιΟΔΩΡΟΥ

       ΥΓΟ⁻Γ   ιΙΔΩΡΟΥΚΑΛΛΙ

d ΚΡΑΤΕΥΣΤΟΥΑΓΟΛΛΩΝΙΟΥΓΑΡΡΑΣΙΟΥΤΟΥΓΑΡΡΑΣιυι

   ΜΗΤΡΟΔΡΟΥΤΟΥΑΡΙΣΤΟΔΗΜΟΥΑΛΚΙΣΟΕΝΕΥΣΤΟυ

20 ΑΝΥΤΟΥ ΚΑΙΔΙΑΚΟΥΣΑΝΤΕΣΑΥΤΩΝΕΝΤΕΡΟΔΩΙΕΝ

   ΤΟιΙΕΡΩιΤΟΥΔΙΟΝΥΣΟΥΚΑΙΕΓΙΤΑΣΧΩΡΑΣΤΑΣΑΜϕΙΣΒι

     ΝΑΣΕΦΑΝΕΓΑΓΑΓΟΝΑΜΕΕΚΑΤΕΡΟΙΚΑΙΕΓΙΤΟΥ

     ΟΥΟΚΑΛΕΙΤΑΙΚΑΡΙΟΝΚΑΙΕΝΕΘΕΣΩΙΕΝΤΩΙΙΕΡΩΙ

        ΔΟΣΕΓΟ   ιΓΡΙΣΙΝΚΑΤΑΤΑΥϕ

25   ΟΡΑΜΕ   ιΑΜΕΝΕΙΝ ?

e Supplied from a copy made by Mr. Newton from the stone, which was not brought from
Priene : see Cursive Text. The left return face contained No. cccc *f*.

f Supplied imperfectly by conjecture : see Cursive Text.

g (1) Supplied by a copy made by Mr. A. S. Murray from the stone, which was not brought
from Priene. The left return face contained No. cccc *b* (1).

g (2)   ΤΟΥ∠∠

   ΓΡΙΑι   ΣΜΕΤΑΜΕλιι   Inscribed on the return of cccc *b* (2).

   ΜΙΑΝΕ   ϛΤΑΣΙΟΣΔΕΓΓ

h (1) ι   Inscribed on the return of No. cccc *c*.

   ΓϹ

50 *h* (2) ΤΟΥ

     ΣΙΟΥΣ   Inscribed on the return of No. cccc *d*.

     ΝΟΣΚ

i (1) Supplied from a copy made by   *i* (2)   ΔΕΙΚι

     Mr. Murray from the return   ΧΩΡΙΣι

     of No. cccc *e* : see Cur-   55   ΑΥΤΟΙΣΕ

     sive Text.   ΣΘΑΙΑΥΤι

                            ΣΑΥΤΟΙΣΘι

                            ΟΝΥΓΕΡΑΥ

                            ΔΕΚΟΛΟϕΩΝΙΣ

60 *k* ΑΝΑΙΑ

   ΥΓΕΡ⁻

   ΕΝΕϕ   --

   ΒΑΛΛ   ϕΛΣ

   ΤΟΥΤΟΤϼΙΣ ?

65 *l*   ΕΤΑΛΑΘΗΝΑΓΟΡΑΝΣΥΜϕΥΓΕΙΝΕΙΣΤΟΚ   ϽΝϕΡΟΥΡΑΡΧΟΥΝ

   ΟΣΤΩΝΓΟΛΙΤΑΝΚΑΙΤΟΝΤΕϕϼΟΥΡΑΓ   ιΚΑΙΤΟΥΣϕΥΛΑ

   ΔΙΑΤΟΛΙΡΕΙΣΘΑΙΤΑΤΟΥΤΥΡΑΝΝΟϛΓΑϼ ιϼϛΔΙΑϕΘΕΡΑΙΚΑΙ

   ϼΤΟΥΤΩΝΕΓΕΔΕΙΚΝΥΟΝΨΑϕΙΣι   ΟΑΡϹ   ΛΛΕΝΓΟΤΙ

70   ϽΥΣΥΡΟΤΩΝΓΕΡΙΤΟΝΤΥΡΑΝΝΟ   ΑΙΤΑΨΑϕΙΣΜΑιιΤΑ

   ιΛΕΝΤΑΓΟΤΑΥΤΟΥΣΚΑϕΟϞΚΑΙΡΟΝΗΣΑΝΕΚΓΕΡιι∠

   ΓΟΤΩΝΓΕΡΙΤΟΝΤΥΡΑΝΝΟϞϞΑΙΣΥΜΓΕϕ   ΓΟΤΕϛϛ

m (1) ΕΙΣΤΟΚΑΡΙΟΝΑΗΝΥΓΟΓΛΕΙΟΝΩΝΓΟΛΙΩΝΑΓϵ   *m* (2) (The endings

   ΔΕΙΚΝΥΟΝΑΔΕΚΑΙΤΟΨΑϕΙΣΜΑΟΕΓΡΑΨΑΝΓΟΤΙΤϹ   of these lines

75   ΟΔΙΩΝΕΟΝΤΕΣΕΝΤΩΙΚΑΡΙΩΙΥΓΕΡΤΟΥΚΑΤΑΓΑΓΕ   are supplied

   ΤΑΝΓΟΛΙΝΚΑΙΓΡΙΑΝΕΩΝΓΟΤΙΤΟΥΣΒΑΣΙΛ   in the cursive

   ΛΥΣΙΜΑΧΟΝΥΓΕΡΑΥΤΩΝ   ΚΑ   from a copy

   ΓΑΡΑΡΟΔΙΩΝΥΓΕΡΤΟΥΚΑΤΑϕΥ⁻Ε   made by Mr.

   ΛΟΥΓΕΡΟΓΛΩΝΔΟΣΙΟΣΚΑΙΓΟΤΙΡΟΔΙΟΥΣΥΓ   Newton from

80   ΧΡΗΜΑΤΩΝΕϕΑΣΑΝΔΕΚΑΤΑΛΥΘΕΙΣ   a stone now

                                                lost.)

```
·ΙΔΟΣΛΕΙ Ε      ΙΤΙΙΑΚΑΤΕΛ꜀ΟΥΝΤΙΣΕΚΤΟΥΚΑΡΙΟΥΕΣΤΑΜ   н(2)
·²ΟΛΙΝΕΓ⌐Σ Τ    ΝΑΦΟΡΟΥΑΥΚ꜀Ο꜀ΚΑΙΤΟΦ·ΡΟΥΡΙΟΝΕΧΕΙΝΚΑΘΑ
ΚΑΙΓΓΟΤΕΡΟ·  ²ΑΙΤ    ·꜀ΩΡΑΝΝΕΜΕΣΘΑΙΚΑΙΜΕΤΕΝΙΑΥΤΟΝ
ΕΓΙΣΤΕΦΑΝΑ       ΛΙΣΤΡΑΤΟΥΤΑΣ ΛΓΟΛΕΙΓΟΜΕΝΑΣ
ΤΩΙΤΟΓΩΙΑ        ·⌐²ΑΖΑΓ   Ο²Γ  ΜΕΡΗΤΙΝΑΔΙΕΛΟΝ
                 ⌐ΟΥΣΤΡΙΑΚΟΝΤΑΕ⌐ΤΑΚΑΙΓΑΡΕΔΕΙΚ
                 ΛΛΑⱵΛΦΙΣΜΑΤΑΥΓΑΡΧΟΝΤΑΕΝΤΩΙΙΕΡ
    ΛΛΧΟ. . ΤΡΙΑΚΟΝΤΑΚΑΙΕ⌐ΤΑΚΛΑΡΩΝΚΑΙ
                 ⌐ΤΙΑΓΟΚΑΛΛΙΣΤΡΑΤΟΥΓΕΜΓΤΟΣ
                 ΑΛΛΟΥΣΚΛΑΡΟΥΣΓΕΝΤΕ⊷ΕΦΑ
                 ΡΙΟΝΑΥΤΩΝΓΑΡΑΙΡΗΣΘΑΙΚΑ·
   (il to the     ΑΓΟΣΤΕΛΛΟΝΤΕΣΓΟΤΙΛΥ
   surface        ΦΡΟΥΡΙΟΝΑΥΤΩΝΓΑΡΑΙΡ
   is utterly      ΟΥΤΥ⌐ΑΝΝΟΥΚΑΤ
   destroyed)      ꜀ΝΑΓΟΣΤΕΙΛΑΙΓΟΤ
                  ΤΙΛΥΣΙΜΑΧΟ
/  (a broad course) and y (a narrow course) are lost : see Plan.
/(1)  ΣΑΜ꜀ΥΓΑΡΕ·     ΙΟΝΔΕΚΑΙΚΛΟ꜀ΝΙ Α. ΡΟΝ
  ΕΓΙΣΤΟΛΑΣΥΓΟΑΓΗΣΑΡΧΟΥΕΝΑΙΣΥΓΕΡΜΕΝΙ⌐ΛΙ²⌐
  ΚΑΙΤΑΣΓΕΡΙΤΟΚΑΡΙΟΝΧΩΡΑΣΟΥΘΕΙΣΑΜΦΕΣΒΑΤΕΙ
  ΤΩΝΓΡΟΔΙ꜀ΩΝΕΓΚΑΛΟΥΝΤΑΣΟΤΙΧΩΡΑΣΤΕΡΛΗΘ
  ΚΑΡΙΟΝΥΓΕΡΟΥΝΥΝΔΙΑΚΡΙΝΕΣΘΛΙΟΙΔΑΕΣΑΜΙꜾ
  ΚΑΘΑ ⌐ΑΙΕΓΙΤΑΣΚΡΙΣΙΟΣΤΑΣΥΓΕΡΤΟΥΒΑΤΙΝΗΤΟΥΑΓΟ
  ΤΟΚΑΡΙΟΝΚΑΙΑΓΕΡΙΤΟΥΤΟΧ꜀ΟΡΑΑΥΤꜾΟΙΣΕΡΙ. ΛΛ
  ΧꜾΟΡΑΝΛΑΧΕΙΝΑΥΤΟΙΚΑΡΙΟΝΚΑΙΑΡΥΟΥΣΣΑΝΚΑΤΑΤΑ
  ΛΗΣΙΟΥΙΣΤΟΡΙΑΙΣΚΑΤΑΚΕΧꜾΟΡΙΣΜΕΝΑΔΙΟΤΙΛΑΧΟ     r(2)          \ⱵⱵin
  ΤΑΝΓΕΝΟΜΕΝΑΝΑΝΑΥΤΟΙΣΓΟΤΙΓΓΙΑΝΕΙΣΕΓΙΔΡΥΙΚΑΙΝΙⱵΑΣΚΡΙΣΙΝΕΧΕΙΝ       ΤΑ  ꜾΝΘΗΚΑΙΣ
  ΑΥΤΩΝΓΕΝΕΣΘΛΙΟΡΙΣΑΣΘΛΙΓΑΡΓΟΤΑΥΤΟΥΣ꜀Ο꜀ΣΥΔΑΤΩΝΓΟΛΙΚΛΙΓΑΡ      ⌐ΦΟΥΣ ΟΥΣΜΑΡΤΥ
  ΡΟΥΝΤΑΣΑ⌐      ꜾΟΤΙΜΕΝΤΟΚΑΡΙΟΝΕΛΛΑΧΟΝΜΕΤΑΤΟΝΜΕΛΙΑΚΟΝΓΟΛ       ΔΙꜾΟΡΙΞΑΝΤΟΡΟΤΙΤΟΥΣ
  Ρ̅ꜾΒΙΑΙΝⱵ       Ꜿ꜀ΥΑΓꜾΩΝΑΤΕΚΑΙΟΛΥΜΓΙΧΟΝΚ  ΛΟΥΡΙ        ΕΦΑΣΑꜾ ΝΑΥΤΩΝΚΑΤΑ
  ꜀ΛꜾΔΕΣ꜀ΟΑΙ⌐ⱵΙΑΝꜾ    ²    Ꜿ꜀ΩΝΤΑΣΥ⌐. Τ
  ΕΞΟΥΟΡΜΟΥΜΕΝΟΥΣΚΑΤΑΤΡΕΧΕΙΝΚΑΙꜾΚΑΚΟΓΟΙΕΙΝΤΟΝΤΕΙΕ             ΤΑΤΩΙΙΕΡΩΝΙΑΙΡΕ
  ΤΑΣΧΟΝΤΑΣΕΤꜾΤΡΙΑΚΑΤΕΛΘΕΙΝΕΙΣΤΑΜΓΟΛΙΝΕΚΓΟΛΙΟΡΚΗΘΕΝΤΟΣΤΟΥΤΥΡΑΝΝΟΥΤΟΥΕΝΤ⌐Ιι
  ΜΗΚΕΤΙΓΓΟΕΣꜾΟΛΙ⌐ΓΙΑΝΕΙΣΛΛΛ   ΕΙΝΕΣΤΕΚΛΙΤΟΝΝΥΝΧΡΟΝΟΝ⌐⌐       ΟΥΣΑΥΤΩΝΤΑΣΔΕΧꜾ
  ΤΟΑΡΣΕΣΘΛΙΑ:ꜾΤΟΥΣΕΓΙΒΑΙΝΕΙΝΚΛΘΟΝΚΑΙΡΟΝΚΑΤΕΛΘΟΝΤΕΣ             ΟΔΟΚΙΜΑΖΙΑΝΓΕΡΟΙ
  ΘΛΙΓΑΝΤΑΣΣΑΜꜾΟΥΣΚΑΙΑΓΟΓΡΑΦΑΝΤΑΣΤΕΕΝΤΑΙΝΑΣꜾΙΚΑΙΤΑΣ. Ν...Γ·Ρ        ΓΕΝΕ
  ΤΟΥΣΑΜΦΙΣΒΑΣΙΑ꜀ΔΙΑΤΟΕΚΓΛΕΙΟΝΟΣΧΡΟΝΟΥΤΑΝΑΓΟΓΡΑΦΑΝΓΟΙΕΙΣΘΛΙΛΑΒΟΜ         ΝΕΙΣΕΓΕΜΒΑΙ
  ΝΕΙΝΤΑΣΧꜾΟΡΑΣΑΥΤ꜀ΟΝΟΘΕΝΛΙΟΝΤΟΔΕΙΝΑⱵΟΔꜾΟΘΘΜΕΙΝΤΟΝΕΞΑΡΧΑΣΜΕΝΙΛΙ         ΟΝΚΛΑΡΟ
  ΥΣΤΕΡΟΝΔΕΓΑΡΑΙΡΕΣΕΝΤΑΥΓΟΓΓΙΑΝΕꜾΩΝΑΜΕΣΔΕΟΕΔΡΟΥΝΤΕΣΤΟΥΣΓΡΑⱵΑΝΤΑΣΤΟΜ        ΜΕΛΙΑ
  ΚΟΝΚΑΙΤΑΝΔΙΑΙΡΕΣΙΝ⌐ΛΣΧꜾΟΡΑΣΤΟΥΣΜΕΝΑΛΛΟΥΣΓΑΝΤΑΣⱵΑΜΕΝΟΥΣΕΚΤΑΣꜾΔΙΑΙΡΕΣΙΟΣΛ...Ο
  ΦΥΓΕΛΛΑΚΑΙΓΕΡΟΝΤΑΣΤΕΣΣΕΡΑΣΜΕΝΣΑΜΙΟΥΣΟΥΛΙΑΔΗΝΚΛΙΟΛΥΜΓΙΧΟΝΚΑΙΔΟΥΓΙΝΚΛΙΕΥΑΓꜾΟΝΛΔΥΟΔΕΕΦΕΣΙΟΥΣ
  ΚΡΕꜾΟⱵΥΛΟΝΚΑΙΕΥΛΛΚΗΧΙΟΝΔΕΘΕΥΓΟΜΓΟΝΟΥΣΓΑΝΤΑΣΕΝΤΑΙΣΣΤΟΡΙΑΙΣΕΥΡΙΣΚΟΜΕΝΚΑΤΑΚΕΧꜾΡΙΚΟΤΑΣⱵΙΟΤΙΕⱵ
  ΦΥΓΕΛΑΜΟΝΟΝⱵΕΕΝΤΑΙΣΕΓΙⱵΓΕΓΡΑΜΜΕΝΑΙΣΜΑΙΑΝⱵΡΙΟΥΤΟΥΜΙΛΗΣΙΟΥΙΣΤΟΡΙΑΙΣΚΑΤΑΚΕΧꜾΡΙΣΜΕΝΟΝⱵΙΟΤΙΕΛΛΧꜾ
  ΣΑΜꜾΟΙΚΑΡΙΟΝΚΛΙΔΡΥΟΥΣΣΑΝΛΑΙΣΓΟΛΛΟΙΤΩΝΣΥΓΓΡΑⱵΕꜾΩΝΛΝΤΙΓΡΑΦΟΝΤΙⱵΑΜΕΝΟΙⱵΙ      ⌐ΙΓΡΑΦΟ⌐ΣΕΙΜΕΙΝ
/  (as ruled upon a narrow course) is lost : see Plan.
u(t)   ꜾΙΕΚΓ
  ·ΛΥΚΟΥ  ΕΣΤΙΑΓΟΜΑΚ.              u(2)          ΕΙΛΛΙΥΓΕ  ꜾΥΒΑΤΙΝΗΤꜾ
     ⌐    ꜾⱵΟΘΕΟΥΤΟΥ·                            ΔΕΚΑΤΟΣΚΛΙΑΓΟΚΗΝΟΥΤΟΥΧΡΟΝΟΥ
           ΤꜾ·   Ꜿ꜀ΝΚΑΙΤΑⱵ                      ΓΓΑΚꜾΤꜾΩΝΚΛΑΡΟΥΤΕΣΣΑΡΑΚΟΝΤΑ
           ΑΙΤΟΥΣΣΑΜꜾ                           ΕΣΒΕΙΑΝΕΓΚΑΛΟΥΝΤΑΣΕΓΙΤΟΙΣΔΙΑΙ
           ΒΑΣΙΛΣΜ⌐·                            ΑΡΟΡΦΛΣΤΟΥΣΕΚΤΟΥΚΑΡΙΟΥΟΥΚΛΜΦΕΣ
                                                ΛΛΕΝΤΙⱵΛΦΙΣΜΑΤΙΓΕΓΡΑΦΘΛΙⱵΙΟΤΙ
                                                ΙΛΥΣΙΜΑΧΟΥΚΡΙΣΙΝΓΕΓΟΝΕΙΝΛΙΔΙΑ
  . . . . . . . . . . . . .                     ꜾΟΜΕΝꜾΩΝΓΕΡΙΑΥΤΟΥΣΚΛΙΡ꜀꜀ΩΝⱵΥΣΧꜾ
           ΝΓΛΕΙΟΝꜾꜾꜾ·                          ΕΝΕΚΛΛΟΥΝΥΓΕΡꜾΔΕΚΑΡΙΟΥΟΥΘΕΝ
           ΤΟΥΣΣΑΜꜾꜾ                            ΟΥΣΤΟΝΛΛΟⱵΙΚΕΙΟΝΓΟΛΕΜΟΝΕΝ꜀ΩΙ
                                                ΤΑΥΤΟΥΣΕΓΙΣΤΑΤΑΣΙΜ꜀ΩΝΟΣΟ[ΝΧ
  .Χ                                            ΤΑΣΟΥΣΙΑΣΚΑΤΑΓΑΓΕΙΝΕΙΣΤΑΜΓΟ
                                                ꜾΤΟΝΓΕΝΟΜΕΝΟΝⱵΙΑⱵΟΧΟΝΤΑΣΒΑΣΙΛΕΙΑΣΦΙ
```

ΠΟΔΟΜΕΙΝΤΑΝΧΩΡΑΝΑΝΕΧΟΝΤΕΣΕΞΕΓΕΣΟΝΥ
ΘΟΝΤΕΣΔΕΕΙΣΤΑΝΠΟΛΙΝΝΕΜΕΣΘΑΙΤΑΝΧΩ
ΒΑΙΝΟΝΤΑΣΤΑΣΧΩΡΑΣΤΑΣΟΜΟΡΟΥΣΑΣΑΥ
ΓΠΙΤΑΣΑΝΤΙΓΟΝΟΥΒΑΣΙΛΕΙΑΣΟΘΕΝΚΑΙΑ
ΟΥΝΤΑΣΤΟΙΣΠΡΙΑΝΕΥΣΙΔΙΟΤΙΠΑΡΟΡΙΖΟΝ
ΝΣΑΙΚΑΙΑΠΟΣΤΕΙΛΑΙΠΡΕΣΒΕΙΑΝΠΟΤΙΑΝΤΙ
ΓΕΠΑΡΟΡΙΣΕΣΘΑΙΑΥΤΩΝΚΑΙΤΑΝΕΝΤΩΙ
ΓΡΑΨΑΙΠΟΤΑΥΤΟΥΣΔΙΟΤΙΚΡΙΝΕΙΕΡΙΜΕΝ
ΝΔΡΟΥΔΙΑΒΑΝΤΟΣΕΙΣΤΑΝΑΣΙΑΝΕΝΕΜΟΝ
ΤΟΥΣΠΡΕΣΒΕΥΤΑΙΣΤΟΥΣΠΑΡΑΤΩΝΣΑΜΙ
Ο   ΑΝ ΤΑΝΧΩΡΑΝΑΝΚΑΙΕΡΑΝΤ
           ΤΑΙΣΒΑΣΙΛΙΚΑΙΣΕΥΡΕ
ΧΟιιΤΟΜΒΑΣΙΑΗΥΓ   ΤΑΣΚΡΙιιΟΣ
ΑΜΟΝΕΥΟΝΤΑΣΚΑΙΓΑ ΙΝΕΠΑΝΤΙΟΧΟΥΤΟΥΒΑΣΙΛΕΩΣ
ΡΤΟΥΓΑΡΟΡΙΣΕΣΘΑΙΤΑΙΧΩΡΑΝΥΓΕΡΤΟΥΦΡΟΥΡΙΟΥΟΥΘ Ν
ΓΙΟΧΟΝΤΟΝΥΓΟΒΑΣΙΛΕΩΣΠΤΟΛΕΜΑΙΟΥΤΕΤΑΓΜΕΝΟΝ
ϽΥΟΥΘΕΝΕΙΡΗΚΟΤΑΣΚΑΙΔΙΑΤΑΣΑΛΛΑΣΑΙΤΙΑΣΤΑΣΚΑΤΑ
ΛΦΟΥΤΑΜΠΟΛΙΝΟΙΚΟΥΝΤΙΠΑΡΑΔΕΙΚΝΥΝΤΑΣΟΤΙΚΑΙΤΩΑΦΡΟΥΡΙΟΝ
ΛΝΤΑΔΙΚΑΙΑΤΑΕΙΡΗΜΕΝΑΥΓΟΡΠΡΙΑΝΕΩⁿ
ΓΟΦΡΟΥΡΙΟΝΧΩΡΑΝΕΙΜΕΙΝΠΡΙΑΝΕΩΝ

ΟΥΣΔΕΑΓΕΔΕΙΣΑΜΕΝΤΑΣΤΕΣΑΜΙΑΣΚΑΙΓΡΙΑι
ιΤΑΣΑΝΙΔΕΙΑΝΤΟΓΩΝΩΣΔΕΡΡΙΑΝΕΙΣΑΡΟΘ
ΞΝΟΝΥΓΕΡΤΑΕΡΓΑΣΙΜΑΛΕΦΟΥΚΑΙΟΡΟΝΕΠΕΚΓ
ΛΡΑΓΞΑΑΝΑΦΕΡΟΥΣΑΡΑΡΑΤΑΣΡΓΑΣΙΜΑΑΣΜΕˉ
ΡΕΚΟΛΑΨΑΜΕΝΩΣΤΕΤΑΜΕΝΥΠΟΤΟΝΑΛΟΦΟΝ
ΙΔΕΥΓΕΡΤΟΝΑΟΦΟΝΚΑΙΤΑΝΦΑΡΑΓΓΑΚΑΙΤΟΥ   ΘΕΝΤ
ΟΥΑΠΟΔΕΙΘΘΕΝΤΟΣΟΣΕΣΤΙΥΨΗΛΟΤΑΤΟΣΑΛ   ΙΟΡΟΝΕΡΕΚΟΛ
ΨΘΕΙΑΣΑΛΛΟΝΕΘΗΚΑΜΕΝΟΡΟΝΑΡΟΔΕΤΟΥΤΟΥΕΡΕΥΘΕΙΑΣΓΑΛΙ
ΕΣΤΕΤΟΝΟΡΟΝΟΝΕΘΗΚΑΜΕΝΡΑΡΑΤΑΛ ΑΡΑΓΓΑΑΡΟΔΕΤΟΥ
ΚΟΛΑΨΑΜΕΝΕΙΣΤΟΝΠΕΤΡΟΝΑΠΟΔ_ΤΟΥΤΟΥΕΝΤΩΙΡΕΤΡ
ΡΑΦΕΡΕΙΠΑΡΑΤΟΝΒΟΥΝΟΝΕΙΣΤΟΛΠΟΛΗΓΟΝΑΥΤΟΥΟΡΟΥΣΕΡΕΚΟΛι
ΙΝΤΙΒΟΥΝΟΝΤΟΝΛΑΕΡΡΟΝΕΘΗΚΑΜΕΝΡΟΝΚΑΙΑΠΟΤΟΥΤΟΥΓΑΡΑΤΟΝ
ΕΤΟΥΤΟΥ   ΤΑΝΚΑΤΕ   ΟΥΟΡΕΥΣΔΙΑΒΑΝΤΩΝΤΟΝΠ

ΔΥΟΕϴΟΙΣΙΣ̣Ι
ΥΕΦΑΣΑΝΓΕΝ ꞈ
ϽΔΙΩΝΑΡΟΣˉ ᵝ
9½ in.

	∠ Ϲ		ΗΣ			ε			ΝΙΑΓ
	ιΧΩΡ			ϽΕΙΣ			Σ			ΛΙΓΛΛΓ
	ΤΗΙΓ						ιΓΓΟ			6½ in.
2⅜ in.				5 in.			2⅜ in.			

a   Πριηνέω[ν καὶ Σ]αμίων.
Εὐφανίσκος Καλλιξείνου καθ' ὑοθ[ε-
σίαν δὲ Νικασιδάμου, 'Αγήσανδρο[ς
Εὐδάμου, Τιμαγόρας Πολεμαρκλεῦς [Νι-
5   κόστρατος Τεισύ[λλου ?...]νδρος Ἑ[κα-
τωνύμου αἱρεθέν[τες ὑπὸ το]ῦ δά[μου
ὁ τοῦ 'Ροδίω[ν ἀποφαίνεσθαι περὶ τᾶ]ς χώρα[ς ὑπὲρ
ᾶς ἀμ[φισβατοῦντι Σάμιοι ποτὶ Πριανέ]ας, ὡς ποθ-
ἀκει ? ἑαυτ]οῖς, καὶ τοῦ φρουρίου ὃ καλεῖται Κ[ά-
10   ριον ὑπὲρ οὗ ἀμφισβατοῦντι Σάμιοι καὶ Πριανεῖς,
ἀξιωθέντος τοῦ δάμου ὑπὸ Σαμίων καὶ Πριανέων ἄνδρας ἀποδεῖξαι οἵτινες κρινοῦντι καὶ ὁρί-
ξουντι καὶ ἀποφαινοῦνται ἢ συλλύσουντι δικαιολο-
γησ[αμένω]ν τῶν αἱρεθέντων ὑπὸ μὲν Σαμίων

ϲ   (Here followed about five lines upon a narrow course, containing a list of the
names of the Samian and some of the Prienian delegates: there were perhaps six
on either side.)

15 . . . . Σω . . . . . . [τοῦ
'Αγα]θίωνος, [ὑπὸ δὲ Πριανίων] 'Απολλοδώρου
d το]ῦ Ποσε[ιδωνίου. . . . . . 'Αρτεμ]ιδώρου, Καλλι-
κράτευς τοῦ 'Απολλωνίου, Παρθασίου τοῦ Παρθασίου,
Μητροδώρου τοῦ 'Αριστοδήμου, 'Αλκισθένευς τοῦ

20 'Ανύτου· καὶ διακούσαντες αὐτῶν ἔν τε 'Ρόδῳ ἐν
τῷ ἱερῷ τοῦ Διονύσου, καὶ ἐπὶ τᾶς χώρας τᾶς ἀμφισβα-
τευμέ]νας ἐφ' ἃν ἐπάγαγον ἀμὲ ἑκάτεροι, καὶ ἐπὶ τοῦ
φρουρί]ου ὃ καλεῖται Κάριον, καὶ ἐν 'Εφέσῳ ἐν τῷ ἱερῷ
τᾶς 'Αρτέμι]δος, ἐπο[ιησάμεθα τὰν] κρίσιν κατὰ τὰ ὑφ'

25 ἁμῶν ἐφε]οραμέ[να ? . . . . . . διεκρί]νομεν . . . . . . [τ-
ε ὁ φρούριον ὃ κα]λεῖται Κάριον κα[ὶ τ]ὰμ [περὶ
αὐτὸ χώ]ραν ἐπείμειν Πριανέων· τὰν δὲ ἀπόφα[σιν
δόν]τες ὑπὲρ τούτων καὶ ποιήσαντες ἀντίγραφα [θ-
ύο] ἐδώκαμεν τὸ μὲν ἐν τοῖς πρυτάνεσι τοῖς Σαμίων

30 Πρωτομάχῳ Τρίτωνος, Σιμαλίωνι Εὐφράνορος, Θεο-
μνήστῳ 'Ισοκράτευς, 'Ηγεπόλει 'Αντιπάππου, Λυσιμά-
χῳ Διονυσίου, καὶ τῷ γραμματεῖ τᾶς βουλᾶς Μενίπ-
π]ῳ Κλέωνος, ὡς μὲν 'Ρόδιοι ἄγοντι ἐπ' ἱερέως Πρατο-
f [φάνευς, μηνὸς . . . . . νος . . . . . ϙ, ὡς δὲ Σάμιοι]

35 [ἐπὶ δαμιουργοῦ τοῦ δεῖνος, μηνὸς . . . . νος]
[. . . . . ϙ, τὸ δὲ ἄλλο ἐδώκαμεν τῷ γραμματεῖ]
[τᾶς βουλᾶς τᾶς Πριανέων ? τῷ δεῖνι τοῦ δεῖνος,]
[. . . . . ἐπὶ στεφαναφόρου . . . .]
g (1) ου τοῦ Φιλοτίμου καὶ Λυκίππῳ 'Αντιόχου . . . .

40 . 'Α]πολλοδώρου, Εὐφά[νει] 'Αρτεμιδώρου, Διο . . . . . . ['Α-
π]ολλοδώρῳ Ποσειδωνίου, Σωτ . . . . [τῷ δεῖνι Φι-
λ]ώτα παμμενον (sic = 'Επαμείνονι ?) ὡς μὲν 'Ρόδιοι ἄγοντι μηνὸς
Παναμου ἐνάτᾳ . . . . . . ὡς δὲ Πριανέων ὑπο [(sic) ? = ἄγοντι μηνὸς . . .
λωνο[ς . . . . . . ϙ. "Εφασαν δὲ οἱ Σάμιοι

45 τὰν Βατ[ινατίδα ? . . . .
g (2) . . . . τοὺς δ . . . .
Πριαι[εῖ]ς μετὰ Μελιέ[ων . . . . πόλιν
μίαν ἔ[χειν], στάσιος δὲ γε[νομένης . . . .

h (1) (Here there followed over a dozen lines, inscribed upon the return
of No. cccι, c, d. But only two lines of No. cccι, c, have their ends
complete; and there only the letters ΓΟ can be recovered on the return
of line 20. These letters I give below, to make it clear.)

. πο . . . .

50 h (2) τοῦ . . . . [Μιλη- ?
σίους . . . .
νος κ . . . .
i (1) . . . . Κάριον καὶ Δρυοῦ[σσαν, καὶ ἐπε]δείκν[υον ἐν ταῖς   i (2)
Μαιανδρίου τοῦ Μιλησίου ἱστο[ρίαις κατακε]χωρισμ[ένον διότι

55 καὶ ἁ] λοιπὰ χώρα ἁ Μελιὰς [ἐπικλαρωθείη] αὐτοῖς ε . .
μετὰ τὸμ πόλεμον τὸμ Με[λιακὸν ? . . . .]σθαι αὐτὰ[ν . .
. παρὰ μὲν Μιλησίων αι[. . . . . τοῖ]ς αὐτοῖς θη[. . . Μ-
αραθήσιον καθὼ[ς . . . .]αν ὑπὲρ αὐ[τῶν . .
. . Πανιωνίοις [. . . . . παρὰ] δὲ Καλοφωνίω[ν . .

60 k 'Αναια . . . .
ὑπὲρ τ . . . .
ἐνεφ[άνισαν ? . . . . ἐπί-
βαλλ[ε· ἔ]φασ[αν δὲ . . . .
τοῦτο τοῖς . . . .

(The remaining seven or eight lines of k are lost; immediately after which
followed l.)

65 . . . . [ἐπὶ στεφαναφόρου Μακαρέως
l τοῦ μ]ετὰ 'Αθηναγόραν συμφυγεῖν εἰς τὸ Κ[άρι]ον φρουραρχοῦν-

τοῦ ἐν]ὸς τῶν πολιτᾶν καὶ τόν τε φρούραρ[χο]ν καὶ τοὺς φύλα-
κας] διὰ τὸ αἱρεῖσθαι τὰ τοῦ τυράννου πάντας διαφθε(ῖ)ραι· καὶ
ὑπὲ]ρ τούτων ἐπεδείκνυον ψάφισμ[α τ]ὸ ἀπο[στ]αλὲν ποτὶ
αὐτ]οὺς ὑπὸ τῶν περὶ τὸν τύραννο[ν, κ]αὶ τὰ ψαφίσματα τὰ
ἀποστ]αλέντα ποτ' αὐτοὺς καθ' ὃν καιρὸν ἦσαν ἐκπεπ[τω-
κότες ὑ]πὸ τῶν περὶ τὸν τύραννον καὶ συμπεφ[ευ]γότες

| εἰς τὸ Κάριον, ἃ ἦν ὑπὸ πλειόνων πολίων ἀπε[στα]λμένα· ἐπ-   м (2)
ε]δείκνυον δὲ καὶ τὸ ψάφισμα ὃ ἔγραψαν ποτὶ τὸν δᾶμον τὸν
'Ρ]οδίων ἰόντες ἐν τῷ Καρίῳ ὑπὲρ τοῦ καταγαγε[ῖ]ν αὐτοὺς εἰς
τὰν πόλιν, καὶ Πριανέων ποτὶ τοὺς βασιλ[έας Δη]μήτριόν τε καὶ
Λυσίμαχον ὑπὲρ αὐτῶν [δύο ψαφίσματα ?] καὶ] ἄλλο ψάφισμα
παρὰ 'Ροδίων ὑπὲρ τοῦ καταφυγε[ῖν το]ὺς περὶ [τὸν τ]ύραννον, καὶ ἄλλο ὑπὲρ ὅπλων ὅσσιος καὶ ποτὶ 'Ροδίους ὑπὲρ δανεισμοῦ
χρημάτων· ἔφασαν δὲ καταλυθεῖσας τὰς τυραν-

) νίδος ἃ ἐπέ[σχεν ἔτ]η τρία κατελθόντες ἐκ τοῦ Καρίου ἐς τὰμ   н (2)
πόλιν ἐπὶ στ[εφα]ναφόρου Λύκου καὶ τὸ φρούριον ἔχειν καθὰ
καὶ πρότερο[ν κ]αὶ τ[ὰν] χώραν νέμεσθαι· καὶ μετ' ἐνιαυτὸν
ἐπὶ στεφανα[φόρου Καλ]λιστράτου τὰς ἀπολειπομένας
ἐν] τῷ τόπῳ δ[ιαιροί:?ντες ?] χώρας ἀπ[οδ]όσθ[αι] μέρη τινὰ διελόν-
τες εἰς κλά]ρους τριάκοντα ἑπτά, καὶ ἀ μεδείξ[ινου . . . . . .
ἄ]λλα ψαφίσματα ὑπάρχοντα ἐν τῷ ἱερ[ῷ τᾶς 'Αθανᾶς περὶ τοῦ
λάχο[υς] τριάκοντα καὶ ἑπτὰ κλάρων· καὶ [ἐπὶ στεφαναφόρου
. . . . . ὅς ἐσ]τι ἀπὸ Καλλιστράτου πέμπτος
. . . ἀποδόσθαι] ἄλλους κλάρους πέντε.—Ἔφασαν δὲ Σάμιοι ?
. . . . . . τὸ φρού]ριον αὐτῶν παραιρῆσθαι καὶ . . . .
. . . . ἀποστέλλοντες ποτὶ Λυ[σίμαχον
. . . . τὸ] φρούριον αὐτῶν παραιρ[ῆσθαι . . . . .
. . . ἐκπολιορηθέντος ? τ]οῦ τυράννου κατ[ελθόντας . . .
. . . . ον ἀποστεῖλαι ποτ[ὶ . . . . .
. . . . πο]τὶ Λυσίμαχο[ν . . . . . .

φ   (Here followed some seventeen or eighteen lines inscribed on a broad and a
narrow course of masonry, now lost: see the Plan.)

1) Σάμιοι παρε . . . . ιον δὲ καὶ καθ' ὃν [κ]α[ι]ρὸν . . . . .
ἐπιστολὰς ὑπὸ 'Αγησάρχου ἐν αἷς ὑπὲρ μὲν ἰδίων[ικῶν ἀμφισβασιῶν ἐλέγετο, ὑπὲρ δὲ τοῦ Καρίου   r (2)
καὶ τᾶς περὶ τὸ Κάριον χώρας οὐθεὶς ἀμφεσβάτει· [νῦν δὲ τοὺς Σαμίους ἀποστεῖλαι πρὸς τὸν δᾶμον
τὸν 'Ροδίων ἐγκαλοῦντας ὅτι χώρας τε πλῆθ(ο)ς νέμοιντο Πριανεῖς παρὰ τὸ δίκα(ιον) καὶ μάλιστα τὸ
Κάριον ὑπὸ οὗ νῦν διακρίνεσθαι. Οἱ δὲ Σάμιο(ι τά τε) [τᾶν ἱστ(ο)ρι(ο)γράφω(ν) μαρτύρια ὑφαγ(ήσαντο)
καθὰ καὶ ἐπὶ τᾶς κρίσιος τᾶς ὑπὲρ τοῦ Βατινήτου ἀπὸ [τούτων π(ειρώ)μενοι (δεικνύειν διότι)
τὸ Κάριον ἀεὶ ἃ περὶ τοῦτο χώρα αὐτοῖς ἐπι(κ)λα[ρωθείη, καὶ καθ' ὃν καιρὸν διαιροῦντο τὰν τῶν Μελιέων)
χώραν λαχεῖν αὐτοὶ Κάριον καὶ Δρυοῦσσαν κατὰ τὰ [ἐν ταῖς ἐπ](ι)γραφομέναις Μαιανδρίου τοῦ Μι-)
λησίου ἱστορίαις κατακεχωρισμένα διότι λάχο[ιεν Κάριον καὶ Δρ](υοῦσσαν, μετὰ δὲ τὰν παράτ)αξιν
τὰν γενομέναν αὐτοῖς ποτὶ Πριανεῖς ἐπὶ Δρυὶ καὶ νίκας ἔχοιεν [καὶ] (ταύταν τὰν χώραν ἐν τα[ῖς σ]υνθήκαις
αὐτῶν γενέσθαι, ὁρίσασθαι γὰρ ποτ' αὐτοὺς ὡς ὑδάτιον ῥοᾷ· καὶ παρ[είχ](οντο ἱστοριογρ)άφους (τ)οὺς μαρτυ-
ροῦντας αὐ[τοῖς] ὅτι μὲν τὸ Κάριον ἔλαχον μετὰ τὸν Μελιακὸν πόλ[εμον ὅτε ?] διωρίξαντο ποτὶ τοὺς
Πριαινέ[ας . . . .] Εὐάγωνά τε καὶ 'Ολύμπιχον κ[αὶ] Δοῦρι[ν, τι, τὸ] (δὲ Κάριον) ἔφασαν [ἐὸ]ν αὐτῶν κατα-
s λαβέσθαι Πριανέ[ας τ]οὺς ἐπι]εσόντας ὑπ[ὸ] τοῦ 'Ιέρωνος τοῦ προσποιησαμένου τὰν τυραννίδα καὶ τῶν περὶ αὐτὸν
ἐξ οὗ ὁρμωμένους καταρχέμεν καὶ κακοποιεῖν τόν τε 'Ι[έρωνα καὶ τὰ ὑπάρχο]ντα τῷ 'Ιέρωνι· αἱρεῖθεν δὲ κα-
τισχύοντας ἔτη τρία κατελθεῖν εἰς τὰμ πόλιν ἐκπολιορηθέντος τοῦ τυράννου τοῦ ἐν τῷ [πόλει· τὸ δὲ
μηκέτι προίεσθαι Πριανεῖς ἀλλ' [ἔχ]ειν ἔς τε καὶ τὸν νῦν χρόνον [τοὺς ἐκγόνους αὐτῶν· τᾶς δὲ χώ[ρας
τὸ ἄρξασθαι αὐτοὺς ἐπιβαίνειν καθ' ὃν καιρὸν κατελθόντες [εἰς τὰν πόλιν ἐπόθον?] δοκιμασίαν πεποι[ῆσ-
θαι πάντας Σαμίους καὶ ἀπογραφὰν τᾶς τε ἐν τῷ νάσῳ καὶ τᾶς [ἐ]ν [τᾷ] π[ε]ιρ[αία γᾶς, ὥστε μὴ] γενέ[σθαι πωθ' αὐτοὺς ἀμφισβασίαν διὰ τὸ ἐκ πλείονος χρόνου τὰν ἀπογραφὰν ποιεῖσθαι· λαβομ[ένους δὲ Πρια]νεῖς ἐπεμβαί-
νειν τᾶς χώρας αὐτῶν, ὅθεν ᾤοντο δεῖν ἀποδοθῆμειν τὰν ἐξ ἀρχᾶς μὲν ἰδίαν αὐτῶν γενόμεν]ον κλάρο[ν
ὕστερον δὲ παραιρεθεῖσαν ὑπὸ Πριανίων ἀμὲ δὲ θεωροῦντες τοὺς γράψαντας τὸμ [πόλεμον τὸν] Μελιακὸν καὶ τὰν διαίρεσιν τᾶς χώρας τοὺς μὲν ἄλλους πάντας φαμένους ἐκ τᾶς διαιρέσιος λ[αχ]ό[ντας Σαμίους
Φύγελα, καίπερ ἐόντας τέσσαρες μὲν Σαμίους Οὐλιάδην καὶ 'Ολύμπιχον καὶ Δοῦριν καὶ Εὐάγωνα δύο δὲ 'Εφεσίους
Κρεώφυλον καὶ Εὐάλκη, Χίον δὲ Θεόπομπον, οἱ πάντες ἐν ταῖς ἱστορίαις εὑρίσκομεν κατακεχωρικότας διότι ἔλαχον [Σάμιοι
Φύγελα, μόνον δὲ ἐν ταῖς ἐπιγεγραμμέναις Μαιανδρίου τοῦ Μιλησίου ἱστορίαις κατακεχωρισμένον διότι ἔλαχον
Σάμιοι Κάριον καὶ Δρυοῦσσαν, αἷς πολλοὶ τῶν συγγραφέων ἀντιγράφοντι φάμενοι ψ[ευδέ]πιγράφους εἴμειν.

/   (Here some seven or eight lines, inscribed on a narrow course of masonry, are lost: :ce Plan.)

1) κ]αὶ ἐκπιεσεῖν μὲν Καρσὶ . . . . οσια καὶ) [. . . . . κατελθεῖν ἐπὶ στεφαναφό-]

125 (ρο)ν Λύκου (ὅτ) ἐστι ἀπὸ Μακα(ρίως τέταρτος· ποτὶ δὲ τὸν Λυσίμαχον ἀ)(ποστ)|εῖλαι ὑπὲ[ρ τ]οῦ Βατινῆτο[υ ἐπὶ στε-
(φαναφό)ρ(ου τ)οῦ θεοῦ τοῦ μ(ετὰ Νίκανδρον, ὅς ἐστι ἀπὸ Λύκου πεντε)[και]|δέκατος καὶ ἀπὸ κήνου τοῦ χρόνου
(ἐχόντων αὐτῶν καὶ) τὸ φ(ρούρ)ιον καὶ τᾶς (χώρας τᾶς περὶ τὸ φρούριον) [πε]|πρακότων ἐλάχους τετετράκοντα
(καὶ δύο, οὐκ ἀγανακτῆσ)αι τοὺς Σαμί(ους, οὐδ' ἀποστεῖλαι ποτ' αὐτοὺς π)[ρ]|εσβείαν ἐγκαλοῦντας ἐπὶ τοῖς διφ-
(εημένοις, ἀλλ' ἀμφισ)βασίας μὲ(ν ποθ' αὑτοὺς ἰδιωτικὰς γεγονείαν) [π]|αρορίας τοὺς ἐκ τοῦ Καρίου,— οὐκ ἀμφισ-
130 (βατήκειν τοὺς Σαμίους, ἀλλὰ τοὐνάντιον ἐν τῷ ποτὶ Λυσίμαχον ἀ)(ποστ)|αλέντι ψαφίσματι γεγράφθαι διότι
(Πριανεῖς ἔχοντι τὰν αὐτῶν χώραν· μετὰ δὲ τὰν ἀναφερομέναν) [ἐπ]|ὶ Λυσίμαχον κρίσιν γεγονείν δια-
(γενομένων ἐτῶ)ν πλειόνων, (βασιλεύοντος Ἀντιόχου τοῦ Ἀντιόχου), [γε]|νομένων περὶ αὐτοὺς καιρῶν δυσχε-
(ρῶν), πέμψαι ποτ' αὐ)τοὺς Σαμίο(υς [πρέσβεις λέγοντας ὅτι] ἐν παρορίᾳ) | ἐνεκάλουν ὑπὲρ δὲ Καρίου οὐθὲν
εἰρηκότας] . . . . (θα περὶ) [αὐτ]|οὺς τὸν Λαοδίκειον πόλεμον ἐν ᾧ
135 . . . . (τ) . . . . [πο]|ἰ' αὐτοὺς ἐπὶ στασίμων ὅσο[ν χ-
x ρόνον] . . . . τὰς οὐσίας καταγαγεῖν εἰς τὰμ πό[λιν
. . . . ποτ]ὶ τὸν γευόμενον διάδοχον τᾶς βασιλείας Φίλιππον? . . . . ἀ]ποδόμειν τὰν χώραν ἂν ἔχοντες ἐξέκισον ὑ-
πὸ τῶν περὶ τὸν τύραννον? . . . . κατελ]θόντες δὲ εἰς τὰν πόλιν νέμεσθαι τὰν χώ-
140 ραν . . . . παρα]βαίνοντας τὰς χώρας τὰς ὁμόρους δι αὐτῷ . . . . ἐ]πὶ τᾶς Ἀντιγόνου βασιλείας ὅθεν καὶ α-
. . . . ἀμφισβατ]οῦντας τοῖς Πριανεῦσι διότι παρορίζον-
ται . . . . ἀγανακτ]ῆσαι καὶ ἀποστεῖλαι πρεσβείαν ποτὶ Ἀντίγονον? . . . .]ε παρορίζεσθαι αὐτῶν καὶ τὰν ἐν τῷ
145 . . . . γράψαι ποτ' αὐτοὺς διότι κρίνει ἐπιμεῖν-
ειν . . . . Ἀλεξά]νδρου διαβάντος εἰς ταν Ἀσίαν ἐπιμον-
το . . . . τοὺς πρεσβεύτα(ι)ς τοὺς παρὰ τᾶν Σαμίων . . . .]ο . . [αὐτ]ὰν τὰν χώραν ἂν καὶ ἐπ' Ἀντιγόνου . . . . ἐν ταῖς ἐπιστολαῖς ταῖς βασιλικαῖς εὑρέ-
150 y θέντα? . . . . Λυσίμα]χον τὰμ βασιλῆ ὑπ[ὲρ] τᾶς κρίσιος
. . . . ἀπομν]αμονεύοντας καὶ πά[λ]ιν ἐπ' Ἀντιόχου τοῦ βασιλέως
. . . . ὑπὲ]ρ τοῦ παρορίζεσθαι τὰν χώραν ὑπὲρ τοῦ φρουρίου οὐθ[ὲ]ν
εἰρηκότας . . . . Ἀν?]τίοχον τὸν ὑπὸ βασιλέως Πτολεμαίου τεταγμένον
. . . . ὑπὲρ τοῦ φρουρί]ου οὐθὲν εἰρηκότας καὶ διὰ τὰς ἄλλας αἰτίας τὰς κατα-
155 κεχωρισμένας . . . .]ἀφ' οὗ τὰμ πόλιν οἰκοῦντι παραδείκνυνται ὅτι καὶ τὸ φρούριον
καὶ ἁ περὶ τὸ φρούριον χώρα . . . . π]άντα δίκαια τὰ εἰρημένα ὑπὸ Πριανέων (καὶ κατακεχωρισμένα . . . κρίνομεν τὸ φρούριον καὶ τὰν περὶ] τὸ φρούριον χώραν εἶμεν Πριανέων.

x(1) Ὅρους δὲ ἀπεδείξαμεν τᾶς τε Σαμίας καὶ Πριαν[ίδος χώρας, ἀρχόμενοι, ὡς μ]ὲν Σ[άμιοι ποτ']αγορεύοντι, ἀπὸ τῶν
κατὰ Σανιδείαν τόπων, ὡς δὲ Πριανεῖς ἀπὸ Θ[ινίχου πάγου, τὸν δὲ πρᾶτ]ον λόφον [τὸ]ν πετρώδη τὸν ὑπερκεί-
160 μενον ὑπὲρ τὰ ἐργάσιμα, ἐφ' οὗ καὶ ὅρον ἐπεκε[λάψαμεν, ἐφ' ὃν ἀνα]τείνει ἁ ἐκ τοῦ παραπειμένου ποταμοῦ
φάραγξ ἁ ἀναφέρουσα παρὰ τὰ ἐργάσιμα ἃς με[ταξὺ καὶ τοῦ προγεγ]αμμένου λόφου ἄλλον ὅρον ἐπὶ πέτρας
ἐπεκολάψαμεν, ὥστε τὰ μὲν ὑπὸ τὸν λόφον [καὶ τὰμ φάραγγα καὶ] τοὺς ἐπικολαφθέντας ὅρους εἶμεν Σαμίων,
τ]ὰ δὲ ὑπὲρ τὸν λόφον καὶ τὰν φάραγγα καὶ τοὺ[ς ἐπικολαφ]θέντας ὅρου[ς εἶμεν Πριανέων. Ἀπὸ δὲ τοῦ λόφου τοῦ
πράτο]υ· ἀποδειχθέντος ὅς ἐστι ὑψηλότατος ἐλ[λο]ν ὅρον ἐπεκολ[άψαμεν ἐ]ν τῷ καταλήγοντι τοῦ λόφου· ἀπὸ δὲ τούτου
165 ἐπ' ε]ὐθείας ἄλλον ἐθήκαμεν ὅρον· ἀπὸ δὲ τούτου ἐπ' εὐθείας [ἀλ]ν ἐθήκαμ[εν ὅρον· ἀπὸ δὲ τούτου ἐπ' εὐθεία[ς] ἁ [φάραγξ
ὁρίζ[ει] ἔστε τὸν ὅρον ὃν ἐθήκαμεν παρὰ τὰν [φ]άδραγγα· ἀπὸ δὲ τού[του καὶ αἰναίνουσι ποτὶ τὰν πετρῶν[α ἄλλον] ὅρον
ἐπε]κολάψαμεν εἰς τὸν πετρῶνα· ἀπὸ δὲ τούτου ἐν τῷ πετρ[ῶνι ἄλλον] ὅρον ἐπεκολάψαμε[ν· ἀπὸ] δὲ τούτου δὲ
πα]ραβρέντι παρὰ τὸν βουνὸν εἰς τὸ ἀπάλογον αὐτοῦ ὅρους ἐπεκολά[ψαμεν· ἀπ]ὸ δὲ τὰν ἐγκολαπτ[ὸν ὅρων ε]ἰς τὸν ἀπέναντι βουνὸν τὸν λειπὸν ἐθήκαμεν ὅρον· καὶ ἀπὸ τούτου παρὰ τὸν [βουνὸν ἔστε] καὶ τὰν φάραγγα ἐ[θήκαμεν ἄλλο]ν ὅρον· ἁ
170 δὲ τούτου [παρ' αὐ]τὰν κατέ[ναντι τ]οῦ ὄρεος διαβάντων τὸν π[οταμὸν ἄλλον ἐ]θήκαμεν [ὅρον· ἀπὸ δὲ τούτου ἀποσ]τρεψάν-
των . . . . .]

Fragments of uncertain position:

αα . . . δύο ἐν οἷς . .   ββ . . . τὰ]ν χώρ[αν . .
. . ου ἴφασαν γεν[έσθαι   . . . . τῃ . .
. . Ῥοδίων ἀποστ[αλ . . .

This is the award made by Rhodes concerning the disputed lands Karion and Dryussa, and is in favour of Priene. For an account of this document see the Introduction; the arrangement of the various portions is shewn by the Plan, p. 7. I add here a few notes.

The fragment *i* (2) is in the Museum, and appears to read into *i* (1), as given in the cursive. *r* (1) is in the Museum; the endings of lines 99, 100, are merely an improvement of the conjectures of Böckh

and Waddington, but may be trusted to give the sense fairly enough. The endings of lines 101–109 are from a copy made by Le Bas from a stone afterwards broken up, of which a small fragment is now in the Museum, namely the underlined portion of *r* (2). The portions here given from Le Bas' copy only are indicated by being enclosed within curved brackets ( ). Lines 102, 111, πειρούμενοι, ὁρμουμένους : of this Doricism other examples are found; see C. I. 2525 c, line 10, τιμοῦντες, and C. I. 5491, line 16, τιμεῖν. In line 108 I dissent from Le Bas, his reading being contradicted by the extant portion of the marble. Πριαινε[ῖ̈, line 109, must be a blunder for Πριανε[ῖ̈. Lines 110, 111. The Hieron here mentioned is probably the tyrant whom Pausanias, vii, 2, § 7, speaks of as having endangered the very existence of Prienè at some unspecified date. Line 113, τὸ δὲ (sc. Κάριον) μηκέτι προίεσθαι. 'The Prienians' (say the Samians) 'no longer permitted the Samians to retain possession as before, but even seized now the land round it as well (τὰς δὲ χώρας).' In line 114, if τὸ is the article, it is used pleonastically. The place named Φύγελα in line 120, was a little town upon the coast more often called Πύγελα. The right-hand portion of the slab, u (2), is in the Museum. The left-hand portion, u (1), is given from the copy of Le Bas: the stone was marked to be sent to England, but was broken up in its transit to Smyrna. The few fragments of u (1) which reached the Museum are given in the uncial text, and are underlined in the cursive. In lines 125 foll., [ἐπὶ στε]φαναφόρου τοῦ θεοῦ τοῦ μετὰ Νίκανδρον is an interesting phrase. The divinity meant would be Apollo; compare Waddington-Le Bas, Part v, Nos. 252–299 (Iasos), which are headed ἐπὶ στεφανηφόρου Ἀπόλλωνος τοῦ μετὰ τὸν δεῖνα, or ἐπὶ στ. Ἀ. τοῦ τετάρτου μετὰ τὸν δεῖνα, and so on ; C. I. 2677, 2855. Similarly in C. I. 189, Πολιὰς Ἀθηνᾶ stands first in a list of πρυτάνεις. These examples explain the statement of Livy xxxii, 25: mos erat comitiorum die primo, velut ominis causa praetores pronuntiare Jovem Apollinemque et Herculem. In several decrees, Nos. ccccxv–ccccxvi, post, an eponymous hero is named as στεφανήφορος. Line 135, ΝΧ are from an impression made before the stone left Prienè ; it suffered some injury in its conveyance to England. ΕΠΙΣΤΑΤΑΣΙ seems a lapidary's blunder for ΕΠΙΣΤΑΣΙ : see also ΔΙΑΦΘΕΡΑΙ, line 68 ; ΠΡΕΣΒΕΥΤΑΙΣ, line 147. In line 134 the Prienian case is brought down to the most recent event, viz. the 'war about Laodikè' (see Introduction). Then the argument harks back to the exile and restoration, and refers to the reign of Antigonos Monophthalmos B.c. 306–301. The phrase ἐπὶ στασίμων must mean 'without disturbance,' 'in statu quo,' or the like. x, y. The general tenour of these lines is not hard to follow, although one half is gone. It is better however not to fill up the blank with mere conjectures. z. In several places the stone has been broken and injured since the copy given by Böckh (C. I. 2905) was made. The restorations are chiefly therefore from him. As to the historians referred to in lines 109, 120, 121, see ante p. 4.

Thucydides (iii, 19) records how, during the Peloponnesian War (B.c. 428), the Athenian commander Lysikles, who had been sent out to gather arrears of tribute, landed at Myus in the gulf of Latmos. Thence he attempted to cross the valley of the Maeander northward and advanced μέχρι τοῦ Σανδίου λόφου, where the Karians and the Samian exiles (oligarchs) from Anaea attacked him from their vantage ground on the hill, and killed Lysikles and many of his expedition. We may, with Waddington, identify ὁ Σάνδιος λόφος with οἱ κατὰ Σανιδίαν τόποι of the inscription (line 159). On its situation see Rayet, Le Golfe Latmique, i, p. 27. The Prienians called this height ὁ Οἴνιχος λόφος : is it fanciful to conclude that the exiled historian got his information from the oligarchical Samians who had been at Anaea ?

CCCCIV.

A wall-stone of blue marble, of which the bottom and right edge are entire, and the top edge is preserved just enough to give us the height, viz. 20 in.; the present length is 22 in.; from the temple of Athenè Polias, Prienè. Published C. I. 2905 G ; Waddington-Le Bas, Part v, No. 199; presented by the Society of Dilettanti, 1870.

```
                    _ΤΙΝΚΑΙΡΕϜ
                  ͺϜΑΘΟΙΚΑΙΦΙΛΟΙϜΑ
                 ͺΝΤΕΑΝΕΝΕΩΣΑΝΤͺ
                ϽΕΝΑΙΕΙΣΕΚΕΙΗΝΤΗΝΧΩΡΑΝΙͺ
       5        ͺΖΣΙΝΚΑΙΟΣΑΚΡΙΤΗΡΙΑΚ▣ΑΚΡΙΜΕΝΑΕΙΣ
                ΞΩΘΗΚΑΙΦΙΛΑΝΘΡΩΡΩΣΤΕΑΥΤΟΙΣΑΡϽΚΡΙ
                ΣΑΥΤΑΕΤΗΚΑΤΕΧΕΙΝΕΚΕΙΝΗΣΤΗΣΧΩΡΑΣ
             ͺΙ ΡΙΚΑΣΙΝΟΥΤΩΣΔΟΚΕΙΔΕΙΝΕΙΝΑΙΕΙΔΕΤΙΕΣΤΙΝ
                ͺΟΝΟΥΕΣΤΙΝΟΥΤΩΦΑΙΝΕΤΑΙΔΕΙΝΕΙΝΑΙΞΕΝΙΑΤΕΑΥΤ
      10        ΜΩΝΣΗΣΤΕΡΤΙΟΝΕΚΑΤΟΝΕΙΚΟΣΙΠΕΝΤΕΚΑΘΕΚΑΣΤΗΝ
```

. . . . ἔ]στιν καὶ περ[ὶ ὧν οἱ
ἀφικόμενοι παρὰ Πριηνέων πρεσβευταὶ ἄνδρες καλοὶ καὶ ἀ]γαθοὶ καὶ φίλοι πα[ρὰ δήμου
καλοῦ καὶ ἀγαθοῦ καὶ φίλου λόγους ἐποιήσαντο συμμαχία]ν τε ἀνενεώσαντο
. . . . ἐληλυ]θέναι εἰς ἐκείνην τὴν χώραν . . . .
5   . . . . ωσιν καὶ ὅσα κριτήρια κεκριμένα εἰς
. . . . ἀνεν]εώθη καὶ φιλανθρώπως τε αὐτοῖς ἀποκρίνασθαι . . . . το]σαῦτα ἔτη κατέχειν ἐκείνης τῆς χώρας
. . . . κ]ε[κ]ρίκασιν, οὕτως δοκεῖ δεῖν εἶναι · εἰ δέ τί ἐστιν
. . . . ονου ἐστίν, οὕτω φαίνεται δεῖν εἶναι· ξένιά τε αὐτ-
10   οῖς τὸν ταμίαν ἀποστεῖλαι ἕως ἀπὸ νό]μμων σηστερτίων ἑκατὸν εἴκοσι πέντε καθ' ἑκάστην
πρισβείαν].

The restorations in lines 9, 10, are from the end of No. cccv. The precise occasion and reference of this Senatusconsultum cannot be determined in its present mutilated condition. It seems closely allied to No. cccv, and a conjecture has been hazarded in the Introduction, p. 5, as to its probable import. The height of the block being 20 in., we may suppose it to have formed part of the next course but one above No. ccccv *a* (1) and *a* (2): see the Plan.

CCCCV.

Fragments of wall-stones of blue marble; for their arrangement and measurements see Plan. *a* (1) is inscribed on the right-hand of the same block as No. cccciii *j*; *b* (1) is on the same block as No. cccciii *a* (2); *b* (2), which is entire only at the top, measures 1 ft. 1¾ in. in length by 9 in. in height. It seems to have come in beneath the extreme right of No. ccccv *a* (2). Presented by the Society of Dilettanti, 1870. *a* (1) published C. I. 2905 F; Waddington-Le Bas, Part v, No. 195; *a* (2) ibid. 196: *b* (1), *b* (2), ibid. 197, 198.

a (1)

KAΘΩΣANAYTΩIEKT

ΔΟΓΜΑΤΟΚΟΜΙΣΘΕΝΠΑΡΑΤΗΣΣΥΙ
ΣΕΡΟΥΙΟΣΦΟΛΟΥΙΟΣΚΟΙΝΤΟΥΥΙΟΣΣΤ
ΡΩΝΠΕΝΤΕΕΙΔΥΙΩΝΦΕΒΡΟΑΡΙΩΝΓΡΑΦΟΝ
ΚΑΜΕΛΛΙΑ ΛΕΥΚΙΟΣΑΝΝΙΟΣΛΕΥΚΙΟΥΓΟ   5
ΑΝΔΡΕΣΚΑ ΔΙΑΓΑΘΟΟΙΚΑΙΦΙΛΟΙΠΑΡΑΔΗ 10
ΚΑΤΑΡΡΓ   ΠΡΓ ΠΡΙΗΝ ΙΣΡ ΙΡΑΣ

a (2)

ΛΙΝΗΙΑΙ ΔΟ±Ε

ΙΩΝΑΠΟΣΤΑΛΕΝΤΩΝΠΡΕΣΒΕΥΤΩΝΥΠΕΡΤΩΝΠΡΟΣΣΑΜΙΟΥΣ
ΓΑΤΟΣΤΗΙΣΥΓΚΛΗΤΩΙΣΥΝΕΒΟΥΛΕΥΣΑΤΟΕΓΚΟΜΕΤΙΩΙΠΡΟΗΜΕ
ΗΣΑΝΛΕΥΚΙΟΣΤΡΕΜΗΛΙΟΣΓΝΑΙΟΥΚΑΜΕΛΛΙΑΓΑΙΟΣΑΝΝΙΟΣΓΑΙΟΥ
ΡΙΩΝΣΑΜΙΟΙΠΡΕΣΒΕΥΤΑΙΤΗΛΕΜΑΧΟΣΜΑΤΡΩΝΟΣΛΕΩΝΛΕΟΝΤΟΣ
ΚΑΙΑΓΑΘΟΥΚΑΙΦΙΛΟΥΣΥΜΜΑΧΟΥΤΕΗΜΕΤΕΡΟΥ ΛΟΓΟΥΣΕΠΟΗΣΑΝ
ΚΑΩΩΣΓΝΑΙΟΙΣΜΑΝΛΙΟΣΚΑΙΟΙΔΕΚΑΠΡΕΣΒΕΥΤΑΙΔΙΕΤ
ΣΟΥ ΑΝΔ ΤΙ

b (1)   ΗΝΟΔΟΤΟΣΑΡ
        10   ΛΟΓΟΥΣΕΠΟΗΣΑΙ
             ΕΚΑΤΕΡΩΝΘΕΛΟΝ
             ΘΕΙΝΑΙΟΟΔΗΜΟΣΟ
             ΕΜΜΕΙΝΩΣΙΝΤΟΥΤ
             ΑΠΟΣΗΣΤΕΡΤΙΓ
        15   ΚΑΘΩΣΑΝΑΥΤΩ

b (2)   ΜΑΧΟΥΤΕ
        10   ΙΚΑΘΩΣΟΔΗΜΟΣΟΡΟΔΙΩΝ
             ΚΕΥΧΕΡΕΣΕΙΝΑΙΕΣΤΙΝΜΕΤΑ
             ΚΡΙΜΑΤΙΚΑΙΤΟΥΤΟΙΣΤΟΙΣΟΡΙΓ
             ΣΕΚΑΣΤΗΝΠΡΕΣΒΕΙΑΝΕΟ
             ΤΑΜΙΑ ΑΠΟΣΤΕΙΛΑΙΚΕ

Close to the upper edge of the marble are these words from the conclusion of a Senatusconsultum, which must have occupied the broad course immediately above ccccv; see Plan.

. . καθὼς ἂν αὐτῷ ἐκ τ[ῶν δημοσίων πραγμάτων] βέλτιστον φ]αίνηται . Ἔδοξε[ν.

a (1) Δόγμα τὸ κομισθὲν παρὰ τῆς συγ[κλήτου Ῥωμαίων, ὑπὸ] τῶν ἀποσταλέντων πρεσβευτῶν ὑπὲρ τῶν πρὸς Σαμίους.
Σερούιος Φολούιος, Κοίντου υἱός, στ[ρατηγὸς ὕ]πατος τῇ συγκλήτῳ συνεβουλεύσατο ἐγ κομετίῳ πρὸ ἡμε-
ρῶν πέντε εἰδυιῶν Φεβροαρίων· γραφομ[ένῳ παρ]ῆσαν Λεύκιος Τρεμήλιος Γναίου Καμελλία, Γάιος Ἄννιος Γαίου
Καμελλία, Λεύκιος Ἄννιος Λευκίου Πο[λλίᾳ· πε]ρὶ ὧν Σάμιοι πρεσβευταὶ Τηλέμαχος Μάτρωνος, Λέων Λέοντος,   5
ἄνδρες κα[λοὶ κ]αὶ ἀγαθοὶ καὶ φίλοι παρὰ δήμο[υ καλοῦ] καὶ ἀγαθοῦ καὶ φίλου συμμάχου τε ἡμετέρου λόγους ἐποήσαντο
κατὰ πρόσ[ω(ωπον) πρό(ς) Πριην[ε]ῖς π[ερὶ χ]ώρας [καὶ ὁρίων ὅπως ὦσι] καθὼς Γνᾱῖο(ς)ε Μάνλιος καὶ οἱ δέκα πρεσβευταὶ διέταξ
[μετὰ τὸν Ἀντιόχειον πόλεμον] καὶ περὶ ὧν Πριηνεῖς πρεσβευταὶ ὁ δεῖνα . . . . .]ρου, Ἀνα . . . .
b (1) Ζηνόδοτος Ἀρ[. . . . . ἄ]γ[νδρες καλοὶ καὶ ἀγαθοὶ καὶ φίλοι [παρὰ δήμου καλοῦ καὶ ἀγ[αθοῦ] συμ]μάχου τε [ἡμετέρου   10
λόγους ἐποήσα[ντο κατ᾿](ὰ πρόσω[πον πρ]ὸτ Σαμίου[ς] περὶ χώρας καὶ περὶ ὁρίων, ὅπως οὔτω[ς ὦ]σι)ν καθὼς ὁ δῆμος ὁ Ῥοδίων
ἑκατέρων θελόν[τ](ων ἐκρινεν· περὶ τούτου τοῦ πράγματο[ς ἀποκρι]θῆναι οὔ[τ]ως ἔδοξεν ἡμῖν οὐ)κ εὐχερὲς εἶναί ἐστιν μεταθεῖναι ὃ ὁ δῆμος ὁ (᾿Ροδίων ἑκατέρων θελόντων κέκρι[κε κ]αὶ ὁρ[ισμὸν] πεπόηνται, τοῦ(sic) μ]ὴ] τούτῳ τῷ) κρίματι καὶ τούτοις τοῖς ὁρίι
ἐμμείνωσιν· τούτ(ῳ τε τῷ κρίματι καὶ τοῦ[τοις τοῖς ὁρίοις ἐμμένει]ν καθὼς τούτοις τε ξένιον εἰ]ς ἑκάστην πρεσβείαν ἔω(ς)
ἀπὸ σησττερτίω(ν νόμων ἑκατὸν εἴκοσι [Σερούιος Φ]ολ[ο]ύιοτ Κοίντου ὕπατος τὸν) ταμίαν(ν) ἀποστείλαι κε[λεύσῃ   15
καθὼς ἂν αὐτῷ (ἐκ [τ]ῶν δημοσίων πραγμάτων [βέλτιστα φαίνη]τ[αι]. Ἔδοξεν.)

The subject of this document, a Senatusconsultum, is explained fully in the Introduction, pp. 4, 5, *ante*.

a (1). In line 3 στ[ρατηγὸς ὕ]πατος is the certain restoration of Mommsen, Ephemeris Epigraphica, 1872 p. 156. It is known that in the second century B.C. the usual Greek equivalent of Consul was στρατηγὸς

ὕπατος (Marquardt, Röm. Alt. iv, p. 380); Mommsen (Eph. Ep. p. 223) considers it the literal translation of praetor maximus, the older designation of the Consul. He cites C. I. 1770, 1325, 3800 (Waddington-Le Bas, Part v, No. 588), in all of which στρατηγὸς ὕπατος stands for Consul. Gradually the abbreviation ὕπατος was adopted, the oldest example being the

Thisbæ Senatusconsultum, B.c. 170 (Hicks, Manual of Historical Inscriptions, No. 195). Meanwhile the longer form occasionally lingered in use; in Polybios, as in this inscription, both forms are found. Mommsen adds that Servius Fulvius, Cos. B.C. 135 (A.U.C. 619), was probably son of Quintus Cn. f., Cos. B.C. 180 (A.U.C. 574). It is singular that the Milesian award in the dispute between Sparta and Messenè took place under sanction of the Senate this very year; see Archäologische Zeitung, 1876, p. 128, and 1878, p. 104 (Hicks, Manual, No. 200). For in line 41 of that award, if we read στρατηγὸς [ὕπατος] Κόϊντος Καλπόρνιος, we have the name of the colleague of Servius Fulvius in the consulate. In line 5 the tribe must be Pollia, there not being sufficient space for Popillia, or Poblilia. The beginnings and endings of the lines in δ (1), δ (2), are in the British Museum. The portions included within curved brackets are given from the copy of Le Bas, made from the stone when in a more perfect condition. ΓΝΑΙΟΙΣ, line 7. is a manifest blunder of the lapidary. The reading at the end of line :1 is undoubtedly εὐχερὶς εἶναί ἐστιν κ.τ.λ. Perhaps in the original MS. draft the scribe had first written εἶναι and then added ἐστιν by way of correction, forgetting to erase εἶναι; the lapidary therefore inscribed both. For the formulæ of this document compare a Senatusconsultum concerning a treaty with Astypalæa, C. I. 5879, where the Latin reads: munusque eis ex formula locum lautiaque Q(uæstorem) Urb(anum) eis locare mittere[que juberent], and the Greek copy thus (line 25): ξένιά τε αὐτοῖς κατὰ τὸ διάταγμα, τόπον, παροχήν τε τὸν ταμίαν τὸν κατὰ πόλιν τούτοις μισθῶσαι ἀποστεῖλαί τε κελεύωσιν.

CCCCVI.

Portion of a wall-stone of blue marble, entire on left and at bottom; 2 ft. 4½ in. long, 10 in. high. From the temple of Athenè Polias, Prienè. Given less accurately but more completely by Waddington-Le Bas, Part v, Nos. 203, 204, from which the endings of the lines are restored; the portions between curved brackets were read by Le Bas. Presented by the Society of Dilettanti, 1870.

Uninscribed.

```
᾿ΔΕΤΟΥΤΟΥΚΑΤΑΒΑΝΤΕΣΕΙΣΤΗΝΚΟΙΛΑΔΑΤΟΝΜΕΝΥΠΟ
ΙΡΟΝΤΕΣΚΑΙΑΥΤΟΙΤΗΝΛΙΜΝΗΝΕΝΤΗΙΓΡΙΗΝΙΔΙΑΠΟΔΕΤΟΥΤΟΥ
ΤΕΘΕΝΤΑΟΡΟΝΕΠΙΤΟΜΕΤΕΩΡΟΝΟΛΙΣΘΗΜΑΤΟΑΙΓΙΛΩΔΕΣΟΥΧΕΥ
ΥΠΟΡΟΔΙΩΝΤΕΘΕΝΤΑΟΡΟΝΟΥΧΕΥΡΟΜ᾿ΝΑΥΤΟΙΔΕΕΘΗΚΑΜΕΝΑΙ
ΤΟΝΜΕΝΥΠΟΡΟΔΙΩΝΤΕΘΕΝΤΑΟΡΟΝΟΥΧΕΥΡΟΜΕΝ/
```

5

δὶ τούτου καταβάντες εἰς τὴν κοιλάδα τὸν μὲν ὑπὸ ('Ροδίων τεθέντα ὅρον ὑπὲρ τὴν λίμνην οὐχ εὕρομεν), [αὐτοὶ δὲ ἐθήκαμεν καθόντες καὶ αὐτοὶ τὴν λίμνην ἐν τῇ Πριηνίδι· ἀπὸ δὲ τούτου (ἐπ' εὐθείας δι[αβ]άντων [τὸ βου]νίον τὸ καλούμενον 'Ανδρεκᾶς?) [τὸν μὲν ὑπὸ 'Ροδθέντα ὅρον ἐπὶ τὸ μετέωρον ὀλίσθημα τὸ αἰγιλωδὲς οὐχ εἴ(ρομεν αὐτοὶ δὲ) [ἐθήκαμεν) ἀπὸ δὲ τούτου.......] (αν ἐπ' εὐθείας)..... [τὸν τὸ 'Ροδίων τεθέντα ὅρον οὐχ εὕρομεν, αὐτοὶ δὲ ἐθήκαμεν' ἀ[πὸ δὲ τούτου?.............] (ὑπέρκειται)........... .... τὸν μὲν ὑπὸ 'Ροδίων τεθέντα ὅρον οὐχ εὕρομεν α[ὐτοὶ δὲ ἐθήκαμεν κ.τ.λ.

Probably another part of the document in Waddington-Le Bas, Nos. 206, 207; see Nos. cccvII, ccccvIII. Αἰγιλωδὲς, in line 3, means 'covered with αἴγιλος,' a plant mentioned in Theokrit. v, 128, perhaps the same as αἰγίλωψ, see Theophrastos, Hist. Plant. viii, 7, 1, etc.: Sibthorp, Flora Græca, 1806, I, p. 74, Pl. 93. With the irregular δι[αβ]άντων (for διαβάντες), line 2, compare No. ccccIII, line 170.

CCCCVII.

Wall-stone of blue marble, 4 ft. 0½ in. long, 11¼ in. high, and therefore belonging to a narrow course : see Plan, p. 7. From the temple of Athenè Polias, Prienè. Entire on the upper, right, and lower edge. Unpublished. Presented by the Society of Dilettanti, 1870.

```
᾿ΑΙΟΡΙΖΟΝΤΑΤΑΠΡΟΣΒΗΣΣΑΝΕΧΡΗΣΑΝ   ΘΑΟ  ΔΙΑΥΤΩΙΤΩΙΠΟΤΑΜΩΤΩΙΕΟΝΤΙΔΙΑΤΗΣΜΕΓΑ
ῥΑΝΕΣΤΙΝΤΟΗΡΑΚΛΕΙΟΝΚΑΘΟΤΙΚΑΙΡΟΔΙΟΙΑΠΟ᾿ΞΤΗΣΣ᾿ΝΒΟΛΗΣΤΩΝΠΟΤΑΜΩΝΠΟΡΕΥΘΕΝΤΕΣΔΙΑΤΟΥΠ
᾿ΕΡΚΕΙΜΕΝΟΥΛΟΦΟΥΤΟΝΥΠΟΡΟΔΙΩΝΤΕΘΕΝΤΑΟΡΟΝΕ᾿ΡΟΜΕΝΑΠΟΔΕΤΟΥΤΟΥΕΠΙΤΟΝΕΧΟΜΕΝΟΝΒΟΥΝΟΝΠΑΡΑΤ
᾿ΜΕΝΑΠΟΔΕΤΟΥΤΟΥΕΠΙΤΟΕΛΑΣΣΟΝΒΟΥΝΙΟΝΤΟΠΑΙ   ΤΗΝΑΦΑΡΑΓΓΑΕΛΘΟΝΤΕΣΤΟΝΜΕΝΥΠΟΡΟΔΙΩΝΤΕΘΕΝΤ
ΕΤΟΥΤΟΥΔΙΑΒΑΝΤΕΣΤΗΝΜΕΙΖΩΦΑΡΑΓΓΑΕΠΙΤΟΜΕΤΕΩΡΟΝΕΠΕΥΘΕΙΑΣΤΟΝΥΠΟΡΟΔΙΩΝΤΕΘΕΝΤΑΟΡΟΝΕΥΡΟ
᾿ΙΤΟΝΠΟΤΑΜΟΝΤΟΝΚΑΛΟΥΜΕΝΟΝΥΠΟΜΕΝΣΑΜΙΩΝΜΑΙΜΑΑΠΟΠΗΥΠΟΔΕΠΡΙΗΝΕΩΝΤΟΝΑΠΟΛΑΙΜΑΣΤΟΡΕΙΑ
ΑΝ᾿᾿ΕΙΝ᾿ΝΤΟΣΕΠΑΝΔ᾿᾿   ᾿ΜΕΝΥΠΟΡΟΔΙΩΝΟΡΟΝΤ᾿᾿ΙΕΝΤΑΟΥΥΕΥΡΟΜΕΝΑΥΤΟΙΔΕΕΘΗΚΑΜΕΝΑΠΟΔΕΤΟΥΤΟΥΕΓ
᾿ΙΩΝΤΕΘΕΙΤ   Υ᾿᾿ΟΜΕΝΑΥΤΟΙΔΕΕ   ᾿ΚΑΜΕΝΑΠ᾿ ΛΕΤΟΥΤΟΥΕΡΕΥΘΕΙΑΣΕΠ᾿᾿ ᾿ΕΤΡΩΔΕΣΕΛΘΟΛ
```

..... ἐλθόντες ἐπὶ τὸν ποταμὸν τὸν] διορίζοντα τὰ πρὸς βῆσσαν ἐχρησάμ[ε]θα ὁ[ρ]ῳ αὐτῷ τῷ ποταμῷ τῷ ἐόντι διὰ τῆς μεγάληφάραγγος οὗ ἐπὶ τῶν ὑπερκειμένων λό]φων ἐστὶν τὸ 'Ηράκλειον, καθότι καὶ 'Ρόδιοι· ἀπὸ δὲ της συνβολῆς τῶν ποταμῶν πορευθέντες διὰ τοῦ π-
:᾿................ ἐπὶ τοῦ ὑ]περκειμένου λόφου τὸν ὑπὸ 'Ροδίων τεθέντα ὅρον εὕρομεν· ὑπὸ δὲ τούτου ἐπὶ τὸν ἐχόμενον βουνὸν παρατ-

σριτθέντις τὸν ὑπὸ Ῥοδίων τεθέντα ὅρον εὕρ]ομεν· ἀπὸ δὲ τούτου ἐπὶ τὸ ἔλασσον βουνίον τὸ παρ[ὰ] τὴν φάραγγα ἐλθόντες τὸν μὲν ὑπὸ Ῥοδίων·
5 ὅρον οὐχ εὕρομεν αὐτοὶ δὲ ἐθίκαμεν· ἀπ]ὸ δὲ τούτου διαβάντες τὴν μείζω φάραγγα ἐπὶ τὸ μετέωρον ἐπ' εὐθείας τὸν ὑπὸ Ῥοδίων τεθέντα ὅρ
μεν· ἀπὸ δὲ τούτου πορευθέντες .... ἐ]πὶ τὸν ποταμὸν τὸν καλούμενον ὑπὸ μὲν Σαμίω Μαιμαλώπη ὑπὸ δὲ Πριηνέων τὸν ἀπὸ Λαιμασ
.... βουνοῦ το]ῦ ἀνατείνοντος ἐπάνω τ[ὸ]ν μὲν ὑπὸ Ῥοδίων ὅρον τεθέντα οὐχ εὕρομεν αὐτοὶ δὲ ἐθήκαμεν· ἀπὸ δὲ τc
εὐθείας πορευθέντες τὸν μὲν ὑπὸ Ῥο]δίων τεθέντ[α ὅρον οὐχ ε]ὕρομεν αὐτοὶ δεο ἐ[θ]ήκαμεν· ἀπ]ὶ δὲ τούτου ἐπ' εὐθείας ἐπὶ τ[ὸ] πετρωδὲς ἐλθὸν[τε

Possibly in line 1 the lapidary has omitted a Ρ by mistake, and we should read τῷ ποταμῷ τῷ [ῥ]έοντι. This inscription and the one before it (No. ccccvi) form part of a specification of landmarks drawn up by order of the Roman Senate, so as to carry into effect the Senatusconsulta Nos. cccciv, ccccv, which

had lately re-affirmed the award of Rhodes (No. cccciii). See Introduction, p. 5. The next document (No. ccccviii) contains part of the dating of this survey. Its date must be B.C. 135. Μαιμαλώπης is from μαιμάω: Λαιμασγορεία was, no doubt, a waterfall (λαίμαργος ῥίω, compare λαιμάσσω, λαμυρός).

CCCCVIII.

Fragments of wall-stones of bluish marble from the temple of Athenè Polias, Prienè. Presented by the Society of Dilettanti, 1870. *a* is given by Waddington-Le Bas, Part v, No. 200. The others are unpublished.

```
a   ιΔΤΕΦΑΝΗϹ
    ΤΟΥΔΗΜΗΤΡΙϹ
    ΝΘΕΣΤΗΡΙΩΝ        Joint on right-hand; bottom bed.   Broken along top
    ΥΛΛΟΥΤΟ           and left-hand.   Height, 6¾ in.; breadth, 6¼ in.
5   ΕΜΙΔΩΡϹ
    ΜΟΥΚΡΙΤ
```

Waddington-Le Bas, No. 201, give a few words (those enclosed within curved brackets in the cursive text below) from another block which joined on the end of *a*. This enables us to restore somewhat as follows :—

'Επ)ὶ στεφανηφ[όρ](ου 'Ηγήμονος τοῦ Οὐλιάδου, [.... ὢν]ος ἕκτη ἀπιόντος), (ἔτι δὲ ἐπὶ στεφανηφόρου τοῦ δεῖνος
τοῦ Δημητρίο[υ], ('Ανθεστηριῶνος τεσσαρεσκαιδεκάτῃ, προσ)(ἔτι δὲ καὶ ἐπὶ στεφανηφόρου τοῦ δεῖνος τοῦ δεῖνος
'Α)νθεστηριῶν(ος πέμπτῃ ἀπιόντος; Τάδε) . .(the report was presented to the Prienians by the following commissioners)
Μιν)ύλλου το[ῦ] (Καλλιμάχου, Δ) ....
5 'Αρτ)εμιδώρο[υ] (τοῦ Εὐβούλου τοῦ Διονυσίου, Διω]γένου?)ς Λέοντο[ς, τῶν αἱρεθέντων ὑπὸ τοῦ ....
δή]μου κριτ[ῶν κα](τὰ τὸ τῆς [συγ]κλήτου διο)[ίκημα ?

Line 1: Οὐλιάδης occurs in No. cccciii, line 120, as the name of a Samian historian. It is here the name of a Prienian. It was a common name at

Iasos (Waddington-Le Bas, Nos. 270, 286, 298), and in all this region. The beginnings of lines 1, 3-5 are complete in the copy of Le Bas.

```
b   ιΑ                         a   .... παρ]ὰ τῇ φάρα[γγι .....
    ΛΤΗΙΦΑΡΑ                       ... το]ῦ πέτρου οὐ .........
    ΥΠΕΤΡΟΥΟΥ                      μὶ]ν ὑπὸ 'Ροδίων ο[ὕρομεν ? ..
    ΝΥΠΟΡΟΔΙΩΝΕ
5   ΑΥΤΟΥΤΟΥϹ              5       αὐτοῦ τοὺς [.............. ἐ-
    ΠΙΤΟΝΑΠΕΝ                      πὶ τὸν ἀπέν[αντι .......... κα-
    ΤΑΒΑΝΤ                         ταβάντ[ες .............. ἀπένα-
    ΝΤΙΤϹ                          ντι το ....
    Ρ
```

Top bed and joint on left alone entire.   Height, 12 in.; breadth, 9¼ in.

```
c   ΑΛΛΟΝΟΡΟΝ                  ..... ἄλλον ὅρον [ἐθήκαμεν .....
    ΝΕΩΣΤΟΥΟΡΟ                  ... ν ἕως τοῦ ὅρο[υ .....
    ΞΝΥΠΟΡΟΔ                    τὸν μ]ὲν ὑπὸ 'Ροδί[ων τεθέντα ὅρον ....
    ΑΠΟΔΕΤ                      .... ἀπὸ δὲ τ .....
```

Top bed alone entire.   Height, 5 in.; breadth, 6¼ in.   Portions of the same survey with Nos. ccccvi, ccccvii.

```
d   ιΤΟΝΠΟΤΑΜ                  ... ἐπ]ὶ τὸν ποταμ[ὸν
    ΤΗΝΡΟΔΙΩΝΑΠΟΦ              ... τὴν 'Ροδίων ἀπόφ-
    ΚΑΤΟΜΝΩΙΜΕΝΑΝ             ασιν ......... 'Ε]κατόμνῳ Μενάν-
    ΟΙΣΔΕΦΡΑΤΥ                 δρου ......... ]οις δὲ Θρασυ[μ ..
```

Joint on right alone entire.   Height, 6 in.; breadth, 8¼ in.   With τὴν 'Ροδίων ἀπόφ[ασιν] compare No. cccciii, lines 13 and 27.

Hekatomnos is a rare name, which is best known as borne by the father of Mausolos: a Milesian of the name won the foot-race at Olympia in B.C. 72

(Krause, Olympia, p. 294). This fragment may belong to the conclusion of the Survey.

CCCCIX.

A number of fragments of bluish marble inscribed in small letters. They are too much broken to be pieced in any way together. The dialect is Doric. From the temple of Athenè Polias, Prienè. Unpublished. Presented by the Society of Dilettanti, 1870.

a			
	NONKAI		.... νον καὶ ....
	OKAPION		...τ]ὸ Κάριον
	ΙΓΡΑΨΑΝ		..ἐπ]ιγραψαν[τ...
	ΩΝΑΡΟΦ		'Ροδί]ων ἀπόφ[ασιν ?
5	ΓΕΛΕΦΕΣ	5	...γεα 'Εφέσ[ιον ? ...
	ΦΟΥΣΣΑ		... ἱστοριογρά]φους Σα[μιο...
	ΥΡΟΜΡΟΝ		... Θε]ύπομπον...
	ΟΙΦΥΓΕΛ		.... οἱ Φύγελ[α...
	ΑΡΙΟΝΚ		.... Κ]άριον κ[αὶ Δρυοῦσσαν...
10	ΓΙΓΡΑ	10	.... ψευδε]πιγρά[φους εἶμεν ....

In this fragment we observe very much the same words as No. ccccIII, lines 120-3, from which indeed it might be possible to restore the connexion of lines 5-10. The edge is entire (a bed) at the top only. Height, 13 in.; width, 4 in.

b	ΛΥΑΤΟΥΝΤΑΣΥΡΕΡΤΟΥΒΑΤΙΝΗΤΣ	... ἀμφ]ισβατοῦντας ὑπὲρ τοῦ Βατινήτο[υ...
	ΝΕΜΡΡΑΓΜΑΣΙΝΑΤΤΟΝΕΙΜΕΝΚ	....ν ἐμ πράγμασιν αὐτὸν εἶμεν κ....
	ΕΜΟΥΓΟΤ΅ΤΑΓΠΟΛΕΙΤ ΗΤΕΚ	...πολ]έμου ποτὶ τὰς πόλεις [μ]ήτε ρ..

Broken all round. Length, 13 in.; height, 4½ in. This also recalls several expressions in No. ccccIII.

c	ΙΓΟΝΟΝ		...'Αντ]ίγονον
	ΕΓΚΛΗΜΑ		...ἔγκλημα
	ϿΑΙΚΑΙ		...θαι καὶ
	ΚΑΤΣΚ		...κατεκ[ριν ?
5	ΥΤΩΝΤΟ	5	....ντων το
	ΚΑΤΑΓΑ		....καταγα[γ ?
	ΥΓΟΤΑ		....ὑπὸ τα...

Bottom bed and right return only entire. Height, 9 in.; width, 4½ in. Right return uninscribed.

d	ΜΑ		...μα....
	ΝΟΝΤϹ		νοντο....
	ΝΑϪ		νας....
	ΓΕΝΟΜΕΝϹ		γενόμενο[ν ....Πρι-
5	ΑΝΕΙΣΚΑΙΤϹ	5	ανεὶς καὶ το...

Left return and bottom bed alone complete. Height, 7 in.; width, 5½ in. This is inscribed on the return of No. ccccx b.

e	ΜΟΥΟΥΔϪ	μου αὐδὶ[ν ....

Left edge (probably return) alone complete. Height, 2 in.; width, 4⅜ in.

f	ΚΑΤΛ		...κατε..
	ΝΕΓΚ		..ε]νεγκ...
	ΟΥΓΟϽ		...ου ποτ...
	ΙΣΡΡΕϽ		...το]ὺς πρέσ[βεις

Bottom bed alone entire. Height, 4½ in.; width, 3 in.

```
TΩIT                              . . τῷ τ . . .
```

Bottom bed alone entire.   Height, 4 in.; width, 2½ in.

```
h  ΙΟΥΡ                          . . . . . φ]ρούρ[ιον
   ΙΝΤΙ                          . . . υντι . . .
   ΕΝΤ                           . . . ιντ . . .
```

Broken on all sides.   Height, 4 in.; width, 2 in.

```
i  ΟΝΑϹ                          . . . . ον Αθ . . .
   ΙΤΕΚΗΝϹ                       . . . τε κηνο . . .
```

Bottom bed alone entire.   Height, 3½ in.; width, 4½ in.   Compare ἀπὸ κήνου τοῦ χρόνου, in No. cccciii, line 126, *ante*.

```
k  ΟΛΛΡΓ
   ΟΗΜΕΙΝΤ                       ἀποδο]θήμειν τ . . . . .
```

Bottom bed entire only.   Height, 2½ in.; width, 4½ in.   Compare the Doric infinitives in the Rhodian award No. cccciii, *ante*, lines 117, 123, 138.

CCCCX.

Fragments of wall-stones from the temple of Athenê Polias, Prienè.   The character of the writing proves them all to belong to the same document.   Unpublished.   Presented by the Society of Dilettanti, 1870.

```
a       ΣΓΑΙ
        ΩΚΑΜΕΝΤΙΜ
        ΟΞΙΝΗΜΑΣΜΕΓ              Height, 10 in.
        ΜΕΝΗΜΕΙΞΕΙΣΤΗΝ           Width, 9½ in.
s       ΝΕΝΗΜΕΡΑΙΣΤΡΙΑ
        ΓΑΡΟΙΚΕΙΝΚΑΙΕΝ
        ΤΨΑΜΕΝΟΙΚΑΤΑΙ
```

```
b    ΥΓΟΛΑΜΒΑΝΟΝΤΕΣΕΓ
     ΚΑΤΑΣΚΕΥΑΞΕΙΝΓΕΔΙΕΥΣ
     ΔΩΚΑΜΕΝΓΕΔΙΕΙΣΔΕΤΙ         Return on right
     ΚΑΙΓΟΛΛΟΥΣΜΕΝΓΡΙΗΝΕΩΝ      inscribed with
10   ΑΞΔΙΗΡΓΑΤ ΑΝΤΩΝΔΕΑΓΩ       No. ccccix d.
            ΤΙΤΟΙΞΓΕΓΓΡΑΓΜΕ     Height, 10½ in.
          ΞΕΝΑΝΤΙΟΙΞ            Width, 14½ in.
          ΑΝΕΦΟΓΙΡΟΝ
```

```
c         ΙΟΙΕΙ
15   ΡΑΨΗΤΑΙΕΝΤΩΙΧΡΟΝ           Height, 7½ in.
Return on ΑΓΑΛΛΑΞΣΟΜΕΝΟΙΓ       Width, 10½ in.
left unin- ΜΑΓΝΗΞΙΑΙΕΙΞΑΓϹ      Thickness, 13 in.
scribed.   ΑΙΚΑΕΙΝΑΙΚΑΤΑΤΑΥΤ
              Uninscribed.
```

```
d   ΑΤΑΚΩΑ    Fragment, bottom bed alone entire; height, 4 in.; width, 5 in.
```

```
a  . . . s πα . . . .
   ἀπεδ]ώκαμεν τιμ[ὴν ? . . . . . . . . . . . . . . . . . . . τοῖς ὠφ-
   ελήκ]όσιν ἡμᾶς μεγ[άλως ? . . . . . . . . . . . . . . . . . . . . .
   . . . μεν ἡμεῖς εἰς τὴν [χώραν ? . . . . . . . . . . . . . . . . .
5  . . ἐν ἡμέραις –ριά[κοντα . . . . . . . . . . . . . . . . . . . .
   . καὶ] παροικεῖν, καὶ ἐν [τούτῳ ? . . . . . . . . . . . . . . κα-
   ταστρ]εψάμενοι κατὰ . . . ὑπολαμβάνοντες ἐπ[ὶ                    b
```

τὸ ἄμεινον τὴν χώραν ταύτην] κατασκευάζειν Πεδιεῦσι[ιν
κατοικοῦσιν αὐτὴν νέμεσθαι? ἐ]δώκαμεν· Πεδιεῖς δὲ τ . .
10 . . . . καὶ πολλοὺς μὲν Πριηνέων
ἀποκτείναντες καὶ τὰς χώρ]ας διήρπασαν, τῶν δὲ ἀπο-
φυγόντων καὶ ἀγανακτησάντων πρὸς αὐτοὺς ἐ]πὶ τοῖς πεπραγμέ-
νοις οὐδένα λόγον ἐποιήσαντο ἀλλ.' αὐτοῖς ὠ]ς ἐναντίοις
ἐχρῶντο? . . . . . . ἐὰν οὖν τις ὧν τὴν χώρ]αν ἔφθειρον
15 c γ]ράψηται ἐν τῷ χρόν[ῳ . . . .
ἀπαλλασσόμενοι[. . . . ἐν
Μαγνησίᾳ εἰσαγό[ντων? . . . . . . τοῖς δὲ φθείρασι τὰ βασι-
λικὰ εἶναι κατὰ ταῦτ[ά, cnd?
d κ]ατὰ κώμ[ας?

These fragments are portions of wall-stones, which made up originally a large inscription. The characters are firm and good, belonging to the third century B.C. It is natural to connect the depredations mentioned in lines 10 foll. with those which were referred to in the decree in honour of Lysimachos, No. cccci. If so, this document can hardly be anything else than an edict of Lysimachos (or perhaps rather of Seleukos) in protection of Prienè. This would account for the first person plural in lines 2, 4, 9. If I have rightly divined the sequence of the fragments (which is very uncertain) the author of the edict first speaks of having made a grant of land in the plain of the Mæander to persons who had rendered him good service (lines 2, 3; 7–9). He next complains (lines 9 foll.) of the violent conduct of these 'dwellers in the plain' (τὸ Μαιάνδρου καλούμενον πεδίον, Strabo, xii, p. 577; see on No. cccci, aute), and appears to promise redress (lines 14 foll.); both γράψηται and εἰσάγειν are judicial terms. I place however no confidence in my suggested restoration of these fragments. d is inscribed close to the bottom of the stone, and must belong to the first line of a new statement.

CCCCXI.

Various fragments from the wall-stones of the temple of Athenè Polias, Prienè. Unpublished. Presented by the Society of Dilettanti, 1870.

a	ΝΤΩΙΗ	ΙΡΟ◆ (a)		a	. ν τῷ η .	προφ[άσει . . (a)
	ΡΟΣΣ	ΙΜ◆Ε			. . ρος σ . .	σ]υμφε[ρον . .
	ΟΛΙ	ΗΗ			. . πολι . . .	. . . ηλ . . .
	ΝΩΙ	ΤΩΙ			. . ρω	. . . τῷ . . .
5	Λ	ΑΤ 5		5	. . . ατ . . .	. . . ατ . . . 5

Corner of a wall-stone inscribed on both surfaces; the endings of a and the beginnings of (a) are therefore entire. The edges are broken and the corner is damaged: height, 5½ in.

b	ΧΟΙ ΓΕΡ	ΙΕΤΑ.ιιΛ (β)		b	. . . ἔχοι περ	. . . μετὰ . . . (β)
	ΗΤΟΝΕΙΣ	ΠΟΝΤΟΝΕ			. . σύγκλ]ητον εἰς	. . . πον τὸν ε . . .
	ΚΕΙΝΟΙ	ΟΙΗΞΟΜΙ			. . . ἐ]κεῖνοι	. . . . . . ποιησομε . . .
		ΤΨΡΗΣΑ				. . . . . . τηρῆσα[ι . . .
		ΤΕ 5				. . . . τε . . . 5

Another corner of wall-stone, evidently connected with the preceding: height, 4 in. The bed at the top is entire, the edge of the corner is mutilated.

c	-ι			c	υσεις .
	ΥΣΕΙΣ				θα
	ΘΑ				

Endings of two lines from the same inscription as a and b. Height, 3½ in.; return on right preserved, but uninscribed.

| d | ΥΙΟΣ ΑΡΧΟ | | | d | . . . ο]υ υἱὸς ἀρχο[ντ . . . |
| | ΝΟΥΣΒΟ | | | | . . . . . . νους βο . . . . |

Another fragment, broken on all sides, except the top, where the bed is preserved: height, 3 in.; breadth, 5¼ in.: from the same inscription as a, b, c.

I append here another fragment of the corner of a wall-stone, from the same temple; the letters of which are larger than the preceding; they are about 1 in. high, and do not match any of the other inscriptions. Both surfaces are inscribed; height of *c*, 11¼ in.: breadth, 7 in.: height of (*r*), 5¾ in.; breadth, 3½ in. Presented by the Society of Dilettanti. Unpublished.

```
              κ
            ΓΑΔΙ
  c         ΥΣΙΟΣ    Ιξ    (r)
            ΛΗΣ      ΑΚ
                     ΔΙΟΝ
```

CCCCXII.

Portions of two wall-stones of blue marble. From the temple of Athenè Polias, Prienè. Presented by the Society of Dilettanti, 1870. Unpublished.

All edges except the bottom broken: height, 5¼ in.
```
a  ⌐ ⌣ΣΗΙΠΡΟΣΤΟ
     ΥΠΕΚΕΙΝΩΝΚΑΙΝ
     ΝΗΙΠΡΟΟΕΣΜΙΑ
     ΛΑΚΙΜΟΥΑΝΤ
5    ΑΣΕΠΙΝΙΚΟ
          Λ
```
Bed of wall-stone: width, 5 in.

Bed of wall-stone: width, 3 in.
```
b   ⌐  ΓΡΑΓΤ,
     ⌐  ΟΙΤΑΓΡΟ
            ς
```
All edges except the top broken: height, 2¾ in.

Bed of wall-stone: width, 10 in.
```
c   ⌐ ΓΡΑΓΦΑΤΗΝΕΓΙΣΤΟΛΗΝ
      ΑΙΣΕΚΑΤΟΝΕΙΚΟΣΙ ΕΡΡΩΣΘΕ
      ΗΝΕΥΣΙΝΟΡΙΑΣΤΗΣΑΤΩΣΑΝ
      ΥΡΝΑΙΩΝΔΗΜΟΣΕΝΑΥΤΟΙΣ
10    ΩΝΓΑΡΑΤΕΜΙΑΗΣΙΩΝΚΑΙΓΡΙΗ
      ΙΓΡΟΝΟΗΘΗΙΙΝΕΚΑΣΤΑΓΡΑΧΘΗΙ
      ΗΜΟΥΚΡΙΣΙΝΚΑΙΕΓΑΧΘΕΝΤΩΝ
      ΟΝΗΒΟΥΛΗΘΗΣΑΝΑΥΤΟΙΧΡΟ
15    ΟΥΔΗΝΚΑΙΦΙΛΟΤΙΜΙΑΝΙΝΑ
      ΕΝΑΓΡΑΓΜΑΤΑΚΑΙΤΟΝΕΝΕ
      ΡΑΝΑΓΟΤΡΙΨΑΜΕΝΩΝΓΑ
```
Right return uninscribed: height, 9 in.

It is pretty certain that *b* belongs to the same block with *c*, and is in its right place to the left of *c*: the bed at the top of each is precisely similar, and the lines exactly range. The bed at the bottom of *a* also corresponds, and the lines range; but it may have stood more to the right or more to the left. I place it above *b*, because it then follows the lines of breakage.

```
       . . . . . . . . . . . . . . . . . .
  a  . . . . εὔσῃ πρὸς τὸ . . . .
     . . ὑπ' ἐκείνων καὶ μ . .
     μέ]νη προθεσμία . . .
     . . . . . Ἀλείμου Ἀντ . . .
  5  . . . . . ας ἐπὶ Νικο . . .
     . . . . . . . . λ . . . . . . . . . . . . . . . . . . . . . [καθάπερ
  b  παραγέ]γραπτα[ι κατὰ ταὐτὰ γέ]γραπφα τὴν ἐπιστολὴν      c
     ποιεῖν μ]οι τὰ πρό[σφορα ἐν ἡμέρ]αις ἑκατὸν εἴκοσι. Ἔρρωσθε.
     Οἱ ὁρι]σ[ταὶ? Μιλησίοις καὶ Πρι]ηνεῦσιν ὅρια στησάτωσαν
10   καθὼς αὐτοῖς διώρισεν τὴν γῆν ὁ Σμ]υρναίων δῆμος, ἐν αὐτοῖς
     τοῖς τόποις· παρόντων πρεσβευτ]ῶν παρά τε Μιλησίων καὶ Πριη-
     νέων, ὅπως ἂν πάσῃ σπουδῇ] προνοηθῇ ἵν' ἕκαστα πραχθῇ
     κατὰ τὴν τοῦ Σμυρναίων δ]ήμου κρίσιν, καὶ ἐπαχθέντων
     ἐκ τῆς ἑκατέρων πόλεως καθ'] ὃν ἠβουλήθησαν αὐτοὶ χρό-
15   νον, ποιουμένων τε πᾶσαν σπ]ουδὴν καὶ φιλοτιμίαν ἵνα
     εἰς τὸ βέλτιον τιθῶσι τὰ γενόμ]ενα πράγματα καὶ τὸν ἐνε-
     στῶτα πόλεμον?, μηδεμίαν ἡμέ]ραν ἀποτριψαμένων πα . .
```

Fragment of a letter about boundaries. The restorations of lines 7–17 must be accepted merely as suggestions of what appears to have been the drift of the meaning: of this we may be fairly sure, without insisting upon the exact words. Lines 12 and 13 give a clue to the original length of the lines. The inscription formed part of the series of documents engraved upon the temple-walls, and seems to belong to the second or third century B.C. It informs us that a dispute had arisen between Prienè and Miletos about the boundary which divided their territories, and that Smyrna had arbitrated as an ἔκκλητος πόλις. It appears also that delay had been shown by one side or the other in carrying out the award of Smyrna, so that application had been made to the king or other potentate who was the writer of this letter. Of the letter only a fragment of the end is preserved (lines 1–8): it appears to fix a time (viz. a hundred and twenty days, i. e. four months), within which active steps must be taken to execute the Smyrna award (compare line 3). All that was wanted was a commission from the two cities concerned, accompanied by competent surveyors (ὁρισταί?), to go over the ground and set up landmarks along the frontier determined by Smyrna. Lines 9 foll. are part of an edict (ἐπιστολήν line 7, i. e. 'injunction') supplementary to the letter, urging all parties to immediate action, and removing pleas for delay. Thus (lines 13, 14) the city authorities are to see that the envoys are conveyed to the spot at such time as they desire ; and the envoys are not to decline (ἀποτριψαμένων line 17, compare Plutarch, Theseus, 26) any day which is proposed for the purpose. If my restoration of lines 16, 17 is right, the quarrel had gone so far that the villagers dwelling on the disputed lands

had come to blows over it. Miletos by this time was hardly more than a second-rate town like Prienè itself, and had long ceased to be what it was in the days before Herodotos, πρόσχημα τῆς Ἰωνίης (Herod. v. 28; compare Strabo, xiv. 635). We can only conjecture from whose hand this letter and edict proceeded. It appears likely that after the war between Antiochos Theos and Ptolemy Euergetes, the peace of B.C. 239 left both Prienè and Miletos in the hands of the Egyptian king (Droysen, Hellenismus, iii, 1, 399). Smyrna, on the other hand, had remained steadfast to the Syrian cause (see the Oxford Historical Inscription, C. I. 3137; and my Greek Historical Inscriptions, No. 176). This attitude however was not held by Smyrna very long. In B.C. 222 Smyrna is spoken of by Polybios (v, 77) as having been for some time allied with the rising dynasty of Pergamon : ἐχρημάτισε (i. e. Attalos I.) τοῖς παρὰ τῶν Σμυρναίων πρεσβευταῖς φιλανθρώπως διὰ τὸ μάλιστα τούτους τετηρηκέναι τὴν πρὸς αὐτὸν πίστιν. There is therefore some plausibility in the conjecture that Ptolemy Euergetes may have been the author of the letter. Finding two cities in his dominion quarrelling about boundaries, he may have encouraged them to submit to the arbitration of a neutral city like Smyrna.

I fail to obtain any clue from the peculiar spelling of [γέγ]ραφα in line 7, which does not seem to point to any particular locality. It is interesting phonetically, as a fresh proof that the Greek φ was not sounded like ƒ, but as a p followed by an aspirate : see Curtius, Griech. Etymologie, 2nd ed., pp. 386–388, and compare the forms σκύπφος and possibly ὄπφις. I think also the use of the first person singular γέγραφα is noticeable. Letters from the Greek kings usually exhibit the first person plural ; the Roman Emperors used the singular.

CCCXIII.

Stelè of blue marble, surmounted by a pediment. Height, 2 ft. 4 in.; breadth, 1 ft. 5½ in. From the temple of Athenè Polias, Priene. Presented by the Society of Dilettanti, 1870. Unpublished.

```
     ΕΔΟΞΕΤΗΙΒΟΥΛΗΙΚΑΙΤΩΙΔΗΜΩΙΕΥΕΤΙ
     ΑΠΟΛΛΩΝΙΟΥΕΙΠΕΝΕΠΕΙΔΗΑΙΡΕΘΕΝΤΕ>
     ΚΕΣΥΓΟΤΟΥΔΗΜΟΥΗΓΗΣΙΑΣΘΡΑΣΥΒΟΥΛΟΥΦΙ
     ΑΠΟΛΛΩΝΙΟΥΣΩΙΛΑΟΣΕΥΑΓΟΡΟΥΚΟΙΝΗΝΕΡΓ
5    ΟΤΗΝΑΡΧΗΓΚΑΙΤΟΥΤΕΣΙΤΟΥΚΑΙ ᵀΩΝΑΛΛΑΣ
     ΚΑΤΑΤΗΝΑΓΟΡΑΝΤΗΝΣΙΤΟΡΩΑΙΝΠΩΛΟΥΜΓ
     ΤΗΝΕΓΔΕΧΟΜΕΝΗΝΕΠΙΜΕΛΕΙΑΝΕᵖΟΙΗΣΑ
     ΤΟΥΣΝΟΜΟΥΣΤΟΥΣΤΕΛΟΓΟΥΣΑΡΕΔΩΚΑΙ
     ΟΡΘΟΥΣΚΑΙΔΙΚΑΙΟΥΣΕΡΗΙΝΗΣΩΑΙΤΕΗΓΗΣΙΑΙ
10   ΛΟΥΦΙΑΙΣΚΟΝΑΠΟΛΛΩΝΙΟΥΣΩΙΑΟΝΕΥΑΓΟΡ
     ΗΡΞΑΝΤΗΝΑΡΧΗΝΔΙΚΑΙΩΣΚΑΙΚΑΤΑΤΟΥΣΝ
     ΣΤΕΦΑΝΩΣΑΙΑΥΤΩΝΕΚΑΣΤΟΝΣΤΕΦΑΝΩΙΧΙ
     ΕΚΤΟΥΝΟΜΟΥΚΑΙΑΝΑΓΓΕΙΑΑΙΑΥΤΩΝΤΟΥΣΣ
     ΕΝΤΑΩΙΘΕΑΤΡΩΙΤΟΙΣΡΩΟ ΙΣΔΙΟΝΥΣΙΟΙᵀΕ
15   ΤΩΙΜΟΥΣΙΚΩΙΔΗΛΟΥΝΤΑΣΔΙΑΤΙΣΑΝΑΓΓ
     ΑΙΤΙΑΣΔΙΑΣΣΤΕΦΑΝΟΥΝΤΑᵀᵀ
     ΜΕΛΗΘΗΝΑΙΤΟΝΑΓΩΝΟΘΕΤ
     ΓΡΑΨΑΤΩΟΝΕΩΓΠΟΙΗᵀ
     ΣΑΤΩΕΝΤΩΙΙΕΡΩΙ
```

Ἔδοξε τῇ βουλῇ καὶ τῷ δήμῳ· Εὑτι[ων
Ἀπολλωνίου εἶπεν· Ἐπειδὴ αἱρεθέντες [σιτοφύλα-
κες ὑπὸ τοῦ δήμου Ἡγησίας Θρασυβούλου Φι[λίσκος
Ἀπολλωνίου Ζωίλος Ε.'αγόρου κοινὴν ἐπο[ιήσαν-
5 τ]ο τὴν ἀρχήν, καὶ τοῦ τε σίτου καὶ τῶν ἄλλω[ν τῶν
κατὰ τὴν ἀγορὰν τὴν σιτόπωλιν πωλουμέ[νων
τὴν ἐγδεχομένην ἐπιμέλειαν ἐποιήσα[ντο κατὰ
τοὺς νόμους τούς τε λόγους ἀπέδωκαν [τῆς ἀρχῆς
ὀρθοὺς καὶ δικαίους· ἐπηινῆσθαί τε Ἡγησίαν [Θρασυβού-
10 λου Φιλίσκον Ἀπολλωνίου Ζωίλον Εὐαγόρ[ου ὅτι
ἦρξαν τὴν ἀρχὴν δικαίως καὶ κατὰ τοὺς ν[όμους καὶ
στεφανῶσαι αὐτῶν ἕκαστον στεφάνῳ χρ[υσῷ τῷ
ἐκ τοῦ νόμου, καὶ ἀναγγεῖλαι αὐτῶν τοὺς σ[τεφάνους
ἐν τῷ θεάτρῳ τοῖς πρώτοις Διονυσίοις ε[ν ἀγῶνι
15 τῷ μουσικῷ δηλοῦντας διὰ τῆς ἀναγγ[ελίας τὰς
αἰτίας δι' ἃς στεφανοῦνται, τ[ῆς τε ἀναγγελίας ἐπιμεληθῆναι τὸν ἀγωνοθέτ[ην· καὶ τὸ ψήφισμα τοῦτο ἀνα-
γραψάτω ὁ νεωποίης [εἰς στήλην λιθίνην καὶ στη-
σάτω ἐν τῷ ἱερῷ [τῆς Ἀθηνᾶς.

Line 4. κοινήν means 'impartial.' Line 7. As Γ
never stands for N before Δ, ἐγδεχομένην is a slip
for ἐνδεχομένην.

We learn from this decree (apparently moved by
a brother of one of the Board) that the Corn-Com-
missioners (σιτοφύλακες) at Prienè were three in
number. They were originally three at Athens
also: see Böckh, Staatsh., 2nd ed., i, 117, 118. The
use of the singular νεωποίης in line 18,—as in Nos.
ccccxv, lines 31, 35, ccccxix, 29, ccccxx, 72,—does
not prove that there was only one temple-warden at
Prienè. Probably ὁ νεωποίης was the chairman of

the Board. At Iasos sometimes the plural was
used, sometimes the singular: C. I. 2671, 2678 compared with 2673, 2675, 2677. We shall find evidence in the dedications from Ephesos (post) that
there the νεωποίαι were twelve in number, elected
annually, two from each tribe. The Ephesian decrees (post) always have the plural, τοὺς νεωποίας.
Their function was to take care of the fabric of a
temple, and to superintend its repairs; or (as here)
to take charge of the erection of any kind of
monument in the building.

CCCCXIV.

Broken slab of blue marble, entire only on the right side towards the bottom. Height, 1 ft. 7½ in.; width, 1 ft. 3¼ in. From
the temple of Athenè Polias, Prienè. Presented by the Society of Dilettanti, 1870. Unpublished.

```
                .ΙΤΩΜΜΕ
            ΕΛΝΔΣΤΙΣΕΚΤΩΝΛΠΑΝι
          ΠΤΑΙΟΙΔΙΚΑΣΤΑΙΤΗΝΔΙΚΗΝΜΗ
        ιΩΡΑΗΜΙΛΗΣΙΩΝΚΑΙΠΡΙΗΝΕΩΝΕΜΦΥΛ
5       ΧΟΝΤΑΣΑΕΙΚΑΤΕΝΙΑΥΤΟΝΠΡΟΝΟΕΙΝΥΠΕΡ
        ΟΙΗΘΕΙΝΑΛΛΗΛΟΙΣ    ΠΕΡΙΔΙΚΩΝ    ΤΑΣΔΙ    ΣΓ
        ΕΡΙΤΩΝΤΟΥΕΜΠΟΡΙΟΥΕΠΙΜΕΛΗΤΩΝΕΜΠΡΙΗΝΙΔΣΕΠ
        ΤΩΝ ΤΟΥΣΔΕΕΓΚΑΛΟΥΝΤΑΣΠΕΡΙΤΙΝΩΝΑΦΟΥΧΡΟ
        ΕΣΩΑΙΜΙΛΗΣΙΟΥΣΜΕΝΕΝΠΡΙΗΝΗΙΠΡΗΝΕΙΣΔΕΕΝΜι
10      ΚΛΗΤΟΥΣΜΙΛΗΣΙΟΙΜΕΝΕΜΠΡΙΗΝΗΙΤΟΙΣΣΤΡΑ
        ΡΙΟΥΕΠΙΜΕΛΗΤΑΙΣΓΡΑΦΟΝΤΕΣΤΟΤΕΟΝΟΛ
        ιΝΠΡΟΦΑΙΝΟΝΤΕΣΤΟΕΓΚΛΗΜΑΓ
                        Λ
                    ΟΝΟΜΑΤΑΓΓ
15                 ΩΝΤΑΙΠΡΟΣΓΡΑΦΕΤΩΣΑΝ<
                 ΛΣΕΚΑΣΤΟΥΜΗΝΟΣΑΠΟΤΗΣΝΟΥΜΗι
                 ΡΑΨΑΝΤΕΣΑΥΘΗΜΕΡΕΙΕΚΤΙΘΕΤΩΣΑΝ.
                 ιΗΡΥΓΜΑΕΦΗΜΕΡΑΣΠΕΝΤΕ
                 ΙΑΠΕΝΗΝΕΓΜΕΝΑΙΤΑΣΔΕΑΛ
20               ΣΑΠΟΤΗΣΕΚΚΑΙΔΕΚΑΤΗΣ
                 ΗΣΔΙΚΗΣ ΕΙΣΑΓΕΤΩΔΕ
                 ΕΝΗΘΙΤΩΝΣΤΡΑ
                 ΝΔΙΔΟΝΑΙΔΕ
                 ΕΜΠΟΡΙ
```

```
. . . . . . . . . . . . . . . . . . . ι τῶμ με . . . . . . . . . .
. . . . . . . . . . . . . . . ἐὰν δέ τις ἐκ τῶν ἄπαν . . . . . .
. . . . . . . . . . . . . . . ωται, οἱ δικασταὶ τὴν δίκην μὴ . . . . . .
. . . . . . . . . . χώρα ἡ Μιλησίων καὶ Πριηνέων ἐμ φυλ[ακῆ ? . . . .
5    . . . . . . . ἀρ]χοντας ἀεὶ κατ᾽ ἐνιαυτὸν προνοεῖν ὑπὲρ . . . . . . . .
. . . . . . β]οιηθεῖν ἀλλήλοις. — Περὶ δικῶν· — τὰς δί[κας ? . . .
. . . . . . . . ἐν Μιλήτῳ μὲν] ἐπὶ τῶν τοῦ ἐμπορίου ἐπιμελητῶν· ἐμ Πριήη δὲ ἐπ[ὶ
τῶν στρατηγῶν τῶν ἐνεστώ ?]των, τοὺς δὲ ἐγκαλοῦντας περὶ νινῶν ἀφ᾽ οὗ χρό[νου
ταῦτα τὰ σύμβολα ἐγένετο δικάζ]εσθαι Μιλησίους μὲν ἱ Πριήνῃ Πριηνεῖς δὲ ἐν Μι[λήτῳ.
10   ἐνδειξάτωσαν δὲ ἑκάτεροι τοὺς ἐγ?]κλήτους Μιλήσιοι μὲν ἐμ Πριήην τοῖς στρα[τηγοῖς
Πριηνεῖς δὲ ἐν Μιλήτῳ τοῖς τοῦ ἐμπο]ρίου ἐπιμελεταῖς, γράφοντες τό τε ὄνομα[ . . . .
. . . . . . . . . . . . . . . . . . . ιν προφαίνοντες τὸ ἔγκλημα . . . . . . . .
. . . . . . . . . . . . . . . . . . . . . . . . . . . . . . . . α . . . . . . . . . .
. . . . . . . . . . . . . . . . ὀνόματα γρ[αφέτωσαν ? . . . . . .
15   . . . . . . . . . . . . . . . . . ω·ται, προσγραφέτωσαν δ[ὲ . . . . . .
. . . . . . . . . . . . . ας ἑκάστου μηνὸς ἀπὸ τῆς νουμην[ίας
. . . . . . . . . . . . . . γράψαντες αὐθημερεὶ ἐκτιθέτωσαν
. . . . . . . . . . κήρυγμα ἐφ᾽ ἡμέρας πέντε
. . . . . . . . . . ἀπενηνεγμέναι τὰς δὲ ἂν
20   . . . . . . . . . . . . . . . . . ας ἀπὸ τῆς ἐκκαιδεκάτης
. . . . . . . . . . . . . . . . . τῆς δίκης· εἰσαγέτω δὲ
. . . . . . . . . . . . . . . . . . . . . ἔνιοι τῶν στρα-
τηγῶν . . . . . . . . . . . . . . . . . . . ] διδόναι δὲ
. . . . . . . . . . . . . . . . . . . . . . . ἐμπορι . . .
```

The document before us is a treaty between Prienè and Miletos, chiefly referring to lawsuits. It was common for two states having intimate relations with each other, to arrange the conditions under which the natives of either city, when sojourning in the other, might obtain justice in the foreign courts. Such lawsuits were called δίκαι ἀπὸ συμβόλων. See Meier, Attisch. Process, p. 773 foll. : Böckh, Staatshaushaltung, i, pp. 72, 529. The treaties were termed σύμβολα, the present inscription being one of the kind. Other examples are the Attic inscription, No. IV of Part I, ante (where see notes), and Waddington-Le Bas, Part v, No. 86, line 24 foll. (from Teos).

No. CCCCXII exhibited Prienè and Miletos as disputing about their boundaries, and submitting their claims to the arbitration of Smyrna. In the present inscription, which appears to be somewhat later, we find the two cities drawing nearer to each other, and cementing their friendship by means of a definite treaty. In lines 4 foll. it seems as if the two cities had made common cause, so as to unite forces for the protection of their territory : if so the arbitration of Smyrna had borne good fruit. I read β]οιηθεῖν in line 6, comparing C. I. 3137, lines 68 and 77 (from Smyrna), and Waddington-Le Bas, Part v, No. 1140 (from Kios), where the same form occurs. Observe that the magistrates before whom a charge was to be made at Miletos, are the Commissioners of the market (lines 7, 11); the interests of Miletos being mainly commercial, these magistrates held an important position. At Prienè the corresponding magistrates are the στρατηγοί, in whose hands the chief executive power was lodged; they had also charge of the police of the city. The στρατηγοί are spoken of in Nos. CCCCXV, 12; CCCCXIX, end. This treaty tends to confirm the conjecture made on No. CCCCXII, that in the latter part of the third century B. C. both Prienè and Miletos were under the patronage of the Egyptian king. It would be to his interest to draw the two cities together, as against both the Syrian and Pergamene monarchies.

CCCCXV.

A stele of white marble, broken at the top. From the temple of Athenè Polias. Prienè. Height. 2 ft. 9½ in.; width, 1 ft. 11½ in. Presented by the Society of Dilettanti, 1870. Unpublished.

```
ΛΛΛΚΗ   ΑΙΣΙΗΣΟΗ οἱ ΑΙΟ ι-   ΗΣΙΛΕΙΣΣΑΛΥΚΣ
ΝΤΙΟΧΟΝΔΕΔΟΣΘΑΙΔΕΑΥΤΩΙΚΑΙΠΡΟΕΔΡΙΑΝΕΜΠΑΣΙΤΟΙΣΑΓΣ
ΚΑΙΕΦΟΔΟΝΕΠΙΤΗΜΒΟΥΛΗΓΚΑΙΤΟΝΔΗΜΟΜΠΡΩΤΟΙΜΕΤΑΤΑΙΕ
ΑΙΣΙΤΗΣΙΝΕΜΠΡΥΤΑΝΕΙΩΙΚΑΙΕΜΠΑΝΙΩΝΙΩΙΚΑΙΑΤΕΛΕΙΑΝΤ
5   ΣΩΜΑΤΟΣΚΑΙΩΝΑΝΕΙΣΑΓΗΤΑΙΗΕΞΑΓΗΤΑΙΕΙΣΤΟΝΙΔΙΟΝΟΙ᾿
ΚΑΙΕΜΠΟΛΕΜΩΙΚΑΙΕΝΕΙΡΥΝΗΙΤΑΥΤΑΔΕΥΠΑΡΧΕΙΓΚΑΙΑΥΤΩΙΚ
ΞΚΡΟΝΟΙΣΑΝΑΓΓΕΙΛΑΙΔΕΤΟΝΣΤΕΦΑΝΟΝΔΙΟΝΥΣΙΟΙΣΤΡΑΓΩΙΔΑ·
ΩΙΠΡΩΤΩΙΑΓΩΝΙΔΗΛΟΥΝΤΑΣΕΞΤΗΙΑΝΑΓΓΕΛΙΑΙ...ΝΕΝΕΚΑΤΕ‾
ΗΤΑΙΤΗΣΔΕΑΝΑΓΓΕΛΙΑΣΕΓΙΜΕᵃΗΘΗ   ΑΙΤΟΝΑΓΩΝΟΘΕΤΗΝΤ
10   ΙΕΚΑΤΑΣΚΕΥΗΣΤΩΝΕΙΚΟΝΛΓΚΑΙ ΗΣΣΤΑΣΕΩΣΟΡΩΣΣΥΝΤ
ΙΕΣΘΗΣΟΝΤΑΙΚΑΤΑΤΑΧΟΣΚΑΙΣΥΜΦΕΡΟΝΤΩΣΕΓΙΜΕΛΕΙΣΘΑΙ‾
```

1

```
:ΝΕΣΤΩΤΑΣΑΕΙΣΤΡΑΤΗΓΟΥΣΙΝΑΔΕΑ ΤΕΤΙΜΑΙΑΙΔΕΔΟΜΕΝ
ΡΙΧΔΙΕΡΙΦΑΝΕΣΤΕΡΑΙΩΣΙΓΚΑΙΤΩΝΑΛΛΩΝΟΙΡΡΟΑΙΡΟΥΜΕΝC
ΓΟΛΕΙΓΑΡΕΧΕΣΘΑΙΤΑΣΧΡΕΙ ΘΕΩΡΩΣΙΝΟΤΙΟΔΗΜΟΣΤΟΙΣΚ
ΛΟΙΣΚΑΙΑΓΑΘΟΙΣΑΝΔΡΑΣΙΝΕΡΙΣΤΑΤΑΙΧΑΡΙΤΑΣΑΓΟΔΙΔΟΝΑΙΚΑΤΑ
ΣΙΑΣΑΝΑΓΡΑΨΑΙΤΟΔΕΤΟΨΗΦΙΣΜΑΕ ΣΣΤΗΛΗΝΛΙΘΙΝΗΓΚΛΙΣΤΗΣΑΙ
ΓΑΡΑΤΗΝΕΙΚΟΝΑΤΑΔΕΑΝΑΛΩΜΑΤΑΤΑΓΕΝΟΜΕΝΑΥΓΗΡΕΤΕΙΝ
ΤΟΥΣΟΙΚΟΝΟΜΟΥΣ

ΕΓΙΣΤΕΦΑΝΗΦΟΡΟΥΙΓΓΟΘΩΝΤΟΣΜΗΝΟΣΜΕΤΑΓΕΙΤΝΙΩΝΟΣΕΔΟΞΕΤΩ
ΔΗΜΩΙΓΝΩΜΗΙΣΤΡΑΤΗΓΩΝΓΕΡΙΤΩΝ‾  ΙΩΝΤΩΜΠΡΟΤΕΡΟΝΕΨΗΦΙΣΜΕ
ΝΩΝΛΑΡΙΧΩΙΤΑΜΕΝΑΛΛΑΕΙΝΑΙΚΑΘ‾ ΓΡΟΤΕΡΟΝΟΔΗΜΟΣΕΨΗΦΙΣΤ
ΣΤΗΣΑΙΔΕΛΑΡΙΧΟΥΕΙΚΟΝΑΧΑΛΚΗΝΕΦΙΓΓΟΥΕΝΤΗΙΑΓΟΡΑΙΑΝΤΙΤΗΣ
ΓΡΟΤΕΡΟΝΕΨΗΦΙΣΜΕΝΗΣΑΥΤΩΙΥΓΑΡΧΕΙΝΔΕΛΑΡΙΧΩΙΑΤΕΛΕΙΑΓΚΑΙΤΩ
ΚΤΗΝΩΓΚΑΙΤΩΝΣΩΜΑΤΩΝΟΣΑΑΝΥΓΑΡΧΗΙΕΝΤΕ‾ΟΙΣΙΔΙΟΙΣΚΤΗΜΑΣ
ΚΑΙΕΝΤΗΙΓΟΛΕΙΟΓΩΣΑΜΦΑΙΝΗΤΑΙΟΔΗΜΟΣΧΑΡΙΤΑΣΑΓΟΔΙΔΟΥΣ
ΛΑΡΙΧΩΙΤΩΝΕΥΕΡΓΕΤΗΜΑΤΩΝΑΞΙΑΣ

ΕΓΙΣΤΕΦΑΝΗΦΟΡΟΥΑΚΑΜΑΝΤΟΣΜΗΝΟΣΑΓΑΤΟΥΡΙΩΝΟΣΑΝΑΞΙΛΑ
ΛΥΚΙΔΕΩΣΕΙΓΕΝΟΓΩΣΑΝΑΙΕΨΗΦΙΣΜΕΝΑΙΥΓΟΤΟΥΔΗΜΟΥΤΙ
ΜΑΙΛΑΡΙΧΩΙΑΝΑΓΡΑΦΩΣΙΝΕΙΣΣΤΗΛΗΝΛΙΘΙΝΗΓΚΑΙΣΤΑΘΗΙΗΣΤΗ
ΛΗΕΝΤΩΙΙΕΡΩΙΤΗΣΑΘΗΝΑΣΔΕΔΟΧΘΑΙΤΗΙΒΟΥΛΗΙΚΑΙΤΩΙΔΗΜΩΙΤΟΙ
ΝΕΩΓΟΙΗΝΛΕΩΜΕΔΟΝΤΑΑΓΕΓΔΟΥΝΑΙΟΓΩΣΣΤΗΛΗΤΕΚΑΤΑ
ΣΚΕΥΑΣΘΗΚΑΙΑΝΑΓΡΑΦΗΕΙΣΑΥΤΗΝΤΑΨΗΦΙΣΜΑΤΑΤΑΕΨΗΦΙΣ
ΜΕΝΑΥΓΟΤΟΥΔΗΜΟΥΥΓΕΡΤΙΜΩΝΛΑΡΙΧΩΙΚΑΙΣΤΑΘΗΙΗΣΤΗΛΗΕΝΤΩ
ΙΕΡΩΙΤΗΣΑΘΗΝΑΣΤΟΔΕΓΕΝΟΜΕΝΟΝΕΙΣ‾ΑΥΤΑΑΝΑΛΩΜΑΥΓΗΡΕΤΙ
ΣΑΙΤΟΝΝΕΩΓΟΙΗΓΚΑΙΑΝΕΝΕΓΚΕΙΝΤΗΙΓΟΛΕΙΕΛΛΟΓΩΙ
```

     . . . . [εἰκόν-

a] χαλκῆ[ν κ]αὶ στῆσαι παρὰ τοὺς [β]ασιλεῖς Σέλευκο[ν καὶ
Ἀ]ντίοχον· δεδόσθαι δὲ αὐτῷ καὶ προεδρίαν ἐμ πᾶσι τοῖς ἀγῶ[σιν
καὶ ἔφοδον ἐπὶ τὴμ βουλὴν καὶ τὸν δῆμομ πρῶτῳ μετὰ τὰ ἱε[ρά,
κ]αὶ σίτησιν ἐμ πρυτανείῳ καὶ ἐμ Πανιωνίῳ, καὶ ἀτέλειαν τ[οῦ
     σώματος καὶ ὧν ἂν εἰσάγηται ἢ ἐξάγηται εἰς τὸν ἴδιον οἶ[κον
καὶ ἐμ πολέμῳ καὶ ἐν εἰρήνῃ· ταῦτα δὲ ὑπάρχειν καὶ αὐτῷ κ[αὶ
ἐκγόνοις· ἀναγγεῖλαι δὲ τὸν στέφανον Διονυσίοις τραγῳδῶ[ν
τῷ πρώτῳ ἀγῶνι δηλοῦντας ἐν τῇ ἀναγγελίᾳ ὧν ἕνεκα τετ[ί-
μ]ηται, τῆς δὲ ἀναγγελίας ἐπιμεληθῆ[ν]αι τὸν ἀγωνοθέτην, τ[ῆς
     δὲ κατασκευῆς τῶν εἰκόνων καὶ [τ]ῆς στάσεως ὅπως συντ[ε-
λεσθήσονται κατὰ τάχος καὶ ξυμφερόντως ἐπιμελεῖσθαι τ[οὺς
ἐνεστῶτας ἀεὶ στρατηγούς· ἵνα δὲ α[ἴ] τε τιμαὶ αἱ δεδομέν[αι Λαρίχῳ ἐπιφανέστεραι ὦσιν, καὶ τῶν ἄλλων οἱ προαιρούμενο[ι τῇ
πόλει παρέχεσθαι τὰς χρεί[ας] θεωρῶσιν ὅτι ὁ δῆμος τοῖς κ[α-
     λοῖς καὶ ἀγαθοῖς ἀνδράσιν ἐπίσταται χάριτας ἀποδιδόναι κατα-
ξίας, ἀναγράψαι τόδε τὸ ψήφισμα ε[ἰ]ς στήλην λιθίνην καὶ στῆσαι
παρὰ τὴν εἰκόνα, τὰ δὲ ἀναλώματα τὰ γινόμενα ὑπηρετεῖν
τοὺς οἰκονόμους.
Ἐπὶ στεφανηφόρου Ἱπποθῶντος, μηνὸς Μεταγειτνιῶνος, ἔδοξε τῷ
     δήμῳ, γνώμῃ στρατηγῶν· περὶ τῶν [τι]μῶν τῶμ πρότερον ἐψηφισμέ-
νων Λαρίχῳ, τὰ μὲν ἄλλα εἶναι καθ[ὼς] πρότερον ὁ δῆμος ἐψήφιστ[αι,
στῆσαι δὲ Λαρίχου εἰκόνα χαλκῆν ἐφ' ἵππου ἐν τῇ ἀγορᾷ ἀντὶ τῆς
πρότερον ἐψηφισμένης αὐτῷ, ὑπάρχειν δὲ Λαρίχῳ ἀτέλειαν καὶ τῶ[γ
κτηνῶν καὶ τῶν σωμάτων ὅσα ἂν ὑπάρχῃ ἔν τε τοῖς ἰδίοις κτήμασ[ι
     καὶ ἐν τῇ πόλει ὅπως ἀμ φαίνηται ὁ δῆμος χάριτας ἀποδιδοὺς
Λαρίχῳ τῶν εὐεργετημάτων ἀξίας.
Ἐπὶ στεφανηφόρου Ἀκάμαντος, μηνὸς Ἀπατουριῶνος, Ἀναξίλα[ς
Λυκιδέως εἶπεν· ὅπως ἂν αἱ ἐψηφισμέναι ὑπὸ τοῦ δήμου τιμαὶ Λαρίχῳ ἀναγραφῶσιν εἰς στήλην λιθίνην καὶ σταθῇ ἡ στά-
     λη ἐν τῷ ἱερῷ τῆς Ἀθηνᾶς, δεδόχθαι τῇ βουλῇ καὶ τῷ δήμῳ τὸν
νεωποίην Λεωμέδοντα ἀπεγδοῦναι ὅπως στήλη τε κατα-
σκευασθῇ καὶ ἀναγραφῇ εἰς αὐτὴν τὰ ψηφίσματα τὰ ἐψηφισμένα ὑπὸ τοῦ δήμου ὑπὲρ τιμῶν Λαρίχῳ καὶ σταθῇ ἡ στήλη ἐν τῷ
ἱερῷ τῆς Ἀθηνᾶς· τὸ δὲ γενόμενον εἰς ταῦτα ἀνάλωμα ὑπηρετ[ῆ-
     σαι τὸν νεωποίην καὶ ἀνενεγκεῖν τῇ πόλει ἐλ λόγῳ.

Decrees in honour of Larichos for his services to Prienè. They must have been great, to receive such an acknowledgement. For besides the usual grants of προεδρία, of priority of access to the βουλή and ἐκκλησία, and free export and import of commodities at all times, he is awarded an equestrian statue (lines 10, 22), and exemption from taxation for himself (lines 4, 5), his cattle and his slaves (line 24). The name Larichos is very rare, and we may probably pronounce the subject of these decrees to have been a grandson and namesake of the Larichos who was a well-known man at the court of Philip (Arrian, Anab. iii, 6), and whose two sons Laomedon and Eriguios were officers of rank in the army of Alexander (Arrian, Anab. l. c.; Indica, 18; Curt. ed. Zumpt, vi, 10 and viii, 10, § 40). Probably this younger Larichos was the son of Laomedon, who upon Alexander's death received as his portion the satrapy of Syria (Diod. Sic. xviii, 3, 39, 43; Appian, Syr. 52, etc.). Upon the downfall of his father, we may suppose that Larichos entered the service of the Syrian monarchy, for the statue originally voted him (lines 1, 2) was to be set up beside the statues of Kings Seleukos and Antiochos. I take this to refer to Seleukos Nikator and Antiochos Soter; and if it is worth while to add another conjecture, I would connect these decrees with the statement in No. ccccIII, lines 132–3 about the δυσχερεῖς καιροί at Prienè during the reign of Antiochos Theos. This was during the 'Second Syrian War' which came to an end in B.C. 248: in this war the forces of Ptolemy Philadelphos had pressed hard upon the Greek cities of Asia Minor, and Samos the adversary of Prienè had become an Egyptian naval station (see Introduction, p. 4 ante). I imagine Larichos to have been the general of Antiochos Theos, who came to the relief of Prienè.

In lines 19 and 27 it is curious that both the στεφανηφόροι mentioned bear the names of eponymous heroes. The occurrence of two such names together suggests the idea that the office of στεφανηφόρος may have been held by the heroes themselves, just as ὁ θεός occurs in No. ccccIII, line 126, on which see the note. Compare also No. ccccXVI, line 9, [ἐπὶ] στ[εφα]νηφόρου Ἀκάμαντος.

Line 27. 'Απατουριών is already known as the name of a month in Tenos, see ante No. cccLXXVII (C. I. 2338), Kyzikos (C. I. 3661), Olbia (C. I. 2083, Addenda, p. 1000), and elsewhere.

The dative γνώμῃ, in line 20, is very remarkable, the nominative in this connexion being all but universal. Perhaps the few instances of the dative are slips of the lapidary: see however C. I. 2264, 2484.

CCCCXVI.

Fragment of blue marble stelè, from the temple of Athenè Polias, Prienè. Entire only on left. Height, 9½ in.; width, 1 ft. 6 in. Presented by the Society of Dilettanti, 1870. Unpublished.

```
            ΝΤ
              ΛΙΦΙΛΟΤΙΜΩΣΙ
       ]  ΑΛΤΕΣΕΙ ΑΓΑΝΤΑΤΟΓΧΡΟΝΟΝ
       ΤΑΙΑΝΑΓΡΑΨΑΙΤΟΨΗΦΙΣΜΑΤΟΔΕΕΙΣΙ
   5   ΝΗΝΚΑΙΣΤΗΣΑΙΕΙΣΤΟΙΕΡΟΝΤΗΣΑΘΗΝΑΣΤ
       ΩΜΑΥΓΗΡΕΤΗΣΑΙΤΟΕΙΣΤΟΝΣΤΕΦΑΝΟΝΚΑ
       ΤΗΝΣΤΗΛΗΝΚΑΙΤΗΝΑΝΑΓΡΑΦΗΝΤΟΥΨΗΦΙΣΜΑ
       ΤΟΝΝΕΩΠΟΙΗΝΗΡΑΚΛΕΩΤΗΝ

            ΤΤ   ΝΗΦΟΡΟΥΑΚΑΜΑΝΓΟΣΜΗΝΟΣΜΕΤΑΓΕ
   10              ΣΤΑΜΕΝΟΥΑ         ΕΟΥΕΙΠΓ
```

. . . . ΝΤ . . . .
. . . . κ]αὶ φιλοτίμως [τὴν πόλιν εὐεργε-?
τ[ήσ]αντες εἰ[ς] ἅπαντα τὸν χρόνον [μνημονεύαν-?
ται, ἀναγράψαι τὸ ψήφισμα τόδε εἰς σ[τήλην λιθί-
5 νην καὶ στῆσαι εἰς τὸ ἱερὸν τῆς Ἀθηνᾶς, τ[ὸ δὲ ἀνά-
λ]ωμα ὑπηρετῆσαι τὸ εἰς τὸν στέφανον κα[ὶ εἰς
τὴν στήλην καὶ τὴν ἀναγραφὴν τοῦ ψηφίσμα[τος
τὸν νεωποιὴν Ἡρακλεώτην.

   'Επὶ] στ[εφα]νηφόρου Ἀκάμαντος, μηνὸς Μεταγε[ιτ-
10 νιῶνος . . . .]σταμένου, 'Α . . . . ίου εἶπε· . .
. . . .

Fragment of two decrees, of which the first was an honorary one, and the second probably a rider to it. The subject of them cannot be more precisely determined. The date may be the second or third century B.C. Akantas, in line 9, may be the name of a citizen, but is more likely to refer to the hero, who is here elected to the eponymous magistracy, as was Apollo in No. cccciii, line 126; compare No. ccccxv ante.

CCCCXVII.

Fragment of bluish marble stele, from the temple of Athenè Polias, Prienè. Entire only on left. Height, 4½ in.; width, 7⅞ in. Presented by the Society of Dilettanti, 1870. Unpublished.

```
ﻨﻌΘΑΙΟΡΩΣΑΓΑ
ΚΑΙΙΝΑΑΝΑΓΡΑΦΗΤΟΥ
ΝΕΣΤΑΤΩΙΤΟΡΩΙ
ΑΙΤΟΝΔΗΜΟΝ
‐∩‐
```

. . . . [ἐπιμελ-
εἶ]σθαι ὅπως Ἀγα[. . . αἱ διδομέναι τιμαὶ ἀναγγέλλωνται ἐν τοῖς πρώτοις ἀγῶσιν, καὶ ἵνα ἀναγραφῇ τὸ ψ[ήφισμα εἰς στήλην λιθίνην καὶ σταθῇ ἐν τῷ ἐπιφα-νεστάτῳ τόπῳ, [ἵνα πᾶσι φανερὸν ᾖ διότι ὁ δῆμος ὁ . . . . . . ων ἀξίως τιμᾷ κ]αὶ τὸν δῆμον [τὸν Πριηνέων καὶ τοὺς δικαστὰς? κ.τ.λ.

This is a fragment of a decree, containing the usual phrases: compare Nos. ccccxviii, lines 35 foll., ccccxx, lines 33 foll., ccccxxi, lines 29 foll., which justify the conjecture that the decree was sent from some other city to confer honours upon a dikast (Ἀγα . . ., line 1) sent from Prienè. The surface is much worn: the letters are neat, and seem to belong to the third century B.C.

CCCCXVIII.

Tall stele of blue marble, from the temple of Athenè Polias, Prienè. Height, 4 ft.; width, 1 ft. 10 in. Presented by the Society of Dilettanti, 1870. Unpublished.

Within wreath.	Within wreath.	Within wreath.
ΤΟΝ	ΚΛΕ	ΜΟ
ΔΗΜϽ	ΑΝ	ΑΓΕ
Ν	ΔΡΟΝ	ΤΗΝΓΑΥ
	ΚΑΛΛΙ	ΣΑΝΙΟΥ
	ΣΤΡΑΤΟΥ	
	ΦΥΣΕΙΔΕΑ	
	ΛΕΞΙ	
	ΔΟΣ	

```
  ΕΠΙΣΤΕΦΑΝΗΦΟΡΟΥΔΗΜΗΤΡΙΟΥΜΗΝΟΣΓΑΝΗΜΟΥ
  ΤΟΓΑΡΑΕΡΥΘΡΑΙΩΝΤΙΜΩΝΔΙΚΑΣΤΗΙΚΛΕΑΝΔΡΩΙ ΕΔΟΞΕΛ
  ΤΗΙΒΟΥΛΗΙΚΑΙΤΩΙΔΗΜΩΙΣΤΡΑΤΗΓΩΝΕΞΕΤΑΣΤΩΝΠΡΥΤΑΝΕ
  ΩΝΓΝΩΜΗΕΓΕΙΔΗΟΑΠΟΣΤΑΛΕΙΣΔΙΚΑΣΤΗΣΥΓΟΤΟΥΔΗΜΟΥ
5 ΤΟΥΓΡΙΗΝΕΩΝΚΛΕΑΝΔΡΟΣΚΑΛΛΙΣΤΡΑΤΟΥΦΥΣΕΙΔΕΑΛΕΞΙΔΟΣ
  ΕΓΙΤΗΝΔΙΚΗΝΤΗΣΜΗΝΥΣΕΩΣΤΗΝΤΕΔΙΚΗΝΕΔΙΚΑΣΕΝΑΞΙΩΣΤΗΣ
  ΤΕΕΑΥΤΟΥΓΑΤΡΙΔΟΣΚΑΙΤΗΣΗΜΕΤΕΡΑΣΓΟΛΕΩΣΓΟΙΗΣΑΜΕΝΟΣ
  ΤΗΝΚΡΙΣΙΝΑΓΟΤΟΥΔΙΚΑΙΟΥΤΗΝΤΕΕΓΙΔΗΜΙΑΝΕΓΟΙΗΣΑΤΟΑΥΤΟΣΤΕ
  ΚΑΙΟΓΡΑΜΜΑΤΕΥΣΑΥΤΟΥΜΟΑΓΕΤΗΣΓΑΥΣΑΝΙΟΥΑΞΙΩΣΤΗΣΕΝΚΕΧΕΙ
○ ΡΙΣΜΕΝΗΣΑΥΤΩΙΓΙΣΤΕΩΣΟΓΩΣΟΥΝΚΑΙΟΔΗΜΟΣΦΑΙΝΗΤΑΙΜΝΕΙ
  ΑΝΓΟΙΟΥΜΕΝΟΣΤΩΝΚΑΛΩΝΚΑΙΑΓΑΘΩΝΑΝΔΡΩΝΚΑΙΔΙΚΑΙΩΣΚΡΙΝΑΝ
  ΤΩΝΤΗΝΔΙΚΗΝΚΑΙΑΞΙΩΣΤΗΣΕΞΑΓΟΣΤΕΙΛΑΣΗΣΑΥΤΟΥΣΓΑΤΡΙΔΟΣ
  ΟΙΤΕΜΕΤΑΤΟΥΤΟΥΣΓΑΡΕΣΟΜΕΝΟΙΕΙΣΤΗΝΓΟΛΙΝΗΜΩΝΔΙΚΑΣΤΑΙΘΕΩΡΟΥΝ
```

ΤΕΣΑΓΟΔΙΔΟΜΕΝΑΣΥΑΣΚΑΘΗΚΟΥΣΑΣΤΙΜΑῪΤ   ΑΓΑΘΟΙΣΑΝΔΡΑΣΙΝΓΡC
ΙΣΤΩΝΤΑΙΚΑΙΑΥΤΟΙΤΩΝΔΙΚΑΙΩΝΜΕΤΑΓ ᷍πᷘΦΙΛΟΤΙΜΙΑΣ ΤΥΧπιᴎᴉ ᴧΘΗΙ
‒ΕΔΟΧΘΑΙΤΗΙΒΟΥΛΗΙΚΑΙΤΩΙΔΗΜΩΙΕΓΑΙΝΕΣΑΙΜΕΝΤΟΝΔΗΜΟΝΤΟΝ
ΓΡΙΗΝΕΩΝΚΑΙΣΤΕΦΑΝΩΣΑΙΑΥΤΟΝΧΡΥΣΩΙΣΤΕΦΑΝΩΙΟΤΙΥΓΑΡ
ΧΩΝΣΥΝΓΕΝΗΣΚΑΙΦΙᴧΟΣΚΑΙΕΥΝΟΥΣΤΩΙΗΜΕΤΕΡΩΙΔΗΜΩΙΚΑΙ
ᴎΡΟΑΙΡΟΥΜᴇΝᴏᷘΞᴂιᴎΦΥΛΑΣΣΕΙΝΤΗΝΠΡΟΣΤΟΓΛΗΘΟΣΗΜΩΝΕΥΝΟΙΑΝ
ᴧΕΝΔΙΚΑΣΤΗΝΑΝΔΡΑΚΑΛΟΝΚΑΙΑΓΑΘΟΝΚΑΙΑΞΙΟΝΑΜΦΟ
ΡΩΝΤΩΝΓΟΛΕΩΝΕΓΑΙΝΕΣΑΙΔΕΚΑΙΤΟΝΔΙΚΑΣΤΗΝΚΛΕΑΝΔΡΟΝΚΑΛ
ΛΙΣΤΡΑΤΟΥΦΥΣΕΙΔΕΑΛΕΞΙΔΟΣΚΑΙΣΤΕΦΑΝΩΣΑΙΑΥΤΟΝΧΡΥΣΩΙΣΤΕ
ΦΑΝΩΙΕΓΑΙΝΕΣΑΙΔΕΚΑΙΤΟΝΓΡΑΜΜΑΤΕΑΑΥΤΟΥΜΟΑΓΕΤΗΝΓΑΥΣΑΝΙΟΥ
ΚΑΙῪΤΕΦΑΝΩΣΑΙΑΥΤΟΝΘΑΛΛΟΥΣΤΕΦΑΝΩΙΑΡΕΤΗΣΕΝΕΚΕΝΚΑΙΕΥΝΟΙ
ΑΣῚΗΣΕΙΣΤΟΝΔΗΜΟΝΕΙΝΑΙΔΕΑΥΤΟΥΣΚΑΙΓΡΟΞΕΝΟΥΣΚΑΙΓΟΛΙΤΑΣ
ΤΗΣΓΟΛΕΩΣΗΜΩΝΔΕΔΟΣΘΑΙΔΕΑΥΤΟΙΣΚΑΙΓΡΟΕΔΡΙΑΝΕΝΤΟΙΣΑΓΩΣΙΝ
ΟΙΣΑΝΗΓΟΛΙΣΣΥΝΤΕΛΗΙΥΓΑΡΧΕΙΝΔΕΑΥΤΟΙΣΚΑΙΤΑΣΑΛΛΑΣΤΙΜΑΣΑΙ
ΤΙΝΕΣΚΑΙΤΟΙΣΑΛΛΟΙΣΓΡΟΞΕΝΟΙΣΓΑΡΑΤΗΣΓΟΛΕΩΣΥΓΑΡΧΟΥΣΙΝ
ΔΕΔΟΣΘΑΙΔΕΤΑΥΤΑΚΑΙΤΟΙΣΕΚΓΟΝΟΙΣΑΥΤΩΝΤΑΣΔΕΔΕΔΟΜΕΝΑΣ
ΤΙΜΑΣΤΩΙΔΗΜΩΙΤΩΙΓΡΙΗΝΕΩΝΚΑΙΤΩΙΔΙΚΑΣΤΗΙΚΑΙΤΩΙΓΡΑΜΜΑ
ΤΕΙῩΑΤΑΤΟΔΕΤΟΥΗΦΙΣΜΑΑΝΑΓΓΕΙΛΑΤΩΔΕΕΝΤΩΙΘΕΑΤΡΩΙΟ
ᴧΓΩΝΟΘΕΤΗΣΤΩΝΔΙΟΝΥΣΙΩΝΑΓΟΔΕΙΞΑΙΔΕΚΑΙΓΡΕΣΒΕΥΤΗΝ
ῩΤΙΣΑΝΑΔΟΥΣΓΡΙΗΝΕΥΣΙΝΤΟΔΕΤΟΥΗΦΙΣΜΑΓΑΡΑΚΑΛΕΣΕΙΑΥ
ᴖΝΤΑΣΣΥΝΓΕΝΕΙΣΚΑΙΦΙΛΟΥΣΚΑΙΕΥΝΟΥΣΤΟΥΔΗΜΟΥΕΓΙΜΕΛΕΙ
ΘΑΙΟΓΩΣΑΙΔΕΔΟΜΕΝΑΙΤΙΜΑΙΤΩΙΤΕΔΗΜΩΙΑΥΤΩΝΚΑΙ ᴊᴊι
ῙΩΙΓΡΑΜΜΑΤΕΙΑΝΑΓΓΕΛΛΩΝΤΑΙΓΑΡΑΥΤΟΙΣΕΝΤΟΙΣΕΓΙΦⲀ
ῙᴖῙΙΝΟΤΑΝΚΑΙΟΙΑΛΛΟΙΣΤΕΦΑΝΟΙΑΝΑΓΓΕΛΛΩΝΤΑΙΚΑΙΙΝΑ
ΥΗΦΙΣΜΑΕΙΣΣΤΗΛΗΝΛΙΘΙΝΗΝΑΝΑΤΕΘΗΓΑΡΑΥΤΟΙΣ
ῙΑΥΤΑΔΕΕΙΝΑΙΕΙΣΦΥΛΑΚΗΝΤΗΣΓΟΛΕΩΣΓΡΕΣ
ΛΕΩΤΟΥ

	Κλέ-	
	αν-	
	δρον	Μι-
Τὸν	Καλλι-	αγέ-
δῆμον.	στράτου	την Παυ-
	φύσει δὲ Ἀ-	σανίου.
	λέξι-	
	δος.	

Ἐπὶ στεφανηφόρου Δημητρίου· μηνὸς Πανήμου·
Τὸ παρὰ Ἐρυθραίων τιμῶν δικαστῆ Κλεάνδρῳ. Ἔδοξεν
τῇ βουλῇ καὶ τῷ δήμῳ, στρατηγῶν ἐξεταστῶν πρυτάνεων γνώμη· ἐπειδὴ ὁ ἀποσταλεὶς δικαστὴς ὑπὸ τοῦ δήμου
5   τοῦ Πριηνέων Κλέανδρος Καλλιστράτου φύσει δὲ Ἀλέξιδος
ἐπὶ τὴν δίκην τῆς μηνύσεως τήν τε δίκην ἐδίκασεν ἀξίως τῆς
τε ἑαυτοῦ πατρίδος καὶ τῆς ἡμετέρας πόλεως, ποιησάμενος
τὴν κρίσιν ἀπὸ τοῦ δικαίου, τήν τε ἐπιδημίαν ἐποιήσατο αὐτός τε
καὶ ὁ γραμματεὺς αὐτοῦ Μοαγέτης Παυσανίου ἀξίως τῆς ἐνκεχει-
10   ρισμένης αὐτῷ πίστεως, — ὅπως οὖν καὶ ὁ δῆμος φαίνηται μνεί-
αν ποιούμενος τῶν καλῶν καὶ ἀγαθῶν ἀνδρῶν καὶ δικαίως κρινάν-
των τὴν δίκην καὶ ἀξίως τῆς ἐξαποστειλάσης αὐτοὺς πατρίδος,
οἵ τε μετὰ τούτους παρεσόμενοι εἰς τὴν πόλιν ἡμῶν δικασταὶ θεωροῦντες ἀποδιδομένας τὰς καθηκούσας τιμὰς τ[οῖς] ἀγαθοῖς ἀνδράσιν προ-
15   ιστῶνται καὶ αὐτοὶ τῶν δικαίων μετὰ π[ά]σης φιλοτιμίας. — Τύχῃ Ἀγαθῇ·
δεδόχθαι τῇ βουλῇ καὶ τῷ δήμῳ ἐπαινέσαι μὲν τὸν δῆμον τὸν
Πριηνέων καὶ στεφανῶσαι αὐτὸν χρυσῷ στεφάνῳ ὅτι ὑπάρ-
χων συνγενὴς καὶ φίλος καὶ εὔνους τῷ ἡμετέρῳ δήμῳ καὶ
προαιρούμενος διαφυλάσσειν τὴν πρὸς τὸ πλῆθος ἡμῶν εὔνοιαν
20   ἀπέστει]λεν δικαστὴν ἄνδρα καλὸν καὶ ἀγαθὸν καὶ ἄξιον ἀμφο-
τέ]ρων τῶν πόλεων, ἐπαινέσαι δὲ καὶ τὸν δικαστὴν Κλέανδρον Καλλιστράτου φύσει δὲ Ἀλέξιδος καὶ στεφανῶσαι αὐτὸν χρυσῷ στε-

κ

φάνῳ, ἐπαινέσαι δὲ καὶ τὸν γραμματέα αὐτοῦ Μοαγέτην Παυσανίου
καὶ στεφανῶσαι αὐτὸν θαλλοῦ στεφάνῳ ἀρετῆς ἕνεκεν καὶ εὐνοί-
25 ας τῆς εἰς τὸν δῆμον, εἶναι δὲ αὐτοὺς καὶ προξένους καὶ πολίτας
τῆς πόλεως ἡμῶν, δεδόσθαι δὲ αὐτοῖς καὶ προεδρίαν ἐν τοῖς ἀγῶσιν
οἷς ἂν ἡ πόλις συντελῇ, ὑπάρχειν δὲ αὐτοῖς καὶ τὰς ἄλλας τιμὰς αἵ-
τινες καὶ τοῖς ἄλλοις προξένοις παρὰ τῆς πόλεως ὑπάρχουσιν,
δεδόσθαι δὲ ταῦτα καὶ τοῖς ἐκγόνοις αὐτῶν· τὰς δὲ δεδομένας
30 τιμὰς τῷ δήμῳ τῷ Πριηνίων καὶ τῷ δικαστῇ καὶ τῷ γραμματεῖ κατὰ τόδε τὸ ψήφισμα ἀναγγειλάτω δὲ (sic) ἐν τῷ θεάτρῳ ὁ
ἀγωνοθέτης τῶν Διονυσίων, ἀποδείξαι δὲ καὶ πρεσβευτὴν
ὅστις ἀναδοὺς Πριηνεῦσιν τόδε τὸ ψήφισμα παρακαλέσει αὐ-
τοὺς] ὄντας συγγενεῖς καὶ φίλους καὶ εὔνους τοῦ δήμου ἐπιμέλει-
35 αν ποιεῖσ]θαι ὅπως αἱ δεδομέναι τιμαὶ τῷ τε δήμῳ αὐτῶν καὶ [τ]ῷ
δικαστῇ καὶ] τῷ γραμματεῖ ἀναγγέλλωνται παρ' αὐτοῖς ἐν τοῖς ἐπιφανεστάτοις ἀ]γῶσιν ὅταν καὶ οἱ ἄλλοι στέφανοι ἀναγγέλλωνται καὶ ἵνα
ἀναγραφὲν τόδε τὸ] ψήφισμα εἰς στήλην λιθίνην ἀνατεθῇ παρ' αὐτοῖς
ἔν τινι τῶν ἱερῶν,] ταῦτα δὲ εἶναι εἰς φυλακὴν τῆς πόλεως· πρεσ-
40 βευτὴς ὁ δεῖνα Ἡρακ?]λεώτου.

Isolated as the Greek cities were, it is interesting to observe how often they rendered important services one to the other by way of arbitration or jurisdiction in case of quarrels either international or intestine. A good example of arbitration between two cities is found in the award of the Rhodian Commission in the dispute between Prienè and Samos, No. cccciii *ante*. The inscription before us is of a somewhat similar nature. A prosecution had been set on foot in the Ionian city of Erythræ which it was desirable to have tried before a judge beyond suspicion of having any political or personal bias. The Erythræan government accordingly requested Prienè to send a δικαστής from among her citizens. He was sent, and having discharged his duties successfully, he receives public honours and thanks from the Erythræans,—honours in which his native city and his secretary have a share. The case in question is termed (line 6) τὴν δίκην τῆν μηνύσεως, i. e. it was based upon information laid before the government against some officer of state by a person who was either not willing or not competent himself to conduct the prosecution (see Schömann, Antiquitt. Juris Pub. Græc. p. 231).

From the mention of the ἐξετασταί in line 3 nothing can be inferred as to the nature of the charge : Aristotle says that ἐξετασταί was the title given in some states to officers corresponding to the εὔθυνοι at Athens (Polit. vii, 8, § 17 = 1322 B). Ἐξετασταί existed at Halikarnassos (C. I. 2656 : Hellenic Journal, ii, 98), at Smyrna (C. I. 3137, line 88), at Nesos (Droysen. Hellenismus, ii, 2, p. 374), at Chios (Monatsberichte d. Berl. Akad. 1863, p. 265), and at Laodikeia (No. ccccxxi *post*). The political troubles which so often befel the Greek cities made the employment of such foreign δικασταί a frequent necessity, as is witnessed by the large number of inscriptions like the present. Thus we find δικασταί from Alexandria Troas at Karystos (C. I. Add. 2152 *b*), from Andros at Adramyttion (C. I. Add. 2349 *b*), and at Chalkis in Eubœa (C. I. 2147), from Iasos at Kalymna (C. I. 2671 ; compare the Kalymnian fragment, Part ii. No. cclxiii *ante*), from Antandros at Peltæ in

Phrygia (C. I. Add. 3568 *f*), from Klazomenæ at Smyrna (C. I. 3184), and from Lampsakos at Kymè(?) (C. I. 3640 ; compare also Bull. de Corr. Hell. vi, p. 356, and C. I. Add. 2167 *c*, Add. 2264 *l*, and Add. 2334 *b*). Böckh has some interesting remarks on this subject in C. I. ii, p. 1065. C. Bétant (An fuerint apud Græcos judices certi litibus inter civitates componendis : Dissert. inaug. Berl. 1862, pp. 19, 20) cites nearly all the instances given above, and adds the following notices from authors : Herod. iv, 161, v, 28 foll. ; Pausan. iii, 2, 7 ; Xenophon, Hellen. v, 3, 10. Meier also mentions this kind of δικασταί in his essay, Die Privatschiedsrichter und d. öffentlichen Diäteten Athens (Halle, 1846), and therein publishes a similar decree from Megara in honour of Megarian dikasts sent to Orchomenos (see Keil, Sylloge inscrr. Bœotic. p. 19 ff.). Bétant cites these further examples : Waddington-Le Bas, Part v, No. 87, a Teian dikast at Bargylia; Rangabé, Antiq. Hell. ii; No. 768. Also K. Curtius, Inschriften und Studien zur Geschichte von Samos, Lübeck, 1877, publishes p. 35 a decree in honour of Samian dikasts (city unknown). Compare also the note on p. 52 *post*.

In line 2, τιμῶν is a genitive of relation, 'respecting honours.'

In line 31, δὲ must be a mistake.

Few decrees of Erythræ seem to be extant : this is the longest and most perfect. The following may be compared : Waddington-Le Bas, Part v, No. 39, in honour of Konon ; ibid. No. 1536 *a*, treaty with Hermias of Atarneus (now in the British Museum, see Part iv *post*) ; ibid. No. 40, honours to Mausolos ; ibid. Nos. 1537, 1539, 1542 are too imperfect to yield much information. More like the decree before us is a tolerably perfect decree in honour of στρατηγοί, ibid. 1536, which is headed like the present one : [Ἔδοξε τῷ δήμῳ· στρατηγῶν πρυτανε[ων ἐξετασῶν γνώμη]; the conclusion is imperfect. Two more short honorary decrees were published by Curtius, Anecdota Delphica, Nos. 68, 69 (see Rangabé, Antiq. Hell., Nos. 737, 738). These also are headed with the same formula, which seems to imply that these three Boards, representing respectively the military and police, the financial, and the civic administration of the state, formed what was in later Greece termed αἱ συναρχίαι, or a collective committee of magistrates with large powers of initiating measures (compare No. cccci, line 21 *anic*). Like the decree from Prienè, the Erythræan decrees from Delphi conclude with the phrase, ταῦτα δὲ εἶναι εἰς φυλακὴν τῆς πόλεως; which is found in a Salaminian decree, C. I. A. ii, part i, p. 357, and in several of the Attic naval documents, Böckh, Staatshaush. iii, p. 467. Böckh and Rangabé, locc. citt., both discuss the phrase, the former thinking it declares the decree to be urgent, as concerning the defence of the country, a meaning it certainly bears in Waddington-Le Bas, No. 136 *a*, line 27; while Rangabé less probably interprets φυλακή in a passive sense. I would rather regard it as a pious wish, resembling ἀγαθῇ τύχῃ καὶ ἐπὶ σωτηρίᾳ τῆς πόλεως, κ.τ.λ., or the Latin 'quod bene vortat': compare No. ccccxxi, line 34, εἶναι δὲ τὸ ψήφισμα τοῦτο ἐπὶ σωτηρίᾳ τῆς πόλεως.

To the Erythræan inscriptions enumerated above should be added a letter from Antiochos Soter to the people of Erythræ, now in the Museum at Smyrna (Monatsberichte d. Berl. Akad. 1875, p. 554), which states that under Alexander and Antigonos the city αὐτόνομος ἦν καὶ ἀφορολόγητος, and that its liberty, though lost under Seleukos, had been re-

stored by Antiochos. It probably remained independent down to the time of the Macedonian Wars. It was probably free at the time of our decree, which I place about B.C. 200. This is the date of the two decrees from Delphi. The decree about the στρατηγοί (Waddington-Le Bas, No. 1536), which has a similar heading to these others, and therefore is probably of a similar date, distinctly declares that Erythræ was then independent. The στρατηγοί, apparently nine in number, are praised because τά τε κατὰ τὴν ἀρχὴν καλῶς καὶ ἐνδόξως διῴκησαν [τοῦ δὲ πο]]λέμου περιστάντος τὴν πόλιν καὶ τὴν χώραν ἐκτενεῖς ἑα[ὶ προθύ]μους αὐτοὺς παρέσχοντο πρὸς τὴν τῆς πόλεως φυλαε[ὴν οὐδένα οὔ] ε φόβον οὔτε κίνδυνον ὑποστελλόμενοι, προθύμως δὲ ἑα[υ]τοὺς ἐπιδιδόντες εἰς τὸ καὶ λέγειν καὶ πράττειν τὰ τῇ πόλ[ει] | σύμφεροντα, διό[τι] τὴν δημοκρατίαν συνδιετήρησαν τ[ῷ δή]μῳ καὶ πόλιν ἐλευθέραν παρέδωκαν τοῖς μεθ' αὐτοὺς σ[τρ]α[τη γ]οῦσιν. Observe that here again the phrase τὴν τῆς πόλεως φυλακήν occurs, though in a slightly different connexion. The war here spoken of was probably that between Seleukos II and Ptolemy Euergetes (Droysen, Hellen. iii, I, p. 393). Dittenberger, Syll., 159, 160, gives two more decrees from Erythrae. The name Moagetes is very rare. Two tyrants so called reigned in the Kibyratic Tetrapolis in the second and first centuries B.C. Their dynasty was suppressed by Murena B.C. 83; (Marquardt, Röm. Alt. iv, p. 222).

CCCCXIX.

A stelè of white marble, from the temple of Athenè Polias, Prienè. Broken at top. Height, 3 ft. 3½ in.; width, 1 ft. 11 in. Presented by the Society of Dilettanti, 1870. Unpublished.

```
                      .ΙΔΗΟΔΗΜΟΣΟΛ
        ΔΜΑ           ΣΩΙΛΟΥΚΑΙΨΗΦΙΣΜΑΚΑΘΟΕ              ΔΗΜΟΝ
        ΚΑΙΕΓΗΙΝΕΚΕΤΟΥΣΓΑΡΑΓΕΝΟΜΕΝΟΥΣΕΙΣΑΛΕΞΑΝΔΡΕΙΑΝΔΙΚΑΣΤΑΣΑΘΗΝΑΓΟΡΑΝ
        ΕΥΚΤΙΤΟΥΝΥΝΦΩΝΑΚΑΛΛΙΚΡΑΤΟΥΑΡΙΣΤΟΔΗΜΟΝ^ΙΔΩΝΟΣΕΓΕΛΟΩΝΔΕΚΑΙΝΙΚΑΣΑΓΟ
  5     ΡΑΣΕΓΙΤΕΤΗΝΒΟΥΛΗΝΚΑΙΤΗΝΕΚΚΛΗΣΙΑΝΑΚΟΛΟΥΘΩΣΔΙΕΛΕΓΗΙΤΟΙΣΕΝΤΩΙΨΗΦΙΣΜΑΤΙ
        ΚΑΤΑΚΕΧΩΡΙΣΜΕΝΟΙΣ ΟΓΩΣΟΥΝΚΑΙΟΔΗΜΟΣΕΥΧΑΡΙΣΤΩΝΤΕΦΑΙΝΗΤΑΙΤΩΙΔΗΜΩ
        ΤΩΙΑΛΕΞΑΝΔΡΕΩΝΚΑΙΦΙΛΑΝΘΡΩΓΩΣΑΡΟΔΕΔΕΓΜΕΝΟΣΤΟΝΤΕΨΗΦΙΣΜΕΝΟΝ
        ΥΡΑΥΤΟΥΣΤΕΦΑΝΟΝΚΑΙΤΟΝΤΩΝΔΙΚΑΣΤΩΝΕΓΑΙΝΟΝ  ΔΕΔΟΧΘΑΙΤΗΙΒΟΥΛΗΙΚΑΙΤΩΙ
        ΔΗΜΩΙΕΓΗΝΗΙΣΘΑΙΤΟΝΔΗΜΟΝΤΟΝΑΛΕΞΑΝΔΡΕΩΝΕΓΙΤΕΤΗΙΓΡΟΑΙΡΕΣΕΙΗΝΕΧΕΙΕΙΣ
 10     ΤΗΜΓΟΛΙΝΗΜΩΝΑΚΟΛΟΥΘΑΓΡΑΤΤΩΝΤΟΙΣΓΡΟΥΓΑΡΧΟΥΣΙΗΑΜΦΟΤΕΡΑΙΣΤΑΙΣΡ ΛΕΞΙΝ
        ΙΛΑΝΘΡΩΓΟΙΣΚΑΙΔΙΟΤΙΤΗΜΓΑΣΑΝΣΓΟΥΔΗΝΓΡΟΑΙΡΟΥΜΕΝΟΣΓΟΙΕΙΣΘΑΙΥΓΕΡΤΩΝΓΑΡΑ
        ΓΙΝΟΜΕΝΩΝΕΙΣΤΗΜΓΟΛΙΝΔΙΚΑΣΤΗΡΙΩΝΟΡΩΣΙΣΑΚΑΙΔΙΚΑΙΑΓ.._ΙΤΟΙΣΓΟ
        ΡΑΓΙΝΗΤΑΙΔΙΑΤΟΜΑΛΙΣΤΑΔΙΑΤΟΥΤΟΤΗΡΕΙΣΘΑΙΤΗΝΔΗΜΟΚΡΑΤΙΑΝΑΓΟΣΤΑΛΕ
        ΓΡΟΣΑΥΤΟΝΓΑΡΗΜΩΝΔΙΚΑΣΤΩΝΤΟΥΣΜΕΝΓΑΡΑΓΕΝΟΜΕΝΟΥΣΑΝΔΡΑΣΕΙΣΑΛΕΞΑΝΔ. ΕΙΑ
 15     ΕΓΗΝΕΚΕΝΕΓΙΤΕΤΩΙΣΩΦΡΟΝΩΣΚΑΙΑΝΕΓΚΛΗΤΩΣΓΑΡΕΓΙΔΗΜΗΣΑΙΚΑΙΔΙΟΤΙΤΑΣΔΙΚΑΣΙΩΣ
        ΚΑΙΔΙΚΑΙΩΣΑΓΑΣΑΣΕΚΡΙΝΑΝΤΑΣΤΕΤΩΜΓΑΡΑΝΟΜΩΝΚΑΙΤΑΣΤΩΜΒΙΑΙΩΝΤΟΝΔΕΔΗΜΟΝ
        ΕΣΤΕΦΑΝΩΚΕΝΑΡΕΤΗΣΕΝΕΚΕΝΚΑΙΕΥΝΟΙΑΣΤΗΣΕΙΣΤΗΜΓΟΛΙΝΚΑΙΔΙΟΤΙΑΝΔΡΑΣΚΑΛΟΥΣ
        ΚΑΙΑΓΑΘΟΥΣΑΓΕΣΤΕΙΛΕΝΕΓΗΝΗΙΣΘΑΙΔΕΚΑΙΤΟΥΣΑΓΟΣΤΑΛΕΝΤΑΣΕΙΣΑΛΕΞΑΝΔΡΕΙΑΝΔΙ
        ΚΑΣΤΑΣΑΘΗΝΑΓΟΡΑΝΕΥΚΤΙΤΟΥΝΥΜΦΩΝΑΚΑΛΛΙΚΡΑΤΟΥΑΡΙΣΤΟΔΗΜΟΝΦΙΛΩΝΥΣΙΝΑΔΕ
 20     ΤΑΕΨΗΦΙΣΜΕΝΑΥΓΟΛΛΕΞΑΝΔΡΕΩΝΛΑΒΗΙΣΥΝΤΕΛΕΙΑΝΤΟΜΜΕΝΑΓ ΩΝΟΘΕΤΗΝΟΣΑΝΗΙ
        ΤΟΤΕΓΟΙΗΣΑΣΩΑΙΕΓΙΜΕΛΕΙΑΝΜΕΤΑΤΟΥΓΡΑΜΜΑΤΕΩΣΟΓΩΣΟΣΤΕΦΑΝΟΣΑΝΑΓΟΡΕΥΩ
        ΤΟΙΣΓΡΩΤΟΙΣΔΙΟΝΥΣΙΟΙΣΟΤΑΝΤΑΣΘΕΑΣΣΥΝΤΕΛΩΜΕΝΜΕΤΑΤΑΣΣΓΟΝΔΑΣΔΙΟΤΙΟΔΗΜ
        ΟΛΑΛΕΞΑΝΔΡΕΩΝΣΤΕΦΑΝΟΙΤΟΝΔΗΜΟΝΤΟΜΓΡΙΗΝΕΩΝΑΡΕΤΗΣΕΝΕΚΕΝ .ΛΕΥΝΟΙΑ .
        ΤΗΣΕΙΣΑΥΤΟΝΚΑΙΔΙΟΤΙΔΙΚΑΣΤΑΣΑΓΕΣΤΕΙΛΑΑΝΑΝΔΡΑΣΚΑΛΟΥΣΚΑΙΑΓΑΘΟΥΣ
 25     ΑΘΗΝΑΓΟΡΑΝΕΥΚΤΙΤΟΥΝΥΜΦΩΝΑΚΑΛΛΙΚΡΑΤΟΥΑΡΙΣΤΟΔΗΜΟΝΦΙΛΩΝΟΣ   ΤΟΔ
        ΨΗΦΙΣΜΑΤΟΓΑΡΑΛΛΕΞΑΝΔΡΕΩΝΑΝΑΓΡΑΨΑΙΕΙΣΣΤΗΛΗΝΛΙΘΙΝΗΝΚΑΙΣΤΗΣΑΙ
```

ΕΙΣΤΟΙΕΡΟΝΤΗΣΑΘΗΝΑΣ ΥΡΟΓΡΑΨΑΙΔΕΚΑΙΤΟΔ' ΟΨΗΦΙΣΜΑΕΙΣΤΗΝΑΝΑΤ:ΘΕ
ΜΕΝΗΝΣΤΗΛΗΝΤΗΣΔΕΛΑΝΑΓΡΑΦΗΣΤΩ ΗΦΙΣΜΑΤΩΝΚΑΙΤΗΣΕΓΔΟΣΕΩΣΤΗΣΣΤΗ
ΛΗΣΕΓΙΜΕΛΕΙΑΜΓΟΙΗΣΑΣΘΑΙΤΟΝΝΕΩΠΟΙΕΙΝΜΕΛΛΟΝΤΑΧΑΡΜΟΝΕΓΙΣΤΕΦΑΝΗΦΟΡΣ
ΑΡΟΛΛΩΝΟΣΚΑΙΤΟΓΕΝΟΜΕΝΟΝΑΝΑΛΩΜΑΑΝΕΝΕΓΚΕΙΝΕΝΛΟΓΩΙΤΗΙΠΟΛΕΙΑΡΟΣΤΕΙ
ΛΑΙΔΕΚΑΙΞΕΝΙΟΝΝΙΚΑΣΑΓΟΡΑΙΤΩΙΡΑΡΑΓΕΓΟΝΟΤΙΡΡΕΣΒΕΥΤΗΙΤΟΚΑΤΑΤΟΝΝΟΜΟΝΤΟΝ
ΝΕΩΠΟΙΗΝΦΛΕΑΝΤΑ ΙΝΑΔΕΚΑΙΑΣΦΑΛΩΣΓΑΡΑΓΕΜΦΘΗΙΤΟΥΣΣΤΡΑΤΗΓΟΥΣΚΑΙΤΟΥΣ
ΙΓΓΑΡΧΑΣΕΓΙΜΕΛΗΘΗΝΑΙ

 . . . . ἐπ]ειδὴ ὁ δῆμος ὁ Ἀ[λεξανδρέων ἀπέστειλεν ἐφ'
ἡ]μᾶ[ς πρεσβευτὴν Νικασαγόραν] Ζωίλου καὶ ψήφισμα καθ' ὃ ἐ[στεφάνωκε τὸν] δῆμον
καὶ ἐπήνεκε τοὺς παραγενομένους εἰς Ἀλεξανδρείαν δικαστὰς Ἀθηναγόραν
Εὐκτίτου Νύμφωνα Καλλικράτου Ἀριστόδημον Φίλωνος, ἐπελθὼν δὲ καὶ Νικασαγό-
5 ρας ἐπί τε τὴν βουλὴν καὶ τὴν ἐκκλησίαν ἀκολούθως διελέγη τοῖς ἐν τῷ ψηφίσματι
κατακεχωρισμένοις· ὅπως οὖν καὶ ὁ δῆμος εὐχαριστῶν τε φαίνηται τῷ δήμῳ
τῷ Ἀλεξανδρέων καὶ φιλανθρώπως ἀποδεδεγμένον τόν τε ἐψηφισμένον
ὑπ' αὐτοῦ στέφανον καὶ τὸν τῶν δικαστῶν ἔπαινον,— δεδόχθαι τῇ βουλῇ καὶ τῷ
δήμῳ ἐπηρῆσθαι τὸν δῆμον τὸν Ἀλεξανδρέων ἐπί τε τῇ προαιρέσει ἣν ἔχει εἰς
10 τὴμ πόλιν ἡμῶν ἀκόλουθα πράττων τοῖς προυπάρχουσι(ν) ἀμφοτέραις ταῖς π[ό]λεσιν
φ]ιλανθρώποις, καὶ διότι τὴμ πᾶσαν σπουδὴν προαιρούμενος ποιεῖσθαι ὑπὲρ τῶν παρα-
γινομένων εἰς τὴμ πόλιν δικαστηρίων ὅπως ἴσα καὶ δίκαια πᾶ[σ]ι τοῖς πο[λί]ταις παραγίνηται διὰ τὸ μάλιστα διὰ τοῦτο τηρεῖσθαι τὴν δημοκρατίαν, ἀποσταλέ[ντων
πρὸς αὐτὸν παρ' ἡμῶν δικαστῶν, τοὺς μὲν παραγενομέν υς ἄνδρας εἰς Ἀλεξανδ[ρ]εία[ν
15 ἐπήνεικεν ἐπί τε τῷ σωφρόνως καὶ ἀνεγκλήτως παρεπιδημῆσαι καὶ διότι τὰς δίκας ἴσως
καὶ δικαίως ἁπασας ἔκριναν τάς τε τῶμ παρανόμων καὶ τὰς τῶμ βιαίων, τὸν δὲ δῆμον
ἐστεφάνωκεν ἀρετῆς ἕνεκεν καὶ εὐνοίας τῆς εἰς τὴμ πόλιν καὶ διότι ἄνδρας καλοὺς
καὶ ἀγαθοὺς ἀπέστειλεν, ἐπηνῆσθαι δὲ καὶ τοὺς ἀποσταλέντας εἰς Ἀλεξανδρείαν δικαστὰς Ἀθηναγόραν Εὐκτίτου Νύμφωνα Καλλικράτου Ἀριστόδημον Φίλωνος, ἵνα δὲ
20 τὰ ἐψηφισμένα ὑπὸ Ἀλεξανδρέων λάβῃ συντέλειαν τὸμ μὲν ἀγωνοθέτην ὃς ἂν ᾖ
τότε ποιησάσθαι ἐπιμέλειαν μετὰ τοῦ (γ)ραμματέως ὅπως ὁ στέφανος ἀναγορευθ[ῇ
τοῖς πρώτοις Διονυσίοις ὅταν τὰς θέας συντελῶμεν μετὰ τὰς σπονδὰς διότι ὁ δῆμ[ος
ὁ Ἀλεξανδρέων στεφανοῖ τὸν δῆμον τὸμ Πριηνέων ἀρετῆς ἕνεκεν [κ]αὶ εὐνοία[ς
τῆς εἰς αὐτὸν καὶ διότι δικαστὰς ἀπέστειλαν δικαίας ἄνδρας καλοὺς καὶ ἀγαθούς
25 Ἀθηναγόραν Εὐκτίτου Νύμφωνα Καλλικράτου Ἀριστόδημον Φίλωνος,—τὸ δ[ὲ
ψήφισμα τὸ παρὰ Ἀλεξανδρέων ἀναγράψαι εἰς στήλην λιθίνην καὶ στῆσαι
εἰς τὸ ἱερὸν τῆς Ἀθηνᾶς,—ὑπογράψαι δὲ καὶ τόδ[ε τ]ὸ ψήφισμα εἰς τὴν ἀνατιθε-
μένην στήλην, τῆς δὲ ἀναγραφῆς τῶ[ν ψ]ηφισμάτων καὶ τῆς ἐγδόσεως τῆς στήλης ἐπιμέλειαμ ποιησάσθαι τὸν νεωποιεῖν μέλλοντα Χάρμον ἐπὶ στεφανηφόρο[υ
30 Ἀπόλλωνος, καὶ τὸ γενόμενον ἀνάλωμα ἀνενεγκεῖν ἐν λόγῳ τῇ πόλει, ἀποστεῖλαι δὲ καὶ ξένιον Νικασαγόρᾳ τῷ παραγεγονότι πρεσβευτῇ τὸ κατὰ τὸν νόμον τὸν
νεωποιῶν Φλίαντα. ἵνα δὲ καὶ ἀσφαλῶς παραπεμφθῇ τοὺς στρατηγοὺς καὶ τοὺς
ἱππάρχας ἐπιμεληθῆναι.

This is the latter part of another decree concerning dikasts. What remains of it gives a decree of Priene in acknowledgment of certain honours voted by the city of Alexandria Troas to the people of Priene and the Prienian dikasts. Some debased forms occur : line 3, ΕΠΗΝΕΚΕ ; line 5, ΔΙΕΛΕΓΗΙ ; line 15, ΕΠΗΝΕΚΕΝ ; lines 9, 18, ΕΠΗΝΗΙΣΘΑΙ. In line 10 Η for Ν in προυπάρχουσιν and in line 21 Ρ for Γ in γραμματίως are mere blunders of the lapidary. The document cannot be much earlier than the second century B.C. We are enabled, in line 16, to learn the nature of the disputes which the Prienian dikasts were called in to decide : τάς τε τῶμ παρανόμων καὶ τὰς τῶμ βιαίων (δίκας). It is clear that party spirit had run high, and violence had been resorted to : it seemed advisable to call in judges from a friendly, but impartial, state, to hear the lawsuits which had

thus arisen, with a view to restoring tranquillity (see the notes on No. ccccxviii ante).

Line 32. Φλέας is a name not found elsewhere : it may be connected with Φλέων, which occurs as an epithet of Dionysos at Ephesos, see post.

This inscription is an interchange of compliments between Priene and Alexandria Troas ; the latter had voted an honorary crown to the people of Priene (lines 2, 17, 21) for sending such efficient dikasts : this crown was further commemorated by the stelè, No. ccccxxxi, post, by help of which we make sure which Alexandria is referred to. On Apollo as eponymos (line 30), see on No. cccciii, line 126, and compare Nos. ccccxv, ccccxvi.

Concerning the στρατηγοί and ἱππάρχαι, see p. 53, post.

CCCCXX.

A stelè of white marble, from the temple of Athenè Polias, Prienè, surmounted by a pediment on which are three wreaths in low relief. Height, 5 ft.: width, 1 ft. 9½ in. Presented by the Society of Dilettanti, 1870. Unpublished.

```
ΤΟΓΑΡΑΙΑΣΕΩΝΕΔΟΞΕΝΤΗΙΒΟΥΛΗΙΚΑΙΤΩΙΔΗΜΩΙΓΡΥΤΑΝΕΩΝΓΝΩΜΗΓΕΡΙΩΝ
ΕΡΗΑΘΩΝΓΡΩΤΕΑΣΕΡΜΙΟΥΚΑΙΕΚΑΤΑΙΟΣΓΡΟΣΕΙΔΙΓΓΟΥΙΝΑΗΒΟΥΛΗΚΑΙΟ
ΔΗΜΟΣΒΟΥΛΕΥΣΗΤΑΙΤΙΣΙΝΔΕΙΤΙΜΑΙΣΤΙΜΗΘΗΝΑΙΤΟΝΔΗΜΟΝΤΟΝΓΡΙΗ
ΝΕΩΝΚΑΙΤΟΝΓΑΡΑΓΕΝΟΜΕΝΟΝΓΡΟΣΗΜΑΣΔΙΚΑΣΤΗΝΗΡΟΚΡΑΤΗΝΑΝΔΓΙΟΥ
ΑΙΤΟΝΓΡΑΜΜΑΤΕΑΗΓΕΓΟΛΙΝΗΓΙΟΥΔΕΔΟΧΘΑΙΤΗΙΒΟΥΛΗΙΚΑΙΤΩΙΔΗ
ΜΩΙΕΓΕΙΔΗΟΔΗΜΟΣΟΓΡΙΗΝΕΩΝΕΝΤΕΤΟΙΣΓΡΟΤΕΡΟΝΧΡΟΝΟΙΣΕΥΝΟΥΣΩΝ
ΚΑΙΦΙΛΟΣΔΙΕΤΕΛΕΙΕΙΚΑΙΝΥΝΑΞΙΩΣΑΝΤΩΝΗΜΩΝΑΓΟΣΤΕΙΛΑΙΔΙΚΑΣΤΗΝ
ΑΓΕΣΤΕΙΛΕΝΑΝΔΡΑΚΑΛΟΝΚΑΙΑΓΑΘΟΝΗΡΟΚΡΑΤΗΝΑΝΔΡΙGΥΟΣΓΑΡΑ
ΓΕΝΟΜΕΝΟΣΤΑΣΜΕΝΣΥΝΕΛΥΣΕΤΩΝΔΙΚΩΝΟΥΘΕΝΕΛΛΕΙΓΩΝΓΡΟΘΥΜΙΑΣ
ΑΛΛΑΓΑΣΑΝΣΓΟΥΔΗΝΓΟΙΟΥΜΕΝΟΣΙΝΑΣΥΛΛΥΘΕΝΤΕΣΟΙΑΝΤΙΔΙΚΟΙΤΑ
ΓΡΟΣΑΥΤΟΥΣΜΕΘΟΜΟΝΟΙΑΣΓΟΛΙΤΕΥΩΝΤΑΙΤΑΣΔΕΔΙΕΚΡΙΝΕΝΔΙΚΑΙΩΣΤΗΝ
ΤΕΑΛΛΗΝΕΝΔΗΜΙΑΝΕΓΟΙΗΣΑΤΟΑΓΟΓΑΝΤΟΣΤΟΥΒΕΑΤΙΣΤΟΥΑΞΙΩΣΑΜ
ΦΟΤΕΡΩΝΤΩΝΓΟΛΕΩΝΙΝΑΟΥΝΚΑΙΟΔΗΜΟΣΦΑΙΝΗΤΑΙΧΑΡΙΝΑΓΟΔΙΔΟΥΣ
ΤΟΙΣΕΥΕΡΓΕΤΟΥΣΙΝΑΥΤΟΝΚΑΙΟΙΛΟΙΓΟΙΟΙΓΑΡΑΓΙΝΟΜΕΝΟΙΔΙΚΑΞΕΙΝΕΙΣ
ΤΗΝΓΟΛΙΝΣΗΤΩΣΙΝΑΞΙΩΣΕΓΑΙΝΟΥΚΑΙΤΙΜΩΝΓΟΙΕΙΣΘΑΙΤΑΣΚΡΙΣΕΙΣΕΙ
ΔΟΤΕΣΟΤΙΟΔΗΜΟΣΤΟΥΣΚΑΛΟΥΣΚΑΙΑΓΑΘΟΥΣΤΩΝΑΝΔΡΩΝΕΓΑΙΝΕΙΤΕ
ΚΑΙΤΙΜΑΙΕΓΗΝΗΣΘΑΙΤΟΝΔΗΜΟΝΤΟΝΓΡΙΗΝΕΩΝΑΡΕΤΗΣΕΝΕΚΕΝΚΑΙΕΥΝΟΙΑΣ
ΗΣΕΧΕΙΕΙΣΤΗΝΓΟΛΙΝΚΑΙΣΤΕΦΑΝΩΣΑΙΧΡΥΣΩΙΣΤΕΦΑΝΩΙΑΓΟΓΡΟΘΥΣΤΟΥ
ΕΚΤΟΥΝΟΜΟΥΟΤΙΑΙΤΗΣΑΜΕΝΩΝΗΜΩΝΔΙΚΑΣΤΗΝΑΓΕΣΤΕΙΛΕΝΑΝΔΡΑΚΑ
ΛΟΝΚΑΙΑΓΑΘΟΝΕΡΙΤΑΣΚΡΙΣΕΙΣΕΓΗΝΗΣΘΑΙΔΕΚΑΙΤΟΝΑΓΟΣΤΑΛΕΝΤΑΔΙΚΑΣ
ΤΗΝΗΡΟΚΡΑΤΗΝΑΝΔΡΙΟΥΑΡΕΤΗΣΕΝΕΚΕΝΚΑΙΚΑΛΟΚΑΓΑΘΙΑΣΕΓΙΤΩΙΓΡΟΣ
ΣΤΗΝΑΙΤΩΝΤΕΚΡΙΣΕΩΝΚΑΙΤΩΝΣΥΛΛΥΣΕΩΝΙΣΩΣΚΑΙΔΙΚΑΙΩΣΕΓΑΙΝΕ
ΣΑΙΔΕΚΑΙΤΟΝΣΥΝΕΞΑΓΟΣΤΑΛΕΝΤΑΜΕΤΑΥΤΟΥΓΡΑΜΜΑΤΕΑΗΓΕΓΟΛΙΝ
ΗΓΙΟΥΕΓΙΤΩΙΤΗΝΚΑΘΑΥΤΟΝΧΡΕΙΑΝΔΙΟΙΚΗΚΕΝΑΙΕΓΙΜΕΛΩΣΚΑΙΕΥΤΑ
ΚΤΩΣΚΑΙΤΗΝΕΝΔΗΜΙΑΝΓΕΓΟΙΗΣΘΑΙΜΕΤΑΓΑΣΗΣΕΥΤΑΞΙΑΣΚΑΙΣΤΕΦΑΝΩ
ΣΑΙΤΟΜΜΕΝΔΙΚΑΣΤΗΝΧΡΥΣΩΙΣΤΕΦΑΝΩΙΑΓΟΓΡΑΘΟΥΣΤΟΥΕΚΤΟΥΝΟΜΟΥ
ΤΟΝΔΕΓΡΑΜΜΑΤΕΑΘΑΛΛΟΥΣΤΕΦΑΝΩΙΕΙΝΑΙΔΕΑΥΤΟΥΣΚΑΙΓΡΟΞΕΝΟΥΣΤΗΣ
ΓΟΛΕΩΣΓΕΡΙΓΟΛΙΤΕΙΑΣΔΕΑΥΤΟΙΣΤΕΚΑΙΤΟΙΣΕΚΓΟΝΟΙΣΑΥΤΩΝΓΡΟΓΡΑΨ
ΘΑΙΤΟΥΣΓΡΟΣΤΑΤΑΣΕΝΤΟΙΣΕΝΝΟΜΟΙΣΧΡΟΝΟΙΣΕΙΝΑΙΔΕΑΥΤΟΙΣΚΑΙΕΦΟΔΟΝΕΓ
ΤΗΝΒΟΥΛΗΝΚΑΙΤΗΝΕΚΚΛΗΣΙΑΝΓΡΩΤΟΙΣΜΕΤΑΤΑΙΕΡΑΕΛΕΣΘΑΙΔΕΚΑΙΓΡΕΣ
ΒΕΥΤΑΣΟΙΤΙΝΕΣΓΑΡΑΓΕΝΟΜΕΝΟΙΕΙΣΓΡΙΗΝΗΝΤΟΤΕΨΗΦΙΣΜΑΑΓΟΔΩΣΟΥΣΙΝ
ΚΑΙΓΑΡΑΚΑΛΕΣΟΥΣΙΝΑΥΤΟΥΣΤΗΝΑΥΤΗΝΑΙΡΕΣΙΝΕΧΕΙΝΓΡΟΣΤΟΝΔΗΜΟΝ
ΟΣΟΥΣΙΝΑΕΚΑΙΙΝΑΟΙΣΤΕΦΑΝΟΙΑΝΑΓΓΕΛΘΩΣΙΝΕΝΤΩΙΘΕΑΤΡΩΙΤΟΙΣΓΡΩ
ΤΟΙΣΚΑΙΤΟΨΗΦΙΣΜΑΑΝΑΓΡΑΦΗΕΝΙΕΡΩΙΩΙΑΝΑΥΤΟΙΣΦΑΙΝΗΤΑΙΙΝΑ
ΝΗΙΔΙΟΤΙΟΔΗΜΟΣΟΙΑΣΕΩΝΚΑΙΤΑΣΓΟΛΕΙΣΚΑΙΤΟΥΣΑΝΔΡΑΣΤΟΥ
ΑΓΡΑΨΙΛΔΕΤΟΨΗΦΙΣΜΑΚΑΙΓΑΡΗΜΙΝΕΝΤΩΙΕΡΩΙΤΗΣΑΡΤΕ
ΟΗΣΑΝΕΚΑΤΑΙΟΣΓΟΣΕΙΔΙΓΓΟΥΜΕΝΕΣΕΞΕΝΟΣΚΥΔΙΟ·
ΙΣΤΡΑΤΗΓΩΝΕΡΕΙΔΗΙΑΣΕΙΣΦΙΛΟΙΥΓΑΡΧΟΝΤΕΣΤΩ
ΑΓΟΣΤΕΙ  ΝΤΕΣΓ      ΛΓΟΥ    ΙΓΓΟΥ
- - - - - - - - - - - - - - - - - - - - - - ΥΔΙΚΑΣ
                 ΩΝΓΡΟΘΥ·
          ΙΚΟΙΤΑΓΡΟΣΑΥΤΟΥΣΜΕΘΟΜΟΝ
          ΝΔΕΑΛΛΗΝΕΝΔΗΜΙΑΝΕΓΟΙΗΣΑΤΟ,
          ΕΡΩΝΤΩΝΓΟΛΕΩΝΕΓΑΙΝΟΥΣΙΝΤΕΤΟΝΔΗ·
          ΚΑΙΕΥΝΟΙΑΣΗΣΕΧΕΙΕΙΣΤΗΝΓΟΛΙΝΑΥΤΩΝΚΑΙΕΣ,
          ΑΓΟΓΛΗΘΟΥΣΤΟΥΕΚΤΟΥΝΟΜΟΥΟΤΙΑΙΤΗΣΑΜΕΝΩΝΑ  ΩΝΔ
          ΣΙΛΑΕΝΕΓΙΤΑΣΚΡΙΣΕΙΣΑΝΔΡΑΚΑΛΟΝΚΑΙΑΓΑΘΟΝΕΓΑΙSΙ,ΥΣΙΔΕΚΑΙ
          ΑΛΕΝΤΑΔΙΚΑΣΤΗΝΗΡΟΚΡΑΤΗΝΑΝΔΡΙΟΥΑΡΕΤΗSΓ ΚΕΝΚΑΙΚΑΛΟΚΑ
          ΣΕΓΙΤΩΙΓΡΟΣΤΗΝΑΙΤΩΝΤΕΚΡΙΣΕΩΝΚΑΊΤ    ,,ΥΣΕΩΝ,ΩΣΚΑΙΔΙΚΑΙΩΣ
          ΓΑΙΝΟΥΣΔΕΚΑΙΤΟΝΣΥΝΓ ,ΓΟΣΤΑΛΕΝΤΑΜΕΤΑΥΤΟΥΓΡΑΜΜΑΤΕΑΗΓΕΓΟ
          ΛΙΝΗΓΙΟΥΕΓΙΤΩΙΤΗΝ (ΑΘΑΥΤΟΝΧΡΕΙΑΝΔΙΟΙΚΗΚΕΝΑΙΕΓΙΜΕΛΩΣΚΑΙΕΥΤΑΚΤΩ
          ΚΑΙΤΗΝΕΝΔΗΜΙΑ   ΓΟΙΗΣΘΑΙΜΕΤΑΓΑΣΗΣΕΥΤΑΞΙΑΣΚΑΙΣΤΕΦΑΝΩΚΑΣΙΝΤΟΝΜΕΙ
          "ΑΣΤΗΝΥ    _ΩΙΣΤΕΦΑΝΩΙΑΓΟΓΡΑΘΟΥΣΤΟΥΕΚΤΟΥΝΟΜΟΥΤΟΝΔΕΓΡΑΜΜ,
          ΑΛΛΟΥΣΤΕΦΑΝΩΙΓΕΓΟΙΗΝΤΑΙΔΕΑΥΤΟΥΣΚΑΙΓΡΟΞΕΝΟΥΣΤΗΣ ΟΛΕΩΣΓΕΡΙΔΕ
          ,ΛΙΤΕΙΑΣΑΥΤΟΙΣΤΕΚΑΙΤΟΙΣΕΚΓΟΝΟΙΣΑΥΤΩΝΕΓΙΤΕΤΑΧΑΣΙΝΤΟΙΣΓΡΟΣΤΑΤΑΙΣ
          ΓΡΟΓΡΑΨΑΣΘΑΙΕΝΤΟΙΣΕΝΝΟΜΟΙΣΧΡΟΝΟΙΣΔΕΔΩΚΑΝΔΕΑΥΤΟΙΣΚΑΙΕΦΟΔΟΝΕΓΙΤΗΝΒΟΥΛΗΝ
```

```
        ΚΑΙΤΙΙΝΕΚΚΛΗΣΙΑΝΓΡΩΤΟΙΣΜΕΤΑΤΑΙΕΡΑΑΞΙΟΥΣΙΝΔΕΚΑΙΙΝΑΟΙΣΤΕΦΑΝΟΙΑΝΑΓΓΕΛΩ
        ΣΙΝΓΑΡΗΜΙΝΕΝΤΩΙΘΕΑΤΡΩΙΤΟΙΣΓΡΩΤΟΙΣΔΙΟΝΥΣΙΟΙΣΚΑΙΤΟΨΗΦΙΣΜΑΑΝΑΓΡΑΦΗΙ
60      ΕΝΙΕΡΩΙΩΙΑΝΗΜΙΝΦΑΙΝΗΤΑΙΙΝΑΓΑΣΙΝΦΑΝΕΡΟΝΗΙΟΤΙΟΔΗΜΟΣΑΥΤΩΝΚΑΙΤΑΣΓΟ
        ΛΕΙΣΚΑΙΤΟΥΣΑΝΔΡΑΣΤΟΥΣΑΓΑΘΟΥΣΤΙΜΑΙΕΓΕΑΘΟΝΤΕΣΔΕΚΑΙΟΙΓΡΕΣΒΕΥΤΑΙ
        ΕΓΙΤΗΝΕΚΚΛΗΣΙΑΝΔΙΕΛΕΓΗΣΑΝΑΚΟΛΟΥΘΩΣΤΟΙΣΕΝΤΩΙΨΗΦΙΣΜΑΤΙΓΕΓΡΑΜΜΕΝΟΙΣ
        ΣΓΟΥΔΗΣΚΑΙΦΙΛΟΤΙΜΙΑΣΟΥΘΕΝΕΛΛΕΙΓΟΝΤΕΣΕΓΟΙΗΣΑΝΤΟΔΕΚΑΙΤΗΝΕΓΙΔΗΜΙΑΝ
        ΕΥΚΟΣΜΩΣΔΕΔΟΧΘΑΙΤΩΙΔΗΜΩΙΕΓΗΝΗΣΘΑΙΜΕΝΤΟΝΔΗΜΟΝΤΟΝΙΑΣΕΩΝΕΓΙΤΕ
65      ΤΗΙΕΥΝΟΙΑΙΗΙΕΧΕΙΕΙΣΤΗΝΓΟΛΙΝΤΗΝΗΜΕΤΕΡΑΝΚΑΙΕΓΙΤΗΙΕΥΧΑΡΙΣΤΙΑΙΗΜΓΕΓΟΙΗ
        ΤΑΙΕΙΣΤΕΤΟΝΔΗΜΟΝΚΑΙΤΟΝΑΝΔΡΑΤΟΝΑΓΟΣΤΑΛΕΝΤΑΗΓΟΚΡΑΤΗΝΑΝΔΡΙΟΥΚΑΙΤΟΙ
        ΓΡΑΜΜΑΤΕΑΗΓΕΓΟΛΙΝΗΓΙΟΥΚΑΙΑΓΟΚΡΙΝΑΣΘΑΙΑΥΤΟΙΣΔΙΟΤΙΟΔΗΜΟΣΔΙΑΤΗΡΗΣΕΙΚ
        ΞΙΣΤΟΝΑΛΛΟΝΧΡΟΝΟΝΤΗΝΑΥΤΗΝΑΙΡΕΣΙΝΓΡΟΣΤΟΝΔΗΜΟΝΑΥΤΩΝΙΝΑΔΕΚΑΙΤΑΛ
        ΟΥΜΕΝΑΥΓΟΙΑΣΕΩΝΣΥΝΤΕΛΕΣΣΩΗΙΤΟΜΜΕΝΑΓΓΝΟΟΕΘΗΝΟΣΑΝΗΙΤΟΤΕΡΟΙΗΣΑΣΘ
70      ΤΗΝΑΝΑΓΓΕΛΙΑΝΑΥΛΗΤΩΝΤΩΙΑΓΩΝΙΤΩΙΡΑΙΔΙΚΩΙΤΩΝΣΤΕΦΑΝΩΝΟΙΣΕΣΤΕΦ
        ΙΩΚΑΣΙΝΙΑΣΕΙΣΤΟΝΤΕΔΗΜΟΝΤΟΝΗΜΕΤΕΡΟΝΚΑΙΤΟΝΔΙΚΑΣΤΗΝΚΑΙΤΟΝΓΡΑΜ
        ΜΑΤΕΑΤΟΝΔΕΝΕΩΓΟΙΗΝΑΝΑΞΑΓΟΡΑΝΑΡΕΓΑΔΟΥΝΑΙΣΤΗΛΗΝΛΙΘΙΝΗΝΕΙΣΗΝΑΝΑ
        ΡΑΦΗΣΕΤΑΙΤΑΨΗΦΙΣΜΑΤΑΚΑΙΣΤΑΘΗΣΕΤΑΙΗΣΤΗΛΗΑΘΕΝΤΩΙΕΡΩΙΤΗΣΑΘΗΝΑΣ
        Ν ΛΕΞΙΑΤΗΣΕΙΚΟΝΟΣΤΗΣΚΩΜΟΥΤΟΥΤΙΜΟΚΛΕΙΟΥΣΔΟΥΝΑΙΔΕΤΟΝΝΕΩΓΟΙΗΝ
75      ΝΑΞΑΓΟΡΑΝΤΟΙΣΓΡΕΣΒΕΥΤΑΙΣΤΟΙΣΓΑΡΑΙΣΕΩΝΞΕΝΙΑΤΑΕΚΤΚΤΟΥΝΟΜΟΥ
```


Τὸ παρὰ Ἰασέων. Ἔδοξεν τῇ βουλῇ καὶ τῷ δήμῳ· πρυτάνεων γνώμη· περὶ ὧν
ἐπῆλθον Πρωτίας Ἑρμίου καὶ Ἑκαταῖος Ποσειδίππου, ἵνα ἡ βουλὴ καὶ ὁ
δῆμος βουλεύσηται τίσιν δεῖ τιμαῖς τιμηθῆναι τὸν δῆμον τὸν Πριηνέων καὶ τὸν παραγενόμενον πρὸς ἡμᾶς δ:καστὴν Ἡροκράτην Ἀνδρίου
5 κ]αὶ τὸν γραμματέα Ἡγέπολιν Ἡγίου· δεδόχθαι τῇ βουλῇ καὶ τῷ δήμῳ. Ἐπειδὴ ὁ δῆμος ὁ Πριηνέων ἔν τε τοῖς πρότερον χρόνοις εὔνους ὢν
καὶ φίλος διετέλει, καὶ νῦν ἀξιωσάντων ἡμῶν ἀπέστειλεν δικαστὴν
ἀπέστειλεν ἄνδρα καλὸν καὶ ἀγαθὸν Ἡροκράτην Ἀνδρίου, ὃς παραγενόμενος τὰς μὲν συνέλυσε τῶν δικῶν οὐδὲν ἐλλείπων προθυμίας
10 ἀλλὰ πᾶσαν σπουδὴν ποιούμενος ἵνα συλλυθέντες οἱ ἀντίδικοι τὰ
πρὸ αὑτοῖ μεθ' ὁμονοίας πολιτεύωνται, τὰς δὲ διέκρινεν δικαίως, τήν
τε ἄλλην ἐνδημίαν ἐποιήσατο ἀπὸ παντὸς τοῦ βελτίστου ἀξίως ἀμ-
φοτέρων τῶν πόλεων, — ἵνα οὖν καὶ ὁ δῆμος φαίνηται χάριν ἀποδιδοὺς
τοῖς εὐεργετοῦσιν αὐτὸν καὶ οἱ λοιποὶ παραγινόμενοι δικάζειν εἰς
15 τὴν πόλιν ζητῶσιν ἀξίως ἐπαίνου καὶ τιμῶν ποιεῖσθαι τὰς κρίσεις εἰ-
δότες ὅτι ὁ δῆμος τοὺς καλοὺς καὶ ἀγαθοὺς τῶν ἀνδρῶν ἐπαινεῖ τε
καὶ τιμᾷ. ἐπηνῆσθαι τὸν δῆμον τὸν Πριηνέων ἀρετῆς ἕνεκεν καὶ εὐνοίας
ἧς ἔχει εἰς τὴν πόλιν καὶ στεφανῶσαι· χρυσῷ στεφάνῳ ἀπὸ πλήθους τοῦ
ἐκ τοῦ νόμου, ὅτι αἰτησαμένων ἡμῶν δικαστὴν ἀπέστειλεν ἄνδρα κα-
20 λὸν καὶ ἀγαθὸν ἐπὶ τὰς κρίσεις, ἐπηνῆσθαι δὲ καὶ τὸν ἀποσταλέντα δικαστὴν Ἡροκράτην Ἀνδρίου ἀρετῆς ἕνεκεν καὶ καλοκἀγαθίας ἐπὶ τῷ προσ-
(σ)τῆναι τῶν τε κρίσεων καὶ τῶν συλλύσεων ἴσως καὶ δικαίως, ἐπαινέσαι δὲ καὶ τὸν συνεξαποσταλέντα μετ' αὐτοῦ γραμματέα Ἡγέπολιν
Ἡγίου, ἐπὶ τῷ τὴν καθ' αὑτὸν χρείαν διαπεφηκέναι ἐπιμελῶς καὶ εὐτά-
25 κτως καὶ τὴν ἐνδημίαν πεποιῆσθαι μετὰ πάσης εὐταξίας, καὶ στεφανῶσαι τὸμ μὲν δικαστὴν χρυσῷ στεφάνῳ ἀπὸ πλήθους τοῦ ἐκ τοῦ νόμου
τὸν δὲ γραμματέα θαλλοῦ στεφάνῳ, εἶναι δὲ αὐτοὺς καὶ προξένους τῆς
πόλεως, περὶ πολιτείας δὲ αὐτοῖς τε καὶ τοῖς ἐκγόνοις αὐτῶν προγράφ[ας-
θαι τοὺς προστάτας ἐν τοῖς ἐννόμοις χρόνο(ι)ς, εἶναι δὲ αὐτοῖς καὶ ἔφοδον ἐπ[ὶ
30 τὴν βουλὴν καὶ τὴν ἐκκλησίαν πρώτοις μετὰ τὰ ἱερά, ἐλέσθαι δὲ καὶ πρεσβευτὰς οἵτινες παραγενόμενοι εἰς Πριήνην τό τε ψήφισμα ἀποδώσουσιν
καὶ παρακαλέσωσιν αὐτοὺς τὴν αὐτὴν αἵρεσιν ἔχειν πρὸς τὸν δῆμον,
ἀξ]ιώσουσιν δὲ καὶ ἵνα οἱ στέφανοι ἀναγγελθῶσιν ἐν τῷ θεάτρῳ τοῖς πρώτοις Διονυσίοις καὶ τὸ ψήφισμα ἀναγραφῇ ἐν ἱερῷ ῷ ἂν αὐτοῖς φαίνηται, ἵνα
35 πᾶσιν φανερὸ]ν ᾖ διότι ὁ δῆμος ὁ Ἰασέων καὶ τὰς πόλεις καὶ τοὺς ἄνδρας τοὺ[ς
ἀγαθοὺς τιμᾷ, ἀν]αγράψαι δὲ τὸ ψήφισμα καὶ παρ' ἡμῖν ἐν τῷ ἱερῷ τῆς Ἀρτέμιδος. —Ἡιρέ]θησαν Ἑκαταῖος Ποσειδίππου, Μενέξενος Κυδίου.

Ἔδοξεν τῷ δήμῳ· γνώμη] στρατηγῶν· Ἐπειδὴ Ἰασεῖς φίλοι ὑπάρχοντες τῷ
δήμῳ τῷ Πριηνέων καὶ νῦν] ἀποστείλα]ντες Ἑ[καταῖο]ν Ποσ[ειδ]ίππου [καὶ
40 Μενέξενον Κυδίου ἐπαινοῦσιν τὸν ἀποσταλέντα ὑπὸ τοῦ δήμο]υ δικασ-
[τὴν Ἡροκράτην Ἀνδρίου διότι παραγενόμενος πρὸ αὐτοῖ τὰς μὲν συνέλυσε]
τῶν δικῶν οὐθὲν ἐλλείπ]ων προθυ[μίας ἀλλὰ πᾶσαν σπουδὴν ποιούμενος ἵνα

συλλυθέντες οἱ ἀντίδ]ικοι τὰ πρὸς αὐτοὺς μεθ' ὁμον[οίας πολιτεύωνται, τὰς δὲ διέκρινεν δικαίως τὴ]ν δὲ ἄλλην ἐνδημίαν ἐποιήσατο [ἀπὸ παντὸς τοῦ βελτίστου

45   ἀξίων ἀμφοτ]έρων τῶν πόλεων, ἐπαινοῦσίν τε τὸν δῆ[μον τὸν ἡμέτερον ἀρετῆς ἕνεκεν] καὶ εὐνοίας ἧς ἔχει εἰς τὴν πόλιν αὐτῶν, καὶ ἐστ[εφανώκασιν χρυσῷ στεφάνῳ] ἀπὸ πλήθους τοῦ ἐκ τοῦ νόμου ὅτι αἰτησαμένων α[ὐτ]ῶν δ[ικαστὴν
ἀπέστ]ειλεν ἐπὶ τὰς κρίσεις ἄνδρα καλὸν καὶ ἀγαθόν, ἐπαινοῦσι δὲ καὶ [τὸν
ἀποστ]αλέντα δικαστὴν Ἡροκράτην Ἀνδρίου ἀρετῆς ἕ[νε]κεν καὶ καλοκά-
50   γαθία]ς ἐπὶ τῷ προστῆναι τῶν τε κρίσεων καὶ τ[ῶν συλ]λύσεων ἴσως καὶ δικαίως,
ἐ]παινοῦσιν δὲ καὶ τὸν συνε[ξ]αποσταλέντα μετ' αὐτοῦ γραμματέα Ἡγέπολιν Ἡγίου ἐπὶ τῷ τὴν καθ' αὐτὸν χρείαν διῳκηκέναι ἐπιμελῶς καὶ εὐτάκτω[ς
καὶ τὴν ἐνδημία[ν πε]ποιῆσθαι μετὰ πάσης εὐταξίας, καὶ ἐστεφανώκασιν τὸν μὲν
δι]καστὴν χ[ρυ]σῷ στεφάνῳ ἀπὸ πλήθους τοῦ ἐκ τοῦ νόμου τὸν δὲ γραμμα-
55   τέα θ]αλλοῦ στεφάνῳ, πεποίηνται δὲ αὐτοὺς καὶ προξένους τῆς [π]όλεως, περὶ δὲ
π]ολιτείας αὐτοῖς τε καὶ τοῖς ἐκγόνοις αὐτῶν ἐπιτετάχασι · οἷς προστάται
προγράψασθαι ἐν τοῖς ἐννόμοις χρόνοις, δέδωκαν δὲ αὐτοῖς καὶ ἔφοδον ἐπὶ τὴν βουλὴν
καὶ τὴν ἐκκλησίαν πρώτοις μετὰ τὰ ἱερά, ἀξιοῦσιν δὲ καὶ ἵνα οἱ στέφανοι ἀναγγελῶ-
σιν παρ' ἡμῖν ἐν τῷ θεάτρῳ τοῖς πρώτοις Διονυσίοις καὶ τὸ ψήφισμα ἀναγραφῇ
60   ἐν ἱερῷ ᾧ ἂν ἡμῖν φαίνηται, ἵνα πᾶσιν φανερὸν ᾖ ὅτι ὁ δῆμος αὐτῶν καὶ τὰς πόλεις καὶ τοὺς ἄνδρας τοὺς ἀγαθοὺς τιμᾷ, ἐπελθόντες δὲ καὶ οἱ πρεσβευταὶ
ἐπὶ τὴν ἐκκλησίαν διελέγησαν ἀκολούθως τοῖς ἐν τῷ ψηφίσματι γεγραμμένοις
σπουδῆς καὶ φιλοτιμίας οὐθὲν ἐλλείποντες, ἐποιήσαντο δὲ καὶ τὴν ἐπιδημίαν
εὐκόσμως, —δεδόχθαι τῷ δήμῳ ἐπῃνῆσθαι μὲν τὸν δῆμον τὸν Ἰασέων ἐπί τε
65   τῇ εὐνοίᾳ ᾗ ἔχει εἰς τὴν πόλιν τὴν ἡμετέραν καὶ ἐπὶ τῇ εὐχαριστίᾳ ἥμ πεποίη-
ται εἴς τε τὸν δῆμον καὶ τὸν ἄνδρα τὸν ἀποσταλέντα Ἡροκράτην Ἀνδρίου καὶ τὸν
γραμματέα Ἡγέπολιν Ἡγίου, καὶ ἀποκρίνασθαι αὐτοῖς διότι ὁ δῆμος διατηρήσει τ[αῖ-
ς] εἰς τὸν ἄλλον χρόνον τὴν αὐτὴν αἵρεσιν πρὸς τὸν δῆμον αὐτῶν, ἵνα δὲ καὶ τὰ ἀ[ξι-
ούμενα ὑπὸ Ἰασέων συντελεσθῇ τὸμ μὲν ἀγωνοθέτην ὃς ἂν ᾖ τότε ποιήσασθ[αι
70   τὴν ἀναγγελίαν αὐλητῶν τῷ ἀγῶνι τῷ παιδικῷ τῶν στεφάνων οἷς ἐστεφ[α-
νώκασιν Ἰασεῖ τόν τε δῆμον τὸν ἡμέτερον καὶ τὸν δικαστὴν καὶ τὸν γραμματέα, τὸν δὲ νεωποίην Ἀναξαγόραν ἀπεγδοῦναι στήλην λιθίνην εἰς ἣν ἀνα-
γ]ραφήσεται τὰ ψηφίσματα, καὶ σταθήσεται ἡ στήλη ἐν τῷ ἱερῷ τῆς Ἀθηνᾶς
ἐ]πιδείξια τῆς εἰκόνος τῆς Κώμου τοῦ Τιμοκλείους, δοῦναι δὲ τον νεωποίην
75   Ἀ]ναξαγόραν τοῖς πρεσβευταῖς τοῖς παρ' [Ἰα]σέων ξένια τὰ ἐκ τ(κτ)οῦ νόμου.

Another document concerning Dikasts. Lines 1–37 give a copy of an Iasian decree in honour of Prienè and a Prienian dikast and his secretary. Lines 38 foll. contain a decree of Prienè in acknowledgment of these honours. The iota adscriptum is not uniformly given, e.g. lines 17, 20, 64, ΕΡΗΝΗΣΘΑΙ; line 34, ΑΝΑΓΡΑΦΗ. The forms δίδωκαν, line 57, the doubling of the Σ in προστῆναι, line 22, and συντελεσθῇ, line 69, are indications of a late date. In line 75 ΑΙΣΕΩΝ for ΙΑΣΕΩΝ and ΚΤ repeated are errors of the lapidary. The inscription probably belongs to the middle of the second century B.C. In the lists of names from the Iasian theatre published by Waddington-Le Bas we find mentioned Κυβίας Ποσειδίππου (No. 256), Μενέξενος Ποσειδίππου (Nos. 260, 268), Κυβίας Μενεξένου (No. 284): these appear to belong to the same family with Ἑκαταῖος Ποσειδίππου and Μενέξενος Κυβίου of line 37.

This is, I believe, the longest entire decree that we have from Iasos. The πρυτάνεις (line 1) were probably an executive committee of the βουλή, analogous to the prytanes at Athens; from C. I. 2677 it appears they were five in number, like the prytanes at Samos (No. cccciii, lines 29-32, ante). In a decree from Iasos concerning Mausolos (Bull. de Corr. Hell. v, 1881, p. 491) six prytanes are named: I offer no explanation of the discrepancy. A board of προστάται is spoken of in line 29: they are enjoined

to bring a proposal before the βουλή, 'at the proper times,' for the admission of these strangers of Prienè to the citizenship of Iasos. By ἐν τοῖς ἐννόμοις χρόνοις it is probably implied that strangers were not admitted into the body of citizens until after a certain notice had been given, so that anyone who pleased might raise an objection. This however, as we may be sure, was a mere matter of form. A similar notice was formally required at Athens before a grant of citizenship: see Demosthenes, In Neaer., p. 1374, Reiske. The formula ran thus : τοὺς δὲ πρυτάνεις οἳ ἂν πρῶτοι λάχωσιν πρυτανεύειν δοῦναι περὶ αὐτοῦ τὴν ψῆφον εἰς τὴν πρώτην ἐκκλησίαν, τοὺς δὲ θεσμοθέτας εἰσαγαγεῖν αὐτῷ τὴν δοκιμασίαν τῆς δωρεᾶς εἰς τὸ δικαστήριον ὅταν πρῶτον οἷόν τ' ᾖ (C. I. A. ii, 1. No. 312): see my remarks on this custom in the Hellenic Journal, iii, p. 138. The term προστάτης at Athens was applied to any citizen who made himself answerable for the good behaviour of a metoikos, and acted as his patronus or (so to say) political sponsor : see Suidas, s. v.; Aristotle, Politics, iii, 1, 4 = 1275 A ; and commentators on Sophokles, Oed. Rex, 411. In some of the Greek cities there seems to have existed a definite board of προστάται, whose functions resembled those of the individual προστάται at Athens, and who certainly superintended the admission of strangers to the citizenship. They are mentioned in this connexion at Rhodes (Part ii, ante, p. 114)

and at Knidos (see the references *ibid.*). At Kalymna the decrees of politeia are usually headed
γνώμα προστατᾶν (*ibid.*, Nos. ccxxxii, foll.). We find
them in the same connexion at Iasos in the decree
before us; and in another decree of politeia from
Iasos (C. I. 2676) the προστάται are charged to select
the place where the decree shall be inscribed : τόπον
δὲ ἀποδεῖξαι τοὺς προστάτας τὸ[ν ἐπιφανέστ]ατον, [ὅπ]ου
τὸ ψήφισμα ἀναγραφῆσ[ε]ται. At Amphipolis (C. I.

2008) in a decree relating to two citizens who had
been struck off the roll of citizens and banished for
ever, it is ordered τοὺς δὲ προστάτας ἀναγράψαι αὐτοὺς
ἐν στήλην λιθίνην : the προστάται therefore seem to
have been concerned with the expulsion as well as
the admission of citizens. The προστάτης Μολοσσῶν
so often mentioned in the Dodona decrees (see Cara-
panos, Dodone, *passim*) was an officer of a different
kind. See also C. I. A. ii, No. 546, line 36 (Keos).

CCCCXXI.

Stele of blue marble, from the temple of Athenè Polias, Prienè. Height, 2 ft. 5½ in. ; width, 1 ft. 9 in. Just above the decree are
traces of three wreaths. Surface very much worn. Presented by the Society of Dilettanti, 1870. Unpublished.

ΛΛΑΟΔΙΚΕΩΝ

⟨ΥΔΩΡΟΣΔΙΟΝΥΣΙΟΥΕΙΓΕΝΕΓΕΙΔΗΕΚΓΑΣΙΩΝΟΣΣΙΜΟΥΔΙΚΩΝΟΥ
ΞΩΝΛΔΙΚΑΣΤΩΝΠΑΡΗΜΙΝΟΔΗΜΟΣΕΓΙ.....ΗΣΑΞΙΑΝΠΡΟ
ΣΕΥΞΙΝΠΕΡΙΞΕΝΙΚΟΥΔΙΚΑΣΤΗΡΙΟΥΠΟΙΟΥΜΕΝΟΣΥΠΟΛΑΜΒ
5 ΩΝΜΑΛΙΣΤΑΠΡΟΣΤΗΣΕΣΘΑΙΤΩΓΚΑΤΑΤΑΣΔΙΚΑΣΑΥΤΩΝΤΟΥΣΠΑ
ΓΡΙΗΝΕΩΝΑΡΟΣΤΑΛΗΣΟΜΕΝΟΥΣΔΙΚΑΣΤΑΣΕΠΑ...ΙΑΥΤΩΝΤΗΙΒΟ
ΗΙΚΑΙΤΩΙΔΗΜΩΙΟΠΩΣΠΡΟ......ΤΑΙΔΙΚΑΣΤΑΣΤΡΕΙΣΩΣΕΠΙΛ
ΛΕΣΤΑΤΟΥΣΚΑΙΠΕΜΨΑΣΙΓΡΟΣΗΜΑΣΑΠΟΣΤΕΙΛΑΝΤΟΣΤΕΚΑΙΤΟΥΔ
ΜΟΥΓΡΟΣΑΥΤΟΥΣΠΡΕΣΒΕΙΑΝΓΡΙΗΝΕΙΖΟΝΤΕΣΗΜΩΝΦΙΛΟΙΕΠΕΛ
10 ΨΑΝΔΙΚΑΣΤΑΣΜΕΝΙΣΚΟΝΜΗΤΡΟΔΩΡΟΥΑΓΙΑΝΣΙΜΟΥΜΟΛΩΝΑΔΙΑΓ
ΡΟΥΟΙΓΑΡΑΓΕΝΟΛΕΝΟΙΕΙΣΤΗΜΓΟΛΙΝΕΔΙΚΑΣΑΝΤΑΣΔΙΚΑΣΔΙΚΑΙ
ΚΑΤΑΤΟΥΣΓΑΡΧΟΝΤΑΣΗΜΙΝΝΟΜΟΥΣΕΡΕΙΔΕΚΑΛΩΣΕΧΟΝΕΣ
ΤΙΜΑΣΘΑΙΤΟΥΣΕΥΝΟΥΣΑΝΔΡΑΣΤΥΧΗΙΑΓΑΘΗΙΚΑΙΕΓΙΖΩΤΗΡΙΑΙΔΕΔ
ΘΑΙΤΗΙΒΟΥΛΗΙΚΑΙΤΩΙΔΗΜΩΙ.......ΕΡΗΝΗΣΘΑΙΕΓΙΤΩΙΡ..Α
15 .ΡΙΗΝΕΥΣΙΝΠΡΕΣΒΕ..................ΚΑΙΑΓΑΘΟΥΣΤΟΥ
ΔΕΔΙΚΑΣΤΑΣΜΕΝΙΣΚΟΝΜΗΤΡΟΔΩΡΟΥΑΓΙΑΝΣΙΜΟΥΜΟΛΩΝΑΔΙΑΓΟΡΟΥ
ΕΡΗΝΗΣΘΑΙΤΕΚΑΙΚΑΛΕΙΣΘΑΙΥΓΡΩΤΟΙΣΔΗΜΟΥΕΙΣΤΟΘΕΑΤ..ΝΚΑΙΣΤΕΦ
ΛΟΥΣΘΑΙΕΚΑΣΤΟΝΑΥΤΩΝΧΡΥΣΩΙΣΤΕΦΑΝΩΙΚΑΘΕΚΑΣΤΟΝΕΤΟΣΔΙ
ΙΟΥΕΝΤΩΙΑΓΩΝΙΤΩΙΓΥΜΝΙΚΩΙΤΩΙΣΥΝΤΕΛΟΥΜΕΝΩΙΕΝΤΟΙΣΑΝΤΟΧ
20 ΟΙΣΕΡΗΝΗΣΘΩΑΙΔΕΚΑΙΤΟΝΣΥΝΑΡΟΣΤΑΛΕΝΤΑΑΥΤΟΙΣΓΡΑΜΜΑΤΕΑΗΓ
ΓΟΛΙΝΗΓΙΟΥΚΑΙΣΤΕΦΑΝΩΘΗΝΑΙΕΝΤΟΙΣΑΝΤΙΟΧΕΙΟΙΣΕΛΑΙΑΣΣΤΕΦΑ
ΝΩΙΓΕΡΙΔΕΤΟΥΚΑΛΕΙΣΘΑΙΕΙΣΤΗΝΓΡΟΕΔΡΙΑΝΤΟΥΣΔΙΚΑΣΤΑΣΤΗΣ
ΑΝΑΓΓΕΛΙΑΣΤΩΝΣΤΕΦΑΝΩΝΕΓΙΜΕΛΕΙΑΝΓΟΙΗΣΑΣΘΑΙΤΟΝΤΕ
ΑΓΩΝΟΘΕΤΗΝΚΑΙΤΟΥΣΓΡΥΤΑΝΕΙΣΤΟΥΣΕΚΑΣΤΟΤΕΓΙΝΟΜΕΝΟΥΣ
25 ΥΓΑΡΧΕΙΝΔΕΤΟΙΣΔΙΚΑΣΤΑΙΣΚΑΙΕΜΓΡΥΤΑΝΕΙΩΙΣΙΤΗΣΙΝΚΑΙΕΦΟΔΟΝ
ΕΓΙΤΗΝΒΟΥΛΗΝΚΑΙΤΟΝΔΗΜΟΝΓΡΩΤΟΙΣΜΕΤΑΤΑΙΕΡΑΙΝΑΔΕΚΑΙΟΔΗΜΩ
ΟΓΡΙΗΝΕΩΝΕΙΔΗΣΗΙΤΑΕΨΗΦΙΣΜΕΝΑΛΕΣΘΑΙΓΡΕΣΒΕΥΤΗΝΟΣΑΦ
ΚΣΜΕΝΟΣΕΙΣΓΡΙΗΝΗΝΤΟΤΕΨΗΦΙΣΜΑΑΓΟΔΩΣΕΙΚΑΙΤΗΝΤΟΥΔΗΜΟ
ΕΥΝΟΙΑΝΕΜΦΑΝΙΣΕΙΗΝΕΧΕΙΓΡΟΣΓΡΙΗΝΕΙΣΓΑΡΑΚΑΛΕΣΕΙΤ
30 ΑΥΤΟΥΣΓΟΙΗΣΑΣΘΑΙΤΗΝΑΝΑΝΑΓΓΕΛΙΑΝΤΩΝΕΨΗΦΙΣΜΕ
ΝΩΝΣΤΕΦΑΝΩΝΤΟΙΣΤΕΔΙΚΑΣΤΑΙΣΚΑΙΤΩΙΓΡΑΜΜΑΤΕΙ
ΕΝΤΩΙΑΓΩΝΙΤΩΝΔΙΟΝΥΣΙΩΝΟΤΑΝ.ΥΓΥΑΙΓΡΟΓΑΣΗΣ
ΣΓΟΝΔΑΣΚΑΙΙΝΑΛΛΑΝΑΓΡΑΦΗΙΤΟΨΗΦΙΣΜΑΕΙΣΤΗΛΗΝΚΑΙΣΤΑΘΗΙ
ΕΝΤΩΙΙΕΡΩΙΤΗΣΑΘΗΝΑΣΕΙΝΑΙΔΕΤΟΨΗΦΙΣΜΑΤΟΥΤΟΕΓΙΣΩ
35 ΤΗΡΙΑΙΤΗΣΓΟΛΕΩΣ·ΤΟΥΣΔΕΕΞΕΤΑΣΤΑ᷄᷄   ΛΓΡΑΨΑΝΤΑΣ
ΑΥΤΟΕΙΣΛΕΥΚΩΜΑΘΕΙΝΑΙΕΝΤΩΙΑΡ   ΣΘΗΣΑΥΡΟ
ΓΡΕΣΒΕΥΤΗΣΚΥΔΩΡΟΣΔΙΟΝΥΣΙΟΥ

Τὸ παρ]ὰ Λαοδικέων.

*Κύδωρος Διονυσίου εἶπεν· ἐπειδὴ ἐκ Πασίωνος Σίμου δικῶν οὐ-
σῶν ἀδικάστων παρ' ἡμῖν ὁ δῆμος ἐπι[στροφὴ]ἦι(?) ἀξίαν πρό-
σευξιν περὶ ξενικοῦ δικαστηρίου ποιούμενος, ὑπολαμβ[ά-
5   ν]ων μάλιστα προστήσεσθαι τῶν -ατὰ τὰς δίκας αὐτῶν τοὺς πα[ρὰ
Πριηνέων ἀποσταλησομένους δικαστὰς, ἐπα[ινε]ῖ(?) αὐτῶν τῇ βο[υ-
λ]ῇ καὶ τῷ δήμῳ ὅπως προ[βάλλων]ται δικαστὰς τρεῖς ὡς ἐπιμ[ε-
λεστάτους καὶ πέμψας πρὸς ἡμᾶς, ἀποστειλαντός τε καὶ τοῦ δ[ή-*

PRIENÈ.

41

μου πρὸς αὐτοὺς πρεσβείαν Πριηνεῖς ὄντες ἡμῶν φίλοι ἔπεμ-
10 ψαν δικαστὰς, Μενίσκον Μητροδώρου, Ἀγίαν Σίμου, Μόλωνα Διαγ[ό-
ρου, οἱ παραγενόμενοι εἰς τὴμ πόλιν ἐδίκασαν τὰς δίκας δικαί[ως
κατὰ τοὺς ὑπάρχοντας ἡμῖν νόμους, ἐπεὶ δὲ καλῶς ἔχον ἐσ[τὶ
τιμᾶσθαι τοὺς εὔνους ἄνδρας· Τύχῃ Ἀγαθῇ καὶ ἐπὶ σωτηρίᾳ δεδ-
όχ]θαι τῇ βουλῇ καὶ τῷ δήμῳ [τοὺς μὲν] ἐπῃνῆσθαι ἐπὶ τῷ π[αρ]ὰ
15 Π]ριηνεῦσιν πρεσβε[ύσαι ὄντας ἄνδρας καλοὺς] καὶ ἀγαθοὺς, τοὺ[ς
δὲ δικαστὰς Μενίσκον Μητροδώρου, Ἀγίαν Σίμου, Μόλωνα Διαγόρου
ἐπῃνῆσθαί τε καὶ καλεῖσθαι ὑπὸ τοῦ δήμου εἰς τὸ θέατ[ρο]ν καὶ στεφ[α-
νοῦσθαι ἕκαστον αὐτῶν χρυσῷ στεφάνῳ καθ᾽ ἕκαστον ἔτος δι[ὰ
β]ίου ἐν τῷ ἀγῶνι τῷ γυμνικῷ τῷ συντελουμένῳ ἐν τοῖς Ἀντ(ι)οχ[εί-
20 οις, ἐπῃνῆσθαι δὲ καὶ τὸν συναποσταλέντα αὐτοῖς γραμματέα Ἡγ[έ-
πολιν Ἡγίου καὶ στεφανωθῆναι ἐν τοῖς Ἀντιοχείοις ἐλαίας στεφάνῳ, περὶ δὲ τοῦ καλεῖσθαι εἰς τὴν προεδρίαν τοὺς δικαστὰς τῆς [τε
ἀναγγελίας τῶν στεφάνων ἐπιμέλειαν ποιήσασθαι τόν τε
ἀγωνοθέτην καὶ τοὺς πρυτάνεις τοὺς ἑκάστοτε γινομένους,
25 ὑπάρχειν δὲ τοῖς δικασταῖς καὶ ἐμ πρυτανείῳ σίτησιν καὶ ἔφοδον
ἐπὶ τὴν βουλὴν καὶ τὸν δῆμον πρώτοις μετὰ τὰ ἱερά· ἵνα δὲ καὶ ὁ δῆμο[ς
ὁ Πριηνέων εἰδήσῃ τὰ ἐψηφισμένα ἑλέσθαι πρεσβευτὴν ὃς ἀφ[ι-
κόμενος εἰς Πριήνην τό τε ψήφισμα ἀποδώσει καὶ τὴν τοῦ δήμο[υ
εὔνοιαν ἐμφανίσει ἣν ἔχει πρὸς Πριηνεῖς, παρακαλέσει τ[ε
30 αὐτοὺς ποιήσασθαι τὴν (αν)ἀναγγελίαν τῶν ἐψηφισμέ-
νων στεφάνων τοῖς τε δικασταῖς καὶ τῷ γραμματεῖ
ἐν τῷ ἀγῶνι τῶν Διονυσίων ὅταν [θ]ύηται πρὸ πάσης
σπονδᾶς, καὶ ἵνα ἀναγραφῇ τὸ ψήφισμα εἰστήλην καὶ σταθῇ
ἐν τῷ ἱερῷ τῆς Ἀθηνᾶς· εἶναι δὲ τὸ ψήφισμα τοῦτο ἐπὶ σω-
35 τηρίᾳ τῆς πόλεως, τοὺς δὲ ἐξετασθὰς [ἀν]αγράψαντας
αὐτὸ εἰς λεύκωμα θεῖναι ἐν τῷ Ἀρ[τέμιδο]ς θησαυρῷ.
Πρεσβευτὴς Κύδωρος Διονυσίου.

The slab is entire, but the surface of the marble is very much worn; so that only with great pains could the inscription be recovered. Consequently the readings are not always quite certain. The words ἐπὶ[στροφ]ῆτ in line 3, προ[βάλλων]ται line 7, are somewhat conjectural; nor can one be sure of the turn of the phrase in lines 14, 15, about the honouring of the Laodikeian envoys. In [θ]ύηται, line 32, the third letter on the stone seems rather Ε than Η. The form σπονδᾶς, line 33, is perhaps a blunder of the lapidary, who in line 19 wrote ΑΝΤΟΧΕΙΟΙΣ and ΑΝΑΝΑΓΓΕΛΙΑΝ, line 30.

The inscription, as the heading shows, is a copy of a decree of Laodikeia set up at Prienè. The senate and people of Laodikeia, finding it advisable to call in foreign dikasts to settle certain causes which had remained untried ‘since the magistracy of Pasion, son of Simos’ (line 2), applied by embassy to Prienè to select and send dikasts. The names of these dikasts are given in lines 10 and 16. Their secretary Hegepolis, son of Hegias (lines 20, 21) is the same person who is mentioned in No. cccxx as having been secretary to the dikast sent to Iasos.

The subject of this decree is much the same as that of the others of this class, and calls for little remark. For the perennial honours granted to the dikasts in lines 18, 19, we may compare C. I. 3067, line 23, στεφανοῦν Κράτωνα . . . καθ᾽ ἕκαστον ἔτος εἰς ἀεὶ ἐν τῷ θεάτρῳ, κ.τ.λ.; ibid. 3068 B, lines 15 foll., στε- φανοῦν Κράτωνα . . . διὰ βίου ἐν τε τῇ κοινῇ δείπνῳ τῶν συναγωνιστῶν καὶ ἐν τῷ θεάτρῳ, κ.τ.λ. See other ex- amples, Keil, Analecta Onomatol., p. 25. As to the Ἀντιόχεια in line 19, as Laodikeia was founded

by Antiochos Theos about 250 B.C. (Droysen, Hel- lenismus, iii. 2, p. 270), and named after his wife, it is natural that the city should have held a festival in his honour.

We may fairly assume that the Laodikeia of our inscription was the city of that name on the Lykos, i.e. situated in the upper basin of the same Maeander valley which lay at the foot of Prienè. If so, this decree is interesting as almost the only relic of Laodi- keia as it was before the days of Roman dominion. The city was admirably placed by its founder, upon the great highroad, viâ Ephesos, between the Ægean and inner Asia : but with the decline of the Syrian monarchy, the growth of Laodikeia seems to have flagged. Its opportunity however came when Cilicia became a Roman Province (B.C. 103), and Laodikeia, standing on a great official thoroughfare, rapidly developed in wealth and importance : ἡ δὲ Λαοδίκεια (says Strabo, xii, p. 578) μικρὰ πρότερον οὖσα αὔξησιν ἔλαβεν ἐφ᾽ ἡμῶν καὶ τῶν ἡμετέρων πατέρων. The best notice of its later history will be found in Bishop Lightfoot’s Colossians, pp. 5, foll. Our inscription, though hardly much earlier than B.C. 200, seems anterior to Roman influence. A minute comparison of it, with the decrees of a like nature which precede it, will show that it varies in some points from the regular wording of inscriptions of this class : see especially lines 3–4, λεύκωμα, line 36, etc. For πρὸ πάσης σπονδ(ῆ)ς, in lines 32, 33, we should have ex- pected the usual form μετὰ τὰς σπονδάς, compare No. cccxix, ante, lines 21, foll. Ἐλαίας στεφάνῳ, instead of θαλλοῦ στεφάνῳ, though not a solitary instance (see C. I. 3727, and Dittenberger, Syll.,

M

Nos. 251, line 3; 367, line 90), is rare. This may be attributable to the situation of the town, out of the main current of Hellenic life. It is clear, however, that the constitution of the state was after the usual model. There is a βουλή and δῆμος (line 14), and the executive of the βουλή is a board of πρυτάνεις, who change from time to time (line 24), and who enjoy the privilege of σίτησις ἐν πρυτανείῳ (line 25). Its judicial system also is of the ordinary Greek type. The eponymous magistracy, which was held by Pasion (line 2), was probably entitled στεφανηφόρος (see C. I. 3942).

CCCCXXII.

Broken stelè of blue marble, from the temple of Athenè Polias, Prienè; incomplete at top and bottom. Height, 17 in.; width, 19 in. Presented by the Society of Dilettanti, 1870. Unpublished.

```
          ΑΙΝ   Ε        ᴧ  ιΜᴧ
    ΛΕΥΚΟΣΜΙΑΣΑΞΙΩΣΑΜΦΟΤΕΡΑΝΤΑΝΠΟΛΙΩ
    ΑΜΩΕΠΑΙΝΕΣΑΙΜΕΝΤΟΝΔΑΜΟΝΤΟΝΠΡΙΗΝ
    ΝΑΠΟΔΕΙΣΣΑΜΕΝΟΣΑΝΔΡΑΣΚΑΛΟΙΣΚΑΙΑΓ/
5     ΑΜΜΙΚΑΙΣΤΕΦΑΝΩΣΑΙΑΥΤΟΝΣΤ
    ΓΠΑΙΝΕΣΑΙΔΕΚΑΙΤΟΝΔΙΚΑΣΤΑΝΖΗΝΟΔΟΊ
    ΑΞΙΩΣΤΑΣΕΓΧΕΙΡΙΣΘΕΙΣΑΣΑΥΤΩΠΙΣΤ
    ΤΟΥΣΚ^ΤΑΤΑΝΔΙΚΑΣΤΕΙΑΝΟΣΙΩΣΚΑΙΔ'
    ᵥΑΙΣΤΦΑΝΩΣΑᵢΑᵥΤΟΝΣΤΕΦΑΝΩΧΡΥΣΕΩΔΕΔᶜ
10  ΔΕΣΗΝΟΔΟΤΩΤΩΑΡΤΕΜΩΝΟΣΚΑΙΠΟΛΙΤΕΙΑΝΚΑΙΕΙΣ
    ΛΟΥΝΚΑΙΕΓΓΛΟΥΝΚΑΙΕΜΠΟΛΕΜΩΚΑᶦᵀΝΕΙ.^ΝΑΑΣΥΛΕΙΚΑ
    ΓΠΟΝΔΕΙΚΑΙΦΟΔΟΝΕΠΙΤΑΜΒΟΛΑᴧ      ΟΝΔΑΜΟΝΠΡΩ
    ΜΕΤΑΤΑΙΡΑ:ΕΠΑΙΝΕΣΑΙΔΕΚΑΙΤΟΝΣΥΝ    ᵀΟΣΤΑΛΕΝΤΑΤΩ
    ΥΑΣΤΑΓΡΑΜΜΑΤΕΑΑΠΟΛΛΑΝΕΠΙΤΑΚΑΤΑΝΓΡΑΜΜΑΤΕΙΑΝΘΙΛ
15  ΠΟΝΙΑΙΚΑΙΣΤΕΦΑΝΩΣΑΙΑΥΤΟΝΘΑᴧ  ᴜΥΣΤΕΦΑΝΩΙΤΑΝ^
    ᵢΓΓΕΛΙΑΝΤΩΝΣΤΕΦΑΝΩΝΠΟΗΣΑΣΘΑΙΤΟΝΑΓΩΝᶜ
    ᵀΟΣΕΠΡΩΤΟΙΣΔΙΟΝΥΣΙΟΙΣΤΩΑΓΩΝΙΤΩΝΠΑΙΔΩΝ
    ΠΟΛΛΑΤΩΕΠΙΝΙΚΩΚΑΙΠΟΛΕΙΑΝΑΠΟΔΕΙΞΑΙΔΕΚᴧ
    ΟΣΤΙΣΑΦΙΚΟΜΕΝΟΣΕΙΣΠΡΙΗΝΗΝΤΟΤΕΨΗΦΙΣΜΑΤΟˢ
20  ᴸΕΙΚΑΙΕΠΕΛΘΩΝΕΠΙΤΟΥΣΑΡΧΟΝΤΑΣΚΑΙΤΟΝΔΑΜΟΝ
    ΕΣΕΙΠΡΙΗΝΕΑΣΤΑΝΤΕΦΙΛΙΑΝΣΥΝ  ΓΤΕΙΝ ΚΑΙΤΑΝΑΝΑΙ
         ΠΡΟΕᵢ        ΓΕᶦ        ΑΙΚΑΙ ᵀΑΡ^
```

αιν..ε...α..μ

.... μετ]ὰ εὐκοσμίας ἀξίως ἀμφοτέραν τᾶν πολίω[ν
δεδόχθαι τῷ δ]άμῳ ἐπαινέσαι μὲν τὸν δᾶμον τὸν Πριηνέων διότι ταυ⁰]ν ἀποδειξάμενος ἄνδρας καλο(ὺ)ς καὶ ἀγα-
6 θοὺς δικαστὰς ἀπέστειλεν] ἅμμι, καὶ στεφανῶσαι αὐτὸν στ[εφ-
άνῳ χρυσίῳ, ἐ]παινέσαι δὲ καὶ τὸν δικαστὰν Ζηνόδοτ[ον
διακάσαντα μὲν] ἀξίως τᾶς ἐγχειρισθείσας αὐτῷ πίστ[εως
κρίναντα δὲ] τοὺς κατὰ τὰν δικαστείαν ὁσίως καὶ δι-
καίως] καὶ στ[ε]φανῶσαι αὐτὸν στεφάνῳ χρυσίῳ, δεδ[ός-
10 θαι] δὲ Ζηνοδότῳ τῷ Ἀστέμωνος καὶ πολιτείαν καὶ εἴσ-
π]λουν καὶ ἔγπλουν καὶ ἐμ πολέμῳ καὶ ἐν εἰ[ρ]άνᾳ ἀσυλεὶ κα[ὶ
ἀσ]πονδεὶ καὶ [ἔ]φοδον ἐπὶ τὰμ βόλλα[ν καὶ τ]ὸν δᾶμον πρώ[τῳ
μετὰ τὰ ἱρά· ἐπαινέσαι δὲ καὶ τὸν συν[εξα]ποσταλέντα τῷ [δι-
καστᾷ γραμματέα Ἀπό(λ)λαν ἐπὶ τᾷ κατ(τ)ὰν γραμματείαν φιλ[ο-
15 πονίᾳ καὶ στεφανῶσαι αὐτὸν θαλ[λ]οῦ στεφάνῳ, τὰν δ[ὲ ἀ-
ν]αγγελίαν τῶν στεφάνων ποήσασθαι τὸν ἀγωνο[θέτην
τοῖς πρώτοις Διονυσίοις τῷ ἀγῶνι τῶν παίδων, [δεδόσθαι
δὲ Ἀ]πόλλᾳ τῷ Ἐπινίκῳ καὶ πολ(ιτ)είαν· ἀποδείξαι δὲ κα[ὶ πρεσβευ-
τὴν] ὅστις ἀφικόμενος εἰς Πριηνην τό τε ψήφισμα τοῦ [δάμου ἀπο-
20 δώ]σει καὶ ἐπελθὼν ἐπὶ το(ὺ)ς ἄρχοντας καὶ τὸν δᾶμον [παρα-
καλ]έσει Πριηνέας τὰν τε φιλίαν συν[ά]πτειν καὶ τὰν ἀνα[γραφὰν?
...... προ............τι...........ι καὶ παρα...

A decree of some Æolian state in honour of the Prienians and of the dikast and secretary sent by them. See note on No. ccccxviii, *ante*. The iota adscriptum is in most cases omitted, and various blunders are observable in lines 4 (*ἀποδειξάμενος*, καλοῖς), 14 ('Ἀπόλαν), 18 (πολείαν), 20 (Υ for Υ in τούς). The date is probably not earlier than the second century B.C. For the drift of line 2 compare No. ccccxix, line 15, No. ccccxx, lines 12, 25, 53, etc.

CCCCXXIII.

Fragment of blue marble stelè, from the temple of Athenè Polias, Prienè; entire only on right edge. Height, 1 ft. 9 in.; width, 10 in. Presented by the Society of Dilettanti, 1870. Unpublished.

	ΓΟΝΒΙ	ἐπειδὴ ὁ δῆμος .... πρεσβευτὴν ἔπεμψε πρὸς] τὸν βα[σιλέα
	ΑΙΑΞΙΩΣΕΙ	'Αντίοχον ὅστις ἀποδώσει τὸ ψήφισμα κ]αὶ ἀξιώσει [αὐτὸν
	ΥΤΩΙΨΗΦΙΣΜΑ⁻	ἀποστεῖλαι δικαστὴν ὅμοια λέγ ων τοῖς ἐ]ν τῷ ψηφίσματ[ι
	ΚΟΥΣΑΣΑΡΕ	γεγραμμένοις, ὁ δὲ βασιλεὺς 'Αντίοχος ἀ]κούσας ἀπέ-
5	ΙΔΩΡΟΥΓΡΙΗΝΕΑ	5 στειλε δικαστὴν(?) ἡμῖν τὸν δεῖνα 'Αρτεμ]ιδώρου Πριηνέα,
	ΚΑΙΣΡΟΥΔΑΣΩΚ	ὅστις παραγενόμενος εἰς τὴν πόλιν ἡμῶν] καὶ σπουδάζων
	ΙΤΩΝΣΥΜΒΟΛΑΙΩ	. . . . κα]ὶ τῶν συμβολαίω[ν
	ΣΣΥΜΒΟΛΑΙΟΙΣ	. . . . τοῖ]ς συμβολαίοις
	⁻ΟΥΜΕΝΟΥΤΩΝΧΡ	. . . . γουμένου τῶν χρ..
10	ΝΟΣΤΟΥΣΔΕΛΟΙΓΟΥ	10 . . . . νος τοὺς δὲ λοιπού[ς
	ΟΜΕΝΟΙΣΠΑΡΕΧΟΜΕΝ	διέκρινε, τοῖς εἰς τὸ δικαστήριον παραγεν]ομένοις παρεχόμεν[ος
	ΩΙΚΗΣΕΔΥΝΑΤΩΣΤΟ.	ἑαυτὸν δίκαιον, ... δι]ώκησε δυνατῶς το
	ΑΣΑΝΗΜΕΡΑΝΣΥΝΕ	. . . . π]ᾶσαν ἡμέραν συνε-
	ΝΙΣΤΗΝΔΙΑΛΥΘΗΝΑ	χῶς ? . . . .]ιστην διαλυθῆνα[ι
15	ΙΣΕΤΕΕΝΤΗΙΠΟΛΕΙΓΑ	15 . . . . ἐπεδήμ]σέ τε ἐν τῇ πόλει πά[ν-
	ΛΕΩΣΚΑΙΤΗΣΡΟΛΕΩΣΤΗ	τα τὸν χρόνον ἀξίως τῆς ἡμετέρας πό]λεως καὶ τῆς πόλεως τῆ-
	ΥΘΑΠΡΑΤΤΩΝΤΗΙΤΟΥ ΑΣ	ς ἐξαποστειλάσης αὐτὸν ἀκόλο]υθα πράττων τῇ τοῦ [β]ασ-(?)
	ΦΑΙΝΗΤΑΙΟΔΗΜΟΣΕΥΧΑΡ	ιλέως πρὸς τὸν δῆμον εὐνοίᾳ· ὅπως οὖν] φαίνηται ὁ δῆμος εὐχαρ-
	ΓΑΘΗΙΤΥΧΗΙΚΑΙΡΙΣΩΤΙ	ιστῶν τοῖς εὐεργετοῦσιν αὐτόν, 'Α]γαθῇ Τύχῃ κ αὶ σωτη[ρ-
20	ΓΟΝΩΝΑΥΤΟΥΔΕΔΟΧΘΑΙΤΙ	20 ίᾳ τοῦ τε βασιλέως καὶ τῶν ἐκ]γόνων αὐτοῦ, δεδόχθαι τῇ
	ΤΙΟΧΟΝΤΟΝΒΑΣΙΛΕΑΑΡΕ	βουλῇ καὶ τῷ δήμῳ ἐπαινέσαι 'Αν]τίοχον τὸν βασιλέα ἀρε-
	ΙΣΑΤ	τῆς ἕνεκα καὶ εὐνοίας αἷς ἀεὶ ἐχρή]σατ[ο(?) πρὸς τὸν δῆμον
		κ.τ.λ.

Apparently a decree from a city in acknowledgment of the good services of a dikast or other special commissioner from Prienè; his name was recorded in line 5. If lines 7–12 were perfect, we should know more exactly the nature of the difficulties which called for this intervention: the disputes appear to have been civil cases (lines 7, 8). Whatever they were, the stranger from Prienè had dealt with them 'ably' (*δυνατῶς*, line 12), and had persuaded some of the disputants to a compromise (*διαλυθῆναι*, line 14). So far this decree is very similar to those which immediately precede it. In one important point, however, it differs from them; for the application for a dikast (if dikast he were) was not made directly to Prienè, but to 'king Antiochos,' and Antiochos commissioned Prienè to send a citizen (lines 1–5). This peculiarity makes us the more regret the mutilated state of the decree. I have abstained from all conjectural restorations except what was fairly obvious from a comparison of the other dikast decrees. The preamble and the conclusion are both lost. The preamble must have set forth how that the city in question, desiring to have certain cases tried by an absolutely impartial judge, sent an envoy to the king (line 1), and so on. At the close, after due acknowledgment had been paid to the king, we may be sure the dikast himself and his native city of Prienè came in for their share of praise, request being made, as in similar cases, (see Nos. ccccxviii, lines 37–39, ccccxx, line 33, ccccxxi, line 33, etc.,) that this decree may be inscribed at Prienè and set up in the temple of Athenè,—where it was found by Mr. Pullan.

It is probable that the Antiochos here named was Antiochos Theos, B.C. 261–246. The letters would suit that date, and the relations between that monarch and Prienè were such that he might well have paid the city this compliment: see Introduction, p. 4, *ante*. There is nothing to help us even to guess the city which issued this decree.

CCCCXXIV.

Fragments of wall-stones from the temple of Athenè Polias, Prienè: a only in the British Museum. Presented by the Society of Dilettanti, 1870. Unpublished.

a.

Fragment of a wall-stone from a broad course; edge entire at the top and bottom beds, but broken on the other sides. Height, 1 ft. 8 in., by 1 ft. 1 in. The surface below line 9 is broken off.

```
—ι       ι                              .......
ΦΙΛΩΝΤΟΥΣΑΝΑΝΕ          . φίλων τοὺς ἀνανε[ωσαμένους ?
ΕΠΕΙΓΑΡΑΡΙΑΡΑΕ        ...... ἐπεὶ γὰρ Ἀριαράθ[ης ....
ϹΗΔΥΝΗΘΗΔΙΑΤΩΙ          οὐ]κ ἠδυνήθη διὰ τῶν ...
ᵕΑΙΡΩΜΑΙΩΝΤΩΝ      5   ... κ]αὶ Ῥωμαίων τῶν ...
ΓΩΝΟΙΟΜΕΝΩΝ            ... τῶν οἰομένων ...
ΕΡΩΙ ΜΕΤΑΔ             .. ί]ερῷ.  Μετὰ δ[ὲ ..
ᵕΙΜΙΝΑΠΟΚ              .. ἡ]μῖν ἀποκ ...
ΤΑΛΙΝΕϽ               ... πάλιν ἐξ ..
```

b.

Fragment of wall-stone from a broad course of the temple of Athenè Polias, which was not sent to England: copied by Mr. A. S. Murray at Prienè: height, 20 in. Edge complete at top, left and bottom. The surface seems to have been much worn.

```
                                        ΠΟΛΙΝΠΟΛΙΟ
     ΤΗΜΛιΛΣ                            ΔΕΚΑΙΣΩΜΑΤΑ
     ΣΙΑΑΠ                              ΑΦΕΙΣΜΕ
   ΘΑΙΑΟΡΟΦΕΡΝΗΣΕΝΤΩΙΙΕΡΩΙΤ . ΣΑ
5     ΑΥΤΟΙΣΦΙΛΑΝΘΡΩΠ        Ο
   ΣΥΓΚΛΗΤΟΥΟΥΤΕΤΟΥΔΗΜΟΥΕΠΙΘΕΛΠ
   ΟΣ  ΠΕΡΙΤΕΤΟΥΤΩΝΤΩΝΠΡΑΓΜΑΤΩ
   ΑΣΙΛΕΑΑΤΤΑΛΟΝΚΑΙΒΑΣΙΛΕΑΑΡΙΑ
   ΡΟΜΗΣΟΥΤΩΚΑΘΩΣΑΝΑΥΤΩΙΕ
```

```
.................................... πόλιν πολιο[ρκῶν ..
....... κ]τήμα[τ]α σ[υλήσας πολλὰ] δὲ καὶ σώματα [καὶ θρέμμα-
τα πολλαπλά]σια ἀπ[ολέσας ............] ἀφεὶς με ..
.. θαι ἃ Ὀροφέρνης ἐν τῷ ἱερῷ τ[ῆ]ς Ἀ[θηνᾶς παρακατίθετο ἀποκρί-
5   νασθαι] αὐτοῖς φιλανθρώπ[ως .....]ο[........ οὔτε τῆς
συγκλήτου οὔτε τοῦ δήμου ἐπὶ θελπ ..
ος . , περί τε τούτων τῶν πραγμάτω[ν ............ πρὸς
β]ασιλέα Ἄτταλον καὶ βασιλέα Ἀρια[ράθη ..
. ρομης οὕτω καθὼς ἂν αὐτῷ ἐ[κ τῶν δημοσίων πραγμάτων βέλτιστον
10   [εἶναι φαίνηται.  Ἔδοξεν.]
```

The two fragments, although obviously forming part of the same document, cannot be made to read into one another. And although the subject of our inscription receives ample illustration from Polybios and Appian, yet it unfortunately adds nothing to our previous knowledge.

The Ariarathes here mentioned was the fifth king of Cappadocia of that name, and he succeeded his father Ariarathes IV, B.C. 163. He was surnamed Philopator, and seems to have been an excellent prince (Diodor. Frag. lib. xxxi).

Orophernes was a supposititious son of the late king, who was encouraged by Demetrios Soter to attack Ariarathes and urge his claim to the throne. Ariarathes was vanquished and fled to Rome about B.C. 157 (Diodor. ibid.). The Senate restored him to the throne, although apparently Orophernes was still allowed a share in the government (Appian, Syr. 47; Polyb. xxxii, 20). The character of Orophernes was altogether vicious, and his reign was disgraced by profligacy and extortion. Feeling his position insecure, he deposited 400 talents with the people of Prienè as a reserve in case of misfortune, the temple of Athenè, like many other shrines of antiquity, having been made to serve as a bank (Diodor. *ibid.*). Orophernes before long was expelled from the kingdom, and Ariarathes became sole governor. The latter, following up his advantage, demanded from the Prienians the 400 talents, which he contended were deposited by Orophernes as king of Cappadocia, and now should revert to the royal exchequer. The Prienians refused this unfair demand, and although Ariarathes and Attalos II combined to pillage the Prienian territory, they persisted in delivering up the deposit only to Orophernes himself (Polyb. xxxiii, 12). It is uncertain to what stage in these transactions our inscription is to be referred. The deposit made by Orophernes is mentioned in *b*, line 4, and perhaps *a*, line 7; and the combined attack by Ariarathes and Attalos is referred to in *b*, lines 1 and 8. Polybios (*ibid.*) says that Prienè, being in a strait, appealed to Rhodes, and then to the Senate: and this may be the reference of *a*, line 4, and *b*, line 6. It is probable that the two fragments belong to a series of lost documents relating to the Orophernes affair: *b* is the end of a Senatusconsultum, and the wording of it should be compared with Nos. ccccɪᴠ, ccccᴠ. The suggested restorations are merely to indicate the probable drift of the meaning, but I have taken the words almost entirely from Polybios, xxxiii, 12.

In April, 1870, after the completion of the excavations made by the Society of Dilettanti, Mr. Clarke, then resident in the neighbouring village of Soköi, visited the temple of Athenè at Prienè, and found six silver coins of Orophernes which had apparently been deposited originally under the pedestal of a colossal statue. See the account of this discovery in Mr. Newton's Memoir in the Numismatic Chronicle, New Series, xi, p. 19, and his remarks in Antiquities of Ionia, Pt. ɪᴠ, p. 25. He conjectures that the statue and the coins underneath it may have been a dedication made by Orophernes, by way of recognising the service rendered him by Prienè. The coins are described as follows:—

Obv.—Male head to right, beardless, and bound with a diadem.

Rev.—ΒΑΣΙΛΕΩΣ ΟΡΟΦΕΡΝΟΥ ΝΙΚΗΦΟΡΟΥ. Victory moving to left, clad in a talaric chiton, and diploidion, holding in right hand a wreath, in left a palm-branch; in front of her an owl on an altar; below, a monogram.

CCCCXXV.

Lower portion of a blue marble stelè, from the temple of Athenè Polias, Prienè; broken at the top; the sides complete only from line 9 to the end. Height, 1 ft. 9¼ in.; width, 1 ft. 10½ in. Presented by the Society of Dilettanti, 1870. Unpublished.

```
            ΟΥΝΤΕΣΗΜΙ
        ΓΕΜΦΘΕΝΤΕ Α ΤΕΟΙΑΡΩΓ
        ΧΟΜΕΘΑΣΥΝ ΗΙΤΩΝΘΕΩΝΕΥ
        ΟΜΕΘΑΚΟΙΝΙΙ ΤΕΤΩΙΔΗΜΩ ΤΩ  ΙΟΥ
 5      Κ ΙΤΙΔΙΑΝΤΟΙΣΕΝΤΥΓΧΑΝΟΥΣΙ . . . Ε . . ΤΩ
        ΜΕ . . . ΤΕΟ        ΤΩΝΤΙΜΩΜΕΝΩΝ . . . . . ΑΡΟ
        ΑΓΑΘΙΑΝΤΩΝΣΥΓΚΕΚΙΝΔΥΝΕΥΚΟΤΩΝ
        ΤΑΤΟΥΣΚΑΙΡΟΥΣΓΙΣΤΕΩΣΚΑΙΕΥΝΟΙΑΣΑΓΟΔ
        ΑΓΟΔΕΙΣΑΝΤΑΣΚΑΙΕΙΣΤΗΝΕΙΚΟΝΑΤΟΥΔΗΜΟΥΗΜΕ              ΟΛ
 10     ΑΝΑΛΩΣΑ ΤΑΣΑΛΕΞΑΝΔΡΕΙΑΣΔΡΑΧΜΑΣΤΡΙΣΧΙΛΙΑΣ      Α
        ΔΙΑΦΥΛΑΣΣΟΝΤΕΣΤΗΝΓΡΟΣΗΜΑΣ
        ΤΗΣΑΝΑΘΕΣΕΩΣΤΟΥΑΝΔΡΙΑΝΤΟΣΓΡΟΝΟΗΣΑΝΤΕΣΕΡΡΩ  Ο
```

        . εὐνο]οῦντες ἡμῖ[ν . . . .
     . . . . πεμφθέντε[ς] . . . . ἀραγ . . . .
     . . εὐ]χόμεθα σὺν [τ]ῇ τῶν θεῶν εὐ[νοίᾳ ?
     συνηδ]όμεθα κοινῇ τε τῷ δήμῳ τῷ . . . . [καὶ
 5   . . κατ' ἰδίαν τοῖς ἐντυγχάνουσι . . . .
     . . . . . . τεο . . . . . τῶν τιμωμένων . . . . . ἀπο .
     τὴν ἀνδρ]αγαθίαν τῶν συγκεκινδυνευκότων [ἡμῖν καὶ κατὰ τοὺς δυσ-
     χερεσ]τάτους καιροὺς πίστεως καὶ εὐνοίας ἀποδ[ειξιν τὴν μεγίστην
     ἀποδείξαντας καὶ εἰς τὴν εἰκόνα τοῦ δήμου ἡμε[τέρου . . . .
 10 . . ἀναλώσα[ν]τας ᾿Αλεξανδρείας δραχμὰς τρισχιλίας . . .
     καλῶς ποιεῖτε ?] διαφυλάσσοντες τὴν πρὸς ἡμᾶς [εὔνοιαν καὶ φιλίαν
     καὶ περὶ] τῆς ἀναθέσεως τοῦ ἀνδριάντος προνοήσαντες. ἔρρω[σ]θ[ε.

N

Apparently a letter addressed to the people of Priene by some other state. This is confirmed by the use of the first person plural in lines 1, 3, 4. The surface of the marble is much worn, and the readings given in the text were recovered with difficulty. The date is probably the second century B.C. The writers of the letter seem to have received armed assistance (line 7) from certain Prienians (line 2) at a time of need (line 8); and they express gratitude to the Gods (line 3) and to the Prienian people (lines 4, 5). Their Prienian friends had also contributed (line 10) for a statue of the city in question (line 9) to be erected at Priene. The letter closes with thanks to the Prienian people for permitting the erection of the statue (line 12).

CCCCXXVI.

Two fragments of white marble, from the temple of Athenè Polias, Prienè. *a* entire only at the top and left; height, 1 ft. 6 in.; width, 1 ft. 8 in. *b* broken all round; height, 10 in. by 5 in. Presented by the Society of Dilettanti, 1870. Unpublished.

a.

```
        .ΓΑΘΙΤΥΧΗΙΕΓ
        ΚΟΡΥΛΑΝΜΗΝΟΣΛ
        ΙΕΡΩΣΥΝΗΝΤΟ
        ΕΓΑΜΕΙΝΩΝΓ
   5    ΕΓΙΔΕΚΑΤ

        ΞΤΑΙΔΕΤΟΜΒΙΟΝΤΟΝΛ
        ΔΕΙΖΩΝΙΣΥΝΤΕΛΕΙΚ     10
        ΛΤΕΛΗΣΔΕΕΣΤΑΙΓΛ     ΝΚΑΘΑΓΙ
        ΗΣΤΗΛΗΙΑΝΑΓΕΓ      ΙΚΑΙΤΑΑΛΛΛ
  10        ΕΙΝ            ΖΙΚΑΙΕΜΓΡΥΤΑΙ
                          ΖΛΓΟΙΗΙΚΑΙΓΡΟΓ
                          ΝΤΙΧΡΥΣΕΟΝ'
                          ΟΝΦΟΡΕΙΝΧΡ`
                          ΡΑΙΩΝΟΙ
```

b.

```
        ΝΤΛΛ
        ΤΙΟΣΓ...−Ζ
        ΥΗΤΑΙΑΝΛΓΙ Λ
        ΛΛΙΦΙΝΗΕΝΗΚΛ
   5    ΝΑΓΕΓΡΑΦ
        ΖΥΜ−
```

a.

Ἀγαθῇ Τύχῃ· ἐπ[ὶ στεφανηφόρου τοῦ δεῖνος τοῦ μετὰ
Κορύλαν μηνὸς Μ[εταγειτνιῶνος ? . . . . ῃ· ὁ πριάμενος τὴν
ἱερωσύνην το[ῦ Ποσειδῶνος . . . .
Ἐπαμείνων . . . .
5   ἐπιδέκατ[ον . . . . .

Ἱεράσ]εται δὲ τὸμ βίον τὸν α[ὐτοῦ καὶ τὴν θυσίαν τῷ
Πο]σειδῶνι συντελεῖ κ[ατὰ το]ὺς νόμους τοὺς Ἰώνων,
ἀτελὴς δὲ ἔσται πά[ντω]ν καθάπε[ρ καὶ ἐν
τ]ῇ στήλῃ ἀναγέγ[ραπτα]ι καὶ τὰ ἄλλα [ὅσα
10   δίδοται]· εἰν[αι δὲ αὐτ]ῷ καὶ ἐμ πρυται[είῳ
σίτησιν ὅταμ πόλις ἱε]ρὰ ποιῇ, καὶ προε[δρίαν
ἐν τοῖς ἀγῶσιν ἔχο]ντι χρύσεον . . .
. . . . ἱμάτι]ον? φορεῖν χρύ[σεον . .
. . . . πα]ρὰ Ἰώνω[ν . . .

b.

συ]ντελ . . . . .
. . . τιος γίνεσ[θαι ?
. . . . θ]ύηται ἀναγ[γελίαν
. ἐν στήλ]ῃ λιθίνῃ ἐν ᾗ κα[ὶ
5   . . . . . ἀ]ναγεγράφ[θαι ? . . .
. . . . ου μ . . . .

These fragments appear to belong to one document. The document relates to the appointment of a priest, apparently of Poseidon. The Prienians had the privilege of officiating at the Panionian festival of Poseidon, according to Strabo, xiv, p. 639, τὸ Πανιώνιον ....., ὅπου τὰ Πανιώνια κοινὴ πανήγυρις τῶν Ἰώνων συντελεῖται τῷ Ἑλικωνίῳ Ποσειδῶνι καὶ θυσία, ἱερῶνται δὲ Πριηνεῖς. Our inscription may perhaps relate to the appointment of a priest to act on these occasions, although it seems implied by Strabo, viii. p. 384, that a youthful Prienian citizen was appointed year by year for this office, and this would not accord with line 6, unless the practice varied at different dates. Strabo writes as if the Panionian festival was still held in his day near Mykalè, but Diodoros (xv, 49) states that it was afterwards transferred to a spot near Ephesos; and it is thought to have been finally merged in the worship of the Ephesian Artemis (K. F. Hermann, Gottesdienstl. Alt. § 66). This, however, is very doubtful, as the Ionian League of Thirteen Cities survived until quite a late period, and Miletos claimed the headship in it (Marquardt, Röm. Alt. iv, p. 187). The inscription probably belongs to the second century B.C. We might have expected this decree to have been inscribed at the Panionion itself, like the decree concerning the analogous priesthood of Zeus Boulaios and Hera, which was claimed by the Lebedians (C. I. 2909). But perhaps it was first inscribed there, and these fragments belong to a duplicate erected at Prienè. The mention of Ἰωνες, i. e. the delegates of the Panionic Synod (Ἰώνων ἡ βουλή, C. I. 2909, and Ἰώνων τὸ κοινόν, Dittenberger, Syll., No. 137) in a, line 14, and in No. cccxxvii b, lines 3, 4, makes it certain what priesthood of Poseidon is intended.

In lines 1 foll. my restorations are fairly probable.

Priesthoods in Greece were often sold by the state to the highest bidder : see Dionysios of Halikarnassos, Antiq. Rom. ii, 21; and the following inscriptions :—C. I. 2656 (now in the British Museum); Arch. Epigr. Mittheilungen aus Oesterreich (Vienna 1882), vi, p. 8, no. 14 : Revue Archéologique, N. S. xxxiii, pp. 107 foll. ; Monatsberichte d. Berl. Akad. 1877, p. 475. I therefore suggest ὁ πριάμενος : compare No. cccxxvii c, line 5. Possibly Ἐπαμείνων in line 4 (compare No. cccciii, line 42) was the late priest, whose death or resignation had occasioned the vacancy ; and the first clause of the decree. (lines 1–5) may have briefly enacted that the new priest should have the same perquisites from the various sacrifices which Epameinon had enjoyed, and also a tithe (τὸ ἐπιδέκατον) of certain offerings.

The next clause (lines 5–12) is easily restored by a comparison of No. cccxxvii b, where the same phrases recur. The lettering of that inscription is decidedly coarser than the lettering of the one before us ; I therefore suppose it to be rather later in date, and have suggested (ad loc.) what may have been the relation between the two documents.

In lines 12, 13, in what appears to be a specification of the priest's duties and privileges, is an enactment concerning the wearing of gold. · A similar phrase recurs in the next inscription, which so much resembles the present one, that at first sight they might be imagined to be both parts of the same original document. With line 6 compare the wording of the Halikarnassian inscription (C. I. 2656), line 8, ἱεράσεται ἐπὶ ζωῆς τῆς αὐτῆ[s] κ.τ.λ. See also the Iasian law, No. ccccxl post, concerning the priest of Ζεὺς μέγιστος. As to the wearing of gold see the Andania decree, Foucart-Le Bas, Pt. ii, No. 326 a, line 22.

CCCCXXVII.

Four fragments of a white marble stelè, from the temple of Athenè Polias, Prienè : a, broken on all sides, measures 10 in. by 8 in. ; b, entire on right edge only, and with 4 inches blank space at the top, above which are traces of letters on the broken edge, measures 10 in. by 1 ft. 2½ in. ; c, broken all round, measures 9 in. by 5 in. ; d, broken all round, measures 4½ in. by 7½ in. Presented by the Society of Dilettanti, 1870. Unpublished.

a.

```
 ΛΙ ι                              . . . .
ΓΠΑΤΡΟΣΕΩΣΑΝΞ        . . . . το]ῦ πατρὸς ἕως ἂν Ξ . . . . . .

 ΟΙΓΝΩΜΗΣΤΡΑ         Ἔδοξεν τῷ δήμ]ῳ, γνώμη στρα[τηγῶν· ἐπειδὴ
 ΚΥΡΕΩΝΟΣΕΝΤ         Ξε . . . . . . . . Ἰσ]χυρίεινος ἐν τ[ῷ πρίασθαι
5 ΤΟΥΠΟΣΕΙΔ        5  τὴν ἱερωσύνην] τοῦ Ποσειδ[ῶνος . . . .
 ΧΡΥΣΙΟΝΛΓ           . . . . . . . . . . . χρυσίον λο . . . .
 ΛΟΤΩΙΟΠ             . . . . . . . . . . . ἐ]φ' ὅτῳ ὁ π[ριάμενος . .
 Λ ― Ί
```

b.

ΤΟΥΚΑΙΤΗΝΘΥΣΙΑΝ
ΓΟΥΣΝΟΜΟΥΣΤΟΥΣΙΩΝΩ
ΑΠΕΡΙΩΝΕΣΔΕΔΩΚΑΣΙΝ
ιΚΑΙΤΑΛΛΑΟΣΑΔΕΔΟΤΑΙ
ΔΕΑΥΤΩΙΚΑΙΕΜΠΡΥΤΑΝΕΙΩΙ
ˆΑΜΠΟΛΙΣΙΕΡΑΠΟΙΗΙ (Uninscribed.)
‾Υ‾Ο‾ΝΤΙΧΡΥΣΕ‾

'Ιεράσεται δὲ τὸμ βίον τὸν αύ]τοῦ καὶ τὴν θυσίαν [συν-
τελεῖ τῷ Ποσειδῶνι κατὰ] τοὺς νόμους τοὺς 'Ιώνω[ν,
ἀτελὴς δὲ ἔσται καθ]άπερ ‾Ιωνες διδώκασιν·
εἶναι δὲ αὐτῷ] καὶ τἆλλα ὅσα δίδοται,
δεδόσθαι] δὲ αὐτῷ καὶ ἐμ πρυτανείῳ
σίτησιν ὅ]ταμ πόλις ἱερὰ ποιῇ,
καὶ προεδρίαν ἐν τοῖς ἀγῶσιν ἔχ]οντι χρύσεο[ν
κ.τ.λ.]

c.

Θι   . . . θα . . .
ΊΣΥι   ἱερ]ωσύ[νην ? . .
ΑΝΕΣΧΛ   ἱερ]ὰν ? ἐσχά[ραν . .
ΣΟΜΕΝΟΥΜε   . . . σομένου με . .
ˆΩΤΩΙΠΡΙΑΜΕ   διδότ?]ω τῷ πριαμέ[νῳ
ΊΝΗΚΤΗΝ⌐   . . . . ων ἡ κτῆνω[ν
ˆΛΕΤΩΤ   . . . . λετω τ . .
ΓΚΑΙ⍾   . . . . γ καὶ φ . .

d.

ΕΙΕΠΙΚΕΧΛ   . . . ει ἐπικεχά[ρηκε ?
'ΙΝΑΕΙΔΗΞΕ   . . . ἱνα εἴδη Ξε . . . . .
ΥΣΑΝΤΙΟΣ   . . . τῷ θ]ύσαντι ὅσ[α δίδοται ?

That these four fragments belonged to the same monument seems certain upon examining the marble, but it is impossible to make them read into one another. This document closely resembled the preceding one, and referred to the appointment, duties, and privileges of a priest of Poseidon. The date is probably about 200 B.C.

If I am right in believing that the stelè of which these are fragments was inscribed later than No. cccxxvi, we may suppose that the priest appointed under that decree died or resigned before very long : of his name I seem to find traces in *a*, line 4, and *d*, line 2 ; viz. Ξε[. . . . 'Ισ]χυρίωνος. 'Ισχυρίων would be a variant for 'Ισχυρίων (for which see Pape-Benseler's Wörterbuch), analogous to the forms Μιννίων, Μιννίων, in the decrees Nos. 132, 135 in my Manual of Greek Historical Inscriptions. The vacancy thus left I suppose to have been filled up under the terms of the present decree. In *c*, line 5, the letters are all certain except Μ. But τῷ πρια-μέ[νῳ] is probably right, for τῷ Πριανέ[ων, sc. δήμῳ] would be an inadmissible Doricism.

COCCXXVIII.

Fragment of a white marble stelè, from the temple of Athenè Polias, Prienè. Height, 1 ft. 2 in.; width, 1 ft. 1½ in. Presented by the Society of Dilettanti, 1870. Unpublished.

```
  ΟΔΗΜΟΣ
  ϽΥΛΙΑΝΘΕΑΝ
  ΑΛΛΙΤΕΚΝΟΝ
  ΗΝΚΑΙΣΑΡΟΣ
5 ΟΥΣΕΒΑΣΤΟΥ
  ΥΓΑΤΕΡ. Κ^
  ϽΡΩΣΕΝ
```

'Ο δῆμος
'Ϳουλίαν θεὰν
κ]αλλίτεκνον
τ]ὴν Καίσαρος
5   θε]οῦ Σεβαστοῦ
θ]υγατέρ[α] κα[θι.
ερωσεν.

Dedication to Livia, the consort of Augustus, after the death of both: hence the use of θεάν and θεοῦ. By the Emperor's testament she was adopted into the Julian family (Tac. Ann. i, 8), and was thenceforward usually called Julia Augusta. By virtue of her adoption she was also styled, as here, Augusti *filia*; see Velleius Paterculus, ii, 75: conjugem Augusti, ... transgressi ad deos sacerdotem ac filiam; Orelli, Inscr. Lat. No. 615 foll. At her death Tiberius forbade her consecration (Tac. Ann. v, 2), and Claudius first gave her divine honours (Dio Cass. LX, 5: Suetonius, Claud. 11). Coins and inscriptions at once proclaimed the new divinity, and to this period our dedication must be assigned. The epithet καλλίτεκνον marks her as the mother of Tiberius and grandmother of Claudius the reigning emperor.

COCCXXIX.

Fragment of the pedestal of a statue, from the temple of Athenè Polias, Prienè. Height, 9½ in.; width, 1 ft. ¼ in. Joint on the left; broken on the right. Presented by the Society of Dilettanti, 1870. Unpublished.

ι ΝΑΙΠ ϲ   'Αθ]ηνᾷ Πο[λιάδι.

In large characters 2 inches high, probably of the Augustan age. Compare an unpublished dedication in letters 4¼ inches high, copied by Mr. A. S. Murray at Prienè in 1870, from a piece of architrave: it reads— 'Ο] δῆμος 'Αθηνᾷ [Πολιάδι καὶ Καί]σαρι Θεοῦ υἱῷ [Σεβαστῷ.

COCCXXX.

Fragment of bluish marble, from the temple of Athenè Polias, Prienè. Height, 1 ft. 2½ in.; width, 10½ in. Presented by the Society of Dilettanti, 1870. Unpublished.

```
ι ΤΙΣΚΟΥΤΟϜ
  ΔΡΑΑΓΑΘΟΝΓΕ
  ϽΙΝΗΣΥΜΦΕΡΟϜ
  ΚΑΙΕΥΝΟΙΑΣ
```

[Τὸν δεῖνα]
. . τίσκου τοῦ [. . . . . . ἄνδρα ἀγαθὸν γε[νόμενον καὶ κ-
οινῇ συμφέρον[τα ἀρετῆς ἕνεκα
καὶ εὐνοίας.

The top and left edge are entire: there is a blank after εὐνοίας. The iota adscriptum is omitted in line 3. The inscription is probably part of the base of some statue, of a date not earlier than the first century B.C. The name of the person commemorated must have been inscribed upon the pedestal of the statue.

This will be a fitting place to insert several short honorary inscriptions copied by Mr. Murray at Prienè in 1870, but as yet unedited, of which the stones were not brought to England.

(a) 'On a stone with moulding along the top: white marble.'
'Ο δῆμος
Ποσειδώνιον Διονυσίου.

(b) 'Base of blue marble: letters 1 inch high.'
Τὸ . . . .
καὶ α . . . .
Νικα . . . .
ἀρετῆς [ἕνεκα καὶ εὐνοίας
τῆς εἰς ἑ[αυτούς.

(c) 'Apparently a stelè.'
Δημ]ήτριον 'Αθηναῖ[ου,
Δ]ημήτριον 'Αθηναίο[υ,
ἀ]ρετῆς ἕνεκεν καὶ εὐ[ν]ο[ία]ς
τῆς εἰς ἑαυτ[ὸ]ν . . . [sc. ὁ δῆμος].

(d) 'On a base of blue marble.'
Δι ?]όδοτον 'Ισίω ἀρετῆς [ἕνεκεν
καὶ εὐνοίας [τῆς εἰς ἑαυτόν.

CCCCXXXI.

Upper part of a stele of white marble, from the temple of Athenè Polias, Prienè. Width, 1 ft. 11½ in.; height, 11 in. Broken at the bottom. Presented by the Society of Dilettanti, 1870. Unpublished.

ΛΗΜΟΣΟΛΛΕΞΑΝΔΡΕΩΝΤΩΝΑΠΟΤΗΣΤΡΩΙΑΣ
ΝΗΜΟΝ   ΤΟ   ΕΩΝ

'Ο] δῆμος ὁ 'Αλεξανδρέων τῶν ἀπὸ τῆς Τρῳίας
τὸν δ]ῆμον   τὸ[ν Πριην]έων.

A stelè recording that the people of Alexandria Troas have voted a crown in honour of the people of Prienè. No. ccccxix *ante* (see lines 2, 17, 21) has already informed us of the occasion upon which this honour was conferred.

CCCCXXXII.

Fragment of white marble, from the temple of Athenè Polias, Prienè. Height, 7½ in.; breadth, 5½ in. Presented by the Society of Dilettanti, 1870. Entire on the right only.

ΛΕΥΝ	. . . . λευν
ΕΔΙΟΝ	. . . . . π]εδίον
ΜΑΤΟΕΡ	. . . ψήφι]σμα τὸ ἐν
ΙΕΡΩΙ	. . . . τῷ] ἱερῷ
5 ΑΙ	5 . . . . αι
ΡΙ	. . . . πι

A fragment in fine clear letters, not later than the fourth century B.C. The ends of the lines are complete, and above the first line is a blank. I suspect ΛΕΥΝ in line 1 to be the Ionic termination for -λεον, e. g. [ἐκά]λευν for [ἐκά]λεον, Attic [ἐκά]λουν.

CCCCXXXIII.

Fragment of blue marble, from the temple of Athenè Polias, Prienè; broken on all sides. Height, 8½ in.; breadth, 6½ in. Presented by the Society of Dilettanti, 1870.

ΕΝΙι	. . . . . ενι . . .
'ΤΕΜΙϲΩΡ	. . . 'Α]ρτέμιδωρ . .
ΜΕΡΟΣ	. . . . . . μερος
ΙΠΟΣ	. . . . . ιπος
5 ΞΙΟΣ	5 . . . . . . ειος
ΟΣ	. . . . ος

Apparently part of a list of names, in characters which may belong to the early period of Roman ascendancy. The endings of the lines seem to be complete.

CCCCXXXIV.

Fragments of bluish marble, from the temple of Athenè Polias, Prienè; broken all round. Height of *a*, 3 in., breadth 8 in.; height of *b*, 4½ in., breadth 3½ in.; height of *c*, 2½ in., breadth 4 in.; height of *d*, 3½ in., breadth 2½ in. Presented by the Society of Dilettanti, 1870.

(*a*) ΛΛΙΣΤΕΥΟΥΣ . . . κα]λλιστευουσ[α   (*b*) ΝΚ   (*c*) ΙΜΛ   (*d*) ΣΙΝ
ΙΣΤ   . . . . ιστ . . . . . .   ΝΤΙΣ

The characters are probably of the third century B.C., and resemble those of the Rhodian award, No. cccciii *ante*, especially in the portion *i* (2). The appearance of the marble suggests that they formed part of a wall-stone or a base, and not of a stelè; and they may have been splintered from one of the lost wall-stones of No. cccciii.

CCCCXXXV.

A fragment of bluish marble stelè, from the temple of Athenè Polias, Prienè; entire only on right. Height, 9½ in.; width, 9½ in. Presented by the Society of Dilettanti, 1870. Unpublished.

```
ⅬΞΕΤΑΣΤΑⅬ                           ........... τοὺϚ] ἐξεταστὰϚ(?) ....
        ΙΠⲀΡΕΧΕ                     ................. κα]ὶ παριχέ[τω....
ΟΞΑΝΤΟΝ⁻ΑϹΥΟΕΡΟΝΕΚΩΝΑΠΟ             ............... ὃϚ ἂν τὸν ἐλεύθερον ἔκων ἀπο[κ-
ΣΑΡΑΚΟΝΤΑΜΝΑΣΑΡΓΥΡΙΟΥΤΟΣΑⲨ          τείνῃ ........... τισ]σαράκοντα μνᾶϚ ἀργυρίου, τοσαύ-
ΚΑΙΔΕΚΑΜΝΑΣΑΠΟΔΟΤΩΚΑΤΕΛΟΘΕΤΩΔΕ   5  ταϚ δὲ καὶ(?)........] καὶ δίκα μνᾶϚ ἀποδότω, κατελθέτω δὲ
ΤΟΙΣⲆΙΚΑΣΤΗΡΙΟΙ        ΑΣΠΟΛΙΣΑ     ............... τοῖϚ δικαστηρίο:[Ϛ .........]αϚ πόλιϚ
ⲨΑΠΟΚΤΕΙΝΗΙΣΩΕΑΙΣΟΟΝΟΛΟΚ           ............... ὃϚ ἂν δοῦλο]ν ἀποκτείνῃ σωία ζωὸν ἐλόκ-
⁻ΟΝϹΑϹΥΟΕΡΟΝϹΚΩΝϹⲨ                 ληρον(?)..............] τὸν ἐλεύθερον ἔκων ευ(?)
ΜΕΤΑΣΧΟΝΤΑΤΟΥΠ                     ................ μετασχόντα τοῦ π ...
ΞΙΟΥΣΕΙΓΕΝΗΤΑΙ               10     .................. εσίουϚ εἰ γένηται
ΡΙΟΥΤΟΣΑΑΕϚΙ                       ................ ἀργυ]ρίου τόσα & ἐπι..
ⲨΕΩΝΕΣΤΟΥϚ                         ................. λεων ἐϚ(?) τοὺϚ
ΣΙΟΙΣΕΔΓ                           ................. σίοιϚ ἐδε
ΕΞΕ⁻                               ............. τοὺϚ] ἐξετ[αστὰϚ(?)
```

The surface is worn and the letters are inscribed between strongly engraved lines, which make decypherment difficult. The letters are badly formed, and seem never to have been finished. If, as would seem from the context, this inscription is a fragment of a law about murder, it may be a copy of the original made by an unskilful hand at a period much later than the promulgation of the law. The forms ΣΩΕΑ and ΙΟΟΝ, in line 7, are more like blunders of the copyist than correct transcriptions of ancient forms (for σῶν, ζωόν).

CCCCXXXVI.

Fragment of blue marble stelè, from the temple of Athenè Polias, Prienè; entire only on left. Height, 7 in.; breadth, 6 in. Presented by the Society of Dilettanti, 1870.

```
     ΕΤΩΝΠΑΡΑΓΙ            ... ε τῶν παραγ[ενομένων
     ΤⲨ ΕΠΙΚΑΤΑ            .... ἐπὶ κατα ....
     Ω  ⲨΙΤΩΝΠⲨ            ω[ν κα]ὶ τῶν πο[λιτῶν?
     ΤΩⲨΚΤΗΜΑΤΩⲨ           τῶν κτημάτων ........ [ὁ δῆ-²
   5 ΜΟΣΤΟⲨΣ            5  μος τοὺς ....
     ⲨΕΤΑΠⲨΑ               μετὰ πά[σης σπουδῆς?
     ⟨ΑΤΑ                  κατὰ ...
     ΟΥΔΕⲨ                 οὐδεμ[ία
     ΤΟΙΣ                  τοῖς ...
  10 ΄ΔΙ               10  . δι ..
```

A fragment, in small letters, much worn.

CCCCXXXVII.

Two fragments of bluish marble, from the temple of Athenè Polias, Prienè; apparently from the same stelè. a, broken all round, measures 6½ in. in height by 4 in.; b, 6½ in. in height by 3 in., gives the endings of lines. Presented by the Society of Dilettanti, 1870.

a.   *b.*

```
ΜΗΝ               ⁻Ι
⁻ΗΜΑΣ             ΙΜΟΥ
ΥΤΟΤΣ             ΟΓⳞ
ΩΡΙΑΣ             Ρ

... μην ...        .... ει
.. εἰ]ϛ ἡμᾶϚ ..    .. δ]ήμου
.. το]ύτους ...    .... ογη
πολυ]ωρίας? ..     .... ρ
```

Fragments perhaps of an honorary decree, but hardly earlier than Roman times.

CCCCXXXVIII.

Small fragment of bluish marble, from the temple of Athenè Polias, Prienè; entire on right and blank at bottom. Height, 5½ in.; breadth, 3 in   Presented by the Society of Dilettanti, 1870.

ιϑι

CCCCXXXIX.

On the right return of the capital of an Ionic pilaster found in the temenos of the temple of Athenè Polias, Prienè.   The inscribed face measures 1 ft. by 1 ft. 1½ in.   Presented by the Society of Dilettanti, 1870.   See Antiquities of Ionia, Pt. IV, p. 31.

ΟΙΦΥΛΕΤΑΙΠΑΝΔ
ΑΠΟΛΛΩΝΙΔΗΛ
ΑΡΕΤΗΣΕΝΕΚΕΝ
ΑΥΤΟ

Οἱ φυλέται Πανδ[ιονίδος
Ἀπολλωνίδην [τοῦ δεῖνος
ἀρετῆς ἔνεκεν [τῆς εἰς
αὐτο[ύς.

Dedication in honour of Apollonides from the members of his tribe Pandionis : of the third century. It does not surprise us to find that Pandionis should be one of the tribes of this Ionian city. Neither the number nor the names of the other tribes of Prienè are known. Two heroes, well known as eponymous heroes of Attic tribes, are named in Nos. ccccxv,

ccccxvi *ante*, in a manner which suggests that there may have been corresponding tribes Hippothontis and Akamantis. But considering the small size of Prienè we shall hardly be safe in concluding that it had the equivalents of all the ten Attic tribes. At Ephesos we shall find only six tribes, and these were originally only five.

Before leaving the Prienian Inscriptions it may be convenient to group together some details that are furnished by the foregoing documents.

Prienian Months. The following are known, but not their position in the calendar.

    Ἀνθεστηριών, No. ccccviii *ante.*
    Ἀπατουριών, No. ccccxv.
    Βοηδρομιών, C. I. 2906.
    Μεταγειτνιών, Nos. ccccxv, ccccxvi, ccccxxvi a.
    Πάνημος, No. ccccxviii.
    Ταυριών(?), Hellenic Journal, iv, p. 238, and v, p. 61.

Compare also No. cccciii, line 44 (cursive text).

Prienian Tribes. See note on No. ccccxxxix.

Prienian Dikast-decrees. I know of no such series of dikast-decrees from any other state ; but so fragmentary is our knowledge of the municipal history of the Greek cities, that it is hardly safe to base any argument upon this fact. One is tempted however to think that there was something in the political situation of Prienè which appeared to qualify its citizens to undertake this delicate office. Perhaps the independent position of Prienè combined with its comparative obscurity to recommend it, since its name would provoke no jealousies. Aeschines (Fals. Leg. p. 286, Reiske), in speaking of the states that sent delegates to the Amphiktyonic synod, calls Prienè quite a third-rate town : Καὶ τούτων ἔδειξα ἕκαστον ἔθνος ἰσόψηφον γινόμενον, τὸ μέγιστον τῷ ἐλάττονι, τὸν ἥκοντα ἐκ Δωρίου καὶ Κυτινίου ἴσον δυνάμενον Λακεδαι-

μονίοις (δύο γὰρ ψήφους ἕκαστον φέρει ἔθνος), πάλιν ἐκ τῶν Ἰώνων τὸν Ἐρετρία καὶ Πριηνέα τοῖς Ἀθηναίοις, καὶ τοὺς ἄλλους κατὰ ταὐτά. The decrees may be tabulated as follows :—

Number of Dikasts sent from Prienè.	To what Place.	No.
1	Iasos	ccccxx
1	Alexandria Troas	ccccxix
1	Erythrae	ccccviii
Uncertain	Unknown	ccccvii
3	Liodikeia	ccccxxi
1	An Æolian city	ccccxvii
1 (? dikast)	Sent by King Antiochos to some city	ccccxxiii

Since writing the note on No. ccccxviii I have observed two more dikast-decrees : one from Eresos (unpublished) in honour of Eresian dikasts sent to some Ionian city ; another from Assos, in honour of Assian dikasts sent to some Ionian city, published in the Report of the American Investigations at Assos (Trübner), 1882. See also Bull. de Corr. Hell. vi, pp. 239, 245. Many more will probably be brought to light in other quarters.

Prienian Magistrates. The following are mentioned in the inscriptions :—

    1. Ὁ στεφανηφόρος, who was the eponymos. The office of the nine archons at Athens was held to be a στεφανηφόρος ἀρχή, i.e. entitling its holder to wear a wreath, by reason of its sacred character (Aeschin. in Timarch. p. 44, Reiske). But in Asia Minor it

was a common title of the eponymous magistracy, its holder being probably analogous to the ἄρχων βασιλεύς at Athens, for the epithet implies a quasi-priestly position. It is the eponymous magistracy at Iasos (see *post*, No. ccccxli), at Aphrodisias, Tralles, and some twenty towns in Asia Minor. So also at Tenos, *ante*, Nos. ccclxxiv foll.; compare Index to C. I., and Hermann, Gottesd. Alterth. § 24, 11; § 35, 17. It appears also to have been the eponymous office at Tarsos; see Athenæos, v, p. 215: Καὶ Ταρσοῦ δὲ Ἐπικούρειος φιλόσοφος ἐτυράννησε, Λυσίας ὄνομα· ὃς ὑπὸ τῆς πατρίδος στεφανηφόρος αἱρεθείς, τοῦτ᾽ ἔστιν ἱερεὺς Ἡρακλέους, οὐκ ἀπετίθετο τὴν ἀρχὴν (it was probably annual therefore), ἀλλ᾽ ἐξ ἱματίου (the costume of peace) τύραννος ἦν κ.τ.λ.

2. Στρατηγοί, whose number is unknown. They appear to have been the most important members of the executive at Priene. Some idea of their functions and position may be obtained by a reference to the passages where they are mentioned. No. cccxiv, lines 10, 22; No. ccccxv, lines 12, 20; No. ccccxix, line 32; No. ccccxx, line 38; No. ccccxxvii *a*. The important position of the στρατηγοί at Priene entirely accords with what we have observed respecting its independent position.

3. Ἵππάρχαι, mentioned in No. ccccxix, *fin.*, with the στρατηγοί, as charged with the safe escort of an envoy to Alexandria Troas. At the time of this decree, therefore, Priene must have had a force of cavalry; perhaps they were mercenaries.

4. Ὁ γραμματεὺς (τῆς βουλῆς?), compare *ante*, No. ccccxix, line 21. I have supposed a reference to this officer in No. cccciii, in my restoration of line 36.

5. Ὁ φρούραρχος is alluded to in No. cccciii, lines 66 fol. An interesting decree in honour of Nymphon, son of Protarchos, who had twice been commander of the citadel of Priene, was copied by Mr. A. S. Murray in 1870, 'from a stelè at the door of a house at Kelibesch,' and was published by me in the Hellenic Journal, iv, p. 237; see my remarks in that memoir.

6. Σιτοφύλακες, see *ante*, No. ccccxiii, three in number, elected, probably for the year, in the ekklesia. Compare Harpokration, s. v. σιτοφύλακες. Ἀρχή τις ἦν Ἀθήνησιν, ἥτις ἐπεμελεῖτο ὅπως ὁ σῖτος δικαίως πραθήσεται καὶ τὰ ἄλφιτα καὶ οἱ ἄρτοι.

7. Οἱ οἰκονόμοι, No. ccccxv, line 18. They are directed to defray out of the public exchequer the expense of a bronze statue and an inscription in honour of Larichos. We shall find an οἰκονόμος similarly mentioned in one of the decrees of Ephesos of the end of the fourth century B.C. (*post*); it is thought that he was probably rather a steward than a treasurer, and held but a subordinate position. This may be true also of the board of οἰκονόμοι at Priene, if I have rightly decyphered the very much worn letters of No. cccci, line 24 : in that case ὁ

ἐπὶ τῆς διοικήσεως would be the supreme minister of finance.

8. Ὁ νεωποίης, No. ccccxiii, line 18; No. ccccxv, lines 31, 35; No. ccccxvi, line 8; No. ccccxix, lines 29, 32; No. ccccxx, lines 72, 74. See note on No. ccccxiii.

9. Οἱ ἱεροποιοί, only mentioned once, as having to do with the celebration of a public festival, No. cccci, line 25.

10. Ὁ ἀγωνοθέτης, frequently mentior :d in connexion with the Dionysia at Priene.

Prienian names. In addition to the names to be found in the foregoing inscriptions, I have been favoured by Professor Percy Gardner with the following list of all the Magistrates' names known to him on autonomous Prienian coins :—

In the British Museum.		Πολι
Silver.		Δημητριος
Βιασ		Πυρρου
Σπιλο		Σωσιβι
Κλεομ		Διονυσιοσ
Λυσαγο		
Σωσιππος		Mionnet.
		Bronze.
Bronze.		Πατρισκου
Αιαντι		Μενεκρ
Ελικ		Τεραι
Ερα		Λατηςκου (?=Πα-
ΑποΛΛοδωρου		τρισκου)
Αναξιλασ		
Διονυσ		Mionnet Supp.
Ηρωαδησ		*Silver.*
Ηρωι		Πασικαη
Θρασυ		
Χαρησ		*Bronze.*
Μεντω		Λακων
Αχιλαειδησ		Ευμερο

Other Prienian names are Sostratos of Priene, from Sextus Emp. Adv. Gramm. i, 13, ed. Fabr. 1718, p. 281; Athenæos, i, p. 19; vi, p. 244; Leomedon a stephanephoros, Nymphon, son of Protarchos, a phrourarch, and Lysias son of Polychares, from the decree in the Hellenic Journal, already referred to; Timagenes from C. I. A. vol. ii, Pt. ii, No. 963, line 27.

It may be added that the coins of Priene in the British Museum appear to belong (like most of our inscriptions) to about the third century B.C. They show a general similarity to the Athenian coins, some even having an owl standing on an amphora; these may belong to a time of alliance with Athens. The usual type on the coins is the head of Athenò Polias, the tutelary goddess of Priene. Next in frequency is the trident of Poseidon, in reference to the worship of Poseidon at the Panionion (see Nos. ccccxxvi, ccccxxvii). The coins give positive evidence in favour of the independent position of Priene in the days of Alexander's successors.

CHAPTER II.

INSCRIPTIONS FROM IASOS.

[The following Inscriptions, Nos. cccxl—ccccxliv, were taken from the ruins of Iasos during a visit made by the Duke of St. Albans to that site in 1872, and were shipped on board his Grace's yacht 'Xantha' under my superintendence. No. ccccxlii was discovered during that visit by Mr. Albert Grey.—C.T.N.]

CCCCXL.

A slab of blue marble, formerly used as the lintel of a window in a Byzantine building. Height, 1 ft. 1 in.; length, 4 ft. 3 in. Presented by his Grace the Duke of St. Albans, 1872; unpublished.

```
ΚΑΤΑΤΑΔΕΙΕΡΑΣΟΠΟΙΕΡΕΥΣΤΟ ΔΙΟΣ ΤΟΥΜΕΓΙΣΤΟΥΛΛΜΒΑΝΓΤΠΔΕΤΠΝΟΥΟΜΕΝΩΝ
ΣΚΕΛΟΣΞΕΝΟΡΟΙΟΝΑΜΟΕ/ΗΙΣ 'ΝΤ   ΟΣΦ/ΙΠΣΕΚ      ΕΤΑΙ·ΙΟΣ   /ΣΕΙΑΝΤΕΠΟΛΛΑΕΞΑ
ΓΗΙΙΕΡΕΑΕΙΑΝΤΕΕΝΚΛ'ΚΕΦΑΛΗΝΚΛΙΠΟΔΑΣ   ΣΓΛ      ΙΕΤΑΡΤΟΜΜΕΡΟΣΤΩΝΔΕ
ΕΝΟΡΥΠΤΩΝΛΑΜΒΑΝΕΤΩΕΝΑΠΟΠΛΕΚ°  ΙΤΩΙΟΣΙ, Α      ΚΑΤΑΤΑΥΤΑΔΕΚΑΙΠΑ
ΡΑΤΩΝΜΕΤΟΙΚΩΝΠΑΡΑΔΕΤΩΝΞΕΝΩΝ  ΑΜΕΝΑΛΛΑΚΑΘΑΙΑΙΓ\  ΛΤΩΝΑΣΤΩΝΛΑΜΒΑΝΕ
ΤΩΔΕΚΑΙΤΑΔΕΡΜΑΤΑΗΝΔΕΜΙ   Α ΑΤ ΓΕΓΡΑΜΜΕΝΑΠΟΙ ' '      ΡΑΣΟΩΚΑΙΤΟΥ
ΙΕΡΟΕΡΓΕΣΟΩΗΝΔΕΤΙΣ           ΑΦΑΙΙ                  ΓΑΣΧΕΤΩ
ΩΣΙΕΡΟΣΥΛΟΣΤΩΝΔΕΑΝΑΘ  ΜΑ ΩΝΟΣΑΜΕΝΑΡΓ       ΤΩΝΕΣΤΩΤΟΥΙΕΡΕΩ
ΤΑΔΕΑΛΛΑΑΝΑΘΗΜΑΤΑΤΟΥΟΕΟΥ=ΣΤΓΓΠΙΜΓ  ΕΣΘΑΙΔΕΤΩΝΑΝΑΘΗΜΑΤΩΝ
ΤΟΥΣΝΕΩΠΟΙΑΣΚΑΤΑΤΟΝΝΙΟΛ ΟΝ
```

The surface has been intentionally chipped by a chisel over the middle portion, where the imperfect readings I have given were recovered with much difficulty. It needed the greatest caution to distinguish a modern chisel-stroke from the surviving stroke of one of the ancient letters. At either end the surface is beautifully preserved, and the letters are perfectly clear; they are of the best period, and are probably not much later than the Lygdamis-inscription of which the date is about 450 B.C. It will be seen that the diphthong OY is written

O in line 7, but OY elsewhere. The lapidary has forgotten Σ at the end of line 8. The letters were originally painted in with colour, which was very clear when the stone was first brought home, but has now faded almost entirely away: the lines were alternately red and blue, the first being red. In Lykia Fellows found inscriptions in the Lykian character coloured alternately red and blue, and sometimes yellow or green: see his 'Discoveries,' p. 146. The inscription appears to be complete, and reads as follows:—

Κατὰ τάδε ἱεράσθω ὁ ἱερεὺς τοῦ Διὸς τοῦ μεγίστου· λαμβανέτω δὲ τῶν θυομένων
σκέλος ἐν ὁποῖον ἂν θίλῃ σὺν τ[ῇ] ὀσφύι ὡς ἐκ[τέμν]εται ἡ ὀσ[φ]ὺς, ἐάν τε πολλὰ ἐξά-
γῃ ἡ ἱερέα εἰάν τε ἐν, καὶ κεφαλὴν καὶ πόδας [καὶ] σπλ[άγχνων] τέταρτομ μέρος· τῶν δὲ
ἐνθρύπτων λαμβανέτω ἐν ἀπὸ πλεκ[το]ῦ? τῷ θεῷ [κ]α[ὶ ἱερ]ώσυνα?]. Κατὰ ταὐτὰ δὲ καὶ πα-
ρὰ τῶν μετοίκων· παρὰ δὲ τῶν ξένων [τ]ὰ μὲν ἄλλα καθὰ καὶ πα[ρ]ὰ τῶν ἀστῶν, λαμβανί-
τω δὲ καὶ τὰ δέρματα. Ἢν δὲ μὴ [κ]ατὰ τὰ γεγραμμένα ποι[ῇ] μὴ ἱε]ράσθω καὶ τοῦ
ἱερο(ῦ) ἐργίσθω. Ἢν δέ τις [τὴν στήλην] ἀφαν[ίζῃ ἢ τὰ γράμματα?] πασχέτω
ὡς ἱερόσυλος. Τῶν δὲ ἀναθ[η]μάτων ὅσα μὲν ἀργ[- - - - - - - - - -]των ἔστω τοῦ ἱερέω[ς,
τὰ δὲ ἄλλα ἀναθήματα τοῦ θεοῦ ἔστω· ἐπιμέ[λ]εσθαι δὲ τῶν ἀναθημάτων
τοὺς νεωποίας κατὰ τὸν νόμον.

This is a law of the city of Iasos, regulating the perquisites of the priest of Zeus Megistos; and it originally must have occupied a conspicuous position in the temple of Zeus. Inscriptions of this kind, relating to priesthoods, are not uncommon : see *ante* Nos. cccxxvi, cccxxvii. The most complete example is the well-known Halikarnassian decree now in the British Museum (C. I. 2656) concerning the appointment and functions of the priestess of Artemis Pergaia, lines 8-14 of which run thus :—

ἱεράσεται ἐπὶ (ζ)ωῆς τῆς αὑτῆς, καὶ θύσει τὰ ἱερὰ τὰ
δημόσια καὶ τὰ ἰδιωτικά, καὶ λήψεται τῶν θυομένων δημοσίᾳ
ἀφ' ἑκάστου ἱερείου κωλὴν καὶ τὰ ἐπὶ κωλῇ νεμόμενα καὶ
τεταρτημορίδα σπλάγχνων καὶ τὰ δέρματα, τῶν δὲ ἰδιωτικῶν
λήψεται κωλὴν καὶ τὰ ἐπὶ κωλῇ νεμόμενα καὶ τεταρτημορίδα
σπλάγχνων.

We may also compare Rangabè, Antiq. Hellén. No. 816 (from Athens), and a curious calendar of sacrifices discovered at Mykonos, and published in the *Ἀθήναιον*, ii. p. 237. Several phrases quoted above from the Halikarnassos decree illustrate the present document; but our inscription appears to make no distinction between public and private sacrifices: both kinds are probably included under the provisions of lines 1–4. Compare also Dittenberger, Syll. 376.

Several Ionicisms are noticeable: *εἰάν*, lines 2, 3 (but *ἦν* in lines 6–7); *ἐργέσθω* for *εἱργέσθω*, in line 7; *ἱερέα* for *ἱερεῖα*, line 3, like *πλέον* the Ionic for *πλεῖον* the comparative of *πολύς*. It will be remembered that Iasos, though originally a Doric colony from Argos, had been re-colonised from Miletos and made Ionian (Polyb. xvi, 12).

Line 1. The priests of *Ζεὺς μέγιστος* are mentioned in an Iasian decree concerning Mausolos (Bulletin de Corr. Hell. v, p. 497) as eleven in number; either we must imagine a college of ten priests with another at their head, or a change took place in the number between the fifth and fourth centuries B.C. Zeus is not often found worshipped under this title, but the following examples may be referred to: C. I. 1625, line 66 (Bœotia, late), C. I. 2171 (Mitylenè), C. I. 2750 (near Hierapolis), C. I. 4501, 4502 (Palmyra), and perhaps C. I. 1513, 3949.

Line 2. The restoration *ὧν ἐκ*[*τέμν*]*εται ἡ ὀσφύς* is doubtful; I take it to mean 'in cases where it is usual to carve the loin (with the leg, so as to make a hind-quarter),' like *κωλῆν καὶ τὰ ἐπὶ κωλῇ νεμόμενα*

(which depended upon the kind of animal sacrificed, ox, sheep, or lamb, &c.) in the Halikarnassos inscription.

Line 4. *ἔνθρυπτα* seem to be cakes to be eaten sopped in wine or milk, 'rusks;' compare Lobeck, Aglaophamus, ii, p. 1073. Aeschines, according to Demosthenes (De Corona, p. 314, Reiske), used to receive *ἔνθρυπτα* among his perquisites when assisting at his mother's initiations: *μισθὸν λαμβάνων τούτων ἔνθρυπτα καὶ στρεπτοὺς καὶ νήλατα.* Compare Harpokration s. v. If I have rightly read *ἀπὸ πλεε*[*το*]*ῦ*, then *πλικτόν* must mean a wicker-basket: compare *πλέκος, κάνεον*.

Line 7 is much defaced; my restorations however are not mere conjectures, but are suggested by what seem to be strokes of the original letters.

Line 8, also much defaced, certainly distinguished between two classes of dedications (*ἀναθήματα*); of which the former kind are to be appropriated by the priest, the latter to be added to the treasury of the god. If I have rightly decyphered the letters *ΑΡΓ*, of which the *Γ* is pretty certain, then it may have run somewhat thus: *ὅσα μὲν ἀργ*[*ύριόν ἐστιν αὐ*]*τῶν*, i. e. all the dedications made in money are to go to the priest: or, *ὅσα μὲν ἀργ*[*ὰ τῶν ἀναθημά*]*των*, i. e. those which were unwrought bullion.

Line 10. On the *νεωποῖαι* see note on No. CCCCXIII ante.

CCCCXLI.

A door-jamb (parastas) of white marble from Iasos, 6 ft. 11¼ in. high, 1 ft. 11¾ in. wide, 10 in. thick; beautifully inscribed. Part of the jamb is preserved in its entire length; but the upper part has been partially calcined by fire, and about the middle of the stone the surface is much worn and has in parts flaked off. The jamb when seen by Mr. Newton in 1872 was in its original position in an ancient doorway. Le Bas describes this gateway as 'la porte du gymnase': see Chandler, Inscr. ant. Syll., p. ix, No. 58. The upper portion (lines 1–69) is published by Waddington-Le Bas, Pt. v, No. 251: they omit the concluding portion, which I have given in my Manual of Greek Historical Inscriptions, No. 182. The letters within curved brackets in lines 39 foll. are given from Waddington-Le Bas' copy, made when the marble was less damaged; they are no longer visible. The letters of this inscription were originally painted with red, which was perfectly fresh when the stone was first unearthed at Iasos in 1872, and is still traceable in the alternate lines. Presented by his Grace the Duke of St. Albans, 1872. Portions of the first sixteen lines are inaccurately given in C. I. 2679.

```
      ΕΠΙΣΤΕΦΑΝΗϹ    ΟΥΔΗΜΕΟΥΤΟΥΣΤΗΣΙϽΧΟΥ
      ΓΡΑΜΜΑΤΕΩΣ⌐ΞΜΕΝΗΤΟΣΤΟΥΠΟΔϽΝΟΣΓΗΦΟΡΙΩΝΟΣ
            ΨⱵΦΙΣΜΑΤΑΠΑΡΑΡΟΔΙΩΝ
      ΔΟΞΕΝΤΟΙΔΑΜΩΙΠΕΡΙΩΝΙΑΣΕΙΣⱵΥΝΙΕΝΓ  ΚΑΙΦΙΛϹ
   5  ⱵΑΡΧΟΝΤΕΣΤΟΥΔΑΜΟΥΑΠΟΣΤΕΙ        ΤΕΣΥΑΦΙⱵΜΑΚΑΙ
      ΕΣΒΕΥΤΑΣΕΜΦΑΝΙΙΟΝΤΙΤ              ΑΔΙΚΗⱵⱵΤΑΕ
      ΧΩΡΑΙΑΥΤΩΝΥΓϹΠΟΔΙΛΟΥΚΑΙΙ         ΤΙΤΟΝΔΑΜΟΝ
      ΑΠΕΡΚΑΙΕΝΤΟΙⱵΓΠΡΟΤΕΡ          ⌐Τ⌐     ⌐ΥΕ
      ΓϽΝΤΑΝΓΟΛΙΝΤΛΝΙΑΣΕΩΝΚΑΙΝ˙     ⱵϹΝΟΙΑⱵ     ΣΘ
  10  ϽΣΑΤΕΓΟΛΙΣΑΥΤΩΝΕΛΕΥΘΕΡΑΚΑΙΑΥΤΟΝΟϹ ϽΣ    ΝΗ
      ⱵΕΡΙΤΑΓΓΕΓΟΝΟΤΩΝΑΔΙΙΗΜΑΤΩΝΕΓΙΜ ΛΓˋⱵ     ΙΗ
      ΚΑΘΟΤΙΚΑΔΟΞΗΙΤΩΙΔΑΜΩΙΚΑΙΤ      ↗ΡΑΓΕΝΟ   ⌐ΑΡⱵ
      ΫΓΟΛΕΜΑΡΧΟΣΚΑΙΓΛΑΥΚΟΣΕΓⱵ     ΟΝΤΕΣΕΓˋ  ꟼ ΥΑΛ
      ΓΑΝΕΚΚΛΗΣΙΑΝΔΙΕΛΕΓΕΝΑΚΟΛΟΥΘϽΣΤϽΙΣΕΝΤ   ΑΦΙΣ
  15  ΓΕΓΡΑΜΜΕΝΟᵎΣΜΕΤΑΓΑΣΑΣΣΓϽΥΔΑΣΚΑΙΦΙⱵΥΤΙΜ
      ΑΓΓΚΡΙΝΑΣΘΑΙΑΥΤΟΙΣ ΟΤΙΟΔΑΜΟΣΕΙⱵ  Σ  Α  ΞΙΣ
      ΥΓΑΡΧΟΝΤΑΣΤΑΙΓΟΛΕΙΓΡΟΤΕΡΟΝΤΙ
```

ΕΠΙΜΕΛΕΙΑΜΓ ϽΙΟΥΜΕΝΟΣΓ ΙΩΝ
ΟΥΜΕΝΣΣΣΥΓΚΑΤΑΣΚΕΥΑΙ
20 ΤΗΡΙΑΝΤΑΣΓΟΛΙΟΣΑΥΤ Σ
ΟΓῺΣΥΓΕΡΤΕΤΩΝΓ ῺΝ
ΑΔΙΚΑΙΑΓΕΝΗΤΑΙΚΑΙ
ΝΤΕΤΑΓΜΕΝΟΙΣΜΗΘΕΝ
ΑΙΙΑΣΕῺΝΚΑΙΕΙΣΤΟΛΟΙΓΟΝῺΣ
25 ΥΣΑΝΑΥΤῺΙΓΟΤΙΙΑΣΕΙΣ
ΛΣΕΙΤΑΙΤῺ ΙΑΣΕΥΣΙΣΥ
ΡΑΙΑΣΕῺΝΚ ΛΛΕΣΑΙΕΓΙ

ΚΑΙΤῺΙΔΑΜῼΙΟΓῺΣΙΑΣ
⅃ΑΜϽΥΕΙΔΗΣῺΝΤΙΤ⅄
30 ϽΟΔΙῺΝ ΔΕΔΟΧΘ⅄
Τ⅄ΣΗΔΗΔ ΤΟΙΔΕΑΙ
ΙΑΝΤΑΝΥΓ ΡΧΟΥΣΑΝΑΥΤΟ ΙΤῺΙΙ ΟΕ
Τ 'ΚΑΙΕΓ'ΔΕΙΞΑΝΤ ΣΜΕ ΛΥΓ
ΥΓΕΡΤ ΝΓΕΓΕΝΗ ϽΝΑΔΙΚΗΜΑΤῼ
35 ϽΔΙϿ ϽΥΔΗΛΟ(Υ)ⱵΤῺΝΑΥΤΟΙ ΔΑΜϽΣΚΑΙΕΙΣ¯
ΟΥΣ(Α)ΝΑΥΤῼΙΓΟΤΙΙΑΣΕΙΣ ΓΕΝΕΙΑΝΚΑ(ΙΦΙΛ
ΤⱵΙΤῺΝΙΑΣΕΥΣΙΣΥΜΦΦΡΟ Ν ΑΙΡΕΘ(ΕΝ
ϽΥ ΕΓΙΚΡⱵΤΗΣΤΙΜΑΣΙΣ ⱵΤΟΥ

ⱵΜῼΙΕΓΕΙΔΗΙΑΣΕῺΝ Υ ΕΝῺΝΚ(ΑΙΦΙⱵ
40 ϽΟΣΤΕΙⱵ ⱵΥⱵΦΙΣΜΑΚΑΙΓΡΕΣΒF.(ΑΝ.Ο
ΙΤΑΓΕι (ΜΕΝΑ)ΑΔΙΚΗΜΑΤΑΕΙΣΑ(ΥΤΟΥΣΑΓ
ϿΟΟΛΥΙ(ΓΙΧΟΝΚ)ΑιΓΑΙΑΙ (ΤῺΝΤΟ
¯ΑΣΓΟ(ΛΙΟΣΑΥΤῺ)Ι ⱵΑΙΑΓΟΣΤF(ΙΛΑΙΓΡΟΣ
ⱵΓΟⱶ.(ΓΙΣΟΥΜΕΝΟΥΣΓ)ΕΡΙ.ῺΝ
45 (ΑΥΤΟΙΣΤΑΝΓΟΛΙΝΕΛΕΥΘΕΡΑΝ)
(ΟΑ.ΡΕΣΙΝΚΑΙ.Τ)
(ΙΑΣΕῺΝΤΟΥⱵ)
(ΡΑΚΑΛΕΣ)
(Γ Κ Ι)
50 (ΡΑ ΚΑΙΑ ΟΝΟΜ)
(ΑΑΞΙΟΥΜΕΝΑΚΑΙ)
(ΟΣΕΥΧΑΡΙΣΤΟΥΝΤῼ)
(ΤῺΝΓΕΓΕ)
(ῺΝ ΚⱵ)
55 (ΙΑΓΝΟΝ ΣΥΝ)
(ΕΓΟΝ ΜⱵ)
(ΕⱵ ΑΣ)
(ΟΝ)
(ΛΙΓ)
60 (ΡΑΝΑΥΤῼ)
(ΚΑΙΔ)
(ΝⱵ Σ ΑΙΕΝΓΕ)
(ΚΑΙΤΑΛΟΙΓⱵ)
(ΑΙ)
65 (ΟΟΡΙΟΙ)
(ΝΤΑ)
(Ι)
(Ι)
(ΙΑ)

70 . . . .
. . . .
       ΟΝΤ   ΑΝ
      ΓΟΙΑΜ | Α ΤΕΣΤΑΕΓΕΣ
  ΥΓΟΛΙΝ ΑΡΑΚΑΛ   ΑΥΤΟΙΚΛΙΤΟΝΥΓΑΡΛ
75 ΞΓΞΙΝΤΟΙΣΥΦΑΥΤΟΝΤΕΤΑΓΜΕΝΟΙΣΜΗΘΕΝΑΔΙΚΗΜΑ
  ΓΑΙΑΣΕΩΝΑΛΛΑΓΟΤΙΦΕΡΕΣΘΑΙΑΥΤΟΙΣΦΙΛΑΝΘΡΩΓΩΣΚΑΙΣ
  ΕΝΗΜΕΝΩΝΑΔΙΚΗΜΑΤΩΝΓΡΟΝΟΙΑΝΤΙΝΑΓΟΙΗΣΑΣΘΑΙΟΓΩ
  ΛΙΤΑΔΙΚΑΙΑΑΚΟΛΟΥΘΩΣΤΟΙΣΥΓΟΤΟΥΒΑΣΙΛΕΩΣΕΓΙΣΤΑΛΕΙΣ
  ΛΟΤΙΤΟΥΤΩΝΕΓΙΜΕΛΗΘΕΙΣΟΜΟΛΟΓΟΥΜΕΝΑΦΑΙΝΕΙΤΑΙΓΡΑΣΣΩ
80 ΕΤΟΥΒΑΣΙΛΕΩΣΑΙΡΕΣΕΙΚΑΙΤΟΙΣΕΓΙΣΤΕΛΛΟΜΕΝΟΙΣΥΓΑΥΤΟΥΦΙ
  ΡΩΓΟΙΣΓΟΤΙΤΑΝΓΟΛΙΝ ΕΜΦΑΝΙΖΟΝΤΩΝΔΕΑΥΤΩΙΤΟΙΓΡΕΣΒΕΥ
  ΤΙΟΔΑΜΟΣΕΙΔΩΣΙΑΣΕΙΣΕΥΝΟΥΣΥΓΑΡΧΟΝΤΑΣΤΑΙΓΟΛΕΙΚΑΙΓΡΟΛ
  ΜΕΝΟΣΑΥΤΟΙΣΣΥΓΚΑΤΑΣΚΕΥΑΙΕΙΝΓΑΝΤΑΤΑΓΟΤΑΣΦΑΛΕΙΑΝ
  ΣΩΤΗΡΙΑΝΓΡΟΤΕΡΟΝΤΕΕΤΥΓΧΑΝΕΔΕΔΩΚΩΣΓΟΤΙΤΑΓΜΑΤΟΙ
85 ΛΡΧΟΥΣΙΤΟΙΣΑΓΟΣΤΕΛΛΟΜΕΝΟΙΣΥΓΑΥΤΟΥΕΓΙΜΕΛΕΙΣΘΑΙΤΑΣΙΑΣ
  ΚΩΡΑΣΚΙΘΑΓΕΡΚΑΙΤΑΣΤΟΥΔΑΜΟΥΚΑΙΝΥΝΜΝΑΜΟΝΕΥΩΝΤΑΣΥΓ
  ΧΟΥΣΑΣΓΟΤΑΥΤΟΥΣΟΙΚΕΙΟΤΑΤΟΣΟΥΘΕΝΟΣΑΓΟΣ ΣΕΙΤΑΙΤΩΝΣΥ
  ΡΟΝΤΩΝΙΑΣΕΥΣΙΕΙΔΕΚΑΤΟΥΔΑΜΟΥΓΑΣΑΝΣΓΟΥΔΑΝΓΟΙΟΥΜΕΝΟΥ
  ΤΟΥΤΩΝΜΗΔΕΜΙΑΝΕΓΙΣΤΡΟΦΑΝΟΛΥΜΓΙΧΩΞΓΟΙΗΤΑΙΑΛΛΑΑΓΕΡ
90 ΡΗΤΑΓΙΝΟΜΕΝΑΑΔΙΚΗΜΑΤΑΔΗΛΟΥΝΤΟΙΑΥΤΩΙΤΟΙΓΡΕΣΒΕΥΤΑΙΟΤΙ
  ΤΑΜΜΕΝΦΙΛΙΑΝΚΑΙΤΑΝΕΥΝΟΙΑΝΤΑΝΥΓΑΡΛΟΥΣΑΝΑΥΤΩΙΓΟΤΙΒΑΣΙΛ
  ΦΙΛΙΓΓΟΝΔΙΑΦΥΛΑΞΕΙΟΔΑΜΟΣΓΡΑΞΕΙΔΕΑΓΕΓΕΙΣΤΑΙΣΥΜΦΕΡΟΝΤΛ
  ΕΙΜΕΙΝΓΟΤΙΤΑΝΙΑΣΕΩΝΑΣΦΑΛΕΙΑΝ ΑΙΡΕΘΕΝ   ΤΙΜΑΣΙΘΕΟΣ
  ΔΙΟΝΥΣΙΟΥ   ΕΓΙΚΡΑΤΗΣΤΙΜΑΣΙΣΤΡΑΤΟΥ

            Ἐπὶ στεφανηφ[όρ]ου Δημίου τοῦ Στησιόχου,
            γραμματίως δὲ Μίκητος τοῦ Πόδωνος· Γηφοριῶνος·
               Ψηφίσματα παρὰ 'Ροδίων.

  Α Ἔ]δοξεν τῷ δάμῳ περὶ ὦν 'Ιασεῖς συγγενε[ῖς] καὶ φίλο[ι
  5 ὑ]πάρχοντες τοῦ δάμου ἀποστεί[λαν]τες ψάφισμα καὶ
     πρ]εσβευτὰς ἐμφανίζοντι τ[ὰ γεγενημένα] ἀδικήματα ἐ[ν
     τᾷ] χώρᾳ αὐτῶν ὑπὸ Ποδίλου καὶ [παρακαλοῦν]τι τὸν δᾶμον
     καθ]άπερ καὶ ἐν τοῖς πρότερον χρόνοις διατ]ετέλεκεν εὐέ[ρ-
     γε]τῶν τὰν πόλιν τὰν 'Ιασέων καὶ νῦ[ν π]ρόνοιαν [ποιεῖ]σθ[αι
 10 ὅπ]ως ἅ τε πόλις αὐτᾶν ἐλευθέρα καὶ αὐτόνομος [περιγί]η[ται
     καὶ περὶ τῶν γεγονότων ἀδι[κ]ημάτων ἐπιμ[έ]λειά[ν τινα πο]ιή[σασ-
     θαι καθότι κα δόξῃ τῷ δάμῳ, καὶ τ[οὶ π]αραγενό[μενοι] παρ' α[ὐ-
     τῶ]ν Πολέμαρχος καὶ Γλαῦκος ἐπ[ελθ]όντες ἐπὶ [τὰν] β[ο]υλὰ[ν
     καὶ τὰν ἐκκλησίαν διέλεγεν ἀκολούθως τοῖς ἐν τ[ῷ ψ]αφίσ-
 15 ματι] γεγραμμένοις, μετὰ πάσας σπουδᾶς καὶ φιλοτιμι-
     ίας] ἀπ[ο]κρίνασθαι αὐτοῖς· — Ὅτι ὁ δᾶμος εἰδ[ὼ]ς ['Ι]α[σ]εῖς
     εὔνους] ὑπάρχοντας τᾷ πόλει πρότερόν τε [ἀεὶ διατετελ-
     εκὼς ?] ἐπιμέλειαν ποιούμενος π[ερὶ τῶν] συμφερόντων 'Ιασεῦσι ?
     καὶ προαιρ]ούμενος συγκατασκευάζ[ειν πάντα τὰ ποτ' ἀσφά-
 20 λειαν καὶ σω]τηρίαν τᾶς πόλιος αὐτ[οῖ]ς[. τὰν πᾶσαν πρόνοιαν
     ποιησεῖται] ὅπως ὑπέρ τε τῶν γ[εγονότ]ων [ἀδικημάτων ...
     ......τ]ὰ δίκαια γένηται καὶ [ποτίταγμα δώσει τοῖς ?
     ὑφ' αὐτό]ν τεταγμένοις μηθὲν [ἀδίκημα ποιεῖσθαι ἐν τᾷ
     χώρα τ]ᾷ 'Ιασέων καὶ εἰς τὸ λοιπὸν ὡς [μάλιστα διαφυλάξει ?
 25 τὰν ὑπάρχο]υσαν αὐτῷ ποτὶ 'Ιασεῖ[ς φιλίαν καὶ εὔνοιαν καὶ
     οὐθενὸς ἀποστ]ασεῖται τῶ[ν] 'Ιασεῦσι συ[μφερόντων· τοὺς δὲ παρα-
     γενομένους πα]ρὰ 'Ιασέων καλέσαι ἐπὶ [τὸ πρυτανεῖον.

  Β Ἔδοξεν τᾷ βουλᾷ] καὶ τῷ δάμῳ· ὅπως 'Ιασ[εῖς συγγενεῖς καὶ φίλοι
     ὑπάρχοντες τοῦ δάμου εἰδήσωντι τὰ [ἐψαφισμένα φιλάνθρωπα ?
 30 ὑπὸ τοῦ δάμου τοῦ] 'Ροδίων. — Δεδόχθα[ι τᾷ βουλᾷ καὶ τῷ δάμῳ
     ἑλίσθαι πρεσβευ]τὰς ἤδη δ[ύο], τοὶ δὲ ἀ[φικόμενοι ἐμφανιζόν-

C

10 Ἔδοξεν τᾷ βουλᾷ καὶ τῷ δ]άμῳ· ἐπειδὴ 'Ιασίων [σ]υ[υγ]ενῶν κ(αὶ φίλ[ων
ὑπαρχόντων :οῦ δάμου καὶ ἀπ]οστειλ[άντω]ν ψάφισμα καὶ πρεσβε[ί](αν ο[ἵ-
τινες τῷ δάμῳ ἐνεφάνισαν] τὰ γε[γεγν](μένα) ἀδικήματα εἰς α(ὑτοὺς . .
. . . . υ]πρὸ 'Ολύμ(πιχον, κ)αὶ παρα[καλούν](των το)[ὺτ ?
. . . . τ]ᾶς πό(λιος αὐτῶ)ν καὶ ἀποστε(ῖλαι πρὸς
αὐτὸν πρεσβευτὰς τοὺς] ἀπολ[ο](γισουμένους π)ερὶ [τ]ῶν . . . .

45 . . . . (αὐτοῖς τὰν πόλιν ἐλευθέραν) . . .
. . . . (τὰν πρ](οσα[ί]ρεσιν καὶ . τ .) . . . .
. . . . ('Ιασέων τοῦ) . . . .
. . . . (πα]οακαλίσ[αι) . . . .
. . . . (γ . . κ[α]ὶ) . . . .

50 . . . . (ἐλευθέ]ρα[ν] καὶ α[ὐτ]όνομ[ον ?) . . . .
. . . . (τ]ὰ ἀξιούμενα καὶ) . . . .
. . . . (ος εὐχαριστούντω[ν) . . . .
. . . . (τῶν γεγε[νημένων) . . . .
. . . . (ων . . κα .) . . . .

55 . . . . (αγνον . . . συν) . . . .
. . . . (εγον . . . μα) . . . .
. . . . (ἐλ[ευθέρ]ας ?) . . . .
. . . . (ον) . . . .
. . . . (λιπ) . . . .

60 . . . . (ραν αὐτω) . . . .
. . . . (καὶ δ). . . . .
. . . . (να[ί]ς [κ]αὶ ἐν πε) . . . .
. . . . (καὶ τὰ λοιπὰ) . . . .
. . . . (αι) . . . .

65 . . . . (με]θορίοι[ς ?) . . . .
. . . . (ντα) . . . .
. . . . (ι) . . . .
. . . . (ι) . . . .
. . . . (ια) . . . .

70 . . . .
. . . . ον . . . . αν . . . .
στρατη?]γῷ αμ . . . . a[ν]τες τὰ ἐπισ . . . .
τὰ]ν πόλιν [π]αρακαλ . . . . . αὐτοὶ καὶ τὸν ὑπάρχο(ντα . . . .

75 ἐν]έπειν τοῖς ὑφ' αἱτὸν τεταγμένοις μηθὲν ἀδίκεια [ποιεῖσθαι . . .
ἐν] τᾷ 'Ιασίων ἀλλὰ ποτιφέρεσθαι αὐτοῖς φιλανθρώπως, καὶ ἐ[πὶ τῶν γε-
γ]ενημένων ἀδικημάτων πρόνοιάν τινα ποιήσασθαι ὅπω[ς γένη-
τ]αι τὰ δίκαια ἀκολούθως τοῖς ὑπὸ τοῦ βασιλέως ἐπιστολαῖσ[ιν,
κ]α(ὶ)ό(τι) τούτων ἐπιμεληθεὶς ὁμολογούμενα φαινεῖται πράσσων [τᾷ

80 τ]ε τοῦ βασιλέως αἱρέσει καὶ τοῖς ἐπιστελλομένοις ὑπ' αὐτοῦ φι[λαν-
θ]ρώποις ποτὶ τὰν πόλιν· ἐμφανιζόντων δὲ αὐτῷ τοὶ πρεσβευ[ταὶ
ὅ]τι ὁ δᾶμος εἰδὼς 'Ιασεῖς εὔνους ὑπάρχοντα τᾷ πόλει καὶ προα[ιρού-
μενος αὐτοῖς συγκατασκευάζειν πάντα τὰ ποτ' ἀσφάλειαν [καὶ
σωτηρίαν, πρότερόν τε ἐτύγχανε δεδωκὼς ποτίγραμμα τοῖ[ς

85 ἄρχουσι τοῖς ἀποστελλομένοις ὑπ' αὐτοῦ ἐπιμελεῖσθαι τᾶς 'Ιασ[έων
χώρας καθάπερ καὶ τᾶς τοῦ δάμου, καὶ νῦν μναμονεύων τᾶς ὑπ[αρ-
χούσας ποτ' αὐτοὺς οἰκειότατος οὐθενὸς ἀπος[τα]σεῖται τῶν συ[μφε-
ρόντων 'Ιασεῦσι· εἰ δέ κα, τοῦ δάμου πᾶσαν σπουδὰν ποιουμένου [περὶ
τούτων, μηθεμίαν ἐπιστροφὰν 'Ολύμπιχος ποιῆται ἀλλὰ περ[ιο-

90 ρῇ τὰ γινόμενα ἀδικήματα δηλούντω(ν) αὐτῷ τοὶ πρεσβευταὶ ὅτι
τὰμ μὲν φιλίαν καὶ τὰν εὔνοιαν τὰν ὑπάρχουσαν αὐτῷ ποτὶ βασιλ[έα
Φίλιππον διαφυλάξει· ὁ δᾶμος πράξει· δὲ ἃ πέπεισται συμφέροντα
εἶμεν ποτὶ τὰν 'Ιασέων ἀσφάλειαν. Αἱρέθεν — Τιμασίθεος
Διωνυσίου — 'Επικράτης Τιμασιστράτου·

This inscription records certain negotiations which passed between the people of Iasos and Rhodes and ' King Philip' (line 92). There can be no doubt that Philip V of Macedon is the king referred to; and the only question is, when was the attitude of Philip towards Rhodes and cities on the coast like Iasos such as to account for the transactions here recorded ? The relations between Philip and the Rhodians had been uneasy for some time before the open rupture in B.C. 201: the Rhodians knew that their fleet had been burnt through the king's perfidy, and that he had tried to urge Krete to make war upon them (Polyb. xiii, 4; and compare Part ii, ante, p. 113). Nevertheless· to outward appearance the Rhodians made no sign of hostility, and maintained friendly relations with Philip. Rhodes, indeed, the leading commercial power of the Eastern Mediterranean, had nothing to gain by war. Possessed of a thriving trade, regarded by the many Greek maritime cities as their leader and the protectress of their freedom, holding also a considerable territory on the Karian mainland (the Rhodian Peræa, Strabo xiv, p. 651), Rhodes would have preferred to remain at peace (see Mommsen, Hist. of Rome, Book iii, ch. 8, English Translation 1868, ii, p. 236). But when Philip, perfidiously rejecting their friendly offices, showed the utmost severity to Kios, and was marching southward upon the other Greek cities, the Rhodians hesitated no longer to regard him as an enemy (Polyb. xv, 22). At the same time they dispatched envoys to the Roman Senate ' nuntiantes Asiae quoque civitates sollicitari' (Livy xxxi, 2). In the same year, B.C. 201, Philip marched into Karia, robbed the Rhodians of their mainland territory, and placed garrisons in the various towns to make good his advantage, Iasos being one of these (Polyb. xvi, 12; xvii, 2, 8; compare xviii, 27; Livy xxxii, 33; xxxvii, 17).

Now it is clear that our inscription must be placed before B.C. 201, the year of the outbreak of the second Macedonian War; because the Rhodians speak in lines 91 foll. of 'maintaining their existing relations of friendship and goodwill towards King Philip.' But the very terms of this document (see lines 84 foll., 88 foll.) seem to indicate that the situation was full of danger and a rupture all but inevitable. Our inscription may therefore be probably assigned to B.C. 202 or early in 201, just before the war. Philip had hardly yet crossed the Hellespont, but the Olympichos of lines 42, 89 was probably one of his agents or generals who, while his master was busy in the north, was engaged in paving the way for Philip's advance southward. Polybios indeed (v, 90), mentions an Olympichos, a 'dynast of Asia,' who was so far friendly to the Rhodians that he was one of the monarchs who sent them large sums of money to help them after the earthquake had destroyed their city: this was between B.C. 229 and B.C. 226 (Clinton, F. H. iii, p. 425, Appendix, ch. 8). There is no evidence that this dynast is the Olympichos of our inscription; and if he was, it is quite possible that after twenty years' interval he might be found siding with Philip against Rhodes.

The most obvious means of helping Philip's cause would be to encourage dissensions among the free Greek cities. Krete had already been incited by Philip against Rhodes (Polyb. xiii, 4), and now Iasos had a grievance which might be turned to his advantage. The growing power of Rhodes upon the mainland could not fail to excite the envy of the neighbouring states. The Rhodian Peræa (referred to in lines 23, 24, 85, 86), was administered by magistrates sent from the island (lines 75, 85, compare line 23), and one of these governors named Podilos (line 7) had given offence to the Iasians by certain ἀδικήματα (lines 6 etc.), which had been committed within Iasian territory. The nature of these outrages is not specified, but from lines 85, 86 it may be conjectured that the Rhodian governor had winked at robberies, or perhaps merely trespasses committed by Rhodians over the Iasian border. Whatever the grievance was, it was resented by the Iasians as an attack upon their freedom and independence (lines 9, 10), a sentiment which Olympichos, Philip's agent, would be forward to encourage. In fact we may probably regard Iasos as having been made, throughout this affair, the mere tool of Philip.

The defaced condition of the marble prevents us from following the whole of the negotiations; but thus much is evident. The documents inscribed upon this Iasian stele are all copies of decrees of Rhodes, prefaced by a heading and date proper to Iasos itself (lines 1–3). Then comes (A) a decree of the Rhodians, which recites the application of the Iasian envoys to Rhodes and the friendly reply of the Rhodian people (lines 4–27). We learn from lines 80, 81, that the envoys had brought with them a friendly letter of King Philip addressed to the Rhodians. B (lines 28–38) is a decree of the Rhodians appointing two envoys to proceed to Iasos, and deliver the foregoing decree (A), declaring at the same time by word of mouth the good-will of the Rhodian people. The third decree (C, lines 39–94) is the longest and most important of all, as it dealt with the relations between Rhodes and King Philip. It is very disappointing to be unable to decipher more than a half of this document. The remaining portions however are clear enough, and reveal very plainly the state of affairs. Two envoys (lines 93, 94) were appointed, the same who were to go to Iasos (lines 37, 38). They are to proceed (it seems) to Olympichos (lines 44, 89), to assure him that the Rhodians in no way wish to injure Iasos, and that nothing shall be wanting on their part to secure the liberties and interests of Iasos in accordance with Philip's wishes. They have instructed their governors in the Peræa to be very attentive to this point (lines 75 foll.). It seems clear that Philip had paraded his intention of maintaining the liberty and independence of the individual Greek cities as against the predominant power of a state like Rhodes. It marked him as an ill friend to Greek freedom that he should attack federations,—the only means of securing real independence to such small communities against great monarchies like Macedon. Some idea, on the other hand, of the territorial power of the Rhodians may be gained from the fact that they had purchased Kaunos in Karia of the Ptolemies for 200 talents, and had received Stratonikeia, also in Karia, from the Seleukidæ in reward for various services; and they drew from each of these cities a yearly revenue of 120 talents (Polyb. xxxi, 7). Stratonikeia, situated just on the other side of Mount Latmos, was not very far from Iasos, and it was probably from this quarter that the ἀδικήματα here mentioned proceeded. The complaint of the Rhodians before the Roman Senate (Livy xxxi, 2), 'Asiae civitates sollicitari,' may refer not only to the warlike attacks made by Philip on Kios and elsewhere, but also to his endeavours to set the Greek cities at variance with each other, and especially to break up the Rhodian dominion upon the mainland under the plea of 'independence for the Greek cities.'

Perhaps the negotiations recorded here were the last efforts of diplomacy to stave off the inevitable rupture. When the war came, the Rhodians appear to have borne no grudge against Iasos, and one of the articles of the treaty of B.C. 196 provided that Philip should withdraw his garrisons from Iasos and the neighbouring towns (Polyb. xviii, 27; Livy xxxiii, 30).

The Rhodian envoys (lines 38, 94,) are named Timasitheos son of Dionysios, Epikrates son of Timasistratos. It is curious that in the war with Antiochos, ten years later, when the Rhodian fleet rendered valuable help to the Romans, Livy mentions an Epikrates as a Rhodian officer (xxxvii, 13, 14 bis). This may be the Epikrates of our inscription : this conjecture is confirmed when Livy (ibid. 14) mentions another Rhodian officer Timasikrates in close connexion with Epikrates. For the envoys of our inscription appear, from the look of their names, to have been kinsmen ; and if we identify the envoy Epikrates with the Epikrates of Livy, then Livy's Timasikrates may be another member of the same family; and their tree may be guessed to be somewhat like the following :—

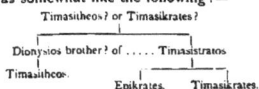

Timasitheos? or Timasikrates?

Dionysios brother? of . . . . . Timasistratos

Timasitheos.   Epikrates.   Timasikrates.

I am unable to discover any difference of dialect

between the Doricism of the Rhodian Award at Prienè (No. cccciii, ante) and the Doricism of these decrees, which are some forty years later in date, except that in the Award οἱ is the plural of the article (line 101), in this document τοί (lines 12, 31, 90). Line 14 : διέλεγεν is for διελέγησαν, as in several Kretan inscriptions, C. I. 3048, 3050, 3052, 3058, and a copy of a Rhodian decree at Kyzikos, C. I. 3050. Similarly αἵρεθεν (ᾑρέθησαν) in lines 37, 93.* Line 26 : ἀποστασείται is the ordinary Doric future middle, as in line 87 : and φαινεῖται in line 79, if not a lapidary's blunder, is a present formed by a false analogy.

The Iasian heading (lines 1–3) furnishes us with the name of an Iasian month Γηφοριών. As this name has been doubted by Ahrens (Rhein. Mus. xvii, p. 356) and other writers on the Greek Kalendar, it should be stated that the letters ΓΗΦΟΡΙΩΝΟ are perfectly legible upon the marble. The only other months of the Iasian calendar known to me are—

Ἀπατουριών, Waddington-Le Bas, Part v, No. 281, fin.; Bulletin de Corr. Hell. v, p. 493 ; Dittenberger, Syll., No. 77, 1.

Ἀφροδισιών, C. I. 2673, 2674.

Ἐλαφηβολιών, C. I. 2675 b, 2677 b.

All the Iasian names that occur in this inscription are known to us from other Iasian documents. Δημέας Στησιόχου, the stephanephoros of line 1, should perhaps be restored in C. I. 2671 lines 5, 6 (. . . τοῦ Στησιόχου), and may be the father of the Στησίοχος Δημέου in Waddington-Le Bas, Part v, No. 270. The name Δημέας occurs ibid. Nos. 267, 275, 276. Μένης Πόθωνος (line 2) the Secretary (of the βουλή?) may be related to the Μένης Τυρταίου of Waddington-Le Bas, No. 281 fin. The name Πόθων occurs ibid. No. 294. Compare Suidas, s. v. Πόθωνος. The names of the Iasian envoys Polemarchos and Glaukos (line 13) recur in Iasian inscriptions : for Glaukos see ibid. Nos. 255, 261, 285; for Polemarchos, ibid. No. 259. Πόθιλος (lines 7, 35) does not seem to occur elsewhere.

In line 4 the Rhodians claim the Iasians as συγγενεῖς, because they were originally a Dorian colony from Argos : compare Livy xxxvii, 17, 'frequentes Rhodios orare institerunt ne urbem (i. e. Iasos) et vicinam sibi et cognatam innoxiam perire sinerent.' This was in the war with Antiochos.

* See Etymol. M. s. v. "Ηγερθεν Αἰολικῶς καὶ Δωρικῶς ἤγερθεν. Of course the termination of the first and second aorist passive in -εν instead of -ησαν is very common in Homer, Pindar, Theokritos and other poets. The same form is also to be found, though very rarely, even in the Attic dramatists : e. g. Euripides, Hippol. 1247 (ἵππου δ' ἐφρύβδεν), but this is in the speech of an Ἐξάγγελος, and has an epic tinge. So also, in an anapæstic tetrameter, and therefore in a quasi-Epic rhythm, in Aristophanes. Wasps. 662 (ἐξ χιλιάσιν, κοῦσιν πλείους ἐν τῇ χώρᾳ κατένασθεν).

CCCCXLII.

A stele of blue marble, broken at the top and bottom. Height, 9¾ in.; breadth, 1 ft. 10 in. Taken from the wall of a bath of the Byzantine period. Presented by His Grace the Duke of St. Albans. 1872. Hicks, *Greek Historical Inscriptions*, No. 174.

```
            IO ⌐ ∧
      ∧Iⲟ∧NKAIAYⲓⲟNⲟMIANΔIAΘYΛAΣΣEINΓEⲅ
    ⲓⲦΛEΘNAKIΣTΛIΔHMΛIⲦEPITOYTΛNAKOΛOYΘAⲅⲢAΣΣΛ∧
    THIΔIAⲦATEP∧NYⲅⲦAPXOYΣHIAYTΛIⲦPOΣTOYΣEΛΛHNAΣ
  5 EYEPⲄEΣIAIOTEΘEⲟΣⲟAPXHⲄETHΣTOYⲅENOYΣTΛM
    BAΣIΛE∧NΣYNEⲄMEMAPTYPHKENTΛIBAΣIΛEIⲦAPAKA
    Λ∧NMEΘOMONOIAΣⲦOΛITETEΣOΛIOΔEΔHMOΣEXΛN
    TAYTHNTHNAIPEΣINⲦOΛYTIMAΛΛONMEⲟOMONOIAΣⲦOΛI
    TEYOMENOΣTAMEⲅIΣTAAⲅAΘAⲅAⲢEIΛHΦΛΣⲦAPATOY
 10 BAΣIΛE∧ΣTAYTAΔIATHPEIINAΔEΦANEPONⲄENHTAITΛITE
    BAΣIΛEIKAITOIΣAΛΛOIΣⲦAΣINHNEXEIΔIAΛHΨINOΔHMOΣ
    ⲦPΛTOMMENYⲅEPBAΣIΛE∧ΣMEⲄAΛOYANTIOXOYKAI
    ЗAΣIΛIΣΣHΣΛAOΔIKHΣ˙KAITΛNTEKNΛΛNAYTΛNⲤⲤⲤEN
```

                    . . . . [τὴν
            δημοκρ]α[τ]ίαν καὶ αὐτονομίαν διαφυλάσσειν, γέγ[ρα-
            φε] πλεονάκις τῷ δήμῳ περὶ τούτων, ἀκόλουθα πράσσων
            τῇ διὰ πατέρων ὑπαρχούσῃ αὐτῷ πρὸς τοὺς Ἕλληνας
      5   εὐεργεσίᾳ, ὅ τε θεὸς ὁ ἀρχηγέτης τοῦ γένους τῷν
            βασιλέων συνγεμαρτύρηκεν τῷ βασιλεῖ παρακα-
            λῶν μεθ' ὁμονοίας πολιτεύεσθαι, ὁ δὲ δῆμος ἔχων
            ταύτην τὴν αἵρεσιν πολύ τι μᾶλλον μεθ' ὁμονοίας πολι-
            τευόμενος τὰ μέγιστα ἀγαθὰ παρειλημφὼς παρὰ τοῦ
     10   βασιλέως ταῦτα διατηρεῖ· ἵνα δὲ φανερὸν γίνηται τῷ τε
            βασιλεῖ καὶ τοῖς ἄλλοις πᾶσιν, ἣν ἔχει διάληψιν ὁ δῆμος
            πρῶτομ μὲν ὑπὲρ βασιλέως μεγάλου Ἀντιόχου καὶ
            βασιλίσσης Λαοδίκης καὶ τῶν τέκνων αὐτῶν ει.εν. . . .

This is part of a decree of the people of Iasos in which they avow their loyalty to Antiochos III, surnamed the Great (line 12), and the Seleukid dynasty. Antiochos the Great married Laodikè (line 13), daughter of Mithradates IV, King of Pontus, by whom he had several children (line 13). It is to be regretted that the document is not complete: happily the portion before us reveals some interesting facts concerning the relations of Antiochos with the Greek cities of Asia.

The preceding inscription (No. CCCCXLI) has already led us to observe the position of Iasos in the war between Rome and Philip V of Macedon. During that war Iasos was among the cities held by the garrisons of Philip: and it was one of the stipulations of the treaty of B.C. 196 that Philip's garrison should be withdrawn (Polyb. xvii, 27). It does not appear however that the Roman Senate made any effort to secure the freedom of the Greek cities thus liberated from Philip; and we read that these cities for the most part fell at once into the hands of Antiochos: διελθούσης δὲ τῆς πανηγύρεως (at the Isthmus of Corinth B.C. 194) πρῶτοι μὲν ἐχρημάτισαν (Flamininus and the Romans) τοῖς παρ᾽ Ἀντιόχου πρεσβευταῖς, διακελευόμενοι τῶν ἐπὶ τῆς Ἀσίας πόλεων τῶν μὲν αὐτονόμων ἀπέχεσθαι καὶ μηδένα πολεμεῖν, ὅσας δὲ νῦν παρείληφε τῶν ὑπὸ Πτολεμαίον καὶ Φίλιππον ταττομένων, ἐκχωρεῖν (Polyb. xviii, 50). Compare ib. 33: γελοῖον γὰρ εἶναι τὰ Ῥωμαϊκὰ ἆθλα τοῦ γεγονότος αὐτοῖς πολέμου πρὸς Φίλιππον Ἀντίοχον ἐπελθόντα παρα-

λαμβάνειν. In the year B.C. 190 we are expressly told by Livy that Iasos was held by a garrison of Antiochos. It was at the moment when both the Romans and the Syrian King were preparing for the decisive conflict which ended in the downfall of the Syrian empire at Magnesia B.C. 190. Æmilius with his whole fleet, assisted by the Rhodians, proceeded southwards along the coast from Samos towards Lykia (Livy xxxvii, 17); many of the Greek cities had by this time taken sides with Rome, but when the fleet reached the bay of Bargylia, the Roman commander stopped at Iasos, which was in the king's hands, and decided to reduce it. He landed and ravaged its territory; but there were with him a number of Iasian exiles, who had been expelled for taking the Roman side: erant Iasensium exsules cum Romanis: ii frequentes Rhodios orare instituerunt, 'ne urbem et vicinam sibi et cognatam innoxiam perire sinerent. Sibi exsilii nullam aliam causam esse, quam fidem erga Romanos. Eadem vi regiorum, qua ipsi pulsi sint, teneri eos qui in urbe maneant. Omnium Iasensium unam mentem esse, ut servitutem regiam effugerent.' Rhodii moti precibus, Eumene etiam rege adsumpto, simul suas necessitudines commemorando, simul obsessae regio praesidio urbis casum miserando, pervicerunt ut oppugnatione absisteretur. This passage, which I have quoted at length from Livy, shows to us, better than our inscription, the true state of parties in Iasos during the war with

K

Antiochos. It appears evident that the inscription is earlier than the circumstances here referred to by Livy, for it speaks of Iasos as αὐτονόμος (line 2): a phrase hardly consistent with the presence of a royal garrison. In short, I place the decree before us a little earlier than B.C. 190, possibly only a few months earlier, at the moment when after considerable struggle the democratic party who sided with the king (line 1), had expelled the opposite faction which advocated alliance with Rome. These are the ' exsules' of Livy, and after their opposition had been thus forcibly silenced, the people of Iasos enjoyed ὁμόνοια (lines 6, 7), or unanimity in favour of Antiochos. Repeated letters had been sent them by the king (lines 2, 3), perhaps during the winter of B.C. 192-1, while he was at Chalkis. At that time he was in correspondence with his partizans all over Greece: in an Ephesian fragment, later in this volume, we shall recognize another letter of his, addressed to the Ephesians concerning Kymè. His letters to Iasos had been accompanied with gifts and promises (line 9), of which we are enabled to conjecture something from the next inscription (No. ccccxliii). The Syrian party at Iasos had further been assisted by an oracular response from Apollo, who had recommended the Iasians to side with the king (lines 5, 6). The oracle of Branchidae is no doubt the one referred to. Apollo was regarded as the divine

progenitor of the Seleukid family (line 4; Justin, xv, 4): it was his oracle at Branchidae which first foretold the greatness of Seleukos I (Appian, Syr. 56; Diod. xix, 90). Seleukos I had been a benefactor of this temple (Pausan. i, 16; viii, 46), and Seleukos II also (C. I. 2852). On the coins of Antiochos the Great, as of others of the Seleukidæ, Apollo appears, seated on the omphalos (compare C. I. 3595, line 26).

With the phrase ὑπαρχούσῃ κ.τ.λ. in line 4, compare Æschin. in Ctes. p. 559, ed. Reiske: δεύτερον δ' ἀπὸ τῶν προγόνων εὐεργεσίαν τιν' αὐτῷ πρὸς τὸν δῆμον ὑπάρχειν. It had been the policy of the Seleukid kings to endeavour to secure the allegiance of the Greek cities of the coast, by allowing them to remain free and independent; see Droysen, Hellenismus, iii. 1, pp. 254, 330, concerning the policy of Antiochos Soter and Antiochos Theos; and compare the language of the Smyrna inscription respecting Seleukos II and Antiochos Theos (C. I. 3137, line 10): καὶ ἐβεβαίωσεν τῷ δήμῳ τὴν αὐτονομίαν καὶ δημοκρατίαν. When Antiochos the Great placed his garrison at Iasos (Livy xxxvii, 17), he would of course say it was to defend the democracy against the enmity of the banished oligarchs and their friends the Romans. And it was historically true that wherever Roman influence was felt, the government was in the hands of the men of wealth and rank,—in other words, the oligarchy.

CCCCXLIII.

A slab of blue marble. Height. 4½ in.; length, 4 ft. 2 in. Presented by His Grace the Duke of St. Albans, 1872. The letters are beautifully inscribed, and the stone is perfectly preserved.

ΟΙΑΙΡΕΘΕΝΤΕΣΤΟΥΤΕΒΟΥΛΕΥΤΗΡΙΟΥΚΑΙΤΟΤΑΡΧΕΙΟΤΕΠΙΜΕΛΗΤΑΙ
ΛΥΣΑΝΔΡΟΣΑΡΙΣΤΟΚΡΙΤΟΥ ΜΕΝΟΙΤΙΟΣΕΥΚΡΑΤΟΥ ΙΕΡΟΚΛΗΣΙΑΣΟΝΟΣ
ΙΕΡΟΚΛΗΣΛΕΟΝΤΟΣ ΑΡΚΤΙΝΟΣΠΟΣΕΙΔΙΠΠΟΤ ΚΑΙΟΑΡΧΙΤΕΚΤΩΝ
ΑΝΑΞΑΓΟΡΑΣΑΠΕΛΛΙΚΩΝΤΟΣΟΜΟΝΟΙΑΙΚΑΙΤΩΙΔΗΜΩΙ

Οἱ αἱρεθέντες τοῦ τε βουλευτηρίου καὶ τοῦ ἀρχείου ἐπιμεληταὶ
Λύσανδρος Ἀριστοκρίτου Μενοίτιος Εὐκράτου Ἱεροκλῆς Ἰάσονος
Ἱεροκλῆς Λέοντος Ἀρκτῖνος Ποσειδίππου, καὶ ὁ ἀρχιτέκτων
Ἀναξαγόρας Ἀπελλικῶντος, Ὁμονοίᾳ καὶ τῷ δήμῳ.

Five commissioners had been appointed by the people of Iasos to repair or restore certain municipal buildings, viz. the council-chamber (bouleuterion) and the official residence of the chief magistrates (ἀρχεῖον); the ἀρχεῖον was also the place where the public records were kept (see Dareste, Bulletin de Corr. Hell. vi, p. 241 foll.). Having fulfilled their task they join with the architect Anaxagoras in making a dedication ' to Homonoia and the People.' If we are right in connecting this phrase with the mention of Homonoia in the preceding decree (No. ccccxlii), then we may interpret the one inscription by the other. Antiochos the Great, whose benefits to the city the Iasians acknowledge in

line 9 of No. ccccxlii, had apparently sent money for the adornment of the town; his gift was laid out upon the βουλευτήριον and ἀρχεῖον, which probably adjoined each other, as did the βουλευτήριον and Μητρῷον (used as the Record-office) at Athens. Ὁμόνοια has been explained on No. ccccxlii: the democratic party which favoured Antiochos had expelled the aristocratic party which favoured Rome; so that the city was now unanimous for the democratic policy. There was a statue to Ὁμόνοια at Thebes (C. I. 1624), an altar at Olympia (Pausan. v, 14, 9), and temples at Miletos and elsewhere. The temple of Concord at Rome is well known. Perhaps our inscription was from the base of a statue, or some other dedication.   Apellikon is an uncommon name, and there is no reason why the Anaxagoras son of Apellikon who designed and executed these works at Iasos may not have been an ancestor of Apellikon the well-known philosopher of Teos.   There was a close connexion between Teos and Iasos (see on No. ccccxliv). An Apellikon of Erythræ is named in a decree of the third century B.C. (Dittenberger, Syll. No. 159).   For the Iasian ἀρχεῖον see C. I. 2672 foll.

Most of the names here given, viz. Aristokritos, Menoitios, Hierokles, Iason, Leon, Poseidippos, were in very common use at Iasos; but I have not been able to identify any of the ἐπιμεληταί with any Iasian mentioned in other inscriptions.   It is a curious fact that most of the Iasian inscriptions hitherto discovered exhibit long lists of names, so that our acquaintance with the nomenclature of Iasos is considerable : see Note on p. 66.

CCCCXLIV.

A stele of blue marble, broken at the top, but with the inscription nearly perfect   Height, 2 ft. 8 in. ; width, 1 ft. 11 in.
Presented by His Grace the Duke of St. Albans, 1872.   Unpublished.

```
ΞΕΝΤΗΙΒΟΥΛΗΙΒΑΧΙΛΕΥΧΧΩΧΙΦΑΝΗΧΣΩΦΑΝΟΥΧΕΙΠΕ
_ΙΔΗΔΥΜΑΧΠΟΗΤΗΧΤΡΑΓΩΙΔΙΩΝΑΕΙΤΙΛΕΓΩΝΚΛΙΓΡΑΦΩΝ
ΛΙΠΡΑΤΤΩΝΑΓΑΘΟΝΔΙΑΤΕΛΕΙΥΠΕΡΤΟΥΙΕΡΟΥΚΑΙΤΗΧΠΟΛΕ
ΛΙΤΩΝΠΟΛΙΤΩΝΗΔΕΒΟΥΛΗΠΡΟΒΕΒΟΥΛΕΥΚΕΝΑΥΤΩΙΠΕΡΙΕ
5   ΧΑΙΧΤΕΦΑΝΟΥΚΑΙΠΟΛΙΤΕΙΑΧ  ΑΓΑΘΗΙΤΥΧΗΙΔΕΔΟΧΘΑ
ΔΗΜΩΙΕΠΑΙΝΕΧΑΙΔΥΜΑΝΤΑΕΠΙΤΗΙΠΡΟΧΤΗΝΠΟΛΙΝΕΥΝΟΙΑΙΚΑΙΧΤΕΦΑ
ΧΑΙΧΡΥΧΩΙΧΤΕΦ  ΝΩΙΔΙΟΝΥΧΙΩΝΤΩΙΑΓΩΝΙΤΗΝΑΝΑΡΡΗΧΙΝΠΟΙΟΥΜΕΝΟΥ
ΟΔΗΜΟΧΧΤΕΦΑΝΟΙΔΥΜΑΝΤΑΑΝΤΙΠΑΤΡΟΥΙΑΧΕΑΧΡΥΧΩΙΧΤΕΦΑΝΟΙΕΥΧ
ΒΕΙΑΧΕΝΕΚΕΝΤΗΧΕΙΧΤΟΥΧΘΕΟΥΧΚΑΙΕΥΝΟΙΑΧΤΗΧΕΙΧΤΟΝΔΗ
10  ΤΗΧΔΕΑΝΑΡΡΗΧΕΩΧΕΠΙΜΕΛΗΘΗΝΑΙΤΟΥΧΠΡΟΕΔΡΟΥΧΚΑΙΤΟΝΑΓΩ
ΟΕΤΗΝΕΙΝΑΙΔΕΑΥΤΟΝΚΑΙΠΟΛΙΤΗΝΜΕΤΕΧΟΝΤΑΠΑΝΤΩΝΩΝΚΑΙ
ΛΛΟΙΠΟΛΙΤΑΙΜΕΤΕΧΟΥΧΙΝΑΝΑΓΡΑΨΑΥΑΙΔΕΤΟΨΗΦΙΧΜΑΕΙΧΤΟΙΕΡΩ
⌐ΗΧΑΘΗΝΑΧ

ΔΟΞΕΝΤΗΙΒΟΥΛΗΙΒΑΧΙΛΕΥΧΘΕΟΤΕΛΗΧΑΡΙΦΑΝΤΟΥΕΙΠΕΝΕΠΕ
15  ΔΥΜΑΧΠΟΗΤΗΧΤΡΑΓΩΙΔΙΩΝΤΑΤΕΠΡΟΧΤΟΥΧΘΕΟΥΧΕΥΧΕΒΩΧΔΙΑ
ΛΕΝΟΧΚΑΙΤΑΠΡΟΧ  ΗΜΠΟΛΙΝΟΙΚΕΙΩΧΚΑΙΦΙΛΑΝΘΡΩΠΩΧΛΕΙΤΙΑ
ΚΑΙΓΡΑΦΩΝΚΑΙΠΡΑΤΤΩΝΑΓΑΘΟΝΔΙΑΤΕΛΕΙΠΕΡΙΤΗΧΗΝΗΧΟΥΚΑΓΑΤΑ
ΧΟΧΤΕΑΠΟΔΕΙΞΙΝΕΠΟΙΗΧΑΤΟΤΗΧΑΥΤΟΥΦΥΧΕΩΧΚΑΙΠΡΑΓΜΑΤΕΙΑΝ▼
ΤΑΧΕΝΕΝΔΡΑΜΑΤΙΤΩΝΔΑΡΔΑΝΟΥΓΡΑΞΕΩΝΤΑΧΜΕΓΙΧΤΑΧΜΝΗΜΧ Χ
20  ΗΔΕΒΟΥΛΗΠΡΟΒΕΒ  ΥΛΕΥΚΕΝΑΥΤΩΙΠΕΡΙΕΠΑΙΝΟΥΚΑΙΧΤΕΦΑΝΟΥ
ΟΥΓΚΑΙΟΔΗΜΟΧΦΑΙΝΗΤΑΙΤΟΥΧΕΥΕΡΓΕΤΟΥΝΤΑΧΑΥΤΟΝΤΙΜΩΝΑΞΙΩ
ΔΙΑΠΑΝΤΟΧ  ΑΓΑΘΗΙΤΥΧΗΙΕΨΗΦΙΧΘΑΙΤΩΙΔΗΜΩΙΕΠΑΙΝΕΧΑΙΔΥΜΑ
ΕΠΙΤΗΙΠΡΟΧΤΗΜΠΟΛΙΝΕΥΝΟΙΑΙΚΑΙΧΤΕΦΑΝΩΧΑΙΑΥΤΟΝΧΡΥΧΩΙΧΤΕ
ΔΙΟΝΥΧΙΩΝΤΩΙΑΓΩΝΙΤΗΝΑΝΑΡΡΗΧΙΝΠΟΙΟΥΜΕΝΟΥΧΟΔΗΜΟΧΧΤΕΦΑΝ
25  ΔΥΜΑΝΤΑΑΝΤΙΠΑΤ  ΟΥΧΡΥΧΩΙΧΤΕΦΑΝΩΙΔΙΑΡΕΤΗΧΕΝΕΚΕΓΛΑΙΕΥΧ
ΙΗΧΕΙΧΑΥΤΟΝΤΗ  ΔΕΑΝΑΡΡΗΧΕΩΧΕΠΙΜΕΛΗΘΗΝΑΙΤΟΥΧΠΡΟΕΔ
ΑΙΤΟΝΑΓΩΝΟΘΕΤΗΝΕΙΝΑΙΔΕΑΥΤΩΙΚΑΙΑΛΛΟΑΓΑΘΟΝΕΥΡΕΧΘΑΙΟΧ
ΟΥΛΗΤΑΙΠΑΡΑΤΟΥΔΗΜΟΥΑΝΑΓΡΑΨΑΥΑΙΔΕΤΟΨΗΦΙΧΜΑΤΟΜΒΑΧΙΛΕΑΙ
ΡΟΝΤΗΧΑΘΗΝΑΧΙΑ, ΕΦΑΝΕΡΟΝΗΙΚΑΙΙΑΧΕΥΧΙΝΟΤΙΟΔΗΜΟΧΤΙΜΑ
30  ΛΟΥΧΚΑΙΑΓΑΘΟΥΧΑΝΔΡΑΧΑΞΙΩΧΤΗΧΑΥΤΩΝΑΡΕΤΗΧΔΟΥΝ
ΨΗΦΙΧΜΑΤΟΜΒΑΧΙΛΕΑΤΟΙΧΠΡΩΤΟΙΧΠΑΡΑΓΕΝΟΜΕΝΟΙΧΘΕΩΡΟΙΧΕ
ΤΟΓΡΑΦΕΝΕΠΙΧΩΧΙΦΑΝΟΥΧΑΝΕΝΕ⌐ΚΕΙΝΤΗΙΒΟΥΛΗΙΚΑΙΤΩΙΔΗΜ
ΧΕΩΝΚΑΙΠΑΡΑΚΕ ΛΗΧΘΑΙΛΑΧ⌐ ΧΕΠΠΜΕΛΗΘΗΝΑΙΩΙΛΟΤΙΜΩΧΙΝΙ
ΗΦΙΧΜΑΤΑΕΝΤΙΝΙΓΩΝΙΕΡΩΝΑΝΑΓ  ΑΦΗΙΚΑΙΟΙΧΤΕΦΑΝΟΙΑΛ
35  ΘΩΧΙΝΕΝΔΙΟ  ΧΙΟΙΧΕΙΔΟΤΑΧΔΙ ΤΙΠΟΙΗΧΑΝΤΕΧΤΑΗΞΙ
ΡΙΟΥΝΤΑΙΤΩΙΧ  ΙΩΙ
```

Ἔδο]ξεν τῇ βουλῇ· βασιλεὺς Σωσιφάνης Σωσιφάνους εἶπε[ν·
ἐπ]ειδὴ Δύμας ποιητὴς τραγῳδιῶν ἀεί τι λέγων καὶ γράφων
κ]αὶ πράττων ἀγαθὸν διατελεῖ ὑπὲρ τοῦ ἱεροῦ καὶ τῆς πόλε[ως
κ]αὶ τῶν πολιτῶν, ἡ δὲ βουλὴ προβεβούλευκεν αὐτῷ περὶ ἐ[παίνου
καὶ στεφάνου καὶ πολιτείας· Ἀγαθῇ Τύχῃ δεδόχθα[ι τῷ
δήμῳ ἐπαινέσαι Δύμαντα ἐπὶ τῇ πρὸς τὴν πόλιν εὐνοίᾳ καὶ στεφα[νῶ-

σαι χρυσῷ στεφ[ά]νῳ Διονυσίων τῷ ἀγῶνι, τὴν ἀνάρρησιν ποιουμένου[ς,
Ὁ δῆμος στεφανοῖ Δύμαντα Ἀντιπάτρου Ἰασέα χρυσῷ στεφάνῳ εὐσ[ε-
βείας ἕνεκεν τῆς εἰς τοὺς θεοὺς καὶ εὐνοίας τῆς εἰς τὸν δῆ[μον,
10   τῆς δὲ ἀναρρήσεως ἐπιμεληθῆναι τοὺς προέδρους καὶ τὸν ἀγω[νο-
θέτην, εἶναι δὲ αὐτὸν καὶ πολίτην μετέχοντα πάντων ὧν καὶ [οἱ
ἄ]λλοι πολῖται μετέχουσιν, ἀναγράψαι δὲ τὸ ψήφισμα εἰς τὸ ἱερὸ[ν
τ]ῆς Ἀθηνᾶς.

Ἔ]δοξεν τῇ βουλῇ· βασιλεὺς Θεοτέλης Ἀριφάντου εἶπεν· ἐπε[ιδὴ
15   Δύμας ποιητὴς τραγῳδιῶν τά τε πρὸς τοὺς θεοὺς εὐσεβῶς δια[γό-
μενος καὶ τὰ πρὸς [τ]ὴμ πόλιν οἰκείως καὶ φιλανθρώπως ἀεί τι λ[έγων
καὶ γράφων καὶ πράττων ἀγαθὸν διατελεῖ περὶ τῆς νήσου, κατὰ τά-
χ]ος τε ἀπόδειξιν ἐποιήσατο τῆς αὑτοῦ φύσεως καὶ πραγματείαν σ[υνέ-
ταξεν ἐν δρήματι τῶν Δαρδάνου πράξεων τὰς μεγίστας μνημοσ[ύνας,
20   ἡ δὲ βουλὴ προβεβ[ο]ύλευκεν αὐτῷ περὶ ἐπαίνου καὶ στεφάνου, [ὅπως
οὖν καὶ ὁ δῆμος φαίνηται τοὺς εὐεργετοῦντας αὐτὸν τιμῶν ἀξίω[ς
διὰ παντός·—Ἀγαθῇ Τύχῃ ἐψηφίσθαι τῷ δήμῳ ἐπαινέσαι Δύμα[ντα
ἐπὶ τῇ πρὸς τὴμ πόλιν εὐνοίᾳ καὶ στεφανῶσαι αὐτὸν χρυσῷ στε[φάνῳ
Διονυσίων τῷ ἀγῶνι, τὴν ἀνάρρησιν ποιουμένους Ὁ δῆμος στεφα[νοῖ
25   Δύμαντα Ἀντιπάτ[ρ]ου χρυσῷ στεφάνῳ ἀρετῆς ἕνεκεν καὶ εὐν[οίας
τῆς εἰς αὑτόν· τῇ[ς] δὲ ἀναβρήσεως ἐπιμεληθῆναι τοὺς προέδ[ρους
κ]αὶ τὸν ἀγωνοθέτην, εἶναι δὲ αὐτῷ καὶ ἄλλο ἀγαθὸν εὑρέσθαι ὅτ[ι ἂν
β]ούληται παρὰ τοῦ δήμου, ἀναγράψαι δὲ τὸ ψήφισμα τὸμ βασιλέα [εἰς τὸ
ἱε]ρὸν τῆς Ἀθηνᾶς· ἵν[α δ]ὲ φανερὸν ᾖ καὶ Ἰασεῦσιν ὅτι ὁ δῆμος τιμᾷ [τοὺς
30   κα]λοὺς καὶ ἀγαθοὺς ἄνδρας ἀξίως τῆς αὑτῶν ἀρετῆς δοῦν[αι τόδε
τὸ] ψήφισμα τὸμ βασιλέα τοῖς πρώτοις παραγινομένοις θεωροῖς, ὅ[τι δὲ
καὶ] τὸ γραφὲν ἐπὶ Σωσιφάνους ἀνενεγκεῖν τῇ βουλῇ καὶ τῷ δήμ[ῳ τῷ
Ἰα]σέων, καὶ παρακε[κ]λῆσθαι Ἰασε[ῖ]ς ἐπιμεληθῆναι φιλοτίμως ἵνα [τὰ
ψ]ηφίσματα ἔν τινι τῶν ἱερῶν ἀναγ[ρ]αφῇ καὶ οἱ στέφανοι ἀν[ακη-
35   ρυχ]θῶσιν ἐν Διο[νυ]σίοις εἰδότας δι[ό]τι ποιήσαντες τὰ ἠξι[ωμένα
χα]ριοῦνται τῷ δ[ήμ]ῳ.

This document is a copy (see lines 29 foll.) of two decrees in honour of a tragic poet named Dymas, a native of Iasos. Readers of the Persæ of Æschylos, or of the Œdipus at Kolonos of Sophokles can well understand how a tragedy might work upon the patriotic feelings of an audience, and will remember how Phrynichos was fined at Athens for his play Μιλήτου Ἅλωσις (Herod. vi, 21). The name of the city which decreed these honours to the poet Dymas is not upon the stone as now extant: but there can be little doubt that it was Samothrace. There are several reasons for this :—(1) Βασιλεύς was the title of the chief magistrate at Samothrace, by whom the year was dated (C. I. No. 2157 foll., and Livy xlv, 5): this accords with lines 1, 14, 28, 31, 32. (2) The state in question was an island (line 17). (3) The argument of Dymas' tragedy (lines 18 foll.) was taken from the adventures of Dardanos, who was said to have come from Samothrace, that island having formerly been called Dardania according to Pausanias (vii, 4, 3). (4) The Iasian θεωροί mentioned in line 31 might very naturally attend at the Samothrakian Mystery-festival.

These are among the very few extant decrees from Samothrace. Apparently the government was of the usual Greek type. The πρόεδροι of lines 10, 26 are the executive committee of the βουλή, analogous to the πρυτάνεις at Athens, and the πρόεδροι of Ephesos (Waddington-Le Bas, Part v, No. 136 a, line 20). Among the inscriptions discovered in Samothrace in 1854 by Messrs. Blau and Schlottmann (Monats-

berichte d. Berl. Akad. 1855, p. 601 foll.) and again copied by Conze (Reise auf den Inseln d. Thrakischen Meeres, p. 60 foll.), are several decrees which illustrate the heading of our inscription : e. g. (Conze, p. 56) Ἔδοξεν τῇ βουλῇ. Βασιλεὺς | Λεωδάρσης Πυθοκλείδου | εἶπεν. Ἐπειδὴ κ.τ.λ. Many of these inscriptions are lists of μυσταί and θεωροί and the states that sent them ; but the name of Iasos does not happen to occur. See also the decrees in Conze, Untersuchungen auf Samothrake, I. p. 40, Nos. 6-7.

In the Bulletin de Corr. Hellén. iv, pp. 345 and 357 are two decrees found in Delos. One is a Delian decree of the 4th century B.C. in honour of an Andrian poet Demoteles son of Æschylos, because ποιητὴς ὢν πεπραγ[μά]τευται περί τε τὸ ἱερὸν καὶ τ[ὴν π]όλιν τὴν Δηλίων, καὶ τοὺς μύθου[ς] τοὺς ἐπιχωρίους γέγραφεν. The other is a later decree (2nd century B.C.) of the Knossians in Krete, in honour of Dioskourides of Tarsos : he had composed 'in Homer's manner' (κατὰ τὸν ποιητήν) a panegyric upon the town of Knossos, and had sent his pupil Myrinos of Amisos to recite his composition. The Knossians reward Dioskourides with citizenship and προξενία, and set up a copy of the decree at Delos ' by permission of the Athenian occupants.' Similar honours are awarded by a vote of the Ætolian League to Irene, a poetess of Smyrna, in a decree published by Rangabè, Antiq. Hell. No. 741. Some account of the dramatic performances at Iasos, the birthplace of Dymas, will be found in Lüders, Die

Dionysischen Künstler, p. 87 foll. There is evidence that the Iasians bestowed especial care upon the celebration of their annual Dionysia. Upon the wall of the ruined theatre at Iasos were found a series of curious inscriptions which are partly lists of subscribers for the repair of the theatre and other expenses of the festival (Waddington-Le Bas, Part v, Nos. 275-299), or else give the names of actors and musicians engaged at the Dionysia together with the names of wealthy citizens who had paid their salaries (*ibid.* 252-274). Some of these Iasian names have reference to the worship of Dionysos, e. g. Νύσιος (No. 283), Νεβρίδης (No. 286). Moreover in No. 252 the second name in the list is the Dymas of our decree : 'Επὶ στεφανηφόρου 'Απόλλωνος τοῦ μετὰ Νημερτέα | οἵδε ἐπέδωκαν ἀγωνοθέτηι 'Απολλόδωρος | Χάρμου Σάσυλον τὸν κωμῳδὸν ἡμέρας δύο, καὶ ἡ [πάρ]οδος εὗρεν δραχμὴν ἡ δὲ θέα ἐγένετο | δωρε[άν]· Δύμας¹ 'Αντιπάτρου, τῆς ἐπιδόσε'ως ἧ[ς ἐπ]ένευσεν χορηγὼν ἐν τῷ ἐπάνω (sic) ἐνιαυτῷ, | Σώ-

συλον τὸν κωμῳδὸν, καὶ ἡ πάροδος εὗρεν | δραχμὴν ἡ δὲ θέα ἐγένετο δωρεάν⁴ κ.τ.λ. This mention of Dymas fixes his date : for amongst the artists mentioned in this series is Kraton the flute-player of Chalkedon (No. 255), who afterwards resided at the court of Eumenes II (C. I. 3067 foll.). In other words Dymas belonged to the early part of the second century B. C., and was a well-known friend of the dramatic artists whose guild lived at Teos under the shadow of the Teian temple of Dionysos, and who not only are known to have furnished performers at the Dionysia at Iasos, the birthplace of Dymas, but also sent θεωροί to the Mystery-festival of the Kabeiroi at Samothrace (Conze, Untersuchungen auf Samothrake, ii, pp. 97-99). It was however not at the Mystery-festival, but at the Dionysia (lines 7, 24) that Dymas was crowned. Whether his tragedy was performed at this festival does not appear ; if so, I am not aware of any other mention of dramatic performances at Samothrace.

CCCCXLV.

A sepulchral monument of blue marble, in the form of a small temple, naiskos, with a pediment at each end, presented by J. Scott Tucker, Esq., 1851. Height, 2 ft.; length, 2 ft. 7 in. On the front there is represented in relief within a sunk panel a male figure draped in a chiton over which is wound a mantle, reclining on a couch and resting on his left elbow : in his left hand is a drinking cup; his right hand is extended, and clasps the hand of a female figure, draped and veiled, who sits at the foot of the couch, and represents his wife. Behind her stands a diminutive male figure, draped to the knees. In front of the reclining figure is a table with cakes ; and immediately below this, on the flat border of the panel, is the inscription. On the right-hand border of the panel is sculptured a laurel wreath. The reliefs are rudely executed, and the heads of the figures are much injured. The upper surface of the marble above the panel is cut away so as to form an oblong sinking, in which are reserved two circular spaces ; on these may have rested some object which fitted into the sinking.

ΕΛΛΑΝΙΩΝΤΑΡΣΕΥΣ

'Ελλανίων Ταρσεύς.

The tomb probably of some merchant from Tarsos : apparently of the third or fourth century | B. C. The name Hellanion is unknown to Pape-Benseler.

Those who may desire to study further the inscribed monuments of Iasos should be reminded that No. cccxx *ante* is an important decree of Iasos, belonging to the second century B.C., which survives only in the copy set up at Prienè. Other Iasian inscriptions will be found in Böckh, C. I. 2671-2690, one of which (2677) gives a list of five | πρυτάνεις. The Iasos inscriptions published by Waddington-Le Bas, Part v, are numerous, but are almost entirely lists of contributors to the Dionysia which were found in the ruins of the theatre (see note on No. ccccxLIV, *ante*). Another Iasian decree, very brief but very important, was discovered in 1880, and was published in the Bulletin de

---

¹ Waddington-Le Bas wrongly read [ι]δύμος in their cursive text.
² The meaning of this formula, which occurs again and again in these lists from the Iasian theatre, has been much disputed ; see Waddington-Le Bas, *ad locum*, and Lüders, Die Dionysischen Künstler, pp. 124, 200. Neither writer, however, appears satisfied with the explanations he suggests. In the absence of any better solution I would translate, 'Dymas, son of Antipater, as part of the subscription which he promised when choragus last year, [engaged at his own expense to perform at the Dionysia] Sosylos the comedian ; now his appearance charged an entrance payment of a drachma [from each spectator], while the performance cost the authorities nothing.' At Athens the charge for admission to the ordinary seats was two obols, one-third of a drachma, payable to the lessee (see on No. xii, Part i, *ante*). At Iasos probably the regular charge was much the same, while the comparative poverty of the state did not allow of a 'theoric fund' to make the entrance free for the poorer citizen. Indeed the celebration of the Dionysia was a burthen which the finances of the state were not always able to bear (see Lüders, *ibid.* p. 87). Accordingly the wealthier citizens and the magistrates connected with the Dionysia (whose office was a λειτουργία) engaged at their own expense certain popular actors or musicians from time to time to add lustre to the festival. Readers of Aristophanes will remember that even in the Birds (203, 665) the poet relied upon the skill of a popular αὐλητρίς to win the favour of his audience. In later days, what we call the 'star-system' was in full vogue, and the presence of a favourite performer at Iasos secured a full house and a high admission-fee ; so that the performance (θέα) was self-supporting. This explanation has the advantage of simplicity, and it gives a proper sense to κώμῳδος and θέα. Much curious information about the history of the Greek stage after the times of the four great dramatists will be found in the Essay of Lüders, already quoted, and in Schäfer, Demosthenes und seine Zeit. i. pp. 214 foll.

Correspondance Hellénique, v, p. 491. It declares the banishment of certain persons who had conspired against Mausolos, and orders the confiscation of their property. The date of it therefore lies between B.C. 367 and 354. Subjoined to the decree is a long list of the various officers of state who sanctioned the confiscation, together with full particulars of the sales. The catalogue enumerates—

(1) Four ἄρχοντες, apparently analogous to the Athenian archons; although at Iasos the eponymous officer was not an archon but was styled stephanephoros (see *ante*, pp. 52, 53).

(2) Four ταμίαι, or treasurers of the civic exchequer.

(3) Two ἀστυνόμοι, whose functions would comprise those of commissioners of police and of a board of works, according to the definition given of ἀστυνομία by Aristotle, Politics vii, 8, 5, = p. 1321 B.

(4) Four συνήγοροι, or public accountants-general, analogous to the Athenian εὔθυνοι and the ἐξετασταί of many Greek towns (see No. ccccxviii *ante*), according to Aristotle, Politics vii, 8, 16, = p. 1322 B: ἐπεὶ δὲ ἔνιαι τῶν ἀρχῶν, εἰ καὶ μὴ πᾶσαι, διαχειρίζουσι πολλὰ τῶν κοινῶν, ἀναγκαῖον ἑτέραν εἶναι τὴν ληψομένην λογισμὸν καὶ προσευθυνοῦσαν, αὐτὴν μηδὲν διαχειρίζουσαν ἕτερον· καλοῦσι δὲ τούτους οἱ μὲν εὐθύνους, οἱ δὲ λογιστάς, οἱ δὲ ἐξεταστάς, οἱ δὲ συνηγόρους. Such synegori are found at Oropos, *ante* Part II, No. CLX, line 26.

(5) Six πρυτάνεις, in contradiction of C. I. 2677, where five prytanes are enumerated. We can only conjecture the reason of this discrepancy; the mutilated commencement of C. I. 2671 affords no sure indication of the number of the Iasian prytanes.

(6) Eleven *priests of Zeus Megistos*; see on No. cccxl.

Several other documents from Iasos have been published by M. Haussoullier, Bulletin viii (1884), pp. 218 foll., and pp. 454 foll. The first-mentioned of these fragments, which was discovered in the island of Karyanda (brought thither perhaps as ballast in a fishing boat) I hope to subject to a more careful study in the Hellenic Journal. It speaks of the νεωποῖαι and the προστάται as officers of importance (see on No. ccccxx *ante*). Another inscription published in the Bulletin, x (1886) p. 267, affords an interesting glimpse of Iasos under the Roman Empire.

Besides the historical interest of these inscriptions, and the new information they furnish concerning the civic institutions of Iasos, they also enrich still further our already large acquaintance with Iasian names. I am favoured by Mr. Percy Gardner with the following list of names which occur upon coins of Iasos of the centuries succeeding Alexander.

SILVER COINS *in the British Museum.*

ΠΑΝΑΙΝΟΣ
ΜΕΝΕΣΘΕ
ΛΑΜΠΙΤΟΣ

BRONZE COINS *in the British Museum.*

ΑΝΑΞΙΠΠΟΣ
ΣΤΗΣΙΟΧΟΣ
Κ]ΤΗΣΙΑΣ

Mionnet.

ΕΡΥΑΞΕ (read ΒΡΥΑΞΙΣ, which occurs frequently in the inscription relating to Mausolos just quoted.)
ΚΤΗΣΙΑΣ
ΜΟΛΠΟΣ
ΠΡΟΞΕΝΟΣ

Mionnet, Suppl.

ΑΡΤΕΜΙΔΩΡΟΣ
ΑΡΥΑΞΙΣ (read ΒΡΥΑΞΙΣ)
ΑΣΤΡΑΙΟΣ
ΕΥΠΟΛΕΜΟΣ (?)

Imhoof-Blumer.

ΕΡΜΙΑΣ

Coins of Iasos are by no means common. The regular types of the autonomous coins are—

Obv. Head of Apollo.

Rev. Youth swimming, holding on to a dolphin; an allusion to the story of Hermias (Pliny, N. H. ix, 8 § 8; Ælian, N. A. vi, 15).

CHAPTER III.

INSCRIPTIONS FROM EPHESOS.

PROLEGOMENA.

THE inscriptions that occupy the remainder of this volume, with only one or two exceptions *, were obtained for the British Museum through the researches carried on at Ephesos by Mr. J. T. Wood in the years 1863-1874. Most of them, together with a few inscriptions which could not be removed to England, were published by Mr. Wood in his *Discoveries at Ephesus*, 1877. The importance of the collection was at once perceived when C. Curtius in 1870 published a few of the inscriptions in the *Hermes*, iv, pp. 174 foll.† Since the appearance of Mr. Wood's book, several of these documents have engaged the attention of scholars: thus No. CCCCLXXVII (*q. v.*) has been illustrated by M. Dareste, who has devoted much attention to the study of ancient law. In particular Droysen, in the new edition of his *Hellenismus*, has made repeated reference to the more important of the Ephesian decrees. Moreover M. Waddington, who took a deep interest in Mr. Wood's researches, was furnished by him with early impressions and copies of many of the newly discovered documents; and has employed them with happy results in his *Mémoire sur la chronologie de la vie du rhéteur Aristide* (1867), and his *Fastes des Provinces Asiatiques* (1872). Other writers who have dealt with the collection will be referred to in the course of the subsequent pages. Some few of these inscriptions had been copied before Mr. Wood removed the originals, and had found their way into Böckh's *Corpus* and Le Bas; *e.g.* Nos. CCCCLXXXII and DCLXXVIII.

Mr. Wood did not attempt to do more than place his inscriptions provisionally before the reader. Not only did much remain to be done for the exact reproduction of the texts, but also a considerable number of inscriptions were left uncopied, and will first see the light in the present volume. In many cases, moreover, a prolonged and repeated handling of Mr. Wood's fragments has enabled me to join the broken pieces together, and to recombine them into a more complete form. Where the evidence of the writing and the appearance of the marble, together with the exact correspondence of the fractured edges, conspired to make the juncture absolutely certain, I have often said nothing of these particulars; being glad, as the reward of much labour, to print an inscription as from one unbroken marble.

The main object which Mr. Wood set before him in his excavations was to discover the Artemision: and this, after great difficulty, he accomplished. The chief results of his labours are familiar to those who have read his book, or have visited the galleries of the British Museum. In the course of his enterprise he of course discovered a great many inscriptions, not only on the site of the temple, but elsewhere. For when delayed in his work at the Artemision, he was commissioned by the Trustees of the British Museum to excavate at the Odeum, at the Great Theatre, and elsewhere. But it did not lie within his power to organize a systematic search for inscriptions in all parts of the ancient site of Ephesos. We are not surprised therefore to find that the Ephesian inscriptions printed in this volume, even if supplemented by the Ephesian documents given in Böckh's *Corpus*, Waddington-Le Bas and other works, fail to present a continuous series. On the contrary, only a few samples (so to speak) have survived to us here and there, to suggest what the inscribed monuments of Ephesos originally were; and whole periods of Ephesian history are unrepresented. Not one document survives from the period of the Peloponnesian War: one tiny fragment (No. CCCCXLVI), inscribed στοιχηδόν in simple characters of the best time, alone represents the momentous fifth century B.C. Of the times before that just one or two curious relics remain. One is the fragment of some augury rules (No. DCLXXVIII), long since published by Böckh, C. I. 2953. We have also some fragments apparently of the columns of the temple destroyed by Herostratos (No. DXVII). No record of Alexander's presence, like his dedication and decree at Priene (Nos. CCCXCIX, CCCC *ante*), has been found at Ephesos. Of the fourth and third centuries B.C. accident has preserved to us a considerable number of documents, the decrees of citizenship and public honours which form the bulk of Section i. Then follows another gap in the series.

---

until the war of Antiochos (No. ccccxxxv), soon after which I place the remarkable law (No. ccccxlix), which must be studied in close connexion with the well-known decree of the Ephesians concerning Mithradates, now at Oxford (Waddington-Le Bas, Part v. 136 a).

When a Greek city, after its incorporation into the Roman Empire, rose into new importance and became a busy centre of Græco-Roman civilization, it nearly always happened that its past history became forgotten. The records of its earlier and purely Hellenic existence suffered neglect or destruction; and the modern scholar in exploring its site finds hardly an inscription referring to the older time : all is Roman. or Græco-Roman*. To a large extent this observation holds good of Ephesos. The greater portion of the Ephesian records in this volume belong to the imperial period. They range from the time of Augustus (Nos. dxxii foll.) down to the fourth century (No. dclxxiii), and the most important results which this collection yields, will be the illustration it affords of the administration and inner life of the province of Asia under the Roman emperors.

As early as 1843 H. Guhl published his Ephesiaca, in which he collected and arranged everything that could be gleaned from ancient literature, and from coins and marbles so far as known, to illustrate the history of Ephesos. This remarkable monograph still retains its value, even after the recent discoveries. The following works must also be consulted by every student of Ephesian antiquities :

Falkener, Ephesus and the Temple of Diana (1862).
Waddington, Fastes des Provinces Asiatiques (1872).
Marquardt, Römische Alterthümer, vol. iv (1872).
E. Curtius, Beiträge zur Geschichte und Topographie Kleinasiens : Abh. der Akademie der Wissenschaften zu Berlin (1872).
E. Curtius, Ephesos ; ein Vortrag (1874).
Zimmermann, Ephesos im ersten Christlichen Jahrhundert (1874).
Head, Coinage of Ephesus (1880).
Menadier, Qua condicione Ephesii usi sint inde ab Asia in formam provinciae redacta (1880).

To each of these treatises we shall have occasion to refer in dealing with the inscriptions which follow. But the essay of Menadier is of peculiar value ; for he has made it his task to illustrate the institutions of Ephesos under the Empire by means of a minute comparison of inscriptions and other records from all the Greek cities of Asia Minor. And yet, after the careful researches of these and other writers, there remain not a few points in the antiquities of Ephesos which await further elucidation. The last word has not yet been said upon Ephesian topography ; for a comparison of the maps of Ephesos appended to the monographs of Curtius, Zimmermann and Wood will show how difficult it

is to assign aright the known names of Ephesian hills and streams. On this subject however I leave those to speak, who have had the advantage of a personal study of the site of Ephesos ; and will confine my attention to the political and social antiquities. In this department there are several questions upon which I shall make a few remarks, before proceeding to the inscriptions themselves.

ON THE EPHESIAN TRIBES AND THOUSANDS
(φυλαί, χιλιαστύες).

We are familiar with the subdivision of the free population of Attika, which remained in its chief features unchanged from the time of the reforms of Kleisthenes. We know the names and order of precedence of the ten tribes (φυλαί), to each of which were assigned a number of villages or districts (δῆμοι) not necessarily contiguous to each other. Each of the four ancient tribes was divided into three φρατρίαι, and each φρατρία comprised (normally) thirty γένη. Each γένος again comprised (normally) thirty families, so that the γένος itself was sometimes called also τριακάς (see Part i, No. xi, and the authorities there quoted). Such were the tribal subdivisions of Attika, about which both authors and inscriptions afford varied information. But we know that similar subdivisions, based upon distinctions of family and race, existed in every Hellenic city, and dated from the earliest times. The language of Homer about the heroic battle-field would hold literally true of historical times (Il. ii, 362-363):

κρῖν' ἄνδρας κατὰ φῦλα, κατὰ φρήτρας, Ἀγάμεμνον,
ὡς φρήτρη φρήτρηφιν ἀρήγῃ, φῦλα δὲ φύλοις.

In fact these subdivisions were the lines upon which the political life of the people, within their own community, moved ; and we gain a valuable insight into the early history and into the inner life of a Greek city, when we can enlarge our knowledge of its tribal and sub-tribal divisions. We expect to find in Attic colonies some traces of the old Ionic tribes ; in Doric colonies, the names of the old Dorian tribes. In illustration of this we may refer to No. ccccxxxix ante, and the note there concerning the tribes of Prienè ; and Part ii, No. clxxviii, on the tribes of Tomis ; compare also Nos. clvi, cccxv, cccxlv, ccclii.

At Ephesos in the time of Ephoros (fl. 340 b.c.) there were five tribes, the names and origin of which he described as follows, according to Steph. Byz. s. v. Βέννα. μία φυλὴ τῶν ἐν Ἐφίσῳ πέντε, ἧς οἱ φυλίται Βενναῖοι, ὡς Ἔφορος· ὅτι Ἄνδροκλος ὁ κτίσας Ἔφεσον, οὗτος Πριηνεῦσι βοηθήσας ἐτελεύτησε καὶ οἱ πολλοὶ Ἐφέσιοι σὺν αὐτῷ. οἱ οὖν καταλειφθέντες Ἐφέσιοι ἐστασίασαν κατὰ τῶν Ἀνδρόκλου παίδων, καὶ βουλόμενοι βοήθειαν ἔχειν πρὸς αὐτοὺς ἐκ Τέω καὶ Καρίνης ἀποίκους ἔλαβον, ἀφ᾽ ὧν ἐν Ἐφέσῳ δύο φυλαὶ τῶν πέντε τὰς ἐπωνυμίας ἔχουσιν· οἱ μὲν γὰρ ἐν Βέννη Βενναῖοι, οἱ δ᾽ ἐν Εὐωνύμῳ τῆς Ἀττικῆς Εὐώνυμοι, οὓς δ᾽ ἐξ ἀρχῆς ἐν Ἐφέσῳ κατέλαβον Ἐφεσίους φασὶ, τοὺς δ᾽ ὕστερον ἐπήλυδας Τηΐους καὶ Καριναίους ἀπο-

---

* See the note on No. ccccxxi ante, respecting Laodicea : and examine e.g. the extant inscriptions of Smyrna and Byzantium. The most promising sites for excavation, if we are in search of purely Greek documents, would be towns like Prienè, or even Lebedos, that had no history under the Roman rule.

καλοῦσι. We shall have occasion frequently to refer to this important passage. Without committing ourselves to its entire historical accuracy, we may safely with Schömann (Griech. Alt. i, 138) accept the conclusion, that the tribe named οἱ Ἐφεσεῖς comprised the original inhabitants whom the Attic colonists found in the land. Οἱ Εὐώνυμοι represented the Attic colonists themselves, Εὐώνυμον being a well-known Attic deme. Τήϊοι and Καρηναῖοι indicate settlers brought in from Teos and Karene*. I take Βέννα to be a blunder for Βέμβινα, due either to Stephanos or to his copyist, and in the gloss above quoted I would write throughout ἐν Βεμβίνῃ and Βεμβιναῖοι. The gloss itself, instead of following the gloss Βέννα· πόλις Θράκης κ.τ.λ., should be placed after the gloss on Βέμβινα· κώμη τῆς Νεμέας. Ἑλλάνικος δὲ Βέμβινον καὶ πόλιν φησίν. ὁ πολίτης Βεμβινίτης, ὡς Σταγειρίτης. παρὰ δὲ Ῥιανῷ Βεμβινάτης. ἔοικεν οὖν Αἰγινάτης καὶ Αἰγινήτης κατὰ τροπήν, ὡς Πανδαεις ἐν Ἡρακλείας πράγη· δέρμα τε θήρειον Βεμβινήταο λέοντος.

καὶ ἄλλος·

καὶ Βεμβινήταο πελώρου δέρμα λέοντος.

τὸ ἐκ τόπου ἐπίρρημα Βεμβίνηθεν, καὶ εἰς τόπον Βεμβίναδε. In the inscriptions we find invariably Βεμβίνης (Βεμβιώτης) or Βεμβειναῖοι. Bembina was a village of Argolis hardly two miles from the Nemean temple (Strabo, viii, p. 377; Theokr. xxv, 202; Pliny, N. H. iv, 6, § 10). It was here that visitors were shown the den of the famous lion (compare Pausan. ii, 15, § 2).

The statements of Ephoros, when thus corrected, concerning the Ephesian tribes, are borne out with slight exceptions by the inscriptions hitherto discovered. In the series of honorary decrees of the third and fourth centuries B.C. (Nos. CCCCXLVII foll.) five tribes only are mentioned, viz. Ἐφεσεῖς, Τήϊοι, Καρηναῖοι, Εὐώνυμοι, Βεμβιναῖοι. In the documents of the Roman period we find six tribes spoken of: see No. DXCIV, where C. Vibius Salutaris dedicates an altar to the 'sex phylais'; and compare his bequest, No. CCCCLXXXI, lines 90 foll. and notes. From No. DLXXVIII we discover that the additional tribe owed its name and perhaps its origin to Augustus: it was called Σεβαστή. This document (No. DLXXVIII) is an important one, for besides other information it supplies a complete list of the tribes. It is highly probable that at Ephesos, as at Athens (Part i, p. 65), the tribes had a recognised order of precedence. If so, their order will be indicated by this document: 1. Ἐφεσεῖς. 2. Σεβαστή. 3. Τήϊοι. 4. Καρηναῖοι. 5. Εὐώνυμοι. 6. Βεμβειναῖοι (Βεμβειναῖοι, Βεμβίνης) †.

The only subdivision of the tribe at Ephesos, so far as the inscriptions inform us, was the Thousand or χιλιαστύς, i. e. a group of a thousand households, corresponding very much to the φρατρία existing in Attica and elsewhere. Similarly at Chios we hear of ἡ χιλιαστὺς ἡ Χαλκιδέων (Rhein. Mus. xxii, p. 326): at Methymna (C. I. Add. 2168 b) ἁ χίλλιαστὺς ἁ Ἐρυθραῖ[ων]: so at Kos (Bulletin de Corr. Hellén. v, 1881, p. 211; compare Part ii, p. 64). In a Samian decree (Hicks, Manual of Greek Historical Inscriptions, No. 135) we read: καὶ ἐπικληρῶσαι αὐτοὺς ἐπὶ φυλὴν καὶ χιλιαστὺν καὶ ἑκατοστὺν καὶ γένος. At Lampsakos (C. I. Add. 3641 b), Byzantion (C. I. 2060), Herakleia (Æn. Polior. 11) we hear of the Hekatostys but not of the Chiliastys. At Kalymna (Part ii, No. CCXXXII, foll.) we read: ἐπικεκλαρῶθη ἐπὶ φυλὰν καὶ δᾶμον· ἴλαχε φυλᾶς Κυθρηλείων, δᾶμου Ἀμφιπετρᾶν etc. At Tenos (Part ii, No. CCCLXXVI): καὶ πρὸς φυλὴν καὶ φρα[τρίαν προσγραφῆναι] ὁποῖαν ἀμ βούλωνται. And these examples may be illustrated by the phrase frequently occurring in Attic honorary decrees: καὶ εἶναι αὐτῷ γράψασθαι φυλῆν καὶ δήμου καὶ φρατρίας ἧς ἂν βούληται (C. I. A. ii, No. 243 and passim; compare Part i, No. xi). The invariable phrase in the Ephesian honorary decrees is: ἐπικληρῶσαι δὲ αὐτὸν καὶ εἰς φυλὴν καὶ χιλιαστύν ‡. Accordingly we may conclude that the Chiliastys was at Ephesos the only subdivision recognised between the tribe (φυλή) and the γένος. It seems unlikely (as Menadier argues, p. 25) that if the Hekatostys existed, it should be entirely omitted from the many surviving records. Menadier has been at pains to draw up a list (p. 24) of all the known Ephesian Chiliastyes; distributing them among the six Tribes. Before his treatise came into my hands I had also done the same; and as my list is made from a fresh examination of the marbles, and is therefore more complete in several particulars, I append it here.

1. Ἐφεσεῖς: Nos. CCCCXLVII, CCCCXLIX, CCCCLII, CCCCLVIII, CCCCLX, CCCCLXI, CCCCLXXI, DLXXVIII, DLXXIX, (DXC).

  (1) Ἀργαδεύς: Nos. CCCCXLVII, CCCCXLIX, CCCCLX.

  (2) Βωρεύς: Nos. CCCCLVIII, CCCCLXXI; Βορεύς, No. DLXXVIII.

  (3) Λεβέδιος: Nos. CCCCLII, DLXXIX.

  (4) Οἰνωπ': Nos. CCCCLXI, DLXXVIII.

  Perhaps [Ἀργαδε]ύς, or [Βωρε]ύς in No. DXC.

2. Σεβαστή: Nos. DLXXVIII, (DXC).

  (1) Λαβάνδιος: Nos. DLXXVIII, DXC.

  (2) Σιεύς: No. DLXXVIII.

  (3) . . . . μηστ: No. DXC.

---

* Καρήνη was a town of Mysia, north of Atarneus, and not far from the coast: see Herod. vii, 42; Diod. Sic. xx, 111. The MSS vary between Καρήνη and Καρήνη, but Steph. Byz. writes it with ῆ s. v. Καρήνη, though with ῑ s. v. Βέννα. No coin or inscription from the place is known, nor is the site identified. The Ephesian tribe is always spelt Καρηναῖοι in the inscriptions.

† In No. DII Mr. Wood (Inscriptions from the Great Theatre, 7) reads φυλῆς Ἀδριανῆς, without any sign of the stone being fractured. At Prusa in the second century A.D. the tribes were still fully recognised, though most of them had been renamed after members of the Imperial house. They were twelve in number, and the ninth was Ἀδριανή (Waddington-Le Bas, Part v, Nos. 1176, 1177).

‡ Other references to the χιλιαστύν will be found in the Bulletin de Corr. Hellén. iv (1880), p. 437; vii (1883), pp. 39, 517 foll. Hesych. s. v. χιλιαστύες· αἱ φυλαί, and s.v. ἑκατοστύες· ὡς χιλιαστύς· συγγένεια: also among his Γλῶσσαι Ἐθνικαί, s.v. Σάμιοι· χιλια τύες (-ιc). At Smyrna, in the decree to incorporate the Magnesians (C. I. 3137, line 73) no mention is made of any subdivision of the tribe: καὶ ποιήσασθαι αὐτοῖς πολίτας πάντας καὶ τοὺς ἐκγόνους μετ᾽ ὧν (ἐφ᾽) ἴσῃ καὶ ὁμοίᾳ τοῖς ἄλλοις πολί[ταις], καὶ εἰς φυλὰς αὐτοὺς ἐπικληρῶσαι καταχωρισθῆναι εἰς ἃς ἂν ἑαυτοὺς λέγωσιν (from the oath of the Smyrnæans).

Τήϊοι: Nos. CCCCLIV, CCCCLXXIII, DXXXIII, DLXXVIII, LXXXVIII (DXC), and the fragment given below*.
(1) Εὐριπόμ[που ?]: No. DLXXVIII.
(2) Ἐχεπτολεμεύς: No. DLXXVIII.
(3) Ἡγητόρειος: Nos. CCCCLIII a, CCCCLIV.
(4) ..—.. εὔντηος, and ..... ος: No. DXC.
4. Καρηναῖοι: Nos. (CCCCLVI), CCCCLIX, CCCCLXIX, (CCCCLXXVI), (DLXXIV), DLXXVIII, DLXXIX, (DXC), DXCIV.
(1) Ἀλθαιμενεύς: Nos. CCCCLIX, DLXXIX.
(2) Ἐχύρειος: No.CCCCLXIX; [Ἐ]χύρηος: No. DXC.
(3) Πεῖος: No. DLXXVIII.
(4) Σιμώνεος: No. CCCCLVI; Σιμώνηος: Nos. DXXVIII, DLXXIV, DXC.
(5) Χηλώνεος: No. CCCCLXXVI; Χηλώνηος: No. DLXXVIII.
5. Εὐώνυμοι: Nos. CCCCLXII, CCCCLXXXI, line 104, DLXXVIII.
(1) Γλαύκηος: Nos. CCCCLXII, DLXXVIII.
(2) Πολί[ελη]ος: No. DLXXVIII.
6. Βεμβίνης: Nos. CCCCL, CCCCLV; Φυλὴ Βεμβινίων: No. CCCCLXXV; [θ]εμβήνης? No. DXXVII; Βεμβειναῖος: (DLXXIV), DLXXVIII; C. I. 2956.
(1) Αἰγώτεος: Nos. CCCCLV, DLXXVIII.
(2) Πελάσγηος: Nos. DLXXIV, C. I. 2956.

Several questions arise in respect of this catalogue. To the Karenaean tribe, and perhaps to the Ephesine and Teian also, we are able to assign as many as five Chiliastyes. Are we to conclude that the other tribes likewise comprised five Chiliastyes each, although their names are at present unknown? Or did the tribes differ in size?

Then again, it is impossible not to speculate upon the origin of the names borne by the Chiliastyes. For these names take us back, if we could but decipher them, to the very roots of the Ionic colony in Asia Minor. The etymology of names is apt to be rather fanciful, but up to a certain point we are here on safe ground.

In the First tribe, 'Εφισεῖς, which seems (see Steph. Byz. s.v. Βέννα) to have comprised the original inhabitants of the locality, the Chiliastyes have names which are intelligible enough. Ἀργαδεῖς was one of the four old Ionic tribes, Ἀργαδεῖς Αἰγικορεῖς Γελέοντες Ὅπλητες. At Miletos the Ionic colony began probably with these four tribes, to which two more were added afterwards (Böckh, on C. I. 2855). The same four tribes were probably retained at Teos (C. I. 3064). The Milesians, when they refounded Kyzikos, carried thither the same four names of tribes, to which two more were added, viz. Βωρεῖς and Οἰνῶπες, making six in all (C. I. 3663 foll.). Three of the names therefore of the Chiliastyes in the first Ephesian tribe are identical with the names of three of the tribes of Kyzikos. There was a tribe

Βωρεῖς also at Perinthos (Bechtel, Inschriften des ion. Diai. p. 135). Böckh on C. I. 3665, p. 952 tries to suggest an etymology for Οἴνωψ and Βωρεύς. Βῶρος is a Homeric name: Il. v, 44; xvi, 177. But Pausanias (ii, 18, § 7) mentions a legendary Boros of Messenia, whose grandson Melanthos being exiled from the Peloponnese, became king of Athens, having dispossessed Thymœtes, the last of the Theseid dynasty. It is clear that three Chiliastyes of the Ephesine tribe bore names which were familiar both at Ephesos and at Miletos in the early days of the Ionic colonies. The fourth, Λεβέδιος, is explained by the historical fact of Lysimachos having transferred to Ephesos the population of Lebedos and Kolophon: συνῴκισε δὲ καὶ Ἐφεσίων ἄχρι θαλάσσης τὴν νῦν πόλιν, ἐπαγαγόμενος ἐς αὐτὴν Λεβεδίους τε οἰκήτορας καὶ Κολοφωνίους, τὰς δὲ ἐκείνων ἀντλῶν πόλεις, ὡς Φοίνικα ἰάμβων ποιητὴν Κολοφωνίων θρηνῆσαι τὴν ἅλωσιν (Pausan. i, 9, § 8; compare vii, 3, § 2; and the Teian inscription in Waddington-Le Bas, No. 86).

Second tribe, Σεβαστή. Excluding the fragmentary.... μηος, we have as names of Chiliastyes Λαβάνδηος and Σιύτ. The latter may perhaps be named, like so many spots in Greece (see Tozer's Lectures on the Geography of Greece, pp. 339 foll.), from the flower which abounded in the locality: for οἶον was a marsh or meadow plant (Theokr. v, 125). Λαβάνδηος seems connected in some way with the Karian worship of Zeus Labrandeus†. Androklos, the founder of Ephesos, is said to have lost his life in 'helping the Prienians'—probably against the Karians, who desired to recover their lands (Ephoros, ap. Steph. Byz. s.v. Βέννα). Herodotos (i, 146) assures us that the most purely Attic of all the Ionic cities, Miletos, had in it a considerable infusion of Karian blood. Pherekydes (Strabo, xiv, p. 632) says the Karians formerly occupied the site of Ephesos. These statements justify the conjecture that at Ephesos also a Karian element was admitted into the body politic, and that their Chiliastys was named Λαβάνδηος to conciliate the favour of the Karian god.

The third tribe, Τήϊοι, besides the fragmentary ... εὔντηος, (which may belong to Λεόντηος, or Γελεόντηος) exhibits these Chiliastyes: Εὐριπόμ[που], Ἐχεπτολεμεύς, Ἡγητόρειος, all of which came evidently from names of men Εὐρύπομπος, Ἐχεπτόλεμος, Ἡγήτωρ, though these names are unknown to the lexicons. It is conceivable that these Chiliastyes were named after leading men among the incorporated Teians. We may believe in this early incorporation as historical, without accepting the circumstantial account of it given above from Ephoros. Nor can we fail to observe the good omen conveyed by each of the three names.

The fourth tribe, Καρηναῖοι. Here the Chiliastys

---

* Apparently part of a base of grey marble, entire at top, right, and probably the bottom, measuring on the inscribed face 9 in. high, 21 in. broad: presented by Mr. Hyde Clark to the University of Oxford, and now in the Ashmolean Museum. The unpublished inscription reads as follows, and may be of the Antonine era: [Τῆς Τ]ηΐων φυλῆς· [μ]ετέθη εἰς ταύτην ['Αν]θρωπος Που ..... The letters are large and clear, but inscribed with ligatures.

† The omitted ρ in Λαβάνδηος occasions no difficulty. The documents in which the word occurs are late, and the spelling may therefore be debased. On the other hand we may compare the forms φαιδντης (C. I. A. iii, 283, 291; C. I. 446), φαιτρια (C. I. A. ii, 599). Λαβρανδεύς was the name of a tribe at Mylasa, C. I. 2731 b.

'Αλθαιμενεύς is manifestly named from 'Αλθαιμένης, a legendary hero of Krete, who fled to Kamiros in Rhodes, and was afterwards worshipped as a hero by the Rhodians (Diod. Sic. v, 59). Another account brought him originally from Argos to Krete, and then to Rhodes (Strabo, x, 479, 481 ; xiv, 653). 'Αλθαιμενίς occurs as the name of a tribe at Kamiros, Part ii, No. cccliii*, where Sir C. Newton considers it to indicate an immigration from Krete to Kamiros. In the same way the existence of the Chiliastys 'Αλθαιμενεύς may point to some infusion of Argive or perhaps of Kretan blood at Ephesos. There were traditions of a settlement of Kretans among the Karians in what was afterwards known as the Milesian territory (Pausan. vii, 2, § 3).

The Chiliastys Πείος occurs only in a list of Νεοποιοί (No. dlxxviii b), the date of which is somewhat doubtful. The characters are certainly not earlier, and I think they are not much later, than the middle of the first century A.D. Other indications discussed in the commentary ad loc. point to a comparatively early date : otherwise there would be no reasonable doubt that Πείος (= Πίος) is simply borrowed from the name of the emperor Antoninus Pius. Such is probably the explanation of the words ΠΕΙΩΝ ΕΦΕΣΙΩΝ (i. e. Piorum Ephesiorum) on the coin of Ephesos described by Mionnet. Suppl. vi, 413–415. I am aware that in the opinion of E. Curtius, who has engraved this coin in his Ephesos (Pl. 1, fig. 4), ΠΕΙΩΝ is the name of the Ephesian hill which modern writers commonly call Prion, deriving it from πρίων, a saw. But although in Strabo (xiv, p. 633) we read Πρηών or Πριών, all the MSS of Pausanias (vii, 5, 5) exhibit Πίων, and so Pliny writes it (N. H. v, 29, 31). Probably E. Curtius is right in deciding for Πίων, but it is another question whether the word on the coin can be referred to the hill Pion. At the same time it is possible that the Ephesians, from being familiar with the name Πίων, were the more ready to adopt the imperial name as an epithet, like Πρώτων 'Εφεσίων, νεωκόρων 'Εφεσίων, also occurring on the coins. The latter indeed is a precisely analogous phrase to Πίων 'Εφεσίων, Νεωκόρων meaning ' devoted to the worship of the emperors,' while Πίοι would mean when applied to the Ephesians, as Pius did when adopted by M. Antoninus, that they (like him) venerated the memory of Hadrian (Spartian. Hadrianus, 24, 27; compare No. bi, infra). But however we prefer to interpret the legend on the coin, there is no reason whatever to connect Antoninus Pius with the name of the Chiliastys. The reader is referred to the commentary on No. dlxxviii, where the conjecture is hazarded that the Chiliastys derived its name from the hill Pion.

Three more names of Chiliastyes in this tribe remain,—'Εχύρεος, Σιμώνεος, Χηλώνεος : such seem the older forms, the later documents give the terminations in -ηος. These names may recall certain leading men among the immigrants from Karene, 'Εχυρος,

Σίμων, Χείλων. That Χείλων (Χίλων) might be written Χήλων we learn from the forms Νειλεύς, Νηλεύς (Lobeck, Pathologia Græci Sermonis, pp. 474–5).

In the fifth tribe, Εὐώνυμοι, only two Chiliastyes are known. Πολυῆ[κλη]ος may enshrine the memory of some early leader among the Attic colonists, Πολυκλῆς. Γλαύκηος recalls the statement of Herodotos (i, 147), that in some of the Ionian cities there had been 'kings' who claimed descent from Glaukos of Lykia, the Trojan hero. It has often been suggested (Jebb, Introduction to Homer, p. 127) that this circumstance may account for the prominent part assigned to the Lykians in the Iliad (Il. vi), and the incident between Glaukos and Bellerophon may have been suggested by the close relations subsisting in the early days of the Ionic colonies between the ruling families of Ionia and the ruling families of Lykia.

Sixth tribe, Βεμβειναῖοι, φυλὴ Βεμβίνης (? genitive of Βεμβίνη), φυλὴ Βεμβινέων (? genitive pl. of Βεμβινεύς). The Chiliastyes known are Αἰγώτεος, Πελάσγηος. It is expressly stated by Herodotos (i, 146), that in the case of all the Ionic colonies, except perhaps Miletos, the immigrants from Greece brought with them a large non-Attic element. In particular he names the 'Arkadian Pelasgians' as among those who accompanied the Attic colonists to Ionia. Now we have already seen that the name of this tribe (Βέμβινα) connects it with the Peloponnese ; and we further find it to comprise two Chiliastyes which also recall Peloponnesian memories. Πελάσγηος speaks for itself. Αἰγώτεος may be connected with Αἴγυς, an ancient Arkadian city on the Lakonian border, which was very early destroyed and absorbed by Lakedæmon (Pausan. iii, 2, § 5 ; viii, 34, § 3). Is it fanciful to conjecture that some of the fugitives from Ægys may have joined the Attic emigrants to Ephesos, and that from them this Chiliastys derived its name ? The gentile adjective of Αἴγυς was Αἰγώτης, and the land was termed Αἰγῶτις ; and how naturally an Æolic υ might be represented by an Ionic ω is shown by such examples as χελύνη χελώνη, κύμη κώμη.

THE EPHESIAN BOULÊ.

In the organisation of a Greek city on a democratic basis, the most important feature was the βουλή. For the constitution of the boulè determined the character of the government. We are fully informed of the arrangements at Athens. Here the boulè of five hundred was made up of fifty citizens from each of the ten tribes, appointed yearly by lot : each fifty in turn acting as a sort of executive committee or 'government' (πρυτάνεις), meeting daily at the prytaneion, preparing measures for the ekklesia (προβουλεύματα), where the prytanes presided. It is instructive to see how minutely the organisation of the boulè is defined in the constitution of Erythræ (about 450 B.C., C. I. A. i, 9: Hicks, Manual, No. 23). Not less significant is the fact that the Athenian oligarchs in B.C. 411 began by

* An inscription full of interest in connexion with our present subject, the subdivisions of the φυλή. At Kamiros the φυλή was subdivided into φρατρίαι (= χιλιαστύες), and the φρατρία into πάτραι (= γένη).

reconstructing the boulè (Thucydides viii, 68); so did the Thirty, B.C. 404 (Xen. Hellen. ii, 3, § 11).

At Ephesos the constitution was after the Attic model during the period of Greek freedom. Only in one point was the ordinary nomenclature different; the officer who was styled πρύτανις at Ephesos corresponded to the Athenian ἄρχων and gave his name to the year (see Nos. CCCCLXXVII, CCCCLXXXI), in accordance with the statement of Aristotle (Politics vii, 8, 20 = 1322): καλοῦσι δὲ οἱ μὲν ἄρχοντας τούτους (as at Athens) οἱ δὲ βασιλεῖς (as at Samothrace, see No. CCCCXLIV) οἱ δὲ πρυτάνεις (as at Ephesos). Neither are we quite sure that the πρόεδροι who are mentioned in the Ephesian decree about Mithradates (Waddington-Le Bas, Part V, 136 a : my Manual, 205) corresponded in all respects to the πρόεδροι or the πρυτάνεις of Attika. When we quit Athenian soil and inquire into the polity even of so prominent a city as Ephesos, it is startling to discover how slight is our knowledge. What was the number of the bouleutai? How many were chosen from each tribe, and how? Who were the officers of the boulè, besides the γραμματεὺς τῆς βουλῆς mentioned in the decree last cited? How often did the boulè meet, and what was the system of presidency? To these and similar questions we can give only doubtful answers, and must be content to infer that probably the Ephesian arrangements closely resembled those of the mother city.

The close of the Peloponnesian War found Ephesos an ally of Sparta, and governed by a dekarchia of Lysander's appointment. The victory of Konon, B.C. 394, brought the oligarchical régime to a sudden end, and Ephesos with most of the cities of Ionia and the islands reverted to the Athenian alliance (Pausan. vi, 3, § 6). The fatal Peace of Antalkidas however in 387 B.C. destroyed all hopes of liberty, and Ephesos, like the rest of Ionia, was left at the mercy of the Persian king. Such a condition of things was favourable to the growth of oligarchies and tyrannies, and the middle of the fourth century B.C. has been called a Second Age of Tyrants. We hear of 'tyrants' at Ephesos, and the city was governed by an oligarchical dynasty at the moment when it was surrendered to Alexander, B.C. 334.

Ephesos now enjoyed a precarious freedom, and under the patronage of Antigonos and his son Demetrios Poliorketes we shall find democratic institutions flourishing (see Nos. CCCCLVIII, CCCCLII, CCCCLIII). Free government however was for a while suspended, in reality if not in form, during the supremacy of Lysimachos (see Nos. CCCCXLIX, CCCCLXX and notes). He even changed the name of the city to Ἀρσινόη in honour of his wife: but his death, B.C. 281, swept away these new arrangements, and the democratic forms reasserted themselves during the next two centuries, however much the city might be under the power of the kings, until Ionia passed under the yoke of Rome*.

We shall have occasion presently, in discussing the origin and nature of the Ephesian Gerousia, to estimate the influence of Lysimachos upon the institutions of the city. Far more serious and permanent was the change which the Roman conquest produced upon the Ephesian constitution, and in particular upon the boulè. The provincial cities were allowed municipal rights, and therefore retained their old forms of government; but it was the deliberate policy of Rome to entrust the wealthiest and best-born citizens of a dependent state with the largest share in its administration. And even apart from deliberate purpose, it was inevitable that the Roman administrators would see in the boulè of a Greek city something resembling the Roman Senate, and would proceed to reorganize it with this in view. The Roman senate was essentially timocratic and oligarchical. When from these general considerations we proceed to inquire into details, there is reason to regret the scantiness of our information. In regard to one province, it is true, we are fairly well informed. The official correspondence which passed between the younger Pliny and the emperor Trajan (Pliny was his commissioner in Bithynia probably from September 17, A.D. 111 to the end of January 113) affords minute and authentic indications of the polity of the Bithynian cities. From the day in which Bithynia became a Roman province, the Lex Pompeia (B.C. 63) had caused the boulè in every city to be filled up by censors (τιμηταί) after the manner of the senate (Pliny to Trajan, 112). In another point also the boulè had been assimilated to the senate; for all who had held magistracies were, by the Lex Pompeia, entitled to become bouleutai (ibid. 79, a letter full of significance as revealing the oligarchical drift of Roman influence: quia sit aliquanto melius honestorum hominum liberos quam e plebe in curiam admitti, etc.). Changes like these in Bithynia must have ensued in various measure throughout Greece when it passed under Roman dominion, although no such exact evidence exists elsewhere. For, indeed, alterations of this kind might be made without any great change of external forms. The number of the boulè might remain unchanged. The boulè would meet as before. Its functions, and its relations to the ekklesia remained untouched. Pliny shows (ibid. 81, 110) that the outward form of the polity remained what it had ever been; and numerous extant decrees from every quarter of Asia Minor tell the same story. And yet everywhere, the result of Roman influence was that the old republican forms of government were undergoing an unnoticed but essential change: they were made the instruments of timocracy and oligarchy.

Various tendencies would assist this development. Already before Roman policy exerted any influence, even at Athens, the boulè and its decrees were more and more concerned with questions of ritual and of compliment, and its members and the prytanes were gradually assuming the character of a religious cor-

---

* The best account of the history of Ephesos, apart from Droysen's Hellenismus and Guhl's Ephesiaca, is perhaps to be found in Mr. Head's History of the Coinage of Ephesus.

poration. I have had occasion to remark upon this tendency in the Journal of Hellenic Studies, iii, pp. 138 foll. Again, in declining Greece there was everywhere the direst poverty, and very many of the Greek cities were in a state of bankruptcy: the decree of Tenos (C. I. 2335; Hicks, Manual, No. 204), now at Cambridge, is one example out of many that illustrate this. In such a state of things, it was a necessity to select wealthy men, whenever possible, to hold public offices and direct the government of the state. If this was the direction in which the Greek states were already drifting, the deliberate policy of Rome hastened the transformation. And, of course, the change was chiefly felt in the modification of the boulè.

What change took place in the Ephesian boulè? and at what date? Do the new inscriptions help to answer the question?

Marquardt (Röm. Alt. iv, pp. 518, 519) thinks that in the province of Asia the constitution of the boulè remained unaltered in form down to the era of the Antonines. This Menadier denies (p. 30, etc.), and would make the alteration as early, or nearly as early, as the Roman domination. From that time, according to him, the Ephesian boulè became a close corporation: its members were appointed for life, and entirely without regard to the Ephesian tribes. Even the number of the bouleutai was not fixed. It becomes necessary to say something upon this question.

It must be owned that the epigraphical evidence is rather negative and inferential, than direct and positive. Certainly the old forms are preserved, and the decrees (ψηφίσματα) of boulè and of ekklesia are couched in terms which reveal nothing of any organic change (see No. CCCCLXXXII, and the first document of No. CCCCLXXXI). It is expressly stated in the Salutaris bequest (No. CCCCLXXXI, lines 129-132) that the boulè in A. D. 104 comprised 450 members: and it is quite clear that this number is a fixed one, since the bequest assigns just 450 denarii for annual distribution among them, one apiece. We are not told the number of the Ephesian boulè in præ-Roman times; and it is quite possible that the number had never been altered, except by the addition of another 75, when the number of tribes was increased from five to six (see above). It is at least a suggestive fact that the tribes in Salutaris' day being six in number, 6 multiplied by 75 make 450, i. e. 75 members from each tribe. Are we to conclude then that the boulè was, as late as A.D. 104, filled up κατὰ φυλάς? Certainly the Salutaris inscription, with its minute directions for the doles, proves that the tribal division of the Ephesian citizen-body counted for a great deal in the civic life of the people. Nor am I prepared to deny that, even so late as this, each tribe may have furnished its equal contingent of 75 to the boulè. The numbers and tribal proportion may have been retained, however greatly the mode of appointment was altered. In the Oxford Colleges before 1854, when the head and fellows formed a close corporation and filled up vacancies by cooptation, the statutes of most colleges compelled them to select from certain counties of England in certain proportions. Until now the aldermen of the city of London are a fixed number, and are appointed for life; yet each is appointed by a particular ward.

We are thus led to ask, in what manner were the bouleutai selected? Certainly no longer by lot, as in republican Athens, and probably in republican Ephesos: although Marquardt (Röm. Alt. iv, p. 519) thinks even this to be conceivable. On the other hand there is no evidence whatever of the existence of τιμηταί or censors, like those of Bithynia and Pontus described by Pliny (*l. c.*) as charged with the nomination of members to the boulè. In the absence of any evidence, I should conjecture that, as vacancies occurred, they were filled by cooptation; the selection being made from among citizens who had held public offices, and had been munificent in the various 'liturgies,' etc. In fact the Ephesian boulè resembled one of our old unreformed corporations. Whether any account was taken of the tribes, remains doubtful.

No. CCCCLXXXVII is a letter of the emperor Hadrian (date probably A. D. 129-130), in which he requests the magistrates and boulè of Ephesos to admit one Lucius Erastos, a citizen of Ephesos, into the boulè. The emperor leaves them the task of inquiring into the man's claims (δοκιμασία), and if nothing disqualifies Erastos from receiving the honour, Hadrian himself engages to furnish the usual fees payable by persons who were made bouleutai. It is plain how this example confirms the idea that the boulè was filled up by cooptation. The emperor requests the boulè to coopt his nominee: but he does not appoint him. The δοκιμασία in this case would probably be little more than a form: but no doubt the boulè valued the power of excluding whom they pleased. Inquiry would be made into a candidate's personal and pecuniary qualifications. Had he a good character? Had he sufficient means? That character was considered is obvious; and it is expressly stated by Cicero (pro Flacco xviii, 43) concerning Temnos in the province of Asia, and by Pliny (to Trajan, 114) concerning the cities of Bithynia, that there were causes for which, at the periodical revision of the boulè, names could be struck off the list of members. But probably the possession of ample means was a primary recommendation; it was expected of bouleutai, that they should be generous givers (Pliny to Trajan, 39); see note on No. CCCCLXXXVII.

But here another question arises. If at the request of the emperor a fresh bouleutes might any day be added to the roll, what became of the fixed number of bouleutai spoken of above? Moreover it is known to have become no uncommon thing at Ephesos, and in other cities, for eminent strangers to be enrolled among the bouleutai. In old days the freedom of the city (πολιτεία) was granted with some show of discrimination to distinguished strangers who had done the city service (Nos. CCCCXLVII, foll.). But now grants of citizenship had grown so common, that a grant of incorporation into the boulè was often superadded (C. I. 3206, 3426; Waddington-

Le Bas, Pt. v, Nos. 1620 a, 1652 b; C. I. A. iii, 129; post, Nos. DCXV, DCXVII; and Röhl in Mittheilungen, ii, 223). These inscriptions show that it was a common thing for a successful athlete to be made πολίτης καὶ βουλευτής in city after city. If so, how could the bouleutai remain a fixed number?

I feel sure that here a strong enough line has not been drawn by writers on this subject, between what we may term 'honorary' and 'ordinary' members of the boulè. Perhaps the co-existence of honorary and actual Fellows in an Oxford College, and the honorary degrees granted by the University will help to illustrate the distinction. Like the honorary freedom of a city, they carry with them no right of voting and no emoluments: they confer only a certain social distinction. Just so did the number of the Ephesian boulè remain fixed; whereas there was no limit to the number of persons who might be made honorary bouleutai, provided that the emperor permitted what might easily have become a scandal. For there was a strong temptation to a boulè to multiply its honorary members for the sake of the entrance fees paid by such persons, and also because it flattered a city's vanity to confer such distinctions upon men of note. Pliny (to Trajan, 112) says of his own province: Lex Pompeia, domine, qua Bithyni et Pontici utuntur, eos qui in bulen a censoribus leguntur dare pecuniam non jubet (i. e. 'ordinary' bouleutai): sed ii quos indulgentia tua quibusdam civitatibus super legitimum numerum adicere permisit et singula milia denariorum et bina intulerunt (i. e. the honorary members paid £40 or even £80 in fees for admission). To the same effect is the language of Dio Chrysostom: οἱ δὲ ἐλογοποίουν ὅτι τοῖς Σμυρναίοις παμπόλλας δωρεὰς δοίη καὶ χρήματα ἀμύθητα πέμψειε μετὰ τῶν Νιμέσεων, καὶ νὴ Δί' ὡς ἄλλου τινὸς διαλεχθέντος μυρίους μὲν ἂν αὐτῷ συνεχώρησε βουλευτάς, χρυσίου δ' ἐκέλευσε ποταμὸν εἰς τὴν πόλιν τραπῆναι καὶ μυριάδες ἄπειροί τινες ἐδόθησαν (De Concordiâ, ii, p. 165 Reiske).

To the further question, whether the boulcutai at Ephesos were appointed (under the Empire) for a year, or for a term of years, or for life, the new inscriptions give no safe answer. It is possible Roman usage sometimes prevailed so far as to make the boulè resemble the senate of an ordinary Roman colonia or municipium, in having lifelong members (Marquardt, Röm. Alt. iv, p. 501 foll.). But I fail to see any real proof that it was true of Ephesos. Certainly at Athens it was not so, as the lists of prytanes prove (C. I. 189 foll.); nor at Kyzikos (see the lists of prytanes, C. I. 3663, 3664); nor perhaps at Mileto (C. I. 287è; compare Mar-

quardt, Röm. Alt. iv, p. 519). Menadier indeed says on this (p. 30): 'quam permutationem eo maxime expressam, quod buleutae honor aeque ac decurionatus et reliqui honores municipales titulis exhibetur,' etc. But this surely is a mistaken argument. The inscriptions repeatedly describe a person as νεοποιὸς and βουλευτής, and by other titles (e. g. No. DLXXVIII): but I shall show presently that the νεοποιοί were certainly annual down to a late period. And if the neopoios, why not the bouleutes? The vanity of the 'Græculi' would sufficiently account for the mention of every possible title, even if Roman usage had not taught them to inscribe a man's 'cursus honorum.'

On the whole we are led to conclude that the constitution of the boulè under the Romans differed greatly in different cities. So that while in Bithynia and Pontus (see Pliny ad Traj. passim), at Massilia (Strabo, iv, p. 179) and in Sicily (Cic. Verr. ii, 49, 50, 120, 122, 123), the Greek boulè was very soon reorganized by Rome on an entirely new basis, at Athens, Kyzikos and perhaps at Ephesos, the old forms more or less survived, however much their spirit had fled.

In præ-Roman times the Ephesian boulè was presided over by proëdroi, of whom we have spoken above, much in the same way doubtless as the boulè of Athens. In the times of the Empire the proëdroi are no more heard of, and a βούλαρχος is named in No. DLXXXVI. By boularchos we must understand the chairman of the boulè; and the title was not confined to Ephesos, but was common at this date both in Asia Minor and in Greece proper, as may be seen by a reference to the Index to Böckh's Corpus (and Menadier's references, pp. 33, 34; to which add Bulletin de Corr. Hell. iv, (1880,) p. 154, Teos). It appears that the boularchos was selected annually; for we find the aorist βουλαρχήσας often employed (C. I. 2882, 2930 b, 3419, 3421, 3831 a[1]), and sometimes the boularchos is named to date the year (C. I. 1725, 3424). Similarly we hear τοῦ τότε βουλάρχου at Minoa (C. I. 2264 p.), and at Thyatira a boularchos for life is spoken of as an exception to the rule (C. I. 3494). We may take for granted that the functions and position of the boularchos were the same at Ephesos also.

THE EPHESIAN GEROUSIA [*]

In the Homeric poems the γέροντες appear as a council of the king or chieftain, in such a way as to make it doubtful whether the word is meant to express seniority of age or merely precedence of rank. This Homeric use Euripides had in mind when in

---

* Since the following remarks on the gerousia were in type some important additions have been made to our knowledge of the subject, chiefly by the discovery of the long inscription at Sidyma by the Austrian scholars (Benndorf, Reisen in Lykien und Karien, i, p. 71 foll.). It belongs to the end of the second century A. D., and records how a gerousia, by permission of the proconsul, was established for the first time at Sidyma: it seems as if the institution of a gerousia in one after another of these remoter towns marked the spread of western and Hellenic influences. Mommsen still regards the gerousia as rather a social club than a civic assembly (Provinces, Eng. Tr. pp. 353, 4); and of course such an assembly would have its social side, just as our House of Commons has been styled the best club in London. Mr. Hogarth has recently summed up the arguments against Mommsen's view in an interesting paper (Journal of Philology, 1890, pp. 69 foll.). I have followed Menadier in suggesting that there may be some historical connexion between the gerousia of Lysimachus and the gerousia of Roman times. It has been too hastily assumed that the similarity of name and functions is accidental. It is certainly a curious fact that most of the earlier gerousiai of the Roman time occur in regions which once were subject to Lysimachus.

the Rhesos (lines 401, 936), he employs γερουσία to express a deputation from the γέροντες, with a further allusion also to the etymology of πρεσβευτής. We discern a survival of Homeric days in the Gerousia which existed at Spa.ta, as the council of the kings (see Plutarch, Lykurg. 5; Aristotle, Politics ii, 6, 17 = 1265 a, 35; vi, 9, 9 = 1294 b, 30). Something similar to a gerousia also existed in the constitution of Krete (Aristotle, Politics ii, 10, 6 = 1272 a), and in that of Carthage (ibid. ii, 11, 5 = 1273 a, 8; Strabo x, 484). It has also been pointed out that the Council of the Areopagos at Athens bore an organic resemblance to the Homeric and the Spartan Gerousia.

Accordingly the word gerousia, to the ears of the Greeks of the fifth or fourth centuries B.C., would suggest ideas the reverse of democratic. Thus Demosthenes speaking B.C. 355 (against Leptines, p. 489 Reiske), singles out this feature as characteristic of the Spartan constitution, and as utterly subversive of free government : οὐ γὰρ ἀγνοῶ τοῦθ', ὅτι Θηβαῖοι καὶ Λακεδαιμόνιοι καὶ ἡμεῖς οὔτε νόμοις οὔτε ἔθεσι χρώμεθα τοῖς αὐτοῖς οὔτε πολιτείᾳ . . . . . . ἄλλαι δέ τινες παρ' ἐκείνοις εἰσὶ τιμαὶ, ἃς ἀπεύξαιτ' ἂν ἅπας ὁ δῆμος ἐνταυθοῖ γενέσθαι. τίνες οὖν εἰσὶν αὗται; τὰς μὲν καθ' ἕκαστον ἐάσω, μίαν δ' ἣ συλλαβοῦσα τὰς ἄλλας ἔχει δίειμι. ἐπειδάν τις εἰς τὴν καλουμένην γερουσίαν ἐγκριθῇ παρασχὼν ἑαυτὸν οἷον χρή, δεσπότης ἐστὶ τῶν πολλῶν. Similarly Xenophon (Mem. iv, 4, § 16) speaks of αἵ τε γερουσίαι καὶ οἱ ἄριστοι ἄνδρες. If such were the associations of the word, it is significant that Lysimachos should have deliberately established a γερουσία at democratic Ephesos, the favourite city of his rivals Antigonos and Demetrios, who relied everywhere on the support of the democrats. The changes made by Lysimachos at Ephesos are thus described by Strabo (xiv, p. 640): Λυσίμαχος δὲ τὴν νῦν πόλιν τειχίσας, ἀηδῶς τῶν ἀνθρώπων μεθισταμένων, τηρήσας καταρράκτην ὄμβρον συνήργησε καὶ αὐτὸς καὶ τοὺς ῥινούχους ἐνέφραξεν ὥστε κατακλύσαι τὴν πόλιν· οἱ δὲ μετέστησαν ἀσμένοι. ἐκάλεσε δ' Ἀρσινόην ἀπὸ τῆς γυναικὸς τὴν πόλιν, ἐπεκράτησε μέντοι τὸ ἀρχαῖον ὄνομα. ἦν δὲ γερουσία καταγραφομένη, τούτοις δὲ συνῄεσαν οἱ ἐπίκλητοι καλούμενοι καὶ διῴκουν πάντα. In other words Lysimachos wished the gerousia to be the oligarchical substitute for a boulè, and the ἐπίκλητοι for the ekklesia. We are reminded again of the proceedings of the oligarchy at Athens (see Thuc. viii, 67, 68, and the masterly comments of Grote), with their ' Four hundred' and 'Five thousand,' the former selected by cooptation, and the latter (the phantom of an ekklesia) to be convened only at the pleasure of the Four hundred. We remember also that the terms σύγκλησις and κατάκλησις (near akin to ἐπίκλητοι) were well known at Athens for the extraordinary summoning of the ekklesia (Thuc. viii, 67; Schömann, De Comitiis 28 foll.). The statement of Strabo just quoted is confirmed by the evidence of Nos. CCCCXLIX and CCCCLXX, where see the notes. To what extent Lysimachos did the same in other cities we have no direct information. But as he was an avowed patron of the oligarchical faction, it is highly probable that in many other cities like Ephesos, the triumph of his cause was followed by the establishment of a gerousia, very much as in B.C. 404 Lysander everywhere set up his dekarchies.

What we know for certain is, that in the times of Roman supremacy a gerousia existed in so many of the Greek cities, and in such widely extended regions, as to make us conclude (with Menadier, p. 61) that the Romans deliberately encouraged this institution, just as at Athens they revived the powers of the Areopagos. It is even possible that in some cities besides Ephesos the Romans found a gerousia already existing, a survival from the reign of Lysimachos. Thus Vitruvius (temp. Augusti) speaks of the gerousia at Sardes as an institution of long standing (ii, 8, 10); and Strabo, his contemporary, makes similar mention of τὸ γεροντικόν at Nysa (xiv, 649). An inscription of Lampsakos (now at Oxford), in honour of Livia the widow of Augustus, speaks of a gerousia there also (C. I. 3642)*. The gerousia is likewise mentioned in an inscription from Erythræ (Waddington-Le Bas, Part v, No. 53) which may perhaps be of præ-Roman date. Inscriptions and other documents of the imperial period show the institution to have existed in very many cities of Greece,—in Asia Minor, in the islands, in Thrace, and occasionally in Greece proper †. But the examples given above will suggest that in some cities, at all events, the gerousia had existed long before.

It is not necessary to repeat here the arguments by which Menadier has demonstrated the nature of the later gerousia. He has convincingly shown that it was a public body, as much as the boulè or ekklesia. He has likewise proved that it was distinct from either, and not even a select committee of the boulè, as Böckh had suggested (C. I. 2811) and as C. Curtius had endeavoured to prove (Hermes iv, p. 224). These conclusions will be amply verified by the inscriptions which follow in this volume. It only remains to speak of the status and functions of the gerousia. I shall here confine my remarks to the Ephesian gerousia only, taking it for granted that what is true of Ephesos in this respect, was true in the main of the many other cities of which we lack information.

The civic status of the Ephesian gerousia is incidentally shown in the Salutaris bequest (No.

---

* Böckh, ad locum, inclines to refer the inscription to Julia Domna, wife of the emperor Severus; and adds, titulusque tam male scriptus est vix ut eum Tiberii sæculo vindicare audeam. I have examined the marble recently, and it is inscribed with letters not unworthy of the age of Tiberius : so is C. I. 3643, which likewise speaks of the gerousia at Lampsakos.

† I need not cite all the instances : they are given by Menadier, pp. 60, 61, and may most of them be found in the index to Böckh's Corpus s. v. γερουσία. To the list of Menadier add Kolophon (Μουσεῖον of the Smyrna Evangelical School, 1880, p. 215); Kos (Bulletin de Corr. Hell. v, p. 229); Tralles (ibid. p. 347); Athens (C. I. 185), and the references given in the note on the preceding page 74.

CCCCLXXXI, lines 58 foll., 324 foll., and fragment 1, line 6). In these passages the gerousia is enumerated next after the boulè, as an integral part of the state. Also while the boulè received a capital sum of 5000 denarii for the purpose of an annual dole to its members, the gerousia received 4450 denarii. or only 550 less. The yearly interest on 4450 denarii was 400½ denarii, and therefore if the members of the gerousia had a fixed number, and if the assumption made on p. 137 is admitted, their number may well have been 400. It is clear from all this that the gerousia stood second in dignity to the boulè only among the assemblies of the state. At Sillyon the gerousia occupies the same position in the apportionment of a dole (Bulletin de Corr. Hell. xiii, 1889, p. 491). It was a common practice for members of the gerousia to mention their title γερουσιαστής upon public monuments, evidently as proud of it (No. DXCIX). Also, like the boulè, the gerousia awards public honours (No. DXLIV).

The officers of the gerousia were (1) a γραμματεύς (No. DLXXXVII), who must not be confounded with the γραμματεύς τῆς βουλῆς (No. DXCVI), nor with the still more important γραμματεὺς τοῦ δήμου, of whom see p. 81. (2) In the Salutaris bequest (line 189) where we should expect to read γραμματεὺς τῆς γερουσίας (see Menadier. p. 50), a closer examination of the marble proves that another officer was named as the receiver of the money due to the gerousia. (3) One of the various gymnasia existing at Ephesos was probably built for the use of the members of the gerousia only: thus at Ephesos, as elsewhere, a γυμνασίαρχος of the gerousia is spoken of (see Nos. DLXXXVII, DCIV, and p. 82 post). (4) In Nos. DLXXXIII and DLXXV (?), certain members of the gerousia receive the title of πατρογέρων (see notes ad loc.).

What were the functions of the gerousia? It is suggested by Menadier (p. 63) that the gerousia, as established by Lysimachos at Ephesos and in other cities of his realm, was given the initiative in all matters, whether political or religious: but that upon the defeat and death of Lysimachos, the democratic forms, which had all along been allowed to survive, reasserted themselves, and the boulè and ekklesia assumed their ancient powers. Thus the ἐπίκλητοι were now no more heard of, and the gerousia henceforward was concerned with religious affairs alone. The language of Strabo quoted above in part favours this view. But I hardly think it agrees with the evidence of the inscriptions. They never exhibit the gerousia as concerned with any interests outside of religion, either at Ephesos or elsewhere (Menadier. p. 57; Newton, Essays on Art and Archæology, p. 227). This might indeed be accounted for by the fact that most of the inscriptions that name the gerousia belong to Roman and imperial times. But I wish to point out that the same thing is true of the Ephesian decrees of the time of Lysimachos himself. No. CCCCXLIX, which seems to date from B.C. 302, speaks indeed of the gerousia moving for a grant of citizenship to Euphronios of Akarnania; but we find that his claims to this recognition rest upon his services to the Artemision.

He had interceded with Prepelaos ὑπὲρ τοῦ σταθμοῦ τοῦ ἱεροῦ καὶ τῆς ἀτελείας τῇ θεῷ, and συνδιοίκησεν .... ὅπως ἂν ἡ ἀτέλεια ὑπάρχῃ τῇ θεῷ. In No. CCCCLXX the gerousia makes a similar proposal. But the recipient of the honour is a Bœotian flute-player, and we may reasonably assume that his skilful playing had added lustre to the Artemision festival (see No. DCVI post, and the notes on No. CCCCXLIV ante). I find therefore no proof, beyond the rather vague language of Strabo (l. c.), that the Ephesian gerousia as organized by Lysimachos dealt with any other affairs but those of religion. If so, it may be asked, what interest had Lysimachos in establishing it, especially as we learn from the decrees just quoted that the democratic forms went on just as usual after the revolution mentioned by Strabo, and every psephisma had to pass the boulè and ekklesia before it became law? I think the answer is this. Behind and above the civil government of Ephesos there had ever been the undefined but powerful influence of the ancient hierarchy of the temple. The power of the priesthood rested not upon fixed constitutional rights, but upon prescriptive authority, and the reverence felt for a mysterious and important worship. To this was added the tangible advantage of a right of asylum which one potentate after another was persuaded to confirm and enlarge (see on Nos. DXXIII–DXXVII). Still more, the temple of Artemis was not merely rich in endowments, and in the accumulated gifts of pilgrims and worshippers; but also, beyond this, the inviolable sanctity of the temple and the renown of its hierarchy made it the chief bank of deposit for all Asia (compare No. CCCCXXIV ante). Thus Dio Chrysostom (Rhod. Oratio, p. 595 Reiske) says: ἔστε που τοὺς Ἐφεσίους, ὅτι πολλὰ χρήματα παρ᾽ αὐτοῖς ἐστι, τὰ μὲν ἰδιωτῶν, ἀποκείμενα ἐν τῷ νέῳ τῆς Ἀρτέμιδος, οὐκ Ἐφεσίων μόνον, ἀλλὰ καὶ ξένων καὶ τῶν ὁπόθεν δήποτε ἀνθρώπων, τὰ δὲ καὶ δήμων καὶ βασιλέων, ἃ τιθέασι πάντες οἱ τιθέντες ἀσφαλείας χάριν κ.τ.λ. Dio proceeds to affirm that the Ephesians, however low their public exchequer, would never dream of touching these funds for any emergency, nor even of borrowing from them. Similarly Aristides (Oration 42, De Concordia, p. 522 Jebb): πάντες γὰρ ὡς εἰς πατρίδα αὐτῶν κομίζονται (to Ephesos) καὶ οὐδεὶς οὕτως ἀγνώμων οὐδ᾽ οὕτως σφόδρα ὁμόσε τοῖς φανεροῖς ἰών, ὅστις οὐκ ἂν συγχωρήσειε ταμιείων τε κοινὸν τῆς Ἀσίας εἶναι τὴν πόλιν καὶ τῆς χρείας καταφυγήν. In other words the temple-authorities made loans upon interest to individuals or to communities from the deposits in the Artemision. These writers belong to the second century A.D., but Xenophon (Anabasis, v, 3) evidently regarded the temple as a safe place of deposit, and Cæsar speaks in the same terms (De Bello Civ. iii, 33; compare iii, 105): Ephesi a fano Dianæ depositas antiquitus pecunias Scipio tolli jubebat . . . . . . but Cæsar's intervention Ephesiacæ pecuniæ salutem attulit. Similar evidence is afforded by Plautus, Bacchides 306 foll.; Strabo xiv, p. 640. It would assuredly have been the aim of Prepelaos to bring the whole influence of the Ephesian hierarchy and the weight of such a large pecuniary interest into the scale of his master Lysimachos. It has been thought, not unreasonably, that the sympathy of the temple-authorities, both as a hier- archy and as capitalists, would lean to the oligar- chical side (Droysen, Hellenismus i, 1, 200). With such a powerful alliance at hand, Lysimachos might contentedly suffer the forms of democracy to go on as before. Enough if he established a new oligar- chical senate or gerousia, avowedly to take charge of the banking transactions of the Artemision, and probably to administer also the endowments and private revenues of the goddess. These affairs of themselves formed no mean department of public business; and he might be sure that a corporation which gave constitutional utterance and effect to the opinion of the temple-authorities would have a weighty influence upon the general politics of the city. Such I conjecture to have been the origin of the gerousia at Ephesos, as organized under Lysimachos. The conjecture is confirmed by the fact that the régime of Lysimachos had a marked effect upon the character of the Artemis-worship; its more Asiatic features were thrust into the background, everything must be Hellenized. The transformation is attested by the coinage. 'Now, for the first time, the bee which had for so many ages maintained its place on the obverse of the coinage of Ephesus, as the signet of the high-priest (or king-bee, 'Εσσήν), gives way to a purely Hellenic type, the head of the Greek huntress- goddess, whose bow and quiver occupy the whole field of the reverse' (Head, Coinage of Ephesus, p. 41; Newton, Essays, p. 221). It would be part of this movement, to transfer the administration of the temple-treasures from a semi-oriental hierarchy to a Greek civic board. It must be confessed that we have no direct evidence to connect the Ephesian gerousia of Lysimachos with the gerousia of later times; nor is there any evidence to warrant us in associating the gerousia of other cities with his name. All we can say is that the later gerousia everywhere was certainly, and the earlier gerousia at Ephesos was probably, engaged with matters of religion.

Such a view of the origin of the gerousia cer- tainly fits in with all the indications given by the inscriptions. It helps us to understand in No. CCCCLXXXVI, why the emperor Hadrian takes such vigorous steps to recover certain debts owing to the gerousia: these sums had been lent on interest from the deposits banked at the Artemision, and if the debtors were allowed to repudiate, the financial credit of the Artemision would be gone for ever. We see also why in No. CCCCLXXXIII, where it is agreed to appropriate some of the κοινὰ χρήματα of the gerousia to furnish a festival, such strong ex- cuses have to be pleaded for so exceptional a use of the deposits in the Artemision. (1) The state was too poor itself to furnish the funds, διά τινα ἐκδίαν χρημάτων (line 5), and this confession of poverty agrees with the statement of Dio Chrysostom (l. c.): καίτοι τοὺς Ἐφεσίους οὐκ ἂν εἴποιτε εὐπορωτέρους αὐτῶν.

τοὐναντίον γὰρ ὑμεῖς μὲν (the Rhodians) καὶ πρότερον ἦτε πλουσιώτατοι τῶν Ἑλλήνων καὶ νῦν ἔτι μᾶλλόν ἐστε· ἐκείνους δὲ πολλῶν ἐστιν ἰδεῖν καταδεέστερον πράττοντας. (2) The festival for which the money was required would be in honour of the reigning emperor, and such an end would justify the means. It becomes obvious that a secretary of the gerousia would have as confidential an office as the cashier of a bank: no wonder that in No. DLXXXVII Agatho- pous renders thanks ὅτι πίστιν ἐτήρησα τῇ γερουσίᾳ. When in No. DLXXVII we read of τοῦ ἱερωτάτου συν- εδρίου τὸ μισθωτήριον and its γραμματεῖς, we under- stand a department or office of the gerousia (συνέ- δριον, so in No. DLXX), which received and admini- stered rents from temple-lands. Nor are we sur- prised that the γραμματεῖς of this department took charge of τῆς δειπνοφοριακῆς πομπῆς: on the contrary, we can identify this celebration with the lectisternium voted in No. CCCCLXXXIII from the funds administered by the gerousia. In No. DXLIV the gerousia erects a monument ἐκ τῶν ἰδίων; that is, the expenses were not defrayed out of public moneys of which the gerousia had charge, and which were voted for public purposes in extreme cases (No. CCCCLXXXIII), but out of moneys properly its own. For the gerousia, like other corporations, might receive bequests; probably its members paid entrance money and other fees. Thus out of this privy purse of the corporation itself, the expense of the monument was met (No. DXLIV). In several in- scriptions, as No. DCIV (compare C. I. 3201, from Smyrna), we hear of a ὑμνῳδὸς τῆς γερουσίας. I shall discuss this title in the notes ad locum, where I adopt the suggestion of Menadier (p. 51), that the words ὑμνῳδὸς νεμητήι are to be taken together in the sense of 'Musical Judge,' i.e. awarder of the prize for ὑμνῳδία at the Hadriancia (see p. 79).[*] The inscription harmonizes with the view I take of the gerousia, if we suppose this body to be trustee of the funds which supported the Hadri- ancia, funds which may in part (as at Smyrna, C. I. 3148,) have come from a grant of the emperor himself.

But the most significant passage of all are lines 206–207 of the Salutaris bequest (No. CCCCLXXXI): 'If Salutaris die before the execution of his gift, his heirs shall be bound to pay over the capital sum, together with the interest due upon it, κατὰ τὰ ἱερὰ τῆς θεοῦ καὶ τὰ παρὰ τοῖς πρεσβυτέροις ἐκδανιστικὰ ἔγ- γραφα. That οἱ πρεσβύτεροι is synonymous with ἡ γερουσία may be gathered from No. DLXXXVII, and is proved by C. I. 3417. The ἐκδανιστικὰ ἔγγραφα are registers of public loans, kept by the gerousia; and the loans are made from the treasures of the Artemision. Observe that ἐγγραφή was the technical Attic term for the registration of public debtors, who were ἐγγεγραμμένοι ἐν ἀκροπόλει (Demosthenes, p. 771, Reiske). The financial importance of the gerousia appears also in No. CCCCLXXXI, line 58.

---

[*] Menadier adds 'quem Hesychius interpretatur ὑμνῳδὸν βραβευτήν.' but I have not been able to find such a gloss. True to his view of the gerousia as a social club, Mommsen suggests that the ὑμνῳδὸς merely superintended its musical entertainments (Provinces of the Roman Empire, Eng. Tr. i, p. 354).

Menadier proposes to go further and identify τὰ συστήματα of the Ephesian decree concerning Mithradates (Waddington-Le Bas, No. 136, line 36 foll. ; Hicks, Manual, No. 205) with the gerousia : *ὅσα δὲ ἱερὰ δεδάνεισται πάντας τοὺς ὀφείλοντας καὶ χειρίζοντας ἀπολελύσθαι ἀπὸ τῶν ὀφειλημάτων, πλὴν τῶν ὑπὸ τῶν συστημάτων ἢ τῶν ἀποδεδειγμένων ὑπ᾿ αὐτῶν ἐκδανεισ[τ]ῶν ἐπὶ ὑποθήκαις δεδανισμένων, τούτων δὲ παρεῖσθαι τοὺς τόκους ἀπὸ τοῦ εἰσιόντος ἐνιαυτοῦ ἕως ἂν ὁ δῆμος εἰς καλλίονα παραγίνηται κατάσ[τα]σιν.* Certainly such an interpretation suits the passage very well, and σύστημα (collegium) is actually employed for the gerousia in an inscription from Tralles (C. I. 2930). I had however adopted a different explanation when publishing the Mithradates decree in my Manual ; nor do I see why, if the gerousia simply is meant, the plural συστήματα should be employed.

THE EPHESIAN CALENDAR.

We may take it for granted that the Calendar of Ephesos originally resembled the Calendar of Athens the mother-city. The names of several months were certainly the same in both cities, and in all probability the civil year originally began at Ephesos, as at Athens, at Midsummer. Of these points however we have no direct evidence, either in ancient writers or in inscriptions; and even now we are unable to give a complete list of the names of the Ephesian months.

When we leave the earlier history of Ephesos, of which so few monuments remain, and enter upon the times which followed the conquests of Alexander, it might be expected that fuller information would be obtainable. Here however the evidence is dubious, if not conflicting. It is universally admitted that the Macedonians began their year with the month Dios (October) at the Autumn equinox (Clinton, F. H., Appendix on the Macedonian months). It was to be expected that the extension of Macedonian influence would lead to the adoption of the Macedonian mode of reckoning; and this was the case, as appears from various passages cited by Clinton (*l. c.*). Thus we are not surprised to read in the Letter of the Church of Smyrna concerning the martyrdom of St. Polycarp (A.D. 154-5, according to Waddington, Fastes, p. 221) : *μαρτυρεῖ δὲ ὁ μακάριος Πολύκαρπος μηνὸς Ξανθικοῦ* (the sixth Macedonian month) *δευτέρᾳ ἱσταμένου, πρὸ ἑπτὰ καλανδῶν Μαρτίων.* The writer, living in Asia in the second century, reckons by the Macedonian Calendar. Now it is asserted by Galen (A. D. 130-200) in his commentary on the Epidemics of Hippokrates (Op. xvii. p. 21), that the Macedonian year had been adopted in all (ἁπάσαις) the Asiatic cities. This statement is confirmed by the Hemerologium Florentinum (see Ideler, Handbuch d. Chronol. i, 410). This not only makes the Ephesian Calendar of the imperial times to resemble the Macedonian in commencing the year in the Autumn, but also presents us with a list of the Ephesian months which is contradicted by all the authentic evidence we have.

There are three questions to be answered before we can reconstruct the Calendar of any Greek city: (1) what are the names of the months? (2) Are the months, and is the year, solar or lunar? (3) When did the civil year begin?

In reply to (1), the inscriptions prove that the Ephesians retained as late as the second century A.D. their old Ionic Calendar (see Droysen, Hermes, xv, 1880, p. 363). Whatever other changes may have followed from the extension of Macedonian influence after Alexander, or again through the rectification of the Calendar by the Julian reform of B.C. 46, it remains certain that no radical change took place in the names of the Ephesian months.

As to (2), Bishop Lightfoot (Ignatius and Polycarp, i, pp. 664 foll.) has sufficiently proved, from data partly supplied by myself, that the solar Calendar was early introduced at Ephesos, although the native names of the months were unchanged.

The Ephesian months which occur in the inscriptions are the following :—

Ἀγνηιών : Waddington-Le Bas, No. 1537.
Ἀνθεστηριών : No. ccccLXXXI, line 321.
Ἀρτεμισιών : No. ccccLXXXI *b*, line 17.
Θαργηλιών : No. ccccLXXXI, *passim*.
Ληναιών; No. ccccLXXVII, Col. E; Joseph. Antiq. XIV, 10, 12.
[Μαι]μακτηρ[ιών] : No. DCI *h*.
Μεταγειτνιών : No. DXXVIII.
Νεοκαισαρεών ? : No. DCI *d, m*.
Ποσειδεών (Ποσιδεών) : No. ccccLXXXI, line 303 ; ccccLXXVII, Col. E, F ; C. I. 3028.

We have also ὄγδοος μήν mentioned in a late (funeral?) inscription, C. I. 3005 ; and δωδέκατος μήν in a decree of the age of Commodus, No. ccccLXXXIII *b*. These two instances confirm the statement of Corsini (Fast. Att. ii, 464 foll.) that the Asiatic Greeks occasionally called their months by their numerical order in the Calendar (compare Clinton, Fasti Hell. iii, Appendix, ch. 4, p. 380). The same thing was done in Phokis (see Part ii, p. 20), and elsewhere (see Hermann, Monatskunde, p. 12 ; C. I. 3892).

Hermann (Monatskunde, pp. 123 foll.) in addition to the months named above, includes also in the Ephesian Calendar Ἀπατουρεών and Καλαμαιών. For Ἀπατουρεών I can find no epigraphical or other evidence, and Ahrens omits it when speaking of the Ephesian Calendar in his contributions Zur Griechischen Monatskunde, Rhein. Museum, XVII (1862) pp. 355 foll. Similarly Bischoff, Leipz. Studien, VII (1884), p. 397. Καλαμαιών is a faulty conjecture of Böckh, C. I. 2953 *b*, which inscription is not Ephesian (see p. 67 *note*, and Homolle, Bulletin de Corr. Hell. v, 1881, pp. 25 foll.).

As to (3) it is certain that the Ephesian year did not begin with our January. In the Salutaris decree the First document is dated *Ἐπὶ π[ρυτ]άνεω[ς] T]ιβ. Κλ. Ἀντιπάτρου Ἰουλ[ι]ανοῦ, μη[νὸ]ς] Ποσιδεῶνος ί ἱσταμένου.* Now the sixth Posideon would correspond to the end of December. The Seventh document is dated *Σέξτῳ Ἀττίῳ Σουβουρανῷ τὸ β΄ Μάρκῳ Ἀσινίῳ Μαρκέλλῳ ὑπάτοις* (i.e. A.D. 104) *πρὸ η΄ καλανδῶν Μαρτίων, ἐπὶ πρυτάνεως Τιβ. Κλαυδίου Ἀντιπάτρου Ἰουλιανοῦ, | μηνὸς Ἀνθεσ-*

So that Julianus who was prytanis in December is still prytanis in the following February, the prytanis being the Ephesian Eponymus. Indeed we have in C. I. 3957 *b* what amounts almost to proof of the fact that at least in later times the Ephesian year began on September 24: see Marquardt, Röm. Alt. iv, p. 177 *note*; Waddington, Fastes des Provinces Asiatiques, p. 20. If so, we may arrange the Ephesian months, as far as they are known, in the following conjectural order.

EPHESIAN.	ATTIC.	ENGLISH.
1. Νεοκαισαρεών (?)	Bœdromion	September. October.
2. Unknown	Pyanepsion	October. November.
3. Μαιμακτηριών (?)	Maimakterion	November. December.
4. Ποσιδεών	Posideon	December. January.
5. Ληναιών	Gamelion	January. February.
6. Ἀνθεστηριών	Anthesterion	February. March.
7. Ἀρτεμισιών	Elaphebolion	March. April.
8. Unknown ὀγδοος μήν	Mounychion	April. May.
9. Θαργηλιών	Thargelion	May. June.
10. Unknown	Skirophorion	June. July.
11. Unknown	Hekatombaion	July. August.
12. Μεταγειτνιών, δωδέκατος μήν	Metageitonion	August. September.

Of doubtful position, Ἀγππαίων.

EPHESIAN GAMES AND FESTIVALS.

The following agonistic festivals will be found named in the inscriptions:—

1. Ἁδριάνεια, or Ἁδριάνεια Ὀλύμπια, or Ὀλύμπια ἐν Ἐφέσῳ: held every fourth year like its great original (C. I. 2987 *b*), and celebrated with contests both musical (C. I. 2810, 3208, No. DCIV) and athletic (C. I. 2999, 3000, 3209). Hadrian was commonly worshipped as Olympian Zeus, and games in his honour were therefore styled Ὀλύμπια (Krause, Olymp. p. 202, note 1). Later on however the local celebration of the Olympia at Ephesos must have been made independent of the Ephesian Hadrianeia; for in an Attic inscription of A.D. 250–300 a κῆρυξ enumerates among his victories side by side Ὀλύμπια ἐν Ἐφέσῳ β΄, Βαρβίλληα ἐν Ἐφέσῳ β΄, Ἁδριάνεια ἐν Ἐφέσῳ (C. I. A. iii, 129).

2. Ἀρτεμίσια (Ἀρτεμείσια, Ἀρτεμίσηα); or, more fully, τὰ μεγάλα ἱερὰ Ἀρτεμίσια: held every year in the month Artemision, on which we have a well-known decree, No. CCCCLXXXII. As I have never found this festival named in other than Ephesian inscriptions, I suppose it to have been more famous as a gathering for religion and pleasure than for its games. It certainly however comprised athletic (Nos. LV, DXV) and probably musical competitions. One also of the agonistic inscriptions (No. DCVI) will be seen to be in honour of a boy named Σαρπηδών from Akmonia in Phrygia, παῖς κωμῳδός, who had won a prize for his acting (τῆς περὶ τὴν ὑπόκρισιν ἐμπειρίας) at the Artemisia; it appears therefore that the Artemisia included dramatic competitions also.

3. Βαρβίλληα (Βαρβίλλεια) ἐν Ἐφέσῳ, occasionally Βαλβίλληα, and once (perhaps by mistake, C. I. A. iii, No. 127) Βαρβύ(λ)λεια: a very famous festival, to judge from its frequent mention in agonistic lists from various parts of Greece (see Index to C. I., and to C. I. A. vol. iii). It included athletic and musical contests. Whether it was quinquennial or not, does not appear: of its origin I shall have to speak in dealing with the agonistic inscription, No. DCV.

4. Ἐπινίκεια ἐν Ἐφέσῳ, mentioned only in one of the agonistic lists, No. DCXV, where see notes.

5. Ἐφέσηα (Ἐφέσεια), or Ἐφέσηα τὰ μεγάλα, or τὰ μεγάλα Ἐφέσηα ἱερὰ ἰσελαστικά, celebrated every fourth year, and comprising both athletic and musical competitions. Guhl (Ephesiaca, p. 116) identifies the Ἐφέσεια with the Ἀρτεμίσια as if the identification needed no proof. But in one agonistic list (No. DCV) the κοινὰ Ἀσίας ἐν Ἐφέσῳ, the Μεγάλα Ἐφέσεια and the Ἀρτεμίσια ἐν Ἐφέσῳ are named side by side as if quite distinct. I think it possible however (though there is no evidence for the conjecture) that the Ἀρτεμίσια was a mere local festival confined to the province of Asia, but that every fourth year it was celebrated with exceptional splendour as the Ἐφέσεια, with contests which brought competitors from all parts of Greece.

6. Κοινὰ Ἀσίας ἐν Ἐφέσῳ: a quinquennial festival, comprising athletic, and probably musical contests (C. I. 1720). It was held in turn in the different cities that were seats of the common cultus (Monceaux, De Communi Asiæ, p. 56; Lightfoot, Ignatius and Polycarp, ii, p. 987). This festival I would identify with ἀγῶνες τοῦ Σεβαστοῦ at Ephesos mentioned C. I. 2961 *b*.

At what time of year these festivals were held we do not know, except in the case of the Artemisia. It appears from Nos. DCXX and DCXXI that gladiatorial shows formed part of the attractions of the κοινὰ Ἀσίας: compare notes on No. DCLXX.

Besides the festivals which comprised contests and exhibitions, there were other festivals in honour of the deities chiefly worshipped at Ephesos. Thus Guhl enumerates the Ταύρεια in honour of Poseidon (p. 122), Thesmophoria in honour of Demeter (p. 123; see Herod. vi, 16); and naturally assumes that the Ephesian month Lenæon was so named from a celebration of the Λήναια in honour of Dionysos (p. 128). We are expressly told by Herodotos (i, 147) that the Ephesians and Kolophonians alone among all the Ionian states did not celebrate the Ἀπατούρια—κατὰ φόνου τινὰ σκῆψιν. But whatever the legendary account may have been, this exclusion probably dated from the time when the Ephesian colonists formally placed themselves under the protection of the Asiatic deity afterwards known as the Ephesian Artemis. The Apaturia was the family festival of Athens and her daughter states; and how could a colony that had forgotten Athenè, any longer keep the Apaturia? (see E. Curtius, Ephesos, p. 13.)

Besides the festivals already named, we find also at Ephesos certain solemnities mentioned under the title of Mysteries (μυστήρια). A careful comparison of all the passages, whether of authors or of inscriptions, which speak of mysteries at Ephesos, enables us to classify these celebrations as follows :—
(1) Strabo, xiv, p. 640, describes a mystery-festival celebrated on Mount Solmissos, of which the birth of Artemis formed the central subject. It was managed by a college of priests called Κουρῆτες, who are mentioned in No. CCCCXLIX, and their πρωτοκουρής in No. DXCVI b. It is this festival which is probably referred to in No. DXCVII and C. I. 3002. The latter document speaks of the munificence of a certain Ulpia Evodia Mudianè, and implies that the celebration of the festival in part depended upon the liberality of the principal Ephesians. If No. CCCCLXXXIII refers, as is probable, to the same festival, then in the reign of Commodus it had for some time been in abeyance, and was publicly revived by help of funds furnished by the gerousia (see p. 77). From another inscription (No. DXCVI a) we infer that private munificence was drawn upon for the celebration.
(2) A letter addressed to the proconsul of Asia, L. Mestius Florus, A. D. 83–84 (quoted from a copy of Cyriacus, on No. DVI) informs us that there was at Ephesos a yearly celebration of the mysteries of Demeter, which had from olden times been held with the approval of 'kings and emperors and the yearly proconsuls.' With this agrees the language of Strabo (xiv, p. 633), which implies that the Athenian colonists brought with them to Ephesos the worship of the Eleusinian Demeter. He states that the descendants of Androklos still retained, amongst other privileges, the supervision of the Eleusinian festival : καὶ ἔτι νῦν οἱ ἐκ τοῦ γένους ὀνομάζονται βασιλεῖς ἔχοντές τινας τιμάς, προεδρίαν τε ἐν ἀγῶσι καὶ πορφύραν ἐπίσημον τοῦ βασιλικοῦ γένους, σκίπωνα ἀντὶ σκήπτρου, καὶ τὰ ἱερὰ τῆς Ἐλευσινίας Δήμητρος. Whether this rule was observed in the later times of the Empire is doubtful. Nothing appears of it in No. DVI, where the mysteries of Demeter seem to be alluded to. Some further information is afforded by No. DXCV, which proves that in the times of the Antonines the festival was conducted by a thiasos of Demetriasts, which comprised a priest (ἱερεύς), a hierophant, and a manager (ἐπιμελητὴς τῶν μυστηρίων). There must have been a temple of Demeter at Ephesos, but its locality is unknown. The phrase however in No. DXCV. οἱ πρὸ πόλεως Δημητριασταί, implies that it was outside the walls of the city; (see p. 218 post). The same inscription proves that the myth of Demeter at Ephesos associated Dionysos with the goddess, just as Iacchos at Eleusis (see Part i, p. 177).
(3) That a mystery-festival in honour of Dionysos was held at Ephesos we know from Plutarch (Ant. 27), who speaks of the way in which the citizens and ladies of Ephesos welcomed Antonius as Dionysos, themselves dressed in costume as Fauns, Satyrs, and Bacchants. I have quoted this passage of Plutarch to illustrate No. DC, which may be connected with a similar worship of the Emperor Hadrian as a new Dionysos. The month Lenæon at Ephesos itself

implies a celebration of the Lenæa. The wild procession of maskers described as the καταγώγιον in the Martyrdom of St. Timothy (Phot. Bibl. cod. 254), appears to have more resemblance to a Dionysiac celebration than to the rites of Artemis or of Demeter (see Hermann, Gottesd. Alterthümer, §§ 66, 67); though Lobeck (Aglaoph. i, p. 177) assigns it to Artemis, and Athenæos, p. 394 F, describes καταγώγια at Eryx in honour of Aphrodite.

The office of neopoies or neopoios, although unknown at Athens, was common enough in other parts of Greece, especially in Asia Minor. Already on No. CCCCXIII ante I have spoken of this office at Priene. At Halikarnassos the decree about appointing a priestess of Artemis Pergæa is dated Ἐπὶ νεωποίου Χαρμύλου (C. I. 2656); he may have been the chairman of a board. At Paros (C. I. 2396) the singular is used, to date a dedication, [Ἐ]πὶ νεωποῦ κ.τ.λ. At Aphrodisias (C. I. 2811) we find an ἀρχινεωποιὸν νεωποιῶν τῆς ἐπιφανεστάτης θεοῦ Ἀφροδείτης (compare C. I. 2812, and Waddington-Le Bas, Part v, No. 1596 bis) who has been superintending certain games. From C. I. 2749 this board appears to have been five in number, and they are described laying out the funds of the goddess in buildings. In C. I. 2824, 2826, 2848 it is specified upon tombs that if the heirs of the testator do not fulfil his directions concerning the sepulchre, certain fines shall be payable to the goddess Aphrodite which οἱ κατὰ τὸν καιρὸν νεωποιοί shall recover. At Teos [οἱ ν]εωποῖ[αι] are named in connexion with the temple of Dionysos (C. I. 3062). At Iasos (C. I. 2671) οἱ νεωποῖαι are to inscribe a decree either in the temple of Zeus or of Artemis : at another time (C. I. 2678) they are to inscribe a decree 'in the agora.' In C. I. 2673, 2675, 2677, also from Iasos, ὁ νεωποίης, who must be the chairman of the board, is instructed to inscribe decrees. At Magnesia ad Mæandrum (C. I. 2917) there seems to have been a board.

These examples show what the functions of the neopoioi were; viz. to take care of the fabric and repairs of a temple ; to superintend any addition to its fabric, such as the setting up of inscriptions ; and in some cases (as at Aphrodisias) to take charge of its revenues. At Ephesos the board of neopoioi is frequently mentioned, and naturally they held an important office in having the charge of the fabric of the Artemision. In the series of decrees of the Macedonian time (CCCCXLVII, foll.) οἱ νεωποῖαι are uniformly entrusted with the duty of inscribing decrees in the temple: similarly in No. CCCCXLVII, line 21. Also in Nos. CCCCXLIX and CCCCLXX the neopoiai apply to the boulè (at the instance of the gerousia and ἐπίκλητοι established by Lysimachos) to ask for honours to be granted to persons who have deserved well of the goddess. It is observable that in these earlier inscriptions the word is always spelt νεωποῖαι (from νεωποίης). In the inscriptions of the imperial times the spelling is always νεωποιοί, νεσποιεῖν, &c.   Böckh on C. I. 2810 from Aphrodisias, speaking of documents of Roman times, says ' locis prope omnibus *ΝΕΟΠΟΙΟΣ* est in schedis ex quibus Aphrodisiensia edidi :' but he everywhere corrects it into νεωποιὸς.   The evidence from Aphrodisias is certainly conflicting : but the uniform witness of the Ephesian marbles in favour of νεσποιοί proves that Böckh was wrong in correcting all his copies into νεωποιοί (see C. I. 2782, 2785, 2795, 2837, &c.)*.   From No. DLXXVIII it appears that the board at Ephesos numbered twelve members, two being chosen annually from each tribe ; the first member from the first tribe ('Εφεσεῖς) gave his name to their year (*ibid.*).   Similarly at Iasos the νεωποῖαι were appointed one from each tribe (Hellen. Journal, viii, 1887, p. 105).   The election of neopoioi seems to have been made by the ekklesia (see No. DLXX).   The office was one of some dignity and also of a sacred character, and is accordingly very often mentioned, especially in ex votos and dedications (Nos. DLXVI, foll.).   At Samos likewise the νεωποῖαι repeatedly made dedications to Hera : see note on No. DLXVI.   It is probable that the neopoioi, although theirs was not a liturgy but a magistracy, were expected to be men of considerable means. At least it is clear from No. DLXXIX *b*, and from the similar document there cited from Waddington-Le Bas, that there were occasions when citizens volunteered to serve the office : οἴδε ἐνεσποίησαν . . . αὐθαίρετοι.   It is doubtful whether this merely arose through vacancies caused by death or resignation ; or whether it points to a lack of wealth or of public spirit.   The functions of the board at Ephesos partly appear from the examples already cited, and are further illustrated by the Salutaris bequest (No. CCCCLXXXI) ; where in lines 292 foll., and 391 foll. the neopoioi (or at least two of the board) are directed to accompany the procession of images from the pronaos of the Artemision, and to see that they are safely brought back to the temple.   Also in line 381 it is provided that when the images are cleaned by the proper functionary with plate-powder (ἀργυ-ρωματική), two of the neopoioi must be present.   The reason is obviously that these images formed part of the furniture of the temple, of which the neopoioi were wardens.

'Αγορανόμοι.

It may be assumed that the office of ἀγορανόμος was an important one.   In No. DLXXV it is held by a member of the gerousia, and in No. DLII by another person of some consequence.   In No. DLXXII the aorist ἀγο]ρανομή[σας shows that it was an annual office, and probably elective : so in No. DCCVIII, ἀγορα]νομή[σαντα.   No. DCLVI (see the note) speaks of a tomb being built πρὸς τὸ ἀγορανόμιν : the inscription is a late one, and we may suppose at that period the offices of the agoranomoi were somewhere on the north side of the city, between the north city-gate

and the Artemision.   The general duties of the office appear from the language of Aristotle (Politics vii,/8, § 3 = 1321 *b*, 12) πρῶτον μὲν οὖν ἐπιμέλεια τῶν ἀναγκαίων ἡ περὶ τὴν ἀγορὰν, ἐφ' ᾗ δεῖ τινα ἀρχὴν εἶναι τὴν ἐφορῶσαν περί τε τὰ συμβόλαια καὶ τὴν εὐκοσμίαν,—and he presently classes the ἀγορανόμοι with ἀστυνόμοι.   The decree of the third century in honour of Agathokles of Rhodes (No. CCCCLV) shows that the Ephesian agoranomos superintended the business of the market.   In this decree ὁ ἀγορανόμος is probably the chairman of the board : the market of Ephesos would be too important for one man to superintend it, and in other cities the plural number is used. At Olbia there were five agoranomoi (C. I. 2078); at Athens, Mesambria, Tralles there were two (Böckh, Staatsh. i, 70 ; C. I. 2053 ; Bulletin de Corr. Hell. i, 55).   As we do not hear of any ἀστυνόμοι at Ephesos, it is probable that the agoranomoi, besides being inspectors of the market, of weights and measures, and so on, were also responsible for the police of the streets as well as of the agora.

Στρατηγοί.

The strategoi appear, in the extant documents from Ephesos, solely in the character of civil magistrates.   In the decree respecting Mithradates, B.C. 86, (Waddington-Le Bas, No. 136*a*; Hicks, Manual, No. 205) they are named with the γραμματεὺς τῆς βουλῆς and the πρόεδροι as drafting a decree and proposing it to the ekklesia.   In the Salutaris decrees, A.D. 104, (No. CCCCLXXXI, lines 7, 307) the strategoi exercise the same function, but in company with the γραμματεὺς τοῦ δήμου alone.   They appear in the same connexion in No. CCCCLXXXII *b*, which is dated A. D. 160.   In No. DXXVIII, which is unhappily incomplete, the strategoi are again named in conjunction with the γραμματεὺς τοῦ δήμου as concerned in some contract for public works.   In other words, from the first century B.C. onwards, the strategoi at Ephesos, as in other Greek cities, were the chief civil magistrates. We have no information as to their number, but perhaps, as at Athens, it corresponded to the number of the tribes.   How early their office ceased to be concerned with warfare, we cannot exactly say.   The inscriptions show that at Prienè and at Erythræ the strategoi retained some relics of their original functions together with the powers of the chief civil magistrate (see p. 35 and p. 53 *an/c*).

Γραμματεὶς βουλῆς, γερουσίας, δήμου.

Already in discussing the character of the boulè and gerousia we have had occasion to speak of their γραμματεῖς.   They were themselves members of their respective boards, and possessed of considerable influence.   The γραμματεὺς τῆς βουλῆς is mentioned in the Salutaris bequest (No. CCCCLXXXI, lines 128, 187) and in No. DXCVI *b*.   The γραμματεὺς τῆς γερουσίας is named in Nos. CCCCLXXXVI, DLXXVII ; compare DLXXVII *a*.   The γραμματεὺς τοῦ

---

* Not less irregular is the form ΝΕΟΚΟΡΟΣ, in Nos. D. DXVII (where see notes).

δῆμου, at least in Roman times, was the most prominent of the three. For as the real vigour of the ekklesia declined in the atmosphere of imperial rule, while at the same time the forms of the free republic were retained, it was more and more left to the γραμματεύς to arrange the business of the public assembly. Together with the στρατηγοί he drafted the decrees to be proposed (Nos. CCCCLXXXI, lines 7, 289, 306; CCCCLXXXII b, CCCCXCIX, n). He has the decree engraved (No. CCCCLXXXI, line 300). He takes charge of money left to the people of Ephesos (ibid., line 193). His year of office dates a decree in the Emperor's letter (No. CCCCLXXXIX). Once he is styled ὁ Ἐφεσίων γραμματεύς (No. CCCCLXXXI, line 72). He also superintends the execution of works ordered by the people (Nos. DXXIX, DXXXIII). It is also plain that the γραμματεὺς τοῦ δήμου held a high position in the community: in No. D he holds the title of Asiarch (compare also Wood's Ephesus, Inscriptions from the Great Theatre, 3; and No. DXXVIII, where the γραμματεὺς τοῦ δήμου is also βασιλεύς). It is therefore one example the more of St. Luke's accuracy in speaking of titles, when in Acts xix, 35 foll., he describes the γραμματεύς as possessed of great influence with the assembly, and keenly sensible of his own responsibility.

Πρύτανις.

I have already pointed out (p. 72) that the Ephesian πρύτανις was the eponymous magistrate, and corresponded to the Athenian archon: see Nos. CCCCLXXVII, line 65, &c.; CCCCLXXXI, lines 1, [243], 285, 320; DXXVIII; DLXX; DLXXVIII b. No. DXCVI b exhibits a female prytanis, which proves that the office had long since become merely titular, and was practically a liturgy.

Ταμίαι τῆς πόλεως, ὁ οἰκονόμος.

Οἱ ταμίαι τῆς πόλεως are mentioned in one late sepulchral inscription DCXXXVI. It is remarkable that so little is said in the Ephesian inscriptions about any financial officers. The οἰκονόμος of Nos. CCCCXLVIII, CCCCLXIX was probably a subordinate official. The reason may be that the finances of the state and of the temple were administered by the gerousia.

Of the βούλαρχος I have spoken on p. 74: see No. DLXXXVI.

Ὁ Βασιλεύς.

Concerning ὁ βασιλεύς see No. DXXVIII, and the passage there cited from Strabo.

Παιδονόμος.

Ὁ παιδωνόμος (late form for παιδονόμος) is named in the Salutaris bequest, as exercising discipline over the sons of citizens when they appeared upon public occasions (No. CCCCLXXXI, lines 170, 174). The office is closely allied to that of the γυμνασίαρχος (C. I. 2885, 3185) and of the ἐφήβαρχος. The best exemplification of it is the decree from Stratonikeia (C. I. 2715) instituting a choir of boys. See also Aristotle, Politics, iv, 17, §§ 5. 7 = 1336 a, 32, 40; he

often classes the office with ἡ γυναικονομία, as ibid. vi, 15, § 13 = 1300 a, 4.

Ἔφηβοι, Ἐφήβαρχος.

We may suppose the ἔφηβοι at Ephesos to have been organized and instructed in one or more gymnasia (compare No. DCXVIII, line 18 and No. DCVI) in very much the same way as at Athens, although we have no such ample information from Ephesos, as is supplied by the Attic documents about the Ephebi (see Dittenberger, De Ephebis Atticis; Dumont, Essai sur l'Éphébie Attique). At Ephesos, as at Athens, the ephebi took a prominent part in the religious solemnities of the state; and they are frequently mentioned in the Salutaris bequest (No. CCCCLXXXI, lines 86, 90, 195; Frag. 1, 26). They were under the discipline and guidance of an Ephebarchos (Nos. CCCCLXXXI, line 153; DLXXIX a), corresponding apparently to the Kosmetes of the Attic gymnasium. The Kosmetes was responsible for the discipline and instruction of the ephebi, and on all occasions of state he was their head and representative. His position has been compared to that of the Head of a College in an English University, only his office was annual, and it usually involved a heavy expenditure.

Γυμνασίαρχος.

The number of the Gymnasiarchs is uncertain, and may have varied from time to time. The duties of a Gymnasiarch were financial rather than disciplinary; he had to administer the funds available for the expenses of the gymnasium. These funds were partly furnished by the state, partly by private individuals, but largely also by himself. The office was therefore one of high dignity. In No. D we hear of τῶν] γυμνασιαρχούντων … γυμνασιαρχίας. From No. DLXXXVII b it appears as if one of the Gymnasiarchs was always a member of the gerousia: possibly he was nominated by that body to administer funds voted by the gerousia for the gymnasium. Perhaps we should restore in No. DLII [γυμν]ασίαρχον. One chief expense was the supplying of oil: in many inscriptions accordingly benefactors are praised as ἀλείψαντες the members of the gymnasium, i. e. they had supplied oil at their own expense (see Böckh on C. I. 3616, 3617, 3643, &c.).

Ἀγωνοθέται.

Passing from the gymnasium, which existed for the due education of young citizens, to the athletic contests connected with the public games, we hear of other offices allied to those just mentioned, but yet distinct. An Agonothetes was appointed for each of the agonistic festivals; his duty was to direct and control the actual contests, to keep discipline, and to superintend the award of prizes. Already in this volume we have found the ἀγωνοθέτης of the Dionysia at Prienè (No. CCCCXIII. &c.) and Samothrace (No. CCCCXLIV), and of the Antiocheia at Laodikeia (No. CCCCXX), charged with a proclamation to be made at the games. The Agonothetæ of the various festivals at Ephesos (see p. 79) will frequently be mentioned in the inscriptions that follow.

Πανηγυριάρχης.

Besides the Agonothetes who was concerned with the athletic and other contests, there was a πανηγυριάρχης who superintended the celebration of the festival as a whole. This office is not unfrequently named. Like the ἀγωνοθέτης, the πανηγυριάρχης of a festival was a considerable contributor to its expenses. But it was exceptional for one man to act in both capacities, as did T. Æl. Marcianus Priscus at the Artemision A.D. 160: see No. CCCCLXXXII ℓ where he is styled ἀγωνοθέτην καὶ πα[νηγυριάρχην τ]ῶν μεγάλων Ἀρτ[εμισίων, καὶ] πρῶτον αὐτ[ὸν ποιήσαντα] τὴν πανήγυριν κατὰ τέλεια[ν] κ.τ.λ.

Ἀλείπτης.

In No. DCXI a grateful athlete records, after his victories, the name of his ἀλείπτης, i. e. his trainer. The ἀλείπτης, a paid instructor of athletes, must not be confused with the benefactors of gymnasia who are often termed οἱ ἀλείψαντες (see p. 82).

THE HIERARCHY OF THE ARTEMISION.

I have reserved to the last that portion of the subject which is most likely to stimulate curiosity, although it has received the least attention. The inner organisation of any Greek temple would be an interesting subject for inquiry; but the Ephesian worship has the peculiar interest of uniting in itself both oriental and Hellenic ideas. Partly, perhaps, because of this fact, the worship of Artemis at Ephesos in the first two centuries of our era showed few signs of decline. When St. Paul began teaching at Ephesos, A. D. 55, the Artemis-worship was living, active and enthusiastic. For the moment indeed his spiritual influence alarmed the vested interests of paganism (Acts xix, 26 foll.). But we may regard the Salutaris bequest fifty years later (A. D. 104) and the elaborate provisions connected with it, as marking a reaction against Christianity, which shows no symptom of abatement until perhaps half a century later (A.D. 161, No. CCCCLXXXII).

Long before the Ionian migration* there was a spot in the valley of the Kaÿster, about five miles from the sea, which was sacred to the Ephesian goddess. Two small streams, known to the Greeks afterwards as the Kenchreios and Selinus, flow past it northwards to join the Kaÿster, on either side of a hill which Mr. Wood was inclined to identify with Mount Solmissos. A fortress crowned the hill and protected the shrine below. The shrine, which stood in a grove of trees, was in the hands of a priesthood certainly of oriental, perhaps of Phœnician origin; for the Ephesian goddess was from first to last an oriental divinity. Her image was a many-breasted, hideous idol, reminding us of the monstrous forms of Indian superstition; and under this form she was adored as the mother of life, the nourisher of the creatures of earth, air and sea. About her temple in the valley dwelt the tillers of the soil, paying dues and owing allegiance to their tutelary goddess, and governed by her priesthood (Pausan. vii, 2, § 4: φασουν δὲ καὶ περὶ τὸ ἱερὸν ἄλλοι τε Λεσσίας ἔνεσα καὶ γυναῖκες τοῦ Ἀμαζόνων γένους). Nothing now marks the spot, except a mean village, which still entombs in its Turkish name Ayasoluk (i. c. Ἅγιος Θεολόγος) the memories of St. John the Divine.

We can imagine what ensued upon the Ionian migration. When the legendary Kodrids under Androklos brought their ships to the mouth of the Kaÿster, and driving back the native inhabitants, founded an Hellenic city upon the neighbouring hills Koressos and Pion, the strange worship of the ancient temple, with its emasculate priests and vestal priestesses and other singular features, must have interested them and perhaps repelled them. By degrees the western settlers grew more familiar with the worship; they fancied they could discern in the Ephesian goddess a likeness to their own Artemis. And while they thus lent to the oriental cultus the new charm of Hellenic imagination, they gained for their infant city the distinction and the security of an immemorial shrine, and an inviolable sanctuary (Pausan. vii, 2, § 5: τοῖς δὲ περὶ τὸ ἱερὸν οἰκοῦσι δεῖμα ἦν οὐδὲν κ.τ.λ.). Hither therefore the Ephesian Greeks transferred the legend of Leto's travail; here, they insisted, and not at Delos, was the birthplace of Artemis (Tacit. Ann. iii, 61; compare Nos. CCCCLXXXII, CCCCXLIX). Here accordingly, about a mile's distance N. E. of the city walls, Artemis with her strange priesthood flourished, while Ephesos lived through its long history. For whatever fortunes befell the city, the Artemision was always safe. Xerxes spared it alone of the temples of Greece (Strabo, xiv. p. 634); and Augustus, though he might limit, did not venture to question, its rights of sanctuary (Nos. DXXIII, foll.). As early as the sixth century a temple on a large scale was begun, which, though helped on by the gifts of Krœsos (he gave most of the columns), it took a century to finish (No. DXVIII). Burnt down on the night that Alexander the Great was born, its rebuilding was not complete when he crossed the Ægean (No. CCCCXCIX autc), although all Asia contributed to the restoration (No. DXIX). Two roads led from the city to the shrine, through the Magnesian gate and another (No. CCCCLXXXI, lines 402–405), both roads being favourite sites for tombs. The road however from the Magnesian gate was the most frequented; and its solid marble pavement, thirty-five feet wide, was found deeply worn by wheels into four distinct ruts, testifying to the once busy traffic between the temple and the town (Wood's Discoveries at Ephesus, p. 114). At a mile's distance was the temenos, surrounded with a ring-wall by order of Augustus (Nos. DXXIII, foll.). The pilgrim passed within the temenos, and before him stood the famous temple, entered at the east end through a forest of columns, which were adorned with an oriental magnificence, with life-sized figures in relief: some important fragments of these sculptured columnæ are now in the British Museum. The temple was rich in lands (No. DLXXVII), in fisheries

---

* Pausan. vii, 2, § 4 : πολλῷ δὲ πρεσβύτερα ἔτι ἢ κατὰ Ἴωνας τὰ ἐς τὴν Ἄρτεμιν τὴν Ἐφεσίων ἐστίν.

(No. IIII), and bequests (No. CCCCLXXXI); and was served by a numerous body of sacred officers[c].

It was E. Curtius who first attempted (in his *Beiträge*, p. 9, and *Ephesos*, p. 6) to illustrate the position of the Artemis-worship at Ephesos by comparing with it the temple and priesthood of Ma which existed both at Komana in Kappadokia and Komana in Pontus. In both of these towns, as at Ephesos, there flourished a worship evidently non-Hellenic in origin, however much it was afterwards Hellenized. Here also were numerous and powerful hierarchies, analogous to the priesthood of the Artemision. Strabo, who gives our only information of the two Komanas and their worship, was himself a native of Pontus and connected by family with the old Pontic kings; and one of his ancestors, Dorylaos, had been advanced by his friend Mithradates the Great to the high-priesthood of Ma (xii, 557): so that his statements on this subject are of exceptional interest and value. He tells us that the priest of Ma at either Komana occupied a very important position, and stood second in the country only to the king; and in Kappadokian Komana the priest usually belonged to the royal house. The priest was landlord of a large extent of sacred lands, and ruled with almost absolute sway (like some medieval abbot) over an enormous retinue of temple-ministers and serfs (ἱερόδουλοι), numbering over six thousand in all, of both sexes. The priest and the priestess of Ma lived within the temenos; and besides other rules of sanctity, no swine were admitted into the precinct. To this important priesthood the appointment seems to have been made by the king, and often therefore for political reasons; such at least was the case with Dorylaos, Archelaos, and Kleon mentioned by Strabo (xii, 557-8, 574-5, respecting Pontic Komana; xi, 521, xii, 535, concerning the other Komana). It is obvious that in many points the singular establishment at either Komana throws light upon the Artemision at Ephesos. There was a time, and that not very remote, when the Megabyzos or chief priest of Artemis held a position hardly second to the 'king' (βασιλεύς) of the Greek colony (see No. DXXVIII). And in the days of the Ephesian republic the hierarchy of Artemis formed a compact body, with power only inferior to the civic authority of the state. Of course Hera at Samos or Argos, Asklepios at Epidauros, Dionysos at Teos, Athena at Priene or in her own Athens, were each in a sense supreme in their several cities. But in all these cases the priesthood formed part of the body of citizens, and what we may call Church and State were one and the same. But at Ephesos, although Artemis was to her birth-place all that Athena was to Athens, yet her priestly retinue had a status and a tradition independent of the Ionian colony, and no

lapse of years sufficed to obliterate all traces of the fact.

As at Komana, so at Ephesos, many, if not all, of the temple ministers lived about the Artemision. Mr. Wood traced certain buildings within the temenos, 'for seven hundred feet in a straight line running eastward,' which he thought were the dwellings of the priests (Ephesus, p. 149). And though there is no evidence that the Ephesian establishment can be compared in point of number with the six thousand of Komana, yet the inscriptions reveal to us a numerous body of sacred officials, with an elaborate organization. This will best be seen from a review of the various titles mentioned in our inscriptions or elsewhere.

Μεγάβυζοι.

Strabo (xiv, p. 641) writes of the Artemision: ἱερέας δ᾽ εὐνούχους εἶχον οὓς ἐκάλουν Μεγαβύζους, καὶ ἀλλαχόθεν μετιόντες ἀεί τινας ἀξίους τῆς τοιαύτης προστασίας, καὶ ἦγον ἐν τιμῇ μεγάλῃ· συνιεράσθαι δὲ τούτοις ἐχρῆν παρθένους. νυνὶ δὲ τὰ μὲν φυλάττεται τῶν νομίμων τὰ δ᾽ ἧττον, ἄσυλον δὲ μένει τὸ ἱερὸν καὶ νῦν καὶ πρότερον. In other words the priesthood of Artemis consisted of a number of vestals, presided over by a eunuch-priest. Strabo's words do not necessarily imply that there was only one at a time, and this agrees well with the expression προστασίας. Xenophon (Anab. v, 3, §§ 6, 7) speaks of only one. We may be sure that the office was never held by a Greek; each Megabyzos was imported from abroad, and usually from Persia: hence the name, which seems to have been a titular name, like Cæsar, etc. But this strange priesthood survived until late times; Pliny, N. H. xxxv, § 93 (compare § 132) names it in connexion with Apelles; Plutarch with Alexander the Great, Alex. 42: Plautus, Bacchides ii, 3, 74 names it in a play from Philemon, i. e. of the third century B.C.; Appian (Bell. Civ. v, 9) in connexion with the sojourn of Antony and Cleopatra at Ephesos; later than this we cannot for certain trace it, and Strabo seems to imply that its most repulsive features were a thing of the past (compare Bernays, Die Heraklitischen Briefe, pp. 107, 8). Quintilian however still used the word Megabyzus as a proper name for an eunuch (Inst. Or. v, 12, § 21); in Lucian, Timon, § 22, the word is intended to convey associations of authority.

Vestal priestesses.

The priestesses of Artemis, over whom the Megabyzos presided, are called by Strabo (l. c.) πάρθενοι or Vestals. A curious passage of Plutarch (An seni sit gerenda resp., 795, 34 Reiske) compares them with the Vestal Virgins, and certainly implies that they were not only numerous but also well organized. It

[c] We are tempted to supplement our scanty information by drawing upon the descriptions of Ephesos in the last three books of Achilles Tatius, who has a great deal to say about the temple of Artemis. But I doubt whether this late romancer says anything true of the Artemision which would not be true of any other temple; and his account of the ordeal of the virgins of Artemis in the eighth book is probably a mere invention. The account in Xenophon Ephesius (i, 2) of the procession at the Artemisia is also very general, but may be more authentic: ἤγετο δὲ τῆς Ἀρτέμιδος ἐπιχώριος ἑορτὴ ἀπὸ τῆς πόλεως ἐπὶ τὸ ἱερὸν στάδια δὲ ἦσαν ἑπτά (this is about the true distance) ἔδει δὲ πομπεύειν πάσας τὰς ἐπιχωρίους παρθένους κεκοσμημένας πολυτελῶς καὶ τοὺς ἐφήβους κ.τ.λ. I have preferred however to take nothing from such slippery authorities.

runs thus: καθόλου δὲ ὥσπερ ἐν 'Ρώμῃ ταῖς 'Εστιάσι παρθένοις τοῦ χρόνου διάρισται, τὸ μὲν μανθάνειν, τὸ δὲ δρᾶν τὰ νενομισμένα, τὸ δὲ τρίτον ἤδη διδάσκειν καὶ τῶν ἐν 'Εφέσῳ περὶ τὴν 'Αρτεμιν ὁμοίως ἑκάστην Μελλιέρην τὸ πρῶτον, εἶθ' 'Ιέρην, τὸ δὲ τρίτον Παριέρην καλοῦσιν· οὕτως ὁ τελέως πολιτικὸς ἀνὴρ τὰ μὲν πρῶτα μανθάνων ἔτι πολιτεύεσθαι καὶ μυσθούμενος, τὰ δ' ἔσχατα διδάσκων καὶ μυσταγωγῶν κ.τ.λ. We may translate the three words by 'Novice,' 'Priestess,' 'Senior.' The form ἱέρη, for ἱέρεα (ἱέρεια), is unusual; but it occurs in inscriptions from Kertch (C. I. 2108) and from Ephesos (C. I. 3003). It was further supposed by Guhl (Ephesiaca, p. 108) that these vestals of Artemis were termed Μέλισσαι. For this statement I find no positive evidence; although the bee, as the symbol of chastity, of organization and of beneficent industry, enters often into the religious ideas of Greece, and Lactantius expressly states that certain priestesses of the Great Mother were called Melissæ (Inst. i, 22): so also Hesychios s.v. Μέλισσαι, and E. Curtius, Ephesos, p. 36.

'Εσσῆνες.

Whether the title Μέλισσαι was known at Ephesos or not, the bee was the regular type on the Ephesian coins (see Mr. Head's Coinage of Ephesus), and an important college of priests at the Artemision was entitled οἱ 'Εσσῆνες. Perhaps the title was of oriental, and even of Semitic origin, and Bp. Lightfoot (Colossians, p. 96) may be wrong in considering its resemblance to the name of the Jewish sect of Essenes to be entirely accidental. Popular etymology however derived the word from ἐσμός, and connected it with the type on the coins, with the meaning of 'king-bee.' The Essenes are often named in the inscriptions. Neither their number nor mode of appointment is known. Their office was not for life (No. DLXXVIII c, ἐσσηνεύσας), but for one year only (Pausan. viii, 13, § 1). From what is told us of their duties we gather that they formed a connecting link between the hierarchy and the civic life of Ephesos. It was the Essenes who 'drew the lot that determined the Tribe and the Thousand of a newly admitted citizen: it was as if the goddess herself, by their hands, welcomed him into her city and assigned him his place within it (Nos. CCCCLVII, CCCCLVII, CCCCLXVII). The phrase ran: ἐπικληρῶσαι δὲ αὐτὸν τοὺς 'Εσσῆνας εἰς φυλὴν καὶ χιλιαστύν. In many of the decrees of politeia ἐπικληρῶσαι is used without an expressed subject, and we must understand τοὺς 'Εσσῆνας. In No. CCCCXLVIII they are instructed to offer a sacrifice to Artemis (θύειν εὐαγγέλια) in the name of the state. During their year of office they had to maintain, in various respects, a ceremonial purity; and it was they who superintended the banquets at the Artemision which followed the sacrifices at the Artemisia. This we learn from Pausanias (viii, 13, § 1), whose statement appears the more authentic since the Ionic form ἱστιάτορας gives it local colouring: 'Εν δὲ τῇ χώρᾳ τῇ 'Ορχομενίων ... τὸ ἱερὸν ἐστι τῆς 'Υμνίας 'Αρτέμιδος * * καὶ ἱέρειαν καὶ ἄνδρα ἱερέα. τούτοις οὐ μόνον τὰ ἐς τὰς μίξεις ἀλλὰ καὶ ἐς τὰ ἄλλα ἀγιστεύειν καθέστηκε τὸν χρόνον τοῦ

βίου πάντα, καὶ οὔτε λουτρὰ οὔτε δίαιτα λοιπὴ κατὰ τὰ αὐτὰ σφίσι καθὰ καὶ τοῖς πολλοῖς ἐστιν, οὐδὲ ἐς οἰκίαν παρίασιν ἀνδρὸς ἰδιώτου. τοιαῦτα οἶδα ἕτερα ἐνιαυτὸν καὶ οὐ πρόσω 'Εφεσίαν ἐπιτηθεύοντας τοὺς τῇ 'Αρτέμιδι ἱστιάτορας γινομένους, καλουμένους δὲ ὑπὸ τῶν πολιτῶν 'Εσσῆνας.

Κουρῆτες.

Οἱ Κουρῆτες also formed a priestly college connected with the worship of the Ephesian Artemis: their origin is discussed on No. CCCCXLIX: and a πρωτοκουρής, presumably the head of the college, is named in No. DXCVI b.

'Η ἱέρεια τῆς 'Αρτέμιδος. 'Ιερεῖς.

As the Μεγάβυζος was the chief priest of Artemis, so there was also one priestess distinctively called ἡ ἱέρεια τῆς 'Αρτέμιδος: No. CCCCLXXXI, line 162. In Nos. DLVI(?), DLXXI, DLXXIII we read of ἱερεῖς, who were probably priests of Artemis, but their status is not defined.

Χρυσοφόροι, ἱερονεῖκαι.

A certain number of the priests enjoyed the privilege of wearing gold (compare Nos. CCCCXXVI, CCCCXXVII ante); and as such are classed with the ἱερονεῖκαι or victors at the (Artemisian?) games who were similarly privileged. This appears from the following passages: No. CCCCLXXXI, lines 308 foll. ἐπεὶ οἱ χρυσοφοροῦντες τῇ θεῷ ἱερεῖς καὶ ἱερονεῖκαι ὑπέσχ(ο)ντο κ.τ.λ.; lines 327 foll. τ[οῖς χ]ρυσοφορ[ο]ῦσι τῇ θεῷ 'Αρτέμιδι ἱερ]εῦσίν καὶ ἱερονείκαις πρὸ πόλεως. So C. I. 2963 c, a dedication to Hadrian by Οἱ τὸν ... κόσμον βαστά[ζοντες] τῆς μεγάλης θεᾶς ['Αρτέμι]δος πρὸ πόλ[εω]ς ἱερεῖς [καὶ ἱερ]ονεῖκαι. These appear to have formed a college of themselves, and are described in brief as οἱ χρυσο[φόροι] or χρυσο[φοροῦντες], No. CCCCLXXXI, line 290, which is evidently synonymous with the longer title: while in line 399 the same body is referred to as οἱ ἱερονεῖκαι. It is easy after this to see why a χρυσ]οφόρ[ος is classed with two ἱερεῖς in No. DLXXI, and we can identify the body described in Nos. DCIV, DCXVIII b, as χρυσοφόροι.

'Ακροβάται.

Another order were the ἀκροβάται, whom the present text of Hesychios wrongly calls ἀκριτοβάται s.v. We learn from No. CCCCLXXXI, lines 374–6, that they were twenty in number; and Hesychios says their office was sacrificial. It has been suggested to me to connect this peculiar title with the small bronze figures usually called Lares, which represent a boy moving on tiptoe and holding up a rhyton to pour wine on an altar. The Kouretes who watched over Rhea and the infant Zeus are also represented on tiptoe, and at Ephesos we have Kouretes of Leto and Artemis.

'Ιεροί.

In several inscriptions we hear of another order or grade of temple ministers who may have been numerous at Ephesos. These were the ἱεροί, a title common in other parts of Greece. In No. DLXXXIX *a* we read : 'Ἐπὶ ἀργυρώματος... νίδου ἱεροῦ, and again in *b* : Σπονδοποιοῦντος Θεοπόμπου ἱεροῦ. Also in DLXXVIII : Σπονδοποιοῦντος Θεοπόμπου ἡ τοῦ Μενεκράτους, ἱεροῦ. There is no doubt as to the civic status held by the hieroi at Ephesos ; this is proved (as Menadier points out, pp. 9 foll.) by the enumeration of inhabitants in the Mithradates decree (Waddington-Le Bas, 136 *a*, lines 43 foll.) : εἶναι δὲ καὶ τοὺς ἰσοτελεῖς καὶ παροίκους καὶ ἱεροὺς καὶ ἐξελευθέρους καὶ ξένους ὅσοι ἀναλάβωσιν τὰ ὅπλα καὶ πρὸς το[ὺς] ἡγεμόνας ἀπογράψωνται πάντας πολίτας κ.τ.λ. In this passage the πάροικοι correspond to the μέτοικοι of Athens ; a certain number of whom, being relieved of the μετοίκιον or tax upon aliens, and paying only such taxes as the citizens, were called ἰσοτελεῖς. Next to the aliens stand the hieroi ; and after them the order of freemen, ἐξελεύθεροι. Finally the ξένοι are aliens who have not secured the recognized status of πάροικοι (= μέτοικοι). All these classes, under the provisions of the decree, are offered the full Ephesian citizenship.

The civic status therefore of the hieroi is clear : they were part of the free population, and were in no sense slaves or serfs. They are placed however just above the freedmen, and this helps us to define their status in the Artemision. It is probable that they were persons of both sexes who had been formerly slaves, and had been emancipated by a form of dedication to Artemis. Emancipation in temples appears to have been a common practice in many parts of Greece, and it took various forms. At Delphi the enfranchisement was effected by a fictitious sale of the slave to the god, the master receiving the purchase-money which really came out of the savings of the slave. It does not appear that the Delphian god ever claimed his property in the person thus committed to his care, but the form was of value as placing freedmen under the protection of the Delphian priesthood (Foucart, Sur l'affranchissement des esclaves par forme de vente à une divinité, 1867). In some cases, as at Kalymna (Part ii, pp. 92 foll.), the manumission was merely recorded in a temple, but involved nothing of a religious character. In other cases, as at the temple of Poseidon in Lakonia (Part ii, No. CXXXIX), the slave was enfranchised by simple dedication to the god, without sale : and this form was very common in Bœotia ; see Larfeld's Sylloge Inscriptionum Bœoticarum, Nos. 27 foll., 53 *c* foll., 71 foll., 241. In the case of simple dedication however, the degree of freedom thereby secured might vary. The dedicated slave might become (1) only nominally the property (ἱερός) of the god, and in reality be his own master ; or (2) he might be simply transferred from the service of a mortal to the service of a deity, i. e. he would become a temple-serf (ἱερόδουλος) ; or again (3) the master might still retain a certain claim upon his allegiance, so that at Delos (C. I. 2953 *b*) we hear of Θεόδωρος ὁ αὐτοῦ ἱερός, Theodoros being in a sense free by dedication to the god, yet still bound by a certain tie to his former owner. In some cases the number of ἱεροί attached to a temple and serving as assistants was very large . . . at the Syrian Hierapolis

(Lucian, De dea Syria, § 43). At Eryx and at Corinth the ἱερόδουλοι were really slaves of the goddess, though not under bondage to a mortal ; and they were also under a moral stigma. But the case of Ion as depicted by Euripides proves that the status of a ἱερός or even a ἱερόδουλος might well be free from any tinge of dishonour, and we have seen that the hieroi of Ephesian Artemis were certainly freemen. It is probable that the hieroi formed a numerous class at Ephesos, inasmuch as the descendants of a man thus emancipated by dedication inherited the same status ; see No. DLXXVIII *c* : Θεοπόμπου ἡ τοῦ Μενεκράτους, ἱεροῦ, i. e. Theopompos son of Menekrates, son of Menekrates, son of Menekrates. All these were freemen, or else their names would not be given ; they must all have been ἱεροί, or else the great-grandson would not have been a ἱερός. At Smyrna likewise (C. I. 3394) we read of 'Ικιος 'Ικίου τοῦ Εὐημέρου, ἱερὸς Σμυρναίων : here the grandfather of Ikios had been a public slave of the demos of Smyrna, and had been emancipated by dedication, but the status still clung to each descendant, and Ikios himself was in the third generation under tutelage in some way to the demos. It follows therefore that when a slave by emancipation became a hieros of Artemis, his descendants also inherited the same status. The number therefore must have grown rapidly ; but probably only one member of each generation was attached to the Artemision. The inscription just quoted (No. DLXXVIII *c*) proves that hieroi were actually employed in the service of the temple.

It may be asked why, if the hieroi were so numerous a body at the Artemision, they are so seldom mentioned. But their position qualified them only to accept subordinate offices ; and therefore they would not be likely to leave much trace in the inscriptions.

Σπονδοποιοί.

A σπονδοποιός is spoken of in Nos. DLXXVIII *c*, DLXXIX *b*, DLXXXIX [*a*] and *b*. In each of these passages the name of the σπονδοποιός dates the performance of some act of service to the goddess. He was, what the title implies, superintendent of libations, and we may class him with the temple-officers enumerated in an Ephesian inscription copied by Chandler (C. I. 2983) :

'Επικράτης ἱεροκῆρυξ
'Ονήσιμος ἐπιθυμίατρος
Μητρόδωρος σπονδαύλης
Λ. Κοσίννιος Γαϊανὸς ἱεροσαλπί-
κτης, 'Ολυμπιονείκης.

Φύλακοι, σκηπτουχοί, &c.

While the charge of the temple-fabric and its contents (see p. 81) was entrusted to a civil magistracy, the Νεωποῖαι (temple-wardens), there were subordinate officials continually on duty to guard the temple and its treasures. Such were the φύλακοι of No. CCCCLXXXI, line 400 ; ὁ ἐπὶ τῶν παραθηκῶν *ibid.*, line 385, who may perhaps be identified with ὁ ἐπὶ ἀργυράματος of Nos. DLXXXIX *a*, *b*, and DCII *g* : if so, he might be also an akrobates, see No. DLXXXIX *b*. Order in the temple and its precincts, and in processions, was maintained by σηπτοῦχοι, or vergers, who are named in No. CCCCLXXXI, lines 196, 382, 399: at their head was an ἀρχισκηπταυχος, No. DLXXXI.

In No. DLXXXVIII *a*, a thankoffering apparently is brought to the goddess by one who speaks of himself as τηρήσας δὲ καὶ τὸ ἱερ[ὸν]: this must point to some official guard of the temple. The sacred vessels used for libations and other purposes were kept clean by officers appointed for that purpose, called καθάρσιοι (No. CCCCLXXXI, line 196; compare ὁ τὰ καθάρσια ποιῶν, line 176; and lines 378 foll.).

Of higher dignity than these was the κοσμήτειρα of the goddess, on whom see No. DCLV. There were also attached to the temple θεολόγοι and ὑμνῳδοί, who are mentioned together in No. CCCCLXXXI, lines 191-2, and C. I. 3148. Their number is not known, but their functions are obvious enough. The θεολόγοι were a kind of hierophants, who recited the sacred legends of the goddess; the ὑμνῳδοί were singers of hymns in her praise.

The ἱεροκῆρυξ is named in Nos. DXLIX, DLXXI, DLXXXVII, DXCIII?, DCIV. His duties would comprise the recitation of the forms of prayer or of oaths and imprecations on the occasion of sacrifice or festivals. There may have been several such heralds attached to the temple. The office appears to have been held in high esteem.

Παραφύλαξ.

The office of the παραφύλαξ named in No. DLXXIX *a* is unexplained.

The title also occurs in an inscription from Tralles (Mittheilungen des arch. Inst. in Athen, viii, p. 329) in honour of a wealthy citizen and benefactor : [Γ.] Ἰο[ύλι]ον Κλαυδιανὸν τὸν στεφανηφόρον καὶ γραμματέα τοῦ δήμου, βουλαρχήσαντα, εἰρηναρχήσαντα, ἀγορανομήσαντα, σιτωνήσαντα ἀπὸ ['Αλεξα]νδρείας, δὶς χρυσοφορήσαντα, [πα]ραφυλάξαντα, πα[ηγυ]μιαρχήσαντα, ἀργυροταμιεύσαντα, δεκαπρωτεύσαντα, γραμματεύσαντα καὶ τῆς φιλοσεβάστου γερουσίας κ.τ.λ.: also at Iotape in Cilicia (C. I. 4413 *c*); (apparently) at Ormele in Phrygia (Bulletin de Corr. Hell., ii, p. 262 = C. I. 4366 *x*); at Colossæ (Waddington-Le Bas, No. 1693 *e*); at Nysa (Bulletin de Corr. Hell., vii, p. 272); at Kadyanda in Lykia (*ibid.* x, p. 54); at Sebastopolis in Karia (*ibid.* ix, p. 347). It is therefore characteristic of the Asiatic towns, and usually occurs in lists which record the services of some wealthy citizen in the way both of *officia* and *munera* : among these, it seems to be brought into closest conjunction with ἀγορανομία, γυμνασιαρχία, and σιτωνία. What however the precise functions of the παραφύλακες were, we can only conjecture : perhaps he supplied the pay of the διωγμῖται or gens d'armes of the city (see Mommsen, Provinces of the R. Empire, Eng. Tr. i, p. 351). We could then understand the gloss of Suidas, δεξιολάβοι· παραφύλακες (see Meyer on Acts xxiii, 23).

'Ασιάρχης, 'Αρχιερεύς.

The inscription let into the peribolos-wall built by Augustus, B.C. 5. (No. DXXII) speaks of an Augusteum (Σεβαστῆον) or temple dedicated Romæ et Augusto, as standing together with the Artemision within the sacred precinct. Mr. Wood (Ephesus, p. 153) identified this with a Roman building which he discovered a little to the south-west of the great temple. Similar Augusta existed at other chief cities of the province, which constituted a League of Asia for the worship of the Augusti (κοινὸν 'Ασίας). For each quadriennium a provincial ἀρχιερεὺς τῆς 'Ασίας was appointed, also styled 'Ασιάρχης, by whose bounty the pentaëteric festival of the league was held in one or other of the associated cities in turn (κοινὰ 'Ασίας : see p. 79). Besides the high-priest of the province, there was also in each of the seats of the united cultus a local ἀρχιερεύς, who superintended the local temple of the league. The title of this local priest was either 'Ασιάρχης, or, more strictly, ἀρχιερεὺς τοῦ ἐν 'Εφέσῳ ναοῦ κοινοῦ τῆς 'Ασίας (No. CCCCLXXXI, line 155). At the Augusteum itself we hear of fourteen θεσμῳδοὶ ναοῦ τῶν Σεβαστῶν ἐν 'Εφέσῳ κοινοῦ τῆς 'Ασίας (No. CCCCLXXXI, lines 328 foll.), who appear to be choristers analogous to the ὑμνῳδοί of the Artemision.

Round the subject of the Asiarchate and the provincial high-priesthood there has grown up a considerable literature. Among the more recent discussions of the question I may name : Bishop Lightfoot, Ignatius and Polycarp, ii, pp. 987 foll. (an excellent essay) ; Monceaux, De Communi Asiæ Provinciæ, together with the valuable review of this work by Prof. Ramsay, Classical Review, 1889, p. 174 ; Guiraud, Les Assemblées Provinciales dans l'Empire Romain, 1887.

SECTION I.

DECREES.

CCCCXLVI.

Fragment of white marble stele, entire on left. Height 6 in.; width 5¼ in. Unpublished.

The only interest attaching to this fragment is its antiquity. It is one of the very few relics recovered by Mr. Wood of old Ephesos. The letters are engraved στοιχηδόν, as in the old Attic inscriptions, and the cha-

```
   C I JL
   Π I N C
   A N E
   Σ Λ I
 5 P F
   r
```

racters are not later than the 5th century B.C. It was probably a decree, but even this is doubtful. The last letter in line 4 was certainly *H*: in line 6, part of Ξ. Perhaps line 2 reads τ]ῷ νέμῳ.

CCCCXLVII.

A stele of white marble, entire but with worn surface. Height 4 ft. 5 in.; width 1 ft. 6 in. 'Found in an excavation near the site of the Temple.' Wood, Ephesus, Inscriptions from the City and Suburbs, 16.

```
      ΕΔΟΞΕΝΤΗΙΒΟΥΛΗΙΚΑΙΤΩΙΔΗΜΩ
      ΞΕΝΟΚΡΙΤΟΣΑΡΙΣΤΕΩΣΕΙΡΕΝΕΡΕΙΑ
      ΦΙΛΩΝΔΙΟΝΥΣΙΟΣΙΕΡΟΚΛΗΣΜΕΝΙΓΡ
      ΕΡΑΜΙΟΙΔΙΑΤΡΙΒΟΝΤΕΣΕΝΡΟΔΩΙΠΑΣΑI
  5   ΕΥΝΟΙΑΝΚΑΙΧΡΕΙΑΝΡΑΡΕΧΟΜΕΝΟΙΔΙΑ
      ΤΕΛΟΥΣΙΝΚΑΙΚΟΙΝΗΙΤΩΙΔΗΜΩΙΚΑΙΙΔΙΑΙ
      ⌐ΟΙΣΕΝΤΥΓΧΑΝΟΥΣΙΤΩΜΠΟΛΙΤΩΝΚΑΙ
      ΛΝΑΥΤΟΥΣΕΙϹΑΣΤ  ΡΑΡΑΚΛΛΗΙ
      ΔΟΧΘΑΙΤΗΙ  ΥΛΗΙΚΑΙΤΩΙΔΗΜΩ
 10   ΕΡΑΙΝΕΣΑΙΤΕΑΥΤ ΥΣΕΡΙΤΗΙΕΥΝΟΙΑΙ
      ΗΝΕΧΟΥΣΙΡΡΟΣΤΟΝΔΗ    ΚΑΙΔΕΔΟΣΘΑ
      ΛΥΤΟΙΣΚΑΙΕΚΓΟΝΟΙΣΡ   ΤΕΙΑΝΕΦΙΣΗΙ
      ΚΑΙΟΜΟΙΗΙΚΛΟΑΡΕΡ     Ι   ΙΣΕΥΕΡΓΕΤΑΙΣ
      ϹΡΩΣΡΑΣΙΦΑΝΕ ΟΝΗΙ      ΟΣΟΕΦΙΣΙΩ
 15   ΕΥΧΑΡΙΣΤΟΣΩΝΤΙ       ΛΛΟΥΣΛΝΔΡΑ
      ΕΡΙ ΛΗΡΩΣΑΙΔΕΑ       ΛΙΧΙΛΙΑΣ
      ΤΥΝΤΟΥΣΕΣΣΗ          ΡΔ ΓΛΙΔΕΤΟΔΕ
      ΟΥΗΦΙΣΜΑΤ            ΕΙΣΣΤΗΛΗΝ
      ΛΙΘΙΝΗΝΚΑ Λ          ΙΕΡΟΝΤΗΣ
 20   ΑΡΤΕΜΙΔΟ             ΛΛΔΣΡΟΛΙΤΕΙΑ
      ΝΑΤΙΟΕΔΣΙΝ           ΦΥΛΗΝΕΦΕΣΕΙΣ
      ΛΙΔΕΤΥΝΑ
```

'Έδοξεν τῇ βουλῇ καὶ τῷ δήμῳ'
Ξενόκριτος 'Αριστέως εἶπεν 'Επειδ[ὴ]
Φίλων Διονύσιος 'Ιεροκλῆς Μένιππ[ος]
Κ]εράμιοι διατρίβοντες ἐν 'Ρόδῳ πᾶσα[ν]
5 εὔνοιαν καὶ χρείαν παρεχόμενοι διατελοῦσιν καὶ κοινῇ τῷ δήμῳ καὶ ἰδίᾳ
τοῖς ἐντυγχάνουσι τᾶμ πολιτῶν καὶ
ὅτ]αν αὐτοὺς ἕκαστ[ος] παρακαλῇ·
δε]δόχθαι τῇ [βο]υλῇ καὶ τῷ δήμῳ
10 ἐπαινέσαι τε αὐτ[ο]ὺς ἐπὶ τῇ εὐνοίᾳ
ᾗ·: ἔχουσι πρὸς τὸν δῆ[μον] καὶ δεδόσθα[ι
αὐτοῖς καὶ ἐγγόνοις π[ολι]τείαν ἐφ' ἴσῃ

καὶ ὁμοίῃ καθάπερ [ἂν το]ῖ[ς ἄλλο]ις εὐεργέβαις,
ὅπως πᾶσι φανε[ρ]ὸν ᾖ [ὅτι ὁ δῆμ]ος ὁ Ἐ[φε]σίω[ν
15   εὐχάριστος ὢν τι[μᾷ τοὺς κ]αλοὺς ἄνδρα[ς,
ἐπι[κ]ληρῶσαι δὲ α[ὐτοὺς εἰς φυλὴν κ]αὶ χιλιαστὺν τοὺς Ἐσσῆ[νας, ἀναγ]ράψαι δὲ τόδε
τ]ὸ ψήφισμα τ[οὺς νεωποίας] εἰς στήλην
λιθίνην κα[ὶ] ἀ[ναθεῖναι εἰς τὸ] ἱερὸν τῆς
20   Ἀρτέμιδο[ς οὗ καὶ τὰς ἄ]λλας πολιτεία[ς
ἀ]ρατιθέ[α]σιν· [ἔλαχον] φυλὴν Ἐφεσεῖς,
χι]λιαστὺν . . . . .

A grant of citizenship to four natives of Keramos resident at Rhodes, who had rendered services to Ephesians visiting that island.

Line 4 : Keramos was a town in the gulf of Kos, not far from Knidos ; the gentile adjective was commonly Κεραμῆται (so Strabo. xiv, p. 660). An inscription from Keramos as published by Prof. Babington in the Transactions of the Royal Society of Literature, x, p. 126, No. 35, gives Κεραμητῶν, but Κεράμιοι is the form used in the Athenian tribute-lists (C. I. A. i, No. 226). We have already had occasion to remark, in connexion with an Iasian document (No. ccccxli *ante*), upon the position of Rhodes as a great commercial centre. This it ceased to be from the time when the Roman Senate made Delos a free port, B.C. 166, and thus transferred from Rhodes the commerce of the Mediterranean : see Prof. Jebb, on Delos, Journal of Hellenic Studies, i, p. 32. The present decree belongs probably to the third century B.C., to which date the form of the letters would point.

On the subject of the Ephesian tribes and chiliastyes enough has been said on pp. 68–71 *ante*. On the Ἐσσῆνες, line 17, see p. 85 *ante*; and for the νεωποίαι, line 18, see pp. 80–81. The formula ἐφ᾿ ἴσῃ καὶ ὁμοίῃ, lines 12–13, occurs in all the decrees of citizenship that follow. See on No. ccccxlviii *post*.

CCCCXLVIII—CCCCLXXVI.

DIAGRAM

TO SHOW THE ARRANGEMENT OF THE DECREES INSCRIBED UPON WALL-STONES FROM THE ARTEMISION.

The series of twenty-nine decrees (many of them mere fragments), next following, were inscribed on eight wall-stones which were found by Mr. Wood built into the proscenium of the Great Theatre (Discoveries at Ephesus, pp. 69, 70). The inscriptions themselves testify that these marbles had originally formed part of the walls of the Artemision (ἐπιγράψαι δὲ αὐτῷ τὴν πολιτείαν εἰς τὸ ἱερὸν τῆς Ἀρτέμιδος οὗ καὶ αἱ λοιπαὶ πολιτεῖ[αι ἀ]νηγεγραμμέναι εἰσίν, No. ccccxlix, lines 7, 8, and so in the other decrees *passim*). It is evident therefore that the proscenium must have been repaired after the destruction of the temple. This took place in the third century A.D.: Scythæ autem, hoc est pars Gothorum, Asiam vastabant; etiam templum Lunæ Ephesiæ dispoliatum et incensum est, cujus opes fama satis notæ populis (Trebellius Pollio, Life of Gallienus, ch. 6, in the Hist. Aug. Scriptores). This explains the condition of Block 2, which has been cut about and its surface ornamented with a sort of panel-work in the right-hand bottom corner, all of very coarse design. The right-hand portion of Block 3 has been similarly sloped off. Only two of these wall-stones can be certainly brought into contact with each other, viz. 5 and 6. Also 3 appears to have belonged to the same course of masonry as 4, for they are alike in height. The Block marked 1 is narrower and belonged to a different course. Block 2, when entire, may have ranged either with 3–4, or with 5–6 : it has been purposely cut and shaped at the right hand, as if to serve as a kind of cornice. The slope on the right hand of Block 3 was also purposely made, to fit the marble for its new destination. Block 8 is the corner of a wall-stone, with the bottom bed alone entire ; inscribed on both faces.

In point of palæography the inscriptions upon these marbles are very much alike. The lettering of the upper portion of Blocks 5 and 6 is larger than the characters employed in the rest of the series : but all are manifestly to be referred to the Macedonian period. The iota adscriptum is consistently used, and the execution is careful. But the scratchy incision of the letters, and the dwarf splayed Λ, shew them to be not earlier than B.C. 300,—a date amply confirmed by the subject-matter of the decrees. Of the six (Nos. ccccxlviii—ccccliii) which may be connected with known historical events, the earliest (No. ccccxlviii) perhaps belongs to B.C. 306 ; the latest to B.C. 299 (No. ccccliii). We may with confidence assign the remaining decrees and fragments of the series to about the same time. The blocks, no doubt, originally formed part of the exterior of the cella-wall, like the marbles from Prienè (Nos. ccccxcix—ccccxli *ante*; see p. 7). Probably other blocks from the same position still exist at Ayasoluk, imbedded in Turkish and other buildings.

BLOCK 1.

1 ft. 7 in.

ccccliii. a

1 ft. 6½ in.

ccccliii.

ccccxlviii.

BLOCK 8.

ccccxxii.

ccccxxiii.

ccccxxi.

11 in.

6½ in.

BLOCK 2.

Present length, 2 ft. 2½ in.

1 ft. 10 in.

cccccl.

ccccxliii.

Accurately cut to suit a new building.

Broken edge.

BLOCK 3.

1 ft. 11 in.

ccccli.

cccclviii.

cccclvii.

Accidently cut off.

1 ft. 10 in.

Present length, 3 ft. 6½ in.

BLOCK 4.

3 ft. 11½ in.

cccclxix.

cccclv.

cccclxiv.

ccccliv.

Surface broken.

cccclxviii.

1 ft. 10 in.

BLOCK 7.

12 in.

cccclxx.

BLOCK 5.

BLOCK 6.

Vacat.

cccclxxiv.

cccclxvi.

cccclxvii.

cccclxxv.

cccclix.

ccccclx.

cccclxix.

cccclxi.

cccclxxv, contd.

cccclix, contd.

ccccclx, contd.

cccclxix, contd.

cccclii.

cccclxxvi.

cccclvi.

cccclxii.

cccclxv.

2 ft.

Original length, 3 ft. 3½ in.

3 ft. 8½ in.

Inscribed on Block 1 ; see the diagram on p. 90, where the measurements are given. Originally from the Artemision, but found built into the proscenium of the Theatre. Wood, Inscriptions from the Temple, No. 8 : inaccurate in several places.

```
         ΤΥΓΧΑΝΕΙΓΕΡΙΤⱵ  ΧΕΛΛΗΝΑΧΚΑΙΤΗΜΓⱵΛΙ
         ΑΓΑΘΗΙΤΥΧΗΙΔΕΔΟΧΘΑΙΤⱵΙΔΗΜⱵΙΧΥΝΗΧⱵ
         ΓΕΛΜΕΝΟΙΧΑΓΑΘΟΙΧΤΟΥΒΑΧΙΛΕⱵΧΚΑΙΤΟ
         ΚΑΙΧΤΕΦΑΝΗΦΟΡΕΙΝΕΦΕΧΙΟΥΧΚΑΙΤΟΥΧΚΑΤΟΙⱵ
    5    ΕΓΙΤΟΙΧΕΥΤΥΧΗΜΑΧΙΝΤΟΙΧΕΧΗΓΓΕΛΜΕΝΟΙΧ
         ΑΓΓΕΛΙΑΤΗΙΑΡΤΕΜΙΔΙΤΟΥΧΕΧΧΗΝΑΧΚΑΙ
         ΟΝΟΙΚΟΝΟΜΟΝΚΑΙΕΥΧΕΧΘΑΙΚΑΙΕΙΧΤΟΛΟΙΓΟΝΕΓ
         ΧΘΑΙΔΗΜΗΤΡΙⱵΙΤⱵΙΒΑΧΙΛΕΙΚΑΙΤⱵΙΔΗΜⱵ
         ΙΑΝΤΙΓΟΝⱵΙΚΑΙΔΗΜΗΤΡΙⱵΙΤΟΥΧΧΤΕ
   10    ΝΤΟΥΔΕΑΝΑΛⱵΜΑΤΟΧΤΟΥΕΙΧΤΗΝΟΥ
         Τ...ΙΚΟΝΟΜΟΝΕΓΑΙΝΕΧΑΙΔΕΚΑΙΑΓΟΛΛⱵ
         Τ  ΒΑΧΙΛΕⱵΧΚΑΙΑΝΑΓΓΕΙΛΑΝΤΑΤΗΝΕΥⱵ
         ⱵΧΤⱵΙΔΗΜⱵΙΚΑΙΗΝΕΧΕΙΑΥΤΟΧΓΡΟΧΤΟΜΒΑ
         Δ  ΜΟΝΤΟΝΕΦΕΧΙⱵΓΚΑΙΧΤΕΦΑΝⱵΧΑΙΑΥΤΟΓΧΡ
   15    ΧΡ  ΧⱵΝΕΙΚΟΧΙΤΟΥΔΕΧΤΕΦΑΝΟΥΕΓΙΜΓ
         Δ  ΥΝΑΙΔΕΑΥΤⱵΙΚΑΙΓΟΛΙΤΕΙΑΝΓ
         ΑΘΑΓΕΡΚΑΙΤΟΙΧΑΛΛΟΙΧΕΥΓΓ
         ΗΜΒΟΥΛΗΓΚΑΙΤΟΝΔΗΜ
         ΑΓⱵΧΙΚΑΘΑΓΕΙ
   20    ΔΕΔΟΜΕΝΑΧΑ
         ΤΑΧΑΛΛⱵ
```

> [Ἔδοξεν τῇ βουλῇ καὶ τῷ δήμῳ· ὁ δεῖνα εἶπεν· Ἐπειδὴ Δημήτριος]
> [ὁ βασιλεὺς πολλῶν καὶ μεγίστων ἀγαθῶν αἴτιος ἂν]
> τυγχάνει περὶ τα[ὺ]ς Ἕλληνας καὶ τὴν πόλιν τὴν ἡμετέραν,
> Ἀγαθῇ Τύχῃ δεδόχθαι τῷ δήμῳ συνησθ[ῆ]ναι ἐπὶ τοῖς ἐξηγ-
> γελμένοις ἀγαθοῖς τοῦ βασιλέως καὶ το[ῦ] στρατεύματος;
> 5   καὶ στεφανηφορεῖν Ἐφεσίους καὶ τοὺς κατοι[κ]οῦντας αὐτοῦ
> ἐπὶ τοῖς εὐτυχήμασιν τοῖς ἐξηγγελμένοις, [θύειν δὲ καὶ
> εὐ]αγγέλια τῇ Ἀρτέμιδι τοὺς Ἐσσῆνας καὶ [τὴν ἱέρειαν
> καὶ τ]ὸν οἰκονόμον, καὶ εὔχεσθαι καὶ εἰς τὸ λοιπὸν ἐπ[ὶ πλέον εὖ
> γίνε]σθαι Δημητρίῳ τῷ βασιλεῖ καὶ τῷ δήμῳ, [δοῦναι
> 10   δὲ κα]ὶ Ἀντιγόνῳ καὶ Δημητρίῳ τοὺς στεφάνους τοὺς ἐκ τῶν
> νόμω]ν· τοῦ δὲ ἀναλώματος τοῦ εἰς τὴν θυ[σίαν ἐπιμελεῖσθαι
> τ[ὸν ο]ἰκονόμον· ἐπαινέσαι δὲ καὶ Ἀπολλω[νίδην? τὸν παρὰ
> τ[οῦ] βασιλέως καὶ ἀναγγείλαντα τὴν εὔνοιαν τοῦ βασ-
> ιλέ]ως τῷ δήμῳ καὶ ἣν ἔχει αὐτὸς πρὸς τὸμ βα[σιλέα καὶ τὸν
> 15   δ[ῆ]μον τὸν Ἐφεσίων, καὶ στεφανῶσαι αὐτὸν χρ[υσῷ στεφάνῳ
> χρ[υ]σῶν εἴκοσι· τοῦ δὲ στεφάνου ἐπιμε[λεῖσθαι τὸν οἰκονόμον·
> δ[ο]ῦναι δὲ αὐτῷ καὶ πολιτείαν ἐ[φ' ἴσῃ καὶ ὁμοίῃ
> κ]αθάπερ καὶ τοῖς ἄλλοις εὐερ[γέταις, καὶ πρόσοδον εἰς
> τ]ὴμ βουλὴν καὶ τὸν δῆμ[ον πρῶτῳ μετὰ τὰ ἱερὰ καὶ προεδρίαν ἐν τοῖς
> ἀγῶσι· καθάπερ [καὶ τοῖς ἄλλοις εὐεργέταις· ἀναγράψαι δὲ καὶ τὰς
> 20   δεδομένας α[ὐτῷ δωρεὰς τοὺς νεωποίας ὅπου καὶ ἀναγράφουσι
> τὰς ἄλλα[ς πολιτείας κ.τ.λ.

The Ephesians pass a vote of congratulation upon hearing of the successes of Demetrios Poliorketes. It is conceivable that this was the victory of Demetrios in the sea-fight off Cyprus, B.C. 306, after which Antigonos and Demetrios received the title of kings (Plutarch, Demet. 16, 17, 18). Droysen, however, (Hellenismus ii, 2, p. 213) refers the inscription to certain advantages gained by Demetrios over Lysimachos, B.C. 302 (described by Diodoros xx, 113) in the movements which preceded the battle of Ipsos.

The restoration of the opening lines may be trusted as giving the general sense. Line 3 : στρατεύματος is very probable ; compare No. cccci, line 9 ante : συνησθ[ή]σονται τῷ βασιλεῖ (Lysimachos) ὅτι αὐτός τε ἔρρωται καὶ ἡ δύναμις κ.τ.λ. The same inscription, line 20, illustrates line 4 of our decree. Not only the citizens however ('Εφεσίους), but all residents at Ephesos (τοὺς κατοι[κοῦντας]) are to join in the rejoicings. What classes of persons are included in οἱ κατοικοῦντες may be seen from the passage quoted from the Mithradates decree p. 86

ante. They would be the ἰσοτελεῖς, πάροικοι, ἱεροί, ἐξελεύθεροι, and ξένοι. Line 6: there is much probability in τὴν ἱέρειαν, concerning whom see p. 85 *ante.* The οἰκονόμος of line 7 is mentioned also in No. CCCCLXIX, line 2; compare No. CCCCLIII, line 20, and *infra,* line 17. At Priene also in a decree of about the same period (No. CCCCXV *ante,* line 18) a board of οἰκονόμοι are similarly ordered to furnish public money (see p. 55 *ante*). In the Mithradates decree from Ephesos (Waddington-Le Bas, Part v. No. 136 a, line 28) λογισταί are mentioned as controllers-general, corresponding to the εὔθυνοι of Athens and the ἐξετασταί of some Asiatic cities. We may take the οἰκονόμος to be a subordinate officer of the city, analogous to the οἰκονόμος or steward of a private estate. The nearest parallels are C. I. 2512 (Kos), οἰκονόμος πόλεως; C. I. 2811 (Aphrodisias), οἰκονόμος τῆς βουλῆς: compare C. I. 2717 (Stratonikeia), and 3151 (Smyrna). So also in Romans xvi, 23 (Corinth). C. I. 3777 (Nikomedia) records the enfranchisement of one who had been a public οἰκονόμος, so that he was merely a servus publicus (see C. I. 3793, and Menadier, Qua Conditione Ephesii etc., p. 77): all these references however belong to times long after our decree. In line 11 I restore Ἀπολλω[νίδην], as

it is likely that the messenger of Demetrios was the Apollonides named by Plutarch (Demet. 50) as a friend of the king.

It is interesting to note the considerable colouring of Ionic dialect which survives in this series of Ephesian decrees of about 300 B.C. The following examples occur :—

χρυσέῳ στεφάνῳ *passim* (never χρυσῷ).
ἕνεκιν, Nos. CCCCXLIX, CCCCLXVI.
ἕνεκι, Nos. CCCCLI, CCCCLVII (never ἕνεκα).
ὁμοίη usually; but once or twice ὁμοίᾳ, as Nos. CCCCLI. CCCCLV.
προθυμίης, No. CCCCLVI.
γερουσίης, No. CCCCXLIX, line 4; but γερουσίας, line 2.

Another peculiarity is the aspirate always here employed in the recurring phrase ἐφ' ἴσῃ καὶ ὁμοίῃ: this is no Ionicism, but an idiom of the κοινή, borrowed rather from the Doric. The following references will suffice: ἐφ' ἴσῃ C. I. 3137, line 75 etc., 3rd cent. B.C. (Smyrna, quoted *ante*, p. 69 note); Waddington-Le Bas, Part v. No. 87, line 14 (Teos), ἀφ' ἴσου; C. I. 2439 c, ἐφ' ἴσης (Melos, 1st cent. A. D.); τὸν ἴσον in the Tabulæ Heracleenses, C. I. 5774-5, line 175. The aspirate here is a reminiscence of the digamma.

CCCCXLIX.

Inscribed on Blocks 5 and 6; see Diagram, p. 90. Originally from the Artemision, but found built into the proscenium of the Theatre. Wood, Inscriptions from the Temple, No. 19; Dittenberger, Sylloge, No. 134.

A decree of citizenship to Euphronios of Akarnania, in return for his public services.

In the summer of 302 B.C. Prepelaos, the general of Kassander, was sent to co-operate with Lysimachos against Antigonos. He invaded Asia Minor with brilliant success: nearly the whole of Æolis and Ionia was speedily reduced, and Ephesos, the stronghold of Antigonos' interests, was forced to submit. Hearing of this, Demetrios late in the same year hurried back from Greece to Asia and recovered Ephesos. See Diod. xx, 107, 111, and compare *post,* No. CCCCL. Next year in the spring of B.C. 301 Antigonos was slain at Ipsos, and his Asiatic dominion lost. Lysimachos then became master of Ephesos. Our inscription therefore refers to the summer of 302, when the Ephesian authorities had to make the best terms they could with Prepelaos. He appears to have taken charge of the port of Ephesos, appropriating for his master Lysimachos the import and export duties. The temple-authorities (line 1) complained that the imports and exports of the goddess were now charged with a duty, and not allowed exemption (ἀτέλεια) as heretofore. Their complaint was further complicated by a dispute about the standard weight (line 4), the agents of Prepelaos and Kassander disputing the correctness of the standard used in the Artemision. On the custom of depositing standard weights in temples the reader is referred to the well-known Attic decree, C. I. A. ii, No. 476 and Böckh, Staatsh. (ed. 1851) ii. p. 356; similarly Mr. Newton found

a number of marble weights within the temenos of Demeter at Knidos (History of Discoveries, ii. Pt. 2, p. 804). With the view of settling these disputes an embassy (line 4) was sent to Prepelaos, which was successful in securing ἀτέλεια for the goddess (line 5). But the success of the envoys was greatly due to the friendly offices of one Euphronios of Akarnania, who appears to have used his influence with Prepelaos (line 5). His being an Akarnanian reminds us of the fact that Kassander was at this time in close alliance with that people. For seeing that the Ætolians took the side of Antigonos and Demetrios, and that they were most troublesome neighbours to the Akarnanians, Kassander made overtures to the latter, and entered into alliance with them, prevailing upon them (in B.C. 314) to make a kind of συνοικισμός by which they consolidated their population in a few central towns (see Diod. xix, 67; and Grote, Pt. ii, ch. 24). This friendship of Kassander with Akarnania, may account for the influence of Euphronios with Prepelaos.

I have remarked on the Ionic forms γερουσίης, line 4 (but γερουσίας, line 2), ὁμοίη, line 7, and ἕνεκεν line 6, in the notes on No. CCCCXLVIII. On the allotment of the new citizen into a tribe and thousand (φυλὴν καὶ χιλιαστύν, lines 8, 9), the reader is referred to the Prolegomena, pp. 68, 69 *ante.* The νεωποίαι (line 1) are also there discussed, p. 80.

Οἱ κουρῆτες (wrongly read by Wood as οἰκουρῆτες) are less readily explained. Strabo (xiv. 640) tells the Ephesian legend of the Κουρῆτες, who on Mount

CCCCXLIX.

ΕΔΟΞΕΝΤΗΙΒΟΥΛΗΙΚΑΙΤΩΙΔΗΜΩΙΗΡΟΓΕΙΤΩΝΕΙΠΕΝΠΕΡΙΩΝΟΙΝΕΩΠΟΙΑΙΚΑΙΟΙΚΟΥΡΗΤΕΣΚΑΤΑΣΤΑΘΕΝΤΕΣΔΙΕΛΕΧΘΗΣΑΝ
ΤΗΙΒΟΥΛΗΙΚΑΙΤΟΨΗΦΙΣΜΑΑΝΗΝΕΓΚΑΝΤΗΣΧΕΙΡΟΥΣΙΑΣΚΑΙΤΩΝΕΠ ΙΚΛΗΤΑΝΥΠΕΡΕΥΦΡΟΝΙΟΥΤΡΟΛΙΤΕΙΑΙΣΑΔΕΔΟΧΘΑΙΤΗΙΒΟΥΛΗΙ
ΕΠΕΙΔΗΕΥΦΡΟΝΙΟΣΗΓΗΜΟΝΟΣΑΚΑΡΝΑΝΠΡΟΤΕΡΟΝΤΕΕΥΝΟΥΣΩΝΚΑΙΠΡΟΘΥΜΩΣΔΙΕΤΕΛΕΙΠΕΡΙΤΟΝΔΗΜΟΝΤΟΝΕΦΕΣΙ ΩΝΚΑΙΝΥΝ
ΑΠΟΣΤΑΛΕΙΣΗΣΠΡΕΣΒΕΙΑΣΠΡΟΣΠΡΕΙΓΕΛΑΑΟΝΥΤΟΤΗΣΧΕΙΡΟΥΣΙΗΣΚΑΙΤΩΝΕΠΙΚΛΗΤΑΝΥΠΕΡΤΟΥΣΙΤΑΘΜΟΥΤΟΥΙΕΡΟΥΚΑΙΤΗΣΙΑΤΕΛΕΙ
ΑΣΤΗΙΘΕΑΙΣΧΝΔΙΟΙΚΗΣΕΝΜΕΤΑΤΗΣΤΡΕΣΒΕΙΑΣΟΠ ΩΣΑΝΑΠΑΤΕΛΑ ΑΥΓΓΑΡΚΗΤΙΟΘΕΟΙΚΑΙΤΑΛΟΙΓΑΕΝΑΓΓΑΣΧΙΚΑΙΡΟΙΣΔΙΑΤΕΛΕΙ
ΧΡΗΣΙΜΟΣΛΝΚΑΙΚΟΙΝΗΙΤΟΙΔΗΜΩΙΚΑΙΙΔΙΑΙΤΟΙΣΕΝΤΥΓΚΑΝΟΥΣΙΤ ΑΠΟΛΙΤΑΝΕΓΝΛΣΘΑΙΕΤΛΙΝΕΣΑΙΤΕΕΥΦΡΟΝΙΟΝΕΥΝΟΙΑΣΕΝΕΚΕΝ
ΗΝΕΧΕΙΠΕΡΙΤΕΤΟΙΕΡΟΝΚΑΙΤΗΛΠΡΟΛΙΝΚΑΙΔΑΘΥΝΑΙΑΥΤΑΙΓΟΛΙΤΕ ΝΕΦΩΣΗΙΚΑΙΟΜΘΙΝΑΙΑΥΤΑΙΚΑΙΕΚΓΟΝΟΙΣΑΝΑΓΡΑΨΑΙΔΕΑΥΤΛΙΤΗΜ
ΠΟΛΙΤΕΙΑΝΕΙΣΤΟΙΕΡΟΝΤΗΣΑΡΤΕΜΙΔΟΣΟΥΚΑΙΑΛΛΟΙΓΑΙΓΟΛΙΤΕ ΝΑΓΕΓΡΑΜΜΕΝΑΙΕΙΣΙΝΕΤΙΚΛΗΡΣΣΑΙΔΕΑΥΤΟΝΚΑΙΕΙΣΦΥΛΗΝΚΑΙΕΙΣ
ΧΙΛΙΑΣΤΥΝΟΓΑΣΑΝΕΙΔΛΣΙΓΑΝΤΕΣΧΟΤΙΟΔΑΜΜΟΣΧΟΦΕΣΙΑΝΤΟΥΣΕΥΓΓ ΝΤΑΣΤΟΤΕΙΕΡΟΝΚΑΙΤΗΝΠΟΛΙΝΤΙΜΑΙΑ ΔΕΡΕΑΙΧΤΑΙΣΤΡΟΣΗΚΟΥΣΛΙΣ
ΕΛΑΧΕΦΥΛΗΝΕΦΕΣΕΥΣΧΙΛΙΑΣΤΥΝΑΡΓΑΔΕΥΣ

Ἔδοξεν τῇ βουλῇ καὶ τῷ δήμῳ· Ἡρογείτων εἶπεν· Περὶ ὧν οἱ νεωποίαι καὶ οἱ κουρῆτες κατασταθέντες διελέχθησαν
τῇ βουλῇ καὶ τὸ ψήφισμα ἀνήνεγκαν τῆς χειρουσίας καὶ τῶν ἐπικλήτων ὑπὲρ Εὐφρονίου πολιτείας· δεδόχθαι τῇ βουλῇ·
ἐπειδὴ Εὐφρόνιος Ἡγήμονος Ἀκαρνὰν πρότερόν τε εὔνους ὢν καὶ προθύμως διετέλει περὶ τὸν δῆμον τὸν Ἐφεσίων καὶ νῦν
5   ἀποσταλείσης πρεσβείας πρὸς Πρειγέλαον ὑπὸ τῆς χειρουσίας καὶ τῶν ἐπικλήτων ὑπὲρ τοῦ σταθμοῦ τοῦ ἱεροῦ καὶ τῆς ἀτελείας τῇ θεῷ συνδιῴκησεν μετὰ τῆς πρεσβείας ὅπως ἂν ἥ τε ἀτέλει[α] ὑπάρχῃ τῇ θεῷ καὶ τὰ λοιπὰ ἐν ἅπασι καιροῖς διατελεῖ
χρήσιμος ὢν καὶ κοινῇ τῷ δήμῳ καὶ ἰδίᾳ τοῖς ἐντυγχάνουσι τ[ῶ]ν πολιτῶν· ἐψηφίσθαι ἐπαινέσαι τε Εὐφρόνιον εὐνοίας ἕνεκεν
ἣν ἔχει περί τε τὸ ἱερὸν καὶ τὴν πόλιν, καὶ δοῦναι αὐτῷ πολιτεί[α]ν ἐφ’ ἴσῃ καὶ ὁμοίᾳ, αὐτῷ καὶ ἐκγόνοις, ἀναγράψαι δὲ αὐτῷ τὴν
πολιτείαν εἰς τὸ ἱερὸν τῆς Ἀρτέμιδος οὗ καὶ αἱ λοιπαὶ πολιτεῖ[αι] ἀναγεγραμμέναι εἰσίν· ἐπικληρῶσαι δὲ αὐτὸν καὶ εἰς φυλὴν καὶ εἰς
χιλιαστύν, ὅπως ἂν εἰδῶσι πάντες ὅτι ὁ δῆμος ὁ Ἐφεσίων τοὺς εὐεργ[ετοῦ]ντας τό τε ἱερὸν καὶ τὴν πόλιν τιμᾷ δωρεαῖς ταῖς προσηκούσαις·
10 ἔλαχε φυλὴν Ἐφεσεύς, χιλιαστὺν Ἀργαδεύς.

Solmissos, overlooking Ephesos, *στάντας φασὶ . . τῷ ψόφῳ τῶν ὅπλων ἐκπλῆξαι τὴν Ἥραν ζηλοτύπως ἐφεδρεύουσαν, καὶ λαθεῖν συμπράξαντας τὴν λοχείαν τῇ Λητοῖ.* He goes on to say that an annual festival commemorated this event, and adds: *τότε δὲ καὶ τῶν Κουρήτων ἀρχεῖον συνάγει συμπόσια καί τινας μυστικὰς θυσίας ἐπιτελεῖ.* Now *ἀρχεῖον* must mean here a college or board of officials, and these officials are the *κουρῆτες* of our inscription. They had at their head a *πρωτοκούρης* (No. DXCVI, *b*). They were named after the mythical *Κουρῆτες* with whose festival they had to do. Similarly at Sparta the priestesses of Hilæira and Phœbe were named after the deities they served (Pausan. iii, 16, § 1): *κόραι δὲ ἱερῶνταί σφισι παρθένοι, καλούμεναι κατὰ ταὐτὰ ταῖς θεαῖς καὶ αὗται Λευκιππίδες.* In discussing the Festivals of Ephesos, pp. 79, 80 *ante*, I have identified the celebration which the Kuretes kept up.

The chief interest of this decree (compare No. CCCCLXX *post*) centres in the mention of the *γερουσία* and *ἐπίκλητοι* (lines 2, 4), which illustrates another passage of Strabo (xiv, p. 640), stating that Lysimachos reorganized the government of Ephesos after an oligarchical model: *ἦν δὲ γερουσία καταγραφομένη, τούτοις δὲ συνῄεσαν οἱ ἐπίκλητοι καλούμενοι καὶ διῴκουν πάντα.* I have discussed the nature of these bodies at length, *ante*, pp. 74–78. We might infer from Strabo that these changes were made by Lysimachos after the battle of Ipsos. It appears, however, from this decree, that the *γερουσία* and *ἐπίκλητοι* formed part of the oligarchical changes introduced by Prepelaos, B.C. 302 (compare Droysen, Hellenismus, ii, 2, p. 211).

CCCCL.

Inscribed on Block . ; see Diagram, p. 90. Originally from the Artemision, but found built into the proscenium of the Theatre. Wood, Inscriptions from the Temple, No. 12.

ΟΞΕΝΤΗΙΒΟΥΛΗΙΚΑΙΤΩΙΔΗΜΩΙΑΡΤΕΜΩΝΜΗΤΡΑΔΟΣΕΙΠΕΝΕΠΕΙΔΗΘΡΑΣ
ΟΣΕΙΔΩΝΙΟΥΜΑΓΝΗΣΠΡΟΤΕΡΟΝΔΙΕΤΕΛΕΙΠΡΟΘΥΜΟΣΚΑΙΕΥΝΟΥΣΩΝΤΩΙΔ
ΤΟΥΠΟΛΕΜΟΥΓΕΝΟΜΕΝΟΥΚΑΤΑΤΗΜΠΟΛΙΝΚ. ΛΛΙΣΚΟΜΕΝΩΝΣΩΜΑΤΩΝ
ΤΩΝΚΑΙΕΛΕΥΘΕΡΩΝΚΑΙΟΙΚΕΤΙΚΩΝΠΑΣΑΝ
ΤΩΜΠΟΛΙΤΩΝΚΑΙΤΟΥΣΜΕΝΔΙΕΣΩΙΖΕΤΩ
ΑΠΕΣΤΕΛΛΕΝΤΟΙΣΠΡΟΣΗΚΟΥΣΙΝΒΟΥΛΟΜ
ΤΟΙΣΠΑΡΑΓΙΝΟΜΕΝΟΙΣΤΩΜΠΟΛΙΤΩΙ
ΠΟΣΕΙΔΩΝΙΟΥΜΑΓΝΗΤΙΠΟΛΙΤΕΙΑΝΕΦ
ΝΑΓΡΑΨΑΙΤΟΥΣΝΕΩΠΟΙΑΣΤΑΔΟΘΕΝΤΑ.
.ΑΙΑΙΛΟΙΠΑΙΠΟΛΙΤΕΙΑΙΕΙΣΙΝΑΝΑΓΕ
ΔΗΜΟΣΟΕΦΕΣΙΩΝΧΑΡΙΤΑΣΑΠΟΔΙΔΟΝ
.ΙΑΝΤΩΝΕΥΕΡΓΕΤΗΜΑΤΩΝΕΠΙ
ΑΣΤΥΝΕΛΑΧΕΦΥΛΗΝΒΕΜΒΙ

Ἔδ]οξ(ε)ν τῇ βουλῇ καὶ τῷ δήμῳ· Ἀρτέμων Μητράδος εἶπεν· Ἐπειδὴ Θρασ[. . . . . ?
Π]οσειδωνίου Μάγνης πρότερον διετέλει πρόθυμος καὶ εὔνους ὢν τῷ δ[ήμῳ καὶ νῦν
τοῦ πολέμου γενομένου κατὰ τὴμ πόλιν κα[ὶ] ἁλισκομένων σωμάτων [αἰχμαλώ-
των καὶ ἐλευθέρων καὶ οἰκετικῶν πᾶσαν [προθυμίαν παρείχετο περὶ τῆς σωτηρίας
τῶμ πολιτῶν καὶ τοὺς μὲν διέσῳζε τῶ[ν ἁλισκομένων λυτρωσάμενος ? τοὺς δὲ
ἀπέστελλεν τοῖς προσήκουσιν βουλόμ[ενος . . . .
τοῖς παραγινομένοις τῶμ πολιτῶν· [δεδόχθαι τῇ βουλῇ καὶ τῷ δήμῳ δοῦναι Θρασ . . . .
Ποσειδωνίου Μάγνητι πολιτείαν ἐφ' [ἴσῃ καὶ ὁμοίῃ αὐτῷ καὶ τοῖς ἐκγόνοις, καὶ ἀ-
ναγράψαι τοὺς νεωποίας τὰ δοθέντα [αὐτῷ εἰς τὸ ἱερὸν τῆς Ἀρτέμιδος οὗ
καὶ αἱ λοιπαὶ πολιτεῖαί εἰσιν ἀναγε[γραμμέναι, ὅπως ἂν ἅπαντες εἰδῶσιν ὅτι ἐπίστα-
ται ὁ] δῆμος ὁ Ἐφεσίων χάριτας ἀποδιδόν[αι τοῖς εὐεργετοῦσιν αὐτὸν
κατ' ἀξ]ίαν τῶν εὐεργετημάτων· ἐπι[κληρῶσαι δὲ αὐτὸγ καὶ εἰς φυλὴγ
καὶ χιλι]αστύν. ἔλαχε φυλὴν Βεμβί[νης, χιλιαστὺν . . . . . .

Honours are decreed to a citizen of Magnesia on the Mæander, for releasing Ephesians captured in war.

This document also fits in very well with the capture of Ephesos by Prepelaos, B.C. 302 (Diod. xx, 107). Certainly Diodoros declares that the victor 'let the Ephesians go scot-free' (*τοὺς Ἐφεσίους ἀφῆκε*), i.e. he inflicted upon them neither slavery nor slaughter nor a money-fine. But while this was his treatment of the defeated city as a whole, there may have been many private prisoners of war, and it is these whose lot had been alleviated by the Magnesian citizen honoured by this decree. As there is no mention made in it of either *γερουσία* or *ἐπίκλητοι* (see No. CCCCXLIX), it may have been drafted just before the battle of Ipsos, and immediately after Ephesos had been recovered by Demetrios from its capture by Prepelaos, i.e. in the winter of B.C. 302. Prepelaos made the government oligarchical; this was reversed by Demetrios, but after his victory at

Ipsos Lysimachus again deposed the democracy, and made great changes in the city. It is worth observing, in reference to this benefactor being a Magnesian, that Magnesia, until the battle of Ipsos, belonged to Antigonos, and had been untouched by Prepelaos (Rayet, Milet et le golfe Latmique, i, p. 168). In line 1 the lapidary has omitted an E in the opening word. For the irregular genitive Μητράδος, see note on No. cccclxxvii, line 69. In lines 3, 4 I restore αἰχμαλώτων after Demosthenes Adv. Lept. p. 480 (Reiske); αἰχμάλωτα σώματα δεῦρ' ἤγαγε. In Xenophon, Hellen. ii, 1, § 19, we read ἐλεύθερα σώματα, and in Æschines, In Timarch. p. 42, σώματα οἰκετικά (Lobeck, Phrynichus, ed. 1820, p. 378). The ransom

of captives was a recognised act of charity in ancient Greece, where frequent wars and the ravages of pirates brought continual danger of captivity; compare Aristotle, Eth. N. ix, 2, § 4 : οἷον τῷ λυτρωθέντι παρὰ λῃστῶν πότερον τὸν λυσάμενον ἀντιλυτρωτέον, κἂν ὁτισοῦν ᾖ .... ἢ τὸν πατέρα λυτρωτέον. After the battle of Granikos we hear of Athenian mercenaries, who had been fighting on the Persian side, as being redeemed from slavery by foreign friends of Athens (C. I. A. ii, Nos. 193, 194). In another Athenian decree (C. I. A. ii, No. 314) Philippides the comic poet is thanked for using his interest with Lysimachos to secure the release of Athenian captives taken at the battle of Ipsos.

CCCCLI.

Inscribed on Block 3 ; see Diagram, p. 90. Originally from the Artemision, but found built into the proscenium of the Theatre. Unpublished.

ΛΙΤΛΝΚΑΟΟΤΙΑ ι
ΡΙΔΔιΟΝΑΡΕΤΗΧΕΝΕΚΕΚΛιL
ΥΤΛΙΚΑΙΕΚΓΟΝΟΙΣΕΦΙΣΗΙΚΑ ΜΟΙΔΙΚΛGΛΙΈΡk...ι
ΕΧΧΗΝΑΣΚΙΣΦΥΛΗΝΚΑΙΧΙΛΙΑΣΤΥΝΑΝΑΓΡΑΨΑΙΔΕΤΟΔΕ ι
5 ΓΟΥΚΑΙΤΑΧΑΛΛΑΣΓΟΛΦΤΕΙΑΧΑΝΑΓΡΑΦΟΥΧΙΕΛΑΧΕΦΥΑ

[. . . . . . . καὶ ἰδίᾳ τοῖς ἐντυγχά-
νουσι τῶν πο]λιτῶν καθότι ἄ[ν ἕκαστος αὐτῶν προσκαλέσηται· δεδόχθαι τῇ βουλῇ καὶ τῷ δήμῳ ἐπαινέσαι Ἀ]ριδαῖον ἀρετῆς ἕνεκα καὶ ε[ὐνοίας, ἣν ἔχει πρὸς τὸν δῆμον τὸν Ἐφεσίων, δοῦναι δὲ πολιτείαν α]ὐτῷ καὶ ἐκγόνοις ἐφ' ἴσῃ κα[ὶ ὁμοίᾳ καθάπερ καὶ [τοῖς ἄλλοις εὐεργέταις, ἐπικληρῶσαι δὲ αὐτὸν το-
ὑς] Ἐσσῆνας εἰς φυλὴν καὶ χιλιαστύν, ἀναγράψαι δὲ τόδε [τὸ ψήφισμα τοὺς νεωποίας εἰς τὸ ἱερὸν
5 ὅ]που καὶ τὰς ἄλλας πολ(ι)τείας ἀναγράφουσι. ἔλαχε φυλ[ὴν . . . . . , χιλιαστὺν . . . .

Honours are decreed to [A]ridæos ? for his public services.

The restoration Ἀριδαῖον in line 3 is probable, but not certain. Aridæos was the name of a general of Alexander, who was entrusted with the conveyance of his funeral to Egypt (Diod. xviii, 26). He afterwards was appointed ruler of Hellespontine Phrygia (Diod. ib. 39) : from which he was driven by Antigonos, B.C. 319 (Diod. ib. 51, 52, 57). After this we hear no more of him ; but as he was reckoned a pronounced enemy of Antigonos (Diod. ib. 72, ἐχθρὸν δ' ὄντα τοῖς περὶ τὸν Ἀντίγονον), it may appear unlikely that he should receive honours from a city so devoted to Antigonos and Demetrios as Ephesos was. Yet as his adventures subsequently to B.C. 319 are quite unknown, it is possible that he may have rendered some services to Ephesos, such as to call for an honorary decree. For example, during the campaign of Prepelaos (B.C. 302) when the dominion of Demetrios and Antigonos in Asia for the moment collapsed before Lysimachos, Aridæos may have used his influence on behalf of Ephesos. Or, later on, after the battle of Ipsos, and the establishment of an oligarchy at Ephesos by Lysimachos (B.C. 295), Aridæos may have been rewarded with these honours just because he was a prominent enemy of the defeated kings.

This identification, however, must remain uncertain as long as the precise name of this chieftain is unknown. In Diodoros and Justin (xiii, 4, § 6) he is called Arrhidaios. In the decree of the people of Nesos in honour of Thersippos (Droysen, Hellenismus, ii, 2, p. 374) he is called Ἀβ]ραβαῖος, or Ἀρ]αβαῖος, while Polyænos gives the name as Ἀριβαῖος (vii, 30), if indeed the same general is meant. In this confusion, it may be convenient to note that (1) the name Ἀρριδαῖος (or Ἀριδαῖος) appears to belong to the Macedonian royal line. The grandfather of Philip II was Arrhidaios, spelt Ἐρρίδαῖος in the Treaty of his son Amyntas with the Chalkidians (now at Vienna : Dittenberger, Sylloge Inscriptionum Græc. i, No. 60). (2) Arrhabaios is a name peculiar to the royal house of Lynkestis : Ἀρράβαῖος in C. I. A. i, No. 42, called Ἀρράβαῖος by Thucydides, iv, 79, etc. If therefore the general who conveyed the body of Alexander to Egypt was rightly named Arrhabaios, he belonged probably to this ruling house of Lynkestis, and cannot have been called also Arrhidaios ; so that it would not be he who is honoured in our decree. In that case we must understand some distinguished Macedonian otherwise unknown to history : compare Droysen, Hellenismus, ii, p. 13. In line 5 the Φ in ΓΟΛΦΤΕΙΑΧ is a blunder of the lapidary.

CCCLII.

Inscribed on Block 6; see Diagram, p. 90: the inscription ran on into another wall-stone which fitted on to the right but is now lost. Originally from the Artemision, but found built into the proscenium of the Theatre. Wood, Inscriptions from the Temple, No. 25.

ΕΔΟΞΕΝΤΗΙΒΟΥΛΗΚΑΙΤΩΙΔΗΜΩΙΜΗΤΡΑ ΕΙΠΕΝΕΓΕΙΔΗΑΡΧΕΣΤΡΑΤΟΣΝΙΚΛΝΟΙΧΑΑΚΕΔΛΝΟΙΚΕΙΟΣΛΝΤΟΥΒΑΣΙΛΕΛΣΔ
ΕΓΚΛΑΖΟΜΕΝΑΙΣΙΣΤΡΑΤΗΓΟΣΠΙΧΣΤΟΝΤΕΑΥΤΟΜΓΑΡΕΣΧΗΤΑΙΕΙΣΤΑΤΟΥΒΑΣΙΛΕΛΣΤΡΑΓΜΑΤΑΚΑΙΤΗΙΡΟΛΕΙΤΑΓΛΟΙΑΤΑΧΙΤ
ΚΑΙΤΟΝΔΗΜΟΝΤΟΝΕΦΕΞΙΛΝΚΑΙΧΕΦΑΝΙΧΑΙΧΡΥΧΕΛΙΣΤΕΦΑΝΛΙΚΑΙΑΝΑΓΓΕΙΛΑΙΤΟΙΧΑΙΟΝΥΣΙΟΙΧΕΝΤΛΙΟΕΑΤΡΛΙΤΗΣ
ΚΑΙΕΙΣΦΥΛΗΓΚΑΙΧΛΙΧΙΛΙΑΣΤΥΝΕΙΝΑΙΔΕΑΥΤΛΙΚΑΙΓΡΟΕΔΡΙΑΝΕΝΤΟΙΧΑΓΛΧΙΚΑΙΑΤΕΛΕΙΑΝΛΝΑΝΕΙΧΑΓΗΤΑΙΗΕΞΑΓΗΤ
ΤΟΥΧΝΕΛΓΓΟΙΑΧΕΙΧΤΟΙΕΡΟΝΤΗΧΑΡΤΕΜΙΔΟΙΓΤΟΥΚΑΙΑΙΛΟΓΓΛΙΓΟΛΙΤΕΙΑΙΑΝΑΙΓΕΤΡΑΜΧΕΝΑΙΕΙΧΙΟΓΛΧΑΓΑΝ

Honours are decreed to Archestratos, a general of king D[emetrios Poliorketes], for public services to the Ephesians.

At the end of the lines is a joint of a wall-stone which is lost. The lines are incomplete by at least one third. Underneath line 5 the stone is blank, so that line 5 was the last. I have restored the lost portions by means of the usual formulas, which certainly convey the general tenour of the decree. I take Archestratos to have been a general of Demetrios, who at the time of the conquests of Prepelaos B. C. 302 (Diod. xx, 107) remained loyal to the cause of Antigonos and Demetrios and did good service against Lysimachos and Prepelaos. Diodoros (ib.) says that at that time two generals of Antigonos went over to Lysimachos, by name Dokimos and Phœnix: we learn from this inscription that Archestratos remained faithful (line 2). Diodoros also states that Prepelaos was not able to capture Klazomenæ or Erythræ, because of ἐλθούσης κατὰ θάλατταν βοηθείας, and that he contented himself with ravaging their territory. Our inscription probably refers to this successful defence of Klazomenæ (line 2), and Archestratos may have been in command of the fleet that came to its relief. In line 2 he is thanked for having protected the corn-vessels on their way to Ephesos. This seems to imply that he was in command of a fleet; and moreover Prepelaos had just burned the entire Ephesian fleet in the harbour (Diod. ib.). The decree was no doubt drawn up at the close of B.C. 302, when Demetrios suddenly regained possession of Ephesos, and perhaps was accompanied by this very Archestratos (Diod. xx, 111). Archestratos appears not to be elsewhere mentioned.

CCCLIII, CCCLIII a.

Inscribed on Block 1; see Diagram, p. 90. Originally from the Artemision, but found built into the proscenium of the Theatre. Wood, Inscriptions from the Temple, No. 7.

A grant of citizenship and other honours to Nikagoras, a messenger of Demetrios and Seleukos, who had conveyed a message of goodwill to the Ephesians from the kings.

The date of this decree must be B.C. 300, when shortly after the battle of Ipsos Demetrios entered into an alliance with Seleukos, giving him his daughter Stratonike in marriage. Thus his shattered fortunes were partially recovered, and nowhere would the news be more welcome than at Ephesos, which was always true to the cause of Antigonos and Demetrios. Compare Droysen, Hellenismus, ii, 2, p. 240

cccl.iii a.

LIO^

cccl.iii.

```
ΚΔΟΞΕΗΤΗΙΒΟΥΛΗΚΑΙΤΛΙΔΗΜΛΙΦΙΛΑΙΝΕΤΟΧΦΙΛΟΦΡΟΝΟΧΕΙΓΕΝΕΓΕΙΔΗ
ΝΙΚΑΓΟΡΑΧΑΡΙΧΤΑΡΧΟΥΡΟΔΙΟΧΑΓΟΧΤΑΛΕΙΧΓΑΡΑΤΛΜΒΑΧΙΛΕΛΝΔΗΜΗΤΡΙΟΥ
ΚΑΙΧΕΛΕΥΚΟΥΓΡΟΧΤΕΤΟΝΔΗΜΟΝΤΟΝΕΦΕΧΙΛΝΚΑΙΤΟΥΧΑΛΛΟΥΧΕΛΛΗΝΑΧ
ΚΑΤΑΧΤΑΘΕΙΧΕΙΧΤΟΝΔΗΜΟΝΓΕΡΙΤΕΤΗΧ ΙΚΕΙΟΤΗΤΟΧΤΗΧΓΕΓΕΝΗΜΕΝΗΧ
ΑΥΤΟΙΧΔΙΕΛΕΧΘΗΚΑΙΓΕΡΙΤΗΧΕΥΝ ΧΗΝΕΧΟΝΤΕΧΔΙΑΤΕΛΟΥΧΙΝΕΙΧ
ΤΟΥΧΕΛΛΗΝΑΧΚΑΙΤΗΜΦΙΛΙΑΝΤΗΛ ΓΡΟΤΕΡΟΝΥΓΑΡΧΟΥΧΑΝΑΥΤΛΙ
ΓΡΟΧΤΗΜΓΟΛΙΝΑΝΕΝΕΛΧΔ― ΕΔΟΧΘΑΙΤΗΙΒΟΥΛΗΚΑΙΤΛΙΔΗΜΛΙ
ΛΙΝΕΧΑΙΤΕΝΙΚΑΓΟΡΑΝΕΓΙ ΙΕΥΝΟΙΑΙΗΝΕΧΛΝΔΙΑΤΕΛΕΙΓΡΟΧΤΟΥΧ
ΓΙΛΕΙΧΚΛΙΤΟΝΔΗΜΟΝΚΑΙΧΤΕΦΑΝΛΧΛΙΑΥΤΟΓΧΡΥΧΕΛΙΧΤΕΦΑΝΛΙ
ΝΑΓΓΕΙΛΑΙΤΟΙΧ ΧΕΙΟΙΧΕΝΤΛΙΘΕΑΤΡΛΙΔΟΥΝΑΙΔΕΚΑΙΓΟΛΙΤΕΙΑΝ
ΚΑΙΟΜΟΙΗΙΚΑΘΑΓΕΡΚΑΙΤΟΙΧΛΟΙΓΟΙΧΕΥΕΡΓΕΤΑΙΧΥΓΑΡΧΕΙΝΔΕΑΥΤΛΙ
ΑΝΕΝΤΟΙΧΑΓΛΧΙΝΚΑΙΕΙΧΓΛΟΥΝΚΑΙΕΚΓΛΟΥΝΚΑΙΕΜΓΟΛΕΜΛΙ
ΙΚΑΙΑΤΕΛΕΙΑΝΛΝΑΝΕΙΧΑΓΗΙΗΕΞΑΓΗΙΗΕΙΧΤΟΝΙΔΙΟΝΟΙΚΟΝ
Ι ΛΡΟΥΛΗΓΚΑΙΤΟΝΔΗΜΟΜΓΡΑΤΛΙΜΕΤΑΤΑΙΕΡΑΤΑΥΤΑΔΕΕΙΝΑΙ
ΓΡΑΨΑΙΔΕΤΑ ΔΕΔΟΜΕΝΑΧΑΥΤΛΙΔΛΡΕΑΧΤΟΥΧΝΕΛΓΟΙΑΧ
ΕΓΙΚΛΗΡΛ ΑΙΔΕΑΥΤΟΓΚΑΙΕΙΧΦΥΛΗΓΚΑΙΕΙΧ
ΛΧΑΓΑΝΤΕΧΕΙΔΛΧΙΝΟΤΙΟΔΗΜΟΧΟΕΦΕΧΙΛΝ
ΛΙΕΙΧΤΑΑΥΤΟΥΓΡΑΓΜΑΤΑΓΡΟΘΥΜΟΥΧΟΝΤΑΧ
ΧΔΙΧΑΓΟΧΤΕΙΛΑΙΔΕΚΑΙΞΕΝΙΑΑΥΤΛΙΤΟΝ
ΦΥΛΗΝΕΦΕΧΕΥΧΧΙΛΙΑΧΤΥΝΛΕΒΕΔΙΟΧ
```

Ἔδοξεν τῇ βουλῇ καὶ τῷ δήμῳ· Φιλαίνετος Φιλόφρονος εἶπεν· Ἐπειδὴ
Νικαγόρας Ἀριστάρχου Ῥόδιος ἀποσταλεὶς παρὰ τῶμ βασιλέων Δημητρίου
καὶ Σελεύκου πρός τε τὸν δῆμον τὸν Ἐφεσίων καὶ τοὺς ἄλλους Ἕλληνας
κατασταθεὶς εἰς τὸν δῆμον περί τε τῆς [ο]ἰκειότητος τῆς γεγενημένης
5 *αὐτοῖς διελέχθη καὶ περὶ τῆς εὐν[οία]ς ἣν ἔχοντες διατελοῦσιν εἰς*
τοὺς Ἕλληνας καὶ τὴμ φιλίαν τὴμ πρότερον ὑπάρχουσαν αὐτῷ
πρὸς τὴμ πόλιν ἀνενεώσατ[ο· δ]εδόχθαι τῇ βουλῇ καὶ τῷ δήμῳ
ἐπ]αινέσαι τε Νικαγόραν ἐπὶ [τῇ] εὐνοίᾳ ἣν ἔχων διατελεῖ πρὸς τοὺς
βα]σιλεῖς καὶ τὸν δῆμον, καὶ στεφανῶσαι αὐτὸν χρυσίῳ στεφάνῳ
10 *καὶ ἀ]ναγγεῖλαι τοῖς [Ἐφε]σείοις ἐν τῷ θεάτρῳ, δοῦναι δὲ καὶ πολιτείαν*
ἐφ' ἴσῃ] καὶ ὁμοίῃ καθάπερ καὶ τοῖς λοιποῖς εὐεργέταις, ὑπάρχειν δὲ αὐτῷ
προεδρίαν ἐν τοῖς ἀγῶσιν, καὶ εἴσπλουν καὶ ἔκπλουν καὶ ἐμ πολέμῳ
καὶ ἐν εἰρήνῃ], καὶ ἀτέλειαν ὧν ἂν εἰσάγῃ ἢ ἐξάγῃ (ἢ) εἰς τὸν ἴδιον οἶκον,
καὶ ἔφοδον εἰς τὴ]μ βουλὴγ καὶ τὸν δῆμομ πρώτῳ μετὰ τὰ ἱερά, ταῦτα δὲ εἶναι
15 *καὶ τοῖς ἐκγόνοις· ἀνα]γράψαι δὲ τὰ[ς] δεδομένας αὐτῷ δωρεὰς τοὺς νεωποίας*
ὅπου καὶ τὰς ἄλλας ἀναγράφουσιν] ἐπικληρῶ[σ]αι δὲ αὐτὸν καὶ εἰς φυλὴγ καὶ εἰς
χιλιαστὺν τοὺς Ἐσσῆνας?, ὅπ]ως ἅπαντες εἰδῶσιν ὅτι ὁ δῆμος ὁ Ἐφεσίων
τιμᾷ τοὺς εὐεργετοῦντας κ]αὶ εἰς τὰ αὐτοῦ πράγματα προθύμους ὄντας
δωρεαῖς ταῖς προσηκού]σαις· ἀποστεῖλαι δὲ καὶ ξένια αὐτῷ τὸν
20 *οἰκονόμον· ἔλαχε] φυλὴν Ἐφεσεύς, χιλιαστὺν Λεβέδιος.*

The superfluous H in line 13 is a lapidary's blunder. I restore οἰκονόμον in line 20, from No. cccxlviii. Nikagoras is nowhere else mentioned. A later Nikagoras of Rhodes is named by Polyb. xxviii, 2, § 1.

cccliii a. At the upper edge of Block 1, above No. cccliii, are still traceable the letters . . ειος, from the end of an honorary decree like the others; which we may restore as follows: [ἔλαχε φυλὴν Τήϊος, χιλιαστὺν Ἡγητόρ?]ειος. This appears as No. 6 in Mr. Wood's Inscriptions from the Temple: [. . . ἔλαχε φυλὴν Τήϊος], χιλιαστὺν Γητόρειος. Perhaps the edge of the marble has been injured since Mr. Wood made his copy; probably, however, his copy was at fault.

CCCCLIV.

Inscribed on Block 4 : see Diagram, p. 90. Originally from the Artemision, but found built into the proscenium of the Theatre. Wood, Inscriptions from the Temple, No. 2.

ΕΔΟΞΕΝΤΗΙΒΟΥΛΗΙΚΑΙΤΛΙΔΗΜΛΙΒΡΟΤΑΧΟΣΓΛΑΤΛΝΟΣΕΙΓΕΝΕΓΕΙΔΗΛΕΥ
ΚΙΓΓΟΧΕΡΜΟΓΕΝΟΥΣΟΛΥΝΘΙΟΣΓΑΣΑΝΕΥΝΟΙΑΝΚΑΙΓΡΟΘΥΜΙΑΜΓΑΡΕΧΕΤΑΙ
ΚΑΙΚΟΙΝΗΙΤΛΙΔΗΜΛΙΚΑΙΙΔΙΑΙΤΟΙΣΕΝΤΥΓΧΑΝΟΥΣΙΤΛΜΓΟΛΙΤΛΝΛ   ΟΧΘΑΙΤΗΙ
ΒΟΥΛΗΙΚΑΙΤΛΙΔΗΜΛΙΔΟΥΝΑΙΛΕΥΚΙΓΓΛΙΓΟΛΙΤΕΙΑΝΑΥΤΛΙΚΑΙΕΚΓΟΝΟΙΣΕΦΙΣΗΙΚΑΙΟ
5   ΜΟΙΗΙΕΓΙΚΛΗΡΛΣΑΙΔΕΑΥΤΟΓΚΑΙΕΙΣΦΥΛΗΓΚΑΙΧΙΛΙΑΣΤΥΝΑΝΑΓΡΑΨΑΙΔΕΤΟΔ
ΤΟΨΗΦΙΣΜΑΤΟΥΣΝΕΛΓΟΙΑΣΕΙΣΤΟΙΕΡΟΝΤΗΧΑΡΤΕΜΙΔΟΧΟΓΟΥΚΑΙΤΑΣΛΟΙΓΑ
ΓΟΛΙΤΕΙΑΧΑΝΑΓΡΑΦΟΥΣΙΕΛΑΧΕΦΥΛΗΝΤΗΙΟΣΧΙΛΙΑΣΤΥΝΗΓΗΤΟΡΕΙ

Ἔδοξεν τῇ βουλῇ καὶ τῷ δήμῳ· Βρόταχος Πλάτωνος εἶπεν· Ἐπειδὴ Λεύ-
κιππος Ἑρμογένους Ὀλύνθιος πᾶσαν εὔνοιαν καὶ προθυμίαμ παρέχεται
καὶ κοινῇ τῷ δήμῳ καὶ ἰδίᾳ τοῖς ἐντυγχάνουσι τῶμ πολιτῶν· δ[εδ]όχθαι τῇ
βουλῇ καὶ τῷ δήμῳ δοῦναι Λευκίππῳ πολιτείαν αὐτῷ καὶ ἐγγόνοις ἐφ᾽ ἴσῃ καὶ ὁ-
5   μοίῃ, ἐπικληρῶσαι δὲ αὐτὸν καὶ εἰς φυλὴν καὶ χιλιαστὺν, ἀναγράψαι δὲ τόδ[ε
τὸ ψήφισμα τοὺς νεωποίας εἰς τὸ ἱερὸν τῆς Ἀρτέμιδος ὅπου καὶ τὰς λοιπὰ[ς
πολιτείας ἀναγράφουσι. ἔλαχε φυλὴν Τήϊος, χιλιαστὺν Ἡγητόρει[ος.

A grant of honours to Leukippos son of Hermo-
genes of Olynthos.

Leukippos is not otherwise known. Olynthos was
destroyed by Philip B.C. 348, and never restored.
The surviving members of its population (ὄντας οὐκ
ὀλίγους, Diod. xix, 52) were afterwards settled by
Kassander in his new town Kassandreia in the
Isthmus of Pallene (Droysen, Hellenismus, ii, 1, p.
250). As this inscription has every mark of the
same date as the preceding ones, we may suppose
that Leukippos, feeling himself without a fatherland,
became a soldier of fortune, and probably a follower
of the cause of Demetrios.

CCCCLV.

Inscribed on Block 4 ; see Diagram, p. 90. Originally from the Artemision, but found built into the proscenium of the Theatre. Wood, Inscriptions from the Temple, No. 1.

ΞΕΝΤΗΙΒΟΥΛΗΙ ΛΙΤΛΙΔΗΜΛΙΖΙ ΝΔΙΟΓΕΙΘΟΥΣΕΙΓΕΝΕΓΕΙΔΗΑΓΑΘΟΚΛΗΧ
ΓΗΜΟΝΟΧΡΟΔΙΟΣΧΙΤΟΝΕΙΧΑΓΑΓΛΝΕΙΣΤΗΝΓΟΛΙΝΓΥΡΛΝΕΛΤΕΙΧΜΥΡΙΟΥΣ
ΕΤΡΑΚΙΣΧΙΛΙΟΥΣΚΑΙΚΑΤΑΛΑΒΛΝΤΟΝΧΙΤΟΝΤΟΝΕΝΤΗΙΑΓΟΡΑΙΓΛΛΟΥΜΕ
ΝΟΜΓΛΕΟΝΟΧΔΡΑΧΜΛΝΕΧΧΓΕΙΧΘΕΙΧΥΓΟΤΟΥΑΓΟΡΑΝΛΜΟΥΚΑΙΒΟΥΛΛΜΕΝΟΧ
5   ΧΑΡΙΣΕΧΘΑΙΤΛΙΔΗΜΛΙΕΓΛΛΗΧΕΤΟΝΧΙΤΟΜΓΑΝΤΑΕΥΛΝΟΤΕΡΟΝΤΟΥΕΝ
ΤΗΙΑΓΟΡΑΙΓΛΛΟΥΜΕΝΟΥΔΕΔΟΧΘΑΙΤΗΙΒΟΥΛΗΙΚΑΙΤΛΙΔΗΜΛΙΔΟΥΝΑΙΑΓΑΘΟΚΛΕΙ
ΡΟΔΙΛΙΓΟΛΙΤΕΙΑΝΕΦΙΣΗΙΚΛΙΟΜΟΙΑΙΚΑΙΑΥΤΛΙΚΑΙΕΚΓ ΝΟΙΣΕΓΙΚΛΗΡΛΣΑΙΔΕ
ΑΥΤΟΝΤΟΥΣΕΣΧΗΝΑΣΕΙΣΦΥΛΗΓΚΑΙΧΙΛΙΑΣΤΥΓΚΑΙΑΝΑΓΡΑΨΑΙΑΥΤΛΙΤΑΥ
ΤΑΤΟΥΣΝΕΛΓΟΙΑΣΕΙΣΤΟΙΕΡΟΝΤΗΧΑΡΤΕΜΙΔΟΧΟΥΚΑΙΤΑΣΛΟΙΓΑΧΓΟΛΙΤΕΙΑΧ
10   ΑΝΑΓΡΑΦΟΥΣΙΝΟΓΛΣΑΓΑΤΕΣΧΕΙΔΛΧΙΝΟΤΙΟΔΗΜΟΧΕΓΙΣΤΑΤΑΙΧΑΡΙΤΑΧΑΓΟ
ΔΙΔΟΝΑΙΤΟΙΧΕΥΕΡΓΕΤΟΥΧΙΝΑΥΤΟΝΕΛΑΧΕΦΥΛΗΜΒΕΜΒΙΝΗΧΧΙΛΙΑΣΤΥΝΑΙΓΛΤΚΟΧ

Ἐδο]ξεν τῇ βουλῇ [κ]αὶ τῷ δήμῳ· Δί[ω]ν Διοπείθους εἶπεν· Ἐπειδὴ Ἀγαθοκλῆς
Ἡ]γήμονος Ῥόδιος σῖτον εἰσαγαγὼν εἰς τὴν πόλιν πυρῶν ἐπέτι μυρίους
τετρακισχιλίους, καὶ καταλαβὼν τὸν σῖτον τὸν ἐν τῇ ἀγορᾷ πωλούμε-
νομ πλέονος δραχμῶν ἔχς, πεισθεὶς ὑπὸ τοῦ ἀγορανόμου καὶ βουλόμενος
5   χαρίζεσθαι τῷ δήμῳ ἐπώλησε τὸν σῖτομ πάντα εὐωνότερον τοῦ ἐν
τῇ ἀγορᾷ πωλουμένου· δεδόχθαι τῇ βουλῇ καὶ τῷ δήμῳ δοῦναι Ἀγαθοκλεῖ
Ῥοδίῳ πολιτείαν ἐφ᾽ ἴσῃ καὶ ὁμοίᾳ καὶ αὐτῷ καὶ ἐκγ[ό]νοις, ἐπικληρῶσαι δὲ
αὐτὸν τοὺς Ἐσσῆνας εἰς φυλὴν καὶ χιλιαστὺν, καὶ ἀναγράψαι αὐτῷ ταῦτα τοὺς νεωποίας εἰς τὸ ἱερὸν τῆς Ἀρτέμιδος οὗ καὶ τὰς λοιπὰς πολιτείας
10   ἀναγράφουσιν, ὅπως ἅπα(ν)τες εἰδῶσιν ὅτι ὁ δῆμος ἐπίσταται χάριτας ἀποδιδόναι τοῖς εὐεργετοῦσιν αὐτόν. ἔλαχε φυλὴμ Βεμβίνης, χιλιαστὺν Αἰγώτεος.

Honours are granted to Agathokles a Rhodian merchant, for keeping down the price of wheat at Ephesos. The price of wheat was commonly reckoned by the μέδιμνος, which contained six ἑκτεῖς. The price varied greatly according to circumstances (see Böckh, C. I. ii, p. 124, and Staatsh. ed. 1851, i, 130 foll.). By Demosthenes (Adv. Phorm. p. 918. Reiske, cited on No. ccccLxi *post*,) five drachmas the medimnos is called ἡ καθεστηκυῖα τιμή 'the ordinary price.' It would probably be a good average price. In line 4 the lapidary has written ΕΧΣ for ΕΞ, and in line 10 has omitted Ν. The Ephesian board of Agoranomoi has been discussed on p. 81 *ante*. On No. ccccxLvii something has been said of the commercial importance of Rhodes in the third century B.C., compare also the Rhodian decrees from Iasos, No. ccccxli *ante*. Mr. Head, in his History of the Coinage of Ephesus, p. 53, shows that under the Ptolemies Ephesos and Rhodes, which both owed

allegiance to the Egyptian kings, were drawn into very near relations with each other, the Ephesians even reorganizing their coinage so as to agree with the Rhodian standards. The adoption of this standard by Ephesos proves that 'the markets of Egypt and the Phœnician towns subject to Egypt, which the Rhodians had held almost exclusively in their own hands' were now thrown open to the Ephesians; they were 'thus reestablished as the second commercial state in Greece, Rhodes being still the first.'

The munificence of Agathokles here recorded finds a parallel in the conduct of Protogenes a benefactor of Olbia, who is commemorated in an inscription probably about a century later than our decree (C. I. 2058). Twice, when there had been a scarcity at Olbia (σιτοδεία), Protogenes had furnished money for the public purchase of wheat to supply the people at a reasonable rate. It is worth while also to compare No. ccccLii *ante*.

CCCCLVI.

Inscribed on Block 6; see Diagram, p. 90. Originally from the Artemision, but found built into the proscenium of the Theatre. Wood, Inscriptions from the Temple, No. 11.

ΕΔΟΞΕΝΤΗΙΒΟΥΛΗΙΚΑΙΤΩΙΔΗ⊢
ΕΧΤΙΚΑΙΕΥΝΟΥΧΤΩΙΔΗΜΩΙΚΑ
ΩΝΑΝΔΕΙΗΤΑΙΠΡΟΟΥΜΙΗΧΟΥΘΕΙ
ΑΥΤΩΙΠΟΛΙΤΕΙΑΝΕΦΙΧΗΚΑΙΟΜΟΙΗΚ⌐
5 ΚΑΙΕΚΓΟΝΟΙΧΕΠΙΚΑΗΡΩΧΑΙΔΕΑΥΤΟΝΚ
ΧΙΛΙΑΧΤΥΝΧΙΜΩΝΕΟΧ

Ἔδοξεν τῇ βουλῇ καὶ τῷ δή[μῳ· ὁ δεῖνα εἶπεν· Ἐπειδὴ ὁ δεῖνα χρήσιμός ἐστι καὶ εὔνους τῷ δήμῳ κα[ὶ ἰδίᾳ τῷ ἐντυγχάνοντι τῶν πολιτῶν ὧν ἂν δέηται, προθυμίης οὐθὲν [ἐλλείπων· δεδόχθαι τῇ βουλῇ καὶ τῷ δήμῳ δοῦναι αὐτῷ πολιτείαν ἐφ' ἴσῃ καὶ ὁμοίῃ κα[θάπερ καὶ τοῖς ἄλλοις εὐεργέταις, αὐτῷ 5 καὶ ἐκγόνοις, ἐπικληρῶσαι δὲ αὐτὸν ε[ἰς φυλὴν καὶ χιλιαστύν. Ἔλαχε φυλὴν Καρηναῖος, χιλιαστὺν Σιμώνεος.

An honorary decree like those which precede it. On the form δέηται line 3, compare Part I, No. xv, lines 49, 51, where πρεσβείων (for πρεσβέων) and δωρειῶν occur; so [βοηθεῖν in No. ccccxiv *ante*. Compare δείωνται, C. I. A. ii, No. 119; ἱδρύσεως for ἱδρύσεως, *ib.* 168, dated B.C. 333; βασιλεῖα for βασιλέα, *ib.* 263; ὀγδοίης for ὀγδόης, *ib.* 269. This insertion of

iota is a common feature of Greek of the third and late fourth centuries B.C. At the same time Ε was often in the Macedonian times substituted for ΕΙ: *e.g.* τὰ βασίλεα for βασίλεια, No. ccccLvii; δάνεα for δάνεια, No. ccccLxxvii *post*. The Ionic form προθυμίης, line 3, has been already remarked upon, p. 92.

CCCCLVII.

Inscribed on Block 3, see Diagram, p. 90. Originally from the Artemision, but found built into the proscenium of the Theatre. Wood, Inscriptions from the Temple, No. 11.

ΕΔΟΞΕΝΤΗΙΒΟΥΛΗΙΚΑΙΤⱭΙΔΗΜⱭΙΕΥΓΑΛΟΧΚΡΟΝΙΟΥΕΙΓΕΝΕΓΕΙΔΗΑΥΧΙΚⱭΝΕΥΜΗΛΟΥΘΗΒΑΙΟΧ
ΡΕΧΕΤΑΙΚΑΙΚΟΙΝΗΙΤⱭΙΔΗΜⱭΙΚΑΙΑΙΑΙΤΟΙΧΕΝΤΥΝΧΑΝΟΥΧΙΤⱭΜΓΟΛΙΤⱭΝΚΑΘΟΤΙΑΝΕΚΑΧΤΟΧΑΥΤΟΝ
ΚΑΙΤⱭΙΔΗΜⱭΙΕΓΑΙΝΕΧΑΙΤΕΑΥΧΙΚⱭΝΤΑΑΡΕΤΗΧΕΝΕΚΕΚΑΙΕΥΝΟΙΑΧΚΑΙΧΤΕΦΑΝⱭΧΑΙΑΥΤΟΝΧΡΥΧ
⌐ΛΝΟΘΕΤΗΝΤΟΙΧΔΙΟΝΥΧΙΟΙΧΕΝΤⱭΙΟΕΑΤΡⱭΙΔΟΥΝΑΙΔΕΚΑΙΓΟΛΙΤΕΙΑΝΑΥΤⱭΙΚΑΙΕΚΓΟΝΟΙΧΕΦ
ΝΒΟΥΛΗΝΚΑΙΤΟΝΔΗΜΟΝΜΕΤΑΤΑΙΕΡΑΚΑΙΤΑΒΑΧΙΛΕΑΓΓⱭΤⱭΙΚΑΙΕΙΧΓΛΟΥΝΚΑΙΕΚΓ
⌐ΓΙΚΑΗΡ⌐ Ϝ   ΧΕΧΧΗΝ   Ν   ΚΙΧΦΥΛΗΝΚΑΙΧΙ ΙΑΧΤΥΝ

Ἔδοξεν τῇ βουλῇ καὶ τῷ δήμῳ· Εὔαλος Κρονίου εἶπεν· Ἐπειδὴ Λυσικῶν Εὐμήλου Θηβαῖος [εὔνουν καὶ πρόθυμον ἑαυτὸν π
ρίχεται καὶ κοινῇ τῷ δήμῳ καὶ (i)δίᾳ τοῖς ἐντυγχάνουσι τῶμ πολιτῶν καθότι ἂν ἕκαστος αὐτὸν [προσκαλίσηται· δεδόχθαι τῇ
καὶ τῷ δήμῳ ἐπαινέσαι τε Λυσικῶντα ἀρετῆς ἕνεκε καὶ εὐνοίας, καὶ στεφανῶσαι αὐτὸν χρυσ[ίῳ στεφάνῳ τὸν
ἀ]γωνοθέτην τοῖς Διονυσίοις ἐν τῷ θεάτρῳ, δοῦναι δὲ καὶ πολιτείαν αὐτῷ καὶ ἐκγόνοις ἐφ' [ἴσῃ καὶ ὁμοίᾳ, καὶ ἔφοδον
5 ἐπὶ τὴ]ν βουλὴν καὶ τὸν δῆμον μετὰ τὰ ἱερὰ καὶ τὰ βασίλεια πρώτῳ, καὶ εἰσπλουν καὶ ἐκπ[λουν καὶ ἐμ πολέμῳ καὶ]
ἐν εἰρήνῃ.] ἐπικληρ[ω]σ[αι δὲ τοὺ]ς Ἐσσῆν[ας αὐτὸ]ν [καὶ] εἰς φυλὴν καὶ χι[λ]ιαστύν. [ἔλαχε φυλήν. . . . . , χιλιαστὺν . . .

A grant of citizenship and other honours to Lysikon of Thebes.
Line 5. Τὰ βασίλεια is an Ionicism for τὰ βασίλεια.
(See on No. cccxlI.) The usual expression in
honorary decrees is ἔφοδον ἐπὶ τὴν βουλὴν καὶ τὸν δῆμον
πρώτῳ μετὰ τὰ ἱερά, i. e. the person so honoured has
the right of coming to the boulé or demos, and
making any application he desires immediately after
the opening sacrifice and prayers. taking precedence

of other business. The unusual addition καὶ τὰ
βασίλεια merely means that any business connected
with 'the kings,' e. g. a letter from Demetrios—must
always take precedence of everything after the
prayers: compare the Samian decree in my Greek
Historical Inscriptions, No. 148, line 23 : πρώτῳ μετὰ
τὰ ἱερὰ καὶ τὰ βασιλικά. The name Lysikon seems to
be otherwise unknown.

CCCCLVIII.

Inscribed on Block 3 : see Diagram, p. 90. Originally from the Artemision, but found built into the proscenium of
the Theatre. Wood, Inscriptions from the Temple, No. 10.

ΔΟΞΕΝΤΗΙΒΟΥΛΗΙΚΑΙΤΩΙΔΗΜΜΛΙΞΛΓΥΡΟΧΕΠΕΝΕΠΕΙΔΗΞΛΙΛΟΧΑ
ΕΛΑΙΤΗΣΔΙΑΤΡΙΒΛΝΕΝΤΗΙΠΟΛΕΙΕΥΝΟΥΝΚΑΙΠΡΟΘΥΜΟΝΕΑΥΤΟΝΠΛΡΕΧ
ΚΑΙΤΛΝΙΔΙΛΤΛΝΤΟΙΧΕΓΤΥΓΧΑΝΟΥΧΙΝΑΕΔΟΧΔΑΙΤΗΙΒΟΥΛΗΙΔΟΥΝΑΙΓ
ΧΛΙΛΛΙΕΦΙΧΗΙΚΑΙΟΜΟΙΗΙΚΑΘΑΓΕΡΚΑΙΤΟΙΧΑΛΛΟΙΧΕΥΕΡΓΕΤΑΙΧΕΠΙΚΛΗ
5 ΑΥΤΟΝΚΑΙΕΙΧΦΥΛΗΝΚΑΙΧΙΛΙΑΧΤΥΝΤΑΥΤΑΔΕΥΓΑΡΧΕΙΝΑΥΤΛΙΚΑΕΚΙ
ΑΝΑΓΡΑΨΑΙΔΕΤΟΗΦΙΧΜΑΤΟΥΧΝΕΛΓΟΙΑΧΟΓΟΥΚΑΙΤΑΧΛΟΙΓΑΧΠΟΛΙΤΕΙΑΧΑΙ
ΓΡΑΦΟΥΧΙΝΟΓΛΧΑΠΑΝΤΕΧΕΙΔΛΧΙΝΟΤΙΟΔΗΜΟΧΤΙΜΑΙΤΟΥΧΕΥΕΡΓΕΤΟΥΝΤΑΧΑ
ΕΛΑΧΕΦΥΛΗΝΕΦΕΧΕΥΧΧΙΛΙΑΧΤΥΝΒΛΡΕΥΧ

Ἔ]δοξεν τῇ βουλῇ καὶ τῷ δήμῳ· Ζώπυρος εἶπεν· Ἐπειδὴ Ζωΐλος Ἀ . . . . .
Ἐλαΐτης διατρίβων ἐν τῇ πόλει εὔνουν καὶ πρόθυμον ἑαυτὸν παρέχ[εται τῷ δήμῳ
καὶ τῶν ἰδιωτῶν τοῖς ἐ(ν)τυγχάνουσιν δεδόχθαι τῇ βουλῇ δοῦναι π[ολιτείαν
Ζωΐλῳ ἐφ' ἴσῃ καὶ ὁμοίῃ καθάπερ καὶ τοῖς ἄλλοις εὐεργέταις, ἐπικληρῶσαι δὲ
5 αὐτὸν καὶ εἰς φυλὴν καὶ χιλιαστύν, ταῦτα δὲ ὑπάρχειν αὐτῷ κα(ὶ) ἐκγ[όνοις,
ἀναγράψαι δὲ τὸ ψήφισμα τοὺς νεωποίας ὅπου καὶ τὰς λοιπὰς πολιτείας ἀ[να-
γράφουσιν, ὅπως ἅπαντες εἰδῶσιν ὅτι ὁ δῆμος τιμᾷ τοὺς εὐεργετοῦντας α[ὐτόν.
ἔλαχε φυλὴν Ἐφεσεύς, χιλιαστὺν Βωρεύς.

A grant of citizenship to Zoilos of Elæa.
In line 3 the lapidary has written ΕΓΤΥΓΧ by
mistake : similarly ΕΓΛ- for ΕΝΛ- in No. cccxiii
ante. Elæa was considered as the harbour of
Pergamon. and rose into importance under the
Pergamene kings. Zoilos may have been a merchant

whose business made him reside at Ephesos. Steph.
Byz. s. v. Ἐλαία· πόλις τῆς Ἀσίας Αἰολική, Περγαμηνῶν
ἐπίνειον, ἢ Κιδαινὶς ὠνομάζετο, Μενεσθίας κτίσμα. ἔστι καὶ
ἑτέρα Ἰταλίας διὰ τοῦ ε ψιλοῦ Ἐλία, ἐξ ἧς Ἐλεάται. τῆς
δὲ προτέρας Ἐλαιῖται (leg. Ἐλαῖται).

CCCCLIX.

Inscribed upon Blocks 5-6 ; see Diagram, p. 90. Originally from the Artemision, but found built into the proscenium
of the Theatre. Wood, Inscriptions from the Temple, No. 17.

ΕΥΘΥΔΑΜΩΙΕΥΜΗΔΟΥΧΑΡΚΑΔΙΕΚΚΑΦΥΑΝ   ΟΥΛΗΓΥΡΩΝΕΙΓΕΝΕΓΕΙΔΗΚΕΥΘΥΔΑΜΟΧ
ΓΡΟΟΥΜΟΧΕΧΤΙΓΕΡΙΤΟΝΔΗΜΟΝΤΟΝΕ   ΕΔΟΞΕΝΤΩΙΔΗΜΩΙΕΙΝΑΙΑΥΤΟΝΓΟΛΙΤΗΓΚΑΙ
ΓΡΟΞΕΝΟΝΚΑΙΕΚΓΟΝΟΥΧΚΑΘΑΓΕΡΚ   ΛΑΛΛΟΙΧΕΥΕΡΓΕΤΑΙΧΔΕΔΟΤΑΙΚΛΑΧΚΕΦΥΛΗΝ
ΚΑΡΗΝΑΙΟΧΧΙΛΙΑΧΤΥΝΑΛΟΘΑΙΜΕ   Χ

Εὐθυδάμῳ Εὐμήδους Ἀρκαδὶ ἐκ Καφυᾶν. [Ἔδοξεν τῇ β]ουλῇ· Πύρων εἶπεν· Ἐπειδὴ Εὐθύδαμος
πρόθυμός ἐστι περὶ τὸν δῆμον τὸν Ἐ[φεσίων], ἔδοξεν τῷ δήμῳ εἶναι αὐτὸν πολίτην καὶ
πρόξενον καὶ ἐκγόνοις καθάπερ κ[αὶ τοῖς] ἄλλοις εὐεργέταις δέδοται. ἔλαχε φυλὴν
Καρηναῖος. χιλιαστὺν Ἀλθαιμε[νεύ]ς.

Grant of proxenia and citizenship to Euthydamos an Arkadian, for his public services.

The nature of the services done by this Arkadian to the Ephesians we cannot tell: it may be mentioned however that in B.C. 303, when Demetrios appeared in the Peloponnese as the 'liberator of Greece,' all Arkadia espoused his cause except Mantineia (Plut. Demetr. 25, Reiske ; Droysen, Hellenismus ii, 2, p. 184). Arkadia and Ephesos were therefore at this time both of them pledged to the same cause.

Euthydamos is designated in line 1 as an Arkadian, i.e. a member of the Arkadian League, and in particular as a native of the canton of Kaphyæ. The efforts of Epameinondas to unite the Arkadians into one compact confederation round Megalopolis were only partially successful. The League had no sufficient power of cohesion against the disturbing influences of Achæa, Sparta, Ætolia and Macedon. See my Historical Inscriptions, Nos. 169, 171.

CCCCLX.

Inscribed on Blocks 5–6 ; see Diagram, p. 90. Originally from the Artemision, but found built into the proscenium of the Theatre. Wood, Inscriptions from the Temple, No. 18 ; Dittenberger, Sylloge, No. 315.

ΕΔΟΞΕΝΤΗΙΒΟΥΛΗΙΚΑΙΤΩΙΔΗΜΩΙΕΠΙΚ   ΗΞΕΙΡΕΝΕΓΕΙΔΗΑΝΤΙΦΩΝΑΝΤΙΜΕΝΟΝΤΟΣΙΣΤΙΑΙ
ΕΙΠΡΟΘΥΜΟΣΩΝΕΙΣΤΟΝΔΗΜΟΝΤΟΝΚΦΕ   ΩΝΚΑΤΑΣΤΑΣΕΙΣΤΗΝΒΟΥΛΗΝΚΑΙΤΟΝΔΗΜΟΝ
ΑΙΤΕΙΤΑΙΠΟΛΙΤΕΙΑΝΔΕΔΟΧΘΑΙΤΗΙΒΟΥΛΗ   ΑΙΤΩΙΔΗΜΩΙΔΟΥΝΑΙΑΥΤΩΙΠΟΛΙΤΕΙΑΝΕΦΙΣΗΙ
ΚΑΙΟΜΟΙΗΙΕΠΙΚΛΗΡΩΣΑΙΔΕΑΥΤΟΝΚΑΙΕΙΣΦΥΛΗΝΚΑΙΧΙΛΙΑΣΤΥΝΚΑΙΑΝΑΓΡΑΨΑΙΟΠΟΥΚΑΙΑΙΛΟΙΠΑΙ
ΠΟΛΙΤΕΙΑΙΑΝΑΓΕΓΡΑΜΜΕΝΑΙΕΙΧΙΕΛΑΧΕΦΥΛΗΝΕΦΧΕΥΧΧΙΛΙΑΣΤΥΝΑΡΓΑΔΕΥΧ

     Ἔδοξεν τῇ βουλῇ καὶ τῷ δήμῳ· Ἐπικ[ράτ]ης εἶπεν· Ἐπειδὴ Ἀντιφῶν Ἀντιμένοντος Ἱστιαι-
     ε(ὺς) πρόθυμος ὢν εἰς τὸν δῆμον τὸν Ἐφε[σί]ων, κατασταθὰς εἰς τὴν βουλὴν καὶ τὸν δῆμον
     αἰτεῖται πολιτείαν· δεδόχθαι τῇ βουλῇ [κ]αὶ τῷ δήμῳ δοῦναι αὐτῷ πολιτείαν ἐφ' ἴσῃ
     καὶ ὁμοίῃ, ἐπικληρῶσαι δὲ αὐτὸν καὶ εἰς φυλὴν καὶ χιλιαστὺν, καὶ ἀναγράψαι ὅπου καὶ αἱ λοιπαὶ
5   πολιτεῖαι ἀναγεγραμμέναι εἰσί. ἔλαχε φυλὴν Ἐφεσεῖς, χιλιαστὺν Ἀργαδεύς.

In lines 1, 2 the lapidary has written Ἰστιαιεῖ apparently in the dative by mistake. Histiæa in Eubœa is meant. I restore Ἐπικ[ράτ]ης as the name of the mover, there being just room for these letters ; another possible name is Ἐπικ[ύδ]ης. Observe that Antiphon asks (αἰτεῖται) for the citizenship himself, without the intervention of a citizen. This is unusual, and the grant is made in very brief terms.

CCCCLXI.

Inscribed on Block 5 ; see Diagram, p. 90. Originally from the Artemision, but found built into the proscenium of the Theatre. Wood, Inscriptions from the Temple, No. 24.

ΗΜΕΝΟΙΧΕΚΤΟΥΔΗΜΟΥΕΠΙΤΑΙΧΙΤΑΙΠΟΙΗΧΑΧΘΑΙΠΟΛΙΤΑΧΤΡΕΙΧΕΙΧΤΑΧΥΜΦΕΡΟΝΤΑΤΟΥΔΗΜΟΥ
ΗΧΑΝΑΓΡΑΨΑΙΔΕΤΑΟΝΟΜΑΤΑΤΑΓΓΕΝΟΜΕΝΑΝΠΟΛΙΤΑΝΤΟΥΧΝΕΩΠΟΙΑΧΟΠΟΥΚΑΙΤΟΥΧΑΛΛΟΥΧΠΟΛΙΤΑ
ΝΑΘΗΝΑΓΟΡΟΥΔΙΟΝΥΧΙΟΧΧΑΡΜΟΥΑΠΟΛΛΛΝΙΟΧΕΥΘΗΝΟΥΕΛΑΧΟΝΦΥΛΗΝΕΦΕΧΕΙΧΧΙΛΙΑΣΤΥΝΟΙΝΛΠΕΧ

     Ἔδοξεν τοῖς ᾑρ]ημένοις ἐκ τοῦ δήμου ἐπὶ τῷ σίτῳ ποιήσασθαι πολίτας τρεῖς εἰς τὰ συμφέροντα τοῦ δήμου [δόντας κατὰ τὸ ψήφισ-
     μα τῆς βου]λῆς, ἀναγράψαι δὲ τὰ ὀνόματα τῶν γενομένων πολιτῶν τοὺς νεωποίας ὅπου καὶ τοὺς ἄλλους πολίτα[ς ἀναγράφουσιν.
     . . . . . . τῶν Ἀθηναγόρου, Διονύσιος Χάρμου, Ἀπολλώνιος Εὐθήνου· ἔλαχον φυλὴν Ἐφεσεῖς, χιλιαστὺν Οἰνῶπες.

A grant of citizenship to three persons, for their munificence in a time of scarcity.

The heading of the decree (line 1) is quite exceptional, for it is not a decree of the boulè and demos, but of ' the commissioners appointed to see to the corn-supply.' We may compare the expression οἱ ᾑρημένοι ἐπὶ τῷ σίτῳ with the analogous phrase in No. CCCCLXXVII passim, οἱ ᾑρημένοι ἐπὶ τοῦ κοινοῦ πολέμου, understanding in either case extraordinary commissioners appointed to meet a great emergency. Most cities had regular magistrates like the σιτοφύλακες at Athens and Prienè (No. CCCCXIII ante), whose business it was to watch and regulate the corn-supplies. Ephesos like Athens was to a large extent dependent for its wheat supplies on the harvests of the Crimea and Southern Russia (Part i, No. XV, p. 31); and a war or a bad harvest immediately brought the danger of famine. In No. CCCCLII ante, Archestratos, an admiral of Demetrios, is thanked for protecting the corn-ships on their way to Ephesos from the Euxine. The Ephesian inscriptions never name any title like that of σιτοφύλακες : and it appears from No. CCCCLV, line 4, that the superintendence of the corn-supply formed part of the duties of the ἀγορανόμοι (see ante p. 81). At any rate it may be assumed that the decree before us emanated from a board of extraordinary commissioners. We are to understand that there had been a scarcity, like that spoken of in No. ccccLv, and the ordinary machinery had broken down. The commissioners who have to deal with the emergency are authorized, by a decree of the boulè (lines 1, 2), to offer the citizenship of Ephesos to any resident foreigners (πάροικοι, see p. 86 ante) who will come forward with timely assistance. It is not certain whether a loan, or a gift of money or corn, was asked for : but the lacuna seems to be too short in line 1 to allow of a longer word than [δόντας], which I have accordingly supplied. The grant of citizenship was in reality the act of the boulè, and all the commissioners have to do is to publish the names of the three benefactors. Who the three men were is not said, but probably they were resident aliens. Eutheños is a name hitherto only known from an Ephesian dedication of the fourth century, C. I. 2984. A passage from Demosthenes (Adv. Phorm. 918, Reiske) may serve to illustrate the present inscription and No. ccccLv : σιτηγοῦντες διατετελέκαμεν εἰς τὸ ὑμέτερον ἐμπόριον, καὶ τριῶν ἤδη καιρῶν κατειληφότων τὴν πόλιν, ἐν οἷς ὑμεῖς τοὺς χρησίμους τῷ δήμῳ ἐξητάζετε, οὐδενὸς τούτων ἀπολελείμμεθα, ἀλλ' ὅτε μὲν εἰς Θῆβας Ἀλέξανδρος παρῆει ἐπεδώκαμεν ὑμῖν τάλαντον ἀργυρίου, ὅτε δ' ὁ σῖτος ἐπετιμήθη πρότερον καὶ ἐγένετο ἑκκαίδεκα δραχμῶν, εἰσαγαγόντες πλείους ἢ μυρίους μεδίμνους πυρῶν διεμετρήσαμεν ὑμῖν τῆς καθεστηκυίας τιμῆς, πέντε δραχμῶν τὸν μέδιμνον . . . . πέρυσι δ' εἰς τὴν σιτωνίαν τὴν ὑπὲρ τοῦ δήμου τάλαντον ὑμῖν ἐπεδώκαμεν ἐγώ τε καὶ ὁ ἀδελφός.

CCCCLXII.

Inscribed on Block 6 ; see Diagram, p. 90 : the right hand portion was upon a block now lost. Originally from the Artemision, but found built into the proscenium of the Theatre. Wood, Inscriptions from the Temple, No. 22.

ΔΙΟΔΩΡΟΧΕΙΡΕΝΑΜΦΙΚΤΥΩΝΙΑΧΟΝΟΧΜΥ
ΚΑΙΙΔΙΑΙΓΕΡΙΤΟΥΧΕΝΤΥΓΧΑΝΟΙ
ΕΦΙΣΗΙΚΑΙΟΜΟΙΗΙΕΓΙΚΑΗΡΩΣΑΙΔΕ
ΦΥΛΗΝΕΥΩΝΥΜΟΣΧΙΛΙΑΣΤΥΝΓΛΙ

Διόδωρος εἶπεν 'Αμφικτύων 'Ιασόνος Μυ[τι]ληναῖος εὔνους καὶ πρόθυμός ἐστι τῷ δήμῳ καὶ ἰδίᾳ περὶ τοὺς ἐντυγχάνον[τας αὐτῷ ἐγνῶσθαι πολιτείαν αὐτῷ δοῦναι ἐφ' ἴσῃ καὶ ὁμοίῃ, ἐπικληρῶσαι δὲ [αὐτὸν καὶ εἰς φυλὴν καὶ χιλιαστύν, ἔλαχε φυλὴν Εὐώνυμος, χιλιαστὺν Γλα[ύκηος.

A grant of citizenship to Amphiktyon of Mytilene. In line 1 after εἶπεν the lapidary has omitted ἐπειδή. A glance at the marble shows that he had made a blunder at starting, and has inscribed line 1 again over his blunder ; in so doing he has omitted an important word. I give ἐγνῶσθαι from No. ccccxlix, line 6. The name of the Chiliastys is recovered from the list given, p. 70 ante.

CCCCLXIII.

Inscribed on Block 2 ; see Diagram, p. 90. Originally from the Artemision, but found built into the proscenium of the Theatre. Unpublished.

ΒΟΥΛΗΙΚΑΙΤΩΙΔΗ ΛΙΓΟΧΕΙ Λ
ΤΟΙΣΓΑΧΙΝΕ ΝΟΙΑΓΚΑΙΓ
ΙΚΑΙΙΔΙΑΙΤΟΙΣΕΝΤΥΓΧΑ
ΕΔΟΧΘΑΙΤΗΙΒΟΥΛΗΙΚ
5   ΤΟ

Ἔδοξεν τῇ] βουλῇ καὶ τῷ δή[μ]ῳ· Ποσει[δ]ώ[νιος τοῦ δεῖνος εἶπεν· Ἐπειδὴ ὁ δεῖνα . . . ἐν] τοῖς πᾶσιν ε[ὔ]νοιαν καὶ π[ροθυμίαν παρέχεται καὶ κοινῇ τῷ δήμ]ῳ καὶ ἰδίᾳ τοῖς ἐντυγχά[νουσιν αὐτῷ τῶν πολιτῶν, ἀγαθῇ τύχῃ δ]εδόχθαι τῇ βουλῇ κ[αὶ τῷ δήμῳ δοῦναι τῷ δεῖνι 5 πολιτείαν ἐφ' ἴσῃ καὶ ὁμοίῃ αὐτῷ καὶ] το[ῖς ἐκγόνοις κ.τ.λ.

A grant of citizenship to a man whose name is lost.

CCCCLXIV.

Inscribed on Block 4; see Diagram, p. 90. Originally from the Artemision, but found built into the proscenium of the Theatre. Wood, Inscriptions from the Temple, No. 5. The right hand portion was inscribed upon another block now lost.

```
ΕΔΟΞΕΝΤΗΙΒΟΥΛΗΙΚΑΙ
ΕΙΠΕΝΕΠΕΙΔΗΑΡΤΕΜΙ
ΑΠΟΛΛΟΔΑΡΟΥΠΕΡΙΝΘΙ
ΒΟΝΤΕΣΕΥΝΟΙΕΙΣΙΤΑΙΔΗΛ
5    ΠΡΑΤΤΟΝΤΕΧΑΕΙΤΙΑΓΑ
ΤΗΣΟΙΚΕΙΟΤΗΤΟΣΤΗΣΥΠ
ΑΓΑΘΗΙΤΥΧΗΙΔΕΔΟΧΘΑΙ
```

Ἔδοξεν τῇ βουλῇ καὶ [τῷ δήμῳ· ὁ δεῖνα . . . . . .
εἶπεν· Ἐπειδὴ Ἀρτεμί[δωρος . . . . . καὶ . . . .
Ἀπολλοδάρου Περίνθι[οι πατρικὴν τὴν φιλίαν παραλα-
βόντες εὔνοί εἰσι τῷ δήμῳ καὶ διατελοῦσιν λέγοντες ἢ
5 πράττοντες δεί τι ἀγα[θὸν περὶ τὴν πόλιν καὶ ἄξιον
τῆς οἰκειότητος τῆς ὑπ[αρχούσης αὐτοῖς παρὰ τοῦ δήμου·
ἀγαθῇ τύχῃ δεδόχθαι κ.τ.λ.

A grant of honours to two citizens of Perinthos, who appear to come of a family which had been on friendly terms with the people of Ephesos for a generation or more.

The restorations certainly give the sense, and are in agreement with the usual formulas : compare, for example, No. CCCCXLII *ante.*

CCCCLXV.

Inscribed on Block 6; see Diagram, p. 90. The right hand portion was on another block now lost. Originally from the Artemision, but found built into the proscenium of the Theatre. Wood, Inscriptions from the Temple, No. 23.

```
ΕΔΟΞΕΝΤΗΙΒΟΥΛΗΙΚΑΙΤΛΙΔΗΜΛΙΑΡΙΣΤΕΥΣΕ
ΔΗΜΛΙΚΑΙΤΛΜΠΟΛΙΤΛΝΤΟΙΣΑΦΙΚΝΟΥΜΕΝΟ
ΣΤΑΛΕΝΤΟΣΕΙΣΤΕΛΥΠΟΤΗΣΠΟΛΕΛΣΠΟΛΛΗ
ΦΑΝΗΙΑΡΙΣΤΕΙΔΟΥΣΤΗΙΛΙΠΟΛΙΤΕΙΑΝΑΥΤΛΙΚ
5    ΚΑΙΧΙΛΙΑΣΤΥΝΑΝΑΓΡΑΨΑΙΔΕΤΟΥΝΗΦΙΣΜΑΤΟ
ΓΑΣΑΝΑΓΡΑΦΟΥΣΙΠΟΛΙΤΕΙΑΣΕΛΑΧΕΦΥΛΗΝ
```

Ἔδοξεν τῇ βουλῇ καὶ τῷ δήμῳ· Ἀριστεὺς ε[ἶπεν· Ἐπειδὴ Ἀριστοφάνης Ἀριστείδους Τήϊος πρότερόν τε χρείας παρείχετο τῷ
δήμῳ καὶ τῶν πολιτῶν τοῖς ἀφικνουμένο[ις εἰς Τέω . . . . καὶ νῦν . . . . πρεσβίᾳς ἀπο-
σταλέντος εἰς Τέω ὑπὸ τῆς πόλεως πολλὴ[ν τὴν προθυμίαν ἐποιήσατο, δεδόχθαι τῇ βουλῇ καὶ τῷ δήμῳ δοῦναι Ἀριστο-
φάνη Ἀριστείδους Τήϊῳ πολιτείαν, αὐτῷ κ[αὶ ἐκγόνοις ἐφ' ἴσῃ καὶ ὁμοίᾳ, ἐπικληρῶσαι δὲ αὐτὸν καὶ εἰς φυλὴν
5 καὶ χιλιαστὺν, ἀναγράψαι δὲ τὸ ψήφισμα το[ῦτο τοὺς νεωποίας εἰς τὸ ἱερὸν τῆς Ἀρτέμιδος ὅπου καὶ τὰς λοιπὰς ἀναγράφουσι πολιτείας. . ἔλαχε φυλὴν [. . . . , χιλιαστὺν . . . . .

A grant of citizenship to [Aristo]phanes of Teos, for his public services.

It is difficult to determine the length of the lines. Though the general tenor of the restorations is certain, yet these formulas vary in length in different decrees. The name of the man was probably [Ἀριστο]φάνης : his father was Ἀριστείδης, and it was usual for the son to retain one element of his father's name. We

should like to know on what errand the envoy (?) apparently mentioned in lines 2, 3 was despatched to Teos. Teos is named by Diodoros (xx, 107) as one of the towns which yielded to Prepelaos in B.C. 302 without resistance : so the transaction may refer to that time. The accusative in ω, εἰς Τέω (line 3) is of course strictly regular.

CCCCLXVI.

Inscribed on Block 5; see Diagram, p. 90. The beginnings of the lines were inscribed upon another wall-stone now lost. Originally from the Artemision, but found built into the proscenium of the Theatre. Wood, Inscriptions from the Temple, No. 14.

ΔΝΗΡΑΓΑΘΟΧΚΑΙ
ϽΙΑΓΚΑΙΡΟΘΥΜΙΑΝ
ΗΑΡΕΤΗΧΕΝΕΚΕΝΚΑΙ
˰ΦΑΝˬΧΑΙΑΥΤΟΝΧΡΥΧΕˬΙ
5   ΤΕΧΕΙΔˬΧΙΝΟΤΙΟΔΗΜΟΧ
ΟΝΤΟΥΧΝΕˬΓΟΙΑΧ

Ἔδοξεν τῇ βουλῇ καὶ τῷ δήμῳ· ὁ δεῖνα εἶπεν· Ἐπειδὴ ὁ δεῖνα] ἀνὴρ ἀγαθὸς καὶ
χρήσιμός ἐστι *vel tale aliquid et similia* . . . . εὔν]οιαν καὶ προθυμίαν
παρεχόμενος *vel hujusmodi aliquid* δεδόχθαι τῷ δήμῳ ἐπαινέσαι αὐτὸ]ν ἀρετῆς ἕνεκεν καὶ
εὐνοίας ἧς ἔχει *et cetera* . . . . καὶ στε]φανῶσαι αὐτὸν χρυσέῳ
5   στεφάνῳ *certaminis nescio cujus tempore* . . . . ὅπως ἅπαν]τες εἰδῶσιν ὅτι ὁ δῆμος
τιμᾷ τοὺς εὐεργετοῦντας δωρεαῖς ταῖς προσηκούσαις, καὶ τὸν στέφαν]ον τοὺς νεωποίας
[ἀναγράψαι εἰς τὸ ἱερὸν τῆς Ἀρτέμιδος.]

A golden chaplet is voted to a person unknown, for public services.

CCCCLXVII.

Inscribed on Block 5; see Diagram, p. 90. The beginnings of the lines were on another wall-stone now lost. Originally from the Artemision, but found built into the proscenium of the Theatre. Wood, Inscriptions from the Temple, No. 15.

ΕΥΝΟΙΑΓΚΑΙ
˭ΑΙΔΕΔΟΧΘΑΙΤΗΙ
ΥΤΟΝΤΟΥΧΕΧΧΗΝΑΧ
ΝΑΓΡΑΦΟΝΤΑΙ

Ἔδοξεν τῇ βουλῇ καὶ τῷ δήμῳ· ὁ δεῖνα εἶπεν· Ἐπειδὴ ὁ δεῖνα . . . .] εὔνοιαν καὶ
προθυμίαν . . . . τ]αι· δεδόχθαι τῇ
βουλῇ καὶ τῷ δήμῳ εἶναι αὐτὸν πολίτην ἐφ' ἴσῃ καὶ ὁμοίᾳ καθάπερ καὶ τοὺς ἄλλους εὐεργέτας, ἐπικληρῶσαι δὲ α]ὐτὸν τοὺς Ἐσ
εἰς φυλὴν καὶ χιλιαστὺν, ἀναγράψαι δὲ τὴν πολιτείαν τοὺς νεωποίας εἰς τὸ ἱερὸν τῆς Ἀρτέμιδος ὅπου καὶ αἱ λοιπαὶ πολιτεῖαι ἀ]ναγράφ
5   ἔλαχι φυλὴν . . . . , χιλιαστὺν . . . . .]

A grant of citizenship to a public benefactor. The office of the Essenes (line 3)
has been discussed on p. 85 *ante.*

CCCCLXVIII.

Inscribed on Block 4; see Diagram. p. 90. The inscription was continued on a wall-stone below, now lost. Originally from the Artemision, but found built into the proscenium of the Theatre. Wood, Inscriptions from the Temple, No. 3.

ΕΔΟΞΕΝΤˬΙΔΗΜˬΙΓΙΝΔΑΡΟΧΔˬΡΟΘΕΟΥΕΙΓΕΝΕΓΕΙΔΗΑΓΟΛ
ΚΟΝˬΝΟΧΜΑΓΝΗΧΓΑΧΑΝΕΥΝΟΙΑΓΚΑΙΓΡΟΘΥΜΙΑΝΓΑΡΕΧΟΜΕΝ
ΤΕ   ΓΕΡΙΤΟΝΔΗΜΟΝΤΟΝΦΦΕΧΙˬ   ΙΑ   ΥΓΧΔ

Ἔδοξεν τῷ δήμῳ· Πίνδαρος Δωροθέου εἶπεν· Ἐπειδὴ Ἀπολ[λο . . .
Κόνωνος Μάγνης πᾶσαν εὔνοιαν καὶ προθυμίαν παρεχόμεν[ος δια-
τε[λεῖ] περὶ τὸν δῆμον τὸν Ἐφεσίω[ν καὶ] ἰδ[ίᾳ τοῖς ἐντ]υγχά[νουσι
[τῶν πολιτῶν κ.τ.λ.]

Honours are voted to a citizen of Magnesia (ad Mæandrum) for his services.
Compare No. ccccl *ante.*

CCCCLXIX.

Inscribed on Block 4; see Diagram, p. 90. The ends of the lines were inscribed upon another wall-stone, now lost. Originally from the Artemision, but found built into the proscenium of the Theatre. Wood, Inscriptions from the Temple, No. 4.

KAIΞENIΔ   NOIKONOM
TOYΣEYNOIAMΓAPEKOM
ΓOΛEΛΣTIMAIOΔHMOΣKATΔ
XIΛIAΣTYNEXYPEOΣ

The citizenship is granted to a public benefactor. The office of the οἰκονόμος is mentioned also in No. CCCCXLVIII lines 7 and 11; compare No.

. . . . [ἀποστεῖλαι δὲ αὐτῷ
καὶ ξένια [τὸ]ν οἰκονόμ[ον· ὅπως ἅπαντες εἰδῶσιν ὅτι
τοὺς εὐνοίαμ παρεχομ[ένους περὶ τὰ συμφέροντα τῆς
πόλεως τιμῷ ὁ δῆμος κατα[ξίως. ἔλαχε φυλὴν Καρηναῖος,
χιλιαστὺν Ἐχύρεος.

CCCCLIII, line 20. See the remarks on p. 92, ante. For the Essenes, see p. 85. The name of the tribe is restored from the list given, p. 70.

CCCCLXX.

Inscribed on the fragmentary Block 7; see Diagram, p. 90. Originally from the Artemision, but found built into the proscenium of the Theatre. Unpublished.

ΛΔIΔΣ
HΛ ᴗ ΛHNTΛNNEΛ
TATOYHΦIΣMATHΣΓEP
NEΓIKΛHTΛNYΓEP
5   ᴗΔ ΛYΛHTOYΔEΛOΧΘAI
ΔIKAITΛIΔHMΛIEΓAINEΣ
ΝΑΙΣMHNOΔΛPOYBOIΛTIOΛ
ΝKAIΣTEΦΑΝΛΧΑIAYTON
EΦΑΝΛΛIKAIANAΓ ΚIΛΑI
ITΛ

[Ἔδοξεν τῇ βουλῇ καὶ τῷ δήμῳ·]
ὁ δεῖνα τοῦ δεῖνος εἶπεν· κατασ[ταθ-
έντων ἐπὶ τ]ὴμ β[ου]λὴν τῶν νεα[π-
οιῶν, κα]τὰ τὸ ψήφισμα τῆς γερ[ουσ-
ίας καὶ τῶ]ν ἐπικλήτων, ὑπὲρ . . . .
5   ὦν]ος [τοῦ] αὐλητοῦ δεδόχθαι [τῇ βουλῇ καὶ τῷ δήμῳ ἐπαινέσ[αι . . . . .
ω]να Ἰσμηνοδώρου Βοιώτιον [τὸν αὐλητ-
ὴ]ν καὶ στεφανῶσαι αὐτὸν [χρυσέῳ σ-
τ]εφάνῳ καὶ ἀναγγεῖλαι κ.τ.λ.

A golden chaplet is voted to a Bœotian flute-player by the boulè and demos, upon application made to the boulè by the neopoiai in pursuance of a decree of the gerousia and the epikletoi.

The chief interest of this inscription arises from the mention of the γερουσία and ἐπίκλητοι, and the evidence here furnished that these assemblies existed side by side with the βουλή and ἐκκλησία. For a discussion of these points the reader is referred to pp. 74–78 foll. ante: see also No. CCCCXLIX, the decree referring to Prepelaos. There can be no doubt that both that and the present inscription date from the same period, soon after the defeat of Demetrios at Ipsos and before the death of Lysimachos (B.C. 301–281). In both these decrees the proposal is first sanctioned by the gerousia and epikletoi, and then the application to the boulè is made by the neopoiai in their official capacity as guardians of the Artemision, their request being for a reward to persons who have served the goddess.

In the present instance the recipient of the honour is a musician who no doubt had been engaged at one of the Ephesian festivals (see p. 79, ante), and had lent it additional lustre by his beautiful playing. He is a Bœotian; for Bœotia among the Greeks, like Etruria with the Romans, had almost a monopoly of flute-playing: see Pauly, Real-encyclop. i, p. 2406. The most famous of Greek flute-players was Ismenias the Theban, in the middle of the fourth century B.C., whose name became proverbial. The flute-player of our decree may have been a member of the same family, for his father's name (line 8) is Ἰσμηνόδωρος. Two other Bœotian flute-players are named at Iasos in the series of inscriptions from the Theatre (Waddington-Le Bas, Part v, Nos. 253, 255), Μνασίας Πυρρίλου Βοιώτιος and Σάτυρος Ἀριστοκλείους Βοιώτιος. Something has been said on p. 65 respecting the employment of popular artists at festivals.

CCCCLXXI.

Inscribed on the right-hand return face of Block 8; see Diagram, p. 90. Originally from the Artemision, but found built into the proscenium of the Theatre. Wood, Inscriptions from the Temple, No. 26.

IΛᴗΛI
AΣTYNANAΓPA
ΦIΣMATOYΣNEΛΓO
APTEMIΔOΣOΓOYKΛ
5   IAΧANAΓPAΦOYΣI
ΣΦEΣEYΣXIΛIAΣTYNBᴦ

. . . . [ἐπικλη-
ρ]ῶσαι [δὲ αὐτὸν καὶ εἰς φυλὴν καὶ χιλιαστὺν ἀναγρά[ψαι δὲ τόδε τὸ ψήφισμα τοὺς νεωπο[ίας εἰς τὸ ἱερὸν τῆς
Ἀρτέμιδος ὅπου κα[ὶ τὰς ἄλλας πολι-
5   τείας ἀναγράφουσι[ν· ἔλαχε φυλὴν
Ἐφισεύς, χιλιαστὺν Βω[ρεύς.

Conclusion of an honorary decree, in terms resembling the rest.

CCCCLXXII.

Inscribed on the left-hand face of Block 8; see Diagram, p. 90. Originally from the Artemision, but found built into the proscenium of the Theatre. Unpublished.

ΟΔΗΜΟΣ

ΛΙ~ΕΛΛΧΕΦΥΛΗΝ

. . . . ὅπως ἂν εἰδῶσι πάντες ὅτι] ὁ δῆμος
τιμᾷ τοὺς εὐεργετοῦντας αὐτὸν δωρεαῖς ταῖς προσηκούσ]αις. ἔλαχε φυλὴν
τὴν δεῖνα, χιλιαστὺν τὴν δεῖνα].

A fragment from the end of an honorary decree, similar to the preceding.

CCCCLXXIII.

Inscribed immediately under the preceding (No. ccccLxxii) on Block 8; see Diagram, p. 90. Unpublished.

ΧΓΡΟΜΗΘΙ^ΝΟΣΧΡΗΣΙΜΟΣΕΣΤΙΝ
ΒΟΥΛΗΙΚΑΙΤΛΙΔΗΜΛΙΔΟΥΝΑΙΓΟΛΙΤΕΙ
ΓΚΑΙΧΙΛ ΣΤΥΝΑΝΑΓ᠈ΛΨΑΙΔΕΤΟΔΕ
ωΝΤΙ ΙΛΙΑΣΤΥΝ

Ἔδοξεν τῇ βουλῇ καὶ τῷ δήμῳ· ὁ δεῖνα εἶπεν· Ἐπειδὴ . . . . .]ς Προμηθίωνος χρήσιμός ἐστιν
καὶ κοινῇ τῷ δήμῳ καὶ ἰδίᾳ τοῖς ἐντυγχάνουσιν αὐτῷ· δεδόχθαι τῇ] βουλῇ καὶ τῷ δήμῳ δοῦναι πολιτείαν αὐτῷ ἐφ' ἴσῃ καὶ ὁμοίᾳ, ἐπικληρῶσαι δὲ αὐτὸν καὶ εἰς φυλὴ]ν καὶ χιλ[ια]στὺν, ἀναγράψαι δὲ τόδε
τὸ ψήφισμα ὅπου καὶ αἱ λοιπαὶ πολιτεῖαι ἀναγεγραμμέναι εἰσίν. ἔλαχε φυλὴ]ν Τ[ήϊον], χιλιαστὺν . . . .

A fragment from the conclusion of an honorary decree similar to the others. The end of
line 4 is worn, and the name of the Chiliastys cannot be recovered.

CCCCLXXIV.

Inscribed on Block 5; see Diagram, p. 90. Wood, Inscriptions from the Temple, No. 13.

ΝΕΓΕΙΔΗΝΙΚΗΡΑΤΟΣ
Μ.ΩΙΕΙΝΑΙ
.ΛΟΙΣΕΟΕΡΓΕΤΑΙΣ

Ἔδοξεν τῇ βουλῇ καὶ τῷ δήμῳ· ὁ δεῖνα εἶπε]ν· Ἐπειδὴ Νικήρατος
διατελεῖ εὔνους ὢν εt similia . . . . τῷ δή]μῳ· εἶναι
αὐτὸν πολίτην ἐφ' ἴσῃ καὶ ὁμοίᾳ καθάπερ καὶ τοῖς ἄ]λλοις ἐοεργέταις
δίδοται. ἔλαχε φυλὴν . . . . . . , χιλιαστὺν . . . .].

Fragment of a decree granting Nikeratos the citizenship. The form ἐοεργέταις in line 3 is interesting as the solitary example in this series of decrees of EO for EY. The reader is referred to G. Curtius, Griechische Studien, v, p. 294, for a discussion of this form, which is found in the inscriptions of Asia Minor and of the Chalkidic peninsula between B.C. 400–250. Mr. Head observes in his Coinage of Ephesus, (p. 47) that EO for EY is not found upon the coins after B.C. 280–258. This would agree with the date I have suggested for these inscriptions (p. 89 ante), namely the earlier years of the third century B.C.

CCCCLXXV.

Inscribed on Block 5; see Diagram, p. 90. Wood, Inscriptions from the Temple, No. 16.

ΕΛΔ᠈ΕΦΥΛΗΝΒΕΜΒΙΝΕΩΝΧΙΛΙΛ

ἔ. . . . .
Ἔλα[χ]ε φυλὴν Βεμβινέων, χιλια[στὺν . . . .

The last line of a decree of citizenship similar to the rest.

Inscribed on Block 6; see Diagram, p. 90. Wood, Inscriptions from the Temple, No. 20.

ΑΥΙΟΝΙΡΟΛΙΙΓ
ΧΙΛΙΑΣΤΥΝΧΗΛΛΝΕΟΧ

. . . . [εἶναι δὲ
πολίτη[ν ἐφ᾿ ἴσῃ καὶ ὁμοίᾳ καθάπερ καὶ τοὺς ἄλλους εὐεργέτας, ἐπικληρῶσαι δὲ αὐτὸν καὶ εἰς φυλὴν καὶ χιλιαστύν. Ἔλαχε φυλὴν Καρηναῖος
ττὺν Χηλάνεος.

A fragment of a decree of citizenship, similar to the others. The tribal name Καρηναῖος
is restored from the list given, p. 70.

———————

CCCCLXXVII.

Inscribed on 3 blocks of white marble, 'found in a causeway near the River Caÿster, about two miles north of Ayasalouk.' Published
by Wood, Inscriptions from the City and Suburbs, No. 1. For the measurements of these marbles, and the arrangement of the
inscriptions upon them, the reader is referred to the Diagram. M. Dareste gives the text in cursive only, from fresh impressions;
Une Loi Ephésienne du premier siècle avant notre ère, Paris (Larose), 1877, and in Nouvelle Revue Historique de droit, 1877, pp. 164
foll.; Dittenberger, Sylloge, No. 344, following Dareste; K. F. Hermann, Griech. Antiq. ed. Thalheim, 1884, ii, Pt. 1, pp. 134–149.

DIAGRAM SHOWING THE ARRANGEMENT OF THE INSCRIPTION UPON THE THREE WALL-STONES.

Each of the three blocks is surrounded by a small margin, or depressed edge, 1¼ inch wide and ¼ inch deep. The three blocks appear
to have belonged to the same course of masonry, and probably followed on, end to end; perhaps one additional block at the
beginning and another at the end would make the inscription complete. These marbles probably formed part of the walls of the
Artemision.

BLOCK 1.

7 ft. 10 in.

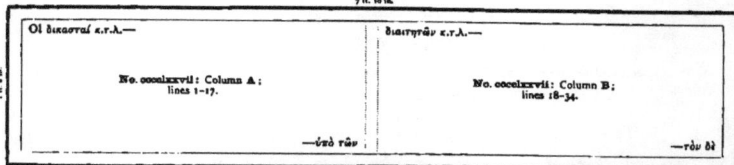

BLOCK 2.

5 ft. 8 in.

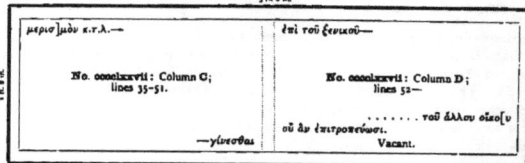

BLOCK 3.

CCCCLXXVII.

Column **A.**

ΟΙΔΙΚΑΣΤΑΙ —— ΕΣΕΙΝΑΙΔΕΤΟΙΣΔΙΚΑΣΤΑΙΣΚΑΝΑΥΤΟΙΣΜΗϘΑΙΝΗΤΑΙΔΙΚΑΣΤΙΚΟΝΕΙΝΑΙΤΟΓΡΑΓΜΑΑΛΛΟ
ΓΕΑΡΓΟΣΓΛΕΟΝΟΣΤΕΤΙΜΗΣΘΑΙΟΔΕΤΟΚΙΣΤΗΣΕΛΑΤΤΟΝΟΣΕΣΕΙΝΑΙΑΥΤΟΙΣΤΙΜΗΣΔΙΟΣΟΥΑΝΔΟΚΗΙΚΑΛΣ
ΕΧΕΙΛ —— ΤΟΥΔΕΧΡΕΟΥΣΜΗΕΙΝΑΙΑΝΤΙΤΙΜΗΣΙΝ —— ΕΑΝΔΕΗΜΕΝΤΙΜΗΣΙΣΣΥΝΟΜΟΛΟΓΗΤΑΙΤΟΔΕ
ΔΑΝΕΙΟΝΔΙΑΜϘΙΣΒΗΤΗΤΑΙΗΤΟΜΕΝΔΑΝΕΟΝ ΟΜΟΛΟΓΗΤΑΙΗΔΕΤΙΜΗΣΙΧΑΝΤΙΛΕΓΗΤΑΙΓΕΡΙΤΟΥΔΙΑΜϘΙ
5 ΣΒΗΤΟΥΜΕΝΟΥΤΗΓΚΡΙΣΙΝΕΙΝΑΙ —— ΔΔΑΝΟΙΔΙΚΑΣΤΑΙΚΡΙΝΛΣΙΝΑΝΑΓΡΑΨΑΝΤΕΣΕΙΧΛΕΥΚΛΜΔΟΙΕΙΣ
ΑΓΛΓΕΙΣΚΑΙΤΑΣΕΓΙΚΡΙΣΕΙΣΤΑΣΤΛΝΔΙΑΙΤΗΤΛΝΑΣΑΝΕΓΙΤΟΥΔΙΚΑΣΤΗΡΙΟΥΣΥΝΟΜΟΛΟΓΗΣΛΣΙΜΓΑΡΑΔΟΤΛ
ΣΑΝΤΟΙΣΕΓΙΤΟΥΚΟΙΝΟΥΓΟΛΕΜΟΥΗΙΡΗΜΕΝΟΙΣ —— ΟΤΑΝΔΕΓΑΡΑΛΑΒΛΣΙΝΟΙΕΓΙΤΟΥΚΟΙΝΟΥΓΟΛΕΜΟΥΗΙΡΗΜ
ΝΟΙΤΑΣΚΡΙΣΕΙΣΚΑΙΤΑΣΔΙΑΙΤΑΣΚΛΗΡΟΥΤΛΣΑΝΕΚΤΛΝΤΡΙΑΚΟΝΤΑΤΛΝΗΙΡΗΜΕΝΛΝΥΓΟΤΟΥΔΗΜΟΥΚΑΘΕΚΑΣΤ
ΓΕΝΟΗΜΕΡΟΝΑΝΔΡΑΧΓΕΝΤΕΔΙΑΙΡΕΤΑΣΤΛΓΚΤΗΜΑΤΛΝΚΛΗΡΟΥΤΛΣΑΝΔΕΚΑΙΤΟΥΣΤΟΓΟΥΣΑΝΑΓΡΑΨΑΜΕ
10 ΝΟΙΟΙΔΕΛΑΧΟΝΤΕΣΔΙΑΙΡΕΙΤΛΣΑΝΚΑΘΟΥΣΑΝΕΚΑΣΤΟΙΤΟΓΟΥΣΛΛΧΛΣΙΝΜΗΔΙΑΣΓΛΝΤΕΣΜΗΤΕΤΑΤΟΥΤΟΚΙΣΤ
ΜΕΡΙΙΙΙΗΤΓΤΑΤΟΥΓΕΛΡΓΟΥΑΛΛΑΤΑΜΕΡΗΤΕΜΝΟΝΤΕΣΣΥΝΕΧΗΑΛΛΗΛΟΙΣΚΑΙΑΓΟΔΙΔΟΤΛΣΑΝΤΗΣΓΗΣΤΟΙΧΤΟ
ΤΑΛΟΓΟΝΕΚΑΤΕΡΟΙΣΤΛΝΕΝΟΝΤΛΓΧΡΗΜΑΤΛΝΣΥΛΛΟΓΙΣΑΜΕΝΟΙΤΟΤΕΔΑΝΕΟΝΚΑΙΤΗΝΤ
ΑΝΔΕΚΕΝΤΗΙΔΙΑΙΡΕΣΕΙΤΗΣΛΡΑΣΟΔΟΥΣΓΡΟΣΤΕΤΑΙΕΡΑΚΑΙΓΡΟΣΤΑΥΔΑΤΑΚΑΙΓΡΟΣΤΑΣ
ΙΣΚΑΙΓΕ ΙΑΙΟΥΣ —— ΕΑΝΔΕΤΙΝΕΣΔΙΑΜϘΙΣΒΗΤΗΣΛΣΙΝΤΗΓΙΓΕΓΕΝΗΜΕΝΗΙΔΙΑΙΡΕΣΕΙΚΓΑΓΓΕΙΛΑΤΛΣΑ
15 ΕΓΙΤΟΥΚΟΙΝΟΥΓΟΛΕΜΟΥΗΙΡΗΜΕΝΟΙΣΚΑΙΤΛΙΕΓΙΤΟΥΔΙΚΑΣΤΗΡΙΟΥΤΕΤΑΓΜΕΝΛΙ —— ΟΔΕΑΓΟΔΕΔΕΙΓΜΕΝΟΣΙ
ΤΟΥΔΙΚΑΣΤΗΡΙΟΥΕΣΑΓΕΤΛΕΓΙΤΟΝΤΟΓΟΝΟΙΔΕΔΙΚΑΣΤΑΙΕΙΛΝΤΙΔΟΚΗΙΑΥΤΟΙΣΜΗΔΙΚΑΙΛΣΔΙΗΙΡΗΣΘΑΙΑΝΙΣΟΥ
ΤΛΣΑΝΚΑΤΑΛΟΓΟΝΕΚΑΣΤΟΙΣΓΡΟΣΝΕΜΟΝΤΕΣΤΟΥΔΑΝΕΙΟΥΚΑΙΤΗΣΤΙΜΗΣΕΛΣΤΟΥΣΔΕΓΕΝΟΜΕΝΟΥΣΥΓΟΤΛΝ

Column **B.**

ΔΙΑΙΤΗΤΛΝΗΤΛΝΔΙΚΑΣΤΛΝΜΕΡΙΣΜϹΟΥΣ ΑΝΕΝΕΓΚΑ ΛΣΑΝΟΙΔΙΑΙΤΗΤΑΙΚΑΙΟΙ
ΔΙΚΑΣΤΑΙΕΓΙΤΟΥΣΗΙΡΗΜΕΝΟΥΣΕΓΙΤΟΥΚΟΙΝΟΥΓΟΛΕΜΟΥΑΝΑΓΡΑΨΑΝΤΕΣΤΑΤΕΟΝΟ
20 ΜΑΤΑΤΛΝΑΝΔΡΛΝΚΑΙΤΟΥΣΤΟΓΟΥΣΚΑΙΤΟΥΣΟΡΟΥΣΤΛΝΜΕΡΙΣΜΛΝ —— ΟΙΔΕΗΙΡΗΜΕ
ΝΟΙΓΡΑΨΑΝΤΕΣΕΙΣΛΕΥΚΛΜΑΤΑΓΑΡΑΔΟΤΛΣΑΝΤΟΙΣΝΕΛΓΟΙΑΙΣΘΕΙΝΑΙΕΓΙΤΟΕΔΕΘΛΟΝ
ΔΟΤΛΣΑΝΔΕΚΑΙΤΛΙΑΝΤΙΓΡΑϘΕΙΤΟΥΤΛΝΑΝΤΙΓΡΑϘΙΝΕΣΗΙΤΛΙΒΟΥΛΟΜΕΝΛΙΤΛΜΓΟ
ΛΙΤΛΝΕϘΟΙΛΝΤΟΥΣΓΕΓΕΝΗΜΕΝΟΥΣΜΕΡΙΣΜΟΥΣΤΛΝΕΓΓΑΙΛΝΚΑΙΚΟΙΝΗΜΕΝΔΙΑΙΡΕΣΙΝ
ΤΑΥΤΗΝΕΙΝΑΙ —— ΑΝΔΕΓΛΣΛΛΛΣΓΡΟΣΑΥΤΟΥΣΑΜϘΟΛΟΓΗΣΛΣΙΝΥΓΕΡΤΗΣΔΙΑΙΡΕΣΕ
25 ΛΣΚΑΙΑΓΟΓΡΑΨΑΝΤΑΙΓΡΟΣΤΟΥΣΕΓΙΤΟΥΚΟΙΝΟΥΓΟΛΕΜΟΥΟΥΤΛΣΑΥΤΟΙΣΕΙΝΑΙΛΣΑΝΟΜΟ
ΛΟΓΗΣΛΣΙΓΡΟΣΑΛΛΗΛΟΥΣΑΝΤΙΓΡΑϘΑΔΕΛΑΜΒΑΝΕΙΝΤΟΓΓΕΛΡΓΟΝΤΛΝΤΟΥΤ
ΤΟΥΤΟΥΑΥΤΛΙΓΡΟΣΚΟΙΝΛΝΟΥΝΤΟΣΚΑΙΤΗΝΤΛΝΤΟΤΙΚΛΝΓΕΛΡΓΟΥΤΟΥΑΥΤ
ΚΟΙΝΛΝΟΥΝΤΟΣΤΙΜΗΜΑΤΛΓΚΑΙΔΑΝΕΙΛΝΚΑΙΕΓΙΤΟΓΟΝΥΓΕΡΟϘΛΝΟΥΚΑΙΤΟΥΣΣΥ
ΝΙΣΤΑΣΟΥΣΑΝΓΑΡΑΛΑΜΒΑΝΛΣΙΝΕΚ ΑΛΛΛΝΔΕΜΗΘΕΝΑΛΛΑΜΒΑΝΕΙΝΜΗΔΕΤΟΥϪ
30 ΕΓΙΤΟΥΤΛΝΤΕΤΑΓΜΕΝΟΥΣΛΙΔΟΝΑΙ ΑΥΤΟΥΣΛΛΜΒΑΝΕΙΝΕΙΔΕΜΗΕΣΛΛΗΕΙΝΑΙ
ΚΑΙΑΥΤΟΝΤΟΝΛΛΑΒΟΝΤΑΚΑΙΟΣΑΝΕΤΕ ΛΙΚΑΙΥΓΟΔΙΚΟΝΕΙΝΑΙΚΑΙΤΟΝΛΛΑΒΟΝΤΑΚΑΙ
ΤΟΝΔΟΝΤΛΣΑΓΕΙΘΟΥΝΤΑΚΑΙΕΓΙΒΟΥΛΕΥΟΝΤΑΤΟΙΣΣΥϘΕΡΟΥΣΙΤΗΣΓΟΛΕΛΣ —— ΟΧΟΙΔΔΕΓΙ
ΤΟΙΣΥΓΕΡΕΧΟΥΣΙΔΕΔΑΝΕΙΚΑΣΙΝΕΙΝΑΙΤΗΓΚΟΜΙΔΗΝΑΥΤΟΙΣΕΚΤΟΥΓΕΡΙΟΝΤΟΣΜΕΡΟΥΣΤΛΙ
ΓΕΛΡΓΛΙΚΑΝΕΙΣΚΑΜΓΛΕΙΟΥΣΛΣΙΤΟΙΣΓΡΛΤΟΙΣΓΡΛΤΟΙΣΚΑΙΤΟΙΣΑΛΛΟΙΣΕΓΕΣΗΣΤΟΝΔΕ

Column **C.**

35 ΙΟΝΕΙΝΑΙΚΑΙΤΟΥΤΟΙΣΚΑΘΑΓΕΡΚΑΙΤΟΙΣΓΡΛΤΟΙΣΔΑΝΕΙΣΑΣΙΝ —— ΕΙΔΕΤΙΝΕΣ
ΝΤΕΣΑΛΛΟΙΣΚΤΗΜΑΤΑΔΕΔΑΝΕΙΣΜΕΝΟΙΕΙΣΙΜΓΑΡΕΤΕΡΑΝΛΣΕΓΕΛΕΥΘΕΡΟΙΣ
ΤΗΜΑΣΙΝΕΣΑΓΑΤΗΣΑΝΤΕΣΤΟΥΣΥΣΤΕΡΟΥΣΔΑΝΕΙΣΤΑΣΕΣΕΙΝΑΙΤΟΙΣΥΣΤΕΡΟΙΣ
ΤΑΙΣΕΣΑΛΛΑΣΛΣΙΤΟΥΣΓΡΟΤΕΡΟΝΔΑΝΕΙΣΤ ΛΣΚΑΤΑΤΟΝΣΥΛΛΟΓΙΣΜΟΝΤΟΥΚΟΙΝΟΥΓΟ
ΕΧΕΙΝΤΑΚΤΗΜΑΤΑΚΑΝΑΔΕΚΝΟϘΕΙΛΗΤΑΙΤΙΑΥΤΟΙΣΕΤΙΕΙΝΑΙΤΗΓΚΟΜΙΔΗΝΤΟΙΣ
40 ΑΙΣΕΚΤΗΣΑΛΛΗΣΟΥΣΙΑΣΤΟΥΡΧΕΙΣΤΟΥΓΑΣΗΣΤΡΟϘΛΙΛΙΛΙΑΝΔΥΝΛΝΤΑΙΑΣΗΜΙΟΙΣ
ΣΙΧΜΙΑΣΑΝΔΕΚΑΙΕΓΓΥΟΣΗΙΕΙΝΑΙΤΗΝΕΚΤΟΥΕΓΓΥΟΥΚΟΜΙΔΗΝΚΑΘΑΓΕΡΕΚΤΛΝ
ΛΡΑΕΓΓΥΛΜΕΝΛΝ —— ΥΓΕΡΤΛΝΕΓΓΥΛΝΤΛΝΕΓΓΥΛΜΕΝΛΝΛΓΡΟΧ
ΤΑΚΤΗΜΑΤΑ —— ΕΑΜΜΕΝΙΣΜΗΙΗΤΙΜΗΤΟΥΚΤΗΜΑΤΟΣΤΛΙΔΑΝΕΙΛΙΓΡΟΧΟ
ΓΓΥΟΣΤΗΙΤΙΜΗΣΕΙΤΗΙΓΡΟΤΟΥΓΟΛΕΜΟΥΓΕΓΕΝΗΜΕΝΗΙΔΙΗΡΛΛΛΣΘΑΙΤΟΝΕΓΓ
45 ΣΕΓΓΥΗΣΕΚΑΝΔΕΓΛΕΟΝΗΙΤΟΟϘΕΙΛΗΜΑΤΗΣΤΙΜΗΣΤΟΥΚΤΗΜΑΤΟΣΤΟΓΛΕΟΝΟϘΕΙ

ˉΙΜΗΧΟΕΓΓΥΟΧΑΓΟΤΙΝΕΤ∧ΚΑΤΑΛΟΓΟΝ∧ΣΓΕΡΟΙΑΛΛΟΙΟΙΤΑΜΕΤΕ∧ΡΑΕΓΓΥ∧
ΜΗΕΓΙΤΕΤΟΚΙΧΜΕΝΟΝΗΙΕΙΧΓ∧ΕΙ∧ΧΡΟΝΟΝΤΗΧΕΝΤΗΙΓΡΑΞΕΙΓΕΓΕΝΗΜΕΝΗΧ
——— ΕΑΝΔΕΕΓΙΤΕΤΟΚΙΚ∧ΧΗΟΔΑΝΕΙΧΤΗΧΓΑΡΑΤΗΜΓΡΑΞΙΝΚΑΙΤΟΝ
∧ΜΟΛΟΓΗΜΕΝΟΝΕΝΤΗΙΓΡΑΞΕΙΧΜΚΑΓΟΤΙΝΕΙΝΤΟΝΕΓΓΥΟΝ∧ΙΓ∧ΕΙΟΝ
ΚΤΟΚ ΜΕΝΟΝΕΑΜΜΗΕΓΕΧΧΗΚ∧ΧΗΙΤΗΝΕΙΧΓΡΑΞΙΝΟΤΟΚΙΧΤΗΧΧΥΜΒΟΥ
ΤΟΥΕΓΓΥΟΥΓΕΡΙΔΕΤΟΥΤΟΥΑΝΑΜΦΙΧΒΗΤ∧ΧΙΓΚΡΙΧΙΝΑΥΤΟΙΧΓΙΝΕΧΘΑΙ

D.

ΕΓΙΤΟΥΞΕΝΙΚΟΥΔΙΚΑΧΤΗΡΙΟΥΑΜΜΗΤΙΥΓΟΤ∧ΝΔΙΑΙΤΗΤ∧ΝΧΥΜΓ
ΤΗΧΔΕΔΙΚΗΧΑΡΧΕΙΝΤΟΝΤΟΚΙΧΤΗΝ ——— ΕΙΔΕΤΙΧΕΓΙΤΡΟΓΟΧΕΝΤΗΙΕΙ
ΛΑΒ∧ΝΑΥΤΟΧΕΚΕΙΧΡΗΜΑΤΑΤ∧ΝΤΟΥΟΡΦΑΝΟΥΤΡΟΓ∧ΙΟΤ∧ΙΟΥΝΤΟΥΤ∧
ΕΙΝΑΙΚΟΙΝΟΝΤΟΜΓΟΛΕΜΟΝ ——— ΟΧΟΙΔΕΦΕΡΝΑΧΟΦΕΙΛΟΥΧΙΘΥΓΑΤΡΙΟΙΧΗ
ΔΕΛΦΑΙΧΤΑΙΧΑΥΤ∧ΝΜΕΜΕΡΙΚΟΤΕΧΕΚΤΗΧΓΑΤΡ∧ΙΑΧΟΥΧΙΑΧΗΕΓΙΤΡΟΓΟΙ
ΥΓΟΓΑΤΡΟΧΚΑΤΑΛΕΛΕΙΜΜΕΝΟΙΗΥΓΟΔΗΜΟΥΗΙΡΗΜΕΝΟΙΤΑΙΧΟΡΦΑΝΑΙΧ
ΤΑΙΧΥΓΑΥΤ∧ΝΕΓΙΤΡΟΓΕΥΟΜΕΝΑΙΧΜΗΑΓΟΔΕΔ∧ΚΑΧΙΤΑΧΦΕΡΝΑΧΑΧΟΙ
ΓΑΤΕΡΕΧΕΤΑΞΑΝΗΓΗΜΑΝΤΕΧΚΑΙ ΔΙΑΛΥΘΕΝΤΕΧΜΗΑΓΟΔΕΔ∧ΚΑ
ΧΙΤΑΧΦΕΡΝΑΧΟΥΧΑΧΑΓΟΔΟΤΟΥΧΚΑΤΑΤΟΝΝΟΜΟΝΤΟΥΤΟΥΧΑΓΟΔΙΔΟΝΑΙ
ΤΑΧΦΕΡΝΑΧΚΑΙΤΟΥΧΤΟΚΟΥΧΚΑΤΑΤΑΧΓΡΑΞΕΙΧΚΑΙΜΗΕΙΝΑΙΑΥΤΟΙΧΥΓΟΛΟ
ΓΙΧΕΧΘΑΙΤΟΓΚΟΙΝΟΝΓΟΛΕΜΟΝΑΛΛΑΤΟΓΕΝΟΜΕΝΟΝΔΙΑΓΓ∧ΜΑΑΝΑΓΑΗ
ΡΟΥΤ∧ΧΑΝΕΙΧΤΗΝΦΕΡΝΗΝΤΑΙΧΟΡΦΑΝΑΙΧΟΙΕΓΙΤΡΟΓΟΙΕΚΤΟΥΑΛΛΟΥΟΙΚΟ
ΟΥΑΝΕΓΙΤΡΟΓΕΥ∧ΧΙ

E.

ΟΧΟΙΔΕΕΓΙΚΤΗ ΑΧΙΝΔΕΔΑΝΕΙΧΜΕΝΟΙΕΙΧΙΝΑΓΟΔΗΜΑΓΟΡΟΥΓΡΥΤΑΝΕ∧ΧΚΑΙΜΗΝΟΧΓΟΧΙΔΕ∧
ΝΟΧΤΟΥΤΟΙΧΤ ΜΜΕΓΚΟΙΝΟΜΓΟΛΕΜΟΝΕΙΝΑΙ∧ΧΓΕΡΚΑΙΤΟΙΧΑΛΛΟΙΧΤΑΧΔΕΤΙΜΗΧΕΙΧΕΙΝΑΙ
ΤΑΓΚΤΗΜΑ ∧ΝΕΝΟΙΧΡΟΝΟΙΧΤΑΔΑΝΕΔΑΚΑΙΑΙΓΡΑΞΕΙΧΓΕΓΟΝΑΧΙΝΟΓ∧ΧΕΙΤΙΝΕΧΚΕΚΑΡΜΕΝΟΙΧ
ΤΟΙΧΚΤΗΜΑ ΙΝΗΤ∧ΝΕΓΑΥΛΙ∧ΝΚΑΘΗΡΗΜΕΝ∧ΝΧΥΝΗΛΛΑΧΑΧΙΝΟΥΤ∧ΧΑΙΤΙΜΗΧΕΙΧΑΥΤ∧Ν
ΓΙΝ∧ΝΤΑΙ∧ΧΔΙΑΚΕΙΜΕΝΟΙΧΧΥΝΗΛΛΑΞΑΝΤΟΙΧΚΤΗΜΑΧΙΝ ——— ΟΧΟΙΔΕΓΓΡΟΔΑΓΟΛΛΑΔΟΧ
ΚΑΙΜΗΝΟΧ ΗΝΑΙ∧ΝΟΧΓΡΑΞΕΙΧΓΕΓΡΑΓΑΧΙΝΕΝΑΝΤΙΑΧΤ∧ΙΚΟΙΝ∧ΙΓΟΛΕΜ∧ΙΜΗΕΙΝΑΙΤΑΧ
ΓΡΑΞΕΙΧΚΥ ΙΑΧΑΛΛΕΙΝΑΙΤΟΥΧΟΦΕΙΛΟΝΤΑΧΤΟΥΤΟΙΧΕΝΤ∧ΙΚΟΙΝ∧ΙΓΟΛΕΜ∧Ι ——— ΟΧΟΙΔΕΑΓΟ
ΜΗΝΟΧΛΗ ΑΙ∧ΝΟΧΚΑΙΑΓΟΛΛ∧ΓΡΑΞΕΙΧΓΕΓΡΑΓΑΧΙΝΕΓΙΤΟΙΧΚΤΗΜΑΧΙΝΤΟΥΤΟΙΧΔΕΙΝΑΙ
ΤΑΧΓΡΑΞΕ ΚΥΡΙΑΧΚΑΙΜΗΕΙΝΑΙΑΥΤΟΙΧΚΟΙΝΟΝΤΟΜΓΟΛΕΜΟΝΕΓΕΙΔΗΕΝΤ∧ΙΓΟΛΕΜ∧ΙΔΙΑΓΙ
ΧΤΕΥΧΑΝˉ ΕΙΧΕΥΓΟΡΗΧΑΝΤΟΚΟΥΧΔΕΑΥΤΟΙΧΕΙΝΑΙΜΗΛΕΙΟΥΧΔ∧ΔΕΚΑΤ∧Ν ——— ΥΓΕΡ
Τ∧ΝΔΑΝΕ ∧ΝΤ∧ΝΕΜΒΕΒΗΚΟΤ∧ΝΕΙΧΚΤΗΜΑΤΑ ——— ΟΧΟΙΜΕΜΓΡΟΜΝΗΝΟΧΓΟΧΙΔΕ∧ΝΟΧ
ΤΟΥΕΓΙΔ∧ ∧ΓΟΡΟΥΕΜΒΑΝΤΕΧΕΙΧΚΤΗΜΑΤΑΚΑΤΑΓΡΑΞΕΙΧΕΧΟΥΧΙΝΤΑΚΤΗΜΑΤΑΚΑΙΝΕΜΟΝ
ΤΑΙΕΙΝΑΙ ΤΟΙΧΚΥΡΙΑΧΤΑΧΕΜΒΑΧΕΙΧΕΙΜΗΤΙΑΛΛΟΕΚΟΝΤΕΓΓΟΧΑΥΤΟΥΧ∧ΜΟΛΟΓΗΚΑΧΙΝΓΕΡΙ
ΔΕΤΗΧΓ ˉΚΤΗΧΙΑΧΑΝΤΙΝΕΧΑΜΦΙΧΒΗΤ∧ΧΙΝΚΡΙΧΙΝΑΥΤΟΙΧΕΙΝΑΙΚΑΤΑΤΟΥΧΝΟΜΟΥΧ
ΟΧΟΙΔΕΕΜ ΒΗΚΑΧΙΝΥΧΤΕΡΟΝΜΗΝΟΧΓΟΧΙΔΕ∧ΝΟΧΤΟΥΕΓΙΔΗΜΑΓΟΡΑΝΕΜΟΜΕΝ∧ΝΤ∧ΝΔΕΔΑ
ΝΕΙΧΜΕΝ ΚΤΗΜΑΤΑΚΑΤΑΤΟΥΗΦΙΧΜΑΚΑΙΚΑΤΗΓΜΕΝ∧ΝΥΓΟΤΟΥΔΗΜΟΥΤΑΜΕΓΚΤΗΜΑ
ΤΑΕΙΝΑ ΝΕΙΧΑΜΕΝ∧ΓΚΑΙΝΕΜΟΜΕΝ∧ΝΤΑΔΕΔΑΝΕΙΑΤ∧ΝΔΑΝΕΙΧΤ∧ΝΤΟΥΜΕΡΙΧΜΟΥ

F.

ΓΕΝΟΜΕΝΟΥΚΑΘΑΓΕΡΚΑΙΤΟΙΧΑΛΛΟΙΧΔΑΝΕΙΧΤΑΙΧ ——— ΕΑΝΔΕΔΙΑΜΦΙΧΒΗΤΗΧ∧ΧΙΝΟΙΔΑΝΕΙ
ΧΑΝΤΕΧΓΡΟΧΤΟΥΧΟΦΕΙΛΟΝΤΑΧΦ∧ΜΕΝΟΙΕΜΒΕΒΗΚΕΝΑΙΓΡΟΤΕΡΟΝΔΗΜΑΓΟΡΟΥΓΡΥΤΑΝΕ∧ΧΚΑΙΜΗ
ΝΟΧΓΟΧΙΔΕ∧ΝΟΧΚΡΙΧΙΝΑΥΤΟΙΧΓΙΝΕΧΘΑΙΚΑΘΑΓΕΡΚΑΙΤΟΙΧΑΛΛΟΙΧΤΟΙΧΕΝΤ∧ΙΚΟΙΝ∧ΙΓΟΛΕΜ∧ΙΕΒΑΔΜ
ΜΕΝΟΙΧ ——— ΕΙΔΕΤΙΝΕΧΜΗΕΜΒΑΝΤ∧ΝΤ∧ΝΔΑΝΕΙΧΤ∧ΝΑΥΤΟΙΝΕΜΟΜΕΝΟΙΤΑΚΤΗΜΑΤΑΕΚΟΝΤΕΧΤΙ
ΧΥΝ∧ΜΟΛΟΓΗΝΤΑΙΓΡΟΧΤΟΥΧΔΑΝΕΙΧΤΑΧΜΗΒΙΑΧΘΕΝΤΕΧΕΙΝΑΙΑΥΤΟΙΧΤΑ∧ΜΟΛΟΓΗΜΕΝΑΚΥΡΙΑ
ΕΑΝΔΕΟΜΕΜΦΗΒΕΒΙΑΧΘΑΙΟ∧ΜΟΛΟΓΗΚΕΝΑΙΑΥΤΟΙΧΚΡΙΧΙΝΓΕΓΙΤΟΥΤ∧ΝΕΝΤ∧ΙΞΕΝΙΚ∧ΙΔΙΚΑΧΤΗΡΙ∧ΙΓΡΟ
ΔΙΑΙΤΑΧΘΑΙΔΕΑΥΤΟΥΧΕΓΙΤ∧ΝΔΙΑΙΤΗΤ∧ΝΚΑΤΑΤΟΝΔΕΤΟΝΝΟΜΟΝ ——— ΟΧΟΙΔΕΕΓΙΚΑΤΑΛΙΓΟΝΤΕΧΤΑ
ΚΤΗΜΑΤΑΔΑΓΗΛΛΑΑΓΜΕΝΟΙΕΙΧΙΝΟΙΔΕΤΟΚΙΧΤΑΙΓΕΓΕ∧ΡΓΗΚΑΧΙΝΕΙΝΑΙΤΑΚΤΗΜΑΤΑΤ∧ΝΤΟΚΙΧΤ∧Ν
ΕΑΝΔΕΒΟΥΛ∧ΝΤΑΙΟΙΟΦΕΙΛΟΝΤΕΧΑΓΟΔΟΝΤΕΧΤΑΑΝΗΛΑΜΕΝΑΤΟΙΧΤΟΚΙΧΤΑΙΧΚΑΙΤΟΚΟΥΧΕΓΙ
ΤΕΧΧΕΡΑΧΚΑΙΔΕΚΑΤΟΥΧΚΑΙΕΙΤΙΑΥΤΟΙΧΑΝΗΛ∧ΤΑΙΕΙΧΤΗΓΓΗΝΗΑΓΟΛ∧∧ΕΤΙΔΙΑΤΗΓΓΕ∧ΡΓΙΑΝ
ΥΓΟΛΟΓΙΧΘΕΙΧ∧ΝΤ∧ΓΓΕΓΕΝΗΜΕΝ∧ΝΓΡΟΧΟΔ∧∧ΜΓΑΡΑΛΑΒΕΙΝΤΑΚΤΗΜΑΤΑΔΕΞΕΙΝΑΙΑΥΤΟΙΧΑΓΟ
ΔΟΥΧΙΝΕΝΕΝΙΑΥΤ∧ΙΤΑΙΕΓΙΔΑΝΑΟΥΜΕΤΕΧΕΙΝΑΥΤΟΥΧΤΟΥΚΟΙΝΟΥΓΟΛΕΜΟΥΚΑΤΑΤΑΥΤΑ
ΤΟΙΧΑΛΛΟΙΧ ——— ΥΓΕΡΔΑΓΓΕΓΕΝΗΜΕΝ∧ΝΚΑΙΜΗΑΓΟ∧∧∧ΟΤ∧ΝΕΝΤΗΙ
ΓΕ∧ΡΓΙΑΙΚΑΙΤΑ∧ΓΡΟΧΟΔ∧ΝΤ∧ΓΓΕΓΕΝΗΜΕΝ∧Ν∧ΝΕΑ∧ΜΜΕΝΤΙΓΡΟΧΑΛΛΗΛΟΥΧΧΥΜΦ∧ΝΗ
Χ∧ΧΙΝΗΧΥΜΓΕΙΧΟ∧ΧΙΝΥΓΟΤ∧ΝΔΙΑΙΤΗΤ∧ΝΤΑΥΤΕΙΝΑΙΕΙΔΕΜΗΚΡΙΧΙΝΑΥΤΟΙΧΕΙΝΑΙΕΓΙΤΟΥ
ΞΕΝΙΚΟΥΔΙΚΑΧΤΗΡΙΟΥΚΑΘΑΓΕΡΚΑΙΤΟΙΧΑΛΛΟΙΧΤΗΧΔΕΔΙΚΗΧΑΡΧΕΙΝΤΟΝΕΓΚΑΤΑΛΙΓΟΝΤΑ
ΤΟΚΤΗΜΑΕΙΔΕΤΙΝΕΧΕΓΙΔΗΜΑΓΟΡΟΥΗΝΜΑΝΤΙΚΡΑΤΟΥΧΑΓΟΛΛΑΔΟΧΕ∧ΧΜΗΝΟΧΓΟΧΙΔΕ∧ΝΟ

ＦＩ

Col. A. οἱ δικασταί. —— Ἐξεῖναι δὲ τοῖς δικασταῖς, ἐὰν αὐτοῖς μὴ φαίνηται δικαστικὸν εἶναι τὸ πρᾶγμα, ἀλλ' ὁ μὲν
γεωργὸς πλέονος τετιμῆσθαι ὁ δὲ τοκιστὴς ἐλάττονος, ἐξεῖναι αὐτοῖς τιμῆσαι ὅσου ἂν δοκῇ καλῶς
ἔχειν· —— τοῦ δὲ χρέους μὴ εἶναι ἀντιτίμησιν —— ἐὰν δὲ ἡ μὲν τίμησις συνομολογῆται τὸ δὲ
δάνειον διαμφισβητῆται, ἢ τὸ μὲν δάνειον [συν]ομολογῆται ἡ δὲ τίμησις ἀντιλέγηται, περὶ τοῦ διαμφι-
5 σβητουμένου τὴν κρίσιν εἶναι· —— ἃ δ' ἂν οἱ δικασταὶ κρίνωσιν ἀναγράψαντες εἰς λεύκωμα οἱ εἰσα-
γωγεῖς καὶ τὰς ἐπικρίσεις τὰς τῶν διαιτητῶν ἃς ἂν ἐπὶ τοῦ δικαστηρίου συνομολογήσωσιν παραδότωσαν τοῖς ἐπὶ τοῦ κοινοῦ πολέμου ᾑρημένοις· —— ὅταν δὲ παραλάβωσιν οἱ ἐπὶ τοῦ κοινοῦ πολέμου ᾑρημένοι τὰς κρίσεις καὶ τὰς διαίτας, κληρούτωσαν ἐκ τῶν τριάκοντα τῶν ᾑρημένων ὑπὸ τοῦ δήμου καθ' ἑκάστην
πενθήμερον ἄνδρας πέντε διαιρέτας τῶν κτημάτων, κληρούτωσαν δὲ καὶ τοὺς τόπους ἀναγραψάμε-
10 νοι· οἱ δὲ λαχόντες διαιρείτωσαν καθ' οὓς ἂν ἕκαστοι τόπους λάχωσιν, μὴ διασπῶντες μήτε τὰ τοῦ τοκιστοῦ
μέρη μήτε τὰ τοῦ γεωργοῦ, ἀλλὰ τὰ μέρη τέμνοντες συνεχῆ ἀλλήλοις· καὶ ἀποδιδότωσαν τῆς γῆς τοῖς τοκισταῖς
καὶ τοῖς γεωργοῖς κα]τὰ λόγον ἑκατέροις τῶν ἐνόντων χρημάτων, συλλογισάμενοι τό τε δάνειον καὶ τὴν τί-
μησιν· ἀφοριζέτωσ]αν δὲ ἐν τῇ διαιρέσει τῆς χώρας ὁδοὺς πρός τε τὰ ἱερὰ καὶ πρὸς τὰ ὕδατα καὶ πρὸς τὰς ἐπαύ-
λια]ς καὶ π[ε]ρὶ τ]ἄφρους· —— ἐὰν δέ τινες διαμφισβητήσωσιν τῇ γεγενημένῃ διαιρέσει, ἐπαγγειλάτωσαν τοῖς
15 ἐπὶ τοῦ κοινοῦ πολέμου ᾑρημένοις καὶ τῷ ἐπὶ τοῦ δικαστηρίου τεταγμένῳ· —— ὁ δὲ ἀποδεδειγμένος ἐπὶ
τοῦ δικαστηρίου ἐξαγέτω ἐπὶ τὸν τόπον· οἱ δὲ δικασταὶ ἐάν τι δοκῇ αὐτοῖς μὴ δικαίως διῃρῆσθαι ἀνισού-
τωσαν κατὰ λόγον ἑκάστοις προσνέμοντες τοῦ δανείου καὶ τῆς τιμήσεως, τοὺς δὲ γενομένους ὑπὸ τῶν

Col. B. διαιτητῶν ἢ τῶν δικαστῶν μερισμοὺς ἀνενεγκά[τ]ωσαν οἱ διαιτηταὶ καὶ οἱ
δικασταὶ ἐπὶ τοὺς ᾑρημένους ἐπὶ τοῦ κοινοῦ πολέμου, ἀναγράψαντες τά τε ὀνό-
20 ματα τῶν ἀνδρῶν καὶ τοὺς τόπους καὶ τοὺς ὅρους τῶν μερισμῶν· —— οἱ δὲ ᾑρημένοι γράψαντες εἰς λευκώματα παραδότωσαν τοῖς νεωποίαις θεῖναι ἐπὶ τὸ ἐδέθλον,
δότωσαν δὲ καὶ τῷ ἀντιγραφεῖ τούτων ἀντίγραφα, ἵν' ἐξῇ τῷ βουλομένῳ τῶν πολιτῶν ἐφορᾶν τοὺς γεγενημένους μερισμοὺς τῶν ἐγγαίων, καὶ κοινὴν μὲν διαίρεσιν
ταύτην εἶναι· —— ἂν δέ πως ἄλλως πρὸς αὑτοὺς ὁμολογήσωσιν ὑπὲρ τῆς διαιρέσε-
25 ως καὶ ἀπογράψωνται πρὸς τοὺς ἐπὶ τοῦ κοινοῦ πολέμου, οὕτως αὐτοὺς ὡς ἂν ὁμο-
λογήσωσι πρὸς ἀλλήλους, ἀντίγραφα δὲ λαμβάνειν τὸν γεωργὸν τῶν τοῦ τ[οκισ-
τοῦ τοῦ αὐτῷ προσκοινωνοῦντος καὶ τὸν τοκιστὴν τῶν τοῦ γεωργοῦ τοῦ αὐτ[ῷ προσκοινωνοῦντος τιμημάτων καὶ δανείων καὶ ἐπίτροπον ὑπὲρ ὀρφάνου καὶ τοὺς ὀρφα-
νιστὰς οὓς ἂν παραλαμβάνωσιν ἕκ[αστοι·] ἄλλων δὲ μηθένα λαμβάνειν μηδὲ τοὺς
30 ἐπὶ τούτων τεταγμένους διδόναι [μηδὲ] αὐτοὺς λαμβάνειν· εἰ δὲ μή, ἑξώλη εἶναι
καὶ αὐτὸν τὸν λαβόντα καὶ ὃς ἂν ἐτ[έρῳ δ]ῷ, καὶ ὑπόδικον εἶναι καὶ τὸν λαβόντα καὶ
τὸν δόντα ὡς ἀπειθοῦντα καὶ ἐπιβουλεύοντα τοῖς συ(μ)φέρουσι τῆς πόλεως· —— ὅσοι δὲ ἐπὶ
τοῖς ὑπέρχουσι δεδανείκασιν, εἶναι τῆς κομιδῆς αὐτοῖς ἐκ τοῦ περιόντος μέρους τῷ
γεωργῷ κἂν εἷς κἂν πλείους ὦσι, τοῖς πρώτοις πρώτοις καὶ τοῖς ἄλλοις ἐφεξῆς, τὸν δὲ

Col. C. 35 μερισ]μὸν εἶναι καὶ τούτοις καθάπερ καὶ τοῖς πρώτοις δανείσασιν. —— εἰ δέ τινες
ὑποθέ]ντες ἄλλοις κτήματα δεδανεισμένοι εἰσὶμ παρ' ἑτέρων ὡς ἐπ' ἐλευθέροις
τοῖς κ]τήμασιν ἐξαπατήσαντες τοὺς ὑστέρους δανειστάς, ἐξεῖναι τοῖς ὑστέροις
δανεισ]ταῖς ἐξαλλάξασι τοὺς πρὸτερον δανειστὰς καὶ τὸν συλλογισμὸν τοῦ κοινοῦ πο-
λέμου] ἔχειν τὰ κτήματα· ἐὰν δὲ ἐνοφειληθῇ τι αὐτοῖς ἔτι, εἶναι τὴν κομιδὴν τοῖς
40 δανεισταῖς ἐκ τῆς ἄλλης οὐσίας τοῦ χρεώστου πάσης τρόπῳ ᾧ ἂν δύνωνται ἀζημίοις
ἀπάσης ζημίας· ἂν δὲ καὶ ἔγγυος ᾖ, εἶναι τὴν ἐκ τοῦ ἐγγύου κομιδὴν καθάπερ ἐκ τῶν
μετ]έωρα ἐγγυωμένων. —— ὑπὲρ τῶν ἐγγύων τῶν ἐγγυωμένων πρὸς
αὑτὰ] τὰ κτήματα· ἐὰμ μὲν ἴση ᾖ ἢ τιμὴ τοῦ κτήματος τῷ δανείῳ πρὸς ὃ
ἂν ᾖ ἔ]γγυος, τῇ τιμήσει τῇ πρὸ τοῦ πολέμου γεγενημένῃ, ἀπηλλάχθαι τὸν ἐγγύ-
45 ον τῆ]ς ἐγγύης· ἐὰν δὲ πλέον ᾖ τὸ ὀφείλημα τῆς τιμῆς τοῦ κτήματος, τὸ πλέον ὀφείλημα τῆς] τιμῆς ὁ ἔγγυος ἀποτινέτω κατὰ λόγον ὥσπερ οἱ ἄλλοι οἱ τὰ μετέωρα ἐγγυώ-
μενοι, ἐὰμ] μὴ ἐπιτετοκισμένον ᾖ εἰς πλείω χρόνον τῆς ἐν τῇ πράξει γεγενημένης
ἐγγύης] —— ἐὰν δὲ ἐπιτετοκικὼς ᾖ ὁ δανειστὴς παρὰ τὴμ πρᾶξιν καὶ τὸν
χρόνον τὸν] ὡμολογημένον ἐν τῇ πράξει, μὴ ἀποτίνειν ὑπὲρ τούτου τὸ πλέον
50 ἢ ἐπιτετοκ[ισ]μένον ἐὰμ μὴ ἐπεισχνηκῇ ᾖ τὴν εἴσπραξιν ὁ τοκιστὴς συμβου-
λομένου] τοῦ ἐγγύου· περὶ δὲ τούτου ἂν ἀμφισβητῶσι, κρίσιν αὐτοῖς γίνεσθαι

Col. D. ἐπὶ τοῦ ξενικοῦ δικαστηρίου ἂμ μή τι ὑπὸ τῶν διαιτητῶν συμπ[εισθῶσι
τῆς δὲ δίκης ἄρχειν τὸν τοκιστήν· —— εἰ δέ τις ἐπίτροπος ἐν τῇ ἐ[πιτροπῇ
λαβὼν αὐτὸς ἔχει χρήματα τῶν τοῦ ὀρφανοῦ τρόπῳ ὁτῳοῦν, τούτῳ [μὴ
55 εἶναι κοινὸν τὸμ πόλεμον· —— ὅσοι δὲ φερνὰς ὀφείλουσι θυγατρίοις ἢ [ἀ-
δελφαῖς ταῖς αὑτῶν μεμερικότες ἐκ τῆς πατρῴας οὐσίας, ἢ ἐπίτροποι
ὑπὸ πατρὸς καταλελειμμένοι ἢ ὑπὸ δήμου ᾑρημένοι ταῖς ὀρφαναῖς
ταῖς ὑπ' αὑτῶν ἐπιτροπευομέναις μὴ ἀποδεδώκασι τὰς φερνὰς ἃς οἱ
πατέρες ἔταξαν, ἢ γήμαντες καὶ διαλυθέντες μὴ ἀποδεδώκα·

60 σι τὰς φερνὰς οὔσας ἀποδότους κατὰ τὸν νόμον, τούτους ἀποδιδόναι
τὰς φερνὰς καὶ τοὺς τόκους κατὰ τὰς πράξεις καὶ μὴ εἶναι αὐτοῖς ὑπολο-
γίζεσθαι τὸν κοινὸμ πόλεμον, ἀλλὰ τὸ γενόμενον διάπτωμα ἀναπλη-
ροῦτωσαν εἰς τὴν φερνὴν ταῖς ὀρφαναῖς οἱ ἐπίτροποι ἐκ τοῦ ἄλλου οἴκο[υ
οὗ ἂν ἐπιτροπεύωσι.   (*Here Column D ends: whether any interval, and if so how much, inter-*
venes between D and E, we cannot determine. For convenience the lines are numbered straight
on, as E and F certainly form a very suitable appendix to the foregoing.)

Col. E. 65 Ὅσοι δὲ ἐπὶ κτή[μ]ασιν δεδανεισμένοι εἰσὶν ἀπὸ Δημαγόρου πρυτάνεως καὶ μηνὸς Ποσιδεῶνος, τούτοις τ[ὸ]μ μὲν κοινὸμ πόλεμον εἶναι ὥσπερ καὶ τοῖς ἄλλοις, τὰς δὲ τιμήσεις εἶναι
τῶν κτημά[τ]ων ἐν οἷς χρόνοις τὰ δάνεια καὶ αἱ πράξεις γεγόνασιν, ὅπως εἴ τινες κεκαρμένοις
τοῖς κτήμα[σ]ιν ἢ τῶν ἐπαυλίων καθηρημένων συνηλλάχασιν οὕτως αἱ τιμήσεις αὐτῶν
γίνωνται ὡς διακειμένοις συνήλλαξαν τοῖς κτήμασιν —— ὅσοι δὲ πρὸ Ἀπολλάδος
70 καὶ μηνὸς [Λ]ηναιῶνος πράξεις πεπράγασιν ἐναντίας τῷ κοινῷ πολέμῳ, μὴ εἶναι τὰς
πράξεις κυ[ρ]ίας ἀλλ' εἶναι τοὺς ὀφείλοντας τούτοις ἐν τῷ κοινῷ πολέμῳ· —— ὅσοι δὲ ἀπὸ
μηνὸς Λη[ν]αιῶνος καὶ Ἀπολλᾶ πράξεις πεπράγασιν ἐπὶ τοῖς κτήμασιν, τούτοις δ' εἶναι
τὰς πράξε[ις] κυρίας καὶ μὴ εἶναι αὐτοῖς κοινὸν τὸμ πόλεμον, ἐπειδὴ ἐν τῷ πολέμῳ διαπι-
στεύσαντ[ες] εἰσηνέχθησαν τόκους δὲ αὐτοῖς εἶναι μὴ πλείους δωδεκάτων. —— ὑπὲρ
75 τῶν δανει[στ]ῶν τῶν ἐμβεβηκότων εἰς κτήματα ——ὅσοι μὲμ πρὸ μηνὸς Ποσιδεῶνος
τοῦ ἐπὶ Δη[μ]αγόρου ἐμβάντες εἰς κτήματα κατὰ πράξεις ἔχουσιν τὰ κτήματα καὶ νέμον-
ται, εἶναι [αὐ]τοῖς κυρίας τὰς ἐμβάσεις εἰ μή τι ἄλλο ἑκόντες πρὸς αὐτοὺς ὡμολογήκασιν περὶ
δὲ τῆς π[αγ]κτησίας ἄν τινες ἀμφισβητῶσιν, κρίσιν αὐτοῖς εἶναι κατὰ τοὺς νόμους.
ὅσοι δὲ ἐμ[β]ε[β]ήκασιν ὕστερον μηνὸς Ποσιδεῶνος τοῦ ἐπὶ Δημαγόρου νεμομένων τῶν δεδα-
80 νεισμένω[ων τὰ] κτήματα κατὰ τὸ ψήφισμα καὶ κατηγμένων ὑπὸ τοῦ δήμου, τὰ μὲν κτήματα εἶναι[ι τῶν δα]νεισαμένων καὶ νεμομένων, τὰ δὲ δάνεια τῶν δανειστῶν, τοῦ μερισμοῦ

Col. F. γενομένου καθάπερ καὶ τοῖς ἄλλοις δανεισταῖς· —— ἐὰν δὲ διαμφισβητήσωσιν οἱ δανεί-
σαντες πρὸς τοὺς ὀφείλοντας φάμενοι ἐμβεβηκέναι πρότερον Δημαγόρου πρυτάνεως καὶ μηνὸς Ποσιδεῶνος, κρίσιν αὐτοῖς γίνεσθαι καθάπερ καὶ τοῖς ἄλλοις τοῖς ἐν τῷ κοινῷ πολέμῳ ἰβλαμ-
85 μένοις· —— εἰ δέ τινες μὴ ἐμβάντων τῶν δανειστῶν αὐτοὶ νεμόμενοι τὰ κτήματα ἑκόντες τι
συνωμολόγηνται πρὸς τοὺς δανειστὰς μὴ βιασθέντες, εἶναι αὐτοῖς τὰ ὡμολογημένα κύρια·
ἐὰν δὲ ὁ μὲμ φῇ βεβιάσθαι ὁ δὲ μή, εἶναι αὐτοῖς κρίσιν περὶ τούτων ἐν τῷ ξενικῷ δικαστηρίῳ, προ-
διαιτᾶσθαι δὲ αὐτοὺς ἐπὶ τῶν διαιτητῶν κατὰ τόνδε τὸν νόμον· —— ὅσοι δὲ ἐγκαταλιπόντες τὰ
κτήματα φυγάδες εἰσὶν οἱ δὲ τοκισταὶ γεγεωργήκασιν, εἶναι τὰ κτήματα τῶν τοκιστῶν·
90 ἐὰν δὲ βούλωνται οἱ ὀφείλοντες ἀποδόντες τὰ ἀνηλωμένα τοῖς τοκισταῖς καὶ τόκους ἐπὶ
τέσσαρας καὶ δεκάτους καὶ εἴ τι αὐτοῖς ἀνήλωται εἰς τὴν γῆν ἢ ἀπόλωλέ τι διὰ τὴν γεωργίαν
ὑπολογισθεισῶν τῶν γεγεωργημένων προσόδωμ παραλαβεῖν τὰ κτήματα, ἐξεῖναι αὐτοῖς ἀπο-
δοῦσιν ἐν ἐνιαυτῷ τῷ ἐπὶ Δαναοῦ μετέχειν αὐτοὺς τοῦ κοινοῦ πολέμου κατὰ ταὐτὰ
τοῖς ἄλλοις· —— ὑπὲρ δὲ τῶν γεγεωργημένων ἀναλωμάτων καὶ τῶν ἀπολωλότων ἐν τῇ
95 γεωργίᾳ καὶ τῶμ προσόδων τῶν γεγεωργημένων ἐὰμ μέν τι πρὸς ἀλλήλους συμφωνή-
σωσιν ἢ συμπεισθῶσιν ὑπὸ τῶν διαιτητῶν, ταῦτ' εἶναι· εἰ δὲ μή, κρίσιν αὐτοῖς εἶναι ἐπὶ τοῦ
ξενικοῦ δικαστηρίου καθάπερ καὶ τοῖς ἄλλοις, τῆς δὲ δίκης ἄρχειν τὸν ἐγκαταλιπόντα
τὸ κτῆμα· εἰ δέ τινες ἐπὶ Δημαγόρου ἢ Μαντικράτους ἢ Ἀπολλάδος ἕως μηνὸς Ποσιδεῶνο[ς . . .

(*The rest of the inscription is lost.*)

Long as this inscription is, it is imperfect at the end and probably at the beginning. For though οἱ δικασταί in line 1 might be taken as a heading or title, it is far more likely to be the subject of a lost verb; and in any case it must have been preceded by some form of preamble and date. We are therefore left to conjecture the occasion and origin of these elaborate enactments. The style of the characters very markedly resembles that of the preceding decrees, and it is difficult to suppose that this inscription was separated from them by any long interval of time. The iota adscriptum is constant, and the Greek is good. Very few blunders occur: as M omitted in line 32 (though the form συφέρουσι might conceivably be intentional). Certain Ionicisms are observable, as in Ephesian

documents of good age: e.g. ἐπαυλίων, line 68 (compare line 14); ἐπεξῆς, line 34; χρείστης for χρήστης, a debtor, line 40, is probably Ionic, compare the Herodotean form χρέω (vii, 111) and Homeric χρείω (Od. viii, 79). With δάνειον for δάνειον, line 4 and' passim compare τὰ βασίλεια for τὰ βασίλεια No. cccclvii, and the Herodotean forms ἐπιτήδεος (ἐπι-τήδειος), ἐπίδεξις (ἐπίδειξις). Also τέσσερας, line 91, is Ionic; and although this form reappeared in late Greek (Winer, Grammar of the N. T., Moulton's English Ed. 1870, p. 46; Westcott and Hort, N. T., Appendix, p. 150), it is more likely in this place to be a survival of older usage. See also the similar forms in No. ccccxl ante, and in the index to Dittenberger's Sylloge, ii, p. 780.

Whatever the date may be, the circumstances which gave rise to this law (τόνδε τὸν νόμον, line 88) are plainly indicated. A desolating war had swept over the Ephesian territory (ὁ κοινὸς πόλεμος *passim*), and had lasted two whole years (see on lines 65-74). From what quarter the invasion had come we are not informed; the phrase ὁ κοινὸς πόλεμος, repeated so often in this inscription, occurs also in a Tenian decree (at Cambridge) of about B. C. 100 (C. I. 2335; Hicks, Manual, No. 204) respecting the attacks of the pirates: καθ' ὃν καιρὸν ἐπιγενόμενος ὁ κοινὸς πόλεμος καὶ συνεχεῖς πειρατῶν ἐπίπλοι τὴν νῆσον οὐχ ὡς ἔτυχεν συνηνάγκασαν ὑπὸ τῶν δανείων ἐπιβαρηθῆναι κ.τ.λ.— a passage which bears a curious likeness to our Ephesian document. Whatever the origin of the war, it had crippled for the time the prosperity of Ephesos. The owners and occupiers of farms were ruined, their crops and farm-buildings had been destroyed by the invaders; lines 67-68: κεκαρμένοις τοῖς κτήμα[σ]ιν ἢ τῶν ἐπαυλίων καθηρημένων. Many of the farms had been mortgaged before the late war began (lines 65-69 and notes), some had now been mortgaged a second time (lines 32-42). And some owners, whose land had been unincumbered before the war, were forced in the general troubles to raise money by mortgage (lines 71-74). Peace was now restored after two years of suffering, but a great deal was wanting before commercial credit and prosperity could be restored. Every one was in need of ready money; creditors were clamorous for payment; landowners had mortgaged their properties up to the fullest value, and the mortgagees were demanding immediate repayment or else immediate possession of the land. The courts were filled with suitors, whose contentions were embittered by pressing personal need. It was an obvious step towards remedying these evils, to call in dikasts from another state (ξενικὸν δικαστήριον, lines 52, 87, 97), who might deal with the suits that had arisen without suspicion of partiality. It is this court, no doubt, that is alluded to in line 1, οἱ δικασταί. Probably the constitution of this court (on which see No. ccccxviii *ante*) had been described in the missing portion at the commencement. The remaining portions record enactments defining the rules that are to guide the dikasts in their decisions.

The Greek law of mortgage, as we know it at Athens, at Tenos (see Part ii, p. 150), and as we may assume it to have been at Ephesos, very much resembled the law of England. It gave the lender power to take possession of the land pledged in security, if the borrower neglected to pay his instalments of interest. But no provision was made for a compulsory sale of the land and the repayment of the creditors out of the proceeds. The mortgagee could simply take possession and hold the property as security for payment. In ordinary times the mortgager would at once sell, and having paid the creditor, would remain possessed of the surplus proceeds; or else he might arrange another loan. But in the present condition of Ephesos, when all credit was bad, and capital was scarce, no one was able or willing to lend, and no property could find

a purchaser. What was wanted was a fair subdivision of properties between borrower and lender, and this could only be done under a special decree. To meet this difficulty the present law was passed, which might be entitled 'An Incumbered Estates Subdivision Act.'

Such is the general scope of the inscription. Before discussing the provisions of it in detail, an attempt should be made to fix the date. M. Dareste, whose knowledge of law makes him a competent guide to the interpretation of our decree, has an ingenious theory respecting its date. He connects it with the decree of the Ephesians against Mithradates (B.C. 86), now at Oxford, published by Waddington-Le Bas, Part v, No. 136 a (No. 205 of my Manual). That decree reveals that the Ephesians, who had taken a prominent part against Rome in the Mithradatic War, as soon as they saw the tide of fortune now turning against the king, themselves turned suddenly round. They passed the decree above-mentioned, protesting their unabated friendship for Rome, and summoning all citizens and residents in Ephesos to take up arms against Mithradates. Various inducements are held out to such volunteers. If they are citizens who have been deprived of civil rights for non-payment of taxes to the state or of loans due to the Artemision, they are to be restored to the citizenship and their debts cancelled. Persons who have raised loans on note of hand from temple-funds, are to be released from their obligations, upon enlistment as volunteers for the war. But it is specially provided that in the case of certain loans upon mortgage, the mortgage is still to be held binding, the interest merely being excused for the present. (Other provisions of the decree I omit as not relevant to the present question.) We know what punishment Sulla meted out to Ephesos, for her share in the Mithradatic revolt. While sparing the lives of the people, he inflicted a very heavy fine; see the striking account of Appian (De Bello Mithrid. 62, 63). M. Dareste places the decree just after the departure of Sulla from Asia. Certainly the circumstances of that time would well suit the provisions of this law. The public funds were exhausted, the citizens impoverished, and the decree which had been passed in the time of panic had proved a very violent and a very partial remedy. It had relieved a large number of debtors by abolishing all claims for debt except those which were secured by a mortgage upon real property. Borrowers upon mortgage were now in a worse case than ever; and the present enactment, M. Dareste thinks, was therefore passed for their relief, and is to be regarded as supplementing the Mithradates decree described above.

I have set forth the view of M. Dareste somewhat fully, as being very ingenious, and *a priori* probable. There are, however, it seems to me, grave objections to it.

(1) The lettering of our inscription so nearly resembles the lettering of the decree No. ccccLXXVI that they cannot differ very greatly in date.

On the other hand the lettering of our inscription must, in the present state of our knowledge of palæography, be assigned to an earlier date than the Oxford decree, which not only has elaborate apices, but exhibits the forms Α Γ Σ.

(2) Again, we find in the Oxford decree indications of late orthography, such as συνφυλάσσων, line 10, and συνφέρειν, line 20 ; πολείται, line 24, and ἐπίτειμα, line 32 ; χρεοφιλέτας, line 53 (see Lobeck's Phrynichus, ed. 1820, 691); also line 38, ΣΥΣΤΕΜΑΤΩΝ, which all the editors alter to συστ[η]μάτων, suspiciously resembles a debased form like ἀνάθεμα, εὕρεμα, ὑπόδεμα κ.τ.λ., concerning which see Lobeck, Phrynichus 249, 445, and Paralipomena Gr. Gr. 417 foll. In our decree nothing of the kind occurs : even the terminal consonant is frequently assimilated, lines 5, 6, etc. What peculiar forms do occur I have already shown to be rather earlier than later.

I am unable therefore to assign this law to so late a date as the time of Mithradates, and should be disposed to place it somewhere between B.C. 200 and 100, say B. C. 150. Whatever its date, the law was enacted to meet a great financial emergency occasioned by a war described as ὁ κοινὸς πόλεμος, an expression which occurs in the Tenian decree already quoted (C. I. 2335 ; No. 204 of my Manual). In that context ὁ κοινὸς πόλεμος appears to be explained by the words καὶ συνεχεῖς πειρατῶν ἐπίπλοι immediately following ; and if so the fighting alluded to must have preceded the suppression of piracy by Pompey B.C. 67. There is, however, no sufficient reason for identifying the κοινὸς πόλεμος of the Tenian decree with the war so designated here. The war is called 'Common,' because it affected all the inhabitants of Ephesos and left no citizens uninjured ; this is clear from lines 54–55 : τούτῳ [μὴ] | εἶναι κοινὸν τὸν πόλεμον, and line 73 : μὴ εἶναι αὐτοῖς κοινὸν τὸν πόλεμον,—phrases which can only be translated 'the war shall not be held to have affected them.' If so, there is no more reason for identifying two wars termed ὁ κοινὸς πόλεμος than two wars termed 'the civil war.' The few facts that we know of the history of Ephesos in the second century show that it fell under the dominion of Antiochos the Great about B.C. 196, and after his final defeat B.C. 190 was handed over by the Romans as an appanage of the Pergamene kingdom. As such it passed again into Roman hands upon the death of Attalos Philometor, B. C. 133, until Mithradates invaded Ionia B.C. 88, and occupied Ephesos with a garrison.

During all this period from B. C. 196 to 88, there were constant wars in Asia Minor from which Ephesos may have greatly suffered. But if asked to name a particular war as having been likely to occasion the disasters described in our inscription, one might suggest the rebellion of Aristonikos against the Romans upon the death of Attalos Philometor as meeting the requirements of the case. The events and dates of this warfare, and the authorities for the facts, will be found fully set forth by Waddington, Fastes, pp. 20, 21, and 28–31 ; compare Clinton, F. H. under B. C. 131–129, and

Marquardt, Röm. Alt. iv, p. 177. It is not actually stated by the historians that Aristonikos devastated the Ephesian territory. But it was natural for him to do so, after he had killed the Roman general in battle; and we know that, while waging his guerilla warfare with hosts of runaway slaves and adventurers, he had a special ground for hating the Ephesians, who had given him his first check in the sea fight off Kyme. Moreover, the duration of his rebellion agrees pretty closely with the duration of 'the Common War' as defined in lines 65–74 (see notes).

The provisions of the law are as follows :—

Lines 1–14. *The official valuation of properties*, with a view to their official subdivision between mortgager and mortgagee. If the valuation of the owner and the usurer differ so much that it is impossible for the court to entertain either (ἐὰν μὴ φαίνηται δικαστικὸν τὸ πρᾶγμα), the court is to decide what is a fair valuation of the farm ; but no re-valuation (ἀντιτίμησις) of the debt itself is to be entertained by the court. In some cases the dispute seems to have been settled by both parties accepting, in the presence of the court, the award proposed by the public arbitrators (διαιτηταί, line 6, compare lines 87–88, 96) before the suit came into court at all. In either case, the judicial valuation is to be entered in an official record (λεύκωμα) by the εἰσαγωγεὶς, and to be laid before the Commissioners of the Common War (οἱ ἐπὶ τοῦ κοινοῦ πολέμου ᾑρημένοι). The term εἰσαγωγεύς may either be, as it was at Athens, a generic title of any magistracy that had the duty of convening the court to try the case, or it may be the title of a special board. The Commissioners of the Common War are obviously an extraordinary executive board elected by the boulè and demos, to see that the decrees which had been passed concerning the complications resulting from the late war were duly carried out : compare οἱ ᾑρημένοι ἐκ τοῦ δήμου ἐπὶ τῷ σίτῳ, No. cccclxi *ante*. The Commissioners, upon officially receiving the valuation, had next to put it into execution by a subdivision of the land. For this purpose the service of scientific experts would be wanted. Accordingly thirty experts in land-measuring are to be nominated by the ekklesia to avoid the suspicion of partiality, and the Commissioners every five days are to ballot for five of these to act as measurers and dividers (διαιρέται) of lands, and also are to determine by ballot which lands among those in question they are to be set to work upon. In subdividing the lands, care is to be taken not to cut up the farms to disadvantage, nor to spoil the approaches to farm-buildings, etc.

Lines 14–20. If the award thus made is disputed, appeal may be lodged with the Commissioners of the War and the magistrate in charge of the ξενικὸν δικαστήριον. The latter is to summon the dikasts to personally inspect the disputed properties and make a final award between the creditor and debtor ; and the awards made by them,—or by the public arbitrators with the sanction of the court,—are to be duly reported with full details to the Commissioners of the War.

Lines 20–32. *Record of awards how to be kept.*

G g

Official copies of all awards are to be delivered to the Temple-wardens of the Artemision, who are to deposit them upon the floor (ἔδεθλον) of the temple. The public Registrar is also to receive copies, so that any citizen may be able at any time to consult the award. If however the debtor and creditor have come to any private agreement, without application to the court, such agreement, if confirmed by the Commissioners of War, shall be valid and copies of the award shall be in the hands of the parties chiefly concerned; trustees for wards whose property is concerned are likewise each to have copies of such awards; but no one else. Anyone transgressing these enactments will be liable to prosecution and heavy penalties.

Lines 32-42. *Concerning second mortgages.* If the landowner, besides the first loan, has contracted a second or more, upon the surplus value of his lands, (ἐπὶ τοῖς ὑπερέχουσι, lines 32, 33), the claims of these subsequent creditors are to be severally satisfied, according to their priority, in the subdivision of the property This provision, however, is to apply only to bonâ fide transactions. If a debtor has raised a loan under false pretences, concealing the fact that his property has a mortgage upon it, then this second mortgagee shall have the right to take possession of the land upon assigning to the first mortgagee such a share of the property as may satisfy his claim, the valuation of the property being in this case, as in the others, reckoned according to its marketable value before the war (κατὰ συλλογισμὸν τοῦ κοινοῦ πολέμου, see line 38). And if, after thus satisfying the first mortgagees, the second mortgagees have something still owing them, they may recover from the rest of the property of the fraudulent debtors, and from any sureties who are parties to the transaction, in the same way as the ordinary law allows a creditor to recover a loan on property affording no adequate security (καθάπερ ἐκ τῶν [μετέ]ωρα ἐγγυωμένων, line 42; compare line 46 and Part II, No. cccxxxvii, lines 76, 77, p. 149; and Dareste, La Transcription des Ventes, Paris. 1884, p. 9).

Lines 43-53. *Of sureties who have given collateral securities in a mortgage.* If the debt does not exceed the value of the mortgaged property as it stood before the war, such surety is to be absolved from all liability. If it exceeds it, such excess is to be paid by the surety—κατὰ λόγον (line 46), i. e. only in so far as the debt is in excess of the value of the land. Also the surety is not to be charged with any interest which had accumulated on the debt before he became surety. If such overcharge is made by the creditor, he is not to be paid, unless he delays the enforcement of his claim with the knowledge and consent of the surety. Any dispute on this head to be decided by the dikastery aforesaid, or by the public arbitrators. Application to the court to be made by the creditor.

Lines 53-64. *Cases in which the valuation of the land is to be reckoned at its present value.* There are certain debts which are to be paid in full, no abatement being made on account of 'the common war.' These cases are those of—

(1) Trustees owing money to their wards;
(2) Parents, guardians, or trustees, who owe dowries to daughters, sisters, or other wards, according to the terms of a will of which they are executors;
(3) Divorced husbands who have not repaid moneys repayable according to marriage-settlements.

Lines 65-74. *Definition of dates between which the war may be held to affect the payment of debts.* It is now well known that the eponymous magistrate of Ephesos, corresponding with the archon at Athens, was always the πρύτανις (see *ante*, p. 72, p. 82). It appears that 'the common war' (which may possibly, as I have ventured to suggest, be the warfare waged against Aristonikos), had lasted from the year of Demagoras to the year of Danaos. It should be noted also that in Asia Minor the civil year began at the autumn equinox. The following dates are here referred to:

Prytanes		B.C.
Demagoras (in Posideon = January, the war breaks out) *circa*	.	132–1?
Mantikrates (the war continues)	.	131–0?
Apollas (in Lenæon = February, the war ends)	.	130–29?
Danaos	.	129–8?

Lines 65-69. In the original document it must have been expressly laid down that all mortgages concluded before January in Demagoras' year may plead 'the common war,' so that the land is to be valued at its market value before the war, the consequent loss to fall upon the lender. This enactment, which is implied throughout the document, is lost; but it is plainly referred to here, when it is provided that even in the case of mortgages concluded after January of Demagoras' year, the borrower may plead 'the common war,' excepting that the valuation shall be lowered in proportion to the injuries sustained by the lands or buildings at the time of the loan.

Lines 69-71. Even when the terms of a mortgage contain stipulations that the borrower shall not plead 'the common war' to obtain a higher valuation of his estate, such stipulations (πράξεις ἐναντίας τῷ κοινῷ πολέμῳ) are cancelled by this enactment, in case of all loans effected before February of Apollas' year; i. e. before the close of the war.

Lines 71-74. Where loans have been raised on the security of land since the month of February in Apollas' year, the agreement is to be binding, and the 'common war' may not interpose to upset it; the debtor, however, in the present state of public credit, is to receive thus much relief that the interest charged upon his debt may not exceed 8¼ per cent. A reason is assigned for thus maintaining the contract, viz. 'that the capitalist who advanced money (εἰσευπόρησεν) during time of war, did so with full knowledge of his risk (διακιστεύσας),' and therefore he could have no reason to complain of being treated as this enactment provides. But it was otherwise with loans contracted since Apollas' year, i. e. in time of peace.

Hitherto the act before us has been dealing with unfulfilled engagements. The remaining provisions deal with cases where the terms of the covenant have been fulfilled. Three cases are supposed, viz.:

Lines 74–85. *Where the creditor has taken possession of the land of the defaulting mortgager.*

(*a*) If he has taken possession before January in Demagoras' year, i. e. before the outbreak of the war, his possession is not to be disturbed, unless any voluntary agreement has been subsequently entered into between the parties, to modify the original contract. If any shall dispute the legality of any such occupation, the case may go before the ordinary courts.

(*b*) If the creditor has taken possession after January in Demagoras' year, although at that time the decree of the demos [this document is only known from this allusion] had granted relief and restoration to such debtors, then the possession of the land is to be conceded to such debtors, but the creditor is allowed his claim for the debt, which is to be repaid him by subdivision of the land according to the provisions of the present act.

(*c*) If a dispute arise as to whether the creditor did or did not take possession before the date above defined, the question shall be determined by the court just like any other question affecting injuries sustained through the war.

Lines 85–88. *Cases where the creditor, instead of taking possession, has made a private agreement with the debtor.* If this agreement has been voluntary on the debtor's part, it shall hold good. If it be disputed whether or no it was purely voluntary, the question shall be settled by the public arbitrators with the sanction of the foreign dikastery, as provided in this act.

Lines 88–98. *Cases where the debtor has surrendered his property for the payment of the debt.* Here the lender shall remain the owner. But if the mortgager desires to recover possession of his land, he may do so by making use of the provisions of this act during the year of Danaos; only, he must give the existing tenant due compensation for his outlay upon the land or for his losses in farming, and interest upon such outlay of 7½ per cent., allowance being made on the other hand for profits made. Any dispute about the estimate of these claims may be settled by help of the public arbitrators or by application to the foreign dikastery. Such application to be made by the debtor who surrendered.

The rest of the provisions are lost.

The names of the four prytanes are (with the exception of Apollas, which is universal) known Ephesian names. See Mr. Head's Coinage of Ephesus (especially p. 83): he tells me however that he has seen reason for changing his opinion that the names stamped on the Ephesian coins were the names of the eponymous prytanes. Observe that we have the genitive Δημαγόρου in line 65, and Δημαγόρα in 79. So 'Απολλᾶ, the usual form, in line 72, and 'Απολλάδου by a false analogy in line 69. With this last form compare Μητράδου in No. cccct, line 1. This formation of the genitive of names in -ᾶς was not uncommon in Ionia, and is no sign of a late date; see Dittenberger, Syll. No. 344, note 28: compare 'Απολλάδου C. I. 3253; so Μηνάδου and other like genitives in C. I. 3141, 3142, 4366ᵛ, and note on 4224ᶠ p. 1120. The mode of adjudicating between debtor and creditor in this law and in the Oxford decree after the Mithradatic war may be compared with the measures adopted by Lucullus to relieve the cities of Asia Minor after the exactions of Sulla; Plutarch, Lucullus, ch. 20.

CCCCLXXVIII.

Fragment of white marble, entire on right only: 6 in. by 3½ in. width. From Mr. Wood's Excavations. Unpublished.

	\ι		. . . . *ι* . .
	ΧΚΑΤΑ		. . *ς* κατα
	ΩΑΙΤΟΙΧΚ		. . . θαι τοῖς κ-
	ΟΙΚΑΙΤΟΙ		. . . . οι καὶ τοῖ-
5	ΠΡΟΝΟΙΑΝ	5	*ς* . . . .] πρόνοιαν
	ΤΕΤΟΛΟΙΠΟΝ		. . . . ἐς] τε τὸ λοιπὸν
	ΑΧΑΝΤΙΛΑΜ		. . . . ας ἀντιλαμ-
	ΕΝΤΕΩ		βαν . . . .]εντεω

Probably part of a decree. In line 8 possibly *ἐν Τέῳ.*

CCCCLXXIX.

Two fragments of white marble, broken all round: *a* measuring 3½ in. by 4½ in.; *b* 1½ in. by 3½ in. From Mr. Wood's Excavations. Unpublished.

(*a*)	ΜΑΙΟΙΧ	(*a*)	. . . 'Ρω]μαίοις . . .
	ΟΝΟΙΑΙ		. . . ὁμ]όνοια[ν . . .
	ΟΝΤϹ		. . . . οντο . . .
(*b*)	ΟΥΑ	(*b*)	. . . . ουα . . .

The letters are very similar to those of the great decree concerning Mithradates (now at Oxford) published by Waddington-Le Bas, Voyage Archéol. Part V, No. 136 a. The letters of our fragments are rather larger than those of the Oxford marble; but there is little doubt that they belong to the same date, and a similar subject.

--- --- ---

CCCCLXXX.

Portions of a white marble stele : *a* is entire only on right, measuring 14 in. in height, 11 in. in greatest width. *b* is inscribed upon the right return of the same marble, being 2 in. wide, and broken to right. *c* is on a different marble, and is broken all round, and measures 7½ in. by 2½ in. From Mr. Wood's Excavations. Unpublished.

	a (front surface)	*b (right return)*	*c*
	ꞏΝ	ΦΑ Ν	ꞏΣꞋ
	ΝΟΥ	ΜΑΓ	ΚΥꞏ
	ΑΡΤΥ	ΝΕΝ	ΑΠΕꞏ
	ΩΝΕΝ	ΤΑΓ	ΙΑΥΤΣ
5	⁻ΟΤΕΤΑ	ΤΑΓ	ΕΥΣΗΙC
	⁻ΡΟΣ	ΡΟΣ	⁻ΩΝΠΙΣ
	ΓΟΡΟ⁻	ΑΝꞋ	⁻ΧΩ
	Νꞌ	ΓΑΡ	ΙΔΩ
	ꞏ∪	Τ.Ωꞏ	ΓΝ
10	ΓΡΑΜ	ΔΙΟΙ	ΓΙ
	Ι	ΔΕκ	ꞏꞏ
	∪ΣΟꞏ	ΠΕΡΓΑ	.ΩΝΕ
	ꞏΤΩΝ	ᴢꞏΑΣΠΡΟΑΓΟ	ΛΗꞏ
	ꝺΝΕ ΣΕΠΙΦΑΝΕΣΤΑΤΗΝΔΟ	ΤΟꞏ	
15	ꞏΝΟ ΠΡΟΓΟΝΟΙΠΡΟΣΑΛΛΗΛΟΥ	ΟΕꞏ	
	ΒΕΙΑΣΕΥΧΑΡΙΣΤΙΑΥΠΕΡ	ΤΗΝ	
	ΝΑΥΤΩΝΤΗ ΤΩΝΠΡΑΓΜΑ	ΣΕꞏꞏ	
	ꞏΞΕΩΝΕΠΙΦΑΝΕΙΑ	ΤΗꞏ	
	ΤΑΠΡΟΑΙΡΕΣΙΝθΥΜΟ	.ΩΝ	
20	ΩΝΔΙΑΤΑ	ΚΑΙ	
	⁻ΤΙΝ⁻Ο	ΚΟΣΣ	
		Νꞏ.Ωꞏ	

	a		*b*
	. . . . . .	ꞏν	φαμ . . .
	. . . . . .	ꞏν	μαρ . . .
	. . . .	ꞏνου	νεν . . .
	. . . . μ]αρτυ-		ταγ . . .
5	ρ . . . .]ων ἐν		ταγ . . .
	. . . . τὸ τετα-		ρος . . .
	γμένον . . . . μ]ὲρος		αν . . .
	. . . . Αὐτοκρά]τορο[ς ?		παρ . . .
	. . . . νт-		τωρ . . .
10	. . . . το-		διο[ι α . .
	. . . . γραμ-		δεκ . . .
	ματ . . . .]ι		ωνε . . .
	. . . . ος ο[. . . . . . ἐ]περγα-		λη . . .
	σάμενον ? . . . .]στων . . . . . σίας προάγο-		το . . .
	ντα ? τὴν πόλιν ἡμετέρ]αν ε[ἰ]ς ἐπιφανεστάτην δό-		θει . . .
15	ξαν, περὶ ἧς ? . . . . . σ]αν ο[ἱ] πρόγονοι πρὸς ἀλλήλου-		τημ . . .
	ς . . . . τῆς εὐσε]βείας εὐχαριστία· ὑπερ-		σει . . . . [σω
	βαλλ ? . . . .]ν αὐτῶν τῇ τῶν πραγμά-		τηρ[ια . . . .
	των ἐπιμελείᾳ ? καὶ τῇ τῶν πρ]άξεων ἐπιφανείᾳ		ων . . .
	. . . . κα]τὰ προαίρεσιν θυμο-		και . . .
20	ῦ . . . . τ]ῶν διατα-		κοσσ . . .
	γμάτων . . . .] ἐσιν το.		νω . . .

c. Line 3 : ἀπ᾽ εὐ[λαβείας or the like. Line 4 : αὐτῶ[ν. Line 5 : -εύσῃ ο . . . Line 6 : τ]ῶν πισ[τ . . .

Fragment 1.

Scale of Feet and Inches.

The original edge of blocks is indicated thus ————
Supposed edge of broken blocks
Broken edges of marble are indicated by thin wavy lines.
Surfaces enclosed by inscription are indicated by - - - - - - - -

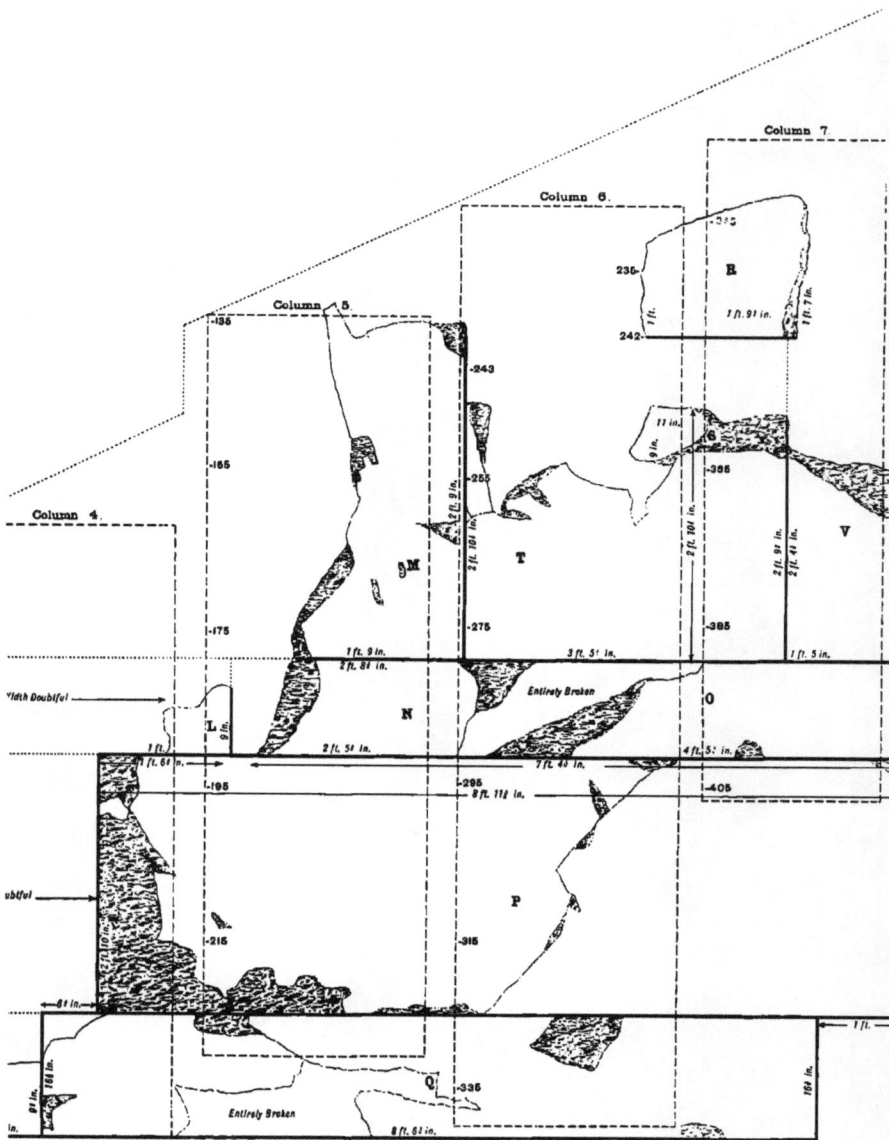

Column 7.

Column 6.

Column 5.

Column 4.

-135

-185

-175

-243

-255

-275

2 ft. 10½ in.

2 ft. 10½ in.

·M

T

·345

235-

242-

R

1 ft.

1 ft. 9½ in.

1 ft. 7 in.

11 in.

1 in.

-365

-385

2 ft. 10½ in.

2 ft. 9½ in.

2 ft. 6½ in.

V

Width Doubtful

L

9 in.

1 ft.

1 ft. 6½ in.

-195

N

2 ft. 8½ in.

2 ft. 5½ in.

1 ft. 9 in.

2 ft. 8½ in.

3 ft. 5½ in.

2 ft. 5½ in.

7 ft. 4½ in.

Entirely Broken

O

-295

8 ft. 11½ in.

4 ft. 5½ in.

1 ft. 5 in.

-405

·315

P

ubtful

-215

6½ in.

1 ft.

-335

Q

Entirely Broken

8 ft. 6½ in.

10½ in.

in.

16½ in.

16½ in.

A decree couched in florid terms and ornamentally inscribed, perhaps in honour of a Proconsul. Similar documents may be found in C. I. 3187 (see Waddington, Fastes, No. 88), 3902 *b*. Probably not much earlier than the Christian era; the restoration Αὐτοκρά]τορος in line 8 is fairly certain. In line 12 we ought possibly to read Περγα[μ . . . and to understand an allusion to Pergamon. Lines 17–18 give a clue to the length of the lines; note the frigid contrast between πράγματα 'affairs,' and πράξεις 'achievements.'

CCCCLXXXI.

A number of inscribed blocks of white marble, which formed the wall on the right flank of the south entrance of the great Theatre, between the ποδ̄ον and the σκηνή. In their original arrangement these blocks formed a nearly complete triangle: see the accompanying diagram, which shows their scale and respective position. Most of them were in their original courses when discovered, and I have had by me while making the diagram a pencil sketch by Mr. Wood 'of the stones found in situ.' The uncial text simply follows the columns of inscription, without regard to the different blocks that contain them; except that the joints of the stones are indicated by a thick line. Nearly the whole of the inscription has been published in cursive by Wood, Discoveries at Ephesos (Appendix), Inscriptions from the Theatre, 1 ; compare ibid. p. 73. He omits block R. A few lines of the opening decree are given by C. Curtius, Hermes iv, p. 201.

Col. 1.

```
                              ΕΠιιι      ιιLι.
                    ιΒ·ΚΑ·ΑΝΤΙΠΑΤΡΟΥΙΟΙ,  ΑΝΟΥ·ΜΝ
                    ΠΟΣΕΙΔΕΩΝΟΣ·Ϛ·ΙΣΤ 'ΑΜΕΝΟΥ
                  ΙΟΣΕΤΗΒΟΥΛΗΚΑΙΤΩΝΕΩΚΟΡΩΔΗΜΩϟ ΙΟΣΕΒΑΣΤϹ
          ⸴ ⸴ΩΝΕΝΕΦΑΝΙΣΑΝΤΙΒ·ΚΑ·ΤΙΒΚΑ·ΑΛΕΞΑ  ϽΥΥΙϹⸯ
                 ϟΦΙΛΟΠΑΤΡΙΣΚΑΙΦΙΛΟΣΕΒΑΣΤΟ    ΟΣΕΥΣΕΒΗⸯ
                ⸻ΟΥΔΗΜΟΥΤΟϬ·ΚΑΙΟΙΣΤΡΑϩΓΟΙϩ  ιιϹ · ΓΩΣΦΙΛΟΣΕ
                      ⸺ΙΛΟΤΕΙΜΟΥΣΑΝΔΡΑΣΤΕΡΙϞ  ΙΝΚΑΙΚΑΤΑ
                       ⸻ΣΤΟΡΓΗΝΓΝΗΣΙΩΝΠΟΛΕΙ     ΜΟΙΒΑΙ
  ιο                    ⸻ΤΟΑΠΟΛΑΥΕΙΝ ΙΕΝΤΟΥΣΕι     ΜϟΑΝ
                            ⸺Α           ΥΛΟΜΕΝΟΙΣΤΕ'
             ΟΜΟΙΑΑΜ               ⸺ΕϞιιϽΥΔΑ  ϽΤΑΣϮΗΜΕΓΙΣϮΝΘΕ
             ΟΝΑΡΤΕΜΙΝ            ⸻ΙΝΕΤΑΙΠΑΣΙΝΤ  ϟΑΛΛΙΣΤΑΚΑΘΗΚΕ
             ΠΑΡΑϮΠΟΛΕ            ΤΕΟΥΙΒΙ       ϽΥΤΑΡΙΟΣΑ
  ι5 ϮΗΡΙΠΠΙΚΗΣΤΑ  ϽΣΓΕΝΕΙΚΑΙΑΣΙΑΔΙΑΣΗΜΟΣΣΤΡΑΤΕΙΑΙΣΤΕΚΑΙ
     ΕΠΙΤΡΟΠΑΙΣ⸴  ΤΟΥΚΥΡΙΟΥΗΜΩΝΑΥΤΟΚΡΑΤΟΡΟΣΚΕΚΟΣΜΗΜΕΝ⸴ϽϹ
     ΠΟΛΕΙϮΗΣΗ⸴  ⸻ΡΟΣΚΑΙΤϹΥΘΟΥΛΕΥΤΙΚΟΥΣΥΝΕΔΡΙΟΥΠΡΟΣΠΑ
        ⸻ ΑΘΗΧΡΩι   ΙΑΘΕΣΙΩΣΚΑΙΤΑΣΑΠΟϮΣΤΥΧΗΣΕΠΙΤΟΥΡ
     ΙΙΡΟΚΟΠΑΣΚΟΣ  ΤΩΝΗΘΩΝΣΕΜΝΟϮΤΙΕΥΣΕΒΩΝΜΕΝΦΙΛΟΕΙ
  20 ϮΝΑΡΧΗΓΕΤΙΗΠϹ  ⸴ΙΣΜΕΝΕΠΙΝΟΙΑΙΣΣΕΣΠΟΥΔΑΚΕΝΠΕΡΙϞΝΘΡΗ⸻
     ⸴ⴱι  ⸺ΜΕΓ⸴ΑΛΟϪΥΧΟϹ  ΚΑΘΙΕΡϽΣΕΣΙΝϩΝΠΟΛΙΝ⸴  ΙΤΑΠΑΝ⸻  ⸻Ε
     ΚΕΝΤΡΟ⸴         ⸴Ν⸴ΙΣϞΝΕΚΚΛΗΣΙΑΝΥΤΕΣΧ⸴
     ΤΕΙΚΟΝΙΣ⸴        ϹΝΜΕΝΧΡΥΣΕΟΝΕΝΩΚΑΙΑΡΓ
     ΕΠΙΧΡΥΣΑΕΤ       ΤΕΙΚΟΝΙΣΜΑΤΑΟΚΤΩ ΕΓ
```

Col. 2.

```
  25      ΚΑΙ   ιϵΙΝΤΟϟ      ΑΣΣΑΡΙΑΙΟΝ
       ΑΙΡΕΘ  ΣΟΜΕΝΩΝΚ       ΝΙΑΥ⸻ϽΝΚΑ
       ϽΝΔΙΑΤΑΞΙΝΑΥΤΟΥϮ      ΣΘΕΟΥι
         ϟΕΣΤΙΝΤΟΥΘΑΡΓΗΛΙϟ  ΣΜΝΟΣΕΚ ΗΙΣΤΑΜΕ
       ιΙΟΛΟΓΗΣΑΣΑΠΟΔΩΣϹ  ΙΤΑΧΡΗΜΑΤ  ΞΑϒΤΟΝΤΑ
  30   ⸻ΡΩΜΕΝΑΟΤΑΝΒΟΥΛΗ  ΗΗΤΟΥΣΚΑ ΜΡΟϞϽϟ
       ϟΓΗΠΟΛΕΙΚΟΜΙΖΟϞ  ϞΩΝΤΩΝΕΚΑ    ΤΟΥΠΡΟ
       ⸴ΡΟΙΣΤΑΜΕΝΩΝΠΕΡι  ΑΠΑΝΤΩΝΔΙΑΤΑ ⸺ΙΝΕΙΣϮι
       ⸴⸴⸴⸻ ϽϟΕΝΕΠΙ  ϽΩΘΗΝ⸴ΙΚ⸴ι⸴Διⴰτ φΙΣΜΑ
                      ΝΤΗΣΕΠΙ⸴      ⸺ΙΑϟ
  35                  ΗΡΚΑΙΕϒΕΡΓΕ  ΙΣΑΚϹ  ΙΑΙ
                      ΣΚΑΙΑφΡΑΝΙ   ϟΦΛΑϽΥΙΑ
                      ιϟΤΡΑΤΗΓϹ      ΠΕΡΒΛΗΤΩ
                                   ϽΝΤΕΣΤΗΝ
                                   ΙΟΛΕΙΤΑΙΙΙ
```

ιι h

ΑΙΔΙΕΠΙΣΤΟΛΩΝ
ΕΥΣΑΙιΩᵀΤΕΔΙ
ΟΝΑΥΤС

Δ   ＿ΥΣΕΒΗ

ꟼΡΟΣ   ⊾ιⳤΔ⳨   ∪ΤΕΙΜΟΝΤΕ

45   ΤΕι   ꟼΑΙᵀ   ⳤ   ⳥ΤΙΣΤΑΙΣΤΙΜ   ΩΝΤΕΑΝΑΣΤΑΣΕ

ΣΙΝΕꟼ ιIΕΡΩΤΗΣΑΡΤΕΜΙΔᴄ   ΣΕΠΙΣΗΜΟΤΑΤΟΙΣ

ΤΟΠΟΙΣΤΗⳤΠΟΛΕΩΣΑΝΑꟽ   ΤΟΝΚΑΙΧꟼΥΣΕΩ

ΣΤΕΦΑΝΩΕΝΤΑΙΣΕΚΚ   ΖΟΝΤΑΚΑΙΦΙΛΑꟼ

ΤΕΜΙΝ Τ̅Ν̅ΔΕꟼᴬᴾ   ΕΓΡΑΜΜΕΝΩΝΙΕ

50   ΡΩΝ   ⳦ΩΝΚΑΙΤΗΝΕ   ΕΡΟΥ̅ΕΙΣΤΟΘΕΑ

ΤΡΟΝΚΑΙΤΗΝΕΚΤΟᐱ   ΤΗΣΑΡΤΕΜΙΔΟΣ

ΤΟΣ

⅄

55   Ⅴ·ΕΝΜ⋿ΝΤΩ⳦ΕΑΤΡΩ

ΑΥΤΟΥΜΑΡΜΑꝶΙⳤ⳦Ⅱⳤ

⳨ΩΕΝΤΟΠΩꟼ ΤΙΤΗⳤΕΙΩΦΙΛΟΤΕΙ

⸱ΚΑΙꟼΕΡΙΤΗ ΙΑΜΟΝⲎΣΤΩΙΚΑΘΙ

ﬨΜΑΤΩΝ·ΤΗᵀꟷΒΟᵞΛΗΚΑΙΤΗΓΕΡᴼ

⸱ΟΙΣΥꟼΕΣΧΕΤΟΑΥΤΟΣΚΑΙᴬ

60   ΙΕΚΔΑΝΙΣΤΗΣΓΕΝΕΣΘΑΙ

Col. 3.

ΓΑΙΟ⅃

ΣΙΝΕΙ⅃

ΕΦΕΣΙⱠ

ΤΑΙΣᵀꝶ

65   ΤΕΜΙΔ

ΤΗΕ⸖

⅄

∪ꟼⱤΩΝΓ·ΚΑΙΕΙΚΩΝ

ΗΣΛΕΙΤΡΩΝΓΝΕΟΚΟΡΩΝΤΑΙꟼΑ

70   ⸗⸖⸱

ΣΛΛΟ   ιΩΙΚ   ⳦ΡΟΚΟΤΙΜΕΤΑΔΕ⳨ΝΣΑΛΟΥΤΑΡΙΟ

ΑΠΟΔΟΘ ΣΙΝΑΙΠΡΟΔΗΛΟΥΜΕΝΑΙΕΙΚΟΝΕΣΤΟΙΕΦΕΣΙΩΝΓΡΑΜΜ

ꟼΡΟΓΕΓꝶ⸳ ꟻΜΕΝΩΙΣΤΑΘΜΩΙΑΠΟΤΩΝΚΛΗꝶΟΝΟΜΩΝΑΥΤΟΥΩ

ΤΑΣΤΙΘΕ   ΘΑΙΕΝΤΑΙΣΕΚΚΛΗΣΙΑΙΣΕΠΑΝΩΗΣΣΕΛΙΔΟΣΗΣΒΟᵞ/

75   ΧΡΥ̅ΣΕ   ΜΙΔΟΣΚΑΙΤΩΝΑΛΛΩΝΕΙΚΟΝΩΝ·ΑꟼΤΕΜΙΣΔΕΧΡᵞ

ΛΕΙΤΡⱠΝΤΡΙΩΝΚΑΙΑΙΤΕΡΙΑΥ̅ΝΑΡΓΥΡΕΟΙΕΛΑΦΟΙΔΥΟΚΑΙΤΑΛ⳽

ΟΛΚⱧⳤΛΕΙΤΡΩΝΔΥΟΟΥΝΚΙΩΝΔΕΚΑΓΡΑΜΜΑΤΩΝΓΕΝΤꟻ ꟾΙ

ꝶꝶ   ΣΙΕΡΑΣΣΥΝΚΛΗ̅ΟΥΟΛΚΗΣΛΕΙΤΡΩΝ Δ̅ΟᵞⲚιⳤ   ⸞ΚΑΙΕꟾ

Ρ   ΣΦΙΛΟΣΕΒΑΣΤΟΥΚΑΙΣΕⲘΝΟΤΑΗ̅ⳤΓΦΕΣΙΩꟼΒΟΥΛΗΣΟ

80   ⸗   Ν̅ΓΡΑΜΑΤΩΝΘ̅ΤΑΚΑ⸱ΑΥΤΑΚΑΘΙΕꝶΩΜΕΝΑΗ̅Τ ΕΑꝶΕ ΜΙΔ ꟾ

ΑΣΤΩΙΕΦΕΣΙΩΝΒΟΥΛΗΙ ΟΜΟΙΩΣΚΑΙ⸝ꝶΥ̅ꝶΕΑΑꝶΕΜΙΣΛΑ

Ρ ⳤΟΛΚΗⳤΑⳅΚΑΙΕΙΚΩΝΑΡΓΥΡΕΑΤΟΥΔΗΜΟΥΤΟΥΡΩΜΑΙΩΝ

Κ⸝ΙΕΙΚΩΝΑΡΓΥΡΕΑΗ̅ΣΦΙΛΟΣΕΒΑΣΤΟΥΓΕΡΟΥΣΙΑΣΟΛΚΗⳤ

ΑⳐΤΑΚΑΘΙΕΡΩΜΕΝΑΤΗ⳨ΑꝶΕΜΙΔΙΚΑΙΗ̅ΕΦΕΣΙΩΝ⳨ΕΡΟΥΣΙΑ

85   ΟΜΟΙΩΣΚΑΙΑΛΛΗΑꝶΕΜΙΣΑꝶΓΥΡΕΑΛΑΜΠΑΔΗΦΟΡΟΣΕ

ꟻΕΝΤꟻΣΕΔꝶΑΤΩΝΕΦꟾΒΩꟾⳤΟΛΚΗⳤⱯΖΟΥΝΚΙΩΝΕꟾΓΡΑΜ

ΚΑΙΕΙΚΩΝΑΡΓΥΡΕΑΤΟΥΙΠꟼΙΚΟᵞΤΑΓ ΜΑΤΟΣΟΛΚΗⳤΑꟽΗ

ΚΙΟΥΓΡΑΜΜΑΤΩΝ ⸱⸱ΛΑΙΛΛΗ̅ΕΙΚΩΝΑΡΓΥΡΕΑΗ̅ΣΕΦΗΒΕΙΑ

ΤΑΚΑΙΑΥΤΑΚΑΘΙ⳨ ΜΕΝΑΗ̅ΕΑΡΕΜΙΔΙΚΑΙΤΟΙΣΚΑꟷΝΙΑᵞΤΟ

90   ΝΕΦꟾΒΟΙⳤ ⸿

⸝ΦΙΑΛΗΝΟΛΚ

ΣΕΒΑΣΤΟᐱ

Col. 4.

95

ΛΕΙ

ΕΠΙ
ΚΑΙ
ΛΓΩΝ ΓΙΑ
ΠΛΕΙΤΑΙΣ
ΛΔΗΦΟ

100

ΙΓΚΑΙΕΙΚΩΝ
ΕΑΡΓΕΜΙΔΙ
ΟΜΟΙ ΚΑΙΑΛΛΗΑΡ
ΩΝ Γ ΗΜΙΤΟΥΣΓΡΑΜΜΑ
ΤΑΦΥΛΗΣΕΥ

105

ΛΘΙΕΡΩΜΕ
ΝΦΥΛΗΣ
ΣΤΑΛΙ
ΙΚΩΝ
ΤΕ

110

ΝΤΗΣΟ
ΟΥΤΩ
ΙΕΡΟΥΡΣ
ΕΠΙΤΩΝ

115

ΕΑΝΚΑΤΑ
ΧΙΕΡΑΤΙ
ΚΑΤΑΣΕ
ΟΙΣΒΑ
ΟΙΕ

120

[*About eight
lines are here
broken away.*]

ΟΥΗΤΑΣΕΙΚΟΝΑΣΠΡΟΣΤΟ
ΤΙΝΙΤΡΟΠΩΙΚΑΚΟΥΡΓΗΘΗΝΑ ΕΠΙ
ΔΕΛΤΩΙΕΡΟΣΥΛΙΑΚΑΙΑΣΕΒΕΙΑΚΑΙΟΥΔΕΝ
ΛΘΜΟΣΕΝΤΟΙΣΠΡΟΓΕΓΡΑΜΜΕΝΟΙΣΛΓΕΙΚΟΝΙΣ

125

ΡΙΑΕΧΟΝΤΟΣΗΝΓΕΡΙΤΟΥΤΩΝΕΚΔΙΚΙΑΝΕΠΑΝΑΝ
ΤΩΝΔΕΚΑΘΙΕΡΩΜΕΝΩΝΥΠΟΣΑΛΟΥΤΑ

Ι. Τ ΛΕΣΕΙΤΟΚΟΝΣΑ   ΛΟΥΤΑΡΙΟΣΔΡΑΧΜΙΑΙΟΝΚΑΘΕΚΑΣΤΟΝΕΝΙ
ΤΑΓΕΙ ΟΜΕΝΑΔΗΝΑΡΙΑΧ   ΛΙΑΟΚΤΑΚΟΣΙΑΑΦΩΝΑΔΩΣΕΙΤΟΓΡΑΜΜΑ
ΟΥΛΗΣΔΗΝΑΡΙΑΤΕΤΡΑΚΟΣΙ   ΝΘΚΟΝΤΑΟΠΩΣΕΠΙΤΕΛΕΙΔΙΑΝΟΜΗΝ

130

ΒΟΥΛΕΥΤΑΙΣΕΝΤΩΙΕΡΩΙΕΝΤ   ΙΩΝΑΩΙΗΙΓΕΝΕ ΙΩΙΗΣΜΕΓΙΣΗΣΘΕΑΣΑΡ
ΙΤΙΣΕΣΤΙΝΜΝΟΣΘΑΡΓΗ   ΛΝΟΣΕΚΗΙΣΤΑΜΕΝΟΥΓΕΙΝΟΜΕΝΗΣΗΣΔΙΑΝΟ
ΛΤΕΜΠΗΣΔΙΔΟΜ   ΚΑΣΤΩ ΤΩΝΠΑΡΟΝΤΩΝΔΗΝΑΡΙΟΥΕΝΟΣ
ΤΟΣΕΞΟΥΣΙΑΝΤΟΥΕΠΙ Ι   ΔΙΑΝΟΜΙΣΑΠΟΝΤΙΔΟΥΝΑΙ ΕΙΑΠΟΤΕΙΣΑ
ΟΥΛΗΙΥΓΓΡΕΚΑΣΤΟΥΟΝΟ   ΜΑΤΟΣ ΩΥΜΠΑΡΑΓΕΝΟΜΕΝΟΥΚΑΙΛΑΒΟΝΟΣ

Col. 5.

135

ΕΛ
ΙΣΑ   ΙΟΙΣ
ΛΝΔ   ΛΑΙΛΩΚΑΙ
ΤΟΥΚ...ΗΡΟΥΓΕΙΝΟΜΕΝΟΥ
ΣΙΛΗΤΟΥΓΓΡΑΜΜΑΤΕΟΣΗΣ

140

ΗΗΑΝΑΓΡΑΦΗΝΜΕΤΛ

```
                              ΤΟΤΕΙΣΑΤΩΠΡΟΣΤΕΙΜоΝ
                              ΟΙΩΣΛΠΟΤΟΥΠΡΟΓΕ
                              ΑΣΤΟΝ·ΚΑΙΤΟΙΣΕΞΦΥ
                              ΚΛΗΡΟΝΤΗΣΠΡΟΓΕΓΡΑΜ
145                           ΣΦΥΛΗΣΕΙΣΟΝΟΜΑΤΑΔΙ
                              ΩΝΛΗΞΟΜΕΝΩΝΑΣΣΑΡΙΑ·Θ
                              ΟΜΕΝΟΣΚΟΛΛΥΒΟΣΥΠΟ
                              ΕΙΤΑΣΚΛΗΡΟΥΣΘΑΙ
                              ΤΟΚΣΥΚΑΤΕΝΙΑΥΤΟΝ
150                           ΣΓΤΙΤΕΛΗΚΛΗΡΟΝ
                              ΗΣΑΡΤΕΜΙΔΟΣ
                              ΩΝΤΩΝΛΗΞΟ
                              ΟΕ ΗΒΑΡΧΟΣΧΩ
                              ΟΥΠΡΟΓΕΓΡΑΜΜΕ
155                           ΣΩΝΑΟΥΚΟΙΝΟΥ
                              ΚΑΤΕΝΙΑΥΤΟΝΕΚΑΣ
                              ΕΟΥΗΜΕΡΑΕΠΙΤΕΛΕΙ
                              ΣΑΡΤΜΙΔΟΣΛΑΜ
                              ΑΝΑΓΡΑΨΑΜΕΝΩΝ
160                           ΝΟΜΕΝΗΣΤΗΣΑΝΑ
                              ΕΙΑΠΟΤΟΥΠΡΟΓΕΓΡΑ
                              ΗΙΕΡΕΙΑΤΗΣΑΡΤΕΜΙΔΟΣ
                              ΙΤΗΣΑΡΤΕΜΙΔΟΣΕΙΣ
                              ΙΑΠΟΤΟΥΠΟΓΕΓΡΑΜ
165                           ΗΣΙΑΝΔΥΣΝΝΕΟΠΟΙ
                              ΣΘΑΙΕΚΤΟ ΤΡΟΝΑΟΥ
                              ΘΕΟΥΚΑΙΤΑΣΕΙΚΟΝΑΣΚΑΙ
                              ΥΕΙΣΤΟ ΝΠΡΟΝΑΟΝΑΤΘΗΜΕ
                              ΣΕΙΑΠΟΤ ΟΥΠΡΟΓΕΓΡΑΜΜΕ
170                           ΩΝ ΚΑΙΤΟΙΣ ΛΙΔΩΝ ΜΟΙΣ
                              ΞΙΩΤΗΣΣΕΟΥΗΜΕΡΑΕΠΙΤΕΛΕ
                              ΤΩΝΕΙΣΟΝΟΜΑΤΑ·ΜΘ·ΛΑΜΒΑΝΟΝ
                              ΗΜΕΡΑΕΝΤΩΙΕΡΩΤΗΣΑΡΤΕΜΙΔΟΣ
                              ΙΤΩΝΚΑΙΤΩΝΠΑΙΔΩΝΟΜΩΝΧΩΡΙΣ
175                           ΛΟΙΩΣΔΩΣΕΙΑΠΟΤΟΥΠΡΟΓΕΓΡΑΜ
                              ΑΥΤΟΝΤΩΤΑΚΑΘΑΡΣΙΑΠΟΙΟΥΝΤΙΠΑΡΕ
                              ΤΑΛΟΙΠΑ·ΔΗΤΡΙΑΚΟΝΤ ΩΣΤΕΚΑ
                              ΣΤΟΙΕΡΟΝΑΠΟΦΕ ΗΤΑ ΤΑΛΑΠΕΙΚΟΝ
                              ΔΙΑΥΤΑΕΙΣ ΙΟΝΠΡΟΝΑΟΝΤΗΣΑΡΤΕ
180                           ΙΔΙΑΝΠ ΟΛΙΡΕΣΙΝΑΓΟΡΑΣΗ
                              ΗΘΗΔΙΔΟΣΘΑΙΚΑΘΕΚΑΣΤΟΝΕΝΙ
                              ΩΝΤΑΠΡΟΓΕΓ ΛΜΜΕΝΑΔΗ.ΧΙΛΙΑ
               ΛΤΑΚ           ΔΙΛΤΑΞΙΝΕΙΣ ΕΝΚΕΙΝΜΔΕΝ
               ΕΛΑΣΣ          ΛΛΑΠΡΟΣΑ ΦΛΑΙΟΜΕΝΟΥ
185            ΕΑΝΔΕΤ         ΗΘΗΔΕΑΠΟΔΟΥΝΑΙ ΛΛΞΙΟΝΤΑΤΙΣ
               ΚΑΘΙΕΡΩ        Λ.ΕΞΕΣΤΑΙΑΥΤΩΔΕΠΑΝΑΝΚΗΛΗΨΟΜΕ
               ΝΩΤ            ΤΗΣΒΟΥΛΗΣΤΑΓΕΙΝΟΜΕΝΑΥΠΕΡΤΩΝ
               ΚΑ ΙΕΡΩ        ΑΡΧΑΙΟΥ·ΔΗ ΠΕΝΤΑΚΙΣΧΙΛΙΑ
               ΟΜ ΙΩΣΚΑ       ΙΑΤΩΝΤΗΣΓΕΡΟΥΣΙΑΣΤΑΓΕΙΝΟΜΕΝΑ
190   ΥΠΕΡΤΩΝΚΑ ΘΙΕΡΩΘ ΩΝΤΗΓΕΡΟΥΣΙΑ ΔΗ ΤΕΤΡΑΚ
      ΛΙΑΤΕΤΡΑΚΟΣΙΑΠΕΝΤΗΚΟΝΤΑ ΟΜΟΙΩΣΚΑΙΤΟΙΣΘΕΟΛΟΓΟΙΣ
      ΚΑΙΥ ΝΩΔΟΙΣΤΑΓΕΙΝΟΜΕΝΑΥΠΕΡΤΗΣΚΑΘΙΕΡΩΣΕΩΣΑΡΧΑΙΟΥ
      ΔΗ·ΔΙΑΚΟΣ ΑΠΕΝΤΗΚΟΝΤΑΠΕΝΤΕ· ΟΜΟΙΩΣΤΩΓΡΑΜΜΑΤΕΙ
      ΤΟΥΔΗΜΟΥΤΑΛΟΙΠΑΓΕΙΝΟΜΕΝΑΤΟΥΑΡΧΑΙΟΥΥΠΕΡΤΗΣΚΑΘΙΕΡΩ
195   ΣΕΩΣΤΩΝΕΙΣΤΟΥΣΠΟΛΕΙΤΑΣ ΚΛΗΡΩΝΚΛΙΕΦΗΒΩΝΚΑΙΝΕΟ
      ΠΟΙΩΝ ΚΑΙΣΚΗΠΤΟΥΧΩΝ·ΚΑΙΚΑΘΑΡΣΙΩΝ·ΔΗ·ΜΥΡΙΑΔΙΑΚΟΣΙΑ
      ΕΒΔΟΜΗΚΟΝΤΑΠΕΝΤΕ ΟΠΩΣΕΚΔΑΝΙΖΩΣΙΝΑΥΤΑΕΠΙΤΟΚΩ
      ΑΣΣΑΡΙΩΝΔΕΚΑΔΥΟΑΡΓΥΡΩΝΑΔΙΑΠΤΩΤΑ ΚΑΙΕΠΙΤΕΛΗ
```

ΤΑΙΚΑΘΕΚΑΣΤΟΝΕΝΙΑΥΤΟΝΑΠΟΤΟΥΤΟΚΟΥΤΑΔΙΑΤΕΤΑΓΜΕ
200 ΝΑ · ΙΝΥΠΕΡΘΕΤΩΣ · ΩΣΠΡΟΓΕΓΡΑΠΤΑΙ ~ ΕΑΝΔΕΠΡΟΤΟΥΑΠΟ
ΔΟΥΝΑΙ · ΤΑΔΙΣΜΥΡΙΑ ΔΗ · ΗΔΙΑΤΑΞΕΣΘΑΙΑΠΟΠΡΟΣΟΔΟΥ
ΧΩΡΙΩΝΔΙΔΟΣ ΑΙ~ΟΝΤΟΚΟΝΑΥΤΩΝΗΤΕΛΕΥΤΗΣΕΙ
ΣΑΛΟΥΤΑΡΙΟΣΥΠΟΚΕΙΣΘΩΣΑΝΟΙΚΛΗΡΟΝΟΜΟΙΑΥΤΟΥΤΗΕΥ
ΛΥΚΕΙΤΩΝΚΑΘΙΕΡΩΜΕΝΩΝ ~ ΔΗ ~ ΔΙΣΜΥΡΙΩΝ ~ ΚΑΙΤΟΙΣΕΠΑ
205 ΚΟΛΟΥΘΩΣΑΣΙΤΟΚΟΙΣΜΕΧΡΙΤΗΣΕΥΛΥΤΗΣΕΟΣΥΠΟΚΕΙ
ΜΕΝΩΝΑΥΤΩΝΤΗΠΡΑΞΕΙΚΑΤΑΤΑΙΕΡΑΤΗΣΘΕΟΥ ~ ΚΑΙΤΑΠΑ
ΡΑΤΟΙΣΠΡΕΣΒΥΤΕΡΟΙΣΕΚΔΙ ΝΙΣΤΙΚΑΕΝΓΡΑΦΑ ~ ΥΠΕΣΧΕΤΟ
ΛΕΣΑΛΟΥΤΑΡΙΟΣΩΣΤΕΑΡΞ ΣΘΑΙΤΗΝΦΙΛΟΤΕΙΜΙΑΝΑΥΤΟΥ
ΤΔΕΝΕΣΤΩΤΙΕΤΕΙ ~ ΕΝΤΗΓΕΝΕ ΩΤΗΣΘΕΟΥΗΜΕΡΑ ΔΩΣΕΙ
210 ΔΗ ~ ΧΕΙΛΙΑΟΚΤΑΚΟΣΙΑ ~ ΕΙΣΤΑΣΠΡΟΓΕΓΡΑΜΜΕΝΑΣΔΙΑΝΟΜΑΣ
ΚΛ ΛΗΡΟΥΣ ~ ΜΗΔΕΝ ΔΕΕΞΕΣΤΩΑΡΧΟΝΤΙΗΕΚΔΙΚΩΗΙΔΙΩ
ΤΗΡΙ ΣΑΙΤΙΑΛΛΑΞΑΙΜΕΤΑΘΕΙΝΑΙΗΜΕΤΟΙΚΟΝΟΜΙΣΑΙΗΜΕΤΑ
ΨΗΦΙ ΑΣΘΑ ΤΩΝΚΑΘΙΕΡΩΜΕΝΩΝΑΠΕΙΚΟΝΙΣΜΑΤΩΝΗΤΟΥ
ΑΡΓΥΡΙJΗΤΗΣ ΡΟΣΟΔΟΥΑΥΤΟΥΜΕΤΑΘΕΙΝΑΙΕΙΣΕΤΕΡΟΝΠοΡοΝ
215 ΗΑΝΑ ΩΜΑΗΑΛ ΟΤΙΠΟΗΣΑΙΠΑΡΑΤΑΠΡΟΓΕΓΡΑΜΜΕΝΑ · ΚΑΙΔΙΑ
ΤΕΤ ΜΕΝΑ · ΕΠΕΙΤΟΓΕΝΟΜΕΝΟΝΠΑΡΑΤΑΥΤΑΕΣΤΩΑΚΥΡΟΝ
ΟΔΕΠΕ ΣΑΣΠΟΙΗΣΑΙΤΙΥΠΕΝΑΝΤΙΟΝΤΗΔΙΑΤΑΞΕΙΗΤΟΙΣ
ΥΠΟΤ Β~Υ ΗΣΚΑΙΤΟΥΔΙΜΟΥΕΨΗΦΙΣΜΕΝΟΙΣΚΑΙΕΠΙΚΕΚΥ
ΡΩΜΕΝ ΤΑΥΤΗ~ ΙΣΔΙΑΤΑΞΕΩΣ · ΑΠΟΤΕΙΣΑΤΩΕΙΣ
220 ΠΡΟΣΚ ΗΣΜΕ ΗΣΘΕΑΣΑΡΤΕΜΙΔΟΣ · ΔΗ · ΔΙΣΜΥΡΙΑ
~Α · ΣΕΒΑΣΤΟΥΦΙΣΚΟΝΑΛΛΛ · ΔΗ ~ Μ/Ε
ΩΚΥΡΙΑΕΙΣΤΟΝΑΠΑΝΤΑΧΡΟ
ΟΣΠΡΟΚΛ ~ ΤΗΣ
225 Σ · ΚΑΙΑΦΡΑΝΙΟΣΦΛΑΟΥΙΑΝΟΣΟΚΡΑΤΙΣΤΟΣΠΡΕΣΒΕΥΤΗΣ
Α Ι ΑΤΗΓΟΣΔΙΑΕΠΙΣΤΟΛΩΝΠΕΡΙΤΑΥΤΗΣΤΗΣΔΙΑΤΑΞΕ
ΩΣΕΠΕΚΥΡΩΣΑΝΚΑΙΩΡΙΣΑΝΤΟΠΡΟΓΕΓΡΑΜΜΕΝΟΝΠ ΩΣΤΣ ΝΟΝ
ΓΛΙΟΣΟΥΕΙΒΙΟΣΓΑΙΟΥΥΙΟΣΩΦΕΝΤΕΙΝΑΣΑΛΟΥΤΑΡΙΟΣ ~ ΕΙ ΕΝΗΝΟΧΑ
ΤΗΝΔΙΑΤΑΞΙΝΚΑΙΚΑΘΙΕΡΩΣΑΤΑΠΡΟΓΕΓΡΑΜΜΕΝΑ~

Col. 6.

C
230 ΙΗΤΑΙ
εΜΗΣΑΙΜΕ
ΣΚΑΙΜΕΓΙC
ΓΩΝ · ΚΑΙΗΣ
ΙΑΣΚΑΙΚΛΗ
235 ΕΦΟΙΣΗΔΗ
ΣΧΡΙΝΑΙΤΗΤΕ
ΕΙΑ · ΑΠΡΟΣ
ΝΕΣΑΙΤΕΤΟΝ
ΜΑΡΤΥΡΙΑΣ
240 ΔΥΝΑΤΑΠΡΟ
ΡΟΥΜΕΝΑΧΡΗ
ΞΕΙΚΟΝΑΣΗΙC

ΕΠι
ΑΦ
245 ΟΥ
...ΛΤ ΟΖ
ΛΙΤΟΥΑΡΙΣ
ΟΣΤΩΝΟΙΚΙο
ΛΟΣΕΝΠΟΛΑΟΙC
Α ΝΩΣΕΧΕΙΠΡΟΣ
Τ
250 ΙΕ ΗΤΗΝΕΑΥΤΟΥ

i i

```
          |ΑΤ                                    ΤΗΝΠΟΛΙΝΕΧΕΙ
        ϛ |ΑΛ                                    ΠΡΕΠΟΝΤΩ
        Τ |ΕΒ                                    ϞΟΣΜΕ
        Κ |ΑΙΣ                                      Γ        ϞΑΙ
235     Ε |ΠΙΣ                                              _ΕΠΙ
        Φ |ΑΝΕϟ                                              ϽΚΡΑΤΟ
        Ρ |  ΝΔ_                   ΜΑΤΩΝΑΦΙΕΓ⌣             ϵΙΜΟϓ
        Μ |ΕΝΟϓ                    ΑΙϓΜΕΙΝΤΕΠΕΡΙΤΑΝϟℲ⌣⌣    ΤΙΣΩΝ
        Π |ΡΙϓΜ             ΑΙ  ΙΜΗΝϓΣΑΙΜΑΡΤΥΡΗΣΑΙΤϵ       ϛΦΗΜΙΑΤΗ
260     Π |ΡΟΣΗΚϽ          ΑΥΤΟΝ ΠΕΡΥΜΩΝΑΜΕΙϓΑΣΘΑΙΟΣ       ΥΤΩΚΑΙΠΑ
        Γ |  4Γι.    ΛΕΣΘΑΙΛΟΜΙΖΩΠΡΟΣΤΟΚΑΙΠΑ              ΣΕΙΝΑΙ·ΤΟϓϹ
          |  ΟΙΩΣΠ     ϛΜΟϓΛϵΝΟϓΣ·ΕΙΟΥΤΟΣΦΑΙΝΟΙΤ         ΗΣΚΑΤΑΤΗΝ
          |Ξ ΙΑΝΑΜΟΙΒΗΣ ΙΥΝΧΑ ϟ     ϵΠΙΔΑΝΚΑΜΟΙΕ ι ΤΟΙΣΜΑΛΙΣΤΑ
          |ΕΧΑΡΙΣΝΕΝΟΝΚΑΙΗΔΙΣ   ϽΝ·ΕΙΟΝΕΞΑΙΡΕΤΩΣΤΩΝΦΙΛΩΝ
265     |ΕΙΜΩ·ΚΑΙΣΤΕΡΓΩΠΑΡΥΜΞΙΝΟΡΩΚΜΜΑΡΤΥΡΙΑΣΚΑΙΤΕΙΜΗ
          |ΑΞΙΟϓΜΕΝΟΝ ꞏ ΠΕΡΙΜΕΝΤΟΙΓ⌐ ꞏꞏΨΣΤΩΝΧΡⱽᴴ ꞏꞏꞏꞏΩΔΙΑΤᴀ
          |Ξ ΕΩΣΚΑΙΤΩΝΑΠΕΙΚΟΝΙΣΜΑΤΩ...ꞏꞏϹΘϵϒΤϞ ΙΤΩϻΕΙΚΟΝΩΝ
          |ΟΠΩΣΑΥΤΟΙΣΔΕΗΣΕΙΧΡΗΣΘΑΙΚΑΙΕΙΣΤΗΤΙ ΛΟΙϞΟΝΟΜΙΑΝ
          |Α ΝΔΡΑΤΕΤΑΧΘΑΙ·ΑϓΤΩΝΤΕΤΟΝΑΝΑΤΙΘϵΛ ꞊ ΕΙΣΗΤΗΣΛΣΘΑΙ
270     |ΝΟΜΙΖΩΕΥΛΟΓΟΝΕΙΝΑΙ·ΚΑΙΥΜΑΣΟϓ꞊ Ͱ̵ΗΦΙΣΑΣΘΑΙΕΠΕΙ
          |ΔΙΝΔΕϓΠΟΤΕΑϓΤΟϓΤΟϓΚΑΘΙΕΡΟϓΝΤΟΣΚΑΙΥΜΩΝΑϓΤΩΝΚϓΡΩ
          |ΘꞏΗΤΑΔΟΞΑΝΤΑΒΟϓΛΟΜΑΙΤΑΥΤΑΕΙΣΑΕΙΜΕΝΕΙΝΕΠΙΤΩΝΑϓΤΩΝ
          |Α ꞏΠΑΡΑΛΛΑΚΤΩΣ ꞊ ϓΠΟΜΗΔΕΝΟΣϻΔΕΜΙΑΝΠΑΡΕΝΧΕΙΡΗΣΕΙΑϓ
          |Ο ΜΕΝΑΗΜΕΤΑΤΙΘΕΜΕΝΑ · ΕΙΔΕΤΙΣΠΕΙΡΑΘΕΙΗΟΠΩΣΟΥΝΗΣͰꞋ̈
275     |ΒΟϓΛΕϓΣΑΙΤΙΤΟΙΟϓΤΟΝΗΕΙΣΗΓΗΣΑΣΘΑΙ · ΠΕΡΙΤΗΣΜΕΤΑΘΕΣΕ
          |ΩΣ · ΚΑΙΜΕΤΑΔΙΟΙΚΗΣΕΩΣ · ΤΩΝΝΥΝϓΠΟΤΕΑΥΤΟΥΚΑΙϓϕϓ
          |Μ ΩΝΚϓΡΩΘΗΣΟΜΕΝΩΝ · ΤΟϓΤΟΝΑΝΥΠΕΡΘΕΤΩΣΒΟΥΛΟΜΑΙ
          |Ε ΣΜΕΝΤΟΤΗΣΜΕΓΙΣΤΗΣΘΕΛΣΑΡΤΕϻ ΙΔΟΣΙΕΡΟΝΚΑΤΑΘΕΣ
          |ΘΑΙΠΡΟΣΤΕΙΜΟϓ꞊ꞏΔΗꞏϻꞏΠΕΝΤΑΚΙΣ ꞏΔΙΔ꞊ΕΙΣΔΕΤΟΝΤΟϓ
280     ꞏꞏꞏꞏ
          ΓΕΡϹ                                   ΣΧΙΛΙΑ
          ΚΑΘ                                     ϓΠΑΤΟΣ
          ΚΑΙΙ                                    ΙΣΤΟΛΗΣ
          ΕΓ                                      ΡΡΩΣΘΕ꞊
285     ϵπιΡ                               ꞏΟϓΙΟΥΛΙΑΝΟϓ

          Ϝ                          ϛΦΑΝΙΣΑΝ ΤΙ꞊ΚΛΑΥ꞊
                                     ΦΙΛΟΠΑΤΡΙΣΚΑΙΦΙΛΟ
                                     ΣΤΟϓΔΗΜΟϓ꞊ΤΟꞏΒꞏΚΑΙΟΙ
290                                  ΛΣΤΟΙ꞊ ΟΠΩΣΕΞΗΤΟΙΣΧΡΥΣΟ
                                     ϵΚΚΛΗΣΙΑΣꞏΚΑΙΤΟΥΣΑΓΩΝΑΣ
          ΤΑΛΑΠΕΙϞΟΝΙΣΜΑΤꞏΚΑΙΕΙϞΟΝΑΣΤΑϞꞏΛΘΙΕΡΩΜΕΝ        ϓ
          ΟϓΕΙΒΙϹϓΣΛΑΟϓΤΑΡΙΟϓꞏΕΚΤΟϓΠΡϹΝΛΟϓΤΗΣΑΡΤΕΜΙΔⱽϹ   ΣΥΝ
          ΕΠΙΜΕΛΟϓΜΕΝΩΝΚΑΙΤΩΝΝΕΟΠΟΙΩΝϓΝΠΑΡΑΛΑΜΒΑΝΟϻΤϽΝΚΑΙΤϽΝ
295       ΕΦΙΒϧΩΗΑΠΟΤΗΣΜΑΓΝΗΤΙΚΗΣΠϓΛΗΣΚΑ ΣϓΝΗΠΟΠΕΜΠΟΝΤΩΝ
          ΜΕΧΡΙΤΗΣΚΟΡΗΣΣΙΚΗΣ ΠϓΛΗΣ꞊ΔΕΔΟ ꞏΑΙΤΗΒΟϓΛΗΦΙΛΟΣΕ
          ΒΑΣΤΩꞏΚΑΘΟΤΙΠΡΟΓΕΓΡΑΠΤΑΙ꞊ ΤΙΒ ꞏΛΑϓꞏΠΡΩΡΕΣΙΟΣ
          ΦΡΗΤΩΡΙΑΝΟΣΦΙΛΟΣΕΒΑΣΤΟΣ·ΔΕΔΟΓΜΑΤ ꞏΑΦΗΚΑ꞊ΜΑΡΚΟΣ
          ΚΑΙΣΕΛΑΙΟΣΜΑΡΚΙΑΝΟΣ·ΦΙΛΟΣΕΒΑΣΤΟΣ·ꞏ ΔΟΓΜΑΤΟΓΡΑΦΗΚΑ
300       ΤΙΒꞏΚΛΑϓꞏΙΟϓΛΙΑΝΟΣΦΙΛΟΠΑΤΡΙΣΦΙΛΟΣΕΒΑΣΤ ΣΑΓΝΟΣΕϓΣΕΒΗΣ⌣
          ꞏꞏΟΓΡΑΜΜΑΤΕϓΣꞏΤΟϓΔΗΜΟϓꞏΤΟꞏΒꞏΕΧΑΡΑΞΑꞏ
          ΕΠΙΠΡϓΤΑΝΕΩΣ꞊ΤΙΒꞏΚΛꞏ⸗ϓΤΙΠΑΤΡΟϓΙΟϓΛΙΑΝΟϓ
          ꞏΜΗΝΟΣꞏ ΠΟΣΕΙΔΕΩΝΟΣꞏ
          Ϛ ΔΟΣΕΤΗΒΟΥΛΗΦΙΛΟΣΕΒΑΣΤΩΠΕΡΙΩΝΕΝΕΦΑΝΙΣΑΝ꞊ΤΙΒꞏ
305       ΚΛꞏΤΙΒꞏΚΛꞏΑΛΕΞΑΝΔΡΟΥꞏΥΙ ΚϓΡꞏΙΟϓΛΙΑΝΟΣꞏΦΙΛΟΠΑΤΡΙΣ
          ΚΑΙΦΙΛΟΣΕΒΑΣΤΟΣΑΓΝΟΣΕϓΣΕΒΗΣΓΡΑΜΜΑΤΕϓΣΤΟϓΔΗΜΟϓϓΒ
          ꞊ ΚΑΙΟΙΣΤΡΑΤΗΓΟΙΤΗΣΠΟΛΕΩΣΦΙΛΟΣΕΒΑΣΤΟΙ꞊
          ΕΠΕΙΟΙΧΡϓΣΟΦΟΡΟϓΝΤΕΣΤΗΘΕΩ꞊ΙΕΡΕΙΣΚΑΙΙΕΡΟΝΕΙΚΑΙϓΠϵϹ
```

ΧΕΝΤΟΦΕΡΕΙΝΚΑΙΑΥΦΕΡΕΙΝΤΑΑΠΕΙΚΟΝΙΣΜΑΤΑ · ΤΑΚΑΘΙΕΡΩ
ΘΕΝΤΑ · ΥΠΟ · ΟΥΕΙΒΙΟΥΣΑΛΟΥΤΑΡΙΟΥΗΤΗΣΑΝΤΟΤΕΤΟΠΟΝ
ΕΝΤΩΘΕΑΤΡΩ · ΤΗΝΠΡΩΤΗΝΣ ΛΙΔΑΟΠΟΥΗΕΙΚΩΝΤΗΣΟΜΟΝΟΙΑΣ
ΔΕΔΟΧΘΑΙΕΧΕΙΝΕΑΥΤΟΥΣΤΟΝ ΟΠΟΝΚΑΘΙΖΕΙΝΔΕΠΡΟΣΤΗΝΕΥ
ΣΕΒΕΙΑΝ · ΑΥΤΟΥΣΑ ΥΧΕΙΜΟΝΟΥΝΤΑΣ – ΔΕΔΟΧΘΑΙΤΗΒΟΥΛΗ·
ΦΙΛΟΣΕΒΑΣΤΩΓΕΝΕΣΘΑΙ – ΚΑΘΟΤΙΠΡΟΓΕΓΡΑΠΤΑΙ –
Γ · ΑΥΦΙΔΙΟΣΣΙΛΟΥΑΝΟΣ ΡΙΛΟΣΕΒΑΣΤΟΣ · ΔΕΔΟΓΜΑΤΟΓΡΑΦΗΚΑ
Λ · ΜΟΥΝΑΤΙΟΣΒΑΣΣΟΣΦΙΛΟΣΕΒΑΣΤΟΣ · ΔΕΔΟΓΜΑΤΟΓΡΑΦΗΚΑ
ΝΗΡΕΥΣΘΕΟΦΙΛΟΥ · ΦΙΛΟΣΕΒΑΣΤΟΣ · ΔΕΔΟΓΜΑΤΟΓΡΑΦΗΚΑ

ΣΕΞΤΩ · ΑΤΤΙΩ – ΣΟΥΒΟΥΡΑΝΩ – † Β ΜΑΡΚΩΑΣΙ
ΝΙΩ · ΜΑΡΚΕΛΛΩ · ΥΠΑΤΟΙΣ · ΠΡΟ · Η · ΚΑΛΑΝΔΩΝ · ΜΑΡΤΙΩΝ
ΕΠΙΠΡΥΤΑΝΕΩΣ – ΤΙΒ · ΚΛΑΥΔΙΟΥΑΝΤΙΠΑΤΡΟΥΙΟΥΛΙΑΝΟΥ
– ΜΗΝΟΣ · ΑΝΘΕΣΤΗΡΙΩΝΟΣ · Β · ΣΕΒΑΣΤΗ –
ΓΑΙΟΣΟΥΕΙΒΙΟΣ · Γ · ΥΙ · ΟΥΩΦΕΝΤΕΙΝΑ · ΣΑΛΟΥΤΑΡΙΟΣ · ΦΙΛΑΡ
ΤΕΜΙΣΚΑΙΦΙΛΟΚΑΙΣΑΡ – ΔΙΑΤΑΞΙΝΕΙΣΦΕΡΕΙΚΑΤΑΤΟΠΡΟΓΕ
ΓΟΝΟΣΨΗΦΙΣΜΑΠΕΡΙΩΝΠΡΟΣΚΑΘΙΕΡΩΚΕΤΗΜΕΓΙΣΤΗΘΕΑΕΦΕ
ΣΙΑΑΡΤ ΜΙΔΙ · ΚΑΙΤΗΦΙΛΟΣΕΒΑΣΤΩ – ΕΦΕΣΙΩΝΒΟΥΛΗ

ΚΑΙΤΗΦΙΛΟΣΕΒΑ ΣΙΑ · ΚΑΙΤ ΡΥ
ΣΟΦΟΡ ΥΣΙΤΗΣ ΕΥΣΙΝΚΑΙΙΕΡΟΝΕΙΚΑΙΣΠΡΟ
ΠΟΛΕΩΣΚ ΕΣΙΩΝΠΑΙΣΙ · ΚΑΙΘΕΣ
ΜΩΔΟΙΣ · ΝΑΙ ΩΚΟΙΝΟΥΤΗΣΑΣΙΑΣ · ΚΑΙ
ΑΚΡΟΒΑΤΑΙΣΤΗΣ ΙΟΙΣΔΙΚΑΙΟΙΣΚΑΙΠΡΟΣΤΕΙ
ΜΟΙΣ · ΩΣΕΝΤΗΠΡΟ ΑΤΑΞΕΙΗΣΦΑΛΙΣΤΑΙ ∽ ΕΙΚΟ
ΝΩΝΑΡΓΥΡΕΩΝΔΥΟ Λ ΣΩΝΩΣΤΕΑΥΤΑΣΕΙΝΑΙΣΥΝΤΟΙΣ
ΑΠΕΙΚΟΝΙΣΜΑΣΙΝΤΗΣΘΕΟΥΑΡΙΘΜΩΤΡΙΑΚΟΝΤΑΚΑΙΜΙΑΝ
ΚΑΙΑΡΓΥΡΙΟΥΑΛΛΩΝ · ΔΗ · ΧΕΙΛΙΩΝΠΕΝΤΑΚΟΣΙΩΝ – ΜΕΤΕΣΙΝΑΙ
ΑΥΤΑΣΥΝΤΟΙΣΠΡΟΚΑΘΙΕΡΩΜΕΝΟΙΣ · ΔΗ · ΜΥΡΙΟΙΣΧΙΛΙΟΙΣΠΕΝ
ΤΑΚΟΣΙΟΙΣ – ΕΦΩΕΙΚΩΝΑΡΓΥΡΕΑΑΘΗΝΑΣΠΑΜΜΟΥΣΟΥΟΛΚΗΣ
ΣΥΝ ΣΠΑΡΓΥΡΩΤΗΣΒΑΣΕΩΣΑΥΤΗΣ · ΛΕΙΤΡΩΝΕΠΤΑ · ΗΜΙΟΥΝ
ΚΙΟΥ – ΓΡΑΜΜΑΤΩΝΟΚΤΩ · ΗΚΑΘΙΕΡΩΜΕΝΗΤΗΤΕΑΡΤΕΜΙΔΙ · ΚΑΙ
ΤΟΙΣΑΙΕΙΕΣΟΜΕΝΟΙΣΕΦΕΣΙΩΝΠΑΙΕΙΤΙΘΗΤΑΙΚΑΤΑΠΑΣΑΝΝΟ
ΜΙΜΟΝΕΚΚΛΗΣΙΑΝΕΠΑΝΩ ΤΗΣΣΕΛΙΔΟΣΟΥ ΙΠΑΙΔΕΣΚΑΘΕ ΤΑΙ

Col. 7.

ΘΕΟΦΙΛ
ΗΣΕΦΕΣΙΩΝΠΟ
ΤΟΥΕΡΜΙΟΥΙΕΡΟΥΤΗΣ
ΤΟΣΚΑΙΣΥΝΠΑΡΑΛΛΑ
ΤΗΣΑΡΤΕΜΙΔΟΣΤΟΥ
ΥΠΕΡΔΕΤΩΝΠΡΟΣΚΑΘΙΕ
ΛΙΩΝΠΕΝΤΑΚΟΣΙΩ
ΤΑΡΙΟΣΔΡΑΧΜΙΑΙΟΝ
ΤΑΓΕΙΝΟΜΕΝΑ · ΔΗΝΑΙ
ΤΩΓΡΑΜΜΑΤΕΙΤΗΣΕΦ
ΟΠΩΣΚΛΗΡΟΝΕΠΙΤΕΛΗ
ΙΣΤΑΜΕΝΟΥΤΟΥΘΑΡΓΙ
· Ε̅ · ΟΥΤΟΙΤΕΟΙΛΑΧΟΝΤ
ΤΗΑΡΤΕΜΙΔΙΤΗΕΚ
ΤΗΣΘΕΟΥ · ΑΓΟΡΑΖΟ
ΕΠΤΑΗΜΙΣΟΥΣ · ΚΑΤ
ΔΑΠΑΝΗΣΟΥΣΙΝ
ΔΟΣ – ΕΙΣΤΗΝΟ

ΟΤ
Τ

```
. . . .
. . . .
_ΣΙΚΟΛ
ΕΝΤΩΙΕΡΩΤΗΣΑΡΤ
365    ΝΟΜΕΝΩΝΚΑΤΑΑΛΝΑ
ΕΑΝΔΕΤΙΝΕΣΤΩΝΛΑΧΟΙΙΙΩ
ΤΑΣΘΥΣΙΑΣΜΗΘΥΩΣΙΝΗΜΕΤ_
ΙΕΡΩΩΣΔΙΑΤΕΤΑΚΤΑΙ·ΑΠΟΔΟΤΣ
ΚΟΣΜΗΜΑΤΗΣΑΡΤΕΜΙΔΟΣ·ΔΗ·τ
370    ΟΜΟΙΩΣΔΩΣΕΙΑΠΟΤΟΥΠΡΟΓΕΓΡΑΜΜΕΝΟι
ΚΑΙΤΟΙΣΘΕΣΜΩΔΑΟΙΣΕΙΣΔΙΑΝΟΜΗΝ·ΔΗ·Ζ
ΩΣΤΕΛΑΜΒΑΝΕΙΝΑΥΤΟΥΣΕΝΤΩΙΕΡΩΤΗΣΑΡΤΕ
ΜΙΔΟΣ·ΤΗΓΕΝΕΣΙΩΤΗΣΘΕΟΥ·ΑΝΑ·ΑΣΣΑΡΙΑ·Θ·
ΟΜΟΙΩΣΔΩΣΕΙΑΠΟΤΟΥΠΡΟΓΕΓΡΑΜΜΕΝΟΥΤΟΚΟΥ
375    ΚΑΙΤΟΙΣΑΚΡΟΒΑΤΑΙΣΤΗΣΘΕΟΥΕΙΣΔΙΑΝΟΜΗΝ
·ΔΗ·ΙΕ_ΩΣΤΕΕΛΑΑΝΒΑΝΕΙΝΑΥΤΟΥΣΤΗΓΕΝΕΣΙΩ
ΤΗΣΘ·ΟΥ·ΑΝΑ·ΑΣΣΑΡΙΑ·ΔΕΚΑΤΡΙΑ·ΗΜΙΣΥ
ΠΡΟΣΔΕΤΟΜΕΝΕΙΝΤΑΑΠΕΙΚΟΝΙΣΜΑΤΑΠΑΝΤΑ
ΚΑΘΑΡΑΕΞΕΣΤΩΟΣΑΚΙΣΑΝΕΝΔΕΧΗΤΑΙ
380    ΕΚΜΑΣΣΕΣΘΑΙΓΗΑΡΓΥΡΩΜΑΤΙΚΗΥΠΟΤΟΥ
ΛΙΕΙΕΣΟΜΕΝΟΥΕΠΙΤΩΝΠΑΡΑΘΗΚΛΝΠΑΡΟΝ
ΤΩΝΔΥΟΝΕΟΠΟΙΩΝΚΑΙΣΚΗΠΤΟΥΧΟΥ_
ΕΤΕΡΑΔΕΥΛΗΜΗΔΕΜΙΑΕΚΜΑΣΣΕΣΘΑΙ·ΚΑΙ
ΤΑΛΟΙΠΑ·ΔΗ·ΟΚΤΩ·ΔΟΘΗΣΕΤΑΙΚΑΘΕΚΑΣΤΟΝ
385    ΕΝΙΑΥΤΟΝΤΩΕΠΙΤΩΝΠΑΡΑΘΗΚΩΝΕΙΣΤΗΝ
ΕΠΙΜΕΛΕΙΑΝΤΩΝΑΠΕΙΚΟΝΙΣΜΑΤΩΝΚΑΙΤΟΝ
ΑΓΟΡΑΣΜΟΝΤΗΣΑΡΓΥΡΩΜΑΤΙΚΗΣΓΗΣ=
ΥΠΕΣΧΕΤΟΔΕΣΑΛΟΥΤΑΡΙΟΣΔΩΣΕΙΝΚΑΙ·ΔΗ_
ΕΚΑΤΟΝΤΡΙΑΚΟΝΤΑΠΕΝΤΕ=ΩΣΤΕΑΡΣΑΣΘΑΙ
390    ΤΗΝΦΙΔΟΤΕΙΜΙΑΝΑΥΤΟΥΤΩΔΕΝΕΣΤΩΤΙΕΤΕΙ

ΤΗΓΕΝΕΩΤΗΣΕΟΥ·ΗΜΕΡΑ Ͽ

ΤΑΣΔΕΠΡΟΓΕΓΡΑΜΜΕΝΑΣΕΙΚΟΝΑΣΚΑΙΤΑΣ
ΠΡΟΚΑΘΙΕΡΩΜΕΝΑΣΕΝΤΗΠΡΟΤΑΥΤΗΣΔΙΑ
ΤΑΞΕΙ·ΚΑΙΤΑΑΠΕΙΚΟΝΙΣΜΑΤΑΠΑΝΤΑΤΗΣΘΕΟΥ
395    ΦΕΡΕΤΩΣΑΝΕΚΤΟΥΠΡΟΝΑΟΥΚΑΤΑΠΑΣΑΝΕΚΚΛΗ
ΣΙΑΝΕΙΣΤΟΘΕΑΤΡΟΝ·ΚΑΙΤΟΥΣΓΥΜΝΙΚΟΥΣ·ΑΓΩ
ΝΑΣΚΑΙΕΙΤΙΝΕΣΕΤΕΡΑΙΥΠΟΤΗΣΒΟΥΛΗΣΚΑΙΤΟΥ
ΔΗΜΟΥΟΡΙΣΘΗΣΟΝΤΑΙΗΜΕΡΑΙ·ΕΚΤΩΝΝΕΟΠΟΙ
ΩΝΔΥΟ·ΚΑΙΟΙΙΕΡΟΝΕΙΚΑΙ·ΚΑΙΣΚΗΠΤΟΥΧΟΣ·ΚΑΙ
400    ΦΥΛΑΚΟΙ ᵛΛΙΠΑΛΙΝΑΠΟΦΕΡΕΤΩΣΑΝ·ΕΙΣΤΟ
ΙΕΡΟΝ·ΚΑΙ     ΑΤΙΘΕΣΘΩΣΑΝΣΥΝΠΑΡΑΛΑΜΒΑ

ΝΟΝΤΣᵛΚΑΙΤΩΝΕΦΗΒΩΝΑΠΟΤΗΣΜΑ ΝΗ
ΤΙΚΗΣΠΥΛΗΣ·ΚΑΙΜΕΤΑΤΑΣΕΚΚΛΗΣΙΑΣ
ΣΥΝΠΡΟΠΕΜΠΟΝΤΩΝΕΩΣΤΗΣΚΟΡΗΣΣΙΚΙ
405    ΠΥΛΗΣ·ΚΑΘΩΣΚΑΙΕΝΤΟΙΣΠΡΟΓΕΓΟΝΟΣᵔΙ·
ΨΗΦΙΣΜΑΣΙ·ΗΒΟΥΛΗ·ΚΑΙΟΔΗΜΟΣΩΡΙΣ II
```

FRAGMENTS.—1.

ΛΓΓΥΡΛΣΕΙ	ΤΟΥΥ ΡΙΟΥΗΜΩΝΑΥ
ΝΕΡΟΥΛΤΡΑΙΑ	ᵀᴾΑΣιΟΥΓΕΡΜΑΝΙΚΟΥ
ΤΗΣΙΕΡΩΤΑΣ	ΩΤΞΙΝΗΣΚΑΙΤΗΣΙΕΡ
ΚΑΙΤΟΥΡΩ	ΤΩΣΚΑΙΔΗΜΟΥ
5 ΡΙΣΕΙΚΟΝ	ΝΗ̄Ν̄ΤΟΛΙΝΠΡΟΣ
ΟΥΔ ΙΜ	ΒΟιι ᴵΣΚΑΙΓΓ
ΒΕΙ	ΞΤΟΥ ΝΚ
ι	ᵛΛ·

```
10   MET
     ON
     YΠO
     TAΓ
     TA
     I
15   Φ

        ͻ

     TϹ
20   Δ
     ϵ
     TY
     Ɛ

25   Ω.            ΔιON
     NΩN      ιι  ϹAΙΔΙAΔ
     TΙΚΗϹ    ͺΦΗΒΩΝ ΠOΤΗϹ
     TONAY⁻   ⸂ΝΙΛΛΡΧ
```

2.

Broken all round.   9¼ in. by 4½ in.

```
     ΚΑΘΙ
     ΣΘΑΙ·Τ ι
     ϹΒΑΣΤOϒ
     ϹOΕΑΤΡO

     Π Α Τ

     ΣΤΡΑ
     ΙΡΕΤϹ
    ⁻Δ⁻
```

3.

Broken all round.   14⅛ in. by 4½ in.

```
     ͻΝ·Τι
     ΜΕΝ·ΚΑΤ
     ΑΤΑΤOϒΣ
     Ɛ·ΚΕΙΜΕΝϹ
     ΓΕΓΑΡΗ
     ͻΣ·ΚΑΙΤ
     ͻ·ΑͻΚͱ
     ΩΝΙΣΤͺ
     ΑΤOϒ⸱Γ
     OΙΝͺ
     ϹΕΙΚ
     Ν·Α
    ⸓ΡΙ
```

4.

Broken all round.   7 in. by 7 in.

```
     ΓͻΙΛΟͺͺ
     ΜΩΝΑϒΤOΙΚͺͺ
     ΝΗΔOΜΕΝͻ
     ΝΕΙΣΕΝϜ
    ͺΙΓ
```

5.

Broken all round and defaced.   1 ft. by 8½ in.

```
                            ⸌
     λ
     ΝΘΑΣΕΩΝ    Γ
     ΓΕΠΑΡΑ⁻⁻Θ   ΝΑ
     OϒΛΙͻΝOϒ
     ΜΙΔOΣΙ
    ⁻ΚΑΙ
 θ   ΣΠΑ
     Ν  λ
```

6.

Broken all round ; pieced together out of two bits : partly defaced.   11 in. by 6½ in.

```
     ͱΙΣΗΤ
    ͺOΜΕΝͱ  ι
     ΙΕΙOΤΕ⁻ ΙOΙΗ
     ΣΠΡͻ   ΚOΣ
    ⁻Oϒͱ   ΙOϒΚ
           ⁻O
```

7.

Broken all round and defaced.   8 in. by 7 in.

```
                      ΑΙ
     ΓΑΞΙΝͺ      ΡΑϹ
       OΑ        ⸎
```

8.

Broken all round.   3 in. by 9½ in.

```
     ͻΡΩΙΔΗΜΩΙΦΙΛOΣΕ
     ΠΤΑΙ
```

Blank.

9.

Broken all round and defaced.   6 in. by 5½ in.

```
             ιιͺ
             ΔΜΕ
    ͺΣΙΛΝΒ
     ΔΕΝΤΩΙ
     ΔΝΕΠΙΓΕΓ
     ΙΑΤΑΞΕΙΒ
    ͻΔϒΘͱΝ
    ͺΓ
```

10.

Broken all round.　5 in. by 5 in.

ΙΩΝΤΣ
ΕΤΟΦΑΝ
ΕΓΛΛΟΨΥΥ
ΟΥΓΕ

11.

Broken all round.　5¼ in. by 6 in.

ΕΛ
Σ · Δ̄ 　 · ι
ΔΗ̄ > ΜΕ · Ι
ΠΡΟΚΛΟ

12.

Broken bottom and right.　8½ in. by 4½ in.

ΕΤΟΥΣΟΥΣ
ΜΕΝΑ ΣΙΕΡΑ
ΣΓΡ　ΕΙΩΝ
⌒

13.

Broken top and right.　6 in. by 5¾ in.

ΜΟΤΕ ι
ΡΩΜΕΝΣ
ΚΑΙΠΟΛ
ΕΠΙΤΟΥ⟩

14.

Upper edge only entire.　8 in. by 8½ in.

ΤΟΝΝΑΟΝΤΗΣΑΙ
ΩΝΚΑΘΗΚΟΝΤΩ
ΤΟΥ·ΚΥΡΙΑΝΓΙΝ
ΩΝΕΙΣΤΟΝ
·ΤΕΑΡΧΟ
ΣΜΑ

15.

Broken all round.　4 in. by 4 in.

ΙΑ　ΔΟ
ΟΓΕΓΡΑΛ
ι　ΝΕΙΛ

16.

Broken all round.　3½ in. by 3 in.

ΡΕΣ
ΚΑΙΠΑ
ΙΤΩ

17.

Broken all round.　3 in. by 4 in.

ΑΙ
ΙΠΑΥ

18.

Entire only at top.　3 in. by 6 in.

ΙΘΕΚΑΣΤΟΛ
ΟΥΧΟΝΚΑΙΤΟΥ

19.

Entire only at top.　3½ in. by 3½ in.

ΙΙΣι
ΙΝΟΜ
ΗΡΙΩΝ

20.

Entire only at top.　3 in. by 5½ in.

ΝΜΗΝΑι
ΗΣΙΑΙΣΚΑ
ΙΙΤ

21.

Broken all round.　3½ in. by 4 in.

ΩΚΟ
· ΑΝΑ · ⎯
ΝΤΟ

22.

Joint only on right.　11 in. by 4 in.

ΛΙΕΥΜΕΝ
ΙΤΟΥΣΥΓ
ΟΥΙΕΡΟΥΤ
ΙΙΣΜΑΤ
ΝΟΥΜι
ΟΤΩΝΚΑ
ⵔ ΒΑΣΕΙΣ
ΣΙΑΣΕΦΗ
ΑΣΑΠΟΦ
ΙΔΟΣΚΑ
ΤΩΝΝΕΟ
ΛΘΙι

23.

Broken all round.　6 in. by 4 in.

ΕΣ
ΝΔΙΕ ,
ΟΥΣΕΛΛ ι
ΟΣ · ΝΥΝ
ΣΑΡΧΗ
ΕΙΟΝ

24.

Broken all round.　2 in. by 4 in.

ΙΑΣΗΣΟ
ΟΜΕΝΟ

25.

Broken all round.　3 in. by 4 in.

ΛΣΕι
ΞΕΟΥΕΞ
ΜΒΑΝΟι

26.

Broken all round.　6 in. by 3 in.

ΑΙ ΛΑιϹ
ΞΙΚΑΙΤΟΥ
ΣΤΕΚΑΙΤ
ΛΟΣ
ΤΕΠΟ
ΟΥΚ

27.

Entire only at bottom　4½ in. by 3½ in.

ΛΟΜΕΙ
ΡΓΥΡΕⵔ
ⵔΚΑΙ

28.

Broken all round.　7 in. by 3½ in.

ΗΣ
ΟΛΕ
ΛΑΤΟⁿ
ΥΡΕΑΓ
Γ · ΗΜ
Ις

First Document.

Decree in honour of C. Vib. Salutaris.

Col. 1.

Ἐπὶ π[ρυτ]άνεω[ς
Τ]ιβ. Κλ. Ἀντιπάτρου Ἰουλ[ι]ανοῦ, μην[ὸς
Ποσειδεῶνος ς̄ ἱσταμένου,
Ἔ]δοξε τῇ βουλῇ καὶ τῷ νεωκόρῳ δήμῳ φ[ι]λοσεβάστ[ῳ·
5 πε]ρὶ ὧν ἐνεφάνισαν Τιβ. Κλ. Τιβ. Κλ. Ἀλεξά[νδρ]ου υἱὸς [Κυρ.
Ἰουλιανὸ]ς φιλόπατρις καὶ φιλοσέβαστο[ς ἀγν]ὸς εὐσεβὴς
γραμματεὺς τ]οῦ δήμου τὸ β̄, καὶ οἱ στρατηγοὶ τῆ[ς] πό[λ]εως φιλοσέ-
βαστοι· ἐπειδὴ τοὺς] φιλοτείμους ἄνδρας περὶ τὴν π[όλ]ιν καὶ κατὰ
πάντα ἀποδειξαμένους] στοργὴν γνησίων πολει[τῶν ἀ]μοιβαὶ
10 ἴκαναὶ περιμένουσιν, εἰς] τὸ ἀπολαύειν [μ]ὲν τοὺς εὖ [ποι]ήσαν-
τας, ἀποκεῖσθαι δὲ τοῖς φιλοτιμεῖσθαι βο]υλομένοις, πε[ριμένει δὲ
ὁμοία ἀμ[οιβ]ὴ παρ' ἡμῶν τοὺ]ς ἐσπουδα[κ]ότας τὴν μεγίστην θεὸν Ἄρτεμιν [εὐσεβεῖν ἐξ ἧς γε]ίνεται πᾶσιν τ[ὰ ἄ]ελλιστα καθήκε[ι, δὲ
παρὰ τῇ πόλε[ι τὰ ἄριστα, ἐπειδή] τε Οὐίβι[ος Σαλ]ουτάριος ἀ-
15 νὴρ ἱππικῆς τά[ξ]εος γένει καὶ Ἀσίᾳ διάσημος στρατείαις τε καὶ
ἐπιτροπαῖς ὑ[πὸ] τοῦ κυρίου ἡμῶν Αὐτοκράτορος κεκοσμημένος,
πολείτης ἡ[μέτε]ρος καὶ τοῦ βουλευτικοῦ συνεδρίου, πρὸς πα[ιρ-
δὲ ἀγ]αθῇ χρώ[μενος δ]ιαθέσει ὡς καὶ τὰς ἀπὸ τῆς τύχης ἐπὶ τὸ κρ[εῖ-
ττον] προκοπὰς κοσ[μῶν τῇ] τῶν ἠθῶν σεμνότητι, εὐσεβῶν μὲν φιλοτεί-
20 μως] τὴν ἀρχηγέτιν πο[ικίλ]αις μὲν ἐπινοίαις ἐσπούδακεν περὶ τὴν θρη[σ-
κείαν] μεγαλόψυχος, [καὶ] καθιερώσειν τὴν πόλιν κατὰ πάν[τα] τε[τείμη-
κεν, προσ[έτι δὲ καὶ νῦν παρελθ]ὼν εἰς τὴν ἐκκλησίαν ὑπέσχε[το ἐννέα ἀ-
πεικονίσ[ματα καθιερῶσαι], ἐν μὲν χρύσεον ἐν ᾧ καὶ ἀργ[ύρεα
ἐπίχρυσα, ἕτ[ερα δὲ ἀργύρεα ἀ]πεικονίσματα ὀκτὼ ἐπ[ίχρυσα,

Col. 2.
25 Καὶ [τε]λεῖν τόκ[ον δραχμιαῖον] ἀσσαριαῖον
δι]αιρεθ[η]σομένων κ[αθ' ἕκαστον ἐ]νιαυτὸν κα-
τὰ] τὴν διάταξιν αὐτοῦ τ[ῇ γενε]σ[ίῳ τῆ]ς θεοῦ [ἡμέρᾳ
ἥτι]ς ἐστὶν τοῦ Θαργηλιῶ[νο]ς μηνὸς ἕκ[τ]η ἱσταμ[ένου,
ὁ]μολογήσας ἀποδώσε[ιν] τὰ χρήματ[α] ἑαυτοῦ τὰ [καθ-
30 ι]ερωμένα ὅταν βουλη[θ]ῇ ἢ τοὺς κληρονόμ]ους αὐτοῦ τῇ πόλει κομιζομ[έ]νων τῶν ἑκάσ[σ]του προ[θύμως?
π]ροϊσταμένων, περὶ [ὧν] ἁπάντων διάτα[ξ]ιν εἰση[γησάμε-
νος ἰδ(ίᾳ) ἠξί]ωσεν ἐπι[κυ]ρωθῆ[ν]αι καὶ διὰ ψ[η]φ[ί]σ[μ]ατος τῆς
βουλῆς καὶ τοῦ δήμου, καὶ νῦ]ν τῆς ἐπα[ρχ]εί[α]ς [ἡγε-
35 μονεύων?· ὁ κράτιστος ἀν]ὴρ καὶ εὐεργέ[τη]ς Ἀκο[υΐ]λλι-
ος Πρόκλος ὁ ἀνθύπατο]ς καὶ Ἀφράνι[ο]ς Φλαουϊανὸς ὁ κράτιστος ἀντι]στράτηγο[ς ἀνυ]περβλήτῳ
τῇ φιλανθρωπίᾳ . . . .]οντες τὴν
. . . . π]ολείται π-
40 . . . . κ]αὶ δι' ἐπιστολῶν
. . . . ἐβούλ]ευσαν ὥστε δι-
. . . . ον αὐτο.
Δ[εδόχθαι Γάιον Οὐείβιον Σαλούταριον ἄνδρα] εὐσεβῆ
ὄντα] πρὸς [τοὺς θεοὺς εἰς] δὲ [τὴν πόλιν φιλ]ότειμον τε-
45 τει[μῆσ]θαι [ταῖ]ς [κρ]ατίσταις τιμ[αῖ]ς εἰκόν[ω]ν τε ἀναστάσε-
σιν ἔν [τε τῷ] ἱερῷ [τῆ]ς Ἀρτέμιδο[ς καὶ ἐν τοῖ]ς ἐπισημοτάτοις
τόποις τῆς πόλεως, ἀναγ[γεῖλα]ι δὲ αὐ]τὸν καὶ χρυσίῳ
στεφάνῳ ἐν ταῖς ἐκκ[λησίαις σπουδά]ζοντα καὶ φιλάρ-
τεμιν· τὴν δὲ παρ[απομπὴν τῶν προγ]εγραμμένων ἱε-
50 ρῶν [δόσε]ων, καὶ τὴν ἐ[κ τοῦ προνάου τοῦ ἱ]εροῦ εἰς τὸ θέατρον καὶ τὴν ἐκ τοῦ [θεάτρου εἰς τὸ ἱερὸν] τῆς Ἀρτέμιδος

```
. . . . . . . . . . . . . . . . . . . . . ῳ ἐν τόπῳ ἐπιτηδείῳ φιλοτει-
μίας ἕνεκα ? . . . . . ] καὶ περὶ τῆ[ς δ]ιαμονῆς τῶ(ν) καθι-
ερωμένων χρ]ημάτων τῇ τε βουλῇ καὶ τῇ γερο-
υσίᾳ μελήσειν], οἷς ὑπέσχετο αὐτὸς καὶ δ[ηναρίων ?
```
60   . . . . ἐκβανιστὴς γενίσθαι.

SECOND DOCUMENT.
Salutaris' first deed of gift.

Col. 3.

```
        Γάιος [Οὐείβιος Γαίου υἱὸς Ὀφεντείνᾳ, Σαλουτάριος ταύτην τὴν διάτα-
        ξιν εἰσ[φέρει περὶ ὧν καθιέρωκε τῇ Ἀρτέμιδι καὶ τῇ φιλοσεβάστῳ
        Ἐφεσίω[ν βουλῇ κ.τ.λ.  (Compare seventh document.) . . . . . . . . . . .
        ταῖς ὑπ[ . . . . . . . . . . . . . . . . . . . . . . . . . . . Ἀρ-
```
65   τέμιδ[ι . . . .
```
        τῇ Ἐφ[εσι . . . . . . . . . . . . . . . . . . . . . . . . . Ἐ-
        φ[εσι . . . . . . . . . . . . . . . . . . . . . . . . . . . . . . . .
```

(Six or seven lines are here lost.)

```
        . . . . . . . . . . . . . . . . . . . . . . . . [ἐφ' ᾧ εἰκὼν] . . . . . . . . .
        . . . . . . . . . . . ] οὐνκιῶν γ, καὶ εἰκὼν [τῆς ἐν Ἐφ-
```
70   ίσῳ [ἱερᾶς γερουσίας? ὁλκ]ῆς λειτρῶν γ νεοκοσμῶνται παρ[ὰ αὐτῇ
```
        Σαλο[υταρίῳ] τῷ κ[αθι]ερωρτι, μετὰ δὲ τὴν Σαλουταρίο[υ τελευτὴν
        ἀποδοθ[ῶ]σιν αἱ προδηλούμεναι εἰκόνες τῷ Ἐφεσίων γραμματεῖ τῷ
        προγεγραμμένῳ σταθμῷ ἀπὸ τῶν κληρονόμων αὐτοῦ, ὀ[ρίσθω δὲ αὐ-
        τὰς τίθε[σ]θαι ἐν ταῖς ἐκκλησίαις ἐπάνω τῆς σελίδος τῆς βουλ[ῆς μετὰ τῆς
```
75   χρυσέας [Ἀρτέ]μιδος καὶ τῶν ἄλλων εἰκόνων. Ἄρτεμις ⟨δὲ⟩ χρυ[σέα, ὁλκῆς
```
        λειτρῶν τριῶν, καὶ αἱ (sic) περὶ αὐτὴν ἀργύρεοι ἔλαφοι δύο καὶ τὰ λο[ιπὰ ἀργύρεα,
        ὁλκῆς λειτρῶν δύο, σύνκιων δέκα, γραμμάτων πέντε· [κ]αὶ ε[ἰκὼν ἀργυ-
        ρέ[α τῆ]ς ἱερᾶς συνκλήτου ὁλκῆς λειτρῶν δ, σύνκιω[ν] β· καὶ εἰ[κὼν ἀργυ-
        ρ[έα τῆ]ς φιλοσεβάστου καὶ σεμνοτάτης Ἐφεσίων βουλῆς, ὁ[λκῆς λει-
```
80   τ[ρῶ]ν δ, γραμ(μ)άτων θ· τὰ καὶ αὐτὰ καθιερωμένα τῇ τε Ἀρτέμιδι [καὶ τῇ φι-
```
        λοσεβ]άστῳ Ἐφεσίων βουλῇ. Ὁμοίως καὶ ἀργύρια Ἄρτεμις λα[μπαδηφό-
        ρ[ος], ὁλκῆς λζ· καὶ εἰκὼν ἀργυρία τοῦ δήμου τοῦ Ῥωμαίων, [ὁλκῆς λ . .,
        καὶ εἰκὼν ἀργυρία τῆς φιλοσεβάστου γερουσίας, ὁλκῆς [λγ, τὰ καὶ
        αὐτὰ καθιερωμένα τῇ τε Ἀρτέμιδι καὶ τῇ Ἐφεσίων γερουσίᾳ.
```
85   Ὁμοίως καὶ ἄλλη Ἄρτεμις ἀργυρία λαμπαδηφόρος ἐ[μφερὴς
```
        τῇ ἐν τῇ ἐξέδρᾳ τῶν ἐφήβων, ὁλκῆς λζ, σύνκιῶν ε, γραμ[μάτων . . .,
        καὶ εἰκὼν ἀργυρία τοῦ ἱππικοῦ τάγματος, ὁλκῆς λγ ἥ[μισυ, οὐνκι-
        κίου, γραμμάτων . .· καὶ ἄλλη εἰκὼν ἀργυρία τῆς ἐφηβεία[ς, ὁλκῆς λ . .,
        τὰ καὶ αὐτὰ καθιε[ρω]μένα τῇ τε Ἀρτέμιδι καὶ τοῖς κατ' ἐνιαυτὸ[ν ἑκαστο-
```
90   ν ἐφήβοις. Ὁ[μοίως . . . . εἰκὼν? . . . ἔχουσ-
```
        α φιάλην, ὁλκ[ῆς . . . . . . . . . . . . . . . . . . . . . . . . . .
        φιλο?]σεβάστου . . . . . . . . . . . . . . . . . . . . . . . . . .
```

(Here is a lacuna of seven or eight lines at the bottom of which the third column ends.)

(A good deal is lost from the top of Column 4: if it began at the same level with Column 5, then some 50 lines are lost, but probably it did not begin so high. The fragment at the end about the statues of Trajan and Plotina may perhaps have come in here.)

Col. 4.

```
        . . . . . . . . . . . . . . . . . . . . . . . . . . . . . . . μεν
```
95   . . . . ἐπὶ
```
        . . . . . . . . . . . . . . . . . . . . . . . . . . . . . . . . καὶ
        . . . . . . . . . . . . . . . . . . . . . . . γραμμά]των γ τὰ
        καὶ αὐτὰ καθιερωμένα τῇ τε Ἀρτέμιδι καὶ τοῖς π]ολείταις
        πᾶσιν. Ὁμοίως καὶ ἄλλη ἀργυρία Ἄρτεμις λαμπ]αδηφό-
```
100   ρος, ὁλκῆς . . . .]γ· καὶ εἰκὼν
```
        . . . . . . . . . . . τὰ καὶ αὐτὰ καθιερωμένα τῇ τ]ε Ἀρτέμιδι
        καὶ . . . . . . . . . . . ]. Ὁμοί[ω]ς καὶ ἄλλη Ἄρ-
```

τεμις ἀργυρέα λαμπαδηφόρος, ὁλκῆς λζ, σύνκι]ῶν γ, ἡμίσους γράμμα-
τος· . . . . εἰκὼν ἀργυρ]έα φυλῆς Εὐ-
105 ωνυμέων, ὁλκῆς . . . . τὰ καὶ αὐτὰ κ]αθιερωμέ-
να τῇ τε Ἀρτέμιδι καὶ . . . . Ὁμοίως καὶ εἰκὼ]ν φυλῆς
Βεμβεινέων ? . . . . σταλι
. . . . ε]ἰκὼν
. . . . τε
110 . . . .
. . . . ν τῆς θ[εοῦ ?
. . . . τ]αύτῳ
. . . . ἱεροῦ τῆς
Ἀρτέμιδος . . . .] ἐπὶ τῶν
115 . . . . ἐὰν κατὰ
. . . . ἀρ]χιερατι-
α . . . .] κατὰ σε
. . . . τ]οῖς βά-
θροις ? . . . . τὰ καὶ αὐτὰ ? κα]θιε-
120 [ρωμένα τῇ τε Ἀρτέμιδι καὶ . . . .]

(A lacuna of about eight lines.)

. . . . ου ἡ τὰς εἰκόνας πρὸς τὸ
. . . . τινι τρόπῳ κακουργηθῆνα(ι) ἐπι
. . . . ω ἔστω ἱεροσυλία καὶ ἀσέβεια καὶ οὐδὲν
. . . . στ]αθμὸς ἐν τοῖς προγεγραμμένοις ἀπεικονίσ-
125 μασιν . . . .]ρια ἔχοντος τὴν περὶ τούτων ἐκδικίαν ἐπ' ἀνάν-
κῃ . . . .] Τῶν δὲ καθιερωμένων ὑπὸ Σαλουταρίου χρημάτων] τ[ε]λέσει τόκον Σαλουτάριος δραχμιαῖον καθ' ἕκαστον ἐνι-
αυτὸν] τὰ γει[ν]όμενα δηνάρια χ[εί]λια ὀκτακόσια, ἀφ' ὧν δώσει τῷ γραμματεῖ τῆς β]ουλῆς δηνάρια τετρακόσι[α π]εντήκοντα ὅπως ἐπιτελεῖ (sic) διανομὴν
130 τοῖς] βουλευταῖς ἐν τῷ ἱερῷ ἐν τ[ῷ π]ρ]ονάῳ τῇ γενε[σ]ίῳ τῆς μεγίστης θεᾶς Ἀρτέμιδος, ἥ]τις ἐστὶν μηνὸς Θαργη[λι]ῶνος ἕκτῃ ἱσταμένου, γεινομένης τῆς διανομῆς τῇ]ς πέμπτης, διδομ[ένου ἑ]κάστῳ τῶν παρόντων δηναρίου ἑνός,
ἔχον]τος ἐξουσίαν τοῦ ἐπὶ τ[ῆ]ς διανομῆς αὐτῶν δοῦναι, εἰ ἀπύτεισα-
ι τῇ β]ουλῇ ὑπὲρ ἑκάστου ὀνόματος τοῦ μὴ παραγενομένου καὶ λαβόντος.

[Here a few lines are lost at the top of Column 5, which contained directions for the payment of a certain share of the interest yearly
to the treasurer τῆς γερουσίας (see line 189) for distribution among the γερουσιασταί, and also directions for similar payments to be made to
the θεολόγοι and ὑμνῳδοί. The opening lines as they stand appear to have referred to certain penalties for fraud in the distribution.]

Col. 5.

135 . . . . Ἐὰ[ν δέ τις . . . .
. . . . ἀπυτε]ισά[τω πρόστειμον ? τ]οῖς
. . . . Ἐ]ὰν δ[έ τις . .]αιλω καὶ
. . . . τοῦ κλήρου γεινομένου
. . . . σία ἡ τοῦ γραμματέος τῆς
140 βουλῆς . . . .]ην ἡ ἀναγραφὴν μετα-
τιθ . . . . ἀ]ποτεισάτω πρόστειμον
. . . . Ὁμοίως ἀπὸ τοῦ προγεγραμμένου τόκου δώσει κατ' ἐνιαυτὸν ἕκ]αστον καὶ τοῖς ἐξ φυ-
λάρχοις δη. ἑξακόσια ὅπως ἐπιτελῶσι] κλῆρον τῆς προγεγραμ-
145 μένης καθιερώσεως ἕκαστος ἐξ ἑκάστη]ς φυλῆς εἰς ὀνόματα διακόσια πάντων τῶν πολειτῶν τ]ῶν ληξομένων ἀσσάρια θ̅
καθ' ἕκαστον· ἐὰν δὲ μείζων ᾖ ὁ γεν]όμενος κόλλυβος ὑπὸ
τῶν φυλάρχων ἔξεσται καὶ ἄλλους πολ]είτας κληροῦσθαι.
Ὁμοίως δώσει ἀπὸ τοῦ προγεγραμμένου] τόκου κατ' ἐνιαυτὸν
150 ἕκαστον τῷ ἐφηβάρχῳ δη. . . . . ὅπω]ς ἐπιτελῇ κλῆρον
τῆς προγεγραμμένης καθιερώσεως τῇ γενεσίῳ τ]ῆς Ἀρτέμιδος
ἡμέρᾳ εἰς ὀνόματα . . . . . ἐκ τῶν ἐφήβων ἀπάν]των τῶν ληξομένων ἀσσάρια . . καθ' ἕκαστον ἐν ᾧ ἂν] ὁ ἐφήβαρχος χω-
ρήσῃ τόπῳ. Ὁμοίως δώσει ἀπὸ τ]οῦ προγεγραμμέ-

νου τόκου τῷ ἀρχιερεῖ τοῦ ἐν Ἐφέ]σῳ ναοῦ κοινοῦ
τῆς Ἀσίας δη. . . . .]κατ' ἐνιαυτὸν ἕκαστον ὅπως ἐν τῇ γενεσίῳ τῆς θ]εοῦ ἡμέρᾳ ἐπιτελεῖ (sic)
κλῆρον ἐν :ῷ προνάῳ τοῦ ἱεροῦ τῆ]ς Ἀρτ[έ]μιδος λαμ-
βανόντων ἀσσάρια . . . . τῶν] ἀναγραψαμένων

160 εἰς ὀνόματα . . . . γει]νομένης τῆς ἀναγραφῆς κατ' ἐνιαυτόν. Ὁμοίως δώσ]ει ἀπὸ τοῦ προγεγραμμένου τόκου κατ' ἐνιαυτὸν ἕκαστον τ]ῇ ἱερείς τῆς Ἀρτέμιδος
δη. . . . . . . τῇ γενεσίῳ ἡμέρᾳ] τῆς Ἀρτέμιδος εἰς
θυσίαν ? . . . . 'Ομοίως δώσ]ει ἀπὸ τοῦ π[ρ]ογεγραμ-

165 μένου τόκου κατὰ πᾶσαν νόμμον ἐκκλ]ησίαν δυσ[ὶ]ν νεοποι-
οῖς καὶ σκηπτούχοις δη. . . ὥστε φέρε]σθαι ἐκ το[ῦ] προνάου
εἰς τὸ θέατρον τὰ ἀπεικονίσματα τῆ]ς θεοῦ καὶ τὰς εἰκόνας καὶ
αὖ φέρεσθαι αὐτὰ ἐκ τοῦ θεάτρο]υ εἰς τὸν πρόναον αὐθήμε-
ρον . . . . 'Ομοίως δώ]σει ἀπὸ [τ]οῦ προγεγραμμέ-

170 νου τόκου κατ' ἐνιαυτὸν ἕκαστ]ον καὶ τοῖς [π]αιδων[ό]μοις
δη. . . . . . . ὅπως ἐν τῇ γενι]σίῳ τῆς θεοῦ ἡμέρα ἐπιτελέ-
σωσιν κλῆρον τῶν παίδων πάν]των εἰς ὀνόματα μδ, λαμβανόν-
των . . . . . ταύτῃ τ]ῇ ἡμέρᾳ ἐν τῷ ἱερῷ τῆς Ἀρτέμιδος
. . . . τῶν καὶ τῶν παιδωνόμων χωρὶς

175 . . . . 'Ο]μοίως δώσει ἀπὸ τοῦ προγεγραμμένου τόκου καθ' ἕκαστον ἐνιαυτὸν τῷ τὰ καθάρσια ποιοῦντι παρε
. . . . τὰ λοιπὰ δη. τριάκοντα ὥστε καθαρὰ ἐκ τοῦ θεάτρου εἰ]ς τὸ ἱερὸν ἀποφ[ε]ρητα[ι] τὰ ἀπεικονίσματα καὶ ἀποκαθίστητ]αι αὐτὰ εἰς τὸν πρόναον τῆς Ἀρτέ-

180 μιδος. Ἐὰν δέ τις κατὰ τὴν] ἰδίαν π[ρ]οαίρεσιν ἀγοράσῃ
τὴν κληρονομίαν ταύτην ἢ προνο]ηθῇ δίδοσθαι, καθ' ἕκαστον ἐνιαυτὸν ἀποτεισάτω ὁ ἀγορά[ζ]ων τὰ προγεγρ[α]μμένα δη. χίλια
ὀ]κτακ[ό]σια, παρὰ ταύτην τὴν] διάταξιν εἰσ[εν]εικεῖν μηδὲν
ἔλασσ[ον μηδενὸς δυναμένου δ]λλὰ προσασφαλί[ζ]ομένου.

185 Ἐὰν δέ τ[ις τῶν κληρονόμων βούλη]θῇ 〈δὲ〉 ἀποδοῦναι τάχειον τὰ τῆς
καθιερώ[σεως τοῦ ἀρχαίου χρήματ]α, ἐξέσται αὐτῷ ἐπ' ἀνάγκη ληψομέ-
νῳ τ[εῖσαι τῷ γραμματεῖ] τῆς βουλῆς τὰ γεινόμενα ὑπὲρ τῶν
κα[θ]ιερω[μένων χρημάτων τοῦ] ἀρχαίου δη. πεντακισχίλια.
'Ομ[ο]ίω[ς κα[ὶ τῷ ἐπὶ ?] τῶν χρημ]άτων τῆς γερουσίας τὰ γεινόμενα

190 ὑπὲρ τῶν καθιεραμ[έν]ων τῇ γερουσίᾳ δη. τετράκε[ις χεί-
λια τετρακόσια πεντήκοντα. Ὁμοίως καὶ τοῖς θεολόγοις
καὶ ὑμνῳδοῖς τὰ γεινόμενα ὑπὲρ τῆς καθιερώσεως ἀρχαίου
δη. διακόσ(ι)α πεντήκοντα πέντε. Ὁμοίως τῷ γραμματεῖ
τοῦ δήμου τὰ λοιπὰ γεινόμενα τοῦ ἀρχαίου ὑπὲρ τῆς καθιερώ-

195 σεως τῶν εἰς τοὺς πολείτας κλήρων καὶ ἐφήβων καὶ νεοποιῶν καὶ σκηπτούχων καὶ καθαρσίων δη. μύρια διακόσια
ἑβδομήκοντα (sic) πέντε—ὅπως ἐκδανίζωσιν αὐτὰ ἐπὶ τόκῳ
ἀσσαρίων δεκαδύο ἀργυρῶν ἀδιάπτωτα, καὶ ἐπιτελῆ-
ται καθ' ἕκαστον ἐνιαυτὸν ἀπὸ τοῦ τόκου τὰ διατεταγμέ-

200 να ἀνυπερθέτως ὡς προγέγραπται. Ἐὰν δὲ πρὸ τοῦ (ἀ)πο-
δοῦναι τὰ δισμύρια δη. ἡ διατάξεσθαι (sic) ἀπὸ προσόδου
χωρίων δίδοσθαι: τὸν τόκον αὐτῶν 〈ἢ〉 τελευτήσει (sic)
Σαλουτάριος, ὑποκείσθωσαν οἱ κληρονόμοι αὐτοῦ τῇ εὐ-
λυτήσει τῶν καθιεραμένων δη. δισμυρίων καὶ τοῖς ἐπα-

205 κολουθήσασι τόκοις μέχρι τῆς εὐλυτήσεος, ὑποκει-
μένων αὐτῶν τῇ πράξει κατὰ τὰ ἱερὰ τῆς θεοῦ καὶ τὰ παρὰ τοῖς πρεσβυτέροις ἐκδανιστικὰ ἔνγραφα. Ὑπέσχετο
δὲ Σαλουτάριος ὥστε ἄρξ[α]σθαι τὴν φιλοτιμίαν αὐτοῦ
τῷ ἐνεστῶτι ἔτει ἐν τῇ γενε[σί]ῳ τῆς θεοῦ ἡμέρᾳ δώσει(ν)

210 δη. χίλια ὀκτακόσια εἰς τὰς προγεγραμμένας διανομὰς
κα[ὶ] κλήρους. Μηδεν[ὶ] δὲ ἐξέστω ἄρχοντι ἢ ἐκδίκῳ ἢ ἰδιώ-
τῃ π[ειρᾶ]σαί τι ἀλλάξαι ἢ μεταθεῖναι ἢ μετοικονομῆσαι ἢ μετα-
ψηφί[σ]ασθα[ι] τῶν καθιεραμένων ἀπεικονισμάτων ἢ τοῦ
ἀργυρίου ἢ τῆς [π]ροσόδου αὐτοῦ ἢ μεταθεῖναι εἰς ἕτερον πόρον

215 ἢ ἀνά[λ]ωμα ἢ ἄλ[λ]ο τι ποιῆσαι παρὰ τὰ προγεγραμμένα καὶ δια-
τετ[αγ]μένα, ἐπεὶ τὸ γενόμενον παρὰ ταῦτα ἔστω ἄκυρον.
'Ο δὲ πε[ιρά]σας ποιῆσαί τι ὑπεναντίον τῇ διατάξει ἢ τοῖς

ὑπὸ τ[ῆς] βου[λ]ῆς καὶ τοῦ δήμου ἐψηφισμένοις καὶ ἐπικεκυ-
ρωμέν[οις περὶ] ταύτης [τ]ῆς διατάξεως ἀποτεισάτω εἰς
320 προσκ[όσμημα τ]ῆς με[γίστ]ης θεᾶς Ἀρτέμιδος δη. εἰσμύρια,
πεν]τα[κισχίλια καὶ εἰς τὸν] Σεβαστοῦ φίσκον ἄλλα δη. Μ/Ϛ.
Ἡ δὲ προγεγραμμένη διάταξις ἔστ]ω κυρία εἰς τὸν ἅπαντα χρόνον ἐν πᾶσιν, καθάπερ καὶ Τ. Ἀκουίλλι]ος Πρόκλ[ος ὁ ε]ὐ[εργ]έτης
καὶ ἀνθύπατο]ς καὶ Ἀφράνιος Φλαουϊανὸς ὁ κράτιστος πρεσβευτὴς
325 κ[αὶ ἀντιστρ]άτηγος διὰ ἐπιστολῶν περὶ ταύτης τῆς διατάξεως ἐπεκύρωσαν καὶ ὥρισεν τὸ προγεγραμμένον π[ρ]όστε[ιμ]ον.
Γάϊος Οὐίβιος Γαίου υἱὸς Ὠφεντείνᾳ Σαλουτάριος εἰ[σ]ενήνοχα
τὴν διάταξιν καὶ καθιέρωσα τὰ προγεγραμμένα.

(End of Salutaris' First Deed of Gift.)

THIRD DOCUMENT.

Decree of formal assent to the διάταξις?

(How much is lost from the top of Column 6 is uncertain.)

Col. 6.

```
. . . . . . . . . . . . . . . . . . . . . . . . . . . . . . . . . . . . ς
330 . . . . . . . . . . . . . . . . . . . . . . . . . . . . . . . ηται
. . . . . . . . . . . . . . . . . . . . . . . . . διαν]εμῆσαι με
. . . . . . . . . . . . . . . . . . . . ταῖς κρατίσταις καὶ μεγίσ-
ταις τιμαῖς? . . . . . . . . . . . . . . . . ]εων, καὶ τῆς
. . . . . . . . . . . . . . . . . . . . . . . . διανομ]ὰς καὶ κλή-
335 ρους . . . . . . . . . . . . . . . . . . ] ἐφ᾽ οἶς ἤδη
. . . . . . . . . . . . . . . . . . . . . . . . ς χρῆναι τῇ τε
. . . . . . . . . . . . . . . . . . . . . . . εια ἀπροσ-
δόκητ . . . . . . . . . . . . . . . . . . ἐπαι]νέσαι τε τὸν
. . . . . . . . . . . . . . . . . . . . . . . μαρτυρίας
340 . . . . . . . . . . . . . . . . . . . . . . δυνατὰ προ
. . . . . . . . . . . . . . . . . . καθιε]ρούμενα χρή-
ματα καὶ τὰ ἀπεικονίσματα τῆς Ἀρτέμιδος καὶ τὰς] εἰκόνας, ἥτις
. . . . . . . . . . . . . . . . . . . . . . . . . . . . . .
```

(A lacuna of at least 6 or 8 lines, perhaps more.)

FOURTH DOCUMENT.

Letter from the Proconsul T. Aquillius Proculus approving of the Ephesian decrees, and fixing the amount of the fines for transgressing them.

Ἐπὶ [πρυτάνεως Τιβ. Κλ. Ἀντιπάτρου Ἰουλιανοῦ
Ἀφ[ρανίου Φλαουιανοῦ πρεσβευτοῦ καὶ ἀντιστρατήγ-
345 ου [Τ. Ἀκουίλλιος Πρόκλος ὁ κράτιστος ἀνθύπ]ατος
λέγει· . . . . πο]λίτου ἀρίσ[τ-
ου . . . .]ος τῶν οἰκιο-
. α . . . . λος ἐν πολλοῖς
. τ[. . . . εὔμε]νῶς ἔχει πρὸς
350 ὑμ]ε[τέραν πόλιν . . . .] ἢ τὴν ἑαυτοῦ
π]ατ[ρίδα . . . .] τὴν πόλιν ἔχει
φαν . . . . πρεπόντω[ς
τε β . . . . κοσμε[ῖν τε
καὶ σ[εμνύνειν . . . .] καὶ
355 ἐπισ . . . . ἐπι-
φανεσ[τατ . . . .]τε[. . . . . Αὐτ]οκρατό-
ρ[ω]ν, δσ[ρεῶν καὶ χρη]μάτων ἀφιερώ[σει καὶ τἄλλα φιλοτ]ειμου-
μένου· [διὸ βούλομαι ὑμεῖν τε περὶ τἀνθρὸς [ἄξια] τίσων
π[ε]ρὶ ὑμ[ῶν τε] ἀ[ντ]ιμηνύσαι μαρτυρῆσαί τε, [καὶ ε]ὐφημίᾳ τῇ
360 προσηκο[ύσῃ] αὐτὸν [ὑ]πὲρ ὑμῶν ἀμείψασθαι δσ[α αὐ]τῷ καὶ παρ᾽ [ὑ]μῶ[ν ὀφείλ]εσθαι νομίζω, πρὸς τὸ καὶ πλ[είου]ς εἶναι τοὺς

ὁ]μοίως π[ροθ]υμουμένους εἰ οὗτος φαίνοιτ[ο τ]ῆς κατὰ τὴν
ἀ]ξίαν ἀμοιβῆς τυγχάνων· ἐπειδὰν κἀμοὶ ἐ[ν] τοῖς μάλιστα
κ]εχαρισμένον καὶ ἥδισ[τ]ον εἰ ἂν ἐξαιρέτως τῶν φίλων

265   τ]ειμῶ καὶ στέργω παρ' ὑμεῖν ὁρῶην μαρτυρίας καὶ τειμῆ[ς
ἀξιούμενον. Περὶ μέντοι γε τῆς τῶν χρημ[ά]των διατάξεως καὶ τῶν ἀπεικονισμάτων τῆς θεοῦ κ[α]ὶ τῶν εἰκόνων
ὅπως αὐτοῖς δεήσει χρῆσθαι καὶ εἰς (τ)ήντι[ν]α οἰκονομίαν
ἄνδρα τετάχθαι, αὐτόν τε τὸν ἀνατιθέντ[α] εἰση(γ)ήσασθαι

270   νομίζω εὔλογον εἶναι καὶ ὑμᾶς οὕ[τω] ψηφίσασθαι· ἐπει-
δ(ὰ)ν δὲ ὑπό τε αὐτοῦ τοῦ καθιερούντος καὶ ὑμῶν αὐτῶν κυρω-
θῇ τὰ δόξαντα. βούλομαι ταῦτα εἰσαεὶ μένειν ἐπὶ τῶν αὐτῶν
ἀπαραλλάκτως, ὑπὸ μηδενὸς μηδεμιᾷ(ν) παρενχειρήσει λυ-
όμενα ἢ μετατιθέμενα· εἰ δέ τις πειραθείη ὁπωσοῦν ἢ συν-

275   βουλεῦσαί τι τοιοῦτον ἢ εἰσηγήσασθαι περὶ τῆς μεταθέσε-
ως καὶ μεταδιοικήσεως τῶν νῦν ὑπό τε αὐτοῦ καὶ ὑφ' ὑ-
μῶν κυρωθησομένων, τοῦτον ἀνυπερθέτως βούλομαι
ε[ἰ]ς μὲν τὸ τῆς μεγίστης θεᾶς Ἀρτέμιδος ἱερὸν καταθέσ-
θαι προστείμου δὴ. Μ πεντακισ[χ]ίλια, εἰς δὲ τὸν τοῦ

280   [Σεβαστοῦ φίσκον ἄλλα δὴ. Μ πεντακισχίλια, καὶ τῇ]
γερο[υσίᾳ τῇ Ἐφεσίων ἄλλα δὴ. Μ πεντακι]σχίλια
καθ . . . . [ἀνθ]ύπατος
καὶ . . . . [δι' ἐπ]ιστολῆς
ἔγ[ραψα? . . . . τ]ῤῥωσθε.

FIFTH DOCUMENT.

Decree of the Boulè, authorizing the χρυσοφοροῦντες to bear the images and effigies from the Temple
to the Theatre.

285   Ἐπὶ πρ[υτάνεως Τιβ. Κλ. Ἀντιπάτ]ρου Ἰουλιανοῦ·
[μηνὸς . . . . .]·
Ἔ[δοξε τῇ βουλῇ φιλοσεβάστῳ περὶ ὧν ἐν]εφάνισαν Τι. Κλαυ.
[Τιβ. Κλ. Ἀλεξάνδρου υἱ. Κυρ. Ἰουλιανὸς] φιλόπατρις καὶ φιλοσέβαστος ἀγνὸς εὐσεβής, γραμματεὺ[ς τοῦ δήμου τὸ β̄, καὶ οἱ

290   στρατηγοὶ τῆς πόλεως φιλοσέβ]αστοι· ὅπως ἐξῇ τοῖς χρυσο-
φοροῦσιν φέρειν εἰς τὰς] ἐκκλησίας καὶ τοὺς ἀγῶνας
τὰ ἀπεικονίσματ[α] καὶ εἰκόνας τὰ καθιερωμέν[α ὑπὸ Γαΐο]υ
Οὐειβίου Σαλουταρίου ἐκ τοῦ προνάου τῆς Ἀρτέμιδος [ἅμα] συν-
επιμελουμένων καὶ τῶν νεοποιῶν, συνπαραλαμβανόντων καὶ τῶν

295   ἐφήβω[ν] ἀπὸ τῆς Μαγνητικῆς πύλης κα[ὶ] συντροπευιόντων
μέχρι τῆς Κορησσικῆς πύλης—Δεδό[χ]θαι τῇ βουλῇ φιλοσεβάστῳ καθότι προγέγραπται. Τιβ. [Κ]λαυ. Πρωφόσιος
Φρητωριανὸς φιλοσέβαστος δεδογματ[ογ]ράφηκα· Μάρκος
Καισέλλιος Μαρκιανὸς φιλοσέβαστος [δε]δογματογράφηκα·

300   Τιβ. Κλαυ. Ἰουλιανὸς φιλόπατρις φιλοσέβαστ[ο]ς ἀγνὸς εὐσεβὴς
ὁ γραμματεὺς τοῦ δήμου τὸ β̄ ἐχάραξα.

SIXTH DOCUMENT.

Another decree of the Boulè, granting the χρυσοφοροῦντες mentioned in the previous decree a particular
seat in the Theatre.

      Ἐπὶ πρυτάνεως Τιβ. Κλ. Ἀντιπάτρου Ἰουλιανοῦ·
μηνὸς Ποσειδεῶνος·
Ἔδοξε τῇ βουλῇ φιλοσεβάστῳ περὶ ὧν ἐνεφάνισαν Τιβ.

305   Κλ. Τιβ. Κλ. Ἀλεξάνδρου υἱ. Κυρ. Ἰουλιανὸς φιλόπατρις
καὶ φιλοσέβαστος ἀγνὸς εὐσεβής, γραμματεὺς τοῦ δήμου τὸ β̄,
καὶ οἱ στρατηγοὶ τῆς πόλεως φιλοσέβαστοι·
Ἐπεὶ οἱ χρυσοφοροῦντες τῇ θεῷ ἱερεῖς καὶ ἱερονεῖκαι ὑπέσ-
χ(ο)ντο φέρειν καὶ αὖ φέρειν τὰ ἀπεικονίσματα τὰ καθιερω-

310   θέντα ὑπὸ Οὐειβίου Σαλουταρίου, ᾐτήσαντό τε τόπον
ἐν τῷ θεάτρῳ τὴν πρώτην σ[ε]λίδα ὅπου ἡ εἰκὼν τῆς Ὁμονοίας·

Δεδόχθαι ἔχειν ⟨ε⟩αὐτοὺς τὸν [τ]όπον καθίζειν δὲ πρὸς τὴν Εὐσέβειαν αὐτοὺς λ⟨ε⟩υχειμονοῦντας· Δεδόχθαι τῇ βουλῇ
φιλοσεβάστῳ γενέσθαι καθότι προγέγραπται.

315   Γ. Αὐφίδιος Σιλουανὸς φιλοσέβαστος δεδογματογράφηκα·
Λ. Μουνάτιος Βάσσος φιλοσέβαστὸς δεδογματογράφηκα·
Νηρεὺς Θεοφίλου φιλοσέβαστος δεδογματογράφηκα.

SEVENTH DOCUMENT.

Supplementary διάταξις of Salutaris, bequeathing additional images and more money.

Σέξτῳ Ἀττίῳ Σουβουρανῷ τὸ β̄ Μάρκῳ Ἀσι-
νίῳ Μαρκέλλῳ ὑπάτοις· πρὸ η̄ Καλανδῶν Μαρτίων,
320   ἐπὶ πρυτάνεως Τιβ. Κλαυδίου Ἀντιπάτρου Ἰουλιανοῦ,
μηνὸς Ἀνθεστηριῶνος β̄ Σεβαστῇ·
Γάιος Οὐίβιος Γ. υἱ. Οὐηφεντείνα Σαλουτάριος φιλάρ-
τεμις καὶ φιλόκαισαρ διάταξιν εἰσφέρει κατὰ τὸ προγε-
γονὸς ψήφισμα περὶ ὧν προσκαθιέρωκε τῇ μεγίστῃ θεᾷ Ἐφε-
325   σίᾳ Ἀρτ[έ]μιδι καὶ τῇ φιλοσεβάστῳ Ἐφεσίων βουλῇ
καὶ τῇ φιλοσεβά[στῳ Ἐφεσίων γερου]σίᾳ καὶ τ[οῖς χ]ρυ-
σοφορ[ο]ῦσι τῇ θ[εῷ Ἀρτέμιδι ἱερ]εῦσιν καὶ ἱερονείκαις πρὸ
πόλεως κ[αὶ τοῖς αἰεὶ ἐσομένοις Ἐφ]εσίων παισὶ καὶ θεσ-
μφδοῖς ναο[ῦ τῶν Σεβαστῶν ἐν Ἐφέσ]ῳ κοινοῦ τῆς Ἀσίας καὶ
330   ἀκροβάταις τῆς [Ἀρτέμιδος ἐπὶ] τοῖς δικαίοις καὶ προστεί-
μοις ὡς ἐν τῇ προ[γεγραμμένῃ δι]ατάξει ἠσφάλισται.— Εἰκόνων ἀργυρίων δύο ἐ[πι]χ[ρύ]σων ὥστε αὐτὰς εἶναι σὺν τοῖς
ἀπεικονίσμασιν τῆς θεοῦ ἀριθμῷ τριάκοντα καὶ μίαν,
καὶ ἀργυρίου ἄλλων δή. χειλίων πεντακοσίων ὥστε εἶναι
335   αὐτὰ σὺν τοῖς προκαθιερωμένοις δή, μυρίοις χιλίοις πεν-
τακοσίοις.—ἐφ᾽ ᾧ εἰκὼ ἀργυρία Ἀθηνᾶς Παμμούσου ὁλκῆς.
σὺν τῷ ἐπαργύρῳ τῆς βάσεως αὐτῆς λειτρῶν ἑπτὰ ἡμιουν-
κίου γραμμάτων ὀκτὼ, ἡ καθιερωμένη τῇ τε Ἀρτέμιδι καὶ
τοῖς αἰεὶ ἐσομένοις Ἐφεσίων παι(σ)ὶ, τίθηται κατὰ πᾶσαν νό-
340   μιμον ἐκκλησίαν ἐπάνω τῆς σελίδος οὗ [ο]ἱ παῖδες καθέζ[ο]νται.

Col. 7.   (It is uncertain how much is lost from the top of Column 7.)

. . . .
... Νηρεὺς ?] Θεοφίλ[ου (see line 317) ...
. . . τ]ῆς Ἐφεσίων πό[λεως ? . . . .
του Ἑρμίου ἱεροῦ τῆς [θεοῦ συνπροπένπον-?
τος καὶ συνπαραλαν[βάνοντος ἀπὸ τοῦ προνάου
345   τῆς Ἀρτέμιδος του . . . .
Ὑπὲρ δὲ τῶν προσκαθιε[ρωμένων δηναρίων χι-
λίων πεντακοσίω[ν τελέσει τόκον Σαλουτάριος δραχμιαῖον [καθ᾽ ἕκαστον ἐνιαυτὸν
τὰ γεινόμενα δηνάρ[ια ρλε, ἀφ᾽ ὧν δώσει
350   τῷ γραμματεῖ τῆς Ἐφ[εσίων βουλῆς? δηνάρια ρε
ὅπως κλήρου ἐπιτελῇ [τῶν ἱερέων εἰς ὀνόματα . .
ἱσταμένου τοῦ Θαργη[λιῶνος μηνὸς ἡμέρᾳ
ε̄· οὗτοί τε οἱ λαχόντ[ες θυσίας θύσουσιν
τῇ Ἀρτέμιδι τῇ ἕκ[τῃ ἡμέρᾳ τῇ γενεσίῳ
355   τῆς θεοῦ, ἀγοράζο[ντες . . . .
ἑπτὰ ἡμίσους κατ . . . .
δαπανήσουσιν . . . .
δος εἰς τὴν θ[υσίαν ? . . . .

(A lacuna of 8 or 10 lines.)

οτ . . . .
360   τ? . . . .

. . . .
ἐ]ξήκον[τα . . . .
ἐν τῷ ἱερῷ τῆς Ἀρτ[έμιδος τῶν διανομῶν? γει-
365 νομένων κατὰ ἀνα[λογίαν? . . . .
Ἐὰν δέ τινες τῶν λαχόντω[ν ἱερέων
τὰς θυσίας μὴ θύσωσιν ἢ μὴ εὐ[ξωνται ἐν τῷ
ἱερῷ ὡς διατέτακται, ἀποδότω[σαν εἰς τὸ
κόσμημα τῆς Ἀρτέμιδος δη. ͞ς.
370 Ὁμοίως δώσει ἀπὸ τοῦ προγεγραμμένου [τόκου
καὶ τοῖς θεσμῳδοῖς εἰς διανομὴν δη. ζ
ὥστε λαμβάνειν αὐτοὺς ἐν τῷ ἱερῷ τῆς Ἀρτέμιδος τῇ γενεσίῳ τῆς θεοῦ ἀνὰ ἀσσάρια ͞θ.
Ὁμοίως δώσει ἀπὸ τοῦ προγεγραμμένου τόκου
375 καὶ τοῖς ἀκροβάταις τῆς θεοῦ εἰς διανομὴν
δη. ͞ιε, ὥστε λαμβάνειν αὐτοὺς τῇ γενεσίῳ
τῆς θ[ε]οῦ ἀνὰ ἀσσάρια δεκατρία ἥμισυ.
Πρὸς δὲ τὸ μένειν τὰ ἀπεικονίσματα πάντα
καθαρὰ ἐξέστω ὁσάκις ἂν ἐνδέχηται
380 ἐκμάσσεσθαι γῇ ἀργυρωματικῇ ὑπὸ τοῦ
αἰεὶ ἐσομένου ἐπὶ τῶν παραθηκῶν παρόντων δύο νεοπειῶν καὶ σκηπτούχου,
ἑτέρᾳ δὲ ὕλῃ μηδεμιᾷ ἐκμάσσεσθαι, καὶ
τὰ λοιπὰ δη. ὀκτὼ δοθήσεται καθ' ἕκαστον
385 ἐνιαυτὸν τῷ ἐπὶ τῶν παραθηκῶν εἰς τὴν
ἐπιμέλειαν τῶν ἀπεικονισμάτων καὶ τὸν
ἀγορασμὸν τῆς ἀργυρωματικῆς γῆς.
Ὑπέσχετο δὲ Σαλουτάριος δώσειν καὶ δη.
ἑκατὸν τριάκοντα πέντε ὥστε ἄρξασθαι
390 τὴν φι(λ)οτειμίαν αὐτοῦ τῷ ἐνεστῶτι ἔτει
τῇ γενε[σί]ῳ τῆς [θ]εοῦ ἡμέρᾳ.
Τὰς δὲ προγεγραμμένας εἰκόνας καὶ τὰς
προκαθιερωμένας ἐν τῇ πρὸ ταύτης διατάξει καὶ τὰ ἀπεικονίσματα πάντα τῆς θεοῦ
395 φερέτωσαν ἐκ τοῦ προνάου κατὰ πᾶσαν ἐκκλησίαν εἰς τὸ θέατρον καὶ τοὺς γυμνικοὺς ἀγῶνας καὶ εἴ τινες ἕτεραι ὑπὸ τῆς βουλῆς καὶ τοῦ
δήμου ὁρισθήσονται ἡμέραι ἐκ τῶν νεοποιῶν δύο καὶ οἱ ἱερονεῖκαι καὶ σκηπτοῦχος καὶ
400 φύλακοι, καὶ πάλιν ἀποφερέτωσαν εἰς τὸ
ἱερὸν καὶ [παρ]ατιθέσθωσαν, συνπαραλαμβανόντων καὶ τῶν ἐφήβων ἀπὸ τῆς Μα[γ]νη-
τικῆς πύλης καὶ μετὰ τὰς ἐκκλησίας
συνπροπεμπόντων ἕως τῆς Κορησσικῆ[ς
405 πύλης, καθὼς καὶ ἐν τοῖς προγεγονόσι
ψηφίσμασι ἡ βουλὴ καὶ ὁ δῆμος ὥρισ[α]ν.

FRAGMENT 1 (perhaps from top of Column 4).

d]ργυρέας εἰ[κόνας] τοῦ κ[υ]ρίου ἡμῶν αὐ[τοκράτορος
Νερούα Τραϊα[νοῦ Σ]εβασ[τ]οῦ Γερμανικοῦ [Δακικοῦ, καὶ
τῆς ἱερωτάτ[ης θεοῦ Πλ]ωτείνης, καὶ τῆς ἱερ[ᾶς συνκλήτου,
καὶ τοῦ Ῥω[μαίων ὀνόμα]τος καὶ δήμου [τοῦ Ῥωμαίων, χω-
5   ρὶς εἰκόν[ων τῶν Ἐφεσίω]ν τὴν πόλιν προσ[ωποποιουσῶν,
τ]οῦ δήμ[ου τοῦ Ἐφεσίων καὶ βο[υλῆ]ς καὶ γε[ρουσίας καὶ ἐφη-
βεί[ας . . . .]του[. . . . .]νκ . . . .
. . . . καὶ . . . .
μετ . . . .
10   ον . . . .
ὑπὸ . . . .
να . . . .
τα . . . .
15   φ . . . .

```
          o  . . . . . . . . . . . . . . . . . . . . . . . . . . . . . . . . . .
             . . . . . . . . . . . . . . . . . . . . . . . . . . . . . . . . . .
          το . . . . . . . . . . . . . . . . . . . . . . . . . . . . . . . . . .
    20    δ  . . . . . . . . . . . . . . . . . . . . . . . . . . . . . . . . . .
          ε  . . . . . . . . . . . . . . . . . . . . . . . . . . . . . . . . . .
          τη . . . . . . . . . . . . . . . . . . . . . . . . . . . . . . . . . .
          ε  . . . . . . . . . . . . . . . . . . . . . . . . . . . . . . . . . .
                                  . . . . . . . . . . . . . . δ[ύ]ο νέ[οποι-
    25    ω[ν . . . . . . . . . . . . . . . . . . .] καὶ διαδ[εχομέ-
          νων [καὶ συνπροπεμπόντων τῶν] ἐφήβων [ἀ]πὸ τῆς [Μαγνη-
          τικῆς [πύλης εἰς τὸ θέατρον κ]αὶ ἀπὸ τοῦ θε[άτρου κατὰ
          τὸν αὐτ[ὸν τρόπον . . . . . . . .]νια ἀρχ . . . . . .
```

The inscription consists of a series of public documents relating to a bequest made to the Ephesians by Caius Vibius Salutaris, a Roman knight (line 15) of the tribe Oufentina ('Ωφεντίνᾳ, Οὐωφεντίνᾳ lines 227, 322), a naturalized citizen of Ephesos (line 17) and member of the βουλή. The date is fixed by the mention of the consuls for A.D. 104 in lines 318–319, *Sextus Attius Suburanus* ii, and *Marcus Asinius Marcellus*, concerning whom see Mommsen, Hermes iii, p. 126 foll. The whole of the documents fall within a period of three months, the first six documents being dated ' the 6th of Poseideon,' i.e. December, and the seventh bearing date ' A. d. VIII. Kal. Mart.' or ' 2nd of Anthesterion ' = February.

FIRST DOCUMENT. Decree of the senate and People of Ephesos in honour of C. V. Salutaris, in acknowledgment of his munificence. This was probably drawn up by some rhetorician of the time, who avoids the ordinary phrases of honorary decrees (which are usually verbose enough) translating them into an absurd bombast which even obscures the sense : e. g. in line 17, καὶ τοῦ βουλευτικοῦ συνεδρίου is for καὶ βουλευτής or καὶ βουλῆς ὤν. Lines 1–8 are restored by a comparison of the headings of the Fifth and Sixth Documents. [Κυρ.] is from line 304, and is abbreviated for Κυρείνᾳ, i. e. Quirina ' of the (Roman) tribe Quirina.' Lines 8 foll. : The restorations are suggested as conveying what certainly was the general sense ; but in some cases we cannot be sure of the exact words. Line 15 : The appointments held by Salutaris, here vaguely alluded to, are more fully rehearsed in his inscription upon the altar No. DXCIV. τά[ξ ε]ος or τά[ξε]ος for τάξεως is perhaps rather a debased late form than a survival of an Ionic form : compare γραμματίος line 139, εὐλυτήσεος line 205. Line 16 : The Emperor of course is Trajan. Line 18 : We are familiar in this and other late inscriptions with ει for ι and ι for ει : with διαθίσι = διαθέσει compare ἐπιδάν line 263 ; πλί for πλεί in the letter of Hadrian No. CCCCLXXXVII, line 7. Line 20 : Perhaps πα[λλ]εῖς would do as well. Line 22 : ἐννέα is probably right. The number of images dedicated by Salutaris by his first bequest must have been altogether 29, since with the two dedicated later the number was raised to 31 : see Seventh Document. But ἐννέα will refer to the nine more valuable images first named in the Second Document, which are either of solid gold, or of silver overlaid with gold (ἐπίχρυσα). These nine are what Salutaris especially promised in his first proposal to the ἐκκλησία, line 22. The gold image (line 23) was an Artemis with two silver stags, described in lines 75–76. The images dedicated by Salutaris are spoken of as εἰκόνες and ἀπεικονίσματα, words which are frequently repeated in the course of this inscription. Of the two, ἀπεικόνισμα seems generally to describe a copy of a recognised type, e. g. a representation of Artemis ; and this suits the etymology of the word. On the other hand εἰκών is used for the representation of abstract ideas, where more was left to the invention of the artist, as in the representations of the βουλή and δῆμος, etc., or of 'Αθήνη Πάμμουσος as the patroness of the general education of the young (see Seventh Document). Line 25 : Besides these images Salutaris dedicates δισμύρια δηνάρια, as is specified in the Second and Seventh Documents ; although here the clumsy rhetoric of the drafter prefers vagueness to exact statement. Reckoning the δηνάριον as 10d., 20,000 denarii would be equal to about 835l. Salutaris and his heirs (line 30) are to be at liberty to retain the capital sum in their own hands if they please, paying yearly 9 per cent. interest (about 75l.) to the Ephesians, τόκ[ον δραχμιαῖον] ἀσσαριαῖον, on which see lines 197 foll. and notes. Or they may discharge themselves of this liability whenever they like (ὅταν βουληθῇ, line 30) by the transfer of the capital. This arrangement, vaguely here described, is set forth in detail towards the end of the Second Document. The yearly interest thus accruing is to be spent chiefly in doles (διανομαί) to members of the Ephesian Boulè and Gerousia, to citizens, ephebi, and temple-ministers (διαιρεθησομένων, line 26) ; and the distribution is to take place on the ' birthday of the goddess, the 6th of Thargelion (= end of May), in accordance with the terms of the διάταξις or Will of Salutaris which forms the Second Document. Lines 31 foll. : ' The officers in charge of each department (concerned in this bequest) duly receiving their share of the capital sum dedicated.' The meaning is made clear by the Second Document, lines 185 foll. Line 33: The proposals of Salutaris thus personally made (ἰδίᾳ, see Uncial text), were to be formally approved by a decree. This ψήφισμα must be that of which I have recovered the fragment at the top of Column 6 ; see the Third Document, and R in the Diagram.

Line 34 : The Proconsul of Asia, T. Aquillius Proculus (concerning whom see Waddington, Fastes, p. 171, No. 113) is also applied to: he is requested to fix the amount of the fines for neglect of the Will, and at the same time to lend the transaction the dignity of his name and approval. His letter forms the Fourth Document. Line 49 : The manner of conveying the images to and from the theatre is carefully provided for in the Fifth and Sixth Documents; compare also the Seventh. In lines 54 foll. the statues to be erected in honour of Salutaris (line 45) are more particularly described. Line 57 : Wood reads διανομῆς, but the letters are quite clear; elsewhere in this inscription I have corrected his readings without remark. Lines 59 foll. may mean that Salutaris will lend the βουλή and γερουσία certain sums to defray the costs of the transfer of capital etc., or they may imply a promise that Salutaris will assist and advise those bodies in the safe investment of the dedicated capital if handed over to them at once (compare Second Document, lines 200 foll.).

SECOND DOCUMENT. *Bequest (διάταξις) of Salutaris.* Next follows the διάταξις or formal deed whereby Salutaris makes over his bequest. It is fairly perfect, though with several serious lacunae, and occupies the 3rd, 4th, and 5th columns. It is signed at the close thus :— Γάιος Οὐείβιος Γαίου υἱὸς Ὀφεντείνᾳ Σαλουτάριος εἰσενήνοχα τὴν διάταξιν καὶ καθιέρωσα τὰ προγεγραμμένα. The document is drawn up in a business-like manner, and is very different from the bombastic decree that preceded it. Lines 61 foll. perhaps named the several public bodies and persons who were to profit by the bequest. The enumeration of the gifts themselves opened (lines 68 foll.) with a list of images consecrated, compare above, line 23. It is stipulated that certain of the images, instead of being deposited at once in the pronaos of the temple with the rest, shall be kept in the custody of the donor himself during his life, and then shall be surrendered by his executors. Which statues these were does not appear, nor how many. They were perhaps favourites of Salutaris, who seems to have had the tastes of a connoisseur. They must have been certain of the statues mentioned in lines 75 foll., where the list strictly speaking begins, the golden Artemis standing first. If the image weighing 3 lb. in line 70 be that of the γερουσία, we may restore ȳ in line 83, which just suits the space : in line 70 νεοκορεῖν for ' to take religious care of,' is interesting. Line 74 : I do not exactly see where the images were to be placed : 'above the row of seats (σελίς, compare line 310) occupied by the Boulé,' and perhaps supported on temporary bases or pillars. Line 75 : δέ is superfluous, as also in line 185. The following lines 75-90 contain the subjoined list :—

1. Golden Artemis, with 2 silver stags	dedicated to Artemis and the Boulé.
2. Silver image of Roman Senate	
3. Silver image of Ephesian βουλή	
4. Artemis with torch, in silver	dedicated to Artemis and the γερουσία.
5. Silver image of Roman people	
6. Silver image of Ephesian γερουσία	
7. Artemis with torch, in silver	dedicated to Artemis and the Ephebi of each year.
8. Silver image of the *ordo equester*	
9. Silver image of the Ephesian ἐφηβεία	

In the preceding decree, lines 23, 24, nine images are mentioned, one being certainly the golden Artemis of line 75 ; and the remaining eight are probably the others of this list. These representations of Artemis are, it is to be presumed, from two well-known types : see the woodcut in Wood's Ephesus, p. 269, from the Ephesian Diana of the Museo Nazionale at Naples; the torch-bearing Artemis was more common. In lines 90-108, although the stones are much broken, we trace a continuation of the list of dedicated statues ; but if so, they must have been many more than 'nine.' Perhaps we may explain lines 23, 24 by supposing that the decree only specified the nine which Salutaris originally ' promised' (ὑπέσχετο), whereas the διάταξις here enumerates all that he actually dedicated. His intention seems to have been that each Section of the Ephesian commonwealth which was to receive a dole of money from his bequest, should receive at least one image of Artemis and a representation of the Section or Order itself—βουλή, δῆμος, ἐφηβεία, etc. We may suppose that the lines here lost enumerated images of each of the six Ephesian tribes, in accordance with lines 144 foll. The tribe Εὐώνυμοι is certainly named in line 104, and as this was the last but one in order of precedence, the φυλή of line 106 was probably the last in order, viz. Βεμβιναίων (see, on the Ephesian tribes, pp. 68, 71). We know that Salutaris dedicated an additional pair of silver statues of Artemis and the Karenæan Tribe (see No. DXCIV), probably because as a citizen of Ephesos he belonged to that tribe. And if in the list before us we suppose that each tribe received a similar recognition, then six statues of Artemis and one of each tribe will make 12, the statues of Trajan and Plotina mentioned in Fragment 1 make 14; and the nine named in lines 75-90 bring them up to 23, a number not far under the 29 spoken of in the Seventh Document. Nearer than this we cannot get, in the broken condition of the stones. Lines 121-125 : The list of images having ended, penalties were enacted against any one who should injure or steal them. At line 126 a new paragraph begins, dealing with the moneys dedicated. If Salutaris chooses to retain the capital sum in his own hands (see lines 25 foll. and note), then until the transfer of the dedicated capital, he engages to pay τόκον δραχμιαῖον. The capital sum was 20,000 denarii (see lines 201, 204 and notes on lines 185-199): the yearly interest is stated in line 128 to be 1,800 denarii, or 9 per cent. I shall attempt presently to explain how τόκος δραχμιαῖος, which usually means 12 per cent. came to be used for 9 per cent. Lines 128 foll. : *How the yearly dividends are to be distributed.* Unfortunately there is a lacuna at the top of column 5; but by comparison of lines 187-197 we can make out the following list :—

MONEYS DEDICATED BY SALUTARIS.

FIRST GIFT.

Recipients.	Capital.	Approximate Interest.	Exact Interest (9 p. c.)	Dols for each individual.	Number of recipients.	Lines of the document referring thereto.
1. Βουλή	5000 d.	450	450	1 den.	450	129 foll., 187 fol.
2. Γερουσία	4450	400	400·5	probably 1 den.	probably 400	189 foll.
3. Θεολόγοι } Ὑμνῳδοί }	255	23	22·95	perhaps 1 den.	perhaps 23	191 foll.
4. 200 citizens from each of the 6 tribes }	[6665]	[600]	[599·85]	9 asses=½ den.	1200	142 foll., 195
5. Ἔφηβοι					unknown for whom?	149 foll., 195
6. Ἀρχιερεύς						154 foll.
7. Priestess					1	161 foll.
8. 2 Νεωποιοί Σκηπτοῦχοι }	[3630]	[327]	[326·7]	{ 297 lump sum for distribution }	unknown	164 foll., 195 fol.
9. 49 boys					49	169 foll.
10. 1 Καθάρσιος				30 den. (balance)	1	175 foll., 196
	20,000	1800	1800			

SECOND GIFT.

Recipients.	Capital.	Approximate Interest.	Exact Interest (9 p. c.)	Dols for each individual.	Number of recipients.	Lines of the document referring thereto.
1. Ἱερεῖς		[105]	[105]	unknown	unknown	350 foll.
2. Θεομῳδοί of Augusteum }	1500	7	7	9 asses=½ den.	14	370 foll.
3. Ἀλεμβάται		15	15	13½ asses	20	374 foll.
4. Keeper of the Silver }		8 (balance)	8 (balance)	8 den.	1	384 foll.
	1500	135	135			

The custom of leaving bequests to public bodies, for an endowment to be spent in annual doles, was a feature of Græco-Roman society that deserves more attention than it has yet received. Instances of it are frequent in the inscriptions; the reader may compare two examples from Tralles (Mittheilungen, viii, pp. 321, 329). One reads: Ἡ βουλὴ καὶ ὁ δῆμος ἐτίμησεν Μ. Αὐρ. Εὐάρεστον ... ἀναθέντα τῇ κρατ(ίστῃ) Κλ(αυδίᾳ) βουλῇ εἰς νομὴν ἐπὶ τῇ γενεθλίῳ ἡμέρᾳ (his own birthday), ἥτις ἐστὶν μη(νὸς) Περειτίου ἐνάτῃ, δην. γτλ[γ] = 3333. The other founds an annual dole of a denarius for each member of the βουλή on new year's day. Line 132: as each βουλευτής was to receive one denarius, we discover that the βουλή at Ephesos numbered 450, at this period. Whether the number was always the same is doubtful. At Athens under the Romans the numbers of the βουλή varied (see Part I. No. XIX, p. 39); and it may have been so at Ephesos. It was a common thing in imperial times to adopt distinguished strangers not only as citizens, but also as members of the βουλή: see the letter of Hadrian No. CCCCLXXXVII, and p. 73 ante. But such honorary βουλευταί would not be reckoned in the constitutional number, and would have no share in the doles. As the Boulè numbered 450 members, and there were six Ephesian tribes (see on No. DXCIV), we might infer that each tribe was represented by 75 members: but the whole question has been discussed already, p. 74. In lines 131-2 the expression γεινομένης τῆι διανομῆι τῆς πέμπτης implies that the dole to be distributed out of the bequest of Salutaris was not the only one enjoyed by the βουλή. On this sixth of Thargelion another dole had usually been received, to which that of Salutaris is now added. Thargelion (corresponding to our May and June) was the ninth month of the Ephesian civil year, which began at the autumn equinox; and in the preceding eight months there had been already four doles. These, like the one now instituted, most probably arose from the proceeds of money or land bequeathed to the βουλή by individuals. Such endowments were not uncommon; but besides these, donations to the Boulè for an extraordinary dole were quite frequent. Pliny, speaking of Bithynia, says: Qui virilem togam sumunt vel nuptias faciunt vel ineunt magistratum vel opus publicum dedicant, solent totam bulen atque etiam e plebe non exiguum numerum vocare binosque denarios vel singulos dare, etc. (Ep. to Trajan, CXVII). The first lines of column 5 are lost or mutilated: from lines 189 foll. it appears that after the specification of the doles to the βουλή there came the doles to the γερουσία, and then those for the θεολόγοι and ὑμνῳδοί. Lines 190-1 give the capital sum dedicated for the γερουσία as 4450 denarii, only 50 less than the share of the βουλή: this would yield at 9 per cent. 400½ denarii yearly. In the table given above it is assumed that when the exact interest comes to a fraction of a denarius the next whole number is taken. Assuming further that the members of the Gerousia received, like the members of the Boulè, one denarius each, then they numbered 400. As to the constitution and functions of the γερουσία, see pp. 74-79. As it received a bequest only slightly less than that of the βουλή, we may infer something of the comparative dignity of the two councils. Next came the doles of the θεολόγοι and ὑμνῳδοί: who were these? Doubtless some kind of priests at the Artemision. Their high rank is shown by their being named so early in this catalogue, and the smallness of the sum bequeathed to them (line 193, but see note *post*), suggests that the recipients of the dole were selected yearly by ballot. The fragmentary lines 135 foll. appear to refer to a ballot, and to prescribe penalties for fraud. Θεολόγοι καὶ ὑμνῳδοί are mentioned together in C. I. 3148 as instituted at Smyrna by Hadrian (at the same time that Smyrna was allowed the title δὶς νεωκόρος τῶν Σεβαστῶν) to increase the dignity of the Augusteum there. We may safely render ὑμνῳδοί 'choristers,' 'choirmen' of the Temple of Artemis; but θεολόγοι seem to have to do with the celebration of mysteries (C. I. 3199, 3200, 3803). There were 'mysteries' celebrated in connexion with the worship of the Artemision (see pp. 79-80, *ante*), and these θεολόγοι were perhaps something like hierophants (see the documents just cited from Smyrna, except 3803). Lines 142-148: Dole to the citizens: compare line 195, where the capital assigned to them is included with others in a lump sum. The recipients of the dole (which is 9 assaria) are to be selected by lot out of each tribe: the numeral at the end of line 145 can hardly be anything except δ[ιακόσια], which would make a total number of 1200 citizens to receive. But it seems that at this time at Ephesos the as was equivalent to ¹⁄₁₆ instead of ¹⁄₁₀ of a denarius; this appears certain from Document Seventh, q. v., and it is confirmed by the amount of the dole being 9 asses (= ½ denarius), and bearing no relation to a denarius of 16 asses. If this be so, the number would be for 200 citizens from each of the six tribes, and the dividend required for the purpose of this dole will be 600 denarii. This sum again will require us to assume a capital of 6665 denarii. It is true that 6665 denarii at 9 per cent. would yield strictly speaking 599.85 denarii yearly. But according to the assumption we have made above, the fraction being so large, the next whole number, 600, is taken to be its equivalent. In lines 147-8 I have supplied what makes a probable sense: if at any time the rate of exchange was so far in favour of silver that the 600 denarii would change for more than 10800 assaria, then more citizens might be balloted for instead of increasing the dole per man. Lines 149-153 specified the doles to the ἔφηβοι: the recipients are to be balloted for, but the figures are all wanting: the capital sum is lumped with others in line 195. Lines 154-161 assigned a yearly share of the dividend to the ἀρχιερεύς at Ephesos, who had charge of the Augusteum: out of it he was to pay doles to certain persons chosen by ballot who had registered their names for the purpose. The figures are lost, nor can we gather who the recipients were: perhaps they were Ephesians belonging to the κοινὸν 'Ασίας. The dole cannot have been an important one, as it is omitted (like the dole to the priestess of Artemis, line 162, and to the παῖδες, lines 170 foll.) in the enumeration of capital sums, lines 193 foll. Lines 164-9: Concerning the νεωποιοί see pp. 80, 81; they evidently had control over the fabric

and furniture of the temple — 'temple-wardens' or surveyors. The σκηπτοῦχοι were merely 'vergers,' and their office was a menial one; see the Seventh Document, and p. 87 *ante*: they were especially concerned with the custody of the Temple. Lines 166-8 are restored by comparison of the Fifth and Sixth Documents. Lines 170-5: Compare Document Seventh. The form παιδωνόμοι was probably an established barbarism, like νεωποιός; the office is chiefly known as part of the system of Lykurgos (Xen. Resp. Lac. ii, 2; Plut. Lycurgus 17); but παιδονόμοι are mentioned in inscriptions of later times, as at Astypalæa (Bull. de Corr. Hellén. vii, p. 478), at Stratonikea, Branchidæ and Smyrna (C. I. 2715, 2885, 3185). I suppose that in those towns, as at Ephesos, the παιδονόμοι were magistrates who took cognisance of the sons of free citizens and kept discipline among them on occasions of public games and religious processions. We learn from Document Seventh that οἱ παῖδες had a recognised place reserved for them at every lawful assembly held in the Theatre: when of course the office of the παιδονόμοι would be necessary. But they were only present as visitors, like those who are admitted to the strangers' gallery of our House of Commons, or (to cite a closer parallel) as the Westminster boys were allowed, down to the close of the last century, to enter the House. The number of boys balloted for is 49,—an unlikely number, but as 7 × 7 = 49 perhaps seven boys were selected from each of seven divisions. Lines 175-180: The enumeration of doles is now complete, with a balance of 30 denarii to spare: this sum is to be handed over to the Temple officer who sees to the cleaning of the Temple and its furniture, τῷ τὰ καθάρσια ποιοῦντι. From line 196 it seems as if he had people under him to do the work; and this accounts for the comparatively large sum assigned to him. The construction of ὥστε = ὅπως ἄν with subjunctive is barbarous. Lines 180-4: I have restored the sense by conjecture: 'If anyone shall purchase of Salutaris or his heirs the properties chargeable with these payments, or if anyone contrive to become possessor thereof without purchase, he shall pay these annual sums without any diminution.' Lines 185-200. *Provision for the transfer of the capital, whenever Salutaris or his heirs may choose*: comp. lines 29 foll. The δέ in line 185 is superfluous: and τάχειον must not be translated too strictly, as no fixed time was named at or before which the capital must be transferred. The authorities of the state however are obliged (ἐπ' ἀνάγκῃ) to receive the capital whenever the owners choose to transfer it. The table given above, and the notes on lines 128 foll. will sufficiently explain this part of the Document. In line 197 however a correction should probably be made. If the capital sums named in these lines are added together they amount to 19.980 denarii, i. e. 20 short of the known total 20,000 denarii (line 204 etc.). The mistake was probably made in the addition of the various sums lumped together in lines 193-197. For ἐβδομήκοντα in line 197 read ἐνενήκοντα, then 102(9)5 will be the correct total of items 4-10 in our table of endowments. Line 197: The nominative τὸ ἐκδανίζωσιν is all the recipients of capital sums mentioned in the lines preceding. The phrase ἐπὶ τόκῳ ἀσσαρίων δεκαδύο ἀργυρῶν is peculiar: ἀδιάπτωτα means 'not likely to fail,' 'on good security.' The as or ἀσσάριον was of course a copper coin, so that ἀργυρῶν can only be rendered 'payable in silver:' a good reason for this provision lay in the fact deduced from line 147, that the rate of exchange was in favour of silver, or, in other words, that one denarius (silver) was worth more than the usual 16 asses (copper). In C. I. 3599, which deals with the investment of money at Novum Ilium, it is stipulated that the interest shall be paid half in silver. Similarly at Olbia (C. I. 2058, A. 70, B. 41) a merchant who has advanced money to the state in gold, is praised for accepting payment partly in copper. But of this more will be said on Document Seventh. We know from the figures that are given that the interest was at 9 per cent., viz. 1800 denarii upon a capital of 20,000 (compare lines 182-3, 204, 210). And the phrase ἐπὶ τόκῳ ἀσσαρίων δεκαδύο can only be made to mean 9 per cent. by supposing that 12 asses per month were to be paid on every 100 denarii. This would explain the curious phrase in line 25 τόκ[ον δραχμιαῖον] ἀσσαριαῖον, (compare line 347 in Seventh Document). τόκος ἐπὶ δραχμῇ or δραχμιαῖος usually meant 12 per cent., or 1 drachma per mina monthly, i. e. 12 drachmæ per mina yearly. Apparently τόκος δραχμιαῖος was loosely used at Ephesos in those days to signify interest of 12 asses monthly payable upon 100 denarii, the denarius being reckoned as = 16 asses. In line 25 ἀσσαριαῖον is added to explain the phrase: 'interest of 12 for the 100,—i. e. 12 assaria (per 100 denarii monthly).' In the Seventh Document we shall find reason to believe that at this time the denarius could be exchanged at Ephesos for 18 asses. But in calculation of interest the assarion is taken at its nominal value, ¹⁄₁₆ of a denarius: although by ordering that the interest shall be paid in silver (ἀργυρῶν) the payee gets the advantage of the superiority of silver. Line 202 : ᾗ is superfluous. Lines 206-7 : 'According to the sacred privileges of the goddess, and the registers of interest in the hands of the elders': a reference to the fact that the Artemision was used as a bank of deposit, and had therefore its customs and rules based on experience in money transactions. Thus Dio Chrysostom (Rhod. Or. xxxi, p. 327, ed. Reiske) in a speech composed about the time of our inscription says : ἔστε που τοὺς Ἐφεσίους, ὅτι πολλὰ χρήματα παρ' αὐτοῖς ἐστι τὰ μὲν ἰδιωτῶν, ἀποκείμενα ἐν τῷ νεῷ τῆς Ἀρτέμιδος οὐκ Ἐφεσίων μόνον ἀλλὰ καὶ ξένων καὶ τῶν ὁπόθεν δήποτε ἀνθρώπων, τὰ δὲ καὶ δήμων καὶ βασιλέων, ἃ τιθέασι πάντες οἱ τιθέντες ἀσφαλείας χάριν κ.τ.λ. The πρεσβύτεροι of line 207 are simply the γερουσία, in whose hands apparently were placed the banking transactions of the Temple of Artemis : comp. No. ccccLXXXIII ; and for πρεσβύτεροι see No. DLXXXVII. Line 211 : 'no magistrate, nor public pleader, nor private person :' for ἔκδικος see No. ccccLXXXIII line 20 : ἄρχων at Ephesos always has the general sense of 'magistrate,' and must never be rendered 'archon' (see p. 72 ante). Line 221 : For the cypher Ṁ = δισμύρια compare C. I. 3148. Lines 223 foll. : The letter of Aquillius Pro-

cūlus forms the Fourth Document. It appears as if the Ephesians were not doing anything out of the way in asking the proconsul of the province to give his approval to this endowment and to fix the amount of the fines : observe that a heavy fine was to be paid into the emperor's privy purse (line 221). It is clear from the correspondence of Pliny with Trajan (Epp. cxvii, cxviii) that διανομαί of this kind were not encouraged by the Roman government; also in the letter of Antoninus Pius (No. ccccXCI *post*) we shall find διανομαί similarly deprecated.

THIRD DOCUMENT. *Decree of formal assent to the preceding διάταξις* (?) The fragment I have placed at the top of column 6 is inscribed on the same stone with the fragment at the top of column 7. As there is no doubt of the position of the latter (see notes *ad loc.*), we are equally certain of the position of the present fragment. I take this Third Document to have been the decree referred to in Document First, lines 32-33 : περὶ [ὧν] ἀπάντων διατα[ξ]ιν εἰση[γησάμε]νος ἰδ(ίᾳ) ἠξ(ί)ωσεν ἐπι[κυ]ρωθῆναι καὶ διὰ ψ[η]φίσμα[τος κ.τ.λ. Also compare lines 217 foll. : τοῖς | ὑπὸ τ[ῆς] βου[λ]ῆς καὶ τοῦ δήμου ἐψηφισμένοις καὶ ἐπικεκυ[ρωμέν[οις περὶ] ταύτης [τ]ῆς διατάξεως. The deed of gift (Document Second) was followed up by a ψήφισμα in which the Ephesians gave their assent to its provisions. It is too fragmentary for restoration. Lines 232 foll. : One is tempted to restore [τῆς πρώτη]ς καὶ μεγίσ[της μητροπόλεως τῆς Ἀσίας καὶ νεωκόρου τῶν Σεβασ]τῶν. With [διανομὰ]ς καὶ κλή[ρους] in line 234 compare lines 210-211. Line 235 : ἐφ' οἷς is perhaps explained by [ἐπὶ] τοῖς δικαίοις καὶ προστείμοις of the Seventh Document. The word [ἐπαι]νέσαι, line 238, shows that this document took the form of an honorary decree : perhaps the proconsul and his propraetor received thanks for their services in the matter.

FOURTH DOCUMENT. *Letter from the Proconsul T. Aquillius Proculus, and the Propraetor Afranius, congratulating the Ephesians upon the munificence of Salutaris, and fixing the amount of the fines payable by those who should infringe the preceding regulations.* The first few lines are hopelessly mutilated. From line 256 I have attempted a restoration which is at least plausible. Notice the use of μαρτυρία in the sense of 'praise' 'favourable testimony,' a common New Testament usage. Translate: 'I desire, while intending to deal justly by Salutaris, to give evidence and testimony concerning yourselves also, and with becoming commendation to reward him on your behalf with all the praise that I am sure he deserves at your hands.' On the subject of this letter, lines 266 foll., see note on lines 223 foll. Line 270 : I suppose ψηφίσασθαι to refer to the Third Document. For the fines prescribed in lines 278 foll. compare line 220, where however no fine payable to the γερουσία is mentioned.

FIFTH DOCUMENT. *Decree of the βουλή authorizing οἱ χρυσοφοροῦντες to bear the images and effigies from the Temple to the Theatre.* This decree belongs to the same year as the other documents, but the month is lost : the opening phrases are restored from Document Sixth. It appears from the concluding lines (compare the Sixth Document) that the γραμματεὺς τοῦ δήμου and the στρατηγοί laid the matter before the βουλή, then a definite ψήφισμα was proposed in the names of several senators; ἐχάραξα in line 300 means ' engraved upon the stone.' This decree is supplementary to the foregoing documents. In Salutaris' own regulations (lines 164–169 : comp. 196–197) it had been arranged that two of the temple-wardens assisted by the temple-vergers should carry the images backwards and forwards. They would still remain officially responsible for this task as before (lines 294, 398), but a request had been made by οἱ χρυσοφοροῦντες τῇ θεῷ ἱερεῖς καὶ ἱερονεῖκαι that they might have the honour of bearing the images; and their request is granted. At the same time (lines 294–5) it is directed that when the sacred images have been brought from the Artemision to the city, and have reached the Magnesian gate, the Ephebi shall meet the procession and accompany them to the Theatre. From the Seventh Document (lines 399 foll.) we learn that after the assembly broke up the images, before being taken back to the Temple, were borne in procession from the Theatre to the Koressian gate, the Ephebi accompanying them thus far. By this arrangement the images thus would make a circuit of the chief streets of the city. After the discovery of this inscription in the Theatre Mr. Wood was guided by these passages in it to seek for the Magnesian and Koressian gates, assured that by working from them he would discover the site of the Temple. He accordingly found the Magnesian gate[1], and following the road (' Via Sacra') leading from it, he ultimately struck upon the *peribolos* or ring-wall of the Temple-precinct, and so arrived at the Artemision itself (see Wood's *Ephesus*, pp. 80, 116, 129, 132 foll.). As to the part taken by the Ephebi, it will be remembered that at Athens the Ephebi escorted the bearers of the Eleusinian relics from Eleusis to the Akropolis and from the Akropolis to Eleusis (Part I. Attika, No. XIX). In both cases the Ephebi acted as a guard of honour : ὡς ἂν κόσμο[ς] τε πλείων καὶ φρουρὰ μείζων ἶ[περὶ] τὰ ἱερὰ ὑπάρχῃ[ι] ibid. line 12. Little is known of the ' gold-wearers' who are the subject of the decree: see *ante* p. 85. It was not usual for men among the Greeks and Romans to wear ornaments of gold, and even in the East it appears

[1] As to the site of the Magnesian gate there is no dispute, and Mr. Wood is to be congratulated upon its discovery. But in placing the Koressian gate on the N. of the city, he is opposed to all modern scholars and apparently all ancient evidence. He assumes that the procession described in the text, after passing through the principal streets, made its exit through the NE. gate, and so returned to the Temple. On the strength of this assumption he names the hills on the E., Koressos, and the hills on the S., Prion (Pion). But it is nowhere said that the Ephebi marched in procession *back to the Temple*, but only μεχρὶ τῆς Κορησσικῆς πύλης (line 396), i.e. so far and no further. Nothing therefore in the text forbids us to identify the Koressian gate with the gate marked by Mr. Wood in the W. wall, and leading to the sea. Moreover the gates of ancient cities were usually named with reference to the places to which they led. Thus the ' Magnesian ' gate led to Magnesia, and similarly the ' Koressian ' gate would be so named not merely because it lay beneath Mount Koressos (which I take with Curtius and others to be the range of hills on the S.), but because it led to that locality by the harbour which was also called ὁ Κορησσός (Herod. v. 100 ; Xen. Hell. i, 2, § 7) : see an interesting *Étude sur la chorographie d' Éphèse* by G. Weber in the *Movσεῖον καὶ Βιβλιοθήκη τῆς ἐυαγγελικῆς Σχολῆς*, ··(,ι 1880–4), παρ. iv, p. 1.

to have been a privilege belonging to the royal family or granted to distinguished individuals : see 1 Maccab. x, 89; xi, 58; xiv, 43, 44. In later Greece we occasionally find χρυσοφορία or χρυσοφορεῖν μετὰ πορφύρας granted by decree of the state to eminent benefactors: see C. I. 2929 (Tralles); C. I. A. iii, 623, χρυσοφορίᾳ διὰ βίου τετιμημένον (Athens). But sometimes χρυσοφορία was a privilege enjoyed *ex officio* by certain priesthoods and magistracies : see Artemidor. Oneirocrit. ii, 9 : πλουσίων δὲ τοὺς μὲν χρυσοφορεῖν μέλλοντας διά τινα ἀρχὴν ἢ ἱερωσύνην οὐ βλάπτει (ὁ κεραυνὸς) ἀλλὰ ἐπισημοτέρας ἄρξαι ἢ ἱεράσασθαι προαγορεύει. Thus it had to be specified in the Andanian inscription that the ἱεραί must not wear gold (Dittenberger, Sylloge, No. 388, line 22). And it is this kind of χρυσοφορία which is meant in the only other passages where it is mentioned at Ephesos, viz. No. DCXVIII, ἀγωνοθετήσαντα τῶν χρυσοφόρων, and No. DCIV, ὑμνῳδὸς νεηητὴς βουλῆς, γερουσίας, χρυσοφόρων, ἠγωνίσατο ἀγῶνας τρεῖς ἐστεφθὴ δύο. It appears therefore that there were certain contests at Ephesos, the victors in which (ἱερονεῖκαι) had the privilege of χρυσοφορία : the same privilege was enjoyed by certain priests (lines 307, 326). That it did not include the purple (μετὰ πορφύρας) follows from line 313, λ[ε]υχειμονοῦ[ν]τας. πρὸ πόλεως is simply ' outside of the city,' in reference to the site of the Artemision : see C. I. 2963 *c.*, οἱ τὸν [ἱερὸν?] κόσμον βαστά[ζοντες] τῆς μεγάλης θεᾶς [Ἀρτέμι]δος πρὸ πόλ[εω]ς ἱερεῖς [καὶ ἱερ]ονεῖκαι κ.τ.λ.

SIXTH DOCUMENT. *Another decree granting the χρυσοφοροῦντες a particular seat in the Theatre.* The subject of this decree has been discussed in the notes on the Fifth Document. Line 311: πρὸς τὴν Εὐσέβειαν is ' facing the statue of Piety.' This accusative for dative is a mark of debased Greek : compare πρὸς τὸ ἀγορανόμιν, No. DCLVI.

SEVENTH DOCUMENT. *Supplementary διάταξις or deed of gift, making over additional images and more money.* It happens that this is dated according to Roman as well as Ephesian reckoning, so that the names of the consuls fix the date of the whole inscription to the year A. D. 104 : see Mommsen in Hermes, iii, p. 136. The names of the consuls are, as usual, in the dative case, to imitate the Latin ablative (see C. I. 3148). It is interesting to learn from line 319 that the second day of Anthesterion coincided with February 24th, or rather with our February 25th, as A. D. 104 was leap-year. This day A. d. viii. Kal. Mart. is styled Σεβαστή in line 321, an epithet applied to a certain day of the month in several Egyptian inscriptions (C. I. 4715, 4957, line 3 ; also at Trajanopolis in Phrygia, Le Bas-Waddington, No. 1676 ; and at Lagina in Karia, Bull. de Corr. Hellén. xi, p. 29) : but the precise meaning of it is doubtful (see C. I. addenda 5866 *c.*). Line 322 : The προγεγονὸς ψήφισμα is either the Third Document, or perhaps the First. The total number of images dedicated by Salutaris was 31, see notes on lines 75 foll. In line 335 the lapidary has blundered, and we must certainly read ὥστε εἶναι | αὐτὰ σὺν τοῖς προκαθιερωμένοις δή, δισμύρια χίλια πεντακόσια. Line 336 : Ἀθηνᾶ Πάμμουσος is not elsewhere mentioned : the epithet here designates her the patroness of all the arts, and of the education of the boys. On the presence of οἱ παῖδες in the Theatre at public assemblies, see notes on lines 170–5. The νόμιμοι ἐκκλησίαι were fixed by law and custom (though there might be others extraordinarily convened, like the ἐκκλησίαι σύγκλητοι and κατάκλητοι at Athens): the 'town-clerk' in Acts xix, 39 uses the word ἔννομος in the same sense of 'a regular assembly': comp. supr. line 165. Lines 341–358 : This important fragment is not given by Wood. Although the stones will not join, yet the style of the writing and the general sense of the passage makes the position of this fragment certain. It is clear that until line 345 the inscription was occupied with the images now dedicated. directions were given for their conveyance to the Theatre and back again (lines 343–4), and the Θεόφιλ[ος] of line 341 may be the same as in line 317. On the word ἱερός see ante pp. 85 fol. Lines 346 foll. give directions concerning the distribution of the dedicated moneys, viz. 1,500 denarii. Here a difficulty meets us. It is well known that the value of the as under the earlier emperors was ₁₆th denarius (see note on line 197). But some of the doles specified in this Seventh Document clearly show (unless the figures of the lapidary or the MS. draft were wrong) that at Ephesos at this period the as had sunk to ₁₅th denarius. See lines 370–3, and 374–7 : it is impossible if the denarius = 16 asses to subdivide 7 denarii into any number of doles with 9 asses, nor 15 denarii into doles worth 13½ asses each. It is quite possible that the value of the as in the provinces may have fallen below its usual level, though there is no evidence in proof of it. (Compare however Mr. P. Gardner on the Monetary League on the Euxine, Numismatic Chron. N. S. xvi, pp. 307 foll., where pieces stamped 1½ and 4½ asses imply 18 rather than 16 asses to the denarius.) I have therefore assumed that throughout this Salutaris inscription the as is worth ₁₅th denarius. This assumption is confirmed by the dole to the citizens (line 146) being fixed at 9 asses = ½ denarius ; and by the dole to the θεσμῳδοί (line 370). Also 13½ asses (line 377) are ⅔ denarius by this reckoning, but bear no relation to a denarius of 16 asses. Line 349 : The interest on 1,500 denarii at 9 per cent. is 135 denarii yearly (line 389). Line 350: As the total interest yearly amounted to 135 denarii, and 7 + 15 + 8 denarii were appropriated to other doles (see lines 371, 376, 384), there will remain 105 denarii to be received by the γραμματεύς for the priests. The sum is a large one, but part is to go to the purchase of victims etc. for sacrifice (lines 358, 366 foll.); the remainder only is to be distributed to a certain number of priests selected by lot on the 5th of Thargelion (line 353), the eve of the festival. Lines 370–373 : Next to the priests come the θεσμῳδοί, who receive 7 denarii in doles of 9 asses (= ½ denarius) per man : their number was therefore 14. They are styled in lines 328 foll. θεσμῳδοὶ ναοῦ τῶν Σεβαστῶν ἐν Ἐφέσῳ κοινοῦ τῆς Ἀσίας : and we cannot be wrong in supposing them to be similar to the ὑμνῳδοί instituted by Hadrian at the Augusteum at Smyrna (see note on line 192): as however the 'choirmen' of the Artemision were already called ὑμνῳδοί (line 192), the choir of the

Ephesian Augusteum were named θεσμῳδοί. I cannot find the title elsewhere ; θεσμός is used like νόμος for 'a hymn' by Æschyl. Suppl. 1035. Lines 374–377 : The ἀκροβάται receive 15 denarii in doles of 13½ asses (= ⅔ denarius) per man. The ἀκροβάται were accordingly 20 in number : they were among the inferior temple-ministers of the Artemision, and may be identified with the ἀκριτοβάται of Hesychios, defined (s. v.) as ἀρχή τις παρὰ Ἐφεσίοις τῆς Ἀρτέμιδος θυσιῶν. The title occurs again in No. DLXXXIX b, where the keeper of the silver (called below in line 385 ὁ ἐπὶ τῶν παραθηκῶν) is also an ἀκροβάτης. See on these officials pp. 85–87 ante. Lines 378–387 : See preceding note, and note on No. DLXXXIX b. The 'plate-powder' may be the creta argentaria of Pliny, N. H. xvii, 45 ; xxxv, 44, 199; or possibly wood-ashes (see Theophr. Hist. Pl. v, 9, 1–2). The mention of two νεοποιοί here, as in lines 165, 398, suggests the thought that out of the 12 νεοποιοί (see No. DLXXVIII a, b) two were always on duty for a term of two months.

I have appended to the Salutaris inscription a number of fragments which unmistakeably belonged to it, although their exact position cannot be determined. Of these No. 1 is the most important, a block with the edge entire on left, top and bottom, and put together out of a number of smaller bits. It may possibly have come at the top of column 4. At any rate it is interesting as showing that Salutaris, in doing honour to Artemis and the Ephesians, did not forget the emperor, but dedicated silver statues of Trajan and his wife Plotina. Trajan assumed the title Dacicus at the end of A. D. 102 : see Mommsen in Hermes iii, p. 131. Unfortunately the stone is shattered to pieces and the surface of the existing portions injured : my restorations are only plausible conjectures. Little can be made of the other fragments.

Frag. 2. καθι[ερωμένα]. [Σ]εβαστοῦ or [φιλοσ]εβάστου. [τῷ] θεάτρῳ.

Frag. 4. [συ]νηνδόμενο[ς]. Is this a part of Document Third, referring to the congratulations of the proconsul ? . . [διάταξι]ν εἰσινε[νκεῖν ?]: see line 183.

Frag. 5 seems to refer to the custody of the images. [τῶ]ν βάσεων. παρα[τε]θ[ῆ]να[ι]. [Ἰ]ουλιανοῦ. [Ἀρτέ]μιδος.

Frag. 6. [ἱσ]ρομένην. ὅ τε ποιη ? . . . [τῇ]ς προ[ί]κ ὅς ? [τ]οῦ α[ιων]οῦ? κ . . .

Frag. 7. [διά]ταξιν ?

Frag. 8. [δεδόχθαι τῇ βουλῇ καὶ τῷ νεωκ]όρῳ δήμῳ φιλοσε[βάστῳ καθάπερ γίγρ]απται. Compare Document First, line 4.

Frag. 9. ἐπιγεγ[ρα . . . [δ]ιατάξει. [ἀπ]ολυθῆν[αι].

Frag. 10. [μ]εγαλοψυχ[ία]

Frag. 11. . . . ς δ̄[ην̄.] . . . δην̄. μ̄ε. κ . . . Πρόκλο[ς]. This is probably the proconsul.

Frags. 12, 13. These appear to be parts of the same block, but how much is lost between them is uncertain.

ἔτους ουσ . . .
μένα[ι]ς ιερα . . .
Σε[βαστ]είων ? . . .
(lacuna)
μοτε . . . . [καθιε-

ρωμίνω . . . .
καὶ πολ[λ . . .
ἐπὶ τοῦ . . . .
Frag. 14.   τὸν ναὸν τῆς Ἀ[ρτέμιδος].   [τ]ῶν καθηκόν-
τω[ν].   . . . του κυρίαν εἰ̣ν[αι].   . . . ον εἰς τὸν . . . [οἳ] τε
ἀρχο[ντες].
Frag. 15.   [τ]ὸ γεγραμ[μένον].
Frag. 18.   κα]θ' ἕκαστον [ἐνιαυτόν].   [σκηπτ]οῦχον καὶ
τοῦ[τ . . . .]
Frag. 20.   [καθ' ἕκαστο]ν μῆνα?   ἐπι.λ]ησίαις κα . . . ;

Frags. 22–24 perhaps belonged to Document Seventh, and came from the top of column 7. They seem to refer to the dedication of statues, and statue-bases. In frag. 22 perhaps **ō̄ ΒΑΣΕΙΣ** is the remains of **κθ βάσεις**, 29 statue-bases; which would agree well with the Seventh Document, lines 332–3 : also notes on lines 75–90.

Frag. 25.   [. . λα]μβανό[ντων . .]
Frag. 27.   [εἰκὼν ἀ]ργυρία . . . . [ὁλκῆς . . . . .] θ̄ καὶ . . .
Frag. 28.   [εἰκὼν ἀργ]υρία. [ὁλκῆς . . . . .] γ̄ ἡμ̣[ισυνκείου?]

CCCCLXXXII.

A square altar-like base of white marble, once surmounted by a moulded cornice, inscribed on three sides. The monument is broken into two parts about 18 in. from the top.   It originally supported a statue of Cl. Marcianus Priscus, named in C. Only the upper portion of the marble is in the British Museum, having been discovered by Mr. Wood and brought to London in 1867.   It contains A (1), B (1), C (1).   The greatest height of the B. M. portion is 17½ in.; the width of each of the sides is 19 in.   The lower portions of the inscription have been known since about 1719, and B (2) and C (2) have been repeatedly published : see especially Pococke, Inscr. Ant. i, 3, 3, pp. 34, 35 ; Chandler, Inscr. Ant. Pr. i, No. 36, p. 12 ; C. I. 2954 ; Bailie, Fasciculus Inscr. Grœc. (1842), p. 17 foll. gives A (2), B (2), C (2) ; and more accurately, Waddington-Le Bas, Pt. V, No. 137–139. This lower portion of the monument was brought from Ephesos in 1866 by Mr. Hyde Clarke and presented by him to the University of Oxford, where it now is in the Ashmolean Museum.   The whole inscriptions are here for the first time published in a complete form ; but I find that M. Waddington has anticipated me in identifying the two marbles as parts of the same monument ; see his Fastes Asiatiques, p. 224, where he publishes A (1).   B (1) and C (1) have never been edited before.   I have given both the London and the Oxford portions in uncial type, for the reader's convenience.

A (1)   ΠΙΛΛΙΟΣΚΑΡΟΣΠΕΔΓ
                 ΑΝΘΥΠΑΤΟΣ·ΛΕΓΕΙ
                 ΜΑΘΟΝΕΚΤΟΥΠΕΜΦΘΕΝΤΟΣ
                 ΛΕΨΗΦΙΣΜΑΤΟΣΥΠΟΤΗΣΛΑΜΠΡΟΤ
        5   ΤΗΣΕΦΕΣΙΩΝ·ΒΟΥΛΗΣΤΟΥΣ·ΠΡΟΕΜ
                 ΚΡΑΤΙΣΤΟΥΣΑΝΘΥΠΑΤΟΥΣΙΓ
                 ΝΟΜΙΣΑΙ·ΤΑΣΗΜΕΡΑΤΤΥΤ   .π.   A (2)
A (2)   _ :ΑΡΤΓ   ΚΑΙΤΟΥΤΟΔΙΑΤΑ
                 ΓΜΑΤΙΔΕΔΗΛΩΚΕΝΑΙ·ΟΘΕΝΑΝΑΓΚΑΙ
        10   ΟΝΗΓΗΣΑΜΗΝΚΑΙΑΥΤΟΣΑΠΟΒΛΕ
                 ΠΩΝΕΙΣΤΕΤΗΝΕΥΣΕΒΕΙΑΝΤΗΣΘΕΟ̇
                 ΚΑΙΕΙΣΤΗΝΤΗΣΛΑΜΠΡΟΤΑΤΗΣΕΦΕ
                 ΣΙΩΝΠΟΛΕΩΣΤΕΙΜΗΝ·ΦΑΝΕΡΟΝΠΟΙ
                 ΗΣΑΙΔΙΑΤΑΓΜΑΤΙΕΣΕΣΘΑΙΤΑΣΗΜΕΡΑΣ
        15   ΤΑΥΤΑΣΙΕΡΑΣ·ΚΑΙΤΑΣΕΠΑΥΤΑΙΣΕΚΕ
                 ΄ΕΙΡΙΑΣΦΥΛΑΧΘΗΣΕΣΘΑΙ·ΠΡΟΕΣΤΩ
                 ΤΟΣΤΗΣΠΑΝΗΓΥΡΕΩΣ   ·
                 ΤΙΤΟΥ·ΑΙΛΙΟΥΜΑΡΚΙΑΝΟΥ   ΠΡΙΣΚΟΥ
                 ΤΟΥΑΓΩΝΟΘΕΤΟΥ·ΥΟΥ·ΑΙΛΙΟΥ
        20   ΠΡΙΣΚΟΥΑΝΔΡΟΣΔΟΚΙΜΩΤΑΤΟΥΚΑΙ
                 ΠΑΣΗΣΤΕΙΜΗΣ·ΚΑΙΑΠΟΔΟΧΗΣΑΞΙΟΥ

B (1)   ΟΞΕΝΤΗΣΠΡΩΤΗΣΚΑΙΜΕ
)ΠΟΛΕΩΣΤΗΣΑΣΙΑΣΚΑΙΔΙΣΝΕΓ΄
                 :ΤΩΝ·ΚΑΙΦΙΛΟΣΕΒΑΣΤΟΥΕΦΙ
                 ΥΛΗ·ΚΑΙΤΩΔΗΜΩΠΕΡΙΩΝΕΙΣΗ: ι
        5   ΑΒΕΡΙΟΣ·ΑΜΟΙΝΟΣΦΙΛΟΣΕΒΑΣΤΟΣ·ΟΓΡΑΜΝ.
                 ΙΜΟΥ·ΕΠΕΨΗΦΙΣΑΝΔΕΟΙΣΤ ΑΤΗΓΟΙΤΗΣ
                 ΠΟΛΕΩΣ·ΦΙΛΟΣΕΒΑΣΤΟΙ ·
                 ΡΟΕΣΤΩΣΑΤΗΣΙΙΣ ΛΕΓ ΤΥΜΩΝΘΣ ΙΣΑΡΤΕ
                 ΓΝΤΗΕΛΙΤΗΣΠΑ ΡΙΔΙΛΤΙΜΑΤΑΙ·ΗΝΑ
        10   ΓΝ ΛΟΞΟΤΕΡΑΝ·ΔΙΑΤΗΣ·ΙΔΙΑΣΘΕΙΟ Ħ Τ
B (2)   ΛΛΛΚΛΙΙΙΛΙ ιι   Λ ι ΛΘΘΛΟ ιΣΩ
                 ΛΧΟΥ·ΛΝΕΙΣΘΛΙΑΥΤΗΣΙ̣
                 ΑΥΤΗΤΕΕΙΔΙ) ΣΘΑΙ·ΚΑΙΒΩΜΟΥΣ

ΤΑΣΥΠΑΥΤΗΣΓΕΙΝΟΜΕΝΑΣΕΝΑΡΓΕΙΣΕΠ·
15 ΚΑΙΤΟΥΤΟΔΕΜΕΓΙΣΤΟΝΤΟΥΙΙΕΡΙΑ͞ΤΗΝ·ΣΕ
ΜΟΥΕΣΤΙΝΤΕΚΜΗΡΙΟΝΤΟΕΠΩΝΥΜΟΝΑΥΤ
ΕΙΝΑΙΜΗΝΑΚΑΛΟΥΜΕΝΟΝΠΑι·' ΙΝΜΕΝΑΡΤ
ΩΝΑ·ΠΑΡΑΔΕΜΑΚΕΔΟΣΙΝ·ΚΑΙΤΟΙΣΛΟΙΠΟΙΣΕ
ΓΟΙΣΕΛΛΗΝΙΚΟΙΣΚΑΙΤΑΙΣΕΝΑΥΤΟΙΣΠΟΛΕΣΙ
20 ΙΡΤΕΜΙΣΙΟΝΕΝΩΜΗΝΙΠΑΝΗΓΥΡΕΙΣΤΕΚΑΙΙΕι
ΗΝΙΑΙΕΠΙΤΕΛΟΥΝΤΑΙΔΙΑΦΕΡΟΝΤΩΣΔΕΙ·
ΗΜΕΤΕΡΑΠΟΛΕΙ·ΤΗΤΡΟΦΩΤΗΣΙΔΙΑΣΘΕΟΥΗΣΕϟ
Σ·ΠΡΟΣΗΚΟΝΔΕΕΙΝΑΙ·ΗΓΟΥΜΕΝΟΣ·ΟΔΗΜΟΣ
ΦΕΣΙΩΝΟΛΟΝΤΟΝΜΗΝΑΤΟΝΕΠΩΝΥΜΟΝΤΟΥϚ
25 ΝΟΜΑΤΟΣΕΙΝΑΙΙΕΡΟΝ·ΚΑΙΑΝΑΚΕΙΣΘΑΙΤΗΘΕΩ
ΔΟΚΙΜΑΣΕΝ·Δ ΑΤΟΥΔΕΤΟΥΨΗϟΙΣΜΑΤΟϜ
ΑΙΤΗΝΠΕΡΙΑΥΤΟΥΘΡΗΣΚΕΙΑΝΔΙΩ
ΩΝΤΟΝΜΗΝΑΤΟΝΑΡΤΕΜΙΣΙ ΩΝΑΕΙ
ΝΣΗΜΕΡΑΣ·ΑΓΕΣΘΑΙΔΕ·ΕΠΑΥΤΑΙΣΜΗϞ
30 Ε͞ΟΥΣΤΑΣΕΟΡΤΑΣ·ΚΑΙΤΗΝΤΩΝΑΡΤΕΜ
ΥΡΙΝ·ΚΑΙΤΑΣΙΕΡΟΜΗΝΙΑΣ·ΑΤΕΤΟΥΜΗΝΟΣΟ
ΙΟΥΤΗΘΕΩ·ΟΥΤΩΓΑΡΕΠΙΤΟΑΜΕΙΝΟΝΤΗΣ
ΗΣ·ΗΠΟΛΙΣΗΜ   ΝΔΟΞΟΤΕΡΑΤΕ·ΚΑΙΕΥΔ
ϟ ΕΙΣΤΟ   ΝΤΑ·ΔΙΑΜΕΝΕΙ·Χ

C (1)   ΗΠΑΤΡΙΣ
T·ΑΙΛΙΟΝ·Τ·ΥΙΟΝΚΛ
ΜΑΡΚΙΑΝΟΝΠΡΙΣΚϚ
ΑΓΩΝΟΘΕΤΗΝ·ΚΑΙΠΛ
5   ΩΝΜΕΓΑΛΩΝΑΡΤ
ΠΡΩΤΟΝΑΥΤ
C (2)   ΤΗΝΠΑΝΗΓΥΡΙΝΚΑΙΑΙΕΛΕΙΩ
ΚΑΙΕΚΕΧΕΙΡΙΑΣ·ΕΙΣΟΛΟΝΤΟΙ
ΣΠΩΝΥΜΟΝΤΗΣΘΕΟΥΜΗΝΑ
10   ΤΥΧΟΝΤΑ·ΚΑΙΤΗΝΑΡΤΕΜΙΣΙ
ΑΚΗΝΚΡΙΣΙΝ·ΚΑΤΑΣΤΗΣΑΝΤ/
ΚΑΙΤΑΘΕΜΑΤΑΤΟΙΣΑΓΩΝΙΣ
ΤΑΙΣΑΥΞΗΣΑΝΤΑ·ΚΑΙΑΝΔΡΙ
ΑΝΤΑΣΤΩΝ ϝ ΝΙΚΗΣΑΝΤΩΝ
15   ᴗ ΑΝΑΣΤΗΣΑΝΤΑ ᴗ
ΤΗΝΤΕΙΜΗΝΑΝΑΣΤΗΣΑΝΤϚ
Λ·ΦΑΙΝΙΟΥΦΑΥΣΤΟΥ·
ΤΟΥΣΥΝΓΕΝΟΥΣΑΥΤΟΥ

A (1)   —. Πο]πίλλιος Κᾶρος Πέδω[ν
ἀνθύπατος λέγει·
Ἔ]μαθον ἐκ τοῦ πεμφθέντος [εἰς ἐ-
μὲ ψηφίσματος ὑπὸ τῆς λαμπροτ[ά-
5   της Ἐφεσίων βουλῆς τοὺς πρὸ ἐμ[οῦ
κρατίστους ἀνθυπάτους ἱε[ρὰς
νόμισαι τὰς ἡμέρας τῆς [πα]νη[γύρεως
A (2)   τ]ῶν Ἀρτ[εμισίων] καὶ τοῦτο διατά-
10   γματι δεδηλωκέναι· ὅθεν ἀναγκαῖον ἡγησάμην καὶ αὐτὸς ἀποβλέ-
πων εἴς τε τὴν εὐσέβειαν τῆς θεοῦ
καὶ εἰς τὴν τῆς λαμπροτάτης Ἐφεσίων πόλεως τειμὴν φανερὸν ποιῆσαι διατάγματι ἔσεσθαι τὰς ἡμέρας
15   ταύτας ἱερὰς καὶ τὰς ἐπ' αὐταῖς ἐκεχειρίας φυλαχθήσεσθαι· προεστῶ-
τος τῆς παηγύρεως
Τίτου Αἰλίου Μαρκιανοῦ Πρίσκου

A (2)

τοῦ ἀγωνοθέτου, υἱοῦ Αἰλίου
20   Πρίσκου, ἀνδρὸς δοκιμωτάτου καὶ
πάσης τειμῆς καὶ ἀποδοχῆς ἀξίου.

B (1)   ῎Εδ]οξεν τῆς πρώτης καὶ με[γίστης
μητρ]οπόλεως τῆς ᾽Ασίας καὶ δὶς νεωκ[όρου τῶν
Σεβα]στῶν καὶ φιλοσεβάστου ᾽Εφε[σίων πόλεως
τῇ βο]υλῇ καὶ τῷ δήμῳ περὶ ὧν εἰσήγγ[ηται
5   —. Λ]αβέριος ᾽Αμοινος φιλοσέβαστος, ὁ γραμμ[ατεὺς
τοῦ δ]ήμου· ἐπεψήφισαν δὲ οἱ στ[ρ]ατηγοὶ τῆς
πόλεως φιλοσέβαστοι·
᾽Επειδὴ ἡ π]ροεστῶσα τῆς πόλεως ἡμῶν θεὸς ῎Αρτε[μις
οὐ μόνον] ἐν τῇ ἑαυτῆς πατρίδι ἀτιμᾶται, ἣν ἀ[λλων
10   ἀπασῶν πόλεων] ἐνδοξοτέραν διὰ τῆς ἰδίας θειότητ[ος
B (2)   πεποίηκεν, ἀ]λλὰ καὶ παρὰ [῞Ελλησίν τε κ]αὶ [β]αρβάρ[ο]ις, ὥ[στε
πολλ]αχοῦ ἀνεῖσθαι αὐτῆς ἱε[ρά τε καὶ τιμάς· ἀξία δέ ἐστιν
αὐτή τε εἰδρύσθαι καὶ βωμοὺς [αὐτῇ ἀνακεῖσθαι διὰ
τὰς ὑπ᾽ αὐτῆς γεινομένας ἐναργεῖς ἐπι[φανείας·
15   καὶ τοῦτο δὲ μέγιστον τοῦ περὶ αὐτὴν σε[βασ-
μοῦ ἐστιν τεκμήριον, τὸ ἐπώνυμον αὐτ[ῆς
εἶναι μῆνα καλούμενον παρ᾽ ἡ[μ]ῖν μὲν ᾽Αρτ[εμισι-
ῶνα παρὰ δὲ Μακεδόσιν καὶ τοῖς λοιποῖς ἔ[θνεσιν
τοῖς ῞Ελληνικοῖς καὶ ταῖς ἐν αὐτοῖς πόλεσι[ν
20   ᾽Αρτεμίσιον, ἐν ᾧ μηνὶ πανηγύρεις τε καὶ ἱερ[ο-
μηνίαι ἐπιτελοῦνται, διαφερόντως δὲ ἐν [τῇ
ἡμετέρᾳ πόλει τῇ τροφῷ τῆς ἰδίας θεοῦ τῆς ᾽Εφ[εσί-
α]ς· προσῆκον δὲ εἶναι ἡγούμενος ὁ δῆμος [ὁ
᾽Εφεσίων ὅλον τὸν μῆνα τὸν ἐπώνυμον τοῦ θ[είου
25   ὀ]νόματος εἶναι ἱερὸν καὶ ἀνακεῖσθαι τῇ θεῷ
ἐ]δοκίμασεν δ[ι]ὰ τοῦδε τοῦ ψηφίσματος [κατα-
στῆσ]αι τὴν περὶ αὐτοῦ θρησκείαν· διὸ [δεδόχθαι
ἱερ]ὸν τὸν μῆνα τὸν ᾽Αρτεμισιῶνα εἶ[ναι πάσας
τ]ὰς ἡμέρας, ἄγεσθαι δὲ ἐπ᾽ αὐταῖς μῆν[α ὅλον
30   δι·] ἔτευς τὰς ἑορτὰς καὶ τὴν τῶν ᾽Αρτεμ[ισίων πανηγυ-
ριν καὶ τὰς ἱερομηνίας, ἅτε τοῦ μηνὸς ὅλου ἀνακειμέ-
νου τῇ θεῷ· οὕτω γὰρ ἐπὶ τὸ ἄμεινον τῆς [θεοῦ τιμωμέ-
ν]ης ἡ πόλις ἡμ[ῶν ἐ]νδοξοτέρα τε καὶ εὐδ[αιμονεστέρα
εἰς τὸ[ν ἅπα]ντα διαμενεῖ χ[ρόνον.

C (1)   ῾Η πατρὶς
Τ. Αἴλιον Τ. υἱὸν Κλ[αύδιον
Μαρκιανὸν Πρίσκο[ν τὸν
ἀγωνοθέτην καὶ πα[νηγυριάρχην
5   τ]ῶν μεγάλων ᾽Αρτ[εμισίων,
καὶ] πρῶτον αὐτ[ὸν ποιήσαντα
C (2)   τὴν πανήγυριν κατὰ τέλειο[ν,
καὶ ἐκεχειρίας εἰς ὅλον τὸν
ἐπώνυμον τῆς θεοῦ μῆνα
10   τυχόντα, καὶ τὴν ᾽Αρτεμισι-
ακὴν κρίσιν καταστήσαντα,
καὶ τὰ θέματα τοῖς ἀγωνισ-
ταῖς αὐξήσαντα, καὶ ἀνδρι-
άντας τῶν νικησάντων
13   ἀναστήσαντα·
τὴν τειμὴν ἀναστήσαντο[ς
Λ. Φαινίου Φαύστου
τοῦ συνγενοῦς αὐτοῦ.

Although the lower portion of the monument is not in the British Museum, it seemed best to print the whole of each inscription in uncials, a careful copy having been made by me from the stone in the Ashmolean. *Text of* A. *Line* 1 : The space shows that the proconsul's first name is wanting : cp. A, line 5. *Line* 7 : The marks upon the stone prove that the line originally read thus : ΤΗΣ[ΠΑ]- ΝΗ[ΓΥΡΕΩΣ. *Line* 8 : Though only fragments of letters remain, yet we may make sure of the letters

T.ΝΑΡΤΕ.

Text of B. There is little room for 'doubt about readings, as the surface is well preserved. Line 9 : previous editors have read ΤΙΜΑΤΑΙ wrongly (for ἀτιμᾶται), which quite reverses the sense. The endings of the lines (excepting 11, 12, 25, 26, 28–34) are restored, not from conjecture, but from earlier copies made when the stone was less injured. In line 11 [Β]ΑΡΒΑΡ[Ο]ΙΣ may be considered certain; the remains of letters will allow of no other word but this. The restoration of these lines (11 foll.) cannot therefore be far from correct. Line 25 : ὅλον or πάντα is suggested by Röhl (Schedae Epigraph. p. 11) to fill up the line at the end. Line 26 : [διατιθέν]αι seems to be a conjecture of Muratori's, accepted by Böckh. Line 32 is restored by the conjecture of Röhl, *ibid.* One or two minor corrections have been made also.

Text of C. Line 6 : ποιήσαντα or a similar word must be restored. Line 7 : Böckh reads καὶ ἀτελεί[ᾶ]ν i. e. exemptions, governed by τυχόντα. But the stone reads Ο, not Ω : κατὰ τέλειο[ν] sc. τρόπον resembles κατὰ ἑκούσιον in St. Paul's Epistle to Philemon, 14, where see Bp. Lightfoot's note, and compare Lobeck, Phryn., p. 4.

M. Waddington, Fastes Asiatiques, p. 224, points out that Popillius Carus Pedo was consul suffectus A. D. 148, and probably proconsul Asiae for the proconsular year A. D. 160–1, the last year of Antoninus. This then is the date of our inscription, which Böckh had connected with the reign of Tiberius ('factum fortasse tum cum asylorum examinarentur jura, Tac. Ann. iii, 61').

The three inscriptions all refer to the same affair. It appears from several expressions in them, that Pedo the proconsul had given offence to the Ephesians by transacting public business (possibly holding his conventus) at Ephesos on some of the holy days of the month Artemision (= March). This act was not only injudicious, but also contrary to the custom and express injunctions of previous proconsuls (A, lines 3–9). Accordingly the Ephesian senate made a formal protest by ψήφισμα (A, lines 3–5), to which Pedo very courteously replies in A. He owns his mistake, and reaffirms the ordinance of his predecessors that the sacred days in question shall not be profaned by business (ἱεσχειρία, justitium). In compliment to the Ephesians he dates his reply by naming in flattering terms the ἀγωνοθέτης or president of the Artemision for that year. It does not appear however that the Ephesians had ever claimed more than *some* of the days of the month Artemision as holy days. The phrase πάσης ἀποδοχῆς ἄξιος (line 21) is very common in later Greek, especially in Diodoros : see Field, Otium Norvicense, Part iii, on 1 Timothy, i, 15.

B is a decree of the boulè and demos, following up the reply of the proconsul, though without directly mentioning it. The decree is moved by the γραμματεὺς τοῦ δήμου Laberius Amoenus, whom we find named in No. DLVII as also the prytanis. On the γραμματεὺς τοῦ δήμου I have spoken on p. 81. The decree itself begins by complaining that the Ephesian goddess, whose worship had hitherto been universally recognised, was now being set at nought in her own native city (πατρίδι, line 9, τροφῷ τῆς θεοῦ, line 22; see Strabo, xiv, p. 639 *fin.*), so that a similar neglect might be expected to be shown elsewhere. Therefore by way (it would seem) of reparation to the goddess, and to prevent such neglect in the future, it is enacted by this decree that henceforth not only some but all the days of the month Artemision shall be public holidays, and the entire month, as its name suggested be dedicated absolutely to Artemis. The parallel to this dedication in the Mary-month of the modern Roman Calendar has been often noted. It is evident that the ordinance of Pedo (A) was extended by this ψήφισμα, inasmuch as he had only provided that all sacred days in the month Artemision should be marked by a justitium: the ψήφισμα brought every day of the month under this provision. The term ἱερομηνίαι (line 21) is thus explained by the scholiast on Pindar. Nem. iii, 1 : ἱερομηνίαι δὲ λέγονται αἱ ἐν τῷ μηνὶ ἱεραὶ ἡμέραι, οἰαιδήποτε θεοῖς ἀνειμέναι. Compare Hermann, Monatskunde, p. 17 foll.

C naturally occupies the front of the base, as explaining the significance of the statue which it originally supported. Here we recover the full name of the ἀγωνοθέτης whose year had been made memorable by this vindication of the goddess, and this extension of her festival (lines 1–10). His other services are enumerated in lines 10–15. He appears to have marked this year's festival by increasing the money-prizes (θέματα) of the victors, and by setting up statues of them at his own expense. The words καὶ τὴν Ἀρτεμισιακὴν κρίσιν καταστήσαντα are obscure. It is very fanciful to explain this κρίσις as the ordeal undergone by maidens who were to be dedicated to the goddess. (So Zimmermann, Ephesos, p. 109.) The ordeal is mentioned only by Achilles Tatius (viii, 6, 12), who is probably romancing, and the κρίσις of our inscription must refer to the management of the Artemisian contests. Most probably the improvement in the κρίσις or adjudgment of the prizes which is thus delicately alluded to, was the increased salary of the judges through the generosity of this ἀγωνοθέτης.

The names of the Ephesian months, and their position in the Calendar, have been discussed on pp. 78 foll. The language in B, lines 17 foll., is curious as calling attention to a well known dialectical difference in the Greek names for months. Among the Ionians the names of the months usually terminate in -ιών : but in -ιος among the Aeolians and Dorians, and therefore also among the Macedonians, whose language so far as it was Hellenic was nearest akin to Doric.

The language of B, lines 1 foll., recalls the speech of Demetrius in Acts xix, 27–28. If we may suppose the Salutaris decrees (A.D. 104), which are all but contemporaneous with Pliny's correspondence with Trajan, to mark a wave of reaction against the advance of Christianity in Asia Minor, then we may further interpret the present document as an involuntary confession of the subsequent decline of the Artemis-worship under the growing influence of the new faith.

A–B A large wall-stone of white marble. Height 2 ft. 11½ in., width 2 ft. 9½ in.   'Found in the Great Theatre,' see Wood, Ephesus,
p. 71 (he there describes it).   Published by C. Curtius, Hermes iv, p. 197, foll. ; not given by Wood in his Appendix of inscriptions.
Line 19 is sunk below the surface of the stone.   C is another wall-stone, unpublished, but obviously belonging to the same. It
measures 1 ft. 11 in. by 2 ft. 2½ in. ; edge enure only on right.

A

```
        ΔΟΓΗ      ι ΡΑΦ    Α      ΜΑι ΚΟΣΚΑιΣΕΛΑι
        ΜΡΤC     ΙΦΗΚΑ            ΓΑΙΟΣΦΛΑΒΙΟΣΛΟ
```

B

```
                        - ΑΓΑΘΗ  ᴗ  ΤΫΧΗ ·

        ΩΘΕΝΥΠΟΤΟΝΟΙΚΙΣΜΟΝ - ΤΗΣΠΟΛιΩΣ
        ΤΑΝΤΑ - ΠΕΡιΤΕΜΥΣΤΗΡΙΩΝ · ΚΑΙΘΥΣΙΩΝ
        ΘΙΑΙΔΡΥΣΑΜΕΝΟΝΔΕΚΑΙΝΕΩ - ΚΑΙΑΓΑΛΜΑ - ΣΩΤΕΙΡ
        ΤΑΣ - ΕΚΤΩΝΚΟΙΝΩΝ - ΤΗΣΓΕΡΟΥΣΙΑΣΧΡΗΜΑΤΩΝ - ΕΚΙ
   5    ΠΙΠΛΕΙΣΤΩΝ - ΔΙΑΤΙΝΑ - ΕΚΔΙΑΝ - ΧΡΗΜΑΤΩΝ - ΕΤΕΣΙΝ
        ΥΤΟΥΣΥΝΕΔΡΙΟΥΗΜΩΝ - ΤΗΣΑΥΤΟΥΕΠΙΜΕΛΕΙΑ - ΕΞ
        ΝΥΓΕΡΟΥΣΙΑΝ · ΕΥΣΕΒΕΙΝ · ΚΑΙΘΥΕΙΝΤΗΤΕΠΡΟΚΑΘΗΓΕΙ
        ΥΤΟΚΡΑΤΟΡΙΚΑΙΣΑΡι · Μ · ΑΥΡ · ΚΟΜΜΟΔΩ · ΑΝΤΩΝΕΙΝΩ
        ΟΝΜΗΕΛΑΤΟΝΑΝΑΛΙΣΚΕΙΝ · ΕΙΣΤΗΝΕΥΩΧΙΑΝ · ΑΤ
   10   ΑΝΑΛΩΜΑ · ΤΟΥΔΕΙΠΝΟΥ · ΕΞΩΘΕΝ · ΚΑΙΕΚΤΗΣΤ᷉
        ΥΡΩΣΑΙ - ΚΑΙΝΟΜΟΘΕΤΗΣΑΙ · ΕΙΣΑΕΙΔΙΑΤΟΥΔΕΤ
        ΜΕΝΗΕΥΣΕΒΕΙΑ · ΝΟΜΟΘΕΣΙΑΝ · ΩΣΑΙ
        ΟΤΕΙΜΟΥΜΕΝΟΥΤΟΥΕΚΔΙΚΟΥ · ΙΣΤΗ
        ΚΕΝΔΕΤΑΙΣΚΑΤΑΚΛΙΣΕΣΙΝ · ΚΑΤΕ
   15   ΟΡΟΙ · ΕΠΙΤΑΙΣΟΜΟΙΑΙΣ - ΕΥΩΧΙΑΣ
        - ΤΟΙΣΙΡΟΥΠΑΡΧΟΥΣΙΝΠΟΡΟΙΣ
        Σ · ΠΕΡΙΤΟΝΝΑΟΝ · ΤΗΣΣΩΤΕΙΡ
        ΑΣΤΗΝ - ΤΟΥΔΩΛ-᾿ ΤΟΥΜΗΝΣ
        Ν · ΑΡΙ
```

C

```
   20       ΣΙΩΤΟ      ΤΕΕΚΔΙΚΟΥ ᴗ
        ΟΙΝΗ ΙΑΝΤΑΗΓΕΡΟΥΣΙΑ · ΤΩι
        ᵕᴵΥΠΕΥΘΥΝΟΝΑΥΤΟΝΚΑΤΕΣΙΙ
        ΟΝΤΑΣ · Ει    ΕΔΟΞΕΝΤΟΝΚΑΘΕΤΟ
        ΝΔΙΔΟΝΑ ΩΑΝΚΟΙΝΗΠΑΣΑ · Η
   25        ᴖ ΕΥΣΕΒΕΙᴬ
        ΓΡΑΜΜΑΓΕΥΟΝΤΟΣ · ΤΩΝΠΡ
```

A

```
.........................................................
... δε]δογμ[ατο]γράφ[ηκ]α·   Μάρκος Καισέλ(λ)ιος Μαρκιανὸς φιλοσέβαστος
δεδογ]ματο[γρ]άφηκα·        Γάιος Φλάβιος Λο[..... φιλοσέβαστος δεδογματογράφηκα.
```

B

```
        Ἀγαθῇ   τύχῃ.
.............................. κυρ]ωθὲν ὑπὸ τὸν οἰκισμὸν τῆς πόλεως
............................. πάντα περί τε μυστηρίων καὶ θυσιῶν
............. θια ἱδρυσάμενον δὲ καὶ νεὼ καὶ ἄγαλμα Σωτείρ[ας
.............................. τας ἐκ τῶν κοινῶν τῆς γερουσίας χρημάτων ἐκα
   5    ............................. ἐ]πὶ πλεῖστ(ο)ν διά τινα ἐκδίαν χρημάτων ἔτεσιν
........................... υ τοῦ συνεδρίου ἡμῶν τῆς αὐτοῦ ἐπιμελεία(ς) ἐξ
.................... τὴ]ν γερουσίαν εὐσεβεῖν καὶ θύειν τῇ τε προκαθηγ[ε]τιδι
τῆς πόλεως θεᾷ Ἀρτέμιδι καὶ Α]ὐτοκράτορι Καίσαρι Μ. Αὐρ. Κομμόδῳ Ἀντωνείνῳ
............................. ον μὴ ἐλατ(τ)ον ἀναλίσκειν εἰς τὴν εὐωχίαν ατ
   10   ........................... ἀνάλωμα τοῦ δείπνου ἔξωθεν καὶ ἐκ τῆς τ
............................ κυ]ρῶσαι καὶ νομοθετῆσαι εἰσαεὶ διὰ τοῦδε τ-
αῦ ψηφίσματος ................... ] μένη εὐσεβείᾳ νομοθεσίαν ὥς αι
.......................... φιλ]οτειμουμένου τοῦ ἐκδίκου ιστη
.......................... κεν δὲ ταῖς κατακλίσεσιν κατε
   15   ......................... οροι ἐπὶ ταῖς ὁμοίαις εὐωχία(ι)ς
```

```
.................................. τοῖς προυπάρχουσιν πόροις
.................................. ς περὶ τὸν ναὸν τῆς Σωτείρ[ας
.................................. Σεβ]αστὴν τοῦ δωδεκά[τ]ου μηνὸ[ς
.................................. ν αρι..................
```

(*How much is here lost is uncertain.*)

jamb of wall stone.

```
C  20    .... εἴτε ἰ]διάτο[υ εἴ]τε ἐκδίκου ο .....   ......................
        ..... κ]οινῇ πάντα ἡ γερουσία τῶ[ν ....     ......................
        ...... καὶ ὑπεύθυνον αὐτὸν κατεστ[η ...     ......................
        ....... οντας ε[ὖ?] ἔδοξεν τὸν καθ᾽ ἕτο[ς   ἐνιαυτὸν] .............
        ....... ν διδόνα[ι] ᾧ ἂν κοινῇ πᾶσα ἡ ..    ......................
  25                     ςν εὐσεβεία[ς  ἕνεκα?]
        γραμματεύοντος τῶν πρ[εσβυ-   τέρων τοῦ δεῖνος ..].........
```

A-B. As this is a wall-stone, the inscriptions engraved upon it were continued upon other slabs, and we cannot determine the exact arrangement of the lines. This slab is entire on the top, bottom, and right. It contains part of two inscriptions.

A is the conclusion of a decree of the senate of Ephesos, and receives illustration from two decrees in the Salutaris inscription which have similar signatures at their foot. Indeed one of those signatures is the same as one of these, Μάρκος Καισίλ(λ)ᾳ[ος Μαρκιανός: so that the date of A will be about the same as the Salutaris inscription, viz. *circa* 104 A.D.

B-C is rather later in date, belonging to the reign of Commodus (line 8) A.D. 180-192. It deals with the celebration of certain sacrifices, lectisternia etc. in honour of ' the saviour goddess,' also entitled ἡ προκαθηγέτις, and of the Emperor. This expression in lines 7, 8 resembles C. I. 4332 (an inscription from Phaselis in Lykia) where we read [ἱερα]τε[ύο]αντα [τῆ]ς προκαθ[ηγ]έ[τι]δος τῆς πόλεος θεᾶς Ἀθηνᾶς [Πολ]άδος καὶ τῶ[ν θ]εῶν Σε[β]α[σ]τῶν. Curtius accordingly restores this line as it is given in the cursive text ; and this may afford some clue to the probable length of the lines. The preamble (lines 1-4) speaks of certain ancient sacrifices and mysteries which had been celebrated from the time of the foundation of Ephesos in connexion with a shrine and image of τῆς Σωτείρας, the expense being defrayed out of the 'public moneys of the γερουσία.' Lines 5, 6 speak of these ceremonies as having been intermitted for some years owing to lack of funds. It is resolved (lines 7-10) that the traditional celebrations shall be revived in honour of the goddess and of the reigning Emperor Commodus, without stinting expense. In line 11 it is resolved to put the festival upon a new and permanent footing by fresh enactments. In line 18 we seem to have the date of the festival, viz. ' in the 12th month.'

Such is the outline of an inscription which, if not so mutilated, would be very interesting. There are several points which call for remark. The lapidary seems to have made some mistakes. ἐ]πὶ πλεῖστ(ο)ν is probably intended in line 5, and ἐπιμελεία(ς) in line 6 ; certainly εὐωχία(ι)ς in line 15, and ἔλα(τ)τον line 9. Accordingly it is doubtful whether ἐκδίαν in line 5 is a debased form of ἐκδίκαν, or a lapidary's blunder. In line 3 νεώ is a later variant for νεών:

compare Lobeck's Phrynichus p. 186 and C. I. 3148, line 19. In A we may restore Καισίλ(λ)[ος.

Line 1. κυρ]ωθέν is a mere conjecture ; cp. line 11. We should understand οἰκισμὸς τῆς πόλεως to signify the founding of Ephesos by Androklos. Line 2. As we cannot help identifying the Σώτειρα of lines 3 and 17, and the προκαθηγέτις of line 7 with the Ephesian Artemis, we must further conclude that these mysteries and sacrifices were in her honour. Similarly in No. DLXXXVII *post* ἡ κυρία Σώτειρα is manifestly Artemis.

The inscription, C. I. 3002, in honour of a priestess of Artemis at Ephesos sufficiently proves that her worship included μυστήρια. And Strabo (xiv, p. 640) speaks of τινὰς μυστικὰς θυσίας which were yearly celebrated at Ephesos in memory of the birth of Artemis and the travail of Leto. When Strabo (*ibid.*) speaks of the εὐωχίας and συμπόσια which accompanied that festival, one is inclined to suppose it to be the very festival mentioned in our inscription. Moreover the ἄγαλμα and ναός of line 3 might well be sought among the πλειόνων ναῶν with ἀρχαῖα ξόανα referred to by Strabo (*ibid.*) as standing on Mount Solmissos. For a further discussion of this festival see above pp. 79-80.

Line 4. γερουσία is probably another name for συνέδριον line 6, and πρεσβύτεροι line 26. The relation of this body to the βουλή and δῆμος,—from which it was certainly distinct.—has been fully discussed on p. 75. Line 13. An ἐκδικος (or σύνδικος) was a lawyer employed by a state to represent its interests and plead its cause, as plaintiff or defendant, before some foreign power: see Marquardt, Röm. Alterth. iv, p. 522; and C. I. 1732 (an award of land at Daulis, temp. Hadrian). Thus Cicero (Ad Fam. xiii, 56) speaks of ἔκδικοι to be sent from Mylasa to Rome to dispute a claim upon the town funds for debt. But it is not clear what such an ἔκδικος has to do with our inscription. Waddington-Le Bas (on No. 1602 a and 1176) endeavours to distinguish between the functions of the ἔκδικοι and σύνδικοι: but I think Menadier (Qua condicione Ephesii, etc., p. 97) is right in pronouncing them identical. In line 18 I restore [Σεβ]αστήν sc. ἡμέραν comparing No. CCCCLXXXI, line 320, where the second of Anthesterion is entitled Σεβαστή i. e. sacred to the Emperor. The middle letters of δωδεκά[τ]ου are broken, but enough is preserved to make the word certain. The proper name of the 12th Ephesian month is not known. We find the expression ὄγδοος μήν in C. I. 3005, and the designation of months by numerals is not uncommon (see index to Böckh's C. I. p. 46 foll. and p. 78 *ante*).

C is a fragment of the same decree, and probably followed close after B, very much as it is placed in the cursive text. It appears to contain the end of the document. Line 23 : καθ' ἔτος is a common form ; compare C. I. 2347 c, line 48 ; 2693 c; Addenda 3641 b, line 5 ; 3902 b, 4252 b, etc. It may be compared with ἐφ' ἴσῃ which is common enough in the Ephesian decrees. Nor is ὁ καθ' ἔτος ἐνιαυτός for 'annus quisque' without parallel: see C. I. Addenda, 3641 b, lines 5 and 38.

The ceremony of lectisternia, frequently met with in Roman religion, was widely known among the Greeks also under the name of Θεοξένια (see Deneken, De Theoxeniis). At Athens a decree of the commencement of the third century B. C. (C. I. A. ii, Pt. 1, No. 305) awards praises to certain citizens who

—— ἔθ[υον τάς τε θ]-

[υ]σίας τῶ[ι Διὶ τῷ Σωτῆρι καὶ τ]ῇ 'Αθη[νᾷ τῇ]
[Σω]τείρ[ᾳ καὶ τῶν ἄλλων ἐπεμε]λήθησα[ν μετὰ]
[το]ῦ ἱερ[έως καλῶς καὶ φιλοτίμω]ς, ἐπεμελήθη-
[σα]ν δὲ [καὶ τῆς στρώσεως τῆς κλί]νης καὶ τῆς κ-
[οσ]μή[σεως τῆς τραπέζης· ἀγαθῇ]ι τύχῃ, δεδόχ-
[θα]ι κ.τ.λ.

Again, in C. I. A. ii, Pt. 2, Nos. 948 and 949, similar lectisternia to Pluto are spoken of : Τούσδε ἐπιώψ[ατο] ὁ ἱεροφάντης [τὴν κλίνην στρῶ]|σαι τῷ Πλούτων[ι] καὶ τὴν τράπ[εζαν κοσμῆσαι] ἱκατὰ τὴν μα[ν]τείαν τοῦ [θεοῦ]· κ.τ.λ. And τούς ἐπιοφθ[έντας τήν τε]| κλίνην στρῶσαι τῷ [Πλού-τωνι καὶ τὴν]| τράπεζαν κοσμῆσα[ι κατὰ τὴν μαντείαν]| τοῦ θε[οῦ]· κ.τ.λ. The date of these two documents is about 300 B. C. Compare Köhler, Hermes vi, p. 107.

CCCCLXXXIV.

Fragment of a stelē of white marble : the moulding which surmounted it has been chiselled off. Unpublished. Height 10 in., width 11½ in.

ϽΣΕΛ∪_
ΒΟΥΛΗΚΑΙ
Λ∩ΦΟΥ

[Τῆς μεγίστ-]
[ης 'Εφεσίων]
πόλε]ως ἔδοξ[εν
τῇ] βουλῇ καὶ
τῷ δή]μῳ· Φοῦ[σκος vel simile quid.
κ.τ.λ.

Probably from the heading of a decree.

SECTION II.

LETTERS FROM KINGS AND EMPERORS.

CCCCLXXXV.

Fragment of a stelè of white marble; height 10½ in., width 12½ in. Unpublished. Discovered by Mr. Wood.

```
            ΜΑΙ
    ΤΙΟΧΟΣΕΦΕΣΙΩΝΤΗ
  ΡΟΣΗΜΑΣΚΥΜΑΙΟΙΠΡΟΤΕΡ
  ΙΜΙΝΩΝΙΔΙΟΞΕΝΟΣΕΜΦΑ
  ΑΘΥΣΤΕΡΕΙΝΚΑΙΜΗΔΓΜ
```

Περὶ (?) Κυ]μαί[ων·

Βασιλεὺς 'Αν]τίοχος 'Εφεσίων τῇ [βουλῇ καὶ τῷ δήμῳ χαίρειν· οἱ ἀφικόμενοι? π]ρὸς ἡμᾶς Κυμαῖοι πρότερ[ον . . . . καὶ νῦν ὁ δεῖνα . .
. . . . . ἡμῖν ἃν ἰδιόξενος ἐμφα[νίζει ὑμᾶς . . . .
. . . . μὴ κ]αθυστερεῖν καὶ μηδεμ[ία . . . . .

Part of a royal letter, probably of Antiochos III, perhaps written towards the beginning of his struggle with Rome.

We may conjecture that this was one of the many letters despatched by Antiochos from his winter quarters at Chalkis, B.C. 192–1, like the letter to Iasos, No. CCCCXLII ante. Ephesos was at this time the central point of the king's interests in Asia (see Livy, xxxvii, 10–11). We may be sure that the Asiatic cities watched with an eager and personal interest the course of the king's campaign in Greece proper; and naturally in most of the towns there was a Roman party ready to turn to the best account any grievance against the king or his allies. A year later (B.C. 190), after the defeat of Antiochos at Thermopylæ, Kymè was on the side of Rome. But later on in the same summer, upon the success of the king's admiral Polyxenidas, Kymè went over to Seleukos, who held the chief command by land in those regions for his father (Livy, xxxvii, 11). In 189 B.C., when the Romans settled the affairs of Asia at the close of the war, Kymè was one of the cities which were allowed their freedom,—a privilege which it owed not only to its old renown, but perhaps also to the influence of the strong Roman party within its walls (Livy, xxxviii, 39).

If this view of the contemporary politics of Kymè be correct, we can the better divine what were its relations with Ephesos, and what impelled Antiochos in the winter of B.C. 192–1 to write this letter to Ephesos. Probably the Roman party at Kymè had been making capital out of some grievance between the Kymeans and Ephesos. Envoys had come to Antiochos from Kymè, making complaint (line 3): upon which the king writes to the Ephesians to bespeak their consideration for Kymè, and to remove the grievance which threatened to alienate that city from his cause.

CCCCLXXXVI.

On a large marble slab, surmounted by a moulding: height 2 ft. 6½ in.; width 4 ft. 3½ in. Found in the Great Theatre. C. Curtius, Hermes, iv (1870), p. 178; Wood, Ephesus, p. 71; Appendix, Inscriptions from the Great Theatre, No. 17; Waddington, Fastes p. 191; Dittenberger, Sylloge, No. 284.

```
    ΛΛ _ ΙΡΘεΟΥΤΡΑΙΝΟΥΠΑΡΘΙΚΟΥ – ΥΙΟΣ
    ΙΩΝΟΣΤΡΑΙΑΝΟΣΛΛΡΙΑΝΟΣΣΕΒΑΣΤΟΣ
    ΙΕΓΙΣΤΟΣΔΗΜΑΡΧΙΚΗΣΕΞΟΥΣΙΑΣ  ΤΟ  Δ
    Ο . Γ - ΕΦΕΣΙΩΝΤΗΙΓΕΡΟΥΣΙΑΙ . ΧΑΙΡΕΙΝ
  5 ΜΟΔΕΣΤΟΣΟΚΡΑΤΙΣΤΟΣΕΥΕΠΟΙΗΣΕΝΤΑΔΙΚ
```

ΝΕΙΜΑΣΕΝΤΗΙΚΡΙΣΕΙΕΠΕΙΔΕΠΟΛΛΑΟΥΣΕΔΗΛ
ΣΦ   ΄ΕΣΘΑΙΧΡΗΜΑΤΑΥΜΕΤΕΡΑΟΥΣΙΑΣΤΩΝΔΕΔΑΝΙΣ
ΝΩ   ΑΤΕΧΟΝΤΑΣΟΥΦΑΣΚΟΝΤΑΣΔΕΚΛΗΡΟΝΟΜΕΙΝΤΟΥ͞
ΚΑΙ   ΤΟΥΣΧΡΕΩΣΤΑΣΟΝΤΑΣΠΕΠΟΜΦΑΥΜΩΝΤΟΑΝ͞
10   ΤΟΥΨΗΦΙΣΜΑΤΟΣΚΟΡΝΗΛΙΩΙΠΡΕΙΣΚΩΙΤΩΙΚΡΑΤΙΣΤΩΙ
ΑΝΘΥΠΑΤΩΙΙΝΑΕΙΤΙΤΟΙΟΥΤΟΝΕΙΗΕΠΙΛΕΞΗΤΑΙΤΙΝΑ
ΟΣΚΡΙΝΕΙΤΕΤΑΜΦΙΣΒΗΤΟΥΜΕΝΑΚΑΙΕΙΣΠΡΑΞΕΙΠΑΝΤΑ
ΟΣΑΑΝΟΦΕΙΛΗΤΑΙΤΗΙΓΕΡΟΥΣΙΑΙ   ΟΠΡΕΣΒΕΥΩΝΗΝ
ΚΑΣΚΕΛΛΙΟΣΓ   ΤΙΚΟΣΩΙΤΟΕΦΟΔΙΟΝΔΟΘΗΤΩΣΕΙΓΕΜΗ
15   ΠΡΟΙΚΑΥΠΓ   ΓΟΠΡΕΣΒΕΥΣΕΙΝ - ΕΥΤΥΧΕΙΤΕ - π̄̄.Ε.Κ.ΟΚΤΩΒΡΙΩΝ
ΠΛΙΟΥΡΟΥΤΕΙΛΙΟΥΒΑΣΣΟΥ

Αὐτοκράτωρ] Κα[ῖ]σαρ, θεοῦ Τραϊ(α)νοῦ Παρθικοῦ υἱός,
θεοῦ Νερούα υ[ἱ]ωνός, Τραιανὸς Ἀδριανὸς Σεβαστός,
ἀρχιερεὺς] μέγιστος, δημαρχικῆς ἐξουσίας τὸ δ,
ὕπατος τ]ὸ γ̄, Ἐφεσίων τῇ γερουσίᾳ χαίρειν.

5   Μέττιος] Μόδεστος ὁ κράτιστος εὖ ἐποίησεν τὰ δί[αια
ὑμῖν? κατα]νείμας ἐν τῇ κρίσει. Ἐπεὶ δὲ πολλοὺς ἐδηλ[ώσατε
σφ[ετερί]ζεσθαι χρήματα ὑμέτερα, οὐσίας τῶν δεδανισ[μέ-
νω[ν κ]ατέχοντας οὐ φάσκοντας δὲ κληρονομεῖν, τοὺς [δὲ
καὶ [αὔ]τοὺς χρεώστας ὄντας, πέπομφα ὑμῶν τὸ ἀντ[ίγραφον
10   τοῦ ψηφίσματος Κορνηλίῳ Πρείσκῳ τῷ κρατίστῳ
ἀνθυπάτῳ, ἵνα, εἴ τι τοιοῦτον εἴη, ἐπιλέξηταί τινα
ὃς κρινεῖ τε τἀμφισβητούμενα καὶ εἰσπράξει πάντα,
ὅσα ἂν ὀφείληται τῇ γερουσίᾳ. Ὁ πρεσβεύων ἦν
Κασκίλλιος [Πον?]τικός, ᾧ τὸ ἐφόδιον δοθήτω, εἴ γε μὴ
15   προῖκα ὑπέ[σχε]το πρεσβεύσειν. Εὐτυχεῖτε. Πρ(ὸ) ῑ Κ(αλανδῶν) Ὀκτωβρίων.

Γραμματεύοντος Πο]πλίου Ῥουτειλίου Βάσσου.

The heading of the letter is easily restored by the comparison of similar documents; e. g. No. CCCCLXXXVII. It is a letter of Hadrian to the γερουσία of the Ephesians; dated, as we learn in lines 3 and 15, September 27, A. D. 120,—that year being the 4th of Hadrian's tribunicia potestas.

The stone is but slightly injured, and the restorations pretty certain. Line 1: the lapidary omitted the Α in Τραΐ(α)νοῦ, and in line 7 ΔΕΔΑΝΙΣ- is a late spelling for ΔΕΔΑΝΕΙΣ-. Line 5: Wood, after Waddington (Fastes, p. 189) reads [Μέττιος] Μόδεστος; M. Waddington makes him proconsul of Asia towards the end of Trajan's reign or the beginning of Hadrian's: he occurs as proconsul of Asia in a bilingual inscription from za Æni in Phrygia, C. I. 3835 (compare Addenda, p. 1064), and more perfectly given by Waddington-Le Bas, iii, 860–3, and C. I. L. iii, No. 355. Lines 5–6: Curtius writes τὰ διε[ασθέντα], which is hardly probable. I read τὰ δίκ[αια ὑμῖν κατα]νείμας, and suppose Modestus as proconsul to have given a judgment in favour of the γερουσία, charging the debtors with the principal and due proportion of interest thereon. On the γερουσία I have spoken at length, ante pp. 74–79. In the Bull. de Corr. Hellén. xi (1887), p. 108, M. Radet publishes three letters of Hadrian to the city of Stratonicea, dated A. D. 127. His article is an interesting study of Imperial letters generally.

The drift of the Emperor's letter is as follows. The Ephesian gerousia appears to have lent certain moneys to various persons, and finding the borrowers to be slack in their repayment, has obtained a judg-ment, τῇ κρίσει (line 6), in its favour from Modestus. As, however, much difficulty was still found in recovering the debts, the gerousia applies directly to the Emperor by means of a ψήφισμα (line 10 and ἐδηλώσατε, line 6), sending it to him by an Ephesian citizen Cascellius (line 14), by whom also the Emperor returns this reply. M. Waddington (Fastes, p. 191) restores the cognomen as [Ἀτ]τικός: but there is space for three letters, and the remains of the first letter suggest Π. It appears that while some of the debtors were the original borrowers of the money (αὐτοὺς χρεώστας ὄντας, line 9), a difficulty had arisen in other cases by the fact that the original borrowers were dead, and those who had come into possession of their property now repudiated the debt, refusing to own themselves the heirs and legitimate representatives of the deceased (οὐ φάσκοντας κληρονομεῖν, line 8). At the end of line 8 Dittenberger wrongly follows Waddington in reading τού-[των δέ]; the Σ however is visible on the stone. The Emperor assures them that he has sent a copy of their application to the proconsul of Asia, Cornelius Priscus, directing him to make enquiry and appoint some one to enforce the payment of debts due to the γερουσία (lines 9 foll). For Cornelius Priscus, see Waddington, Fastes, p. 191. He was probably the Priscus whom Pliny mentions in several letters (Ep. iii, 21, heading; v, 20, 7, where he is styled consularis). Marquardt (Römische Alterth. iv, p. 406) accepts it as proved that Cornelius Priscus was consul (i. e. suffectus) A. D. 103, and proconsul Asiæ A. D. 120-1, according to the date of this inscription. Menadier (Qua condicione Ephesii usi sint, p. 55) compares C. I. 2987 δ, an Ephesian inscription in honour of a Roman citizen who is described as δοθέντα [λογιστὴ]ν ὑπὸ θεοῦ Ἀδριανοῦ [τῇ φιλ]οσεβάστῳ γερουσίᾳ. This then was the commissioner appointed in pursuance of lines 11-12 of the Imperial letter: ἐπιλέξηταί τινα | ὃς κρινεῖ τε τὰμφισβη-τούμενα καὶ εἰσπράξει πάντα, | ὅσα ἂν ὀφείληται τῇ γερουσίᾳ. In line 16 I take P. Rutilius Bassus to be the γραμμα-τεύς of the gerousia : see pp. 77 and 82 *ante*. It is possible that No. ccccxcvii *post* is a letter of Hadrian to the proconsul Mettius Modestus on this very affair.

NOTE ON Nos. CCCCLXXXVII, CCCCLXXXIX, CCCCXCI—CCCCXCIII.

DIAGRAM TO SHOW THE ORIGINAL SIZE OF THE SLABS, AND THE ARRANGEMENT OF THE INSCRIPTIONS.

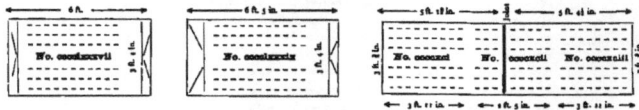

N.B.—The width of this last slab may have been slightly greater, as the fragments composing it are not quite certainly placed.

These five imperial letters were discovered by Mr. Wood in excavating the Odeum at Ephesos, on the southern slope of what he terms Mount Koressos [1]. The dado of the proscenium, consisting of white marble slabs, about an inch in thickness (crustae), had fallen upon the stage, and was broken into little fragments of which more than 150 were found. (Wood, Ephesus, p. 43). ‘ The fragments . . . . were taken down to Smyrna piece by piece as they were found, and almost the only amusement in the evening which I then allowed myself, was to put together the pieces of this marble puzzle ’ (*ibid.* p. 45). ‘ By the end of March (1864), nearly the whole of the fragments of the inscriptions from the proscenium of the Odeum had been found, and these, on being put together in their relative positions, were seen to consist of five inscriptions, four of which ’ (the four last) ‘ were letters addressed by the Emperor Antoninus Pius to the people of Ephesus. Two (?) of them bear the date of the eighth tribunitian power of that Emperor, A. D. 145-6; another was written during his thirteenth tribunitian power, A. D. 150-1. . . . . The fifth inscription ’ (the first) ‘ is a letter addressed by the Emperor Hadrian to the people of Ephesus’ (Wood, *ibid.* p. 44). M. Waddington, who received early copies of these documents, published three of them, Nos. ccccLxxxix, ccccxci, ccccxcii, in his monograph, Sur la vie du rhéteur Aristide, pp. 8, 51. The diagram given above will show the size of the four slabs containing the inscriptions, and the arrangement of the inscriptions upon them. I have succeeded in fitting into their places several fragments omitted before. It must remain doubtful whether the dado contained more inscriptions than these five : see notes on No. ccccxcm.

CCCCLXXXVII.

On a slab of white marble facing, pieced together from a number of fragments : for the measurements see Diagram. Wood, Ephesus, Appendix, Inscriptions from the Odeum ; Dürr, Die Reisen des Kaisers Hadrian, 1881, p. 124 ; Dittenberger, Sylloge, No. 285.

Αὐ[το]κράτωρ Καῖσαρ θεοῦ [Τραϊανοῦ
Παρθ[ι]κοῦ υἱὸς, θεοῦ Νερ[οῦ]α υ[ἱ]ων[ὸς,
Τραϊα[ν]ὸς, Ἀδριαν[ὸ]ς Σεβασ[τὸς ἀρ]χιερεὺ[ς
μέγισ[το]ς, δημαρχ[ικῆ]ς ἐξουσί[ας τὸ ι]γ̄, ὑπατος τὸ γ̄,
5   πατὴ[ρ πατ]ρίδος, Ἐφ[εσί]ων τοῖς ἄ[ρ]χουσι[ι καὶ τῆ β]ουλῇ χαίρειν·
Λ. Ἔ[ρ]αστος καὶ πολ[εί]της ὑ[μ]ῶν [ε]ἶναί φ[ησι, κ]αὶ πολλ[άκις
πλῖ καὶ τ[ὴ]ν θάλασ[σαν, καὶ δ]σα ἀπὸ τοῦ[του δυν]ατὸς [ἐστι
χρήσιμ[ο]ς γενέσ[θαι τῇ πατρ]ίδι, καὶ τοῦ ἔθν[ους τ]ο[ὺς] ἡγεμόνας ἀεὶ δι[α]κομ[ίζειν· ἰμ]οὶ δὲ δ[ὶς] ἤδη συ[νέπλευ]σεν,
10   τὸ μὲν πρῶτον εἰς Ῥόδον ἀπὸ τῆς Ἐ[φέ]σου κο[μιζ]ομέ[νῳ,
νῦν δὲ ἀπὸ Ἐλευσεῖνος πρὸς ὑμᾶς ἀφικ[ν]ουμέν[ῳ, εὔ]χεται[
δὲ βουλευτὴς γενίσθαι, κἀγὼ τ[ὴν] μὲν [δοκι]μασία[ν ἐφ'] ὑμεῖν
ποιοῦμαι· εἰ δὲ μηδὲν ἐνποδών [ἐστιν αὐτῷ ἀλλ' ἐστὶ τι]μῆς ἄξ[ι]ος,
τὸ ἀργύριον ὅσον διδόασιν οἱ βουλεύοντες [δώσω τῆς ἀρχαι]ρεσίας [ἕ]νεκα.
15   Εὐτυχεῖτε.

A letter of the Emperor Hadrian to the Ephesian magistrates and boulê (line 5), recommending L. Erastos for admission to the boulê. The text is here more accurately given than before : several fresh fragments having been fixed into their places in the earlier lines, and the reading of lines 6–14 checked by comparison with No. CCCCLXXXVIII. [Εὔ]χεται also is given in line 11, part of X appearing on the stone. In line 7 πλῖ is a degenerate spelling of πλεῖ (see Franz, El. Epigr. Gr. p. 249) ; Dittenberger wrongly alters it, the reading of the marble being certain. In line 9, instead of Wood's συ[νέβαινε], I restore with Dittenberger συ[νέπλευσ]εν. Line 14 is restored by comparison of the next inscription.

The thirteenth year of Hadrian's tribunicia potestas lasted from Dec. 10, A.D. 128, to Dec. 9, A.D. 129. The Emperor speaks of 'his recent journey from Eleusis to Ephesos' (line 11, νῦν δέ), but we are informed where he was when he wrote this letter. A letter of his to the city of Astypalæa, dated like the one before us [δημαρχικῆς ἐξο]υσίας τὸ ιγ̄, was despatched [ἀπὸ Λαοδι]κείας τῆς ἐπὶ Λύκω[υ] ; it was discovered at Astypalæa, and published by Dubois, Bulletin de Corr. Hellén. vii (1883), p. 407. These inscriptions enable us to determine the date of Hadrian's second visit to Athens, viz. the winter of A.D. 128-9, the date already suggested by Dittenberger C.I.A. iii, No. 735 [1]. In the spring of A.D. 129 Hadrian embarked at Eleusis and proceeded to Ephesos ; and in No. DI post we can trace a memorial of his visit. From Ephesos during the same year 129 he journeyed up the Mæander Valley to Laodicea, and from thence into Syria.

The earlier visit to Ephesos alluded to in line 10 (τὸ μὲν πρῶτον εἰς Ῥόδον ἀπὸ τῆς Ἐφέσου κομιζομένῳ) probably took place A.D. 125, at the close of Hadrian's first tour in Egypt and Asia Minor, when he was on his way through the Ægean islands to Athens ; see Spartianus in Hist. Aug. Vita Hadr. 13 : post hæc per Asiam et insulas ad Achaiam navigavit et Eleusinia sacra exemplo Herculis Philippique suscepit. That first visit of Hadrian to Athens is probably to

be dated A.D. 125-6 (Dittenberger, Hermes vii, (1873), p. 213; C.I.A. iii, No. 735).

Lucius Erastus, the subject of this Imperial letter, appears to have been a shipowner who had twice had the honour of conveying the Emperor upon his vessel. He claims to have done the same honourable service continually to τοὺς ἡγεμόνας τοῦ ἔθνους (line 8), i.e. the proconsuls of the province of Asia, and in this way had deserved well of his native city. In connexion with this statement it should be remembered that official etiquette required each proconsul of Asia to enter upon his province by landing at the port of Ephesos; see Ulpian, ap. Digest, i, 16, 4, § 5 : quædam provinciæ etiam hoc habent, ut per mare in eam provinciam proconsul veniat, ut Asia, scilicet usque adeo, ut imperator noster Antoninus Augustus ad desideria Asianorum rescripserit proconsuli necessitatem impositam per mare Asiam applicare καὶ τῶν μητροπόλεων Ἔφεσον primam partem attingere. Ephesian coins of the imperial times are found with the legend : ΕΦΕΣΙΩΝ Α ΚΑΤΑΠΛΟΥΣ in allusion to this privilege, which was highly valued as a distinction and as a source of profit. No doubt the same rule was observed by all Roman officials and persons of note.

The words ἡγεμόνας and ἔθνους are doubtless meant as synonyms respectively of ἀνθυπάτους and ἐπαρχίας. This choice of generic terms in preference to specific may perhaps be set down to the taste of the time and to a certain intentional courtliness in the letter of Hadrian. Aristides the rhetor does indeed use ἡγεμών for ἀνθύπατος (i, p. 532, Dindorf) ; but even in Dio Chrysostom ἡγεμών is quite commonly used in its older and proper meaning of 'a leading man,' not necessarily holding an official rank. This was the use of the word in Thukydides viii, 89 ; and later on ἡγεμών translated the Latin princeps, both words implying personal importance apart from official status (Dio Chrys. 40th and 45th orations passim ; and H. Pelham, Journal of Philology, 1879, p. 323 foll.). That ἔθνος occasionally was employed for ' province ' is proved by an inscription in Waddington-Le Bas (P[1]. v, No. 1219 from Bubon in Lykia), where ἄρχοντες τοῦ Λυκίων ἔθνους stands for

---

[1] In Part i, p. 39, this visit of Hadrian to Athens is dated by a misprint, A.D. 132.

Λυκιάρχαι ; see also C. I. 2802 (ἐν τῷ τῆς Ἀσίας ἔθνει), and several other instances in the passages cited by Marquardt, Röm. Alterth. iv, p. 374, *note* 5.

From lines 12 foll. we see (what is well known from other sources) that in imperial times the Greek cities granted membership of their βουλή as an honorary distinction. Dio Chrysostom was thus honoured by many cities after his return from exile (see Orat. 41, Ad Apamenses, p. 180 Reiske): καὶ ἴσως οὐδὲν ἐποιεῖτε θαυμαστόν· οὐ γὰρ μόνον αἱ λοιπαὶ πόλεις, ἀλλὰ καὶ τῶν ἰσοτίμων ὑμῖν αἱ πλεῖσται σχεδὸν ὅπου γέγονα καὶ πολιτείας καὶ βουλῆς καὶ τῶν πρώτων τιμῶν οὐδὲν δεομένῳ μετέδωκαν, οὐκ ἀνωφελῆ ἢ σφισι νομίζοντες οὐδὲ ἀνάξιον τιμᾶσθαι. Compare also Nos. DCXV, DCXVII ; C. I. 5913. Line 14 refers to the fees payable by those

who received this distinction ; Hadrian makes himself responsible for the payment of all such fees on behalf of Erastus ; compare Pliny's letter to Trajan XL : Claudiopolitani quoque in depresso loco, imminente etiam monte, ingens balineum defodiunt magis quam ædificant, et quidem ex ea pecunia quam buleutæ additi beneficio tuo aut jam obtulerunt ob introitum aut nobis exigentibus conferunt. The δοκιμασία which the boulè of Ephesos is permitted to exercise (line 12) dealt, we may be sure, as much with the position and wealth of the candidate as with his character. The nature and position of the boulè at Ephesos and elsewhere under the empire has been discussed *ante*, pp. 71 foll.

CCCCLXXXVIII.

A broken slab of white marble, entire only at the top and on the right. Height 2 ft. 6 in. ; width 1 ft. 3½ in. Discovered by Mr. Wood. Published by C. Curtius, Hermes iv, p. 181.

```
        ΑΡΘΙΚΟΥ.
        ΔΡΙΑΝΟΣ
        ‹ΙΚΗΣΞΞΟΥ
        ΟΣΕΦΕΣΙΩΝ
   5    ഗ
        ΣΙΝ . ΚΑΙΠΟΛ
        ΥΤΟΥΔΊΗΑ
        ΛΙΤΟΥΕΘΝΟὙϲ
        ΔΙΣ · ΗΔΗ
  10    ·ΠΟΤΗΣ
        ΞΕΙΝΟΣ
        ΥΛΕΥΤΗΣ
        ϸΥΜΕΙΝ
        ϽΑΛΛ
  15    ·ΛΟ
```

This is manifestly a duplicate of the preceding letter of Hadrian. It is not necessary to give it in cursive again. Which of the two is the original, and which is the copy ? Probably this is the original, being inscribed on a separate stelè, from which I

suppose a copy was made to adorn the marble facing on the proscenium of the Odeum. By comparison of the two copies we are enabled to restore : εἰ δὲ μηδὲν ἐμποδών [ἐστιν αὐτ]ῷ ἀλλ' [ἐστὶ τι]μῆτ ἀξί[ο]τ.

CCCCLXXXIX.

From the proscenium of the Odeum, inscribed upon crustæ ; see note on p. 151 *ante*. Published by Waddington, Sur la vie du rhéteur Aristide, p. 51 ; Wood, Ephesus, Appendix, Inscriptions from the Odeum, No. 2.

```
   ΑΥΤΟΚΙ                          ΡΙΑΝΟΥ
   ΥΙΟΣΘΕϹ                            ΟΣ
   ΘΕΟΥΝΕΡ                          ΑΝΟΣ
   ΑΝΤΩΝΕΙι                        ΓΙΣΤΟΣ
 5 ΔΗΜΑΡΧΙΚΗ                        ΥΠΑΤΟΣ
   ΤΟ ‹ ῙΠΑΤΗΡΠ⁄                     ΒΟΥΛΗΙ
                         ΟΙ₄
                       ιΜΕιΧΑΙι
   ΠΕΡΓΑΜΗΝΟ      ‗ΑΜΗΝΕΝΤΟΙΣΙ⸳⸳  ⸳      ιΑΜΜΑΣΙΝ
```

```
       ΧΡΗΣΑΜΕΝϹ      ιϹΟΝΟΜ ΣΙΝΟΙΣΕΓΩΧΡΗΣΘΑΙΤΗΝΠΟΛΙΝ
  10   ΤΗΝΥΜΕΤΕΡΑΙ    ΕΦ ΝΑΜΗΚΟΙΜΑΙΛΕΚΑΙΣΜΥΡΝΑΙΟΥΣΚΑΤΑ
       ΤΥΧΗΝΠΑΡΑι     ΟΙΠΕΝΑΙΤΑΥΤΑΕΝΤΩΠΕΡΙΤΗΣΣΥΝΘΥΣΙΑΣ
       ΨΗΦΙΣΜΑΤΙΤΟ ΓΛΟΙΠΟΥΔΕΕΚΟΝΤΑΣΕΥΓΝΩΜΟΝΗΣΕΙΝΕΑΝ
       ΚΑΙΥΜΕΙΣΕΝΤΟΙΣΠΡΟΣΑΥΤΟΥΣΓΡΑΜΜΑΣΙΝΟΝ  ΡΟΣΗΚΕΙ
       ΤΡΟΠΟΝΚΑΙΚΕΚΡΙΤΑΙΤΗΣΠΟΛΕΩΣΑΥΤΩΝ       ΣΜΕΜΝΗ
  15   ΣΝΟΙ.ΤΟΨΗΦΙΣΜΑΕΠΕΜΨΕΝΣΟΥΛΠΙΚΙΟΣΙΟΥ  ΝϹ  ΡΟΠΟΣΜΟΥ
                                         ΕΥΤΥΧΕΙΤΕ
       ΛΕΨΗΦΙΣΜΑΕΠΟΙΗΣΕΝΓΡΑΜΜΑΤΕΥΩΝΠΟΥΗΔΙΟΣΑΝ      ιΝϹ
```

Αὐτοκ[ράτωρ Καῖσαρ θεοῦ Ἀδ]ριανοῦ
υἱὸς, θεο[ῦ Τραϊανοῦ Παρθικοῦ υἱων]ὸς,
θεοῦ Νερ[ούα ἔκγονος, Τίτος Αἴλιος Ἀδρι]ανὸς
Ἀντωνεῖν[ος Σεβαστὸς, ἀρχιερεὺς μέ]γιστος,
5 δημαρχικῆ[ς ἐξουσίας τὸ . . , αὐτοκράτωρ τὸ β̄,] ὕπατος
τὸ γ̄, πατὴρ πα[τρίδος, Ἐφεσίων τ]οῖς [ἄρχουσι καὶ τῇ] βουλῇ
καὶ τῷ δή]μῳ χαίρ[ειν.
Περγαμηνο[ὺς ἀπεδε]ξάμην ἐν τοῖς π[ρὸς ὑμᾶς γρ]άμμασιν
χρησαμένο[υς το]ῖς ὀνόμ[α]σιν οἷς ἐγὼ χρῆσθαι τὴν πόλιν
10 τὴν ὑμετέρα[ν ἀπ]εφ[η]νάμην οἶμαι δὲ καὶ Σμυρναίους κατὰ
τύχην παραλ[ελ]οιπέναι ταῦτα ἐν τῷ περὶ τῆς συνθυσίας
ψηφίσματι, τοῦ λοιποῦ δὲ ἕκοντας εὐγνωμονήσειν ἐὰν
καὶ ὑμεῖς ἐν τοῖς πρὸς αὐτοὺς γράμμασιν ὃν [π]ροσήκει
τρόπον καὶ κέκριται τῆς πόλεως αὐτῶν [φαίνησθ]ε μεμνη-
15 μ]ένοι. Τὸ ψήφισμα ἔπεμψεν Σουλπίκιος Ἰου[λια]νὸ[ς ἐπίτ]ροπός μου.
Εὐτυχεῖτε.
Τὸ] δὲ ψήφισμα ἐποίησεν γραμματεύων Πο. Οὐήδιος Ἀν[τωνε]ῖνο[ς.

A letter from the Emperor Antoninus Pius to the magistrates and people of Ephesos (Ἐφεσίων τοῖς ἄρχουσι καὶ τῇ βουλῇ, line 6). Line 14 : [ἀεὶ ἦτ]ε, Wood; but I restore [φαίνησθ]ε from the duplicate copy, No. cccxxc b.

The date is fixed by the mention of the third consulship of Antoninus, line 6. He was consul for the third time A. D. 140, and for the fourth time A. D. 145. The letter therefore must fall between 140–144. It deals with an interesting subject, viz. the jealousy between Ephesos and Smyrna about titular precedence. Such rivalries were not unknown between other cities, but they were the more likely to occur in the province of Asia, where Ephesos, Smyrna, Pergamon, and other chief cities enjoyed the title of μητρόπολις. These three cities which are named together in this letter, are also brought together by the rhetor Aristides (i. pp. 771–777 Dind.) as the three chief cities of the province. But it was Smyrna that disputed the preeminence of Ephesos. Marquardt (Röm. Alt. iv, p. 188) cites most of the passages referring to this quarrel. The oration of Dio Chrysostom, Ad Nicomed. (Or. 38) deals with a similar quarrel περὶ πρωτείων between Nikomedia and Nikaia, the former claiming the sole use among Bithynian cities of the titles πρώτη καὶ μητρόπολις τῆς Βιθυνίας, Nikaia being styled πρώτη but not μητρόπολις. The quarrel was, says Dio (ibid.), περὶ ὀνόματος μόνον : it involved no more serious consequences than the right of precedence in the procession which opened the yearly festival in each province in honour of the Emperor (κοινὰ Ἀσίας, Βιθυνίας, etc.). It may be compared with the old controversy in James I's time between the two English Universities about their respective antiquity ; but though the Romans

might sneer (Dio Chrys. ibid.) and though their own more sensible countrymen (Dio Chrys. and Aristides) might remonstrate, the Greek cities, in the absence of greater political interests, carried their emulation about these trifles beyond all reason. In the province of Asia the Roman government fully recognized the precedence of Ephesos ; and in the procession of the κοινὰ Ἀσίας Ephesos took the first place. But Smyrna made no secret of her jealousy, and claimed a virtual if not formal equality. Dio Chrysostom, under Nerva and Trajan, speaks of it as a standing feud (Orat. 34, Tarsica Altera, p. 59 Reiske) : καὶ εἴτε Αἰγαῖοι πρὸς ὑμᾶς εἴτε Ἀπαμεῖς πρὸς Ἀντιοχεῖς εἴτ' ἐπὶ τῶν πορρωτέρω Σμυρναῖοι πρὸς Ἐφεσίους ἐρίζουσι, περὶ ὄνου σκίας, φασὶ, διαφέρονται. It appears from the present inscription and the next that Antoninus had to use his authority to settle the dispute. A passage from Ulpian, already cited on p. 152, states that Caracalla had to intervene later with a rescript requiring the proconsul invariably ' per mare Asiam applicare καὶ τῶν μητροπόλεων ῎Εφεσον primam attingere.' Antoninus had confirmed the right of Ephesos to a precedence in rank—ἡ πρώτη καὶ μεγίστη μητρόπολις τῆς Ἀσίας. On the other hand Smyrna certainly gained from Antoninus some new distinction. Philostratos (who speaks as if the jealousy were a thing of the past, Lives of the Sophists, p. 50 Kayser) says : ἤριζεν ἡ Σμύρνα ὑπὲρ τῶν ναῶν καὶ τῶν ἐπ' αὐτοῖς δικαίων, ξύνδικον πεποιημένη τὸν Πολέμωνα ἐς τέρμα ἤδη τοῦ βίου ἥκοντα . . . . . καὶ ἀπῆλθεν ἡ Σμύρνα τὰ πρωτεῖα νικῶσα. What Smyrna claimed was that she was the most beautiful of all the cities of Asia, and possessed the most beautiful temple or temples belonging to the κοινὸν Ἀσίας. Such seems to be the right interpretation of Philostratos' words, taken in connexion with Aristides (i, pp. 771-776, Dind.), who claims for Smyrna only the priority of beauty. If Aristides in his letter to M. Aurelius (i, p. 767) is referring to this contention, it was carried before the Emperor and the senate (?). Polemo was selected to plead the claim of Smyrna (Philostratos, l. c.), and that city carried the day by 400 votes to 7. We may take it to be the result of this decision that in inscriptions of the time of Commodus (C. I. 3202 foll.) Smyrna is entitled ἡ πρώτη τῆς Ἀσίας κάλλει καὶ μεγέθει, καὶ λαμπροτάτη καὶ μητρόπολις τῆς Ἀσίας. We learn from the present letter that the people of Smyrna had been reproved by the Emperor, at the instance of the Ephesians, for omitting in a decree addressed to Ephesos certain titles belonging to that city; probably they had left out all or part of the words πρώτη καὶ μεγίστη μητρόπολις τῆς Ἀσίας. The people of Smyrna pleaded that the omission was a mere accident, and the Ephesians are requested to accept this apology (lines 11 foll.). The right of Ephesos to the title had been confirmed by the authority of the Emperor (line 10).

There are no means of learning what was the occasion of the συνθυσία (line 11), or joint sacrifice on the part of the Asiatic cities. It may perhaps refer to the celebration of the κοινὰ Ἀσίας at Smyrna : or it may have been a common rejoicing at the victory of Antoninus in Britain at the end of A. D. 139, after which he assumed the title of Imperator II (see line 5).

Line 15 informs us that the Ephesian ψήφισμα, to which the Emperor is replying, had been forwarded to him by his procurator Sulpicius Julianus, (Procurator Caesaris in the Proconsular Province of Asia): it had been drawn up and moved originally (line 17)

by the γραμματεύς of Ephesos, P. Vedius Antoninus, of whom the following documents will say more. He is also mentioned in an honorary inscription ' From the city and suburbs ' of Ephesos (Wood, Ephesus. Appendix, No. 9) : Πόπλιον Οὐήδιον Παπιανὸν Ἀντωνεῖνον τὸν κράτιστον κληρονόμῳ χρησάμενον τῇ ἁγιωτάτῃ θεῷ Ἐφεσίᾳ Ἀρτέμιδι ἡ πατρὶς ἀνενεώσατο. Also ibid. No. 4 (' from a pedestal in a building near the Odeum ') : Πο. Οὐήδιον | Ἀντωνῖνον, | τὸν κτιστὴν | τῆς Ἐφεσίων | πόλεως, | ἡ συνεργασία | τῶν λαναρίων (= Hermes vii, p. 31). His grandfather, who was also a Roman citizen, is commemorated in the following (Hermes vii, p. 32), where our Vedius Antoninus is styled ὁ κράτιστος : [Π.] Οὐήδιον Π. υἱὸν | Κυρ[ε]ίνᾳ | [Ἀ]ντωνεῖνον, πάππον | Οὐηδίου Ἀντωνείνου [τ]οῦ κρατίστου, | [οἱ] ἀ[λ]ηρόνομο[ι] | .... αμίνου | ... αθ ... In the following (Hermes vii, pp. 32, 33 = Μουσεῖον καὶ Βιβλιοθήκη τῆς Εὐαγγελικῆς Σχολῆς, iii, 1880, p. 179) we seem to read both of his father and his grandfather : ... Οὐήδιον Ἀντωνεῖνον συνκλη(τ)ικὸν, | [υἱὸν Μ. Κλ. Πο. Οὐηδίου Ἀντωνείνου Φαίδρου Σαβεινιανοῦ συνκλητικοῦ, | ἔκγονον Μ. Κλ. Πο. Οὐηδίου Ἀντωνείνου | Σαβείνου ἀρχιερέως τῆς Ἀσίας ἐν | πολλοῖς καὶ ἀναγκαίοις χρησίμου. See also on No. DV.

M. Waddington suggests that the reconciliation effected by this Imperial letter gave occasion to the coin struck by the Ephesians as follows (Mionnet, Ionie, Nos. 289, 1291) :

Obv.　Τ. ΑΙ. ΚΑΙCΑΡ. ΑΝΤΩΝΕΙΝΟC. Head of Antoninus with bay-wreath.
Rev.　ΖΜΥΡ. ΠΕΡΓ. ΕΦΕCΙΩΝ. ΟΜΟΝ. Ephesian Artemis standing between Asklepios and Nemesis.

CCCCXC.

Two fragments of a white marble stelk, unpublished. A measures 8¾ in. by 2 ft. 8 in.; B measures 5¼ in. by 15 in. Discovered by Mr. Wood at Ephesos.

a.

```
                      ΗΡΩΣ
ΜΕΝΟΥΣ . ΙΟ       ΟΝΟΜΑΣΙΝ . ΟΙΣΕΙ Σ
Ν . ΤΗΝ . ΥΜΕΤΕΓ ΙΝ . ΑΠΕΦΗΝΑΜΗΝ .
ΝΑΙΟΥΣ . Κ        ΤΥΧΗΝ . ΠΑΡΑΛΣ
```

b.

```
ΡΟΣΗΚΕΙΤΡΟΥ
ΝΦΑΙΝΗΣΩ
```

Obviously fragments of the original inscription of which the preceding (No. CCCCLXXXIX) was a copy. | It is not necessary to reproduce the whole in cursive characters again.

CCCCXCI.

From the proscenium of the Odeum; see *ante*, p. 151. Published by M. Waddington, Sur la vie du rhéteur Aristide, p. 8 ; Wood, Ephesus, Appendix, Inscriptions from the Odeum, No. 3. On the same slab of crustæ with the left half of No. CCCCXCII.

```
            ?ΚΑΙⁱ      ΡΘΓ       ΡΙ      Υ
            ΑΝC        ΙΚΟ       ΝΟΣ
            ΚΓΟΝ       ΑΙΛΙC    ΑΝ )Σ
            ΣΤC        ⁻Ρ        1ΑΡ
  5    ΄              ΓΟ·Η·Α           )·Β·ΥΠΑ·Ο..·
       ΤΗΡΠ          .ΩΝΤΟΙΣ   ΛΟΥΣΙΚΑΙⁱ  ΒΟΥΛΗΚΑ'
              ΜΙΡΕ        ΗΝΦΙΛΟΓΙΜΙΑΝΗΝΟΙΛΟΤΙΜ'
              ΑΣ C         ⁻ΑΝΤΩΝΕΙΝΟΣΕΜΑΘΟΝΟΥΧΟΥΙ.  .Κ
       ΙΩΝΥΜΕΤΕ·ω       ΜΑΤΩΝΩΣΕΚΤΩΝ         ΕΙΝΟΥΒΟΥΛC  ΜΕ
  10   ΝΟΣΓΑΡΠΑΡΕμΟΥΓΥΧΕΙΝΒΟΗΘΕΙΑⁱ            ΙΚΟΣΜΟⁿΤΩΝ
       ΕΡΓΩΝΩΝΥΜΕΙΝΕΠΗΝΓΕΙΛΑΤΟΕΔΗⁱ           ΝΙΗΑΙⁱΑΟΙ
       ΚΟΔΟΜΗΜΑΤΑΠΡΟΣΤΙΘΗΣΙΝΤΗΠΟ/            ΕΙΣΟˋ  ΟΡ
       ΘΩΣΑΠΟΔΕΧΕΣΘΕΑΥΤΟΝΚΛΓΩΚΑΙΣˋ           ˋΤΟ    Σ
       ΑΗΤΗΣΑ⁻  ΛΑΙΑΠΕΔΕΞΑΜΗΝΟΤⁱ    ΓΟΝι        ΝΠΟ
  15   ΛΕΙΤΕΥΟΜΕΝΩΝΤΡΟΠΟΝΟΙΤΟΥ      ΑΧΡιⁱˋ      ΣΙΝΧΑ
       ΙΝΕΙΣΘΕΔ  ΑΙΔΙΑΝΟΜΑΣΚΑΙΤΑΤΩ              ΛΙι
       Νⁱhⁱ     ΙΑΝΑΛΛΑΔΙΟΥΠΡΟΣΤΟ              εΜΝΟ
                ΣΕΙΝΤΗΝΠΟΛΙΝΠΡΟΗΡ·            ΜΨΕⁱ
                ΛΙΑΝΟΣΟΚΡΑΤΙΣΓCΣΑΝΟˋ            Σ
```

Αὐτοκράτω]ρ Καῖσ[α]ρ θε[οῦ Ἀδ]ρι[ανο]ῦ
υἱὸς, θεοῦ Τραι]ανο[ῦ Παρθ]ικο[ῦ υἱω]νὸς,
θεοῦ Νερούα ἔ]κγον[ος, Τίτος] Αἴλιο[ς Ἀδριανὸς
Ἀντωνεῖνος Σεβα]στὸ[ς, ἀρχιερεὺ]ς μ[έγιστος, δη]μαρ-
5 χι]κ[ῆς ἐξουσίας] τὸ η̅, α[ὐτοκράτωρ τ]ὸ β̅, ὕπατος [τὸ δ̅, πατὴρ π[ατρίδος, Ἐφεσί]ων τοῖς [ἄρ]χουσι καὶ [τῇ] βουλῇ καὶ
τῷ δήμῳ χ]αίρε[ιν· Τ]ὴν φιλοτιμίαν ἣν φιλοτιμ[εῖται
πρὸς ὑμ]ᾶς Ο[ὐήδιος] Ἀντωνεῖνος ἔμαθον οὐχ οὕτω[ς ἐ]κ
τῶν ὑμετέρω[ν γραμ]μάτων ὡς ἐκ τῶν [ἐκ]είνου βουλόμε-
10 νος γὰρ παρ' ἐμοῦ τυχεῖν βοηθείας [εἰς τὸ]ν κόσμον τῶν
ἔργων ὧν ὑμεῖν ἐπηγγείλατο, ἐδήλ[ωσεν ὅσα κα]ὶ ἡλίκα οἰ-
κοδομήματα προστίθησιν τῇ πόλ[ει, ἀλλ' ὑμ]εῖς ο[ὐκ] ὀρ-
θῶς ἀποδέχεσθε αὐτόν· κἀγὼ καὶ συ[νέλαβον α]ὐτὸ[ς ὅσ-
α ἠτήσατ[ο] καὶ ἀπεδεξάμην ὅτι [οὐ] τὸν [πολλῶν τῷ]ν πο-
15 λειτευομένων τρόπον, οἳ τοῦ [παρ]αχρῆ[μα εὐδοκιμ?]εῖν χά-
ρ]ιν εἰς θέα[ς κ]αὶ διανομὰς καὶ τὰ τω[ν ἀγώνων θέματα? δαπανῶ[σιν?
τὴ]ν φι[λοτιμ]ίαν, ἀλλὰ δι' οὗ πρὸς τὸ [μέλλον συνοίσει?, σ]εμνο-
τέραν ποιήσειν τὴν πόλιν προῆρ[ηται. Τὰ γράμματα ἔπε]μψεν
Κλ. Ἰου]λιανὸς ὁ κράτιστος ἀνθύ[πατος. Εὐτυχεῖτ]ε.

A letter of the Emperor Antoninus Pius to the boulé and demos of the Ephesians.

The date of the letter is A. D. 145. Its subject is the same Vedius Antoninus who was named in No. CCCCLXXXIX as γραμματεύων, i. e. probably γραμματεὺ τοῦ δήμου : on that passage I have noted other references to the same man. It appears that he was encouraged by the Emperor to spend large sums on the improvement and erection of public buildings at Ephesos, receiving help for the purpose from his Imperial patron whose name he bore (lines 10-11, 13-14). It is possible that the Odeum, in which this series of letters was inscribed, was one of the buildings reared by Vedius Antoninus. But his munificence apparently was not welcomed by the Ephesians with the gratitude it deserved ; he was obstructed in his work, and both Vedius and the Ephesian authorities laid the matter before the Emperor (lines 12-13, 8-9). I follow M. Waddington in restoring ἀλλ' ὑμ]εῖς ο[ὐκ] in line 12 ; we might also read ἀλλ' ὑμ]εῖς ο[ὖκ] and make ἀποδέχεσθε imperative, but the meaning would be much the same. The Emperor accordingly sends this letter to strengthen the hands of Vedius against the obstructives. Five years later we find the Ephesians writing to the Emperor to acknowledge the bounty of Vedius, a tardy gratitude which the Emperor very coldly acknowledges (No. CCCCXCII). The last seven lines are so mutilated that only the general drift can be recovered. Of this I am pretty confident, although the precise words cannot be certainly restored.

In those days, as now, any alterations in public buildings were liable to be received with much criticism and some strong opposition. Dio Chrysostom gives an amusing account of the opposition made to his schemes of improvement at Apamea (Oratio XL, De Concordia, p. 162 Reiske) : λόγοι δὲ ἐγίγνοντο πολλοὶ μὲν, οὐ παρὰ πολλῶν δὲ, καὶ σφόδρα ἀηδεῖς, ὡς κατασκάπτω τὴν πόλιν, ὡς ἀνάστατον πεποίηκα σχεδὸν ἐξελαύνων τοὺς πολίτας, ὡς ἀνῄρηται πάντα, συγκέχυται, λοιπὸν οὐδέν ἐστι· καί τινες ἦσαν οἱ σφόδρα ὀδυρόμενοι τὸ χαλεπίον τὸ τοῦ δεῖνος, χαλεπῶς ἔχοντες, εἰ μὴ μενεῖ ταῦτα τὰ ὑπομνήματα τῆς παλαιᾶς εὐδαιμονίας, ὥσπερ τῶν Ἀθήνησι Προπυλαίων κινουμένων ἢ τοῦ Παρθενῶνος ἢ τὸ Σαμίων Ἡραιον ἡμᾶς ἀνατρέποντας ἢ τὸ Μιλησίων Διδύμιον ἢ τὸν

νεὼν τῆς Ἐφεσίας Ἀρτέμιδος κ. τ. λ. If I am at all right in the suggested restorations of lines 14–18, it is interesting to find the Emperor deprecating the popular rage for θεὰς καὶ διανομάς, which is a Greek equivalent for ' panem et Circenses.' For the nomen gentilicium and date of the proconsul Julianus see Waddington, Fastes, p. 211. In the last line of our inscription, the name can be clearly read [... Ἰου]-λιανός : the marble has been injured since its first discovery.

A glance at the correspondence between Pliny and Trajan will further illustrate our inscription, by showing how common was the custom of founding games, and giving shows, or endowing doles, and also what a personal interest the Emperors took in the material improvement and public buildings of the Asiatic cities.

CCCCXCII.

From the proscenium of the Odeum ; see Diagram, p. 151. Published by M. Waddington, Sur la vie du rhéteur Aristide, p. 8 δ ; Wood, Ephesus, Appendix, Inscriptions from the Odeum, No 4. There is a joint in the marble slab down the middle of this letter : the left portion is on the same marble with No. cccxci, the right portion is on the same marble with No. cccxciii.

```
        ΓΟΚΡΑΤΩ        ᵀΑΡΘ
   ΑΔΡΙΑΝΟΥΥ Ο. ΙΕΟΥΤΡΑΙ/
       Π ΘΙΚΟΥ ΙΩΝΟΣΟΕΟΥΙ

       ΟΥΑΕΚΓΟΝΟΣΤ              ΔΡΙΑΝΟΣ
  5    ΙΝΤΩΝΕΙΝΟΣΣΕΒΑᵤ          ΡΧΙΕΡΕΥΣ
       ΙΕΓΙΣΤ  ΗΜΑ·ΧΙΚΗ         ΟΥΣΙΑΣΤΟ
       ΙΓΑΥΤΟ. ΙΑΤΟ? Ο ̄        ΤΤΟΑ
       ΠΑΤΗΡΠΑΤΙ
       ΑΡΧΟΥΣΙΚΑΙΤΗ৳            ΤΩΔ৳        Ι
 10          ΧΑΙ
       ΕΙΔΟΤΙΜΟΙΔΗΑС           ΙΟΤΙ
       ΗΝΟΥΗ ΙΟΣΑΝΤ     ΙΙ    ΣΦΙΛΟΤΙΜΕΙ
       ΤΑΙΠΡΟΣΥΜΑΣΟ  ΓΕΚΑ      ΤΠΦΡΕΜΟΥ
       ΧΑΡΙΤΑΣΕΙΣΤΟΝ    ΜΟΝ.ι  ΗΣΠΟ
 15          ΛΕΩΣ           ΓΕΟΕΤΟ
       ΟΥ ΙΦΙˣ               ΞΜΨΕΝ · ΦΛ
       ΤΙ                   ᵀΟ? XEI
```

Αὐ]τοκράτω[ρ Καῖσ]αρ θ[εοῦ Ἀδριανοῦ υ[ἱ]ὸς, [θ]εοῦ Τραϊα[νοῦ Π[αρ]θικοῦ [υ]ἱωνὸς, θεοῦ [Νερ-οὐα ἔκγονος Τ[ίτος Αἴλιος Ἀ]δριανὸς
5 Ἀντωνεῖνος Σεβασ[τὸς, ἀ]ρχιερεὺς μέγιστ[ος δ]ημαρχικῆ[ς ἐξ]ουσίας τὸ ιγ, αὐτο[κρ]άτωρ [τ]ὸ [β, ὕπατο]ς τὸ δ, πάτηρ πατρί[δος, Ἐφεσίων τοῖς ἄρχουσι καὶ τῇ β[ουλῇ καὶ] τῷ δή[μῳ χαί[ρειν·
10 Εἰδότι μοι δηλο[ῦτε τὴν φι]λοτι[μίαν ἣν Οὐή[δ]ιος Ἀντ[ω]ν[εῖνο]ς φιλοτιμεῖ-ται πρὸς ὑμᾶς ὅ[ς] γε κα[ὶ τὰς] παρ' ἐμοῦ χάριτας εἰς τὸν [κόσ]μον ἁ[πάσ]ης πό-
15   λεως [κα]τέθετο.
Τ]ὸ ψήφισ[μα ἐπ]έμψεν ΦΛ . . . . .
. . τι[. . . . . ἐπίτρο]πος. [Εὐτυ]χεῖτε

A letter from the Emperor Antoninus Pius in acknowledgment of a decree (line 16) of the Ephesians respecting Vedius Antoninus; addressed to the magistrates, boulè and demos.

The mention of the 13th year of the tribunicia potestas of Antoninus fixes the date of the letter, viz. A. D. 150 (line 7). I have been able by patiently piecing together a number of tiny fragments, to present this letter in a more complete state than previous editors; the only doubt is about the position of the fragment containing ΧΕΙ at the end of line 17. Unfortunately the name of the ἐπίτροπος, or Procurator Cæsaris in Asia, is mutilated: cp. No. ccccLxxxix fin., and Pauly's Real-Encyclop. s. v. Procurator. For the subject of this letter see the preceding, No. ccccxci.

CCCCXCIII.

From the proscenium of the Odeum, see on p. 151. Referred to by Wood, Ephesus, Appendix, Inscriptions from the Odeum No. 5, as 'too fragmentary for publication.' The end of the inscription containing the date is given by Waddington, Fastes Asiatiques, p. 225, but I question the certainty of his restoration : see below.

```
   ΥΤΟΚΡΑ            ΣΑΡΘΕΟΥ ΑΖ ΙΑΝC
  ΤΟΥΤΡΑΙΑ           ΤΑΡΘΙΚΟΥΥ       Ν
  ϽΕΟΥ ΕΡϹ          ΄ Γ  ΝΟΣ   (b)          (d)
    ΑΔΡΙΑΝΟΣΑΝΤΩΝΕ       ΒΑΣˉ     (c)    ΕΥΣ
5   ΜΓΙΣΤΟΣΔΗΜΑΡΥΙΚΗΣ ε    ΑΣΤϹ  ΥΤΟΛ    Τ ˉ
        Ο Δ ΠΑΤΙ      ΠΙΔ      ΠΙΤΗΣΔ
        Γ Ν ΚΔ        ΜΕΝ
    ΕΨΕΖΙϹ ΝΚΑΙΣΕΜΙΝ       Ι
    ΑΥΤΗΠΟΛΕ  ΙΛΟΝΓ     ΛΣΠ
10  ΛΝΔΡΑΣΙΝΤΟΙ ΥΠΕ     ΣΙΝϹ
    ΑΙΕΠΙΤΑΙΣΠΟΛΕΣΙΝ    ΣΠΡΟΕΟ
    Π      ΝΙ  ΕΙΚΟΣΗΣΘΗΝΑΙΤΗΙΕϹ
    ΠΡ    ΣΕΦΓΣΙΟΙΣΜΕΓΑΛΟΨΥΧΙΑ            (e)
        ΤΙΙΝΕΙΛ      ΕΡΓΕΣΙ              ΛΙΕΙ
15    ΕΠΡΑΞ ΑΥΤ    ΝΕΛΛ    ΛΑ   (f)   ΛΛΥΣ
Uninscribed  ΤΗΣ       ΚΑΙΚΟ    Ι ΤΗ   Uninscribed
        ΗΦΙΣΜ ΓΓ   Ν ΠΟΠΙΛ    ΕΙΣΚΟΣΟ   (g)  ΤΙΣ
          ΤΟ       ΤΟΣ Uninscribed   ΤΥΧΕΙΤΕ
```

(e) Entire only on right : measures 3 in. by 5 in.   (f) Broken all round : but vacant at bottom :
     measures 8 in. by 8½ it.   (g) Broken all round : measures 3 in. by 4 in.

Α]ὐτοκρά[τωρ Καῖσαρ θεοῦ Ἀδ[ρ]ιανο[ῦ υἱὸς,
θ]εοῦ Τραια[νοῦ] Παρθικοῦ υ[ἱω]ν[ὸς,
θεοῦ [Ν]ερ[ο]ύα ἔ]αγ[ο]νος, [Τίτος Αἴλιος
Ἀδριανὸς Ἀντωνεῖνος Σε]βαστ[ὸς, ἀρχιερ]εὺς
5   μέγιστος, δημαρχικῆς ἐ[ξουσί]ας τὸ ˉ., αὐτοκ[ράτωρ] τ[ὸ] ,
ὕπατος τ]ὸ δ̄, πατ[ὴρ πα]τρίδ[ος, τοῖς ἐ]πὶ τῆς Ἀ[σίας Ἑλ-
λησιν χαίρ[ε[ι]ν κα[λὸν] μὲν . . . .
Ἐφεσίων καὶ σεμν[ὸν . . . . τοι-
αύτη πόλε[ι φ]ίλον γ[ὰρ ἰσ]ως π[. . . . . ὥσπερ
10   ἀνδράσιν τοῖς ὑπε[ρέχου]σιν ο[ὕτω . . . .
. κ]αὶ ἐπὶ ταῖς πόλεσιν [ταῖ]ς προεχ[ούσαις . . . . . .
π . . . . . . η . . νη . . εἰκὸς ἠσθῆναι τῆ τε ὀ[νομασθείση? ἐν τοῖς
προ[στέροι]ς Ἐφεσίοις μεγαλοψυχία [καὶ τῆ Ποπλίου Οὐη-
δίου Ἀ]ντωνείν[ου ε]νεργεσί[α ἐν τῷ παρόντι χρόνω; κ]αὶ ἐ[γ-
15   ὼ συν]έπραξα αὐτ[ῷ καὶ σ]υνέλα[βον ὡ]ς α[ὐ]ξοντι τὸ κ]άλλον
τῆς [πόλεως] καὶ κό[σμου] τῆ[ς Ἀσίας?
Τὸ] ψήφισμα ἐπ[εμψε]ν Ποπίλλ[ιος Πρ]είσκος ὁ [κρά]τισ-
το[ς ἀνθύπα]τος.
[Ε]ὐτυχεῖτε.

A letter from Antoninus Pius, dated in his fourth consulate (line 6), but the year of the tribunicia potestas is lost (line 5), so that the exact date is doubtful. The fourth consulship of this Emperor was in A. D. 145, and he must have written the letter between A. D. 145 and 161, the year of his death. Assuming it to be later than the preceding, dated A. D. 150. we may limit the present document to A. D. 150-161.

This inscription, like the others from the Odeum,

is pieced together from a number of fragments. The position of these is made quite certain by the exact tallying of the fractured edges; except only in the case of the fragments marked in the uncial text as *b, c, d, e, f, g.* Of these there is little doubt about *b, c, d.* Although we cannot be mechanically sure of their position, yet they read on with perfect ease, and their general appearance is in favour of the arrangement assigned to them.

My restoration of the address of the letter (line 6): [τοῖς ἐ]πὶ τῆς Ἀ[σίας Ἕλλησι], is amply justified by C. I. 3957 (a decree from Apamea, temp. Augusti) which begins: Ἔδοξεν τοῖς ἐπὶ τῆς Ἀσίας Ἕλλησιν,—and by C. I. 3187 (a decree from Smyrna, temp. Neronis, see Waddington, Fastes, p. 133), which also begins: Ἔδ]οξεν τοῖς ἐπὶ τῆς Ἀσίας [Ἕλλησιν]. I imagine that the friends of Vedius Antoninus in the chief cities of the province of Asia, had endeavoured to strengthen his hands in carrying out his plans at Ephesos by addressing a vote of thanks to the Emperor (τὸ ψήφισμα, line 17) for his bounty in assisting Vedius (compare Nos. cccxci, ante). The purport of their address was to congratulate the Emperor on the improvements which had been effected by Vedius at Ephesos, through the Emperor's assistance, improvements which rejoiced the whole province. The Emperor's reply (lines 7 foll.) is so much mutilated that we can hardly divine its drift. He may have expressed pleasure at seeing the whole province interested in the improvement of its capital (Ἐφεσίων ... [τοι]αυτῇ πόλε[ι]), especially in view of the rivalry between the three chief cities (see on No. ccccLxxxix). There certainly was a comparison drawn in lines 10, 11 between the mutual sentiments of great men and the feelings entertained for each other by great cities. The remainder (lines 12 foll.) is less obscure: 'I quite understand your gratification,' the Emperor goes on (εἰκὸς ἡσθῆναι). This phrase is a sort of formula in this connexion. It recurs in an imperial

letter (C. I. 2743) ascribed by Böckh to Diocletian and Maximian, and assigned to A. D. 286; it is in reply to the congratulations of the people of Aphrodisias: εἰκὸς ἦν ὑμᾶς .... ἡσθῆναι μὲν ἐπὶ τῇ καταστάσει τῆς βασιλείας τῆς ἡμετέρας, θυσίας δὲ καὶ εὐχὰς ἀποδοῦναι δικαίας.

The fragment *e* certainly came at the end of a line, and seems to read easily into the place assigned to it; but its position is quite conjectural. The position of *f* and *g* is equally conjectural, for the edges of the fragments do not fit into the rest of the slab. It must be confessed however that we are led by strong general indications to place them as suggested. M. Waddington (Fastes, p. 225) cites the last lines thus: Τὰ γράμματα ἔπεμψε]ν Ποπίλλ[ιος Πέδων | ὁ κράτιστος ἀνθύπα]τος. For this we may certainly restore: Τὸ] ψήφισμα ἔπ[εμψε]ν Ποπίλλ[ιος ...... ὁ κρά]τισ | το[ς ἀνθύπα]τος. But what was the name of the proconsul? M. Waddington, led by the gentile name Popillius, identifies him with the Popillius Carus Pedo of No. ccccLxxxii, and assigns his proconsulate to A. D. 161. On the other hand the fragments *f* and *g* appear to read into the letter very satisfactorily where I have placed them, and if so we must assume another proconsul, Popill[ius Pr]iscus. In a private letter on this subject M. Waddington reminds me that several years about this time are still vacant in the proconsular fasti; there is therefore no difficulty in supposing Popillius Priscus, a man otherwise unknown, to have been one of the many consules suffecti of this period, and afterwards proconsul of Asia. He may have been a brother of Popillius Pedo.

In lines 12 foll. I would not place too much reliance on the suggested restorations, but of the general drift we may be fairly certain. Observe that μεγαλοψυχία (line 13) was used in later Greek as an equivalent for μεγαλοπρέπεια ' magnificence.

CCCCXCIV.

The following fragments, discovered by Mr. Wood at Ephesos, appear to have come from the Odeum; all but the last (No. g) may be unidentified portions of the five imperial letters noticed p. 131; each is about ⅜ of an inch in thickness. The characters especially resemble No. ccccxci. It is possible however that some or all of these fragments belong to a sixth letter; and if so, M. Waddington may be right in relegating to this sixth letter the fragment marked *f* in No. ccccxci.

1.

Broken all round: measures 4 in. by 1½ in.

ΥΙι
ΚΑΙΤΗ
ΠΑΝ

If we assumed a sixth letter, we might conjecture:— ... ὕπ[ατος το͞·. πατὴρ πατρίδος, Ἐφεσίων τοῖς ἄρχουσι] καὶ τῇ [βουλῇ καὶ τῷ δήμῳ χαίρειν] κ. τ. λ.

Broken all round: measures 2½ in. by 2½ in.

ΥΣΥ

5.

Broken all round: measures 1¾ in. by 3 in.

εΙΙ

6.

Broken all round: measures 1½ in. by 2 in.

ΠΟ

7.

Broken all round: measures 2 in. by 2½ in.

Ϛᴅ

—

8.

Broken all round: measures 2½ in. by 3½ in.

ᴀᴄ

Space uninscribed.

Characters rather larger than preceding.

9.

From the top right hand corner of a slab; measures 3 in. by 3½ in.

´ᴀᴇ

The last fragment (No. 9) is thicker than the others, being ⅜ inch thick ; the characters are also smaller. I have no proof that it came from the Odeum, but for convenience I place it here. Perhaps it is from the heading of a letter: [Αὐτοκράτωρ Καῖσαρ θεοῦ Ἁδριανοῦ υἱὸς, θεοῦ Τραϊανοῦ Παρθικοῦ υἱωνὸς, θεοῦ Νερο]ύα ἔ|[κγονος] κ. τ. λ.

OCCCXCV.

White marble stelè, broken on all sides. Height 2 ft. 8 in.; width 1 ft. Excavated by Mr. Wood at Ephesus. Unpublished.

```
            ᵎΜΑΙΙΙΙ
           ΟΥΕΥΣΕⱵ
           ΚΟΥΚΑΙΘ
           ΣΠΕΡΤΙΝΑⱵ
    5      ᵎΣΜΕΓΙΣΤΟΣᴀ
           ΑΤΡΙΔΟΣΑΝΘ
           ᵎΒΟΥΣΠΕΡΤ
           ΕΟΥΜΑΡΚΟ
           ΝΤΩΝΙΝΟΥ
    10     ΙΚΟΥΚΑΙΘΕϹ
           )ΣΕΥΣΕΒΗΣ
           ΥΠΑ
```

[Αὐτοκράτωρ Καῖσαρ θεοῦ Μάρκου Ἀντωνείνου Εὐσεβοῦς]
Γερμανικοῦ Σαρ]ματι[κοῦ υἱὸς, θεοῦ Κομμόδου ἀδελφὸς,
θεοῦ Ἀντωνεί]ου Εὐσεβ[οῦς υἱωνὸς, θεοῦ Ἀδριανοῦ ἔγγονος,
θεοῦ Τραϊανοῦ Παρθι]κοῦ καὶ θ[εοῦ Νερούα ἀπόγονος, Λούκιος
Σεπτίμιος Σεουῆρο]ς Περτίναξ [Εὐσεβὴς Σεβαστὸς Ἀραβικὸς
5   Ἀδιαβηνικὸς, ἀρχιερε]ὺς μέγιστος, [δημαρχικῆς ἐξουσίας τὸ ῑ, αὐτοκράτωρ τὸ ῑᾱ, πατὴρ π]ατρίδος, ἀνθ[ύπατος, ὕπατος τὸ ῑ, καὶ Λ.
Σεπτιμίου Σεουήρου Εὐσε]βοῦς Περτ[ίνακος Σεβαστοῦ Ἀραβικοῦ
Ἀδιαβηνικοῦ υἱὸς, θ]εοῦ Μάρκο[υ Αὐρηλίου Ἀντωνείνου
Εὐσεβοῦς υἱωνὸς, θεοῦ Ἀ]ντωνείνου [Εὐσεβοῦς καὶ θεοῦ Ἀδριανοῦ
10 καὶ θεοῦ Τραϊανοῦ Παρθ]ικοῦ καὶ θεο[ῦ Νερούα ἀπόγονος, Μάρκος
Αὐρήλιος Ἀντωνεῖν]ος Εὐσεβὴς, [Εὐτυχὴς Σεβαστὸς,
ὕπα[τος, κ. τ. λ.

Probably the heading of a letter from Septimius Severus and Caracalla in the year of their joint consulship, A. D. 202.

The name of Septimius Severus (Lucius Septimius Severus Pertinax) occurs in lines 4 and 7. The earlier portion may be restored by comparison of other documents relating to this Emperor, e. g. C. I. 2878, 3878, Add. 3837, 5891. It was a weakness of this great man to covet the distinction of imperial lineage. Accordingly, A. D. 195, he asserted a fictitious claim to be the adopted son of Marcus Aurelius, and having deified Commodus in 196, he thenceforward styled himself ' son of M. Aurelius and brother of Commodus :' see Böckh on C. I. 1736 ; Eckhel, Doct. Num., vii, 173 ; De Ceuleneer, Essai sur la vie et règne de Sept. Sévère, p. 108. In line 6 ὕπατος τὸ ῡ would be expected to precede πατὴρ πατρίδος : but the stone does not seem to admit of it

Either the lapidary made a slip, or else ὕπατος τὸ γ̄ is placed last by way of emphasis, to indicate the joint consulship with Caracalla; see line 12.

The latter portion (lines 7 foll.) refers to Caracalla (Marcus Aurelius Antoninus Pius; compare C. I. 353, etc.). In a letter of Severus and Caracalla to the people of Minoa (Mittheilungen i, p. 349), the lineage of Caracalla is rehearsed just as here, in deference to the taste of Severus. In A. D. 202 Caracalla was his father's colleague in the consulship, hence ὕπα[τος] in line 12. To this year we may therefore assign our inscription. It is probably part of an imperial letter, in answer perhaps to some letter of compliment from the boulè and demos of Ephesos. C. I. 3178 is another letter jointly addressed by 'the Emperors' Severus and Caracalla to the people of Smyrna, which Böckh assigns to about 200 A. D. (compare C. I. 2971). The reader may also refer to Klein, Fasti Consulares, p. 89 reff.; and C. I. L. vi, Pt. i, 1031; and especially vi, Pt. i, 896, from the Pantheon at Rome, which was restored by Severus and Caracalla when colleagues in 202.

CCCCXCVI.

Fragment of white marble wall-stone; broken at the left and bottom, but at the top and at the right edge are joints. Height 5 in.; width 1 ft. 5 in. Discovered by Mr. Wood. Unpublished.

```
ΕΑΥ..ι ▪ ΤΩΝΜΕΝ
‾ΤΗΚΟΤΩΝΑΠΟΕ|
ι ◂ ΕΙΚΟΣ‾
```

... ἑαυτῷ τῶν μὲν
ἀφει]τηκότων ἀπὸ ε-
... εἰκὸς ....

The inscription so much resembles the fragments of imperial letters Nos. ccccLXXXVIII and ccccXC, that it probably should be placed here. The characters are those of the Antonine age.

CCCCXCVII.

A block of white marble, the surface having at each edge a slight rebate of one inch in width; the joints are entire on all sides, showing that the block fitted on to other wall-stones from the same building. Height 9 in.; width 1 ft. ⅜ in. Discovered by Mr. Wood. Unpublished.

```
      ΕΓΕΙΚΩ.\ι,ΟΔΙΚΝΥΕΙΠΑΡΑΣΤΑΙΗι
      Γ ΚΕΙΝΚΕΛΕΥΣΘΗΝΑΙΤΑΚΑΚΩΣΑΠΟΔΣ
      ⊣ΔΟΣΕΙ  ΑΙΔΕΣΥΝΕΧΕΙΣΑΝΑΒΟΛΑΙΤ.
      Ν ΟΠΑΠΠΟΣΑΥΤΟΥΣΑΒΕΙΝΟΣΩΣΦΗΣΕΝΕι
  5   ‾Ι ΩΝΑΣΧΕΔΟΝΑΝΑΓΚΑΙΟΝΠΟΟΥΣΙΚΑΙΣΟΙΤΟΧΙ
      Ι ΤΟΣΥΝΧΩΡΕΙΝ ▪ ΩΣΠΕΡΓΑΡΑΙΔΩΠΟΛΛΗΝΑΝι
      ΞΙΝ ⏀ ΟΥΤΩΣΕΠΕΙΔΑΝΑΥΤΟΙΤΙΝΕΣΑΙΤΙΑΝι
```

.... [δικαίως μὲν ἂν τὰ χρήματα,]
ἃ τ]ετεικὼς ἀποδεικνύει, παραστείη, [καὶ οὐ δεῖ αὐτὸν προσε-
νε]γκεῖν κελευσθῆναι τὰ κακῶς ἀποδο[θέντα οὐδὲ προσθεῖναι
τ]ῇ δόσει· αἱ δὲ συνεχεῖς ἀναβολαὶ τ[ῶν ....
ὦ]ν ὁ πάππος αὐτοῦ Σαβεῖνος, ὡς φής, ἐνι ....
5   . ιωνα, σχέδον ἀναγκαῖον ποοῦσι καί σοι τὸ χρ[ηζόμενον κατὰ τὸ
αὐ]τὸ συνχωρεῖν· ὥσπερ γὰρ αἰδῶ πολλὴν ἀνα[βολαὶ παρέ-
χου]σιν, οὕτως ἐπειδὰν αὐτοί τινες αἰτίαν ἔ[χωσι? ...

Fragment of a letter, perhaps addressed by the Emperor to the proconsul of Asia (lines 4, 5; ὡς φής, καί σοι). The subject is the recovery of certain debts; and unless these debts were owing to some public body, the letter would hardly have been inscribed on a public building, as it appears to have been. It is possible that it refers to the same affair which occasioned the letter of Hadrian to the Ephesian Gerousia (No. ccccLXXXVI, ante). If so, the writer of the present letter is Hadrian, and it may be addressed to Mettius Modestus, proconsul of Asia, shortly before A. D. 120.

We must suppose that Sabinus (line 4) had borrowed moneys of the Gerousia, and his grandson, who is now his representative, is slack in making repayment (see on No. ccccLXXXVI, lines 7 foll.).

If my restorations are at all right, the drift of the letter is somewhat as follows: 'Whatever the debtor in question can prove that he has paid, must be reckoned to his credit (παραστείη, compare παράστασις in L. and S.), however irregularly it was repaid (κακῶς ἀποδοθέντα); it must not be charged to him again. It would be best to compel an immediate settlement; but such perpetual adjournments have been previously allowed, that you are practically compelled to grant this request for postponement also. I know such delays are embarrassing, and make the creditor appear as if in the wrong, but yet there are cases where the creditor has only himself to blame for the necessity of delay,' etc.

T t

SECTION III.

HONOURS TO THE IMPERIAL FAMILY, AND TO PUBLIC BODIES.

CCCCXCVIII.

Stelè of white marble in good preservation, 'from the Castle at Ephesus.' Presented by Mr. Purser of Smyrna, 1870. Height 3 ft. 11 in.; width 2 ft. Journal of Philology, vii, 1876, p. 145; Waddington, Bulletin de Corr. Hellénique, vi, 1882, p. 286.

ΤΟΚΡΑΤΟΡ
ΘΕΩΙ
ΚΑΙΣΑΡΙ
ΣΕΒΑΣΤΩΙΟΥΕΣΠΑΣΙΑΝΩ
ΕΠΙΑΝΘΥΠΑΤΟΥΜΑΡΚΟΥ
ΦΟΥΛΟΥΙΟΥΓΙΛΛΩΝΟΣ
ΟΔΗΜΟΣΟΚΑΙΣΑΡΕΩΝ
ΜΑΚΕΔΟΝΩΝΥΡΚΑΝΙΩΝ
ΝΑΩΙΤΩΙΕΝΕΦΕΣΩΙΤΩΝΣΕΒΑ
ΣΤΩΝΚΟΙΝΩΙΤΗΣΑΣΙΑΣΔΙΑ
ΤΕΙΜΟΘΕΟΥΤΟΥΤΕΙΜΟΘΕΟΥΚΑ
ΜΗΤΡΟΔΩΡΟΥΤΟΥΜΗΤΡΟΔΩΡΟΥ
ΑΡΧΟΝΩΝΚΑΙΔΙΑΜΗΝΟΦΙΛΟΥΤΟΥ
ΑΠΟΛΛΩΝΙΟΥΚΑΙΜΗΝΟΓΕΝΟΥΣ
ΜΗΤΡΟΦΑΝΟΥΚΑΙΜΕΝΕΚΡΑΤΟΥΣ
ΙΟΥΚΟΥΝΔΟΥΕΠΙΜΕΛΗΤΩΝ

ΕΠΙΑΡΧΙΕΡΕΩΣΤΗΣ
ΑΣΙΑΣΤΙΒΕΡΙοΥΚΛΑΥΔΙΟΥ
ΑΡΙΣΤΙΩΝΟΣ

Αὐ]τοκράτορ[ι
θεῷ
Καίσαρι
Σεβαστῷ Οὐεσπασιανῷ
ἐπὶ ἀνθυπάτου Μάρκου
Φουλουίου Γίλλωνος
ὁ δῆμος ὁ Καισαρέων
Μακεδόνων Ὑρκανίων,
ναῷ τῷ ἐν Ἐφέσῳ τῶν Σεβα-
στῶν κοινῷ τῆς Ἀσίας, διὰ
Τειμοθίου τοῦ Τειμοθίου κα[ὶ
Μητροδώρου τοῦ Μητροδώρου
ἀρχόντων καὶ διὰ Μηνοφίλου τοῦ
Ἀπολλωνίου καὶ Μηνογένους
Μητροφάνου καὶ Μενεκράτους
Ἰουκούνδου ἐπιμελητῶν.

Ἐπὶ ἀρχιερίως τῆς
Ἀσίας Τιβερίου Κλαυδίου
Ἀριστίωνος.

Dedication in honour of the deified Vespasian, set up at Ephesos in 'the temple of the Augusti belonging to the community of Asia' (lines 9, 10). This temple must be the Augusteum, the ruins of which were discovered by Mr. Wood within the peribolos of the Artemision, and to the north of the great temple. (Wood's Ephesus, p. 153.) Κοινῷ here agrees with ναῷ, and means 'belonging to τὸ κοινὸν τῆς Ἀσίας.' This was a confederation of the cities of the province for the worship of the Cæsars, on which something has been said on No. CCCCLXXXIX. An association of the kind existed in every province of the Empire, especially in the Eastern provinces (so τὸ κοινὸν τῶν Γαλατῶν, in No. DLVIII). At its head was an ἀρχιερεύς, whose office was an annual one, and therefore served to fix the date (line 17). His wife also had the right to be styled ἀρχιέρεια; and the title of ἀρχιερεύς was retained by a man after his year of office had expired. Every fourth year he had to furnish the funds for the celebration of the provincial games in honour of the Cæsars, κοινὰ

Ἀσίας : owing to this last duty, the ἀρχιερεύς was also styled Ἀσιάρχης, Λυκιάρχης, Γαλατάρχης, etc., as the case might be. The annual festival of τὸ κοινὸν τῆς Ἀσίας was held in turn in one of the principal cities, e. g. Ephesos, Smyrna, Pergamon, Sardes, Kyzikos and Philadelphia, each of which contained one or more temples dedicated to the worship of the Cæsars, and therefore styled itself νεωκόρος τῶν Σεβαστῶν; hence in lines 9, 10, ναὸς ὁ ἐν Ἐφέσῳ τῶν Σεβαστῶν; compare No. CCCCLXXXI, line 155. The ἀρχιερεὺς τῆς Ἀσίας or Ἀσιάρχης, whose office extended to the whole province, is further to be distinguished from the local high-priest of Cæsar-worship appointed annually in every town wherein there was an Augusteum ; at Ephesos this local high-priest was termed Ἀρχιερεὺς (or Ἀσιάρχης) ναῶν τῶν ἐν Ἐφέσῳ (see No. DCIV, DCV). The office and title of the ἀρχιερεύς and the Ἀσιάρχης have been discussed by Waddington-Le Bas, Part iii, No. 885 ; he considers them to be distinct offices. I follow Marquardt, Röm. Alt. iv, 374 foll. (compare Ephemeris Epigraph. i. p. 200 foll.) in identifying them, notwithstanding the inscription found by Benndorf at Sidyma (Reisen in Lykien und Karien, i, p. 71); see Monceaux, De Communi Asiæ Provinciæ, p. 55.

This dedication is made during the proconsulship of M Fulvius Gillo (lines 5, 6), who is also mentioned in an Ephesian inscription published in the Μουσείον καὶ Βιβλ. τῆς Εὐαγγελικῆς Σχολῆς, Smyrna, iv, 1880, p. 180, and by M. Waddington (see heading). That also is a dedication to Vespasian at Ephesos from the people of Aphrodisias in Gillo's year. A Latin inscription of Vespasian's reign dated Dec. 2, A. D. 76, shows M. Fulvius Gillo to have then been consul suffectus (C. I. L. iii, part 2, p. 853). M. Waddington would make him proconsul of Asia under Domitian. Timotheos and Metrodoros (lines 11-13) are magistrates of the dedicating city; Menophilos, Menogenes and Menekrates are commissioned to assist them in the erection of the monument.

The interest of the inscription centres in the name of the city: ὁ δῆμος ὁ Καισαρέων Μακεδόνων Ὑρκανίων (lines 7, 8). It was situated in Lydia in the Hyrkanian Plain, so named from a colony settled there by the Persians from the shores of the Caspian sea: εἶτα τὸ Ὑρκάνιον πεδίον, Περσῶν ἐπονομασάντων καὶ ἐποίκους ἀγαγόντων ἐκεῖθεν (Strabo, xiii, p.629). The site of the town was until lately unknown; its composite name is due to the planting of a colony of Macedonians here, probably a military colony, to serve as a buttress against the Gauls (see Droysen, Hellenismus, iii, 2, p. 278). Pliny, N. H. v, 29, § 120, assigns the town to the Conventus of Smyrna: Zmyrnæum conventum magna pars Æoliæ quæ mox dicetur frequentat, præterque Macedones Hyrcani cognominati et Magnetes a Sipylo. Tacitus names it among the duodecim celebres Asiæ urbes destroyed by earthquake in one night, A. D. 17 (Ann. ii, 47; compare C. I. 3450). It was relieved of tribute for the time, and otherwise helped. It is possible that this was the occasion on which the inhabitants assumed the additional name Καισαρεῖς (line 7). Coins of the town are extant, see Head, Hist. Num. p. 550. C. I. 3181 is a dedication from the same town in honour of the Emperor Gallus and his son Volusianus, A. D. 252 or 253, and appears to have been set up at Smyrna. A similar dedication (to Caracalla ?) is given in the Μουσείον καὶ Βιβλ., v (1885-6), p. 19 (= Bull. de Corr. Hell. xi, p. 91). A Menekrates son of Menophilos is named as one of the strategi.

CCCCXCIX.

Statue-base of white marble; height 3 ft.; width 2 ft. 3 in. Wood, Ephesus, Inscriptions from the site of the Temple, No. 12; compare Waddington, Bull. de Corr. Hell. vi, 1882, p. 287.

```
        ΝΚΛΗΤΟΝ                        Τὴν ἱερὰν σύ]νκλητον
     ΟΚΟΡΟΣ Φ ΣΙΩΝ                     ἡ νε]οκόρος Ἐφεσίων
    ΙΣΚΑΘΙΕΡΩΣΑÑΟΣ                     πό]λις, καθιερώσαντος
   ΠΕΔΑΝΙΟΥΦΟΥΣΚΟΥ                     Πεδανίου Φούσκου
5  ΣΑΛΕΙΝΑΤΟΡΟΣΑΝΘΥ            5       Σαλεινάτορος ἀνθι[πάτου
   ΔΙΑΠΡΕΣΒΕΥΤΟΥΚΑ                     διὰ πρεσβευτοῦ κα[ὶ ἀν-
   ΤΙΣΣΤΡΑΤΗΓΟΥΓ                       τι(σ)στρατήγαν Γ]αίου
   ΑΡΜΙΝΙΟΥΓΑΛΛ.                       Ἀρμινίου Γάλλ[ου,
   ΨΗΦΙΣΑΜΕΝΟΥΤΙΒΕ,                    ψηφισαμένου Τιβε[ρίου
10  ΛΑΥΔΙΟΥΙΟΥΛΙΑΝ◡           10       Κλανδίου Ἰουλιανο[ῦ
   ΙΛΟΠΑΤΡΙΔΟΣΚΑΙΦΙΛΟ                  φ]ιλοπάτριδος καὶ φιλο-
   ΕΒΑΣΤΟΥΤΟΥΓΡΑΜΜΑ                    σ]εβάστου τοῦ γραμμα-
   ΕΩΣΤΟΥΔΗΜΟΥ                         τ]έως τοῦ δήμου.
```

The inscription records the erection of a statue (?) in honour of the Roman Senate (understand ἐτίμησεν in lines 1, 2), by decree of the Ephesian people, and upon the motion of Ti. Cl. Julianus, secretary of the demos. The statue however was actually dedicated (line 3) by Pedanius Fuscus Salinator the proconsul of Asia, his legatus pro prætore C. Arminius Gallus acting as his proxy. Pedanius is known as the colleague of Hadrian in the consulship A. D. 118 (see C. I. 1732). But M. Waddington (Fastes, p. 168), shows that his proconsulship must have been before the end of A. D. 102, as one of his coins of Trajan omits the title Dacicus. Trajan began his reign A. D. 98, so that our inscription falls between A. D. 98-102.

The γραμματεὺς τοῦ δήμου Ti. Cl. Julianus is repeatedly mentioned in the Salutaris inscription (No. CCCCLXXXI ante, lines 7, 305). A. D. 104, as γραμματεύς τὸ β̄. If, as seems probable, he filled the office in two successive years, then his first year would be A. D. 102-3; and this would fix both the date of our dedication and the proconsulship of Fuscus (see Waddington, Bull. de Corr. Hell. l. c.).

This dedication to the Senate, which I thought it best to place amongst the dedications to Emperors, receives illustration from the Asian coins of this period. After observing that the proconsular province of Asia underwent little or no change either in its limits or in its government from the time of Augustus to the reign of Diocletian, M. Waddington

(Fastes. pp. 23, 24) goes on to say that on the coins of Asia proper during this period the effigy of the reigning Emperor is often exchanged for a symbolic head with the legend **ΙΕΡΑ CΥΝΚΛΗΤΟC**, the head representing the Roman Senate. By placing this device upon their coins the towns of Asia rendered homage to the Senate, under whose government they lived in so far that Asia was always a senatorial province. This custom, he observes, was peculiar to the province of Asia.

D.

Stele of white marble ; height 3 ft. 1½ in. ; width 2 ft. 11½ in. ; broken at the bottom and on the lower portion of the right side. Wood's Ephesus, Appendix, Inscriptions from the site of the Temple, No. 13. Compare Waddington, Bull. de Corr. Hell. vi, 1882, p. 288.

```
    ΑΥΤΟΚΡΑΤΟΡΑΚΑΙCΑΡΑ
    ΘΕΟΥΝΕΡΟΥΑ · ΥΙΟΝ · ΝΕΡΟΥΑΝ
    ΤΡΑΙΑΝΟΝCΕΒΑCΤΟΝ · ΓΕΡΜΑ
    ΝΙΚΟΝΔΑΚΙΚΟΝ · ΗΦΙΛΟCΕ
  5 ΒΑCΤΟCΕΦΕCΙΩΝ · ΒΟΥΛΗ
    ΚΑΙΟΝΕΟΚΟΡΟC ΔΗΜΟC · ΚΑ
    ΘΙΕΡΩCΑΝ · ΕΠΙ · ΑΝΘΥΠΑΤΟΥ
    ΒΙΤΤΙΟΥ · ΠΡΟΚΛΟΥ
    ΨΗΦΙCΑΜΕΝΟΥ · Τ · ΦΛΑ
 10 ΑΡΙCΤΟΒΟΥΛΟΥΑCΙΑ
    ΓΡΑΜΜΑΤΕΩC · ΤΟ᾽
    ΥΙΟΥΠΥΘΙΩΝΟC · ΑΡ
    ΓΥΜΝΑCΙΑΡΧΟΥΝΤΩ
    ΓΥΜΝΑCΙΑΡΧΙΑCΕΝ
 15  ‾‾  ΔΟCΤΟ▸Ϛ‾·Φ
    ᾽ΑCΜΥΡΤ
```

```
    Αὐτοκράτορα Καίσαρα
    θεοῦ Νερούα υἱὸν, Νερούαν
    Τραιανὸν Σεβαστὸν Γερμα-
    νικὸν Δακικὸν, ἡ φιλοσέ-
  5 βαστος Ἐφεσίων βουλὴ
    καὶ ὁ νεοκόρος δῆμος κα-
    θιέρωσαν, ἐπὶ ἀνθυπάτου
    Βιττίου Πρόκλου,
    ψηφισαμένου Τ. Φλα[βίου
 10 Ἀριστοβούλου Ἀσιά[ρχου, τοῦ
    γραμματέως τοῦ [δήμου,
    υἱοῦ Πυθίωνος Ἀρ[ιστοβούλου ?
    γυμνασιαρχούντω[ν τούτων τὰς
    γυμνασιαρχίας ἐν [λόγῳ? τῆς Ἀρ-
 15 τέμι?]δος τὸ Ϛ· φ[ιλοσεβάστων ?
    . . . . . ιας Μυρτ . . . . . .
```

Dedication in honour of the Emperor Trajan by the boulè and demos of the Ephesians. The date is fixed within certain limits by the imperial titles employed. The epithet Δακικός (line 4) was not assumed by Trajan till the close of A. D. 102 ; and the title Παρθικός is here omitted, which he adopted A. D. 116. These limits are narrowed still further by the mention of the proconsul Vettius Proculus (line 8), whose year M. Waddington would place about A. D. 112. A coin of Hyreanis in Lydia (see on No. cccxcvIII) struck in his year is in M. Waddington's possession, and it appears to omit the title of Optimus which Trajan received A. D. 114 (Fastes, p. 180 : Bull. de Corr. Hell. vi, 288).

The epithet νεωκόρος which formerly had described the Ephesian city and people in relation to Artemis (comp. Acts xix) was regularly employed by Ephesos and other cities of Asia under the Empire to express their devotion to the Cæsars (see on No. cccxcvIII). The form νεοκόρος is not a lapidary's blunder (comp. No. DXVII), but a debased spelling, like νεοπολὸς or Ἀντονείνος. Marquardt (Cyzicus und sein Gebiet, p. 86) observes that ΝΕΟΚΟΡΟC is more common upon the coins of that city than ΝΕΩΚΟΡΟC down to the reign of Heliogabalus. The form in which this dedication is drafted resembles closely No. cccxcix (probably A. D. 102) and still more two dedications to Sabina the consort of Hadrian, C. I. 2966 (about A. D. 127) and C. I. 2965 (A. D. 135 or 136). In each of these, after the name of the proconsul, the document proceeds ψηφισαμένου τοῦ δεῖνος τοῦ γραμματέως τοῦ δήμου. The reader is referred to p. 81 ante for some remarks on the importance of this officer ; it is clear that he had considerable authority in the proposing of motions, and was generally a man of rank and wealth.

T. Fl. Aristobulos was not only secretary of the demos, but also was or had been an Asiarch (line 10 ; compare note on No. cccxcvIII), and apparently in conjunction with his father (if I understand aright lines 13–14) was for the sixth year discharging the costly duties of gymnasiarch of certain of the gymnasia in Ephesos. How great the expense of this office was, is abundantly proved by inscriptions (Menadier, Qua condicione Ephesii etc., p. 94) : thus at Kibyra (Waddington-Le Bas, No. 1213 A, B) a gymnasiarch who had munificently fulfilled his office, bequeathed a large sum (400,000 Rhodian drachmas, or nearly £16,000) for the perpetual endowment of the gymnasiarchy ; if however any γυμνασιαρχῆσαι θελήσωσιν ἐκ τῶν ἰδίων ἀναλωμάτων and let the endowment accumulate, they can do so. Menadier (p. 91) restores γυμνασιαρχούντω[ν τῆς] γυμνασιαρχίας in the inscription before us (lines 13–14) but the syntax requires the accusative. The plural may perhaps be explained as follows : there were several gymnasia at Ephesos, (see p. 82 ante), and the heavy burthen of their cost was supported by more than one gymnasiarch : at Miletos (C. I. 2885) it is mentioned as something remarkable that one man was γυμνασίαρχος πάντων τῶν γυμνασίων. One of the Ephesian gymnasiarchs seems to have been appointed from the Gerousia

(No. DLXXXVII); perhaps others represented other bodies in the State. It is moreover conceivable that a grant was made annually from the temple funds towards the expenses of certain gymnasia, and I have suggested ἐν [λόγῳ τῆς Ἀρτέμι]δος as meaning that Pythion and his son were at this time relieving Artemis of her share in the cost, and contributing the sums which otherwise would have been charged upon the temple. Thus ἐν [λόγῳ τῆς Ἀρτέμι]δος means 'on account of Artemis.' The phrase ἐν λόγῳ is somewhat similarly used in some of the Prienè decrees (ante, No. ccccxv fin., No. ccccxix, line 30); so εἰς τὸν λόγον τῆς δεῖνος, in a dedication from Phrygia (Hellenic Journal, 1887, viii, p. 233). This burthen Pythion and his son had undertaken on behalf of the goddess six times. Line 16 appears to have contained a proper name. The dedications already cited (C. I. 2965, 2966; compare 2963 c, and No. DXXIX post), after naming the γραμματεὺς τοῦ δήμου, mention who it was who superintended the erection of the monument. Perhaps we might restore line 16 : . . . . . ιας Μυρτ . . . [ἠργεπιστάτησιν.

DI.

Base of white marble, entire only at the bottom and in the lower portion of the right side: height 2 ft. 3¼ in.; width 2 ft. 5½ in. Discovered by Mr. Wood at Ephesos, but not published by him; C. Curtius, Hermes iv, 182.

ΝΑΔΓΙΛ
ΣΕΒΑΣΤΟΝ
ΙΟΝΚΑΙΠΑΝΕΛΛΗΝΙΟΛ
ΚΑΙΠΑΝΙΩΝΙΟΝ
5   ΓΔΙΟΣΔΗΜΟΣΤΡΑΤΟΣΚΑΙΛΙΑΝΟ˙
˙ΩΝΤΕΚΝΩΝΤΟΝΙΔΙΟΝΕΥΕΡΓΕΤΗ
ΚΑΙΣΩΤΗΡΑ

[Αὐτοκράτορα Καίσαρα]
Τραϊανὸ]ν Ἀδρια[νὸν
Σεβαστὸν
Ὀλύμπ]ιον καὶ Πανελλήνιον
καὶ Πανιώνιον
5   Τιβ. Κλα]ύδιος Δημόστρατος Καιλιανὸς
ὑπὲρ αὑτοῦ καὶ τ]ῶν τέκνων τὸν ἴδιον εὐεργέτη[ν
καὶ σωτῆρα.

Dedication in honour of the Emperor Hadrian by a certain Ephesian on behalf of himself and his children. He styles Hadrian his benefactor and saviour, having received from him some substantial marks of favour (compare a similar dedication at Athens, C. I. A. iii, No. 488).

The date is probably A. D. 129, when Hadrian visited Ephesos on his way from Athens eastward : see Hadrian's own reference to this visit in No. cccclxxxvii. The titles Ὀλύμπιος and Πανελλήνιος (lines 4-5) were commonly applied to Hadrian. His object in visiting Athens in the winter of A. D. 128 was to dedicate the newly-built Olympieion: ad orientem profectus per Athenas iter fecit atque opera quæ apud Athenienses cœperat dedicavit, ut Jovis Olympii ædem et aram sibi, eodemque modo per Asiam iter faciens templa sui nominis consecravit (Spartian, Vita Hadr. 13). The coins and inscriptions of many States from this time entitled Hadrian Ὀλύμπιος: compare the singular series of dedications in the Olympieion itself (C. I. 331-335; C. I. A. iii, No. 471 foll.) from a number of cities, including Ephesos. These were probably placed there A. D. 132 (C. I. A iii, No. 471). We may connect with the visit of Hadrian tó Ephesos the agonistic festival Ἀδριανὰ Ὀλύμπια (p. 79 ante). The epithet Πανελλήνιος is ap-

plied to Hadrian in inscriptions from Æzani, Megara and Tegea (C. I. 3833, 1072, 1521) and is supplied by Dittenberger in the Ephesian dedication at the Olympieion (C. I. A. iii, No. 485), by comparison of the document before us. It occurs again post, No. DC. line 3. The name has reference to another building of Hadrian at Athens, the temple of Hera and Zeus Panhellenios (Pausan. i, 18, § 9); in memory of its dedication Hadrian founded a festival at Athens, (Πανελλήνια) mentioned in the agonistic lists, Nos. DCXI, DCXV post. The title Πανιώνιος is not found elsewhere applied to Hadrian. It needs no explanation : but we may remember in connexion with it, that the old Ionic League of Thirteen Cities survived until late times—a κοινὸν Ἰωνίας side by side with the κοινὸν Ἀσίας described in the commentary on No. cccxcviii ante (Marquardt, Röm. Alt. iv, 187).

Curtius edits Αἴλιος in line 5, but the reading is certain. The prænomen is supplied from a comparison of C. I. 2955 : Ἐπὶ πρυτάνεως Τι(β). Κλαυδίου Τιτιανοῦ, Δημοστράτου υἱοῦ κ. τ. λ., with No. DIII post. Apparently the Tib. Cl. Demostratos of the present inscription and of No. DIII is the same man, who in A. D. 129 (or near it) made this dedication to Hadrian, and between A. D. 138-161 was πρύτανις, and who was the father of Tib. Cl. Titianus, afterwards, πρύτανις.

1 U

DII.

Slab of white marble, entire at the top, right, and part of bottom. Height 2 ft. 6 in.; width 1 ft. 11 in. Discovered by Mr. Wood, but not published by him: compare, however, his Ephesus, Appendix, Inscriptions from the Great Theatre, No. 7; C. Curtius, Hermes iv, p. 184 foll.

```
    ΟΚΡΑΤΟΡΑΚΑΙΣΑΡΑ
    ΟΝΑΙΛΙΟΝΑΔΡΙΑΝΟΝ
    ΤΩΝΕΙΝΟΝΣΕΒΑΣΤΟΝ
       ΕΥΣΕΒΗ
       ΤΗΣΚΑΙΜΕΓΙΣΤΗΣ
       ΕΩΣΤΗΣΑΣΙΑΣ
       ΟΡΟΥΤΩΝΣΕΒΑΣΤΩΛ
       ΑΕΟΣΗΒΟΥΛΗΚ
       ΟΝ ΤΙΣΤΗΝ
          ΜΕΛΗ
          ΤΦΛΑ
          ΔΗΜΟΥ
          ΑΝΗΣ
```

```
Αὐ]τοκράτορα Καίσαρα
Τί]τον Αἴλιον 'Αδριανὸν
'Αν]τωνεῖνον Σεβαστὸν
        Εὐσεβῆ,
5  τῆς πρ]ώτης καὶ μεγίστης
   μητροπό]λεως τῆς 'Ασίας
   καὶ δὶς νεω]κόρου τῶν Σεβαστῶν
   'Εφεσίων πό]λεος ἡ βουλὴ καὶ
   ὁ δῆμος, τ]ὸν κτιστήν·
10  ψηφισαμένου καὶ ἐπι]μελη-
   θέντος Γερελλαν]οῦ Φλα-
   βιανοῦ τοῦ γραμματέως τοῦ] δήμου,
   φυλῆς Τηίων 'Αδρι?]ανῆς.
```

Dedication to the Emperor Antoninus Pius by the boulê and demos of Ephesos: the date is therefore between A. D. 138–161.

The phrase employed in lines 5–6 has already been explained in the notes on No. CCCCLXXXIX. Also in the notes on No. CCCCXCVIII, DIII, the expressions νεωκόρος τῶν Σεβαστῶν and δὶς νεωκόρος have been discussed: Ephesos is styled β νεωκόρος on coins and inscriptions of Hadrian's reign onwards. The title κτιστής (line 9) was very commonly ascribed to Emperors by cities which had received favours from them: compare the series of dedications to the Emperors Hadrian, Antoninus Pius and M. Aurelius at Athens (C. I. A. iii, No. 472 foll.). Antoninus, however, had earned the title in this case by his gifts towards the buildings at Ephesos reared by Vedius Antoninus (see Nos. CCCCXCI–CCCCXCIII). Vedius himself is saluted as τὸν κτιστὴν τῆς 'Εφεσίων πόλεως in a dedication given by Wood (Appendix, Inscriptions from the City, etc., 4; C. Curtius, Hermes vii, p. 31). The Emperor is styled σωτὴρ καὶ κτιστής in No. DIV post. Line 8: πό]λεος may be compared with τάξεος in the Salutaris decree No. CCCCLXXXI, line 15. It is clear that there was a growing confusion in pronunciation between Ω and O: we shall find πόλεω[ς] in No. DIV, and we have already noticed νεωκόρος in No. D, and παιδωνόμος in No. CCCCLXXXI, line 174. It is well known that a similar confusion occurs in the oldest Greek MSS. The restoration of line 10 is taken from C. I. 2961 b, 2972, and No. DXXXIII post.

The restoration of the last three lines as given in the text, is suggested on independent grounds, but is partly confirmed by Mr. Wood's inscription referred to in our heading. This is identical with the one before us down to the word Σεβαστῶν. Then it reads on: 'Εφεσίων ἡ πόλις καὶ ἡ βουλὴ | καὶ ὁ δῆμος [ἐπὶ Πεδ. Πρεισκείνου] | ἀνθυπάτου, ψήφισμα προβου[λευ]-θέντος Πο. Γεμελλίνου Φλα|βιανοῦ γραμματέως τοῦ δήμου | φυλῆς 'Αδριανῆς. I was at one time inclined to think this an inaccurate copy of the present dedication, made perhaps from a blurred paper-impression, in which the editor accidentally had confused his own restorations with the readings still extant on the marble. Mr. Wood assures me that this is impossible. There are however various peculiarities in the text as given by Wood. Instead of 'Εφεσίων ἡ πόλις καὶ ἡ βουλὴ κ. τ. λ. we must of course read 'Εφεσίων πόλεως ἡ βουλὴ κ.τ.λ. Next, the order of words in 'Επὶ τοῦ δεῖνος ἀνθυπάτου is unusual; the name of the proconsul far more commonly follows his title when employed as a date, at all events in inscriptions, thus: 'Επὶ ἀνθυπάτου τοῦ δεῖνος. Again προβουλευθέντος is a very unusual expression. Then Wood's Πο. Γεμελλίνου Φλα|βιανοῦ is curiously similar to No. DXXXIII, DXLVI, DLXXIII. Lastly the tribe 'Αδριανή is not otherwise known at Ephesos. On the whole we may conclude that the dedication published by Mr. Wood is distinct from the one before us, but certainly not very accurately copied. I have therefore endeavoured to restore this document independently, without reference to Mr. Wood's inscription. From No. DXXXIII we recover the name of Gerellanus Flavianus and find him to be of the Teian tribe. It is very possible, however, that ΑΝΗΣ in line 13 is the termination of 'Αδρι]ανῆς, and that this epithet was occasionally affected by the Teian tribe in the days of the Antonines; see p. 69 ante. Curtius suggests δαπ]άνης, which is unlikely, and restores the line differently.

DIII.

A small column of white marble (βωμός? line 12), 'found near the City Port:' height 2 ft. ⅜ in.; diameter 1 ft. 4½ in. C. Curtius, Hermes iv, p. 186 foll.; Wood, Ephesus, Appendix, Inscriptions from the City, etc. 12.

ΚΑΙΑΥⲧ Ω	['Αρτέμιδι 'Εφισίᾳ],
ΑΔΡΙΑΝΩ ΑΝΤΩΝΕΙΝΩ	καὶ Αὐτ[οκράτορι Τ. Αἰλί]ῳ
ΚΑΙΣΑΡΙΣΕΒΑΣΤΩΕΥΣΕΒΕΙ	'Αδριανῷ 'Αντωνείνῳ
ΚΑΙΤΗΠΡΩΤΗΚΑΙΜΕΓΙΣΤΗ	Καίσαρι Σεβαστῷ Εὐσεβεῖ,
5 ΜΗΤΡΟΠΟΛΕΙΤΗΣΑΣΙΑΣ	5 καὶ τῇ πρώτῃ καὶ μεγίστῃ
ΚΑΙΔΙΣΝΕΩΚΟΡΟΥ•ΤΩΝΣΕΒΑΣΤΩΝ	μητροπόλει τῆς 'Ασίας
ΕΦΕΣΙΩΝΠΟΛΕΙ•ΚΑΙΤΟΙΣΕΠΙ	καὶ δὶς νεωκόρ(ῳ) τῶν Σεβαστῶν
ΤΟΤΕΛΩΝΙΟΝ•ΤΗΣ•ΙΧΘΥΙΚΗΣ	'Εφεσίων πόλει, καὶ τοῖς ἐπὶ
10 ΠΡΑΜΑΤΕΥΟΜΕΝΟΙΣ	τὸ τελώνιον τῆς ἰχθυϊκῆς
ΚΟΜΙΝΙΑ•ΙΟΥΝΙΑ	10 πραγματευομένοις,
ΣΥΝΤΩΒΩΜΩΤΗΝΕΙΣΙΝ	Κομινία 'Ιουνία
ΕΚΤΩΝΙΔΙΩΝΑΝΕΘΗΚΕΝ	σὺν τῷ βωμῷ τὴν Εἶσιν
	ἐκ τῶν ἰδίων ἀνέθηκεν
ΠΡΥΤΑΝΕΥΟ͆ΤΟ ΗΜ ▪ Λ͆	Πρυτανεύοντα[ς Τιβ. Κλ. Δ]ημ[οσ]τ[ρ]άτ[ου.

A dedication to [Artemis], the Emperor Antoninus Pius, and the city of Ephesus and the farmers of the 'fishery toll-house' (τὸ τελώνιον τῆς ἰχθυϊκῆς): the date is A. D. 138-161.

It is clear from καί in line 2 that another name preceded the Emperor's; this could only be the name of the goddess, as in C. I. 2958: 'Αρτέμιδι 'Εφεσίᾳ καὶ Αὐτοκράτορι Καίσαρι Σεβαστῷ, καὶ Τιβερίῳ Καίσαρι Σεβ. υἱῷ, καὶ τῷ δήμῳ τῶν 'Εφεσίων, κ. τ. λ.

In line 7 ΝΕΩΚΟΡΟΥ is a lapidary's error. The epithet νεωκόρος has been discussed already on Nos. ccccxcviii, D. Originally claimed by the city of Ephesos in 'proud humility' as the 'Sacristan' of Artemis (Acts xix, 35) it was afterwards usually employed in relation to the Cæsars, whose temple, or Augusteum, stood within the temenos of Artemis. In the time of Hadrian it was granted to the Ephesians to style themselves δὶς νεωκόροι τῶν Σεβαστῶν, a privilege granted κατὰ τὰ δόγματα τῆς ἱερωτάτης συγκλήτου (see the inscription in the Hermes, vii, p. 29 foll. = Wood, Ephesus, Inscriptions from the Great Theatre, No. 6). From the time of Severus we find τρὶς νεωκόρος. In the last line I have restored the name of the prytanis by comparison of No. DI ante (where see note) and C. I. 2955. The worship of Isis at Ephesos (line 12) is also referred to in the latter inscription.

By τοῖς ἐπὶ τὸ τελώνιον τῆς ἰχθυϊκῆς (sc. προσόδου) πραγματευομένοις C. Curtius very properly understands the farmers of the fishery customs: τὸ τελώνιον is their office, and πραγματεύεσθαι ἐπί τι is equivalent to περί τινος (see Winer, Grammar of N. T. Part iii, § 49, l). Just as the Abbey of St. Hilda had in old days a tithe from the Whitby fisheries, and a toll from every vessel that passed the town bridge, so Artemis was sole owner of certain fisheries at the mouth of the Kaÿster. A passage of Strabo (xiv, p. 642) illustrates this point: μετὰ δὲ τὴν ἐκβολὴν τοῦ Καΰστρου λίμνη ἐστὶν ἐκ τοῦ πελάγους ἀναχεομένη (καλεῖται ἡ Σελινουσία) καὶ ἐφεξῆς ἄλλη σύρρους αὐτῇ μεγάλας ἔχουσαι

προσόδους, ἃς οἱ βασιλεῖς μὲν ἱερὰς οὔσας ἀφείλοντο τὴν θεόν, 'Ρωμαῖοι δ' ἀπέδοσαν· πάλιν δ' οἱ δημοσιῶναι (the Roman publicani) βιασάμενοι περιέστησαν εἰς ἑαυτοὺς τὰ τέλη, πρεσβεύσας δὲ ὁ 'Αρτεμίδωρος (the geographer of Ephesos, fl. 100 B. C.), ὥς φησι, τάς τε λίμνας ἀπέλαβε τῇ θεῷ . . . . ἀντὶ δὲ τούτων εἰκόνα χρυσῆν ἀνέστησεν ἡ πόλις ἐν τῷ ἱερῷ. The 'great revenues' produced by these λίμναι or lagoons were from their fisheries. The temple authorities let out these fisheries at a certain rental, and the farmers of them are the persons called in the inscription οἱ ἐπὶ τὸ τελώνιον τῆς ἰχθυϊκῆς πραγματευομένοι. It was usual for mines, fisheries, salt-works, and the like, to be the property of the state. But in this and some other instances a fishery is the property of a temple: see Böckh. Staatsh. i, p. 414. In a report of the board of treasurers who managed the property of the Delian temple we find a fishery (τὴν θάλατταν) let out, just as sacred lands and other property were let out, to be farmed (C. I. A. i, No. 283; Hicks, Manual, No. 38, fin.). Similarly Pausanias (i, 38, § 1) tells us that the salt streams called 'Ρειτοί on the way to Eleusis were sacred to Demeter and Korè, and the priests of those divinities were alone permitted to take fish from these waters. The same writer also mentions a sacred lake (λίμνη) belonging to Poseidon at Ægiæ in Lakonia, which men were afraid to fish (iii, 21, § 5); and at Pharæ (vii, 22, § 2) he says: ὕδωρ ἱερόν ἐστι· 'Ερμοῦ νᾶμα μὲν τῇ πηγῇ τὸ ὄνομα, τοὺς δὲ ἰχθῦς οὐχ αἱροῦσιν ἐξ αὐτῆς, ἀνάθημα εἶναι τοῦ θεοῦ νομίζοντες (compare Schömann, Gr. Alt. ii, p. 189). It will be remembered that when Xenophon dedicated his shrine and temenos to the Ephesian Artemis at Skillus, among other points of similarity between his Artemision and its great prototype he is careful to mention the stream and its fishing: Anab. v, 3, § 8: ἔτυχε δὲ διὰ μέσου ῥέων τοῦ χωρίου ποταμὸς Σελινοῦς. καὶ ἐν 'Εφέσῳ δὲ παρὰ τὸν τῆς 'Αρτέμιδος νεὼν Σελινοῦς ποταμὸς παραρρεῖ, καὶ ἰχθύες δὲ ἐν ἀμφοτέροις ἔνεισι καὶ κόγχαι ('and there is salmons in both').

DIV.

Stelè of white marble, entire, but broken at the edges; height 1 ft. 6 in.; width 9 in.   Discovered by Mr. Wood, but unpublished.

N · ᴗ	[Αὐτοκράτορα Καίσαρα]
ΔΡΙΑΝ	[Τίτο]ν [Αἴλι]ο[ν
7ΩΝΕ	'Α]δριαν[ὸν
ΑΣΤΟ	'Αν]τωνε[ῖνον
5 ΤΟΝΣ‸	Σεβ]αστὸ[ν Εὐσεβῆ,
ΛΙΚΤΙΣΤ	5 τὸν σω[τῆρα
ΗΣ · ΕΦΕ,	κ]αὶ κτιστ[ὴν
ΠΩΛΕΣ	τ]ῆς 'Εφε[σίων
	π(ό)λεω[ς.
⟨ΟΙΝΤΟΣ	Κόϊντος . . .
10 ΤΙΟΣΓΑΙΟ	10 τιος Γάϊο[ς
ΕΚΤΩΝΙΔΙ	ἐκ τῶν ἰδί[ων
ὃ ΔΝΕΘΗ	ἀνέθη[κεν.

Dedication in honour of the Emperor Antoninus Pius, A. D. 138-161. He is styled not only the κτιστήρ but also the σωτήρ of the city ; this was a frequent combination of epithets : see the series of dedica-tions to Hadrian and to Antoninus at Athens, C. I. A. iii, No. 472 foll. Compare No. DII ante, where I have referred to the barbarism ΠΩΛΕΩΣ in line 8.

DV.

Plinth of statue in white marble, ' found near the central doorway of the Odeum' by Mr. Wood, together with the statue (see below) : height of the plinth 3½ in. ; diameter 3 ft. 2 in.   Wood, Ephesus, Inscriptions from the Odeum, No. 6, and ibid. p. 47 : C. Curtius, Hermes iv, p. 189; compare Archäol. Zeitung, 1868, p. 82.

ΛΟΥΚΙΟΝΑΙΛΙΟΝΑΥΡΗΛ ᴐΝΚΟΜΜΟΔΟΝΤΟΝΥΙΟΝΤ
ΑΥΤΟΚΡΑΤΟΡΟΣ · ΟΥΗΔΙΟΣΑΝΤΩΝΕΙΝΟΣ

Λούκιον Αἴλιον Αὑρήλ[ι]ον Κόμμοδον τὸν υἱὸν τ[οῦ
Αὑτοκράτορος Οὑήδιος 'Αντωνεῖνος.

From a statue of Lucius Verus, set up in the life-time of Antoninus Pius, and after that Emperor had adopted him along with M. Aurelius, Feb. 25, A. D. 138.

A good article upon Lucius Verus will be found in Smith's Dict. of Biogr. s. v. L. Ceionius Commodus : such was his original name. Upon his father's adoption by Hadrian he became a member of the Ælian gens, and was styled L. Ælius Aurelius Commodus.

The dedication is made by Vedius Antoninus, whose munificence in adding to the public buildings of Ephesos was the subject of several letters from Antoninus Pius to the Ephesian authorities (Nos. ccccxci-cccxciii ante). Some time between A. D. 140-144 Vedius held the office of γραμματεὺς τοῦ δήμου : see on No. ccccLxxxix, where other notices of Vedius are cited. All these Imperial letters just quoted were found inscribed in the Odeum (see p. 151 ante). If we are justified in supposing the Odeum itself to have been one of the buildings erected by Vedius, then it is obvious to conclude that as soon as the Odeum was completed, about A. D. 150 or a little later, Vedius placed in it this statue, in compliment to his patron Antoninus.

The statue, of which 'this was the inscribed base, has had an unfortunate history since its excavation. The legs and part of the trunk of the figure are with the base in the British Museum. The upper portion (excepting the head) was put on board a sailing vessel together with other antiquities from the Odeum ; the vessel was wrecked on the coast near Syra, and these marbles never reached England. The head of the statue had been appropriated by a man at Smyrna, by whom it is said to have been since transferred to the Museum of the Evangelical School (Wood, Ephesus, pp. 47, 50, 78).

DVI.

Part of an altar of white marble, surmounted by a plain moulding, but broken on all sides. Height 1 ft. 11 in.; width 7½ in. From Mr. Wood's excavations; unpublished.

```
       ϽΕΟΙΣΣΕΒ                    Θεοῖς Σεβ[αστοῖς καὶ
       ΜΫΣΤΑΙΣΑ                    μύσταις 'Α . . . . . .
       ΣΕΡΑΠΙΩΝΟ                   Σεραπίωνο[ς υἱὸς
       ΠΟΫΔΗΣ ΣΤ                   Πούδης σὺ[ν καὶ τοῖ-
   5   ΤΑΫΤΟΫΤΕΚ              5    ς αὐτοῦ τέκ[νοις τὸν
       ϽΜΟΝΑΦΙ                     β]αμὸν ἀφι[έρωσεν
       ϹΫΡΟΤΑΜ                     ἀρ]γυροταμ[ιεύσας,
       ⊠-ΟΫΙ-                      ἐπὶ] Πο. Οὐη[δ. 'Αντωνείνου
       ϽΚΟΣΤ                       κήρυ]κος τ[ῶν μυστῶν?
```

Dedication of an altar (line 6) to the 'Divine Augusti' and the mystæ. For the formula Θεοῖς Σεβαστοῖς compare C. I. 480, 2747, etc. The monument belongs to the reign of Antoninus Pius, if I am right in recognizing in line 8 the Vedius Antoninus of the preceding inscription: see also on No. cccclxxxix *ante*. Already on p. 80 of the Introductory Notice I have pointed out that there was at Ephesos a yearly celebration of the Eleusinian Mysteries, not indeed conducted by the State, but in the hands of a private religious society (θίασος) of Demetriasts. In this body Pudens (line 4), who dedicated the altar, had served as treasurer (line 7); and the date of the dedication is given by naming P. Vedius Antoninus who appears to have accepted the office of κῆρυξ (see Xen. Hell. ii, 4 § 20) this particular year among the Ephesian Demetriasts, and to have helped them with his well known wealth and influence. The restoration κήρυ[κος] in line 9 is fairly certain, as a portion of Υ seems visible. Compare No. DXCV, which refers to the same society.

But the best illustration of this subject is afforded by an inscription from Ephesos of which the original appears to be lost but which was published from the copy of Cyriacus of Ancona in the Bull. de Corr. Hell. i, p. 289. It is a letter addressed to the proconsul of Asia, Lucius Mestius Florus (A.D. 83–84: see Waddington, Fastes, p. 155), requesting permission to celebrate the Mysteries. It begins thus :—

```
      Λουκίῳ Μεστίῳ Φλώρῳ ἀνθυπάτῳ παρὰ
      Λουκίου Πομπηίου 'Απολλωνίου 'Εφεσίου·
      Μυστήρια καὶ θυσίαι, Κύριε, καθ' ἕκαστον
      ἐνιαυτὸν ἐπιτελοῦνται ἐν 'Εφέσῳ Δήμητρι
  5   Καρποφόρῳ καὶ Θεσμοφόρῳ καὶ θεοῖς
      Σεβαστοῖς ὑπὸ μυστῶν μετὰ πολλῆς
      ἁγνείας καὶ νομίμων ἐθῶν σὺν ταῖς
      ἱερίαις ἀπὸ πλείστων ἐτῶν συντετηρημένα
      ἀπὸ βασιλέων καὶ Σεβαστῶν καὶ τῶν
 10   κατ' ἐνιαυτὸν ἀνθυπάτων κ. τ. λ.
```

DVII.

Fragment of moulding, probably from the top of a stele: white marble. Measures 9½ in. by 5 in. From Mr. Wood's excavations; unpublished.

```
      ΑΫΡΙ-

      ϽΝΕΙ

      ΙΑΝϹ

      ΑϽ
```

The occurrence of Αὐρή[λιος] in line 1 and Σαρμ]ατ[ικός in line 4, connects the inscription either with M. Aurelius or with Commodus. The restoration of the lines becomes easy if we understand the inscription to have been in honour of Commodus, erected during the lifetime of M. Aurelius. We may read as follows :—

Αὐτοκράτορα Καίσαρα Λούκιον]Αὐρή[λιον Κόμμοδον Αὐτοκράτ·

ορος Καίσαρος Μάρκου Αὐρηλίου 'Αντ]ονεί[νου Σεβαστοῦ
    υἱόν,
θεοῦ 'Αντωνείνου υἱωνὸν, θεοῦ 'Αδρ]ιανο[ῦ ἔγγονον, θεοῦ
    Τραιανοῦ
Παρθικοῦ ἀπόγονον, Γερμανικὸν, Σαρμ]ατ[ικὸν κ. τ. λ.

Compare C. I. 1319: the date will be between A.D. 177–180. Ο for Ω in line 2 is an instance of late spelling.

DVIII.

Fragment of white marble, broken on all sides, height 7¾ in.; width 10½ in.   From Mr. Wood's excavations; unpublished.

```
       ͻ Υ Λ Ι Α ϩ
       ΙΟΙΗϹΑ
       ⊤ · Ř · Υ Ο Σ
```

'Ι]ουλίᾳ Σ[εβαστῇ
νεο]ποιήσα[ς εὐσεβῶς
. . . . Κο(ίντου) υἱὸς [ἀνέθηκεν.

Dedication to Julia Domna, consort of the Emperor Severus, erected in her lifetime.   Another dedication in her honour at Ephesos is given in C. I. 2972; compare 2971.   The name of the giver is mutilated, but he had served the office of temple-warden (νεοποιός, *ante* p. 81); and I have therefore restored line 2 after the model of the numerous dedications from νεοποιοί given in section vii (see Nos. DLXVI–DLXXI).   It is highly probable that this marble, like most of those just referred to, was found by Mr. Wood in the Augusteum.   The date would be between A. D. 175–217.

DIX.

Three fragments of white marble *crusta*, a little over ⅛ an inch thick.   From the sameness of the moulding on the left, and the similarity of the letters and material, it is clear they belong to each other.   *a* is entire at top and left; measures 8 in. by 8½ in.   *b* entire on left only, measures 2½ in. by 5½ in.   *c* entire on left only, measures 4 in. by 4 in.   From Mr. Wood's excavations; unpublished.

a.

```
    Α ι
    ΑΥΤΟΚΡΑ
    ΡΩΑ
```

a.

'Αγ[αθῇ τύχῃ?]
Αὐτοκρά[τορι Καίσαρι Μ. Αὐρ. Σεουή-
ρῳ 'Α[λεξάνδρῳ Σεβαστῷ κ. τ. λ.

b.

```
    ΤΙΒ . ι
    ι ∩
```

b.

Τιβ. [Κλ. ? . . .
. . . .

c.

```
    ΑΥΡ
    ΟΡΔΙ
```

c.

Αὐρ.
'Ορδ[εων? . . .

The restoration of the name of Alexander Severus in *a* is all but certain.   The inscription appears to have been erected in his honour by a person or persons whose names were given below (see *b* and *c*).

DX.

Fragment of white marble: broken on all sides.   Height 3⅞ in.; width 8½ in.   From Mr. Wood's excavations; unpublished.

```
    ΙΣΕΒΑΣˉ
```

. . Σεβασ[τὸν .
. . . . .

There remain traces of a lower line: the characters are firm and chaste enough for the Augustan age.

--- --- ---

DXI.

Fragment of a white marble stelè, entire on right and at top only, surmounted by a moulding; height 6¼ in.; width 2¼ in. From Mr. Wood's excavations; unpublished. Probably from the Augusteum.

```
erasure  ΚΑΙΣΑΡΙ
ΠΟΙΗΣΑΝΤΕΣ ~
       )ΝΟΣ ὁ
```

Σεπτιμίῳ Γέτᾳ] Καίσαρι
οἱ νεο]ποιήσαντες
. . . . . . ωνος (ορ . . ωνος)

The name is intentionally erased from the earlier portion of line 1, and there is much probability that we should restore as I have suggested. It is well known that after the murder of Geta in A. D. 212, Caracalla ordered his name to be obliterated from all public monuments. Sometimes however the name can still be read in spite of the erasure. see C. I. 2091 b (from Olbia): Ἀγαθῇ τύχῃ, Σεπ[τίμιον] Γέταν Καίσαρα ἡ βουλὴ καὶ ὁ δῆμος ὁ Ὀλβιοπολειτῶν. Perhaps a companion stelè originally commemorated Caracalla also (Μάρκος Αὐρήλιος Ἀντωνεῖνος). Lines 3 foll. may have read: ἐπὶ . . . . ωνος | καθιέρωσαν.

DXII.

Fragment of blue-veined marble, entire at the top only; height 7 in.; width 8¼ in. From Mr. Wood's excavations; unpublished. Probably from the Augusteum.

```
ˎΚΑΙΤΟΙ
ΚΟΥΥΙΟ
```

Ἀρτέμιδι Ἐφεσίᾳ] καὶ τοῖς Σεβαστοῖς
. . . . Μάρ]κου υἱὸ[ς . . . . ἀνέθηκεν ?

Compare Nos. DIII, DVI, DXIII. I suppose the monument to have been dedicated to Artemis and the Augusti (M. Aurelius and L. Verus ?).

DXIII.

Part of a circular base of white marble; height 2¼ in.; length 1 ft. 2¼ in. From Mr. Wood's excavations; unpublished.

ΑΡΤΕΜΙΔΙΕΦΕΣΙΑΙΚΑˈ

Ἀρτέμιδι Ἐφεσίᾳ καὶ [Αὐτοκράτορι Καίσαρι Σεβαστῷ κ.τ.λ.

A dedication in honour of Artemis and one of the Emperors, like C. I. 2958 and 2959; compare the preceding inscription.

DXIV.

Fragment of white marble, entire only on the right and bottom edge; probably part of a statue-base. Height 3¼ in.; length 1 ft. 9¼ in. Wood, Ephesus, Inscriptions from the Augusteum, No. 10.

```
ΙΙΛΗ.ΛΙ.ΖΛΓΙΣΕΒΑΣΤΩ
ˎΙΙΝΑΓΝΕΙΑΝΚΑΘΙΕΡΩΣΑΝ
```

Μάρκῳ Αὐρηλίῳ Ἀντωνεί]ῳ Καίσαρι Σεβαστῷ
οἱ νεωποιοί? τηρήσαντε]ς τὴν ἁγνείαν καθιέρωσαν.

I have restored line 1 as if it referred to Marcus | Hadrian; or Τ. Αἰλίῳ Ἀντωνεί]νῳ Κ, Σ., i. e. Antoninus Aurelius. But we might equally well read Αὐτοκράτορι Pius; or Μ. Αὐρηλίῳ Κομμόδῳ Ἀντωνεί]νῳ Κ. Σ. i. e. Τραϊανῷ Ἀδρια]νῷ Καίσαρι Σεβαστῷ, and understand | Commodus; or again, Μ. Αὐρηλίῳ Ἀντωνεί]νῳ Κ. Σ.

i. e. Caracalla (see on No. DXI *ante*). Mr. Wood's editor translates ἁγνείαν ' an expiatory offering,' and makes it depend directly upon καθιέρωσαν. I prefer to understand the monument itself as the object dedicated, while ἁγνεία in all the inscriptions where it occurs (see Röhl's index to C. I.) signifies personal and ceremonial purity. Indeed ἁγνός and ἁγνεία are equivalent to the Latin integer, integritas; and often, as here, refer to the strict discharge of official duty (Waddington, Fastes, p. 96). Nos. DLXXVIII, DLXXXVIII*b post*, are dedications couched in similar terms to this.

DXV.

Fragment of blue marble moulding, evidently from the top of a stelè : measures 6 in. by 6 in.   Entire only at top.   From Mr. Wood's excavations ; unpublished.

ΤΥΧΗΙ
ΑΙ ϝ Α

'Αγαθῇ] τύχῃ
Αὐτοκράτορα Κ]αίσα[ρα
κ. τ. λ.

The iota adscriptum, and the style of the letters, betoken a comparatively early date ; probably 1st century A. D.

DXVI.

Fragment of white marble *crusta* ¾ in. thick : entire at top only : height 2 in.; width 12½ in.   From Mr. Wood's excavations ; unpublished.

Α Τ Ο Ν · Τ ο · Β

. . . . . ὑπ]ατον τὸ β̅ . . . .

From an inscription in honour of an Emperor, set up during his second consulship.

DXVII.

A fragment of white marble wall-facing, 1¾ in. thick, height 4¼ in., width 7 in.   Broken on all sides.   From Mr. Wood's excavations; unpublished.

ΙΕΙ ΙΣ Ι Μι
ΙΔΙΣΝΕΟΚΟΡΟΝ
ΝΑΣΙΑΝΟΙΚΟϤ
Ϥ · ΤΗΝι

Τὴν πρώτην καὶ] μεγίστην[ν μητρόπολιν
τῆς 'Ασίας κα]ὶ δὶς νεοκόρον [τῶν Σεβαστῶν οἱ κατὰ τὴ]ν 'Ασίαν οἰκοῦ[ντες 'Ρωμαῖοι?
. . . . τὴν . . . .

We may append to the preceding dedications in honour of the Imperial family, a ‚dedication in honour of the city of Ephesos. The form ΝΕΟΚΟΡΟΣ is not an accidental blunder, but a degenerate form, which occurs in No. D : so 'Αντ]ονεί[νος, No. DVII. The ' second neokorate ' of Ephesos began in the reign of Hadrian, and lasted till the reign of Severus who granted the title of τρὶς νεοκόρος ; see on No. DIII.

SECTION IV.

PUBLIC WORKS AND BUILDINGS.

DXVIII.

Five fragments of torus-mouldings from the bases of columns, of reddish-coloured marble. Discovered by Mr. Wood in his excavations at Ephesos. A careful examination of these marbles proves that *a b* probably are from the same column, *c d* from another, and *e* from a third. Hicks, Manual, No. 4; Röhl, Inscriptiones Antiq., No. 493 (compare p. 183) gives a good facsimile.

a.	*b.*	*c.*	*d.*	*e.*
Height 2¼ in.; length 5¼ in.	Height 5⅛ in.; length 6⅛ in.	Height 2⅝ in.; length 3 in.	Height 2¼ in.; length 4⅞ in.	Height 2⅛ in.; length 3¼ in.
Κ Ρ	Ͻ Η Κ	Β Α	Α Ν Ι	Ε Ν

Βασιλεὺς] Κρ[οῖσος ἀνέ]θηκ[ε. — *Βα[σιλεὺς Κροῖσος] ἀνέ[θηκε.* — ...... *ἀνέθηκ]εν*

There can be little doubt that these fragments are from the columns of the former temple of the Ephesian Artemis, of which Chersiphron was the architect (Strabo, xiv, p. 640: *τὸν δὲ νεὼν τῆς Ἀρτέμιδος πρῶτος μὲν Χερσίφρων ἠρχιτεκτόνησεν.* Pliny, N. H. xxxvi, 14, § 95: Græcæ magnificentiæ vera admiratio exstat templum Ephesiæ Dianæ cxx annis factum a tota Asia .... operi præfuit Chersiphron). That temple owed much to the munificence of Krœsos, and Herodotos says that he gave most of the columns (i, 92): *Κροίσῳ δὲ ἔστι καὶ ἄλλα ἀναθήματα ἐν τῇ Ἑλλάδι πολλά, καὶ οὐ τὰ εἰρημένα μοῦνα. ἐν μὲν γὰρ Θήβῃσι τῇσι Βοιωτῶν τρίπους χρύσεος, τὸν ἀνέθηκε τῷ Ἀπόλλωνι τῷ Ἰσμηνίῳ· ἐν δὲ Ἐφέσῳ αἵ τε βόες αἱ χρύσεαι καὶ τῶν κιόνων αἱ πολλαί· ἐν δὲ Προνηΐης τῆς ἐν Δελφοῖσι ἀσπὶς χρυσέη μεγάλη. ταῦτα μὲν καὶ ἔτι ἐς ἐμὲ ἦν περιεόντα.* These last words read as if Herodotos had himself seen the name of King Krœsos upon the Ephesian columns. We know that the names of the donors were inscribed upon the columns of the restored temple (see on No. DXIX); if, therefore, the present fragments are from the older temple (which seems nearly certain), then it is more likely than not that they should bear the name of Krœsos.

Only one objection could be made to this conjecture, viz. that the characters are not archaic enough for the middle of the sixth century B.C. But we may reply (1) that these characters are decidedly more archaic than those of the Augury-rules (No. DCLXXVIII *post*), which Kirchhoff places 'about Ol. 80' or earlier, that is, in the middle of the fifth century B.C. (Studien zur Gesch. d. gr. Alphab., 4th ed., p. 13 ff.). So that these fragments are, at the lowest estimate, dated back into the sixth century. (2) It is not necessary, though it would be more natural, to suppose that the inscriptions were actually engraved upon the columns during the reign of Krœsos. The temple was 120 years in building, according to Pliny, i.e. about B.C. 580–460 (Brunn, Gesch. der griech. Künstler ii, p. 345). There seems however no reason why these inscriptions should not be considered contemporary with Krœsos (Kirchhoff, Studien, 4th ed., p. 22). Traces of the older temple were found by Mr. Wood (Ephesus, pp. 174, 261, 263), especially portions of archaic reliefs (Murray, Hist. of Greek Sculpture, i, 111 foll.).

DXIX.

A number of fragments of white marble from the base-mouldings (tori) of the columns of the Artemision. Röhl, Schedæ Epigraphicæ 1876, p. 1; Wood, Ephesus, Inscriptions from the site of the Temple, No. 17.

a.

1.	2.	3.	4.
Γ'	ΣΑΡΔΙΗΝΗΑΡ	ΔΙ	ϽΥΔΟ

(1) Height 5 in.; width 10½ in. (2) Height 8 in.; length 2 ft. 2½ in. (3) Height 4⅓ in.; width 3¾ in.
(4) Height 4½ in.; width 8¼ in.

.... γ .. *Σαρδιηνὴ Ἀρτ[έμι]δι τ[ὸν] οὐδὸ[ν ἀνέθηκεν.*

The letter following Γ was either ι or Η. The letters of α are all between two and three inches in height, and beautifully inscribed; their forms precisely suit the date of the restoration of the temple in the second half of the fourth century B.C. The rebuilding is thus described by Strabo (xiv, 640): ὡς δὲ τοῦτον (the older temple) Ἡρόστρατός τις ἐνέπρησεν, ἄλλον ἀμείνω κατεσκεύασαν συνενέγκαντες τὸν τῶν γυναικῶν κόσμον καὶ τὰς ἰδίας οὐσίας, διαθέμενοι δὲ (selling) καὶ τοὺς προτέρους κίονας· (see on No. DXVIII) τούτων δὲ μαρτυριά ἐστι τὰ γενηθέντα τότε ψηφίσματα. Perhaps the enactments referred to by Strabo as illustrating the way funds were raised for the rebuilding are what are mentioned by Pseud. Aristot. (Œcon. ii, 20) : Ἐφέσιοι δεηθέντες χρημάτων νόμον ἔθεντο μὴ φορεῖν χρυσὸν τὰς γυναῖκας, ὅσον δὲ νῦν ἔχουσι δανείσαι τῇ πόλει· τῶν τε κιόνων τῶν ἐν τῷ νεῷ τάξαντες ἀργύριον ὃ δεῖ καταβαλεῖν (i. e. defining the estimated cost of each column), εἴων ἐπιγράφεσθαι τὸ ὄνομα τοῦ δόντος τὸ ἀργύριον ὡς ἀνατεθεικότος. The statements of both writers however refer to the women of Ephesos only. Our inscription shows that other cities of Asia afforded munificent donors, and thereby confirms the expression of Pliny (N. H. xvi, 40, § 213), tota Asia exstruente, concerning the restored temple, which he proceeds to say, was built 400 years before his own day. The Ionic forms Σαρδιηνή and οὐδό[ν] are interesting. This lady of Sardes appears to have presented not only the column which bore her name, but also the marble step (λάϊνος οὐδός, II. ix, 404, etc.) upon which the column stood. This column, Mr. Wood writes to me, stood in the outer rank on the north side, a little to the east of the centre.

b.

I have grouped under *b* eleven fragments of torus inscribed with letters very similar to each other, well formed and two inches high. We have no information as to the exact quarter of the temple-site where they were found.

1.

Height 6 in. ; length 1 ft. 1½ in.

ΡΙΧΤ)Α

'Α]ριστοά[ναξ? ἀνέθηκε.

This name is found in No. CCCLXXVII, line 98 (*ante* Pt. ii) under the form Ἀριστῶναξ : compare Πλειστοάναξ. The stone is made up of two fragments, recently found to belong to each other.

2.	3.
Height 4½ in. ; width 8 in.	Height 3½ in. ; width 7 in.
ΕΘ⊦	ΡUᐱ
[ἀν]έθη[κε].	. . . ρος [ἀνέθηκε].

Fragment No. 3 is made up of two smaller bits recently joined together.

4.	5.	6.	7.
Height 3½ in. ; width 6 in.	Height 5½ in. ; width 10 in.	Height 5½ in. ; width 6½ in.	Height 6 in. ; width 10 in.
ΤΕᗽ	ᐱΝΤ	ΕΜ	ᐱΡΟΥ
'Αρ]τίμ[ιδι.	'Αντ . . .	['Αρτ]έμ[ιδι].	. . . δρου.

8.	9.	10.	11.
Height 5½ in. ; width 8 in.	Height 2½ in. ; width 6 in.	Height 3½ in. ; width 3½ in.	Height 2¼ in. ; width 4½ in.
ᐱΝΕ	⊦Υ	ΤС	–ιι
ἀνέ[θηκε].	. . ρυ . .	. . . το . . .	['Αρτ]έμ?[ιδι].

c.

The fragments grouped under *c* are inscribed in characters similar to *b* in form and size, and are said to have been found in the north corner of the temple site.

1.	2.	3.	4.
Height 2½ in. ; width 6¼ in.	Height 2¾ in. ; width 4½ in.	Height 3 in. ; width 5 in.	Height 3½ in. ; width 7 in.
ᴇΥΧ	Ε,	ᴋΕ	ΕΘ⊦
. . . ευς . . .	'Αρτ?] έμ[ιδι?	[ἀνέθη]κε.	ἀν]έθη[κε].

d.

The following 4 fragments are said to come from the south corner of the temple site : inscribed with letters very similar to *b, c.*

1.	2.	3.	4.
Height 4½ in.; width 6¼ in.	Height 4 in.; width 7 in.	Height 2¾ in.; width 8¼ in.	Height 3½ in.; width 6½ in.
OP	NEC	TUI	+KE
. . θρ . .	ἀ]νέθ[ηκε].	. . . τομ ? . . .	ἀνέθ]ηκε,

e.

This fragment has a smaller moulding, and different letters, though of the same size as the preceding.

Height 2½ in.; width 2½ in.

ϽΛ

. . . θα . . .; or perhaps Ἀριστ]οδ[να̣ξ, compare *b* 1.

f.

Two fragments closely alike, but in decidedly smaller letters than the rest.

1.	2.
Height 2¾ in.; width 3 in. Letters 1½ in. high.	Height 2½ in.; width 3 in. Letters 1 in. high.
＼ΡΊ	ϽΝΡ
Ἀρτ[έμιδι ?.	. . . ονα . . .

g.

This fragment is said to come from the north-west portion of the temple site. Compare *a.*

Height 3 in.; width 4 in. Letters 2 in. high.

ΝⱵ

ἡ δεῖνα . . . . .]νὴ [ἀνέθηκε.

h.

Discovered by Mr. Wood in 1884.

Letter 1¾ in. high.

Λ

i.

It is doubtful whether this is really a fragment from a column : it certainly differs from the torus-mouldings that have preceded.

Height 3½ in.; width 5 in. Letters about 1½ in. high.

ΜΙΔϹ

Ἀρτέ]μιδο[ς.

Six columns at Euromos in Karia, of Roman times, inscribed with the names of their donors, are described C. I. 2713, 2714 (= Waddington-Le Bas, Nos. 313–318). A curious parallel may be found in some mediæval churches; thus at Whitby Abbey an inscription, now partly obliterated, upon one of the columns in the north transept formerly read thus (date about 1200) : Johannes de Brumpton quondam famulos (*sic*) domino de la Phe has columnas erexit in metum et honerum (*sic*) Beate Marie. The Minstrel Pillar in St. Mary's Church, Beverley, is another instance. Compare also No. DCXVIII, *b*, lines 16 foll.

DXX.

Wall-stone of white marble ; entire on all the edges, except the right which is broken.   Height 1 1½ in. ;   present length 1 ft. 4 in.   Discovered by Mr. Wood; unpublished.   On the left return-face of the stone is inscribed No. DCLXXXVII, *d, post.*

ΓΟΤΕΜΕΝΟΣΞΗΛι
ΓΤΑΝ ΟΣΟΝΕΣΛΓι
ΓΤΑΡΑΒΑΙΝΗΙΑΥΤΟΣ

Τὸ τέμενος τῆς ['Αρτέμιδος ἀσυλόν ἐστι τὸ
πᾶν. 'Όσον ἴσω π[εριβόλου, μὴ ἀδικείν ὃς δ' ἂν
παραβαίνῃ, αὐτὸς [ἀπόλοιτο καὶ τὸ γένος.

Part of an inscription from the temenos of a goddess, warning persons who enter it against certain transgressions. The restorations are merely conjectural.

The letters belong to the later Hellenistic period i. e. the second century B. C. The iota adscriptum is inserted in ΓΤΑΡΑΒΑΙΝΗΙ. The inscription was completed in three lines, as the marble both above and below is uninscribed. Also a glance at the marble suffices to show that it was a wall-stone. Such are the only indications afforded by the monument itself. Mr. Wood has made no note of the spot where it was discovered. We are left to conjecture its origin, and why the left return came to be inscribed with No. DCLXXXVII *d.*

The restorations suggested in the cursive text will show that I believe this marble to have stood originally in the temenos of Artemis, either as part of the peribolos-wall, or else as part of the wall of some building within the temenos. In line 1 I think the foot of Λ or Α is visible after ΤΗΣ : if so the conjecture is made the more probable. It was a common practice to place some kind of caution at the entrance of a sacred precinct ; so Lucian, de Sacrificiis iii, p. 536 (ed. Lehmann): καὶ τὸ πρόγραμμά φησι, μὴ παριέναι εἴσω τῶν περιῤῥαντηρίων, ὅστις μὴ καθαρὸς

ἐστι τὰς χεῖρας. Compare the stelè, set up by Xenophon at Skillus (Anab. v, 3, § 13): 'Ιερὸς ὁ χῶρος τῆς 'Αρτέμιδος κ.τ.λ. ; Dittenberger, Syll. No. 378 : 'Ιερὸν τὸ τέμενα[ς] τοῦ 'Ασκληπιοῦ καὶ τῆς 'Υγιείας κ.τ.λ. My restorations are merely intended to suggest the probable drift of the meaning. With line 3 compare C. I. 2919 (see Hermann, Gottesd. Alt. 10, 16): 'Όρος ἱερὸς ἀσυλος Διονύσο[υ] Βάκχου τὸν ἱκέτην [μὴ] ἀδικεῖ[ν] μηδὲ ἀδικούμενον [περι]οράν· εἰ δὲ μὴ, ἐξώλη εἶναι καὶ αὐτ[ὸν] καὶ τὸ γένος α[ὐ]τσ[ῦ]. Some interesting illustrations of the sanctity of Greek τεμένη are afforded by the lease of τεμένη belonging to the deme of Peiræeus, Pt. i, No. xiii *ante* (compare the similar lease of the deme Æxoneis, C. I. 93) ; and by the decree from Ialysos in Rhodes, Pt. ii, No. CCCXLIX *ante.*

The history of the asylum of the Artemision, and the successive alterations of the peribolos-wall, are so well known (see on No. DXXII *post*), that one is tempted to connect the present inscription with one of these changes in the extent of the temenos. Strabo (xiv, p. 641) names Alexander the Great, Mithridates, and Augustus. But our document is certainly later than Alexander, and probably earlier than Mithridates. It is therefore best to refrain from conjecture.

DXXI.

A wall-stone of white marble, beautifully inscribed with letters 1½ in. high, entire at the top and left : mutilated at the right and at bottom, the marble having been used for some purpose irrespective of the inscription.   Height 1 ft. 8½ in. ;   width 4 ft. 11½ in.   C. Curtius, Hermes, iv, 194 foll. ; Waddington, Fastes, p. 84.

ΜΑΡΚΟΣΕΡΕΝΝΙΟΣ ΠΙΚ ΗΣ ΑΝΘ
ΑΦΑΝΟΥΣΓΕΓΕΝΗΜΕΝΟΥΤΟΥΠι
ΜΑΤΟΣΟΠΕΡΔΗΜΟΣΙΑΙΚΑΤΑΣΚΕ
ΕΦΕΣΙΩΝΜΕΤΑΞΥΤΗΣΑΓΟΡΑΣΚΑ
5 ΝΟΣΓΕΓΟΝΕΝΑΙΣΥΝΕΦΩΝΕΙΤΟ·Ε
ΤΩΝΚΑΙΡΩΝΗΤΟΥΠΟΛΕΜΟΥΠΕ
ΤΕΛΙΑΤΥΝΤΟΥΤΟΝΑΜΕΛΙΑΝΟΙΤ

Μάρκος 'Ερέννιος Πίκης ἀνθ[ύπατος λέγει·
'Αφανοῦς γεγενημένου τοῦ πα[ροικοδομή-
ματος, ὅπερ δημοσίᾳ κατασκε[υῇ ὑπὸ τῶν
'Εφεσίων μεταξὺ τῆς ἀγορᾶς κα[ὶ τοῦ λιμέ-
5 νος γεγονέναι συνεφωνεῖτο, ε[ἴτε ἔν τινι
τῶν καιρῶν ἢ τοῦ πολέμου πε[ριστάσει, εἴτε διὰ τὴν τούτων ἀμέλιαν, οἱ τ[εταγμένοι? κ.τ.λ.

A proclamation of the proconsul Marcus Herennius Picens, concerning the restoration of an old building once existing near the agora, which had entirely disappeared. Picens was consul suffectus Nov. ɪ, ʙ.c. 34 (Ephemeris Epigr. iii, 12), and he was probably sent as proconsul to Asia after his consulship (Waddington, Fastes, p. 85).

The surface of the marble is much worn, but with care a completer text has been recovered than was given by previous editors. M. Waddington is right in claiming for the characters and for the general style of the document a date as early as Augustus. For the formula of line 1 compare No. cccclxxxii, a. It is uncertain what was the structure spoken of in lines 2, 3. Waddington restores πα[λαιοῦ χό]|ματος. I prefer πα[ροικοδομῆ]|ματος or πα[ρατειχίσ]|ματος, as better filling the space. Line 4 : λιμέ]νος is fairly certain. This harbour is not the Panormos mentioned by Strabo (xiv, p. 639 : εἶτα λιμὴν Πάνορμος καλούμενος ἔχων ἱερὸν τῆς Ἐφεσίας Ἀρτέμιδος), but a basin within the city itself, formed by the enlargement of

the bed of the Kaÿster, and immediately adjoining the Agora and Gymnasium. The best account of the buildings in the Agora is to be found in Falkener's work, Ephesus and the Temple of Diana, p. 48 and p. 119 : see also the plans in Wood's Ephesus, and E. Curtius, Ephesos, ein Vortrag. pl. ɪ. The restoration of the last three lines is merely to suggest the connexion of thought. The building in question had been destroyed either in times of revolution or of war, or else through the mere neglect of the proper authorities. Ἀμέλιαν for ἀμέλειαν in line 7 is precisely parallel with τιχισθῆναι in No. dxxii, and ῥῖθρα in Nos. dxxiii, dxxiv, also of the Augustan age. The impersonal use of συνεφωνεῖτο (' everybody said ') in line 5 is curious, and suggests the thought that this document is a too literal translation from a Latin original, which might have run as follows : Pessum dato munimento, quod publico opere ab Ephesiis inter forum portumque factum fuisse consensum est, sive aliqua temporum aut belli calamitate, sive per harum rerum incuriam, etc.

DXXII.

Block of white marble, height 1 ft. 5½ in.; length 5 ft. 9½ in.; found in situ built into the peribolos-wall of the Artemision. Wood, Ephesus, p. 133, and Appendix, Inscriptions from the Peribolus Wall, No. 1 ; Waddington, Fastes, p. 94 ; C. I. L. iii, 6070. The lapidary divides ΣΕΒΑΣ ΤΟΣ in line 5, to allow for a hole in the surface of his marble.

IMP·CAESAR·DIVI·F·AVG·COS·XII·TR·POT·XVIII·PONTIFEX
MAXIMVS·EX·REDITV·DIANAE·FANVM·ET·AVGVSTEVM·MVRO
MVNIENDVM·CVRAVIT·C·ASINIO (Ancient erasure.) ·CVRATORE·
(Ancient erasure.)   SEX·LARTIDIO·LEG·

5 ΑΥΤΟΚΡΑΤΩΡΚΑΙΣΑΡΘΕΟΥΥΙΟΣΣΕΒΑΣ ΤΟΣΥΠΑΤΟΣΤΟΙΒΔΗΜΑΡΧΙΚΗΣΕΞΟΥΣΙΑΣΤΟΙΗ
⁻ΩΝΙΕΡΩΝΤΗΣΘΕΟΥΠΡΟΣΟΔΩΝΤΟΝ ΝΕΩΚΑΙΤΟΣΕΒΑΣΤΗΟΝΤΙΧΙΣΘΗΝΑΙΠΡΟΕΝΟΗΘΗ
ΕΠΙΜΕΛΗΑΣΕΞΣΤΟΥΛΑΡΤΙΔΙΟΥ ΠΡΕΣΒΕΥΤΟΥ

Imp(erator) Cæsar, divi f(ilius), Aug(ustus), cōs(ul) xii., tr(ibuniciæ) pot(estatis) xviii., pontifex
maximus, ex reditu Dianæ fanum et Augusteum muro
muniendum curavit, C(aio) Asinio [Gallo procōs(ule)], curatore
Sex(to) Lartidio leg(ato).

5 Αὐτοκράτωρ Καῖσαρ θεοῦ υἱὸς Σεβαστὸς ὕπατος τὸ ιβ̄, δημαρχικῆς ἐξουσίας τὸ ιη̄,
ἐκ] τῶν ἱερῶν τῆς θεοῦ προσόδων τόν [τε] νεὼ καὶ τὸ Σεβαστῆον τιχισθῆναι προενοήθη,
ἐπὶ ἀνθυπάτου Γαίου Ἀσινίου Γάλλου,] ἐπιμελῆς Σέξστου Λαρτιδίου πρεσβευτοῦ.

Tablet recording the rebuilding of the peribolos of the Artemision by order of Augustus, ʙ.c. 6.

This document is of interest in connexion with the proconsulate of C. Asinius Gallus, lines 3, 6. He was consul ʙ.c. 8, having three years previously married Vipsania, whom Tiberius had divorced ʙ.c. 11, in order to marry Julia. This arrangement, which was due to the commands of Augustus, proves how high Gallus stood in his favour; but Tiberius never forgave the man who had thus married the wife he had loved. M. Waddington (Fastes, p. 96) thinks it may have been by favour of Augustus that Gallus was sent as proconsul to Asia only two years after his consulate. A law of Pompey ʙ.c. 52 had

ordained that consuls and prætors might not obtain the government of a province until five years after the resignation of their civic office (Dio Cassius, xl, chs. 30, 56). This law, which was not strictly observed, was re-enacted by Augustus ʙ.c. 27 (Dio Cassius, liii, ch. 14 ; Suetonius, Octavian, ch. 36) M. Waddington, (Fastes, p. 12) who has made the subject of provincial government his study, can only point to two instances in which Augustus broke through this rule ; one is the case of Asinius Gallus. Our inscription is dated by means of the 12th consulate of Augustus, and his 18th tribunitian power. He was consul xii from January to December ʙ.c. 5 ; and his 18th tribunitian power lasted from June 27 ʙ.c. 6 to

z z

June 26 B.C. 5. Moreover it is well known that the proconsuls of Asia entered upon their office in the spring (about May) of each year. These facts enable us to determine the date of our inscription within the first four or five months of the year B.C. 5.

In this, as in the two next documents (Nos. DXXIII–DXXIV) the name of C. Asinius Gallus has been anciently obliterated from the marble. In line 3, however, the lapidary has done his work carelessly, and the names C. Asinio remain untouched, while beneath the erasure the words GALLO · PROCOS can still be faintly traced. This erasure took place A.D. 30, when the senate sentenced him to death. Dio Cassius tells the story (lviii, 3) : τῷ δὲ δὴ Γάλλῳ ὁ Τιβέριος, τῷ τήν τε γυναῖκα αὐτοῦ ἀγαγομένῳ καὶ τῇ περὶ τῆς ἀρχῆς χρησαμένῳ παρρησίᾳ, καιρὸν λαβὼν ἐπίθετο . . . . ἐν γὰρ τῇ αὐτῇ ἡμέρᾳ παρά τε τῷ Τιβερίῳ εἱστιάθη καὶ φιλοτησίας ἔπιε, καὶ ἐν τῷ βουλευτηρίῳ κατεψηφίσθη, ὥστε καὶ στρατηγὸν τὸν δήσοντά τε αὐτὸν καὶ πρὸς τὴν τιμωρίαν ἀπάξοντα πεμφθῆναι. How Tiberius kept him in prison for three years until death by starvation put an end to his sufferings, is well known to us from the pages of Tacitus (Ann. vi, 23, 25).

We learn from our inscription that the Ephesians had already built an Augusteum, or temple to Augustus, within the precinct of the Artemision. The site of this building was thought by Mr. Wood to be indicated by some Roman ruins discovered by him not far from the s. w. corner of the Temple (Ephesus, p. 153; see note on No. CCCCXCVIII *an(c)*).

This rebuilding of the peribolos has an interesting connexion both with the history of the Artemision, and with the policy of Augustus. We are informed by Strabo (xiv, p. 641) that the limits of the sanctuary had frequently been changed : ἄσυλον δὲ μένει τὸ ἱερὸν καὶ νῦν καὶ πρότερον· τῆς δ᾿ ἀσυλίας τοὺς ὅρους ἀλλαγῆναι συνέβη πολλάκις. Alexander extended the limit to the radius of ⅛ of a mile from the temple. Mithridates rewarded the Ephesians for their support by slightly enlarging this limit (*ibid.*: Μιθριδάτου δὲ τόξευμα ἀφέντος ἀπὸ τῆς γωνίας τοῦ κεράμου καὶ δόξαντος ὑπερβαλίσθαι μικρὰ τὸ στάδιον). Next Antony, whose stay at Epheseos with Cleopatra is described by Plutarch (Anton. § 56, 58), doubled the limit, thereby including within the range of the sanctuary 'a certain portion of the city' (μέρος τι τῆς πόλεως). As the city and the city wall were a mile distant from the Artemision, the extension of the sanctuary to a radius of ¼ mile from the temple cannot literally have embraced a portion of the city. Strabo must therefore be understood to be speaking of the public road from the city to the temple from the Magnesian gate, and perhaps of the suburbs of the city. Such an enlargement however was detrimental to public order, for criminals would plead sanctuary and escape from arrest, even in the public streets; and

accordingly Augustus annulled the grant of Antony (ἐφάνη δὲ τοῦτο βλαβερὸν καὶ ἐπὶ τοῖς κακούργοις ποιοῦν τὴν πόλιν, ὥστ᾿ ἠκύρωσεν ὁ Σεβαστὸς Καῖσαρ). The sanctuary underwent a further revision under Tiberius, A. D. 22 (Tac. Ann. iii, 61). The statement of Strabo is confirmed by this inscription, which proves that Augustus not only defined the sacred precinct afresh, but also surrounded it with a peribolos.

Augustus, the restorer of temples and of religion at home, made a point of restoring also to the shrines of Asia the treasures which Antony had carried off to gratify Cleopatra. In many ways the victory of Actium introduced an era of order and comfort to the Greek towns which had suffered a century of Roman misgovernment, and had of late been alternately pampered and plundered by Antony. Strabo speaks of his carrying off a statue from a shrine of Ajax at Rhœteum in the Troad (xiii, p. 595), and three more statues from the Heraion at Samos (xiv, p. 637). A similar robbery at Ephesos is recorded by Pliny (N. H. xxxiv, 8, § 58) : Fecit (Myro) et Apollinem, quem ab triumviro Antonio sublatum restituit Ephesiis divus Augustus admonitus in quiete. To this and similar acts of restitution Augustus refers in the Monumentum Ancyranum, chap. xxiv (Mommsen, Res gestæ divi Aug. pp. lxxxx, lxxxxi, 95–96): In templis omnium civitatium pr[ovinci]æ Asiæ victor ornamenta reposui, quæ spoliatis tem[plis is] cum quo bellum gesseram privatim possederat : [Ἐν ναοῖ]ς π[ασ]ῶν πόλεω[ν] τῆς [Ἀ]σί[α]ς νεικήσας τὰ ἀναθ[ή]ματα ἀπ]οκατέστησα, [ἃ] εἶχ[εν] ἰ[δίᾳ] ἱεροσυλήσας ὁ ὑπ᾿ [ἐμοῦ] δ[ι]αγωνισθεὶς πολ[έμιος]. It is in keeping with this view of his conduct that Augustus (through the proconsul Gallus) employs the word ἀποκατέστησεν in the next two documents (Nos. DXXIII, DXXIV).

For the accusative νεά, line 6, see L. and S. s. v., and compare the N. T. forms Ἀπολλώ, accusative of Ἀπολλώς, and τὴν Κῶ (Moulton's Winer, p. 72). The forms Σεβαστῆον and ἐπιμελήᾳ are noticeable in an inscription of such good date as this : τιχισθῆναι has been noticed on No. LXXI.

A duplicate of this inscription was found near it, similarly built into the peribolos. The Turkish authorities had stipulated in the firman granted to Mr. Wood, that any duplicates he might discover should be handed over to the Ottoman government. Accordingly Mr. Wood had one of these inscribed stones (the fellow to the present one) conveyed to Smyrna, and formally handed over to the Turkish commissioner who was appointed to watch his proceedings (Ephesus, p. 132). It has now passed into the possession of the German government (Ephem. Epigr.,v, p. 60: 'Hodie adservatur Berolini in museo n. 969, 9 septem versibus disposita ; ex deletis Latinis apparent hæc ; / ASINI / GALLO · PRO · COS et LEC; Græca deleta non leguntur.' *

---

* In the Mittheilungen, x, 1885, p. 401, and the Bull. de Corr. Hell. x, 1886, p. 95, an inscription from Ephesos is published which records the repair of the peribolos-wall (ἀποκατεστάθη τὸ βλαβὲν περιτείχισμα τοῦ Αὐγουστῆου) in the time of the Emperor Titus, A.D. 79–80.

DXXIII.

A stelè of white marble, height 3 ft. 11 in.; width 1 ft. 6 in.; found by Mr. Wood in situ, built into the peribolos of the Artemision. Wood, Ephesus, p. 132 foll.; Appendix, Inscriptions from the Peribolus Wall, No. 2.

	ΑΥΤΟΚΡΑΤΩΡΚΑΙΣΑΡ		Αὐτοκράτωρ Καῖσαρ,
	ΘΕΟΥΥΙΟΣΣΕΒΑΣΤΟΣ		θεοῦ υἱὸς, Σεβαστὸς,
	ΥΠΑΤΟΣΤΟΙΒΔΗΜΑΡ		ὕπατος τὸ ιβ̄, δημαρ-
	ΧΙΚΗΣΕΞΟΥΣΙΑΣΤΟΙΗ		χικῆς ἐξουσίας τὸ ιη̄,
5	ΣΤΗΛΑΣΙΕΡΑΣΤΩΝΟ	5	στήλας ἱερὰς τῶν ὁ-
	ΔΩΝΚΑΙΡΙΘΡΩΝΑΡΤΕΜΙ		δῶν καὶ ῥίθρων Ἀρτέμι-
	ΔΙΑΠΟΚΑΤΕΣΤΗΣΕΝ		δι ἀποκατέστησεν·
	(Two lines anciently erased.)		(Two lines anciently erased.)
10	ΕΠΙΜΕΛΗΑΣΕΞΤΟΥ	10	ἐπιμελήᾳ Σέξτου
	ΛΑΡΤΙΔΙΟΥΠΡΕΣ		Λαρτιδίου πρεσ-
	ΒΕΥΤΟΥ		βευτοῦ.
	ΤΟΡΕΙΘΡΟΝΕΧΕΙΠΛΑ		Τὸ ῥεῖθρον ἔχει πλά-
	ΤΟΥΣΠΗΧΕΙΣΙΕ		τους πήχεις ιε̄.

Inscription recording that Augustus set up afresh B. C. 5 the sacred stelæ marking the roads and canals pertaining to the temenos of Artemis.

The erased lines 8, 9 can be restored from No. DXXII preceding : ἐπὶ ἀνθυπάτου | Γαΐου Ἀσινίου Γάλλου. The notes on No. DXXII will sufficiently explain the purport of this inscription. The date is the same, viz. B. C. 5.

It was ascertained by Mr. Wood, in the course of his excavations, that there were two principal roads leading from the city to the temple and its precinct, one from a gate at the north-eastern corner of the city wall, and the other from the Magnesian gate, more to the south-east of the city. Both roads are clearly marked upon Mr. Wood's 'Plan' (Ephesus, p. 1). He assumes that the final portions of these two are the ὁδοί mentioned in this and the next inscription (No. DXXIV); and he has represented both roads as flanked by a canal along their latter portion as they drew within the temenos. These canals would be the ῥεῖθρα of our inscriptions. It is doubtful, however, whether we are as yet in a position to define the topographical details so closely as this. Mr. Wood himself discovered that the width of the road leading out from the Magnesian gate was 35 feet (p. 114). On p. 129 he describes the same road when it turned to N. E. towards the temenos, as widening to 45 feet. Now the width of the road as stated in this inscription to be 15 πήχεις, or 22½ English feet. In No. DXXIV the combined width of road and canal is given at 30 πήχεις, or 45 English feet. The water-

way therefore and the road were of equal width; and they must have been so closely side by side as to constitute one thoroughfare, or else they would not thus have been measured together. It is possible that the latter portion of the road from the Magnesian gate, when it crossed the bed of the stream called by Mr. Wood the Selinus, and as it neared the temenos, was reduced to half its former width, the other half being occupied by a canal. It is singular at all events that the width of the undivided road as excavated by Mr. Wood is 45 feet, the combined width of road and canal together as given in No. DXXIV. Mr. Wood, however, tells me he did not discover any traces of this road and canal, and his identification of them in the Plan is only conjectural. Equally conjectural is his representation of the other road as flanked by a canal. We can only say that his conjecture is very probable.

Thus much is certain : one or more canals, formed by diverting the waters of the Kaÿster and its tributaries, afforded a water-way to the temple, which thus became accessible to the sea. And that this water-way was in the hands of the temple-authorities we seem to gather from the mention of a priestly college entitled οἱ ναυβατοῦντες, C. I. 2955 (E. Curtius, Beiträge, p. 34 foll., Ephesos, p. 23). Accordingly Mr. Wood and Professor E. Curtius are probably right in supposing that the canal terminated in an ornamental basin, with a landing-quay for pilgrims, before the west front or entrance of the Artemision (see the sketch in Curtius' Ephesos, ein Vortrag, pl. 1).

DXXIV.

Stelè of white marble, height 4 ft. ½ in.; width 1 ft. 6 in.; found by Mr. Wood in situ, built into the peribolos of the Artemision. Wood, Ephesus, p. 132 foll.; Appendix, Inscriptions from the Peribolus Wall, No. 3.

	ΑΥΤΟΚΡΑΤΩΡΚΑΙΣΑΡ	Αὐτοκράτωρ Καῖσαρ
	ΘΕΟΥΥΙΟΣΣΕΒΑΣΤΟΣ	θεοῦ υἱὸς Σεβαστὸς,
	ΥΠΑΤΟΣΤΟΙΒ ΔΗΜΑΡ	ὕπατος τὸ ιβ̄, δημαρ-

ΧΙΚΗΣΕΞΟΥΣΙΑΣΤΟὶΗ   χικῆς ἐξουσίας τὸ ἴη,

5   ΣΤΗΛΑΣΙΕΡΑΣ ΤΩΝ   5   στήλας ἱερὰς τῶν

ΟΔΩΝΚΑΙΡΙΘΡΩΝΑΡ   ὁδῶν καὶ ῥίθρων Ἀρ-

ΤΕΜΙΔΙΑΠΟΚΑΤΕΣΤΗ   τέμιδι ἀποκατέστη-

ΣΕΝ (This line and   σεν· (This line and

the next erased.)   the next erased.)

10 ΕΠΙΜΕΛΗΑ ΣΕΞΣΤΟΥ 10 Ἐπιμελήᾳ Σίξστου

ΛΑΡΤΙΔΙΟΥΠΡΕΣΒΕΥΤΟΥ   Λαρτιδίου πρεσβευτοῦ.

⌐ΔΟΣΕΧΕΙΣΥΝΤΩΙ   ἡ] ὁδὸς ἔχει σὺν τῷ

ιΙΘΡΩΤΟΥΠΟΤΑΜΟΥ   ῥ]είθρῳ τοῦ ποταμοῦ

ΠΗΧΕΙΣ – Λ   πήχεις Λ.

Inscription recording that Augustus set up afresh | combined width of the road and of the water-course
B.C. 5 the sacred stelæ marking the roads and | is set down as ' 30 cubits,' i. e. about 45 feet. We
canals pertaining to the temenos of Artemis. | may infer from this that the road and canal were
This is a duplicate of the foregoing (No. DXXIII), | each of equal width, and lay so near together that
with the exception of the last three lines. Here, | it was natural to include them under one measure-
instead of the width of the watercourse only, the | ment. See the notes on Nos. DXXIII.

DXXV.

Three fragments of white marble, found by Mr. Wood ' at the junction of the roads near the Coressian gate, three or four stadia from
the Peribolus ; but not *in situ.*' Probably they are parts of a wall-stone from the peribolos itself, like Nos. DXXIII–DXXIV. Wood,
Inscriptions from the City and Suburbs, No. 2 ; compare E. Curtius, Beiträge zur Gesch. und Topogr. Kleinasiens, p. 28.

a.   *b.*

Broken on all sides, except bottom ' bed.' Measures 4½ in. by 1 ft. 2 in.   Broken on all sides except bottom ' bed.' Height 5½ in. ; width 8

ΕΚΑΙΔΕΚΑΤΗΝΣ   ΟΣιΗΙΙΕΡΑΙΧΩ

ΛΗΝιΤΡΟΣι∪_ΙΕΡΟΙΣΩΣΗΑΙΜΑΣΙΑΑΝ   ΟΝΤΗΣΣΤΑΘΕΙΣΗ

ΣΤΗΣΑΜΕΝΕΠΤΑΚΑΙΔΕΚΑΤΗΝΣΤΗΛΗΙ   ΟΣΤΟΙΣΟΡΙΟΙΣΤΟΙΣΓ

ΙΠΡΟΕΛΘΟΝΤΕΣΟΜΟΙΩΣΕΕΣΤΗΣΑΜΕΝΟ   ΩΚΑΙΔΕΚΑΤΗΝΣΤι

Ͻ ΩΣΔΕΠΡΟΕΛΘΟΝΤΕΣΕΕΣΤΗΣΑΜ   ΝΝΕΑΚΑΙΛΕΚΑΤΗλ

ΜΕΝΕΙΚΟΣΤΗΝΕΤΗΛΗΝΑΝ   Νι   ΕΙΣ

ΥΤΟΙΣΤΑΥΤΑΔΕΕΤͼ

                       surface broken and defaced.

c.

Broken on all sides ; height 4½ in. ; width 8 in.

ΔΕΚ..

ͺΤΑΤΟΓΕΝΕιΟΝΤοͺ

ΣΕΝΑΤΗΣΣΤΗΛΗΣΚ

ͻΓΔΟΗΣΣΤΗΛΗΣΟ

5   ͼΑΕΕͼΤΥͼΑΜΕ

a.   *b.*

        . . . . ας επω? . . . . .

. . ἐστήσαμεν πεντ]εκαιδεκάτην σ[τήλην πρ]ὸς τῇ ἱερᾷ χώ[ρᾳ· καὶ ἑκκαιδεκάτην·
στή]λην πρὸς το[ῖ]ς ἱεροῖς, ὡς ἡ αἱμασία, ἀν[ὰ λόγ]ον? τῆς σταθείση[ς στήλης· προελθόντες
δὲ ἑ]στήσαμεν ἑπτακαιδεκάτην στήλη[ν πρ]ὸς τοῖς ὁρίοις τοῖς π[ροτέροις·? . . . .
5 κα]ὶ προελθόντες ὁμοίως ἐστήσαμεν ὀ[κτ]ωκαιδεκάτην στ[ήλην . . . .
ὁμ]ο[ί]ως δὲ πρωελθόντες ἐστήσαμ[εν ἐ]ννεακαιδεκάτην [στήλην· ὁμοίως δὲ προελθόντες
ἐστήσα]μεν εἰκοστὴν στήλην ἀν[ὰ λόγο]ν τ[ῆς σταθ]είσ[ης στήλης· . . . .
. . . . το]ύτοις· ταῦτα δὲ ἰσ[ω . . . .

C.

..... ἀπέναντι? τῆς] δεκά[της στήλης· ....
.... κ]ατὰ τὸ γένειον το[ῦ ....
..... ἀπέναντι? τῆ]ς ἐνάτης στήλης· κ[αὶ ....
..... ἀπέναντι? τῆς] ὀγδόης στήλης· ὁ[μοίως δὲ ἐστήσαμεν? ...
5 .... ὁμοίω]ς δὲ ἐστήσαμε[ν ....

Portions of the report of a commission authorized to set up stelæ marking certain boundaries (line 4). There is little doubt that these are the stelæ mentioned in Nos. DXXIII, DXXIV, as having been ' restored' (ἀποκατέστησεν) by Augustus. The character of the writing points decidedly to that date ; the letters are small, but handsome and carefully formed, and the iota adscript is inserted (line 1). Perhaps the report was drawn up by the neopoiai.

The successive changes made in the limits of the Ephesian asylum have been sufficiently described in the notes on No. DXXII, which records how Augustus (n. c. 6) caused the temenos of Artemis to be enclosed with a wall (τειχισθῆναι). That wall, which was discovered by Mr. Wood, is assumed to have also marked the boundary of the asylum. Antony had doubled its extent, which Augustus reduced to its old limits. The area of the temenos was sufficiently large, as limited by Augustus. According to the actual measurements made by Mr. Wood, it was about half a mile square, having the temple nearly in the centre (Wood, Ephesus, Plan ; ibid. p. 162). But it is more than likely that some, if not all, of the roads which led from the town to the temple were (at least for a certain distance from the temenos) regarded as ἱεραὶ ὁδοί, sacred to Artemis. Whichever of these roads are alluded to in Nos. DXXIII, DXXIV as flanked by canals, these roads certainly, with the water-way adjoining them, were under the charge and authority of the Artemision. Only in this way can we explain the expression στήλας ἱερὰς τῶν ὁδῶν καὶ ῥείθρων Ἀρτέμιδι ἀποκατέστησεν, in the two documents just cited. Accordingly when Augustus reduced the sanctuary to its old boundary, and surrounded it with a wall, it was necessary also to define the limits of the authority of the goddess over the thoroughfares which approached her temple. This was the purpose of the ἱεραὶ στῆλαι, which stood at intervals along the road, to mark the width and the length of the roadways claimed by the goddess.

It would be hazardous to attempt to identify the spots mentioned in the present inscription. In a b we read of the restoration of the fifteenth to the twentieth stelæ. The fifteenth was placed πρ]ὸς τῇ ἱερᾷ χώ[ρᾳ (line 2), by which I understand some sacred field near the road, most probably belonging to Artemis. The sixteenth adjoined ' the temples' (πρὸς τοῖς ἱεροῖς, line 3), which may be certain small temples standing near the road. Two such temples are marked in Mr. Wood's Plan, on the south of the northern road, near the temenos ; whether by conjecture, or from actual discovery, is doubtful. Line 3 : ὡς ἡ αἱμασία, 'where the rubble-wall stands,' perhaps the peribolos of the ἱερά just mentioned. I write here, and in line 7, ἀνὰ λόγον τῆς σταθείση[ς στήλης, i. e. at similar distance from the stelè last set up. By ὁρίοις τοῖς =[ροτέροις, line 4, I understand the boundary fixed by Antony.

I suppose c to be a continuation of the report. The enumeration of the stelæ proceeds in the reverse order, from the tenth to the eighth. I imagine that the commissioners are reporting upon their return journey ; having restored the stelæ further and further from the temple on one side of the road, up to the limit of the authority of the goddess, they cross the road and set up stelæ on the other side of the way, opposite (ἀπέναντι?) to each of the aforesaid stelæ. By κ]ατὰ τὸ γένειον το[ῦ ... (line 2) some well-known slope was indicated.

The form of this report is not unlike that of the Rhodian commissioners at Prienè, appended to their Award, No. CCCIII ante, lines 158 foll. ; compare Nos. CCCCVI-CCCCVIII.

DXXVI.

Fragment of white marble, entire only on left. Height 5½ in.; width 8 in. Discovered by Mr. Wood, but unpublished.

ΑΡΟΔΕΤΟΙ .   ἀπὸ δὲ τοῦ ....
ΤΟΝΕΥΔΗΜΟΥΤΑΦ   τὸν Εὐδήμου τάφ[ον ....
ΜΕΝΟΙΤΑΘΡΙΑΔΙΑΛΕΙΠΕ   μενοι τὰ ὅρια διαλείπε[ιν ....
ΡΡΟΧΑΙΓΑΕΙΧΕΙΤΕΝΕΓΚ   πρὸς Αἰγαεῖς. εἶτ' ἐνέγκ[αντες ....
5 ΚΕΙΜΕΝΟΙΧΕΛΧΤΛΝΟΡΛΝ   5 κειμένοις ἕως τῶν ὅρων ....
ΤΟΙΧΑΙΓΑΕΛΝ   ΟΧ°   τοῖς Αἰγαίων .. ος ....

Evidently part of a report of some commission appointed to survey certain boundaries ; compare No. DXXV, which it somewhat resembles in its letter-ing, though its characters are smaller. There is no record of the spot where the fragment was found, nor can we identify the locality called Αἰγαεῖς (lines

3 A

4, 6), nor the 'tomb of Eudemos' (line 2). It should be noted that the roads outside the city, leading from the Magnesian and from the north-western gates in the direction of the temenos, abounded in sepulchral monuments (Wood, Ephesus, pp. 114–125, 128–129). One such was the tomb of Androklos, the founder of Ephesos (Pausanias, vii, 2, § 6 : Ἐφέσιοι δὲ ἀνελόμενοι τοῦ Ἀνδρόκλου τὸν νεκρὸν ἔθαψαν τῆς σφετέρας ἔνθα δείκνυται καὶ ἐς ἐμὲ ἔτι τὸ μνῆμα κατὰ τὴν ὁδὸν τὴν ἐκ τοῦ ἱεροῦ παρὰ τὸ Ὀλυμπιεῖον καὶ ἐπὶ πύλας τὰς Μαγνήτιδας· ἐπίσημα δὲ τῷ μνήματι ἀνήρ ἐστιν ὡπλισμένος). The foundations of this monument Mr. Wood believed himself to have discovered (Ephesus, p. 127).

DXXVII.

Fragment of a block of white marble, broken on all sides. Height 4¼ in. by 3½ in. Discovered by Mr. Wood; unpublished.

ΤΩ
ΥΤΟΠΟΥ
ΩΡΑΣΚΟ
ΣΤΑΠΡΟΣ
5 ΕΜΒΗΝΗΣ
ΑΣΜΑΡ
ΛΕΝΗΣ

```
    . . . . τω . . . .
. . . το]ῦ τόπου . . . .
    χ]ώρας κο . . . .
. . . . ς τὰ πρὸς . . . .
5 . . . . β]εμβήνης ? . . . .
. . . . . . ας μαρ . . . .
. . . . μίνης ? . . . . .
```

Apparently part of a specification of boundaries; compare Nos. DXXV, DXXVI, which the present fragment much resembles in its lettering, though the lines do not range exactly with them. In line 5 β]εμβήνης may be a local name connected in some way with the tribal name Βεμβίνης, Βεμβειναῖοι (ante, pp. 69, 70).

DXXVIII.

Fragments of a white marble stele, of which a and c are in the British Museum, discovered by Mr. Wood in the Ephesian Theatre. It is doubtful however whether this was the original place of the marble, or whether it was brought thither in the 3rd century A. D. from the Artemision, after its destruction by the Goths (see note p. 89 ante on the decrees from the Artemision, Nos. CCCCLVIII foll.). Wood has printed a in a completer form, giving the endings of the lines; the marble has been injured since then (Ephesus, Inscriptions from the Theatre, No. 23). The additional portions taken from Wood are marked b in the cursive text, and are indicated by a bar |; c is not given by Wood. Measurements :—a, entire at top only, 1 ft. 3½ in. high, 1 ft. 4 in. wide : c, broken on all sides, 5½ in. high, 5 in. wide. Wood calls his text of a, b 'uncertain,' but tested by the original of a it is shown to be trustworthy.

a.

ΑΝΔΡΟΥΠΑΣΣ
ΜΕΤΑΓΕΙΤΟΝΙΩΛ
ΨΟΥΤΟΥΣΩΠΑΤ
ΣΤΟΥΔΗΜΟΥΣ
5 ΣΚΑΙΟΙΣΤ
ΘΥΣΙΝ
. . . . . .

c.

ΥΡ
ΛΛΑΕΣ
10 ΓΑΞΕΙΣ
Γ

a.   *b.*

Ἐπὶ πρυτάνεως Ἀλεξ]άνδρου, Πασσα]αλάτα[υ
ἐνιαυτῷ, μηνὸς]Μεταγειτονιῶ]νος ιβ
. . , ὁ δεῖνα . . . . .]ήου τοῦ Σωπάτ]ρου Σιμώ-
νηος ὁ γραμματε]ὺς τοῦ δήμου, ὁ | καὶ αὐτὸς βασιλεὺς
5 ἐκ προγόνων ? καὶ ἱερε]ὺς, καὶ οἱ στ]ρατηγοὶ τῆς πόλεως

```
.......... ρυσιν ....| τὰς περὶ τῶν ὑδάτων
.......... | περὶ αὐτῶν ἔνγραφα
ε.   ... κ]υρω[θῆναι ? .. τὰ] | ψηφίσματα ὑπὸ τοῦ δ[ήμου
            ὅσα δ]λλα ἐσ[τὶ ....κ]| ατὰ τὰς προϋπαρχούσα[ς
10   δια]τάξεις ? ....|ἔνγραφα ...............
.... ε .....|ἀπομερισμὸν τῶν ....
.......... |στε ...........
```

A public document issued by the γραμματεὺς τοῦ δήμου and the στρατηγοὶ τῆς πόλεως (line 4), and dealing with the construction or repair of certain water-courses (τῶν ὑδάτων, line 6).

Line 1 is in rather larger letters than the rest. The position of ε is conjectural; it belongs to the lower portion of the document, since the letters are rather more crowded, and the lines closer together. Wood reads in line 1 Πασσαλατοβ, and in line 6 .. υσιν .. The letter before Υ was almost certainly Ρ. In ε, line 8, the broken letters before and after ΥΡ can hardly be other than Κ and Ω.

The ὕδατα of line 6 might well be some of those canals in connexion with the bed of the Kaÿster and its tributaries, which formed a striking feature in the ground-plan of ancient Ephesos (see E. Curtius, Ephesos, p. 25; and Nos. DXXIII, DXXIV, DXXX). Whether the inscription merely recorded certain alterations or repairs of the canals (compare No. DXXI ante), or whether it dealt with contracts (δια]τάξεις, line 10) for their repairs, we cannot tell, in the existing state of the document. The mention of written documents (ἔνγραφα, lines 7, 10) and of decrees (line 8) does not reveal much. 'Απομερισμός (line 11) is given by Hesychios as a synonym of ἀπονομή ('Απονομή, ἀπομερισμή). And ἀπονομή (Harpokration s. v.) was used by Deinarchos for the letting out of public mines to contractors who farmed each his portion: so that our document may refer to contracts for making or repairing canals. In line 6 we might restore πέ]ρυσιν, or ῥύσιν, or ὕδ]ρυσιν.

Happily the heading can be restored and the date probably recovered, by help of a dedication copied by Mr. Wood from a marble found in the Augusteum (Inscriptions from the Augusteum, No. 11 : it was not sent to England). The copy is imperfect, but may be restored somewhat as follows :—Γάιον Καίσαρα Γερμα]νικὸν Ἰούλιον Τιβερίου, Δρούσου Ἰούλιον Τιβερίου υἱὸν Καίσαρα, Τιβέριον Ἰούλιον Σεβα[στοῦ] υἱὸν Καίσαρα

..... οἱ νεοποιήσαντες ...... ιον Καίσαρα ? ἐπὶ πρυτάνεως 'Αλεξάνδρου τοῦ 'Απολλωνίου, Πασαλλάτου (sic) ἐνιαυτῷ. The recurrence of the peculiar name Πασσάλατος or Πασάλλατος enables us to identify the name of the prytanis 'Αλέξανδρος. On the Ephesian prytanis as the eponymos see pp. 72, 82 ante and reff. Together with the prytanis the name of the first of the college of νεοποιοί is also subjoined to mark the year : Πασσαλάτο[υ] ἐνιαυτῷ (so No. DLXXVIII a, line 3, Δημητρίου ἐνιαυτῷ). The dedication just cited from Wood's copy was, we may conjecture, originally set up in the Augusteum, A.D. 4, immediately after the adoption of Tiberius by Augustus, when Tiberius at the same time, by the Emperor's request, adopted his nephew Germanicus in addition to his own son Drusus the younger. If that dedication belongs to A.D. 4, the year of Alexander as prytanis and of Passalatos as neopoios is recovered, and our inscription also will be assigned to A.D. 4 ; this date would exactly suit the style of the characters. The prominent mention of the name of the neopoios would suggest that the transactions referred to in the document were not unconnected with the Temple and its precinct. Line 2 discovers to us the name of an Ephesian month hitherto unknown : the form Μεταγειτονιών is found in Attic inscriptions of the Imperial time (C. I. A. iii, No. 1197) ; compare ante p. 79.

Line 4 : this γραμματεύς of the demos is also βασιλεύς, a title explained by Strabo xiv, p. 633 : καὶ ἔτι νῦν οἱ ἐκ τοῦ γένους (of the Ephesian founder Androklos) ὀνομάζονται βασιλεῖς ἔχοντές τινας τιμάς, προεδρίαν τε ἐν ἀγῶσι καὶ πορφύραν ἐπίσημον τοῦ βασιλικοῦ γένους, σκίπωνα ἀντὶ σκήπτρου, καὶ τὰ ἱερὰ τῆς 'Ελευσινίας Δήμητρος. Compare Achilles Tat. vii, 12 : ἦν δὲ τοῦ βασιλικοῦ γένους. Menadier (Qua condicione Ephesii, p. 68) remarks that the kingly name survived as a title not only at Athens (ἀρχὼν βασιλεύς) and Ephesos, but in many other cities, e. g. Samothrace (ante No. CCCCXLIV, line 1). On the Ephesian στρατηγοί, see p. 81 ante.

DXXIX.

Two fragments of white marble which read into one another, but do not join ; height 6 in., combined width 10 in. Entire on left and at bottom. Discovered by Mr. Wood ; unpublished.

```
          ..........
ΕΡΙ ͟Ι ΙΣΤ Λ.
ΤΟΥΓ ΑΜΜΑ ͟
ΜΟΥΠ   ΛΓΟΡΟ ͻ
ΘΑΓΟΡΟ   ᵛΠΥϑΑΓϹ
```

```
          ..........
ἐργε[π]ιστα[τήσαντος
τοῦ γραμματ[έως τοῦ δή-
μου Π[υθ]αγόρα[υ τ]ο[ῦ Πυ-
θαγόρο[υ το]ῦ Πυθαγό[ρου.
```

Record of the erection of some public monument under the superintendence of the γραμματεὺς τοῦ δήμου, who is similarly mentioned in Nos. DII, DXXXIII. The word ἐργεπιστασία occurs in C. I. 2779 (Aphrodisias), and 3936 (Laodikeia). Ἐργεπιστατούντων is similarly used in an inscription of Mr. Wood's (From the Theatre, No. 3) which was not conveyed to England; and in a dedication of a statue of Hadrian at Ephesos (C. I. 2963 c), which ends thus: ἐργεπιστατήσαντος Μάρκου | Ἀντωνίου Ἀρτεμιδώρου, πυθοϊνείκου. Our fragment may be from a similar dedication. The characters appear to belong to the Augustan age.

DXXX.

A pedestal of white marble, surmounted by a r..oukling : height 1 ft. 2½ in.; width 1 ft. 11½ in. 'Found near the Magnesian Gate.'

ΤΟ Ϋ Δ Ω Ρ	Τὸ ὕδωρ
ΕΚΤΟΥΚΑΙΝΟΥΜΑΡΝΑΝΤΟΣ	ἐκ τοῦ καινοῦ Μάρναντος
ΤΟΥ·ΕΙΣΑΧΘΕΝΤΟΣ·ΥΠΟ·~	τοῦ εἰσαχθέντος ὑπὸ
ΚΛΑΥΔΙΟΥ · ΔΙΟΓΕΝΟΫΣ	Κλαυδίου Διογένους,
5 ΕΠΙΜΕΛΗΤΟΫ	5 ἐπιμελητοῦ.

Mr. Wood (Ephesus, p. 112) thus describes the finding of this inscription. ' Near the [Magnesian] gate, and outside of it, was found the inscribed pedestal which had probably supported a figure of the River Marnas, and which informs us that the water of that river was here brought into the City. Before the discovery of this inscription we had only known of the existence of this river in the plain of Ephesos by some ancient copper coins of the time of Domitian, and its whereabouts in the plain was unknown. We can now fix its position with tolerable accuracy. It was probably the river which took its rise in the Ephesus Pass, and fell into the river Selinus, somewhere between the Magnesian gate and Ayasolouk. The figure on the coin is helmeted.' The ἐπιμελητής or commissioner of line 5 is not otherwise known ; he may have been commissioned by the proconsul (compare ante Nos. DXXIII foll.) or by the Ephesian authorities. The Magnesian gate, where the marble was found, was perhaps erected in the reign of Vespasian (Wood, Ephesus, p. 112) ; and the inscription appears to belong to the age of the Antonines. For ὕδωρ εἰσάγειν compare C. I. 3146 (Smyrna) ; in C. I. 3147 (Smyrna) we have ὕδατος ἀποκατασταθέντος. The epithet καινός seems to denote the new course given to the Marnas by the aqueduct of Diogenes. In line 1 the dots on either side of Υ are merely decorative, and not like the examples in Part i, No. CXXV, Part ii, No. CCCLXV, and No. CXLIX post. But see Scrivener, Introduction to the Criticism of the N. T. p. 35, for the custom of placing dots over ι and Υ in early uncial MSS.

DXXXI.

Fragment of white marble, entire at top, otherwise broken all round. Height 6 in., width 11 in.; letters nearly 2 in. high. Discovered by Mr. Wood ; unpublished.

```
῾ΗΜΗΤΡΟ
ΚΟΡΟ
```

Ἡ πρώτη καὶ μεγίσ]τη μητρό[πολις
τῆς Ἀσίας καὶ δὶς νεω]κόρο[ς τῶν
[Σεβαστῶν κ.τλ.]

The heading of an inscription to commemorate some public act of the Ephesian city ; like that given by Wood, Inscriptions from the Theatre, No. 3, in which the Ephesians restore the theatre at the public expense.

DXXXII.

Fragment of blue marble, broken on all sides. Height 1 ft. 1 in.; width 8 in. Discovered by Mr. Wood ; unpublished.

ΙΜΗΤ	Ἡ πρώτη καὶ μεγίστ]η μητ[ρό-
ΔΙΣΛ	πολις τῆς Ἀσίας καὶ] δὶς ν[εωκ-
ΙΙ Ϋ	όρος τῶν Σεβαστῶ]ν τ . . . .

Similar to the preceding (No. DXXXI).

DXXXIII.

Fragment of a white marble stelè, entire at bottom and on the right. Height 1 ft. ; width 1 ft. 3½ in. Discovered by Mr. Wood ; unpublished.

```
        ΟΣ                          . . . . . . . . . . . . ος
       ..ΨΗ .                       . . . . . . . . . . . α' ψη-
    ΚΑΙΕΠΙΜΕΛΗΘΕΝ                    φισαμένου] καὶ ἐπιμεληθέν-
    ΕΛΛΑΝΟΥΦΛΑΒΙ                     τος -- Γερ]ελλανοῦ Φλαβι-
 5  ΜΜΑΤΕΟΣΤΟΥΔΗΜc`            5     ανοῦ τοῦ γρα]μματέος τοῦ δήμου,
    ΗΣ , ΤΗΙ Ω̈̀                      φυλ]ῆς Τηΐω[ν.
```

Record of the erection of some public monument at the proposal and under the superintendence of the γραμματεὺς τοῦ δήμου. Compare Nos. cccckcix, D, DII, *ante*. Perhaps the monument was in honour of one of the Antonines. The restorations are suggested by a comparison of Nos. DII, DXLVI, DLXXIII, from which we recover the name Γερελλανόs. For γρα]μματέος, see note on πό]λεος, No. DII, line 8.

DXXXIV.

A block of white marble, injured at the top ; but the inscription appears to be perfect. Height 1 ft. ; width 2 ft. ½ in. The letters are from 3 in. to 3½ in. in height. Discovered by Mr. Wood at Ephesos, but not referred to in his account of his discoveries. Inaccurately published by C. Curtius, Hermes iv, p. 214.

```
    +  ιΜΓ                          +  [Χ]ΜΓ  +
       ΦΟΡΟϹ                           Φόρος
    ΘΕΟΔΟϹΙΑΝΟϹ ϛ                      Θεοδοσιανός.
```

This stone was probably placed over the entrance of a building called 'The Forum of Theodosius.' Suidas *s. v.* Φόρος informs us that the word was a late Greek equivalent for the Latin *forum*; indeed it is often used in this sense by the geographer Ptolemy, see reff. in Pape-Benseler *s. v.* Φόρος. Nothing is known of this Forum, which we may conjecture to have been a work of Theodosius the Great (A.D. 379-395). Unfortunately Mr. Wood has made no note of the spot where he found the marble, so that we cannot identify the site of the building. C. Curtius wrongly understands φόρος in the sense of tribute.

In line 1 one leg of Χ is visible, and we may certainly restore the monogram ΧΜΓ, which is usually found united (as here) with some Christian emblem. Its meaning however is not certainly known. It occurs not unfrequently on Syrian Christian tombs : see C. I. 9144; Waddington-Le Bas, iii, 2145, 2299, 2660, 2663, 2674, 2691. Another instance from Syria is given by Mordtmann, Archäol.-Epigr. Mittheil. aus Œsterr. viii (1884), p. 192 : + ΧΜΓ. [Κ(ύρι)ε] βοήθι τοῦ δ[ού]λου σου Θωδίαν(?). ἔτους ᾱ̄ω̄. ἰνδ. γ̄ = 1 Sept. A. D. 539·40. Two more examples from Syria are given by the Rev. G. Williams, in his introduction to Neale's Patriarchate of Antioch, pp. xxxvii-xxxix. One he copied from a house at Dell Louzeh : + Εἰ θεὸς ὑπὲρ ἡμῶν τίς καθ' ἡμῶ(ν) ΧΜΓ ‡. The spelling is barbarous. The other he copied from a tomb at Deir Sambir : Τοῦ Κυρίου ἡ γῆ καὶ τὸ πλήρωμα αὐτῆς καὶ πάντες οἱ κατοικ(ο)ῦντες ἐν αὐτῇ. † ΧΜΓ. Occa-

sionally it is found elsewhere ; as on a Christian tomb at Kyzikos (Mittheilungen, vi, p. 126) ; in Phœnicia (Renan, Mission de Phénicie, p. 592) ; at Aphrodisias in Karia (C. I. 9273); at Syracuse, in a crypt or catacomb (C. I. 9455); in Attika (Kumanudes, Ἀττικῆς Ἐπιγραφαὶ Ἐπιτύμβιοι, No. 3622). Again, Ch. Bayet, Bulletin de Corr. Hell. ii, p. 32, mentions a brick discovered at Rome in 1870 with ΧΜΓ combined with the name Κασσίου : this resembles Ἀθανασίου ΧΜΓ in C. I. 9455. De Rossi suggests the explanation Χ(ριστὸς) Μ(ιχαὴλ) Γ(αβριήλ), which is not very likely, although Dittenberger, C.I.A. iii. No. 3536, adopts it. M. Waddington interprets Χριστὸς ὁ ἐκ Μαρίας γεννηθείς, and this conjecture is confirmed by another of his inscriptions (No. 2697, from Refâdi in Syria) which exhibits in full : Ἰησοῦς ὁ Ναζωρέων ὁ ἐκ Μαρίας γενν(η)θεὶς ὁ υἱὸς τοῦ Θεοῦ, as the heading of an epitaph. There is however some difficulty in the omission of ἐκ altogether from the monogram if ΧΜΓ means Χριστὸς ἐκ Μαρίας γεννηθείς, and perhaps Χριστὸν Μαρίας γέννημα is more probable.

Wessely (Wiener Studien, ix. 1887, p. 252) calls attention to the occurrence in Egyptian papyri of other forms of ΧΜΓ, viz. χμγι and χμι, which he proposes to explain by χ(εὶρ) μ(ου) γ(ράφει). This may suit the papyri : but the monogram as employed upon the marbles must certainly have a Christian meaning.

SECTION V.

HONOURS TO ROMAN OFFICIALS.

DXXXV.

Fragment of a base (?) of white marble, broken on all sides. The inscribed face, as now preserved, measures 10 in. high, by 11 in. Discovered by Mr. Wood; unpublished.

```
          ..............
 ∪Σ‹Δ›⌐к›∪            χιλιάρχῳ ? λεγεῶν]ος ᴅ Σκυθ[ικῆς,
ΕΒΑΣΤΟΥ·ΔΗΜΑΡ        ....... Σ]εβαστοῦ, δημάρ[χῳ,
ΙΙΚΑΙΑΝΤΙΣΤΡΑΤ⊦      .. πρεσβευτ]ῇ καὶ ἀντιστρατή[γῳ
ΡΟΣΣΕΒΑΣΤΟΥ          .... Καίσα]ρος Σεβαστοῦ ...
ΛΕΝΤ!‹ΥΠΑΤ      5    ... ἀποστα]λέντι, ὑπατ[ικῷ ...
ΝΟΜΕΝΟ!⌐            ...... γε]νομένῳ ......
Α⌐                  ....... αγ .........
```

In honour of a Roman citizen, who had filled offices of distinction in the first century A.D. The iota adscript (line 3) and the style of the letters point to this date; although the Σ has an eccentric form, and is hardly exaggerated by the Σ as printed.

Line 1: The Legio IVᵗᵃ Scythica is not seldom mentioned in inscriptions; see C. I. 1186, 4022, 4023, 4029, 4033, 4034, 4238 c, Addenda 4536 g; Waddington-Le Bas, No. 627 (Sardes); and the Indices to C. I. L. passim. The best account of this Legion is given by Zumpt, Commentatio Epigraphica ii, p. 8. He points out that its name Scythica is at least as old as the reign of Tiberius, under whom it was stationed in Mœsia. Now in B.C. 30 M. Licinius Crassus commanded in Mœsia and conquered the Dacians and Bastarnians (the latter being termed Scythians), inflicting so severe a defeat that in 28 B.C. he was allowed a triumph. As this was about the only time that the Romans did battle with Scythians, the fourth legion probably gained its title Scythica from this event. The legion remained in Mœsia until the reign of Claudius, when it was summoned to Syria to take part in the Parthian war. It was one of the legions under the command of L. Cæsennius Pætus and Domitius Corbulo in A.D. 62 (Tac. Ann. xv, 6). From that time forward it served in Syria, but without any great distinction. If our inscription had been less mutilated we might perhaps have identified the subject of it by his cursus honorum. He had been in command in the Legio IVᵗᵃ Scythica,—then in some capacity under Augustus (?, Σεβαστοῦ, line 2),—then tribunus plebis (δήμαρχος), — then legatus Augusti pro prætore (line 3) in one of the Imperial provinces, the name of which ought to be found at the end of line 4 in the genitive; and for this he was qualified by being a vir consularis (ὑπατικός, line 5; see Marquardt, Röm. Alt. iv, p. 408).

DXXXVI.

A fragment of white marble, broken at top and bottom; the left edge moulded, and the right edge cut off like the joint of a wall-stone, without regard to the inscription. Height 10 in.; width 1 ft. 1 in. Discovered by Mr. Wood; unpublished.

```
1 /\111c·ΑΙΟΔΗΜ          'Η βο]υλὴ καὶ ὁ δῆμ[ος
:ΤΕΙΜΗΣΑΝ              ἐτείμησαν
ΙΟΝΚΛΑΥΔΙΟ             Γά]ϊον Κλαύδιο[ν
(ancient erasure) ΕΠΙΤΡΟΠ‹   ἐπίτροπο[ν
5 ϽΡΟΥΣΕΒΑΣΤΟΥΑΠ   5   . ορου Σεβαστοῦ, ἀπ[ὸ
▼⊤Ϙ4                  ἐπι]στολ[ῶν Ἑλληνικῶν ? κ.τ.λ.
```

Honours from the boulè and demos of Ephesos to a Roman official, whose cognomen has been intentionally erased. The letters appear to belong to the first century A.D.

One letter only seems wanting at the beginning of line 5; the other letters are certain: perhaps π]όρου or φ]όρου should be restored. Usually the Latin ab epistulis Græcis, a rationibus Augusti, etc.

are translated by ἐπί with the genitive ; see Wood, Inscriptions from the Temple, No. 5 (bilingual) : *Tι. Κλ. Οὐειβιανὸν* | *Τέρτυλλον τὸν* | *ἐπὶ* [*τῶν*] *Ἑλληνικῶν* | *ἐπιστολῶν καὶ τῶν* | *καθόλου λόγων τῶν* | *μεγίστων αὐτοκρατόρων κ.τ.λ.* ; which is rendered in the Latin 'ab epistulis Græcis et a rationibus Aug[ustorum']. But *ἀπό* is sometimes found, see C. I. Addenda 1813 *b* : *ἐπιτρόπῳ ἀπὸ τῶν ἀπο*[*δημή*]*σεων ? Σεβαστοῦ.*

DXXXVII.

A square base of white marble: height of inscribed front 2 ft. 1 in. ; width 1 ft. 11½ in.   Discovered by Mr. Wood. C. Curtius, Hermes iv, p. 190 Wood, Ephesus, Inscriptions from the Great Theatre, No. 5.

```
   ΟΔΗΜΟΣΕΤΕΙΜΗΣΑ
   ΓΑΙΟΝΙΟΥΛΙΟΝΒΑΣΙ
   ΛΕΩΣΑΛΕΞΑΝΔΡΟΥ
   ΥΙΟΝΑΓΡΙΠΠΑΝ    ο
5  ΤΑΜΙΑΝΚΑΙΑΝΤΙΣΤΡΑ
   ΤΗΓΟΝΤΗΣΑΣΙΑΣΔΙ
   ΑΤΕΤΗΝΑΛΛΗΝΑΡΕ
   ΤΗΝΚΑΙΤΗΝΕΙΣΤΗΝ
   ΠΟΛΙΝΕΥΝΟΙΑΝ
```

[Ἡ βουλὴ καὶ]
ὁ δῆμος ἐτείμησα[ν
Γάιον Ἰούλιον, βασι-
λέως Ἀλεξάνδρου
υἱόν, Ἀγρίππαν,
5   ταμίαν καὶ ἀντιστρά-
τηγον τῆς Ἀσίας, δι-
ά τε τὴν ἄλλην ἀρε-
τὴν καὶ τὴν εἰς τὴν
πόλιν εὔνοιαν.

Honours to Gaius Julius Agrippa from the boulè and demos.

As the verb is in the plural (line 1), we must restore [Ἡ βουλὴ καὶ], as in No. DXXXVI, etc. The recipient of the honours may be assumed to belong to the Herodian dynasty from the names Alexander and Agrippa. Gaius Julius Agrippa is described as quæstor pro prætore of the province of Asia (Marquardt, Röm. Alt. iv, p. 390), and as son of King Alexander. This prince is identified by Mommsen (Hermes iv, p. 191) with the Alexander son of Tigranes, King of Armenia, great-great-grandson of Herod the Great, who was invested with the sovereignty of the island Elaiussa in Cilicia by Vespasian, at the time that he united Cilicia Trachea

with the rest of the province of Cilicia (compare Marquardt, ibid. p. 227). This took place in A.D. 74, and is referred to by Suetonius (Vesp. 8) : item Trachiam Ciliciam et Commagenen, ditionis regiæ usque ad id tempus, in provinciarum formam redegit ; and by Josephus (Antiq. xviii, 5, § 4) : *γαμεῖ δ' οὗτος* (Ἀλέξανδρος) *Ἀντιόχου τοῦ Κομμαγηνῶν βασιλέως θυγατέρα Ἰωτάπην, νησῖδός τε τῆς ἐν Κιλικίᾳ Οὐεσπασιανὸς αὐτὸν ἵσταται βασιλέα.* His son C. Jul. Agrippa, the subject of our inscription, does not seem to be elsewhere mentioned. It is interesting to find a descendant of Herod the Great serving on the staff of the Roman proconsul. The inscription may be assigned to the reign of Trajan.

DXXXVIII.

Lower portion of a broken base of white marble ; entire only on the right and at the bottom.   Present height of inscribed front 2 ft. 7½ in. ; width 2 ft. 5¼ in.   Discovered by Mr. Wood ; unpublished.

```
              ...ΚΑι
      1  ...ΚΡΑΤΟΡΟΣ
       Λ...ΦΑΙΑΝΟΥΚΑΙΣΑΡΟΣ
         ΤΟΥΓΕΡΜΑΝΙΚΟΥΣΥΡΙΑΣ
5        ΑΛΛΩΝΕΠΑΡΧΕΙΩΝ
         ΤΗΣΕΝΕΚΕΝΚΑΙΤΗΣΠΡΟΣ
         ...ΟΕΟΝΕΥΣΕΒΕΙΑΣΠΡΟΣΤΕ
         ΗΝΠΟΛΙΝΕΥΝΟΙΑΣ  vacant
                vacant
         ΝΑΣΤΑΣΙΝΠΟΙΗΣΑΜΕ
10       ΙΟΥΒΑΣΣΟΥ · ΕΠΙΤΡΟΠΟΥΕ
          ΙΛΙΟΥΒΑΣΣΟΥΤΟΥ
            ΒΑΣ / ΤΩΝΕ
```

[Ὁ δῆμος?]
[Γ. Ἄντιον Αὖλον Ἰούλιον, Αὔλου]
[υἱόν, Κουοδρᾶτον, δὶς ὕπατον,]
ἀνθύπατον Ἀσίας, πρεσβευτὴν] καὶ
ἀντιστράτηγον Αὐτ]οκράτορος
Νερούα [Τ]ραιανοῦ Καίσαρος
Σεβασ]τοῦ Γερμανικοῦ Συρίας
5   καὶ πολλῶν] ἄλλων ἐπαρχειῶν
ἀρε]τῆς ἕνεκεν καὶ τῆς πρὸς
τὴ]ν θεὸν εὐσεβείας πρός τε
τ]ὴν πόλιν εὐνοίας.

Τὴν ἀ]νάστασιν ποιησαμέ-
νων . . .]ιου Βάσσου ἐπιτρόπου ἐ-
10   παρχίας ? καὶ Ποπ]λίου Βάσσου τοῦ
γραμματέως, φιλο]σεβάστων.

Public honours to an eminent Roman officer under Trajan.

Lines 2 foll., and especially line 5. although mutilated. yet sufficiently inform us that the recipient of the honour had served in various provinces and among others in Syria, as legatus pro prætore under Trajan. Moreover as this inscription is set up at Ephesos, we may presume that the subject of it was at the time holding office in Asia, probably as proconsul. This surmise is confirmed by a similar inscription from Pergamon, C. I. 3548 (Waddington-Le Bas, No. 1722 a; compare C. I. 3532 and 4238 d), in honour of C. Antius Aulus Julius Quadratus, who is described as δὶς ὕπατον, ἀνθύπατον Ἀσίας, σεπτεμούρουμ ἐπουλώνων, φράτρεμ ἀρονάλε(μ), πρεσβευτὴν καὶ ἀντιστράτηγον [Πόντου] καὶ Βιθυνίας, πρεσβευτὴν Ἀσίας, πρεσβευτὴν Σεβαστο[ῦ] ἐπαρχίας Καππαδοκίας, ἀνθύπατον Κρήτης Κυ[ρήνης], πρεσβευτὴν Σεβαστο[ῦ καὶ ἀντι]στράτηγον Λυκίας καὶ Παμφυλίας, πρεσβευτὴν καὶ ἀντιστράτηγον Αὐτοκράτορος Νερούα Τραϊανοῦ Καίσαρος Σεβαστοῦ Γερμανικοῦ Δακικοῦ ἐπαρχίας Συρίας (Marquardt, Röm. Alt. iv, pp. 194. 218, 303). It is highly probable that our inscription commemorates the same person; accordingly his name and titles have been restored in the opening lines. The best account of him is given by Waddington, Fastes, p. 172 foll. Julius Quadratus was consul suffectus in July, A. D. 93, and ordinary consul A. D. 105. He was a native of Pergamon, probably being one of those distinguished provincials admitted to the senate by Vespasian and Titus A. D. 74 (Suetonius, Vesp., 9). Under Domitian he was employed in the administration of various provinces (named in the Pergamene inscription just cited), until his first consulate, A. D. 93. After this his promotion appears to have been delayed until the accession of Trajan, who soon after A. D. 102 appointed him to the important province of Syria (line 7). In 104 A. D. he must have returned to Rome to undertake his consulship in the following year. And M. Waddington would place his proconsulship of Asia in A. D. 106. If my restoration of the heading is correct, the present inscription merely singles out the most important distinctions of his career, his two consulships, which, as usual, stand first, his government of Asia and of Syria. His previous appointments are summarily spoken of in line 5 as πολλῶν] ἄλλων ἐπαρχειῶν.

The restorations in lines 10-12 are doubtful: both ἐπιτρόπου ἐ[παρχίας], and τοῦ [γραμματέως] without the addition of τοῦ δήμου, are unusual expressions, but perhaps not more so than the abbreviated description of Quadratus in line 5. The former Bassus would be procurator Asiæ, i. e. charged with collecting and managing the dues to the imperial fiscus in the proconsular province of Asia (see Tacitus, Ann. iv, 15; C. I. 2977 and 2981; Marquardt, Röm. Alt. iv, p. 414). The other Bassus may be the Publius Rutilius Bassus who in A. D. 120 is named as γραμματεύς of the gerousia (?): see No. CCCCLXXXVI ante. There would be a propriety in associating the procurator of Cæsar with the γραμματεύς of the Ephesian people in erecting a statue to the proconsul.

DXXXIX.

A broken slab of white marble; complete at top, bottom, left and lower part of right. Height of a, 1 ft. 3 in.; present width 1 ft. 7 in. Height of b, 1 ft. 8 in.; width (original) 1 ft. 10 in. It is doubtful how much is lost between a and b. Wood, Ephesus, Appendix, Inscriptions from the Temple, No. 7, and postscript to Appendix, ibid. p. 43; but Wood's copy is not quite complete; Kaibel, Epigrammata Graeca, No. 888 a, following Wood's text.

```
a.        ΥΠΑΤΙΚΟΝ
         ΦΠΟΝΤΙΦΙΚΑ ·· Κ
         ΟΥΜΜΙΔΙΟΥΚΟ
         ΠΑ'·ΕΡΑΚΗΔΓ⁻
    5    ΤΩΙ ΘΕΙΟΤ
         ΚΡΑΤ
                              Υ

                ΡΟΣ ι           Ν
b. 10  ΠΑΝΤΟΙΗΣ    Η  ΙΑΘΜΗΝς  ΙΤΟΛΙΝΑΝΔΡΑ
       ΕΞΟΧΟΝΕ ΛΗΝΩΝΠΡΟΚΡΙΤΟΝΑΥΣΟΝΙΩΝ
       ΚΛΕΙΝΟΥΚΟΔΡΑΤΟΙΟΦΙΛΟΝΠΑΤΕΡΩΙΒΑΣΙΛΕΙΟΝ
       ΑΡΜΟΝΙΗΘΑΛΑΜΟΝΠΗΞΑΤΕΠΕΥΓΑΜΙΗΙ
       ΑΔΡΙΑΝΟΣΜΟΥΣΑΙΣΙΜΕΛΩΝΑΝΕΘΗΚΕΣΕΟΥΗΡΟΝ
   15  ΕΙΚΩΧΑΛΚΕΙΗΝΟΥΝΕΚΑΠΡΟΣΤΑΣΙΗΣ
       ΙΛΑΝΔΡΕΣΙΩΝΕΣΑΓΑΛΜΑΤΑΚΑΛΟΝΟΡΑΣΘΑΙ
       ΡΤ⁻Ⱶ            ⁻ΙΩΙΕΝΤΕΜΕΝΕΙ
                                        ━
```

```
a.        ὑπατικὸν,
         ποντίφικα, κ[αὶ ?
         Οὐμμίδιον Κο[δράτου
         πατέρα, κηδε[στὴν
    5    τῶν θειοτ[άτων καὶ
```

κρατ[ίστων . . . . .
. . . .
(δ)   . . . . o]ν
τὸν π]ροσ[τάτη]ν.
10   Παντοίης [ἀρετ]ῆ͜ς σ]τάθμην [δυσί]ππολιν ἄνδρα,
ἔξοχον Ἑ[λ]λήνων, πρόκριτον Αὐσονίων,
κλεινοῦ Κοδράτοιο φίλον πατέρ᾽, ᾧ βασίλειον
Ἁρμονίη θάλαμον πῆξατ᾽ ἐπ᾽ εὐγαμίη.
Ἀδριανὸς μούσαισι μέλων ἀνέθηκε Σεουῆρον
15   εἰκὼ χαλκείην οὕνεκα προστασίης.
τοιῶν]δ᾽, ἄνδρες Ἴωνες, ἀγάλματα καλὸν ὁρᾶσθαι
ἱσταότ᾽ Ἀ]ρτέμ[ιδος πλη]σίῳ ἐν τεμένει.

Although the top of the marble is entire. the inscription is incomplete. We have before us a slab from the base of a statue, and several lines are lost from the marble above, which probably ran thus :—

'Η βουλή καὶ ὁ δῆμος
ἐτείμησαν
[Λ. Κατίλιον ?] Σεουῆρον

(with his cursus honorum).

Of his titles only two remain, ὑπατικόν, ποντίφικα. The person thus honoured is styled by the Ephesians their προστάτης (lines 9, 15), i. e. patronus, it being a common thing under the empire, as under the republic, for foreign cities (and even whole provinces) to place themselves in the relation of client to some distinguished Roman citizen (see Marquardt, Röm. Alt. iv, pp. 400, 505; C. I. 4154. etc.). That his name was Severus we learn from line 14. and Mommsen (see Kaibel, l. c.) identifies him with Lucius Catilius Severus, well known as a trusted administrator under Hadrian (Spartian, Life of Hadrian. 5. 15, 24), and maternal great-grandfather of the Emperor Marcus Aurelius (Capitolinus, Life of M. Antoninus, 2). Our inscription calls him the 'father of' Ummidius Quadratus' (lines 4, 12), who is probably the C. Ummidius Quadratus the friend of Pliny the younger (Epp. vii, 24). grandson of Ummidia Quadratilla, and consul A. D. 118. The name of Quadratus' father is nowhere else given, but there is no difficulty in thus understanding the words of our inscription. L. Catilius Severus served his first consulship under Trajan (Waddington, Fastes, p. 204), and therefore had been a consular (ὑπατικός, line 1), some time when the death of Trajan found him serving under Hadrian in Syria. Hadrian lost no time in restoring the East to peace, and, leaving Catilius Severus governor of Syria, hastened to Rome A. D. 118. Severus

remained in Syria from the autumn of 117 to the autumn of 119, when he returned to Rome for his second consulship, A. D. 120. As his second consulship seems not to be mentioned in our inscription, it would be earlier than A. D. 120 ; and probably was put up during his government of Syria. It was very natural for the Ephesians thus to court the patronage of the new Emperor's trusted friend. Moreover the son of Severus had recently married a lady of royal family (lines 12–13), ' Harmony had built him a royal bridal-chamber ;' so that Severus is styled (lines 4 foll.) 'father-in-law of divine and noble personages.' We can quite understand how the viceroy of Hadrian in Syria, at a moment when the Emperor's policy was rather to conciliate than to conquer, might marry his son to a daughter of one of the Asiatic royal houses.

While the Ephesians are thus voting honours to Severus as their patronus, his royal master Hadrian (line 14) supplies the Ephesians with funds to rear him a bronze statue in the temenos of the temple of Artemis, which was not far from the city (πλησίῳ, line 17). and himself composes this epigram to adorn it (line 14).

The subsequent career of Severus is well known. In one of the years 128–130 he was proconsul Asiæ (Waddington, Fastes, pp. 203, 204). After which Hadrian made him præfect of Rome. Strong in the royal favour Severus entertained hopes of succeeding to the Empire, and was therefore extremely opposed to the adoption of Antoninus. For this he was dismissed from office and from Imperial favour in 138 : Antonini adoptionem plurimi tunc factam esse doluerunt, speciatim Catilius Severus, præfectus urbi, qui sibi præparabat imperium. qua re prodita successore accepto dignitate privatus est (Spartian, Life of Hadrian, 24).

DXL.

A stele of white marble, surmounted by a moulding ; height 3 ft. 5 in. ; width 1 ft. 5¼ in.   'Found in wall on site of the Temple, 8 feet below present surface of ground.'   Wood, Ephesus, Inscriptions from the Site of the Temple, No. 14.

ΛΤΤΙΔΙΟΝΙ ΟΥΣΚΟΝ   Ἀττίδιον (Φ)οῦσκον
ΠΡΑΙΤΟΡΑ   Πραίτορα
ΚΑΙ ΠΡΕΣΒΕΥΤΗΝ   καὶ πρεσβευτὴν
ΓΕΝΕΡΩΣΟΝ ΚΑΙ   γενέρωσον καὶ
5   ΕΥΓΕΝΕΣΤΑΤΟΝ   5   εὐγενέστατον·

ΣΤΕΡΤΙΝΙΟΣΜΑΞΙΜΟΣ
ΕΥΤΥΧΗΣΙΠΠΙΚΟ
ΡΩΜΑΙΩΝ
ΘΥΤΗΣΤΩΝΕΞΗΚΟΝΤΑ
10 ΣΚΡΕΙΒΑΣΛΙΒΡΑΡΙΟΣ
ΚΟΥΑΙΣΤΩΡΙΟΣ
ΤΟΝΙΔΙΟΝΠΑΤΡΩΝΑ

Στερτίνιος Μάξιμος
Εὐτύχητ, ἱππικὸ[τ
'Ρωμαίων,
θύτης τῶν ἑξήκοντα,
10 σκρείβατ λιβράριος
κουαιστώριος,
τὸν ἴδιον πάτρωνα.

In honour of Attidius [F]uscus or [T]uscus, legate of the proconsul of Asia.

In line 1 the lapidary has written ι by mistake for τ or φ, or the loop of φ has been effaced by wear. The letters belong to the Antonine age, and the inscription exhibits an unusual medley of Greek and Latin. Attidius Fuscus, who may be a kinsman of L. Attidius Cornelianus, legatus Syriæ, A. D. 162 (Marquardt, Röm. Alt. iv, p. 265), had been prætor, and at the time of this inscription was πρεσβευτὴς 'Ασίας. His proper title was legatus pro prætore, and his duty was to assist the proconsul especially in the administration of justice (Marquardt, ibid. p. 410). Thus Julius Quadratus (see No. DXXXVIII) had been πρεσβευτὴς 'Ασίας β̄ before his first consulship (C. I. 3532; Waddington, Fastes, p. 173), i. e. he had been assessor to two different proconsuls. The monument was erected by Stertinius Maximus,

described as eques Romanus (ἱππικὸς 'Ρωμαίων) — haruspex (θύτης) de LX (see Marquardt, Röm. Alt. vi, p. 398, who observes that this college of haruspices Augusti contained none but those of equestrian rank)—and scriba librarius quæstorius, or secretary employed in the service of a quæstor. The title scriba librarius appears to be merely the fuller designation of a scriba (Pauly, Real-encycl. vi, Pt. 1, p. 876). There was a large number of these scribæ in the service of the state. The consuls, prætors, censors and higher magistrates selected their own scribæ or secretaries from among the number; the inferior magistrates, e. g. quæstors, had their scribæ appointed by lot. This rule held good of the provincial quæstors also; see Pliny, Ep. iv, 12: cum in provinciam quæstor exiisset scribamque qui sorti obtigerat ante legitimum salarii tempus amisisset, etc.

DXLI.

A stele of white marble, with moulding at top and bottom: height 4½ ft.; width 1 ft. 11 in. C. Curtius, Hermes, iv, p. 191 foll.; Wood, Inscriptions from the Great Theatre, No. 15.

ΤΗΣΠΡΩΤΗΣΚΑΙ
ΜΕΓΙΣΤΗΣ
ΜΗΤΡΟΠΟΛΕΩΣ
ΤΗΣΑΣΙΑΣΚΑΙΒΝΕΩΚΟΡΟΥ
5 ΤΩΝΣΕΒΑΣΤΩΝΕΦΕΣΙΩΝΠΟΛΕΩΣ
ΗΒΟΥΛΗ – ΚΑΙΟΔΗΜΟΣ
ΕΤΕΙΜΗΣΑΝ
Γ ΙΟΥΛΙΟΝΛΟΥΠΟΝ
Τ· ΟΥΕΙΒΙΟΝΟΥΑΡΟΝΛΑΙ
10 ΒΙΛΛΟΝ · ΤΑΜΙΑΝΚΑΙΑΝΤΙΣΤΡΑ
ΤΗΓΟΝΤΡΙΩΝΑΝΘΥΠΑΤΩΝ σ̄
ΤΗΝΕΙΜΗΝΑΝΑΣΤΗΣΑΝΤΩΝ
Μ · ΑΝΤΩΝΙΟΥ
ΕΠΙΤΥΓΧΑΝΟΥ
15 ⌐ΝΚΑΡΠΩΚΑΙΕΠΙΤΥΓΧΑΝΩ ⌐
ΤΟΙΣΤΕΚΝΟΙΣ
ΤΟΝΕΑΥΤΩΝΕΥΕΡΓΕΤΗΝ

Τῆς πρώτης καὶ
μεγίστης
μητροπόλεωτ
τῆτ 'Ασίας καὶ β̄ νεωκόρου
5 τῶν Σεβαστῶν 'Εφεσίων πόλεωτ
ἡ βουλὴ καὶ ὁ δῆμος
ἐτείμησαν
Γ. 'Ιούλιον Λοῦπον
Τ. Οὐίβιον Οὔαρον Λαί-
10 βιλλον, ταμίαν καὶ ἀντιστράτηγον τριῶν ἀνθυπάτων,—
τὴν τειμὴν ἀναστησάντων
Μ. 'Αντωνίου
'Επιτυγχάνου
15 σὺ]ν Κάρπῳ καὶ 'Επιτυγχάνῳ
τοῖς τέκνοιτ,
τὸν ἑαυτῶν εὐεργέτην.

C. Julius Lupus T. Vibius Varus Lævillus—a curious example of that accumulation of names which became fashionable under the Flavian Emperors (see Mommsen, Hermes iii, 70 foll.)—had filled the office of quæstor pro prætore under three proconsuls (lines 10 foll.), and is here honoured by the senate and people of Ephesos. The inscription is certainly later than Hadrian, under whom Ephesos was allowed to assume the title of δὶς νεωκόρος (see on No. DIII ante). The characters are manifestly of

the Antonine era, and it is observable that not only is the name Epitynchanos (line 14) known from the Meditations of M. Aurelius (viii, 25), but also a freedman of that Emperor bore this name (Pauly, Real-encycl. s. v.). 'Επιτύγχανος occurs not unfrequently in the Attic lists of ephebi of the third century A. D. (see Index to C. I. A. vol. iii); but it is less common than 'Επιτυγχάνων. Lines 12–16 are a parenthesis, and ἑαυτῶν refers back to ἡ βουλὴ καὶ ὁ δῆμος.

DXLII.

Fragment of white marble stelè, broken on all sides: height 10 in.; width 5 in.   Discovered by Mr. Wood; unpublished.

```
                            ['Η βουλὴ καὶ]
                            [ὁ δῆμος ἐτείμη-]
      ΖΑΝΤ                  σαν Τ . . . .
      ΛΙΚΙΝ                 Λικίν[ιον
      ΡΟΥΦ                  'Ρουφ[εῖνον
   5    Π                   ▼ . . .
        ͶͰ               5  ὑπ[ατικὼ?
```

Honours to T. Licinius Rufinus.

Nothing seems lost from the beginning of the lines, and the space before Π, line 4, is blank. Whether ΥΠ began line 5 is doubtful, as the edge is broken. In an inscription from Thyatira (C. I. 3499, compare 3500) the guild of tanners honour one Μ. Γναῖον Λικίνιον 'Ρουφῖνον, τὸν λαμπρότατον ὑπατικόν. As however Τ is certain in line 1, our Rufinus is a different person. A son of Gnæus is named, C. I. 3502, but without mention of his prænomen, so he may conceivably be the Rufinus of our inscription. Another member of the family is mentioned in an inscription from Phaselis in the reign of Hadrian (C. I. 4335). The other documents, like the one before us, belong to the time of the Antonines.

DXLIII.

White marble stelè, from the Ephesian theatre, entire. Height 3 ft. 11½ in.; width 1 ft. 11½ in.   C. Curtius, Hermes, iv, p. 216 foll.; Wood, Inscriptions from the Great Theatre, No. 13; C. I. L. iii, No. 6076, where an inscription from Italy is cited, in honour of the same man (C. I. L. vi, No. 1435).

```
      SPLENDIDISSIMAL
      CIVITATISEPHESIORVM
      ΤΗΣΠΡΩΤΗΣ ΚΑΙΜΕΓΙΣΤΗΣ
      ΜΗΤΡΟΠΟΛΕΩΣΤΗΣΑΣΙΑΣ
   5  ΚΑΙ·Β̄·ΝΕΩΚΟΡΟΥΤΩΝΣΕΒΑΣΤΩΝ
      A·IVNIVM·P·F·FABIA·
      PASTOREM·L·CAESENNIVM
      SOSPITEM·LEG·PR·PR·PROVINCIAE
      ASIAEPRAETOREMDESIGNATVM·TR·
   10 PLEB·QVAESTOREM·AVG·TRIBVNVM
      MILITVM·LEG·XIII·GEMINAETRIVM
      VIRVM·AERE·ARGENTOAVROFLANDO
      FERIVNDO·SEVIROTVRMAEEQVITVM
      ROMANORVM·RARISSIMOVIRO
   15 SEX·IVNIVSPHILETVS
      ET·M·ANTONIVSCARPVS
      HONORIS    Ꝋ   CAVSA ▾
            H          C
```

Splendidissimae
civitatis Ephesiorum,
τῆς πρώτης καὶ μεγίστης
μητροπόλεως τῆς 'Ασίας
5 καὶ β̄ νεωκόρου τῶν Σεβαστῶν,
A(ulum) Iunium P(ubli) f(ilium) Fabia
Pastorem L(ucium) Caesennium
Sospitem, leg(atum) pr(o) pr(aetore) provinciae
Asiae, praetorem designatum, tr(ibunum)
10 pleb(is), quaestorem Aug(usti), tribunum
militum leg(ionis) xiii geminae, trium-
virum aere argento auro flando
feriundo, seviro turmae equitum
Romanorum, rarissimo viro
15 Sex(tus) Iunius Philetus
et M(arcus) Antonius Carpus
honoris causa;
h(onoris) c(ausa).

After line 5 the usual formula ἡ βουλὴ καὶ ὁ δῆμος ἐτείμησαν is omitted, perhaps by mere error. Also in line 13 foll. the scribe has written seviro, rarissimo viro, in the dative instead of accusative, misled perhaps by the termination of feriundo just before.

The inscription is in honour of Aulus Junius Pastor Lucius Caesennius Sospes, whom we may identify with the Pastor who was afterwards consul A.D. 163. On his accumulated names see No. DXLI. The inscription was set up while Pastor was legatus pro praetore of Asia, and designated as praetor for the next year, by Sextus Junius Philetus and M.

Ant. Carpus, the second of whom may be the Carpus son of Epitynchanos named in No. DXLI. The other appointments held by Junius Pastor are recited as usual in chronological order. Line 12 : the ' Triumviri monetales aeri argento auro flando feriundo ' (see Pauly, Real-encycl., s. v. and Marquardt) were the Roman masters of the mint, and are often mentioned ; aere in this connexion was an established spelling for aeri. The division of the Equites into six turmae (line 13) was attributed to Servius Tullius, each turma had its commander (sevir).

<hr>

DXLIV.

Stelè of white marble : height 3 ft. 6 in. ; width 2 ft., by 1 ft. 11 in. deep. Entire, but the surface is worn on right. ' From a basilica near the Odeum.' C. Curtius, Hermes iv, p. 215. C. I. L. iii, No. 6078 ; Wood, Inscriptions from the City and Suburbs, No. 7.

	TI.CLAVDIO		Ti(berio) Claudio
	SECVNDO		Secundo
	VIATORITRIBVNIC		viatori tribunic[io,
	ACCENSOVELATOLICTO		accenso velato, licto-
5	RICVRIATOGERVSIAF	5	ri curiato, gerusia h[o-
	NORISCAVSSA··SV/		noris caussa, sua [pecunia.
	ΗΓΕΡΟΥΣΙΑΕΤΕΙΜΗΣΕΝ		Ἡ γερουσία ἐτείμησεν
	ΤΙ·ΚΛΑΥΔΙΟΝΣΕΚΟΥΝΔ		Τι(βέριον) Κλαύδιον Σεκοῦνδ[ον
	ΟΥΙΑΤΟΡΑΤΡΙΒΟΥΝΙΚ		οὐιάτορα τριβουνίκ[ιον,
10	ΑΚΚΗΝΣΟΝΟΥΗΛΑΤΟΝ	10	ἄκκηνσον οὐήλατον,
	ΛΕΙΚΤΟΡΑΚΟΥΡΙΑΤΟΝ		λείκτορα κουρίατον,
	ΕΚΤΩΝΙΔΙΩΝ		ἐκ τῶν ἰδίων.

A bilingual inscription in honour of Ti. Claudius Secundus, who had filled several subordinate Roman offices. He had been one of the 'viatores' or messengers of the tribunes at Rome. All the higher magistrates seem to have had such viatores in attendance upon them (Pauly, Real-encycl. s. v.), the tribuni plebis included (see Tac. Ann. xvi, 12). Next he had been one of the 'accensi velati,' a class who formed part of the Servian constitution, and who still survived as a distinct corporation down to the times of the empire as here. They were mentioned

in many Latin inscriptions, but their precise functions are not clearly ascertained : they appear however to have been connected in some way with the national priesthood, and were very commonly freedmen. The 'lictores curiati,' (line 5) seem to have ranked the highest among the subordinate officers of the priesthood (Marquardt, Röm. Alt iii, 218), and formed a 'decuria lictorum curiatia, quae sacris publicis apparet.' The inscription is erected by the Gerousia (on which see p. 75) and belongs to the times of the Antonines.

<hr>

DXLV.

. square pedestal or column of white marble : height 4 ft. 11 in. ; original diameter 1 ft. 3 in., by 1 ft. 2¾ in. ; pieced together out of two fragments, but the left hand portion is still missing. Present width of inscribed front 11½ in. Inaccurately given by Wood, Inscriptions from the Augusteum, No. 9.

	ΔΙΟΝ		Τι. Κλαύ]διον
	ΔΟΝ		Σεκοῦν]δον
	ΡΙΒΟΥΝΙ		οὐιάτορα τ]ριβουνί-
	ΗΝΣΟΝ·ΟΥ		κιον, ἄκκ]ηνσον οὐ-
5	ΛΕΙΚΤΟΡΑ	5	ήλατον, λ]είκτορα

ΦΙΛΕΦΕΣΙ
ΣΕΠΙΣΗϽΙΣ
ϽΣΜΗΣΑΝΤΑ
ΣΙΩΝΠΟΛΙΝ
10 ΟΙΚΟΝΚΑΙἮΝ
ΠΟΙΚϽΥΣΤΟ
ΤΑ ΛΙΣΚοΥ
‾ ϽΣ - ΤοΥ
ϐ
15 ΕΡΜΙΑΣ
Ν - ΤΟ
ΗΣΑΝΤΩΝ
Ν ͞ ΕΚΤΛΝ
ΣΤΗΣΕΝ ϐ

κουρίατον,] φιλεφίσι[ον,
καὶ ἄλλοι]ϲ ἐπισήμοιϲ
ἔργοιϲ κ]οσμήσαντλ
τὴν Ἐφε]σίων πόλιν,
10 καὶ . . . .] οἶκον καὶ τὴν
ἄγουσαν ἐ]π' οἴκου στο-
ἀν ἱδρύσαν]τα? , αισκου
. . . . ωϲ τοῦ
. . . . . .
13 Τιβ. Κλ.] Ἑρμίας
τὴν τειμὴ]ν—τὸ
ψήφισμα ποι]ησάντων
τῶν Ἐφεσίω]ν—ἐκ τῶν
ἰδίων ἀνέ]στησεν.

Honours to Tiberius Claudius Secundus, already known from No. DXLIV, by comparison of which the first six lines are restored. It appears however that Mr. Wood had before him only the upper part of our inscription, and that when he made his copy the upper lines were less mutilated than they now are. He certainly prints lines 1–7 with no mark of any lacuna.

Secundus, though not of high birth, and probably no more than a freedman (on his appointments, see No. DXLIV), was evidently a man of wealth, and while residing at Ephesos had adorned the city with various monuments and buildings. With lines 7–9 compare Waddington-Le Bas, No. 1598 *bis* : τοῦ πολλοῖς | καὶ μεγάλοις | ἔργοις | κοσμήσαντος | τὴν πόλιν (Aphrodisias). Ἄλλοι]ϲ, line 7, is from Wood's copy;

and it exactly suits the sense. One especial building was described in lines 10–14 which are broken beyond restoration. It was an οἶκος with a στοά adjoining it. Probably some word in line 10 came before οἶκον to qualify it, perhaps [ἱερὸν] οἶκον : compare an inscription from Naples dated A. D. 71, C. I. 5838, line 2, where Franz points out that οἶκος is not unfrequently used to designate a place for religious worship ; so C. I. 2491 c (a document of good age, from Astypalæa): Σωσικράτης Νεομή|νιος Δαμάτριος Θεο|φάνεος ἀνέθηκαν | τῷ Ἀπόλλωνι τὸν | οἶκον κατάσκινο[ν ; and the inscription from Cnidus, Newton, Hist. of Discoveries, ii, Pt. 2, p. 714.

Line 15 : it seems possible that Ἑρμίας is identical with the Τιβ. Κλ. Ἑρμείας of No. DLXII *post.*

SECTION VI.

INSCRIPTIONS IN HONOUR OF PRIVATE PERSONS.

DXLVI.

White marble stele, slightly broken on right. Height 1 ft.; breadth 2 ft. 1 in. Discovered by Mr. Wood; unpublished.

ΟΔΗΜΟΣΝΕΜΕΡΙΟΝι ᴸιΙΛΛᴀ
ΝΕΜΕΡΙΟΥΥΙΟΝΦΛΑΜΜΑΝΔΙΑΤι
ΤΗΝΑΥΤΟΥΚΟΣΜΙΟΝΑΓΩΓΗΝΚΑ
ΤΗΝΤΟΥΠΑΤΡΟΣΑΥΤΟΥΠΡΟΣΕΑ⁊
5   ΕΥΝΟΙΑΝ

'Ο δῆμος Νεμέριον Γεριλλα[νὸν
Νεμερίου υἱὸν Φλάμμαν, διά τε
τὴν αὐτοῦ κόσμιον ἀγωγὴν κα[ὶ
τὴν τοῦ πατρὸς αὐτοῦ πρὸς ἑατ[ὸν
5   εὔνοιαν.

Honours to Numerius Gerillanus, Numerii f., Flamma. The letters appear to belong to the first century A.D. That Νεμέριος is the transcription of Numerius is proved by Dittenberger in his essay 'On Roman names in Greek Inscriptions' (Hermes, vi. p. 297 ; compare C. I. A. iii, No. 197). Ἀτοῦ and ἱατοῦ for αὐτοῦ and ἑαντοῦ became recognised by-forms throughout Greece in the first century B.C., and were extremely common in the Augustan age ; see Keil, Sylloge Inscr. Bœot., p. 144 ; Meisterhans, Grammatik der att. Inschr. 2, pp. 48, 122 ; Dittenberger, Syll. No. 272. I have restored ἀτὸν in lines 27 and 54 of the Tenian decree now at Cambridge, C. I. 2335 (Hicks. Manual, No. 204). For the name Numerius Gerillanus compare No. DLXXIII *post*; see also No. DXXXIII *ante*.

DXLVII.

Portion of a base of bluish marble. entire except at the upper edge: height 10 inches ; length 4 ft. 2 in. Discovered by Mr. Wood ; unpublished.

a.   *b.*

ᴐΝΦΟΝΙΙΙΙ
ΠΕΝΘΕΡΟΝΤΟΝΜΑΡΚΟΥΑΠΠᴼ   π   ΔΙΑΤΗΝΙΙΓΟᴢ ᴏΝ ιΝᴀ
ΙΟΥΤΟΥΤΑΜΙΟΥΔΙΑΤΗΝΕΚΤΟΥΓΑΜ   ΤΗΣΜΑΡΚΟΝΑΠΠΟΛΗΙΟΝ
ΒΡΟΥΑΥΤΟΥΠΡΟΣΤΗΝΠΟΛΙΝΕΥ   ΣΕΞΤΟΥΥΙ   ΟΝΕΥΝΟΙΑΝ
5   ΝΟΙΑΝ

a.   *b.*

[Ὁ δῆμος ?]   [Ὁ δῆμος ?]
... ον Φοντήἰ[ον ... τὸν   [τὴν δεῖνα .. Φοντηίου θυγατέρα]
πενθερὸν τὸν Μάρκου Ἀππο[λ]η-   διὰ τὴν πρὸς [τ]ὸν [ἀ]νδ[ρα αὐ-
ίου τοῦ ταμίου διὰ τὴν ἐκ τοῦ γαμ-   τῆς Μάρκον Ἀππολήιον
βροῦ αὐτοῦ πρὸς τὴν πόλιν εὔ-   Σέξτου υἱὸν εὔνοίαν.
5   νοίαν.

The base of two statues erected to one Fonteius and his daughter. She had married ' M. Appuleius Sexti f. quæstor ', and it is the kindness of Appuleius towards the city of Ephesos and the gratitude with which the Ephesians received this kindness which are assigned as the motive for erecting the statues.

We may identify M. Appuleius with the Appuleius who was quæstor in Asia at the time of Cæsar's murder, and who gave such important help to Junius Brutus A.D. 43 (see Dict. of Biogr. s.vv. Brutus, Appuleius). Is Fonteius conceivably the Fonteius whom Cicero defended B.C. 69? He may have retired with ill-gotten gains to Asia. This early date is justified by the form of the letters, which resemble No. DXXI, and by the transcription Ἀππολήιος (see Dittenberger, Hermes, vi, p. 282).

DXLVIII.

A stele of white marble, broken at the top and on the right; bottom and left entire: height 3 ft. 6¼ in.; width 1 ft. 7½ in. Wood, Inscriptions from the Site of the Temple, No. 11. Kaibel, Epigrammata Graeca, 877 *a*.

```
ᴅU  ᴧΙΙ∠ᴫ
ΤΩΝΜΑΘ
Τ·Φᴧ·ΥΨΙΚᴧΗΣ      ΤΙ
ΡΟΔΙΟΣ      (Erasure.)
Τ·Φᴧ·ΠᴧΑΓΚΙΑΝΣ  ΕΦΕΣΙC_
ΡΟΔΙΟΣ      ΠΡΕΙΣΚΟ
Τ·ΚΑ·ΚΑᴧᴧΙΣΈΝΣ  ΚΙᴧΒΙΑΝΟ
ΙΕΡΑΠΟᴧΙΤΗϹ·Κᴧ·ΣᴧΑΒΙΟΣ
ΑΥΡ·ΑΤΤΑᴧΟΣ  ΦΩΚΑΕΥΣ
ΝΕΙΚΑΕΥΣ·ΑΙΑ·ᴧΥΚΕΙΝΟΣ
ᴧΕΙ·ΜΑΡΚΕᴧᴧΘ·ΑΝΚΥΡΑΝΘ
ΑΝΤΙΟΧΕΥΣ·ΜΕΤΤΙΑΝΟ
ΕΟᴧΩΝ      ΚΑΥΝΙΟ∠
ΔΙΣΜΕΣΟΦΙΣΤΗΝΠΡΩΤΟᴧ
ΑΘΗΝΝΘΕΝΚΑᴧΕΣΑΝΟ
ΣΩΤΗΡΟΝΒΟΥᴧΗΣΔΟΓΜΑ
ΣΙΝΑΝΔΡΟΚᴧΑΙΔΑΙ
ΠΡΩΤΩΔΕΑΝΤΑΡΕΤΗΣΤΕ
ΒΙΟΥΣΟΦΙΗΣΤΕᴧΟΓΟ
ΟΡΙΣΑΝΕΝΤΙΜΑΙΣΜΥΡⁱ
ΔΩΡΑΤΕᴧΕΙΝ
```

[Ψηφισαμένης τῆς ?]
βο[υ]λῆς, κ[αὶ στησάντων
τῶν μαθ[ητῶν .
Τ. Φλ. ' Υψικλῆς,   Τι . . . . . .
' Ρόδιος.   (name erased.)
Τ. Φλ. Πλαγκιανὸς,   Ἐφέσιος·
' Ρόδιος·   Πρεῖσκο[ς,
Τ. Κλ. Καλλίξενος,   Κιλβιανό[ς·
' Ιεραπολίτης·   Κλ. Σάλβιος,
Αὐρ. Ἄτταλος,   Φωκαεύς·
Νεικαεύς·   Αἰλ. Λυκεῖνος,
Λει. Μάρκελλος,   Ἀνκυρανός·
' Αντιοχεύς·   Μεττιανὸ[ς,
Κόλων,   Καύνιος·
Δίς με σοφιστὴν πρῶτον· Ἀθήνηθεν καλέσαντο
Σώτηρον βουλῆς δόγμα σιν 'Ανδροκλίδαι·
πρώτῳ δὲ ἀπ' ἀρετῆς τε | βίου σοφίης τε λόγο[ι,ο
ὥρισαν ἐν τιμαῖς μυρί[α] | δῶρα τελεῖν.

A monument erected to Soteros, a rhetorician, at the cost of his pupils, who append their names, upon the occasion of his being honoured for the second time by a decree of the boulè. This must be the Soteros mentioned by Philostratos (Vit. Soph. ii, 23) as an Ephesian Sophist of little merit: ἄγει με ὁ λόγος ἐπ' ἄνδρα ἐλλογιμώτατον . . . τὸν ἐκ τῆς Ἐφίσου, ὅθεν ἐξρηθσθων Σώτηροί τε καὶ Σῶσοι . . . . . ἀθύρματα γὰρ τῶν Ἑλλήνων μᾶλλον οὗτοι προσρηθεῖεν ἂν ἢ σοφισταὶ λόγου ἄξιοι. The bombastic quatrain below is vaguely expressed : it seems to mean that Soteros enjoyed the distinction (πρῶτον) of having been twice summoned from Athens by the senate of the Ephesians (Ἀνδροκλίδαι) to come and teach at Ephesos. Probably the fragment in C. I. 2998 (= Waddington-Le Bas, No. 158) refers to the first occasion of his receiving public honours : it reads—Σώτηρο[ν] τὸν σοφισ[τὴν] . . . . . κατὰ ψήφισμα. Compare a similar dedication in honour of Φλ. Φιλόστρατον Ἀθηναῖων τὸν σοφιστὴν (Archäol. Zeit. 1878, p. 102) : this was the well-known author of the ' Lives of the Sophists ' quoted above.

The letters are manifestly of the time of the Antonines. The lapidary had made some blunder at the end of line 8, which he then erased : consequently the Ι in Κιλβιανός is inscribed upon the remains of an Ο. So Κ over Β in line 13.

DXLIX.

Fragment of white stele : height 5¼ inches by 10 in.; surmounted by moulded cornice, but broken on all other sides. Discovered by Mr. Wood ; unpublished.

```
ιϹΡΑΙΕΡΟΚΙΡΥΚΟϹ
ΕΩΣΤΗΣΑϹΙ
```

Τὴν δεῖνα τοῦ δεῖνος . . . θυγα]τέρα ἱεροκήρυκος
τῆς πρώτης καὶ μεγίστης μητροπόλ]εως τῆς Ἀσί[ας καὶ
[δὶς νεωκόρου τῶν Σεβαστῶν ἡ βουλὴ καὶ ὁ δῆμος ἐτείμησαν κ.τ.λ.]

Doubtless an honorary inscription; the woman may have been a priestess. Her father was a 'sacred herald' (*ἱεροκήρυξ*) of Artemis, see *ante* p. 87.

The letters belong to the time of the Antonines. Observe the dots in line 1, to indicate the aspirate; compare No. DXXX *ante*, and the references there given.

DL.

Fragment of white marble, entire at bottom and left; height 2 inches by 4. Discovered by Mr. Wood at the S.W. corner of the Temple-site. Unpublished.

| Ηвс | Ἡ βο[υλὴ . . . . . |

Either honorary (*τὸν δεῖνα . . . ἡ βουλὴ καὶ ὁ δῆμος*); or perhaps from the base of a dedication.

DLI.

Fragment of moulding from the top of a white marble stele; broken on all sides: height 4½ in. by 3½ in. Discovered by Mr. Wood; unpublished.

ιͻΛΕ

⌐ι

Τῆς πρώτης καὶ μεγίστης μητρο]πόλε[ως τῆς Ἀσίας
καὶ δὶς νεωκόρου τῶν Σ]ε[βαστῶν ἡ βουλὴ
[καὶ ὁ δῆμος ἐτείμησαν τὸν δεῖνα κ.τ.λ.]

Probably from the heading of an honorary monument like DXLI *ante*, and many others.

DLII.

Fragment of a white marble stele, broken on all sides except the right-hand edge. Height 8½ in.; width 3½ in. Discovered by Mr. Wood; unpublished.

	ΛΣΙΑΡΧΟΝ	. . . . Ἀσίαρχον,
	ΝΜΕΓΑΛΩΝ	ἀγωνοθέτην τῶ]ν μεγάλων
	'ΣΤΟΥ·Α	ἀγώνων τοῦ Σεθα]στοῦ, ἀ-
	ͻΥ·ΚΑΙ	. . . . ου, καὶ
5	.ΙΑΓΟΡΑ	5 . . . ., κα]ὶ ἀγορα-
	ΜΙΑΣ·ΜΕ	νομήσαντα μετὰ φιλοτι]μίας· με-
	ͻΝΟΥ	. . . . αιτου·
	ϚΠΑΣΑΣ	. . . λειτουργίας τὰ]ς πάσας.
	ΜΛ	. . . . μα-
		. . . .

Apparently in honour of an Ephesian citizen who had served various important municipal offices. The letters belong to the second century A.D. In line 1 we might also read *γυμν]ασίαρχον*. With lines 2, 3 compare C. I. 2961 *b* : *τοῦ ἀγωνοθέτου τῶν τοῦ Σεβαστοῦ ἀγώνων*, and *ante* p. 79 ; but my restoration is doubtful. On the *ἀγορανόμος* (line 5) see p. 81. For line 8 compare Nos. DLXIX, DLXXII, DLXXXIII *post.*

DLIII.

A square altar-like base of white marble; height 3 ft. 5 in.; width 1 ft. 9½ in.   Discovered by Mr. Wood, and published by him:
Inscriptions from the Site of the Temple, No. 2.

I L.	ἀρχ]ιέ[ρειαν
ΑΣΙΑΣΝΑΩΝΤΩΝ	'Ασίας ναῶν τῶν
ΕΝΕΦΕΣΩ	ἐν 'Εφέσῳ·
ΤΗΝΤΕΙΜΗΝ·Α	τὴν τειμὴν ἀ-
5 ΝΑΣΤΗΣΑΝΤΩΝ	5 ναστησάντων
ΟΥΕΤΟΥΛΗΝΙΟΥ	Οὐετουληνίου
ΣΑΒΕΙΝΙΑΝΟΥ	Σαβεινιανοῦ
ΑΠΟΧΕΙΛΙΑΡΧΙΑΣ	ἀπὸ χειλιαρχίας,
ΚΑΙΟΥΕΤΟΥΛΗΝΙΟΥ	καὶ Οὐετουληνίου
10 ΑΥΓΟΥΡΕΙΝΟΥ	10 Αὐγουρείνου
ΙΠΠΙΚΩΝ	ἱππικῶν,
ΥΩΝ ΑΥΤΗΣ	υἱῶν αὐτῆς
ΤΗΣΓΛΥΚΥΤΑΤΗΣ	τῆς γλυκυτάτης
ΜΗΤΡΟΣ	μητρός.

The remaining letters of line 1 are upon the moulding; but the moulding is broken and may have been originally inscribed with two lines e. g. 'Η βουλὴ τὴν δεῖνα | ἀρχιέρειαν | κ.τ.λ.   Or the base may have been surmounted by an ornament fixed on with a joint (like No. DLXXVIII), and containing part of the heading.   The lady here honoured was high-priestess of the temples at Ephesos belonging to the κοινὸν 'Ασίας.   We have already spoken of the κοινὸν 'Ασίας, and of the Asiarchs and ἀρχιερεῖς 'Ασίας, whose office extended over the whole province : the wives of the ἀρχιερεῖς were entitled ἀρχιέρειαι (No. CCCCXCVIII ante).   In addition to these provincial highpriests, each town which contained temples in connexion with the league (i. e. Σεβαστεῖα or temples to the Imperial family), had also its local ἀρχιερεύς, whose wife would be entitled ἀρχιέρεια, as here.   Her sons were both of them Roman equites (ἱππικοί, line 11); and one was tribunicius (ἀπὸ χειλιαρχίας, line 8) i. e. he had served as military tribune.   Compare also Nos. CCCCLXXXI, lines 155, 329, DLIV, DCIV, DCV, DCXI.

DLIV.

Two fragments of white marble, discovered by Mr. Wood; unpublished: a entire on the left only; height 5 in.; width 8 in.   b broken
on all sides; height 9½ in.; width 1 ft.

a.	b.	a.	b.
		. . . .	
ΝΑΤΟΝ		να τὸν [. . . . . ἀρ-	
ΧΙΕΡΕΙ	_Ν ΙΣ	χιερέα ['Ασίας να]ῶν [τ]ῶ[ν ἐν 'Εφέσῳ	
	ΛΚΤΩΕΚΤΩΝ	. . σίτῳ ? ἐπεισ]άκτῳ ἐκ τῶν [ἰδίων	
	ΣΑΝΤΑΠΑΣΑΝ	. . . . σαντα πᾶσαν	
5	ΛΟΔΟΞΙΩΝΚΙ	5 . . μετὰ φι]λοδοξιῶν κ[αὶ	
	ΨΥΧΟΝΚΑΙΛ	. . μεγαλό]ψυχον καὶ	

Apparently in honour of some one who had served as local ἀρχιερεύς (compare No. DLIII and reff.), and had in various other ways displayed his munificence.   With line 5 compare C. I. 2781 (from Aphrodisias): τὴν τῶν προγόνων διά τε φιλοδοξιῶν καὶ ἀναθημάτων πρὸς τὸν δῆμον εὔνοιαν.   The lettering appears to belong to the first century A. D.   The letters of a are slightly larger than those of b, and this lends probability to the manner in which I have conjecturally arranged them ; for their edges do not join.

DLV.

A fragment of white marble cornice, from an ornamental stelè. Height 8½ in.; width 10 in. Discovered by Mr. Wood: unpublished.

```
ΙΣΠΡΩΤΗ∠
ΣΤΗΣΜΗΤΡΟΓ
ΑΣΚΑΙΔΙΣ⋃⁻
ΒΑΣΤΩΝΕ⁺
ΒΟΥΛ⋃ᴷ
⁻ᴇ
```

T]ῆς πρώτης [καὶ
μεγί]στης μητροπ[όλεως τῆς
'Ασί]ας καὶ δὶς νε[ωκόρου τῶν
Σε]βαστῶν 'Εφ[εσίων πόλεως
ἡ] βουλὴ κ[αὶ ὁ δῆμος
ἐ]τε[ίμησαν τὸν δεῖνα κ.τ.λ.

Heading of an honorary inscription, of the age of the Antonines.

DLVI.

A fragment of white marble entire on right only ; height 9 in.; width 1 ft. 5 in. Discovered by Mr. Wood ; unpublished.

```
. . . . . . . . . . . . . . . . . . . .
ΝΤΑΤΗΣΑΡΤΕΜΙΔΟΣ
ΦΙΛΟΤΕΙΜΩΣΚΑΙΕΝΤΗ
⁻ΑΣΚΕΥΑΣΑΝΤΑΕΝΤΗ
⋃ΜΠΕΙΩΔΙΙΕΚΙΩΝ
     ⁻ΑΕΝΝΕΑ
     ⁻ΥΓΗ
```

. . . . λη. . . . .
ἱερατεύσα]ντα τῆς 'Αρτέμιδος
ἁγνῶς καὶ] φιλοτείμως καὶ ἐν τῇ
ἱερατείᾳ κα]τασκευάσαντα ἐν τῇ
ἀγορᾷ? τῷ 'Ολ]υμπείῳ Διὶ ἐκ τῶν
ἰδίων λίθινον ἀνδριάν]τα ? ἐννεά-
πηχυν ? . . . . στρατ ?]ηγή.
[σαντα ? . . .

In honour of some person who had been priest of Artemis and a public benefactor. We may conjecture that the statue to Zeus Olympios was erected in the reign of Hadrian, whom it was the fashion to style 'Olympios:' see on No. DI. The epithet ἐννεά[πηχυν, if correctly restored, would indicate a statue of twice the size of life.

DLVII.

Fragment of a stelè of white marble with surface broken all round, but with left edge of the stone entire as indicated. Height 8 in.; width 1 ft. 3 in. Discovered by Mr. Wood ; unpublished.

```
      ΛΗ
 Ι⋅ΛΑΒ⋅⋂ΜΟΙΝ
ΝΕΩΣ⋅ΚΑΙΓΡΑΜΜΑΤΕΣ
ΗΜΟΥ⋅ΚΑ 7⋆ΞΑΝΑΡΥ
ΑΝΤΟΣ⋅ΕΝ
⁺ΗΝΤΕΙ
```

. . . . λη. . . . .
. . . . Γ.? Λαβ. 'Αμοίν[ου πρυ-
τα]νέως καὶ γραμματέω[ς τοῦ
δ]ήμου κα[ὶ π]ᾶσαν ἀρχ[ὴν ἀρ-
ξ]αντος ἐν [τῇ πόλει . . . .
τ]ὴν τει[μὴν ἀναστησάντων? κ.τ.λ.

Apparently an honorary inscription to a relative of Lab. Amœnus ; perhaps his daughter had been a priestess. This Amœnus appears to be the same person who is named in No. ccccLxxxII ante b, line 5 a document probably of a. d. 160–1. His prænomen is either T(ίτος) or Γ(άïος).

DLVIII.

Plain stelè of white marble, broken on the left : height 1 ft. 1 in. ; width 9½ in. Discovered by Mr. Wood ; unpublished.

```
ⵁΤΟΙΑΗΦⵁ
ΕΡΟΝΤΕΙΑ
ⵁΤΟΡΙΓΟΣ
ΔΛΑΤΩΝ
ᴷΑΛΟΚΑ
ΣΕΙΣ
(vacant)
```

. . . . . . οποία Νήφο-
ντος? καὶ . . .]εροντείᾳ
. . . . 'Αδι]ατορίγος
τὸ κοινὸν τῶν Γ]αλατῶν
εὐνοίας καὶ] καλοκά-
γαθίας ἕνεκα τῆ]ς εἰς
αὐτό.]

It appears to be a dedication made at Ephesos by τὸ κοινὸν τῶν Γαλατῶν in honour of two Galatian ladies of high rank who had assisted the association by their bounty. The restorations are not very certain: the name endings in the first two lines are strange, but not more so than many Galatian names. Νήφων occurs in an Attic inscription, Part I, No. XLVII; it is derived from νήφω. The termination -ατοριξ, -οριξ is of frequent occurrence in Galatian names: e.g. Adiatorix, Gezatorix, Ateporix (see Bp. Lightfoot on Galatians, p. 236). The κοινὸν τῶν Γαλατῶν needs little explanation after what was said on No. CCCCXCVIII. Galatia was constituted a Roman province B.C. 25; but already in B.C. 29 Augustus had permitted a temple to be reared 'Romæ et Augusto' at Pergamon and at Nikomedia. From that time forward the worship of the Augusti was extended throughout the eastern provinces and cities of the empire (Marquardt, Röm. Alt. vi, p. 444 foll.). There was a Γαλατάρχης corresponding to the Asiarch, and a κοινόν or league of the Galatians like the κοινὸν Ἀσίας (compare C. I. 4016). Perhaps the best known of all the Augustea or Σεβαστεῖα is the temple at Ankyra erected in honour of Augustus during his lifetime. On the exterior surface of its cella walls is inscribed in Greek and in Latin the 'Index rerum a se gestarum' which Augustus composed and inscribed upon the Mausoleum at Rome. That original is lost, but the document survives in the famous ' Monumentum Ancyranum ' (Mommsen, Res gestæ divi Augusti). Probably the little stelè now before us was set up in the Augusteum near the Ephesian Artemision: the Augusteum would afford a link between Galatia and Ephesos. The style of the letters suggests a date towards the end of the first century A. D.

DLIX.

Two fragments of moulding in blue marble, evidently from the top of the same stelè : *a* entire at top and left; height 5¼ in.; width 4 in.; *b* entire only at top, height 3¼ in.; width 6 in. Discovered by Mr. Wood; unpublished.

a. *b.*

ΑΒΟΥ   ΙΟΔΗΜΕ

F   ΗΣΑΝ

Ἱ⌐

a. *b.*

'Η βου[λὴ κα]ὶ ὁ δῆμο[ς
ἐ[τείμ]ησαν
'Ἰο[ύλιον ? κ.τ.λ. . . . . .

The letters appear to belong to the first century A. D.

DLX.

Fragment of white marble, broken on all sides; height 8¼ in.; width 4¼ in. Discovered by Mr. Wood; unpublished.

Ν Α̅

ᴎΟΥΚ

ᖱΣΛΑ

ΠΟΣ

⌐Υ

5

να
. . δῆ]μον κ[αὶ . . . .
. . τ]ῆς λα[μπροτάτης ? . .
. . . . . Ποσ[ειδ . . . .
. . . . ου . . . .

5

Possibly honorary. The letters belong to the first century A. D. With λα[μπροτάτης in line 3 compare splendidissimæ, No. DXLIII ante. Λαμπροτάτη is very common in honorary inscriptions from Smyrna; e.g. C. I. 3202 etc.

DLXI.

Fragment of white marble, entire only on right. Height 5¼ in.; width 7¾ in. Discovered by Mr. Wood; unpublished.

ΕΤΝΟΙΑΙ

ΔΙΤΟΥΣ

(uninscribed)

ΓΚΛΑΤ

⌐Α

. . . . . .
. . . . . . ἐπὶ τῇ] εὐνοίᾳ
τῇ εἰς . . . . κ]αὶ τοὺς
. . . .
. . . . ο]υ Κλαυ-
[δίου] . . . . .

Part of an honorary inscription. The letters have more apices than are indicated in the uncial type, and seem to belong to the first century A. D. The last two lines contained the name of the person at whose expense the monument was erected.

DLXII.

A plain base of white marble, somewhat broken at the top : height 3 ft. 4½ in. ; width 1ft. 9 in. by 1 ft. 7⅜ in. 'From a pedestal found in excavation on the high ground nearly opposite the Odeum.' C. Curtius, Hermes iv, p. 193 foll. ; Wood, Inscriptions from the City and Suburbs, No. 5.

```
        ..ΝΙΑ..Σι
      ΥΓΑΤΕΡΑΤΙΒΚΛΕΡΜΕ
   ΤΟΥΛΑΜΠΡΟΤΑΤΟΥΥΠΑΤΙΚΟΥ
   ΚΑΙΑΙΛΙΑΣΠΕΙΘΙΑΔΟΣΤΗΣ
5     ΚΡΑΤΙΣΤΗΣΥΠΑΤΙΚΗΣ
     ΑΔΕΛΦΗΝΤΙΒΚΛΔΡΑΚΟΝΤΟΣ
     ΣΩΣΙΠΑΤΡΑΣΘΕΩΝΙΔΟΣ
        ΤΩΝΚΡΑΤΙΣΤΩΝ
     ΑΝΕΨΙΑΝΚΑΙΑΠΟΓΟΝΟΝ
10     ΠΟΛΛΩΝΥΠΑΤΙΚΩΝ
      ΦΛ·ΖΩΤΙΚΟΣΤΗΝΙΔΙΑΝ
        ΠΑΤΡΩΝΙΣΑΝ
```

$$[\,T\grave{\eta}\nu\ \delta\epsilon\tilde{\iota}\nu\alpha\,]$$

τ]οῦ κρατίσ[του
θ]υγατέρα Τιβ(ερίου) Κλ(αυδίου) 'Ερμε[ίου
τοῦ λαμπροτάτου ὑπατικοῦ
καὶ Αἰλίας Πειθιάδος τῆς
5 κρατίστης ὑπατικῆς,
ἀδελφὴν Τιβ(ερίου) Κλ(αυδίου) Δράκοντος,
Σωσιπάτρας, Θεωνίδος,
τῶν κρατίστων,
ἀνεψιὰν καὶ ἀπόγονον
10 πολλῶν ὑπατικῶν,
Φλ(άβιος) Ζωτικὸς τὴν ἰδίαν
πατρώνισαν.

Inscribed beneath a statue erected in honour of a lady by Fl. Zotikos, probably one of her freedmen. Her name is not given, and was perhaps engraved upon the plinth of the statue itself. The first line has been misread by the previous editors. Her father is entitled a consularis (line 3) and her mother is described (line 5) as ὑπατικῆς i. e. the wife of a consular. The word πατρώνισα (πατρώνισσα) for patrona occurs in a Galatian inscription C. I. 4106. The lettering seems to point to the times of the Antonines.

An inscription from a tomb at Teos (C. I. 3109) runs thus : Τιβέμι(ο)ν Κλαύδι(ο)ς 'Ερμείας Ζωτικῷ συντρόφῳ μνείας χάριν. [Ζ]ωτικὲ χαῖρε. This may be the Zotikos of our inscription : if so he was buried at Teos by his patron, whose daughter he had honoured by a monument at Ephesos.

DLXIII.

Two fragments of white marble, probably from the top of the same stele : a entire at top and left ; height 5 in. ; width 6 in. ; b broken all round, height 3¼ in. ; width 4 in. Discovered by Mr. Wood ; unpublished.

```
   a.          b.
 ┌─────
 │ ΤΗΣΙ
 │   "        ΄ΑΙΔΙΣ
                ΣΤ
```

a.   b.

Τῆς [πρώτης καὶ μεγίστης μητροπόλεως τ]ῆ[ς 'Ασίας κ]αὶ δὶς [νεω-
κόρου τῶν Σεβα]στ[ῶν, 'Εφεσίων
[πόλεως ἡ βουλὴ καὶ ὁ δῆμος]
[ἐτείμησαν τὸν δεῖνα κ.τ.λ.]

Probably honorary, and belonging to the end of the first century A. D.

SECTION VII.

DEDICATIONS AND EX VOTOS.

DLXIV.

A square altar of white marble; height 1 ft. 10 in.; height of the inscribed front 1 ft. 4 in.; width 1 ft. 3 in.; injured upon the right only. 'Found near the Magnesian Gate,' by Mr. Wood, and published by him, Inscriptions from the City and Suburbs, No. 17; C. I. L. iii, 6081.

```
        ᴄARINVS
      ʌVG·LIB·TABVLAI
      PROVINC· ASI·
          D · D ·
    5 KATEYXHN · EAPINᴄ
      ΣΕΒΑΣΤΟΥ · ΑΠΕΛΕΥᴄ
      ΡΟΣ · ΤΑΒΛΑΡΙΟΣ · ΕΠΑ·
      ΧΕΙΑΣ - ΑΣΙΑΣ ᴓ
        ᴓ ΑΝΕΘΗΚΕΝ ᴓ
```

Earinus
Aug. lib. tabular[ius
Provinc. Asia[e
d(edit) d(icavit).
5 Κατ' εὐχὴν Ἐαρινο[ς
Σεβαστοῦ ἀπελεύθ[ε-
ρος, ταβλάριος ἐπαρ-
χείας Ἀσίας,
ἀνέθηκεν.

The name Earinus was borne by a favourite of Domitian, (Dio Cass. lxvii, 2; Martial, ix, 11–13); but our inscription is of the age of the Antonines. In Asia, as in other provinces, the Emperor had his procurator (see No. ccccLXXXVII, line 15) to take charge of payments due to the imperial exchequer (fiscus). In an epitaph transcribed at Ephesos by Wood, and published by Mommsen (C. I. L. iii, 6082) a fine is specified as payable to the fiscus by any who shall injure the monument, and then follow the words: [et] sic ara defend[e]tur ab iis, qui sunt in tabularis Ephes[i]. Tabularium therefore was the office of the fiscus; Earinus is one of the tabularii, or secretaries. In C. I. L. iii, 6077 (Wood) mention is made of a 'Collegium Minervium tabulariorum' consisting of 'lib(ertorum) et servorum domini n(ostri) Aug(usti)';

and it is implied that members of the college were frequently engaged at Ephesos. C. I. L. iii, 6075 (found also by Wood at Ephesos) mentions a certain [Ly ?]cus, Augusto[rum ser(vus) a]djutor tabul(ario-rum) pr[ov(inciæ) Asiæ]. Similar examples occur in other provinces; thus, C. I. L. iii, 251: Zeno Augg. lib(ertus), tabularius (of Galatia); ibid. 348: ex tabular(iis), of Phrygia; ibid. 980: Aug(us)ti lib(ertus), tabularius provinc(iæ) [Da]ciæ; ibid. 1993: Diogenes Aug. lib(ertus), tabul(arius) prov(inciæ) Dalm(atiæ); ibid. 3964: Augustinus Augg. n(ostrorum) libertus, tabu(larius) prov(inciæ) i. e. of Pannonia superior; ibid. 4043: Eucarpus Aug(usti) lib(ertus), tab(ularius) p(rovinciæ) P(annoniæ) s(uperioris); compare ibid. 4066; C. I. L. v, 725: Aurelius Aphrodisius, Augg. lib(ertus), tabularius Alpium Cottiarum.

_____

DLXV.

Fragment of white marble; height 1 ft. 2 in.; width 10 in.; entire on left only, though the inscription is complete at the bottom. Discovered by Mr. Wood at Ephesos, but unpublished.

```
  ΚΑΙᴇ
  ΩΝ·Ιᴇ
  ΚΗΣΑΥ
  ΤΕΙΜΗΘ
5 ΣΕΒΕΣΤΑ
  ΑΝΕ
```

[Ὁ δεῖνα]
[γραμματεὺς τῶν . . . .]
καὶ Ἐ[φεσήων τῶν μεγάλ-
ων, ἱε[ρεὺς καὶ ἱερονεί-
κης αὐ[τῆς τῆς Ἀρτέμιδος,
τειμηθ[εὶς ὑπὸ τῆς εὐ-
5 σεβεστά[της βουλῆς (or γερουσίας)
ἀνέ[θηκεν.

The restorations are merely conjectural, and must not be too confidently accepted. The commencement appears to resemble No. DCIV: γραμματεὺς Ἀδριανείων. We have learned from the sixth document of No. CCCCLXXXI (line 307 foll.) that the ἱερεῖς καὶ ἱερονεῖκαι of Artemis formed a college or order by themselves, with the right of wearing gold. No. CCCCLXXXI belongs to the reign of Trajan, A.D. 104. The ἱερεῖς καὶ ἱερονεῖκαι τῆς Ἀρτέμιδος are similarly mentioned in a dedication to Hadrian, C.I. 2963 c. I have accordingly suggested ἱε[ρεὺς καὶ ἱερονεί]κης αὐ[τῆς τῆς θεοῦ or Ἀρτέμιδος] in lines 2-3. This dedication, like the two inscriptions just cited, belongs to the early part of the second century A.D.

DLXVI.

Fragment of moulding of white marble, entire only at top; height 4½ in.; width 6½ in. Discovered by Mr. Wood, but unpublished. Probably from the Augusteum.

ΟΠΟΙΗΣ	Οἱ νε]οποιήσ[αντες ἐπὶ τοῦ δεῖνος
ΑΤΕΥΟΝΤΟ	γραμμ]ατεύοντο[ς τοῦ δήμου κ.τ.λ.

Apparently from a dedication. Concerning the νεοποιοί (or, as they were originally called, νεωποῖαι) see Prolegomena, p. 80. From the frequency with which they appear as making dedications, we might almost conclude that some such act of thanksgiving was expected of them upon laying down their office.

Similarly at Samos the νεωποῖαι of Hera appear to have made a practice, in Roman times, of inscribing their names year by year upon a certain building within the temenos (E. Fabricius, Mittheilungen d. archäol. Inst. in Athen, ix, p. 259).

DLXVII.

Fragment of white marble, entire on right only where the stone is bordered with a slight sinking of 1 inch wide. Height 8 in.; width 6 in. Discovered by Mr. Wood: unpublished.

ΟΥΚΙΟΣ	. . . . . Λ]ούκιος
ΩΝ	. . . . . ων
ΟΙΗ	. . . . νεο]ποιή-
ΙΣΙ	σας . . . . . .]ει

Part of a dedication by a temple-warden. Compare No. DLXVI.

DLXVIII.

Fragment of white marble moulding, entire only at bottom; height 4½ in.; width 5 in. Discovered by Mr. Wood: unpublished.

ΣΟΠΟΙΟΙ	. . . . οἱ ν]εοποιοί . . .

Probably a dedication: see No. DLXVI.

DLXIX.

A fragment of architectural moulding, perhaps the cornice of a wall; greyish marble; height 9 in.; length 1 ft. 10 in. Joint entire at top, bottom, and right; broken on left. Discovered by Mr. Wood; unpublished.

ΣΟΥ · ΝΕΟΠΟΙΟΣ · ΠΑΊ	Ὁ δεῖνα . . .]ου νεοποιός, πατ[ὴρ
ΡΓΩΝ ΝΕΟΠΟΙΩΝ ◄ vacant	πολλῶν λειτου]ργῶν [καὶ] νεοποιῶν.

A dedication by a temple-warden, the father of several sons (πολλῶν or τριῶν or the like, line 2), who held the same office. For λειτουργός compare Nos. DLXXV, DLXXXIII.

DLXX.

Broken stelè of white marble, inscribed on the front *a*, and on the left return face *b*. The right return face is broken off; the back of the stelè is uninscribed: the upper portion and the bottom are broken. Height of *a* 9½ in.; width 1 ft. ⅜ in.; height of *b* 1 ft. 1 in.; width 10½ in. Discovered by Mr. Wood (probably in the Augusteum), but unpublished.

b.   *a.*

```
          AI
         OY·Λ
         ϽΛ·ΜΕ
         ϹΙΜΟ ΕϽΚΙ
    5    ΕΙϹϽΝ ΤΟΙ        ΜϽΝ
         ΚΓϽΝ ϹΙϽ         ϽϹ·ΝΕΟΠ
         ΛΕΤΕΧΟΥϹΙΛ        ΡΑΕΚΛΗϹΙΑ·
         ΛΙΤΟΥ·ΙΕΡϽΤ      ΝΤϽΕΠΙΠΡΥΤΑΝΕ
         ϹΥΝΕΛΡ           ΟΥ·ΕΥΤΥΧΙϽΝΟϹ·ΦΑΥϹΤ      5
                          ϹΥΝΚΑΙΤΗϽΥΓΑΤΡ
                          ϽϽΗ·ΜΑΡΚΕΛΛΗϹ
```

b.   *a.*

. αι
μ]ον, κ[αὶ . . .
ολ. Με . . . . .
Τ]ειμο[θ]έῳ κ[αὶ   . . . . ος νεοπ[οιὸς ἐν τ-
5 Π]είσων[ι] τοῖ[ς   ῇ ἱε]ρᾷ ἐκλησία [αἱρεθεὶς ?
ἐ]κγόν[οι]ς μ[ού·   ἐν τῷ ἐπὶ πρυτάνε[ως . . .
μετέχουσιν   5 ου Εὐτυχιῶνος Φαύστ[ου,
κ]αὶ τοῦ ἱερωτ-   σὺν καὶ τῇ θυγατρ[ί μου Τρυ-
άτου] συνεδρ[ίου.   φ]ῶσῃ Μαρκέλλης, ...

The inscription, which appears to belong to the second century A. D., began on *a* and was continued upon *b*. It is a dedication by a temple-warden, who had held office in the year of the eponymous prytanis (see p. 85) Eutychion Faustus: compare No. DLXVI. The phrase ἐν τῷ ἐπὶ τοῦ δεῖνος (ἐνιαυτῷ *a*, line 4) has been noticed in No. CCCCLXXVII, lines 93, 76, 79. The form ἐκλησία (*a*, line 3) is a barbarism not uncommon in Galatian inscriptions: e. g. C. I. 4028, 4032, and occasionally found elsewhere; as here, and at Mylasa, *Μουσεῖον τῆς Εὐαγγελικῆς Σχολῆς, Περ.* 2, i, p. 51. There is little doubt about αἱρεθεὶς which I

have supplied in *a*, line 3. The word αὐθαίρετοι in No. DLXXIX *b* implies that the temple-wardens were usually elected in one of the assemblies of the state; we here learn that this assembly was the ekklesia. In making the dedication the giver, as was often done, associates with himself various members of his family; they had probably shared the expense of the monument, and claim with him the favour of the goddess. The wife Marcella (*a*, line 7) appears to be dead; and the men named in *b* seem to be the daughter's sons. They are members of the συνέδριον, i. e. of the γερουσία (see p. 77 *ante*, and No. DLXXVII).

DLXXI.

Fragment of white marble stelè; height 1 ft. 8½ in.; width 1 ft. The inscription is entire at the bottom, but the marble is broken on all sides. Discovered by Mr. Wood; unpublished.

```
         ΡΟΥ·                  . . . ρου·
         ΥΛΟϹΙΕΡΟΙ             . . . υλος ιερο . . .
         ϹΝΕΟΙ                 . . . . . . . . ς νεα[ποιὸς, ?
         ΟΦΟΡ                  . . . . χρυσ]οφόρ[ος,
    5    Ͻ⊿ ΕΡΕΥϹ          5   . . . . ος [ἱ]ερεὺς,
         Ξ·ΙΕΡΕ·              . . . . . ς ἱερεύ[ς.
```

A list of priests and sacred officials, probably from a dedication; compare C.I. 2983, cited *ante*, p. 86. For the titles see Prolegomena, pp. 85, 86 *ante*.

DLXXII.

Fragment of white marble stele, broken on all edges, inscribed on both sides *a*, *c*; height 9 in.; width 10 in.; thickness 5 in. Discovered by Mr. Wood; unpublished. *b*, also unpublished, is a similar fragment, of the same thickness; height 4 in.; width 2½ in.

a.	*b.*	*c.*
ΛΕΙΤΟΥΙ		vacant.
ΔΟΥΣ vacant.	' '	ΕΥΤΥΧ!̣Σ
ΑΡ̣ΙΣ vacant.	)ΣΦΙ	vacant.
ΡΑΝΟΜΗ	ΙΣΗ	
vacant.		

a.	*b.*	*c.*
(face.)	(Perhaps part of *a*, but inscribed only on one side.)	(Reverse of *a*.)
λειτουρ-		
γήσας? . . . . . .]δοὺς	. . ος Φι . . .	Εὐτυχῶς.
. . . . τετρ]ακισ-	. . ως μ . . .	
χιλ? . . . . . . ἀγο]ρανομή-		
5 σας . . . .].		

Εὐτυχῶς, perhaps from the close of a dedication like No. DLXXXVII *b*.

DLXXIII.

A large stele of white marble: height 2 ft. 9 in.; width 2 ft. Entire on all sides, but the left. Discovered by Mr. Wood. C. Curtius Hermes iv, p. 205 foll.

a.

ΛΑΥΔΙΟΣΘΕΟΦΙΛΟΣ — . Κ]λαύδιος Θεόφιλος,
ΛΑΥΔΙΟΣΡΟΥΦΟΣ — . Κ]λαύδιος Ῥοῦφος.

Space of 2½ in. vacant.

b.

Μ · ΑΥΡ · ΚΑΛΛΙΣΤΟΣ   Μ. Αὑρ. Κάλλιστος.

Space of 10½ in. vacant.

c.

ΟΥΜΕΡΙΟΣΓΕΡΕΛΛΑΝΟΣ — . Ν]ουμέριος Γερελλανός,
ΥΦΕΙΝΟΣ · ΚΑΙΙΕΡΕΥΣ — . Ῥο]υφεῖνος καὶ ἱερεύς,
ΠΑΤΡΟΓΕΡΩΝ   πατρογέρων.

Space of 3½ in. vacant.

d.

ΓΤΟΥΚΚΙΟCΑΛΕΞΑΝΔΡΟC Γ. Τούκκιος Ἀλέξανδρος
ΚΑΙ ΙΕΡΕΥC   καὶ ἱερεύς,
ΚΑΙ ΙΕΡΕΥ̣C   καὶ ἱερεύς.

Space of 1½ in. vacant.

e.

ΟΣ
Σ · ΚΥΡΕΙΝΑ · ΣΑΤΟΡΝΕΙΝΟΣΦΙΛΟΡΩΜΑΙ   - . . . . ς, Κυρείνα Σατορνεῖνος φιλορώμαιος.

The stele appears to have been originally inscribed only with *a*, *c*, and *e*, probably in the second century A.D. The lettering of *b* seems to be somewhat later; that of *d* appears later and coarser still. The dedicators, Theophilos, Rufus, Gerellanus, and Rufinus, were perhaps νεοποιοί, and this title (or some other) may have been inscribed upon an ornamental cornice surmounting the stele, but now lost (compare No. DLXXVIII): this would account for the καὶ before ἱερεύς in *c*. Later on, Kallistos and, finally, Alexandros (*b*, *d*) added their names to the list. The repeated καὶ ἱερεύς in *d* seems to refer to Kallistos and to Alexandros, in imitation of the phrase in *c*. The title πατρογέρων in *c*, occurs also in No. DLXXV.

The nearest word like it is πατρομύστης, found in two late inscriptions from Smyrna (C. I. 3173, 3195), which Böckh interprets *mystae principes*, or senior members of the society that celebrated the mysteries of Dionysos Breiseus. Similarly πατρογέρων might be senior member of the γερουσία (see p. 76). If however my restorations are right in No. DLXXV, πατρογέρων must rather mean πατρόθεν γέρων, himself a γέρων and his father before him; and to this explanation I incline. Κυρείνα in *e* is the Latin Quirina (sc. tribu); compare e.g. No. CCCCLXXXI, lines 305 etc. The name of Numerius Gerellanus reminds us of No. DXLVI, and DXXXIII.

DLXXIV.

A square block of white marble, probably the base of a statue; height 10 in.; width of inscribed face 1 ft. 6½ in.   Wood, Inscriptions from the Augusteum, No. 13.

```
  ΄ΤΑΝΙΣΠΡΩΤΟΓΕΝΟΥΤΟΥ
   ΙΜΩΝΙΔΟΥΣΙΜΩΝΗΟΣ
   ΄ΣΣΚΛΗΠΙΑΔΗΣΜΕΜΝΟΝΟΣ
   ΄ΡΥΦΩΝΣΤΡΑΒΕΛΑΦΟΣ
5     ΠΕΛΑΣΓΗΟΣ
```

Πρ]ύτανις Πρωτογίνου τοῦ
Σ]ιμωνίδου, Σιμώνηος·
Ἀσσκληπιάδης Μέμνονος
Τρύφων Στραβίλαφος,
5   Πελάσγηος.

The names of two men who dedicated the statue originally placed upon this base; the name of the person so honoured may have been engraved on the plinth of the statue itself. The letters are firm and good, and point to the earlier half of the first century A. D. On the chiliastyes Σιμώνηος and Πελάσγηος see Prolegomena, p. 70 ante. Τρύφων and Στραβίλαφος are merely additional names of As(s)kle-

piades (κατ᾽ ἐπίκλησιν); compare No. DCIX : ὁ ἐπικληθεὶς Γραῦς. The name Στραβίλαφος is new, but an Ἔλαφος of Kos is mentioned by Suidas s. v. Ἱπποκράτης. If Ἔλαφος, like Δόρκας, was supposed to indicate beauty of the eyes, then the earlier part of Στραβίλαφος may be from στραβός, στραβόν, στράβηλος. Hesychios, however, has the following gloss s. v. Στραβαλός· ὁ στρογγυλίας καὶ τετράγωνος ἄνθρωπος. Ἀχαιοί.

DLXXV.

A stelè of white marble; broken at the bottom and on the right. Height 2 ft. 1 in.; width 1 ft. 9 in. Discovered by Mr. Wood; unpublished.

```
     ΑΓΑΘΗΙ · ΤΥΧΗΙ                        Ἀγαθῇ τύχῃ·
     Μ · ΑΥΡ · ΑΡΤΕΜΙΔΣ                   Μ. Αὐρ. Ἀρτεμίδω[ρος
     ΑΤΤΑΛΟΥ · ΦΙΛΟ                       Ἀττάλου, φιλο[σέβαστος,
     ΓΕΡΟΥΣΙΑΣΤΗ⊿                         γερουσιαστής, [νεο-
5    ΠΟΙΟΣΑΓΟΡΑΝΟΙ              5          ποιὸς, ἀγορανόμ[ος
     ΑΓΝΟΣΛΙΤΟΥΡΓΟ                        ἁγνὸς, λιτουργὸ[ς
        ΕΝΔΟΞ                               ἐνδοξ[ος·
     ΚΑΙ · Μ · ΑΥ                         καὶ Μ. Αὐ[ρ . . . . . .
        ΑΡΤΕΜ                             Ἀρτεμ[ιδώρου υἱὸς(?),
10   ΠΑΤΡΟ                     10         πατρο[γέρων(?) γερου-
     ΣΙΑΣΤ                                σιαστ[ής, νεο-
     ΠΟΙΟ                                 ποιὸ[ς . . . . . .
      ΟΛΥ                                 Ὀλυ[μπιονείκης
                                          . . . . . . . . . . . . .
```

A dedication made by M. Aur. Artemidoros and his son (?). Their offices are rehearsed in full. Compare No. DLXXXIII, which suggests φιλο[σέβαστος] in line 3. Line 10 πατρο[γέρων] is from No. DLXXIII,

where see the note; it is here a kind of epithet of γερουσιαστής. The inscription belongs to the second century A. D., although the iota adscriptum is twice given in line 1.

DLXXVI.

Fragment of marble relief, with Rhea standing in centre, and male figure and seated lion to right; on the left was another figure and another seated lion now broken away : beneath, one line of inscription. Compare A. Conze, Arch. Zeitung, 1880, esp. Tafel iii, Nos. 1 and 3; No. 1 is probably from Ephesos or its neighbourhood. Height 9 in.; width 1 ft. 1 in. Discovered by Mr. Wood; unpublished.

ᵇΟΤΙΛΛΑΜΗΤΡΙΦΡΥΓΙΗ

. . . βότιλλα μητρὶ Φρυγίη.

A dedication to the goddess Rhea, or the Phrygian Mother: compare C. I. Addenda 2107 *b* (from Pantikapaeon): *Βασιλεύοντος Παιρισάδου τοῦ Σπαρτόκου* (third century B.C.) *Ἑστιαία ¦ Μηνοδώρου θυγάτηρ ἱερωμένη ἀνέθηκεν μητρὶ Φρυγίᾳ*. Our inscription is of the Macedonian time, as the Ionicism *Φρυγίῃ* indicates. The first letter is somewhat doubtful, and it cannot be ascertained whether the iota adscriptum was inserted at the end of the line. The name . . . *βότιλλα* is pure Greek; compare *Ἀνάξιλλα, Λύσιλλα, Πράξιλλα, Τελέσιλλα κ. τ. λ.*

DLXXVII.

A stele of white marble, inscribed on front *a*, and on the right return *b*. The left, top and perhaps the bottom of *b* are entire: the edges of *a* are entire, except the bottom and parts of the left side which are broken off. Height of *a* 2 ft. 3 in.; width 1 ft. 10 in.; height of *b* 1 ft. 7 in.; width 5 in. *a* edited by C. Curtius, Hermes iv, p. 203; Wood, Inscriptions from the Theatre, No. 19: *b* is unpublished.

a.

ΙΜΑΤΕΥΟΝΤΩΝ	*Γρα]μματευόντων*
ΙΕΡΩΤΑΤΟΥΣΥΝ	*το]ῦ ἱερωτάτου συν-*
ΡΙΟΥΤΟΥΜΙΣΘΩ	*εδ]ρίου τοῦ μισθω-*
Η ΡΙΟΥ·Μ·ΑΥΡ·ΔΙΟ	*τ]ηρίου Μ. Αὐρ. Διο-*
ΥΣΙΚΛΕΟΥΣΚΟΡΒΟΥ	*ν]υσικλέους Κορβού-*
ΩΝΟΣΚΑΙΑΥΡ·ΔΙΟΝΥ	*λ]ωνος καὶ Αὐρ. Διονυ-*
ΣΙΟΥΔΙΣΤΟΥΘΕΩΝΟΣ	*σίου δὶς τοῦ Θέωνος·*
ΣΥΝΕΠΙΜΕΛΗΣΑΜΕΝΩΝ	*συνεπιμελησαμένων*
ΤΗΣΔΕΙΠΝΟΦΟΡΙΑΚΗΣ	*τῆς δειπνοφοριακῆς*
Φ ΠΟΜΠΗΣ ·	*πομπῆς*
Γ·ΙΟΥΛΙΟΥ·ΙΠΠΕΑΧΡΥ	*Γ. Ἰουλίου Ἱππ(άρχο)υ*
ΑΙ·ΑΥΡ·ΑΛΚΙΝΟΟΥ·	*κ]αὶ Αὐρ. Ἀλκινόου*
ΑΙ·Λ·ΣΤΑΤΙΟΥΕΥ	*καὶ Λ. Στατίου Εὐτ[ύχου*
ΝΟΥΝΕ	*Νουνε[χίου*
ΑΙ·ΤΙΒ·ΚΛ	*καὶ Τιβ Κλ. . . . . . .*
· \	*. . . . .*

b.

ΔЄΙΠΝ	*Δειπν[οφόρος*
CΥΝΚΑ	*σὺν κα[ὶ Λ. Στ.*
ЄΥΤΥΧ	*Εὐτύχ[ῳ*
ΥΠΑΙΡЄ	*ὑπ' αἱρέ[σεως*
CΥΝЄΔΡΙ	*συνεδρί[ου*
ΚΥΚΝC	*Κύκνο[ς*
CЄΛΒЄΙΛΙ	*Σελβείλι[ος*
Є\	*Εὔ[τυχος* (or *εὐτυχῶς* ?).

In *a*, line 4, an ι has been erased between Η Ρ: and in line 11 the lapidary has written ΙΠΠΕΑΧΡΥ by a strange mistake. All the letters are perfectly clear.

A dedication (?) dated by naming certain officers of the gerousia, here (as often) styled *τὸ συνέδριον*: a word or two may have been inscribed upon an ornamental cornice, now lost (compare No. DLXXVIII). The officers named are (1) the secretaries of the rent-office of the gerousia (*μισθωτήριον*); (2) the superintendents of the lectisternial procession (*δειπνοφόροι*). The former, as I have shown on p. 77 of the Prolegomena, received the rents payable to Artemis from temple-lands (compare the rentals of the Attic *τεμένη*, Part I, No. XIII). The procession referred to in *a*, lines 9–10, and in *b*, line 1, may be at once identified with the lectisternia specified in the decree of the reign of Commodus, No. CCCCLXXXIII, which were defrayed out of funds administered by the gerousia.

The writing of *a* is coarsely executed, but in large letters of stately form; *b*, evidently of the same date, exhibits the circular Є and C, but it is beautifully inscribed. Cycnus Selvilius had served as a colleague of L. Statius Eutychos Nounechios of *a*, lines 13–14. His name had been accidentally omitted from *a*; he therefore has it afterwards inserted on the return face of the monument, *b*. It is expressly stated here that the *δειπνοφόροι* were chosen (*ὑπ' αἱρέσεως*) by the gerousia. The name *Σελβείλιος* for Servilius is an example of the same *τραυλισμός* (Aristoph. Wasps, 44), which we shall meet with again in *Βάλβιλλος* for *Βάρβιλλος* (No. DCXV), and *Σατορνεῖλος* for *Σατορνῖνος* (No. DXCV).

DLXXVIII.

An altar-like stelè of white marble, surmounted originally by a very ornamental cornice of which only a fragment remains (*a*). This cornice was in a separate piece and joined on to the stelè just above the fourth line of the inscription on the face *a–b*. The right return face is also inscribed (*c*). The stelè and the moulded cornice were found separately by Mr. Wood in the ruins of the Augusteum, and I have recombined them: *a*, Wood, Inscriptions from the Augusteum No. 5; *b*, *ibid.* No. 1; *c*, *ibid.* No. 2. Height of the monument including the cornice, 3 ft.; width of inscribed surface *b* 1 ft. 2½ in.; width of *c* 1 ft. 5½ in. The stelè is slightly injured at the bottom; perhaps it stood originally upon a plinth, now lost.

a.

ΗΒΟΥΛΗ	Ἡ βουλὴ [καὶ ὁ δῆμος ἐτείμη-
ΛΝΤΟΥΣΝ	σ]αν τοὺς ν[εωποιήσαντας
ΤΙΠΠΡΥΤ	ἐ]πὶ πρυτ[άνεως . . . . . .

b.

	ΔΗΜΗΤΡΙΟΥΕΝΙΑΥιιι		Δημητρίου ἐνιαυτῷ·
5	ΦΥΛΗΣΕΦΕΣΕΩΝ	5	Φυλῆς Ἐφεσίων·
	ΔΗΜΗΤΡΙΟΣΜΗΝΟΦΙΛΟΥΤΡΥ		Δημήτριος Μηνοφίλου (τοῦ) Τρύ-
	ΦΩΝΑΣΒΟΡΕΥΣΘΟΑΣΔΡΑ		φων(ο)ς, Βορεύς· Θόας Δρα-
	ΚΟΝΤΟΜΕΝΟΥΣΟΙΝΩΨ		κοντομένους, Οἴνωψ.—
	ΤΒΑΣΤΗΣ ΑΛΕΞΑΝΔΡΟΣ		Σ[εβαστῆς· Ἀλέξανδρος
10	ΙΚΛΗΟΥΣΤΟΥΑΛΕΞΑΝ	10	Σ]οκλῆους τοῦ Ἀλεξάν-
	ΔΡΟΥΛΛΒΛΝΛΗΟΣ ΠΥΘΙ		δρου, Λαβάνδιος· Πυθί-
	ΩΝΠΕΡΙΓΕ ΟΥΓΧ		ων Περιγέ[νους τ]οῦ Ἐχ[άν-
	ΔΡΟΥΣΙΕΥι ΤΗΙΣ		δρου, Σιεύς.—Τήῖο[ς . . . .
	ΑΣΕΡΜΟΛΑΟΥΕΧΕΠΤΟΛΕι		ας Ἑρμολάου, Ἐχεπτολε[μεύς·
15	ΠΧΘΟΔΩΡΟΣΑΠΟΛΛΩΝΙΟΥ	15	Π(υ)θόδωρος Ἀπολλωνίου
	ΤΟΥΑΠΟΛΛΩΝΙΟΥΕΧΕΠΤΟΛΕΜΕΥ		τοῦ Ἀπολλωνίου, Ἐχεπτολεμεύ[ς.—
	ΚΑΡΗΝΑΙΟΙ ΕΥΣΕΒΗΣΔΕΙ		Καρηναῖοι· Εὐσίβης Δει-
	ΚΑΙΟΥΠΕΙΟΣ ΤΡΥΦΩΝΤΓ		καίου, Πεῖος· Τρύφων Τρύ-
	ΦΩΝΟΣΤΟΥΝΕΙΚΑΓΟΡΟΥ		φωνος τοῦ Νεικαγόρου,
20	ΧΗΛΩΝΗΟΣ ΕΥΩΝΥΜΟΙ	20	Χηλώνηος.—Εὐώνυμοι·
	ΨΡΑΚΛΙΤΟΣΗΡΙ ΛΞΙΤΟΥΤΟΥ		Ἡράκλειτος Ἡρα[κ]λείτου τοῦ
	ΑΠΟΛΛΩΝΙΟΥΓΛΑΥΚΗΟΣ		Ἀπολλωνίου, Γλαύκηος·
	ΛΠΕΛΛΑΣΜΗΝΟΔΟΤΟΥΠΟΛΥ		Ἀπελλᾶς Μηνοδότου, Πολύ-
	ιΟΣ ΒΕΜΒΕΙΝΑΙΟΙ		κλη]ος.—Βεμβειναῖοι·
25	ΕΣΒΩΝΤΕΙΜΟΘΕΟΥΤΟΥ	25	Πρ]ίσβων Τειμοθέου τοῦ
	ΜΟΘΕΟΥΑΙΓΩΤΓ		Τει]μοθέου, Αἰγώτε[ος·
			(one more name wanting.)

c.

Inscribed on the right return face.

	ΑΓΑΘΗ · ΤΥΧΗ ·		Ἀγαθῇ τύχῃ·
	ΕΥΧΑΡΙΣΤΩΣΟΙΚΥΡΙΑ		Εὐχαριστῶ σοι κυρία
	ΑΡΤΕΜΙ · Γ · ΣΚΑΠΤΙΟΣ ·		Ἀρτεμι Γ. Σκάπτιος
	ΦΡΟΝΤΕΙΝΟΣ · ΝΕΟΠΟΙΟΣ		Φροντεῖνος, νεοποιός.
	ΙΥΛΕΥΤΗΣ · ΣΥΝΚΑΙΤΗ		β]ουλευτής, σὺν καὶ τῇ
	ΓΥΝΑΙΚΙΜΟΥ · ΕΡΕΝΝΙΑ · ΑΥ		γυναικί μου Ἐριννίᾳ Αὐ-
	ΤΡΩΝΙΑ · ΕΣΣΗΝΕΥΣΑΣ · ΑΓΝΩΣ		τρωνίᾳ, ἐσσηνεύσας ἁγνῶς
	· ΚΑΙΕΥΣΕΒΩΣ ·		καὶ εὐσεβῶς·
	ΠΟΝΔΟΠΟΙΟΥΝΤΟΣ · ΘΕΟ		σ]πονδοποιοῦντος Θεο-
10	ΠΟΜΠΟΥ · Γ · ΤΟΥΜΕΝΕΚΡΑΤΟΥΣ	10	πόμπου ῦ τοῦ Μενεκράτους
	ΙΕΡΟΥ		ἱεροῦ.

The two inscriptions, although engraved on the same marble, have no connexion with each other, and differ considerably in date. It is clear that *a, b* originally stood alone; afterwards, not earlier than the second century A. D. G. Scaptius Frontinus (*c*, lines 3–4) was permitted by his brother neopoioi to inscribe c upon a vacant side of the marble. An exactly similar instance will be found in No. DXC. It will be convenient to deal first with c, and then to examine the original inscription a-b.

c.

c is a thank-offering to Artemis by Frontinus upon having served as neopoios, and in other offices. On the boulé (line 5) see p. 71 foll. ; and on the Essenes, see p. 85. The use of the aorist ἱσσηνεύσας proves that the office was not permanent (p. 85 *aute*). The introductory formula, εὐχαριστῶ σοι κυρία Ἀρτεμι, recurs in a number of these dedications of neopoioi from the Augusteum, Nos. DLXXIX foll. The date is given by naming the σπονδοποιός, who must be the temple minister who assisted Frontinus in offering his libation and gift to the goddess; see Prolegomena, p. 86; and compare Nos. DLXXIX *b*, DLXXXIX *b*. In the latter document the same Theopompos is named as spondopoios ; we may infer that his office was an annual one, and that the two dedications belong to the same year. Theopompos is termed ἱερός, i. e. a temple-freedman. The exact status of the Ephesian ἱεροί has been discussed on p. 85 foll. The term does not imply slavery, for Theopompos is described as ὁ τοῦ Μενεκράτους, i.e. son of Menekrates, son of Menekrates, son of Menekrates. The date of c is probably late in the second century A. D.

a, b.

a, b is an honorary inscription to the neopoioi of a certain year, granted by the boulé and demos. Strictly speaking it should be placed in Section VI (Nos. DXLVI-DLXIII) ; but it is sufficiently like a dedication to accompany the dedication c, which finds here its proper place. The recovery of the heading (lines 1-3) proves this list to contain the names of the neopoioi of the year, τοὺς ν[εοποιήσαντας] line 2 : Menadier, p. 26, had conjectured it to be a list of prytanes. Two neopoioi were appointed from each of the six tribes (see pp. 80 fol.), by open election in the ekklesia (No. DLXX). The board was thus a thoroughly representative one, enabling every portion of the body politic of Ephesos to take part in the custody of the Artemision. A fragment of a list drawn up exactly like the present one will be found in No. DXC. *a*. And these two lists at once explain the fragment C. I. 2956, which speaks of the munificence of a certain Ephesian of the Bembinean tribe : Β]εμβειναίων φυ(λῆς)· ἐν ταύτῃ ἐνεοποίησεν . . . χι(λιαστὸν) Πελάσγιος. Evidently each neopoios was distinctly regarded as the representative of his tribe : compare also No. DLXXIX *b*.

The year is indicated by the eponymous prytanis, line 3, whose name is lost ; appended is the name of the first neopoios in the yearly board, Δημητρίου ἐνιαυτῷ (line 4). This should be compared with Πασσαλάτου ἐνιαυτῷ in No. DXXVIII, see note *ad loc.*

The document is further interesting as giving a complete list of the Ephesian tribes, concerning which see Prolegomena, p. 69.

What is the date of this list (a, b) ? Obviously later than Augustus, after whom the second tribe receives its name, Σεβαστή (line 9). But how much later ? I should decide without hesitation for the first century A. D., if it were not for the name of the chiliastys of the Karenean tribe in line 18, Πεῖος. One might hastily infer that this division of the Ephesian people derived its name from Antoninus Pius, and therefore that the inscription must be as late as the middle of the second century A. D. Several facts, however, point decisively to an earlier date. The writing is highly florid, with apices, and though wanting in the firmness of the Augustan age (see Waddington, Fastes, p. 85), is yet very different from the plain characters of the second and third centuries. It would be equally strange to date the writing of this inscription later than the Salutaris documents of A. D. 104 (No. CCCCLXXXI). Equally strong is the evidence of the names which compose the list. No Roman name appears in it, except Σεβαστή, already explained, and Πεῖος (if it be Roman) now under dispute. The dedications of neopoioi and other officers are numerous enough in the preceding and following documents, most of them obviously of the Antonine period or later ; and a glance shows how hopelessly Greek and Roman names were fused together[1]. Judging from the other inscriptions, it is scarcely conceivable that a list of nearly thirty Ephesian citizens could be drawn up in the third or even the second century without including a single Roman name. Some other facts of less moment point likewise to an earlier date. The phrase which gives the date by naming the prytanis and the first neopoios (lines 3-4), ἐπὶ πρυτάνεως τοῦ δεῖνος, τοῦ δεῖνος ἐνιαυτῷ, occurs only twice elsewhere, in No. DXXVIII and the fragment from Wood there cited (Wood, Inscriptions from the Augusteum, No. 11), and we saw reason to assign both those documents to the first century A. D. In the orthography of our inscription there is nothing which precludes a date about the middle of the first century A. D. The iota adscriptum is omitted in ΕΝΙΑΥΤΩ, line 4 ; *ει* is used consistently for *i* ; and for *i* in Δείκαιος, line 17 : [Σ]ωκλήουϲ for [Σ]ωκλείουϲ (= Σωκλεοῦϲ) line 10. But *ει* for *i* became common in the first century B. C. ; witness πολείται, ἐπίτειμα in lines 21, 33 of the Ephesian decree about Mithradates (Waddington-Le Bas, No. 136 *a*) ; γειν[ο]μένας in line 31 of the Tenos decree, C. I. 2335 ; ὑμεῖν, πολείτης, τειμή, *passim* in C. I. 2737, immediately after Cæsar's murder. Certainly *ει* for *i* (as in Ἀρτεμείσια No. DCV, line 11) is a later usage : but it may well have occurred as early as 50-60 A. D., especially in a proper name. The use of *η* for *ει*, as in [Σ]ωκλήουϲ was a mark of the Augustan time, and

---

[1] Already in the first century Apollonios of Tyana is represented as having taken bitter notice of this confusion in his 71st letter (Hercher, Epistolog. Graeci. Didot), 'To the Ionians' ('Ἴωσιν): Ἕλληνεϲ οἴεσθε δεῖν ὀνομάζεσθαι διὰ τὰ γένη καὶ τὴν ἔμπροσθεν ἀπουσίαν . . . ἀλλ' ὑμῶν γε οὐδὲ τὰ ὀνόματα μένει ταῖς εὐκλείαϲ, ἀλλ' ὑπὸ τῆς νῦν ταύτηϲ εὐδαιμονίαϲ (the prosperous rule of the early empire) ἀπολωλέκατε τὰ τῶν προγόνων σύμβολα. εὐθὺϲ οὖτε τοῖϲ τάφοιϲ ἐστίν ἄξιοϲ ἃ δὴ ἀγνῶτεϲ αὐτοὺϲ γινόμενοι, εἴ γε πρότερον ἡμῶν ἦν ὑπέρατα καὶ πολεμάρχω καὶ ναυμάχω καὶ νομοθετῶν, καὶ οἱ Ἀπολλῶνι τε καὶ θυάρσωνι καὶ Λυκείω τῶν μακεδῶν. ἐμοὶ μὲν εἰς μᾶλλον ὅσαπερ Μίμνερμοι.

reminds us how the Romans often transcribed αι by a Latin ē (Æneas for Αἰνείας). Thus ἐπιμέληα and Σεβαστῆον in Nos. DXXII–DXXIV; τελησέτατον, C. I. 3957a, a decree in honour of Augustus. The termination in -εῖος became -εῖους in Macedonian times (see C. I. A. ii, 168 : ἱδρυσείως : B. C. 333 ; Index to Dittenberger, Sylloge, p. 780; Part i, p. 31) and thus passed into -ήους, hence Σωκλήους. Similarly the termination of the names of the Ephesian chiliastyes in -εος in the earlier decrees (Nos. CCCCXLVIII foll.) becomes usually -ηος in the post-Augustan inscriptions. Βορεύς for Βωρεύς, line 7, is a mark of declining orthography : similarly 'Απολλωνίου, line 16.

It was necessary to set forth clearly the arguments for an earlier date, because the reference of Πείος to the Emperor Antoninus seems so obvious at first sight. It may be questioned, however, whether Greek flattery, if it desired to make a change in its political nomenclature in compliment to the Emperor, would have been content with merely renaming a minor subdivision of the body politic. Nothing less than the name of a tribe would have sufficed ; so Σεβαστή, line 9 ; perhaps 'Αδριανή as an epithet of the Teian tribe (see on No. DII); compare Röhl's Index to C. I. pp. 13 foll. The chiliastys may either be named after some prominent Roman of an earlier time (see Plutarch, Cato, 24), or possibly after the hill Πίων, the name of which has been discussed on p. 71. If the name of the hill is identical with πίων (fat), there was a by-form πίος (see L. and S.) which readily served to name the chiliastys.

The list before us therefore may be assigned to the middle or latter half of the first century A. D. It is even conceivable that the Demetrios, the foreman of the college of neopoioi, is the very Demetrios the silversmith who raised the outcry against St. Paul (Acts xix) in A. D. 57. It is certain that the Demetrios of the Acts was a citizen of considerable influence, and also that the opposition to St. Paul came from the temple-authorities ; if Demetrios were a neopoios, all would be clear. This however is mere conjecture.

One other list of neopoioi remains in a much mutilated state (No. DXC, b) : it resembles the present one in arrangement, and in its lettering, except that it has A, Σ, instead of A, Σ. It is probably only a little earlier in date.

One or two blunders of the lapidary occur in our list. He has omitted τοῦ in line 6, misled by the homœoteleuton in Μηνοφίλου, and writes Τρύφωνας for Τρύφωνος in line 7, and X in Y in Πυθόδωρος, line 15. The name Περιγένης (line 12) occurs in another Ephesian inscription, C. I. 3004; and Heraklcitos son of Apollonios (line 21) may be related to the 'Απο[λ]λωνίου τοῦ 'Ηρακλ[είτου] of C. I. 3010. Εὐσίβης and Δίκαιος (line 17) are both good Greek names : see, for Δίκαιος, Herod. viii, 65 ; C. I. 2267; for Εὐσίβης, see C. I. 2772 ; Hermes, vii, p. 50.

DLXXIX.

A stele of white marble, inscribed on the face a and right return face b; height 2 ft. 4½ in.; width of a 1 ft. 1 in.; of b 1 ft. 3 in. 'From the Augusteum.' a. published by Wood, Inscriptions from the Augusteum, No. 4 : b, ibid. No. 6 (inaccurately).

a. (1)

```
ΑΓΑΘΗ ~ ΤΥΧΗ
:ΑΡΙΣΤΩ · ΤΗΑΡΤΕΜΙΔΙ
ΞΦΑΝΟΣΣΥΝΕΤΟΥ erasure
ΕΤΑΚΑΙΤΟΥΥΙΟΥ
ΞΦΑΝοΥΚΑΙΤΟΥΣΥΝΜΗΝοΥ
ΓΗ·ΑΙΛΙΟΥΠΛΟΥΤΟΓΕΝο
ΛΕΥΤΟΥ·ΚΑΙΕΦΗΒΑΡ
ΤΑΡΑΦΥΛΑΚΟΣ erasure
erasure
```

(2)

```
ΑΓΑΘΗ  ΤΥΧΗ·
ΒΟΛ·ΑΤΕΙΜΗΤΟΣ
.ΠΟΙΗΣΑΤ   ΥΣΕ
᷍Υ          ΣΟΙ
            Ω
            ϕ
```

b.

```
ι
ΟΙΔΕΕΝ
ΚΑΙΤΟΙΣΣΥι
ΘΑΙΡΕΤΟΙ·ΠΡΥ
ΟΥΟΚΩΝΙΑ·ΑΝ
ΙΕΡΑΤΕΥΟΥΣΗΣ·Αι
ΑΝΗΣ·ΙΕΡΟΚΗΡΥΚοϹ
ΑΑΡΚοΥ·ΚΡΑΤΕΡοϹ
ΠΛΙΟΥ·ΦΥ·ΚΑΡΥ
ΜΕΝΟΣ·ΔΙΟΝΥΣ
ΨΣΣΕΩΝ·χ·Ρ
ΑΗΝΟιΓΕΝϹ
ΚΑΙΔΣ ͞·
ΑΓΝΩϹ
ΛΕΣΑΝ

ΣΠΟΛ
ΤΟΥ
ΟΝ
ΑΓ
Τ᷍͞
```

a.

(1)

'Αγαθῇ τύχῃ·
Εὐ]χαριστῶ τῇ 'Αρτέμιδι
Στ]έφανος Συνέτου
μ]ετὰ καὶ τοῦ υἱοῦ
5 Στ'εφάνου καὶ τοῦ Συνμήνου
τοὺ Πο. Αἰλίου Πλουτογένο[υς
βου]λευτοῦ καὶ ἐφηβάρ[χου
καὶ] παραφύλακος·

(2)

10 'Αγαθῇ τύχῃ·
— . . . βολ. 'Ατείμητος
νεο]ποιήσας [ε]ὐσε-
βῶς] σὺ[ν καὶ τοῖ]ς οἰ-
κείοις εὐχαριστ[ῶ
15 [τῇ 'Αρτέμιδι].

b.

'Α[γαθῇ τύχῃ.]
Οἵδε ἐν[εσποίησαν σὺν
καὶ τοῖς συ[νάρχουσιν αὐ-
θαίρετοι· πρυ[τάνεως . . . . .
5 Οὐοκωνία 'Αν . . . . ,
ἱερατευούσης Λα . . . . .
ανῆς, ἱεροκήρυκος . . . .
Μάρκου· Κρατερὸς [Πο-
πλίου φυ(λῆς) Καρη[νέων, χι(λιαστὺν) 'Αλθαι-
10 μένιος Διονύσ[ιος φω.
Ἐ]φεσέων, χι. Λ[εβέδιος· ἐκ-?
μηνοι γενό[μενοι . . . .
καὶ δω[δεκαταῖοι ?
ἀγνῶς [καὶ δικαίως τε-
15 λέσαν[τες τὴν ἀρχήν.

Σπον[δοποιοῦντος . . .
τοῦ . . . .
ον . . . .
απ . .
20 τοῦ . . . .

The two inscriptions on *a* are thanksgivings to
Artemis of the usual kind. Certain erasures are
marked in the uncial text ; line 4 and the beginning
of line 5 are inscribed over similar erasures. Synmenos is described as bouleutes, ephebarchos, and
paraphylax. For the first two titles see Prolegomena,
pp. 71 foll. : p. 82. The meaning of παραφύλαξ is
obscure. The word is employed in the Etym. Mag.,
and by Suidas to explain the dubious term διξιολάβος
(see Commentators on Acts xxiii, 23). Its meaning
is discussed in the Prolegomena, p. 87. The restorations in the second inscription of *a* are fairly certain.

b is a dedication by two men Κρατερὸς and Διονύ-
σ[ιος] (lines 8, 10), who volunteered to act as νεοποιοί
without being elected. We have learned from No.
DLXXVIII.*b*, that the board numbered twelve members,
two from each tribe ; and in No. DLXX we have seen
that they were elected in the ekklesia. Perhaps
when vacancies arose in the course of the year, they
were filled up by cooptation ; and this may be what
is meant by αὐθαίρετοι : see Prolegomena, p. 80. Our
inscription closely resembles Waddington-Le Bas,
No. 152 : οἵ]δε ἐνεσποίησαν αὐ[θ]α[ίρετοι ἐ]πὶ πρυτάνεως
Τιβερίου [Κλ]αυδίου Διοδώρου Ῥωμύ[λο]υ, ἱερατευούσης
[Κλ]αυδίας Οὐαλεριανοῦ [θυγα]τρὸς Βαλεριανῆς, ἱεροκηρυ-
κε[ύοντος κ.τ.λ. I suppose lines 10–12 to have
specified the exact time during which these neopoioi
suffecti held office. For the *iterea* (line 6) and the
ἱεροκῆρυξ (line 7) see Prolegomena, pp. 85, 87. The
two neopoioi are named with their tribe and chiliastys
(lines 8–11), just as in Nos. DLXXVIII *b*, DXC *b*. In
line 5 the tribe, Voconia, is mentioned : so Quirina in
Nos. CCCCLXXXI, line 305, DLXXIII.

DLXXX.

Fragment of white marble moulding from top of a stele. Height 4 in.; width 8 in. Discovered by Mr. Wood ; unpublished.

ΤΥΧΗ
ΓΕΜΙ·Μ·ΤΥΛΛΙ´
ΚΛΩΣ·

'Αγαθῇ] τύχῃ·
Εὐχαριστῶ σοι κυρία "Αρ]τεμι Μ. Τύλλιο[ς
. . . . . . καθὼς . . . .

In an Athenian inscription of the time of the
Antonines (C. I. 247) a successful athlete named
Marcus Tullius recites his victories in various parts

of Greece and Italy : Ephesos is mentioned in the
list. This may possibly be the same person.

DLXXXI.

Slab of white marble; entire except on the right-hand edge. An incised triangle encloses a portion of the inscription. Height 1 ft. 4 in.; width 1 ft. 5 in. Discovered by Mr. Wood; unpublished.

ΑΓΑϬ
ΑΡΤΕΜΙ Ε΄
ΤΟΥϹΟΥ ΠΙΑΡ ΙΙϹ
ΠΟΦΑ ΧΙϹΚΗ Γ
ΠΤΟΥΧ
ΟΥ·ΑΥ·ΠΟ
ϹΕΙΔΩΝ
ΕΥΤΥΧ

Ἀγαθ[ῇ τύχῃ·
Ἄρτεμι . . . . .
τοῦ σοῦ πο[. . . ά-?
ποφα . . . .
Ἐ|πὶ ἀρ|χισκη|πτούχ,ου
Αὐ(ρηλίου) Πο|σειδωνί ίου]
Εὐτύχ[ου.

A dedication, or invocation addressed to Artemis: the letters are late, perhaps of the third century. Every letter is certain, except the letter before ο at the end of line 3, which is broken, and may be read as π or τρ. The letter immediately under this can hardly be anything but Γ. But I am at a loss to restore the ends of the lines. Line 2: possibly μέμνησο.

The year of the inscription is named after the ἀρχισκηπτοῦχος or chief of the vergers (σκηπτοῦχοι) of the Artemision, who are mentioned several times in the Salutaris inscription, No. CCCCLXXXI, lines 196, 382, 399. Similarly in an honorary inscription which Böckh doubtfully assigns to the first century A. D. (C.I. 2987 = Waddington-Le Bas, No. 161), the date is given as Ἐπὶ ἀρχισκηπτούχου Ἑρμίππου. We have met with the name Εὔτυχος in No. DLXXVII ante.

DLXXXII.

Corner of white marble stele, broken everywhere except at the angle; height 6 in. Inscribed on both sides α and b: width of α 3½ in., width of b 4½ in. Discovered by Mr. Wood; unpublished.

a.   b.

ιΕΜΙ   ῆ · ΚϹ
ΟΥ·   ΝΕΟΓ
ΑΙΓΑΜΟ   ΝΙΑϹ

a.
Εὐχαριστῶ σοι Κυρία Ἄρτ]εμι
ὁ δεῖνα . . . .]ου
. . . . αιγαμο

b.
Ἀ[γαθῇ τύχῃ·
Πό(πλιος) Κο[ρνήλιος ? . .
νεοπ[οιήσας εὐσεβῶς τὰς ἱερομη-?
νίας . . . .

evidently votive inscriptions of the usual character. Part of Α is visible in line 1 of b. The restoration of line 3 is suggested by No. DLXXXVIII, b; where see note.

DLXXXIII.

Fragment of white marble, broken on all sides. Height 8 in.; width 5 in. Discovered by Mr. Wood; unpublished.

      ΛΟ
ΡΙΟΣ᾽Α
ΟϹΕΒι
ΡΓΟϹ
5   ΝΤΗΓ
   ᴖΑʻ

Ἀγ]αθ[ῇ τύχῃ·
. . . . ριος Ἀ . . . .
φιλ]οσίβ[αστος, λι-
του]ργὸς, ...
5   . . ν ήγο . . . .

DLXXXIV.

Fragment of white marble stele, entire at top only. Height 1 ft. 3 in.; width 7 in. Discovered by Mr. Wood; unpublished.

ι τ ν χ	Ἀγαθ]ῇ τύχῃ·
ϽΜΠΗ	.... Π]ομπή]ίος ....
ϹΑΥΡ	.... ς Αὐρ[ήλιος?
Μ Ͱ	... ἀγορανο]μή[σας ?

DLXXXV.

Fragment of a block of whitish marble, entire only on left. Height 2½ in.; width 8 in. Discovered by Mr. Wood; unpublished.

_ Ь / .	. . ε . . . . .
ΑΣΚΑΙΔιι	ας καὶ δ . . . .
ϽΤοΝΘΥΣΙ_Ω_.	. . τῶν θυσιῶ[ν . . .
ΥΤΙ	. . . . . θ]υσιῶν . . .

The mention of sacrifices suggests that this may have been a dedication, if not an honorary inscription.

DLXXXVI.

Fragment of white marble. Height 8 in.; width 9 in.; thickness 5 in.; inscribed on both sides, *a*, *b*. The upper edge of *b* is entire, but the left-hand and upper surface is injured in *a*. The edge of the stone is entire both on right and left; but the vertical dotted line indicates a joint, where another stone was united by a cramp, the mark of which is very obvious. This probably formed part of the same slab as No. DLXXII. Discovered by Mr. Wood; unpublished.

a.

. ı .	Εὐχαρ]ισ[τῶ] σοι
ϹΥΡΙΑΑΡ	κυρία Ἀρ[τεμι νεο-
ΠΟΙ	πο[ιήσας κ.]τ.λ.
(uninscribed)	

b.

ΝΕΩ·	Ὁ δεῖνα . . .]νεώ[τεροσ
ΥΛΑΡΧΟΣ	. . . . βο]ύλαρχος.
(uninscribed)	

Both inscriptions seem to belong to the second century A. D. *a* is a dedication of a common type; see No. DLXXVIII *c*. In *b* we are forbidden to restore νεω-[ποιήσας] by the stop inserted after ΝΕΩ·, and for Ω we should then expect Ο. In one other Ephesian inscription, C. I. 2997, Boeckh has restored βου[λαρ]-χοr. The title occurs frequently elsewhere; see Prolegomena, p. 74.

DLXXXVII.

On a stele of white marble, entire at bottom and on the right; but the left edge is somewhat broken, and the top was once surmounted by a moulded cornice, containing some lost lines (as in No. DLXXVIII, *a*). Height 2 ft. 9 in.; width 1 ft. 10 in. Wood, Inscriptions from the Theatre, No. 4.

a.

ΟΚΗΡΥΚΕΥΟΝΤΟΣ	ἱερ]οκηρυκεύοντος . . . .
ΤΟͰΝΕΙΝΟΥ· ΠͰΕΣΒΥΤΕͰΩΙ	Σα]τορνείνου, πρισβυτέρων . . .
(Two lines here anciently erased.)	

b.

(In rather larger letters.)

```
        ΑΓΑΘΗ ~ ΤΥΧΗ ·
      ΑΥΡ·ΑΓΑΘΟΠΟΥΣ·ΕΥΧΑΡΙΣΤΩ
      ‚ΘΕΩ·ΚΑΙΗΚΥΡΙΑΣΩΤΕΙ
      ΙΚΑΙΤΗΤΥΧΗΗΣΓΕΡΟΥ
    5 _ΙΑΣ·ΟΤΙΗΝΠΙΣΤΙΝ·ΕΗ
      ?ΗΣΑ·ΗΓΕΡΟΥΣΙΑΣΥΝΚΑΙ
      ΟΙΣΕΜΟΙΣ·~·ΠΑΣΙΝ
      ϽΑΥΤΟΣΡΓΡΑΜΜΑΤΕΥΣ·
      ΑΙΓΥΜΝΑΣΙΑΡΧΟΣ·
   10    ·ΕΥΤΥΧΩΣ·
```

'Αγαθῇ τύχῃ·
Μ.] Αὐρ. 'Αγαθόπους εὐχαριστῶ
τ]ῷ θεῷ καὶ τῇ κυρίᾳ Σωτεί-
ρᾳ] καὶ τῇ τύχῃ τῆς γερου-
5 σίας, ὅτι τὴν π΄ίστιν ἐτήρησα τῇ γερουσίᾳ σὺν καὶ
τ]οῖς ἐμοῖς πᾶσιν,
ὁ αὐτὸς γραμματεὺς
κ]αὶ γυμνασίαρχος
10 εὐτυχῶς.

In *a* we have the dating of a separate dedication, and not the dating of *b*, as Wood supposes. On the ἱερόκηρυξ see Prolegomena, p. 87. The plural πρεσβυτέρων shows that the name of another officer had preceded the name of the ἱερόκηρυξ by way of giving the date. Both men were members of the gerousia, for we have already seen on lines 206, 207 of the Salutaris inscription (No. ccccLXXXI) that πρεσβύτερος is a synonym for γέρων or γερουσιαστής. A similar dating of a dedication by νεοποιοί occurs in C. I. 2982 (= Waddington-Le Bas iii, No. 152) cited on No. DLXXXIX *b aute*: ἐπὶ πρυτάνεως Τιβερίου [Κλ]|αυδίου Διο-δώρου 'Ρωμύ||[λο]ψ· ἱερατευούσης [Κλ]|αυδίας Οὐαλεριανοῦ [θυγ'α]τρὸς Βαλεριανῆ[ς]| ἱεροκηρυκε[ύοντος τοῦ δεῖνος].

b is a thanksgiving to Artemis Soteira (compare

No. ccccLXXXIII) by M. Aurelius Agathopous after having served successfully the office of secretary and gymnasiarch of the gerousia. With Artemis is associated another deity [τ]ῷ θεῷ, line 5 ; and if the stelè was originally set up in the theatre where it was found, the deity meant is Dionysos. Concerning the offices here mentioned, see Prolegomena, pp. 76, 77, 81 *ante*, for the γραμματεὺς τῆς γερουσίας, and p. 82 and No. υ for the γυμνασίαρχος. The dedicator M. Aur. Agathopous is probably the same who is mentioned in No. DXCVI *a*. It will be seen by refer-ring to Röhl's Index to Böckh's Corpus that the name 'Αγαθόπους was a favourite one with the Greeks of the imperial period, especially in the times of the Antonines.

DLXXXVIII.

Broken cornice of white marble : height 1 ft. ; width 2 ft. 1 in. From the Augusteum. Published inaccurately by Wood, Inscriptions from the Augusteum, No. 3.

a.

```
  Α    ΛΝ ΩΝΤΗΡΗΣΑΣΔΕΚΑΙΤΟΙΕΡΟ
  ΥΠΕΡΤΩΝΩΝΕΚΤΩΝΙΔΙΩΝ
```

b.

```
  ΑΓΑΘΗΤΥΧΗ·ΕΥΧΑΡΙΣΤΩΣΟΙΚΥΡΙΑ
  ΑΡΤΕΜΙ·ΜΗΤΡΟΔΩΡΟΣ·ΔΑΜΑ·Β·ΤϽ
5 ΑΛΕΞΑ·ΦΥ·ΤΗΙΩΝ-Χ·ΕΥΡΥΠΟΜ
  ΕΟΠΟΙΗΣΑΣ·ΕΥΣΕΒΩΣ·ΤΑ▼
  ΗΝΕΙΑΣ·ΜΕΤΑΚΑΙΤΩΝ·⁻
  ΟΥ·ΤΕΚΝΩΝ·ΝΑᴵᴷϽ
  ΛΙΤΟΥΛΛΓΑᴵ
```

a.

. . . . [μετὰ τῶν συν-(?)
α[ρξ]άν[τ]ων, τηρήσας δὲ καὶ τὸ ἱερό[ν
ὑπὲρ τῶν υἱῶν ἐκ τῶν ἰδίων.

b.

'Αγαθῇ τύχῃ· εὐχαριστῶ σοι κυρία
"Αρτεμι Μητρόδωρος Δαμᾶ β̄ τοῦ
5 'Αλεξᾶ, φυ(λῆς) Τηίων, χι(λιαστύος) Εὐρυπομ . . .
ν]εοποιήσας εὐσεβῶς τὰς [ἱερομ-?
ηνίας· μετὰ καὶ τῶν τ[ριῶν ? αὐτο-
οῦ τέκνων (καὶ γυ)ναικ[ὸς αὐτοῦ κ-
α]ὶ τοῦ ἀδελφ[οῦ . . . . .

a (omitted by Wood) is the conclusion of a dedica-tion, probably of the second century. The upper edge of the marble is entire just above line 1 ; we must suppose that another marble originally was joined on at the top, see No. DLXXXVIII, *b*. Perhaps τηρήσαι τὸ ἱερόν expresses the duties of a ναοφύλαξ (Arist. Pol. vi, 8, 19, = p. 1322 *b*) ; Prolegomena, p. 87 *ante*).

b is a thanksgiving to Artemis of the usual type. Δαμᾶ and 'Αλεξᾶ are genitives, and not contractions. The numeral β̄ in line 2 implies that the father of

Damas bore the same name. So C. I. 2186 ἀπύγονον Εὐξένω β̄, and 2653 γυναῖκα δὲ τοῦ πάντα ἀρίστου Μαρ. Αὐρ. Εὐθόξου υἱῷ and passim. In line 8 the lapidary wrote ΝΑΙ by mistake for ΚΑΙ, and so went on with the word (γυ)ναικός. On the νεοποιοί see Prolegomena, p. 80 ; the mention of the tribe and chiliastys in a mere dedication illustrates what was said on No. DLXXXVIII *b* as to the neopoioi being essentially a representative board, twt from each tribe. I suppose Metrodoros to have been appointed as additional neopoios, or as

3 I

neopoios suffectus during the festival of Artemis in
the month Artemision; and I restore lines 4–5 accordingly. The same formula seems to occur in No.
DLXXXII, b. On the ἱερομηνίαι in the month Artemision

see No. CCCCLXXXII, b. The spelling -είας for -ίας
will not surprise anyone who is conversant with inscriptions of this date : compare the forms Ἀρτεμείσια
No. DCXV, line 11 ; Δείκαιος, No. DLXXVIII, b, line 17.

DLXXXIX

Broken stelé of white marble ; inscribed on the face a, and on the return-face, b.   Present height 2 ft. ; width of a 1 ft. 2 in. ;
width of b 9¼ in.   Broken at the top, and on the left of a and right of b.   Discovered by Mr. Wood, probably in the Augusteum ;
but unpublished.

a.

```
ΕΝΚΑΙ·ΜΕΛ   ΙΝΙ              . . . . . . . . . . συ]ν καὶ Μελ[ίτ]ωνι
ΞΙΑΝΗ·ΚΑΙ·ΓΑ·               καὶ τῇ γυναικὶ Λου?]κιανῇ, καὶ Κλ.
ΛΙΤΟΙΣΤΕΚΝΟΙΣ               . . . . . . . . . . κ]αὶ τοῖς τέκνοις
ΟΥΚΙΑ·ΚΑΙΜΕ ΙΤΗ            αὐτοῦ . . . . . . Λ]ουκίᾳ καὶ Με[λ]ίτῃ,
ΥΝΜΗΝΔΜΟΥ              5    σὺν καὶ τῷ ὑῷ Σ]υνμήνῳ μου,
ΤΩΤΩΠΑΝΤΑ                   Ἀρτέμιδι καὶ Σεβασ]τῷ τῷ πάντα
ΑΡΙΣΤΩ                       . . . . . . . . . . εὐχ]αριστω·
ΝΩΤΩΥΩΑΥΤΟΥ                σὺν καὶ . . Συνμή?]νῳ τῷ ὑῷ αὐτοῦ.
ΓΙΑΡΓΥΡΩΜΑ                  [Σπονδοποιοῦντος] ['Ε]πὶ ἀργυρώμα-
   10   ΝΙΔΟΥΙΕΡΟΥ     10   [τοῦ δεῖνος.]         [τος . . .]νίδου ἱεροῦ.
```

b.

(In rather larger letters.)

```
            Ι                 . . . . . . . ι . . . . . .
         ΝΚΑΙΝ                 σὺ]ν καὶ Ν . . . .
         ΔΗΜΟΣΤΡΑ⁻            Δημοστρά[τῳ τῷ
         *ΩΜΟΥΚΑΙ             ὑῷ μου καὶ . . . .
    5    ΩΔΗΜΟΣΤ         3    ῳ Δημοστ[ράτου
         ΦΙΛΟΣΕΒΑ            φιλοσεβά[στῳ καὶ
         ·Λ·ΦΙΔΟΥ            Λ(ουκίῳ) Φίδου [ὑῷ
         ΠΟΥΔΕΝΙ             Πούδεντ[ι φιλο-
         ΣΕΒΑΣΤΩ             σεβάστῳ·
   10    ΕΠΙΑΡΓΥ'ΩΡ     10   'Επὶ ἀργυρ]ώρ[ατος
         ΕΥΤΥΧΟ'ΙΟΥΛ         Εὐτύχου 'Ιουλ[ια-
         ΝΟΥ·Α':ΡΟΒΑ          νοῦ, ἀκροβά[του
         ΣΠΟ ΔΟΠΟΙ           σπο[ν]δοποι[οῦν-
         Τ   ΕΟΠΟΝ            τ[ος Θ]εοπόμ[που,
   15    ΡΟΥ·            15   ἱε]ροῦ.
```

a is a dedication to Artemis and the reigning
Emperor (line 6. if rightly restored), made by a
neopoios (?) whose name is missing from the commencement.   He associates with him Melito and his
wife (? line 2). Claudius and his daughters (lines
2–4), and his own son Synmenos (line 5) ; also, as
an afterthought, his son's son [Synme?]nos (line 8).
The date in the last two lines was given as at the
end of *b.*   The name Σύνμηνος has occurred already
in No. DLXXIX, *a.*

b is a similar dedication ; the name Δημόστρατος
occurred in No. DI, in a dedication to Hadrian. The
date is given as in *a* by naming the temple-officials
who had charge respectively of the libations and of
the silver plate.   We may probably infer that these
appointments were annual ones.   Theopompos was
similarly named as σπονδοποιῶν in No. DLXXXIII, *c ;*
see note *ad loc.*, and Prolegomena, p. 86.   The title

Ἐπὶ ἀργυρ ώματος is probably identical with Ὁ ἐπὶ τῶν
παραθηκῶν which occurs in the Salutaris inscription,
line 385 (compare No. DCII, *y* line 20, and Prolegomena pp. 86–87) ; one of his duties was to clean the
images bequeathed by Salutaris with special plate-
powder (ἀργυρωματικη, ἡ ἀργυρωματικὴ γῆ, No.CCCCLXXXI.
lines 378–387), in the presence of two of the neopoioi and a σκηπτοῦχος.   The name Εὔτυχος occurs
also in Nos. DLXXVII *b*, DLXXXI.   Eutychos is described as an akrobates, a title which has been discussed in the Prolegomena, p. 85, and No. CCCCLXXXI,
lines 373–6.   On the status of the ἱεροί at Ephesos
(*a* line 10, *b* line 15) see Prolegomena *ante* pp. 85
foll.   As the officer Ἐπὶ ἀργυρώματος is not the same
in *a* and *b*, I infer that they belong to two different,
perhaps two succeeding, years : we may not therefore restore [Θεοπόμπου] in *a* line 10.

DXC.

Broken stele of white marble inscribed upon the front *a* and upon the right return face *b*, broken at the top and bottom; *a* has both the right and left edges entire; *b* is entire upon the right-hand edge only. Height 3 ft. 2½ in.; width of *a* 1 ft. 6 in.; width of *b* 4½ in. Discovered by Mr. Wood, who has published *a* inaccurately, Appendix, Inscriptions from the Augusteum, No. 12; *b* is unpublished.

a.

(1)   ..ΚΕιΝ

(Space of three lines vacant.)

(2)   ┤ᴗᴑ ΤΥΧΗ
ΤΩΣΟι·ΚΥΡι

. . . .
ΙΕΟΠΟΙΗΣΑ━━ιᴄ
ΙᴡΑΙΦΙΛΟΤΕΙΜΩΣΜΕ
5   ΓΩΝΤΕΚΝΩΝΜΟΥ·Τ·φΛ
ᴐΥΑΛΕΝΤΟΣ·ΚΑΙ·Τ·φΛ·
φΡΟΝΤΕΙΝΟΥ·ΚΑΙ·φΛ·φΑΥΣ
ΤΕΙΝΙΣΤΗΣΘΥΓΑΤΡΟΣΜΟΥ

(Space of three lines vacant.)

(3)   ΕΠΙΙΟΥΛΙΟΥΤο⁻
ΑΠΟΛΛΩΝΙΟΣΠΟΣΕΙ
ΡΟΣΕΥΝΟΧ

(4)   ΑΓΑΘΗ   ┳
ΕΥΧΑΡΙΣΤ⊂
ΑΡΈΜΙ·ΑΡ
ΕΥΚΛΗΣ
5   ΒΑΣΣC
ΝΕΟΓ

(1)   .. ὁ δεῖνα ἀνέθ]ηκεν.

(2)   'Αγαθῇ̣ τύχῃ·
Εὐχαρισ]τῶ σοι κυρί[ᾳ 'Αρτεμι
. . . .
... ν]εοποιήσας εὐσ[ε-
βῶς] καὶ φιλοτείμως με-
5   τὰ] τῶν τέκνων μου Τ. Φλ.
Οὐάλεντος καὶ Τ. Φλ.
Φροντείνου καὶ Φλ. Φαυσ-
τείνης τῆς θυγατρὸς μου.

(3)   'Επὶ 'Ιουλίου τὸ [β̄ (?)
'Απολλώνιος Ποσει[δ . . ου, ...
ρος Εὔνοχ . . . .

(4)   'Αγαθῇ τ[ύχῃ.
Εὐχαριστῶ [σοι κυρία
'Αρτεμι 'Αρ . . . .
Εὐκλῆς . . . .
5   Βασσο . . . .
νεοπ[οιήσας κ.τ.λ.

b.

(1)   [Φυλῆς 'Εφεσίων·]
['Ο δεῖνα τοῦ δεῖνος]
[τοῦ δεῖνος, ... ηος,]
['Ο δεῖνα . . .]ρι[. . . .
... τοῦ 'Αρ]τε[μιδώ-
'Αργαδ-
ρου?,   or   ὑτ.
Βαρε |

(1)   Ρ₄
ΓΕΙ
∶Σ

(Space for one line.)

(2)   5   ∶ΑΡΙΔΗ
ΔΗΜΟΥ
ΛΗΟΣ
'ΔΡΟΥ
ᴾΑΝΔΗΟΣ
10   (Space for one line.)

(2)   [Σεβαστῆς·]
5   ὁ δεῖνα] Χαριδή-
μου τοῦ . . .]δήμου,
. . . . μηος,
ὁ δεῖνα . . ν]δρου
τοῦ δεῖνος, Λα]βάρδηος·

(3)   ΜΗΤΡΙΟΥ
ΞΟΝΤΗΟΣ
ΛΕΞΑΝ
ΞΝΟΥ
15   ᴐΣ

(3)   10   [Τήιοι·]
ὁ δεῖνα Δη]μητρίου
τοῦ δεῖνος, . . .]εόντηος,
ὁ δεῖνα 'Α]λεξάν-
δρου τοῦ . . .]ένου,
15   'Ηγητόρει?]ος·

(4)   ΙΟΙ
ᴦ-ΤΟΥ
ΧΥΡΗΟΣ
ᴦΧΩΝΟΣ
20   ΛΩΝΗΟΣ

(4)   Καρηνα]ῖοι·
ὁ δεῖνα . . . ο]υ τοῦ
δεῖνος, 'Ε]χύρηος,
ὁ δεῖνα . . υ]χωνος
20   τοῦ δεῖνος, Σι]μώνηος
[5th Εὐώνυμοι
6th Βεμβειναῖοι] wanting.

a contains portions of four distinct inscriptions. Of these (2) and (4) are dedications by neopoioi of the usual type: (1) and (3) are inscribed in characters of a decidedly earlier date, which resemble those on the return face *b*, and cannot be later than the middle of the 1st century A.D. An examination of the marble shows it to be a 'palimpsest'; in order to receive inscriptions (2) and (4) the surface has been dressed anew in the coarse manner of nearly all the inscribed Ephesian marbles of the second and later centuries. All above (2) and from below (2) to above (4) the surface retains its original smoothness; but traces of another line of characters belonging to inscription (3) can be discerned along the first line of (4). In (3) the date of the dedication is given as the [second?] year of Julius, i. e. as prytanis.

It will be at once perceived that *b* was a list of neopoioi resembling No. DLXXVIII *b*; where see the notes. The date is about the same, viz. the middle of the first century A.D. We may assume that the enumeration of the tribes in that list followed their recognised order of precedence. This granted, it becomes easy to restore the present list to something like its original shape. In line 9 we recognize Λα]βάνδηοι, a chiliastys known to us from No. DLXXVIII *b* as belonging to the tribe Σεβαστή: lines 4–9 therefore gave the names of two neopoioi from the tribe Sebastè. These were preceded by a pair of names belonging to the first, or Ephesine tribe; and this would bring us towards the top of the stelè, which would well accord with the appearance of the stone, and with the arrangement of the inscriptions on the front *a*. Lines 10–15 will have given the neopoioi of the Teian tribe; and lines 16–20 those of the Karenaean tribe. The names of the fifth and sixth tribes are missing, as the lower portion of the stelè is mutilated. For a list of the tribes and chiliastyes, see Prolegomena p. 69 foll. The fragment before us adds to our list two unknown chiliastyes; line 7, . . . μηοι, of the tribe Sebastè; line 12, . . . ίοντηοι, of the Teian tribe. It also enables us to assign to the Karenaean tribe the chiliastyes 'Εχύρηοι and Σιμώνηοι, of which the names only were previously known, but not the tribes of which they formed a part.

DXCI.

A very small moulded base of white marble, broken off on the right; height 3½ in.; width 4 in. Discovered by Mr. Wood; unpublished.

```
ΑϹΚΛΗΠΙ.
ΦΙΜΟϹΔΕ
ΤΙϹΘΕΙϹ
```

The letters are not earlier than the second or third century A.D. I would suggest as a possible restoration:—

'Ασκληπ[ῷ καὶ 'Υγιείᾳ Τρό-
φιμοι Δί[εμου καταρ-
τισθείς.

Or perhaps better thus:—

'Ασκληπ[ῷ καὶ 'Υγιείᾳ Τρό-
φιμοι δε[ξιὰν χείρα καταρ-
τισθείς.

Καταρτίζω seems to be the proper medical term for the setting of a bone.

DXCII.

Fragment of a small circular base of white marble: height 2¾ in.; length 5¼ in.; broken off at either end. Discovered by Mr. Wood; unpublished.

```
ΟΝΙΑϹΑΝ
```

. . . . ονίας ἀν[άθημα.

Apparently a dedication made by a woman.

DXCIII.

Fragment of white marble: broken on all sides except the right. Height 4½ in.; width 1 ft. 6 in. Discovered by Mr. Wood; unpublished.

```
,ΑΙΤΙΤΙΑΣ·Μι                    . . κ]αὶ Τιτίας Μ[ητ-
ΑΟΡΑΣ·ΥΟΣ·ΙΕΡ                  ρο]δάρας υἱὸς, ἱερ-
        Τ                       οκῆρυξ? . . . . . ]τ-
```

The letters are well formed. It seems to be part of a dedication, the names being those of the givers. *Τιτίας* is a mythical name (see Pape-Benseler) ; but perhaps we should here write it *Τιτιᾶς* as a contraction for *Τιτιανός*

DXCIV.

A large square base of white marble, surmounted by a plain moulding, found in the theatre ; a good deal broken at the bottom, and to some extent on the left. Inscribed only upon the front. Present height 1 ft. 10 in.; width of inscribed face 1 ft. 11 in. C. Curtius, Hermes iv, p. 218 foll.; Wood, Inscriptions from the Great Theatre, No. 2 ; Mommsen, C.I.L. iii, 6065.

```
         IANAE ϕ  EPHESIAE · Eι
         PHYLE ⋆ CARENAEON
         IBIVS · C · FVOFSALVTA RISPROMAG · PORTVVM
         OVINC SICILIAE · ITEM · PROMAGFRVMENTIMANCIPALIS·
   5     AEFEC · COHOR · ASTVRVM · ETCALLAECORVMTRID·MIL·
         XII · PRIMIGENIAE · P · F · SVBPROCVRATORPROVINC·
         ETANIAE · TINGITANAE · ITEM · PROVINC · BELGICAE
         · · ARGENTEAM·I  M · IMAGINES · ARGENTEASDVAS·VNAΣ
         FTALIM·PHV  S·SVA·PECVNIA·FECIT·ITAVTOMNI·
  10     Ι· ·ΙΤΟ  RADASESPONERENTVR·OBQVAMDE
         ΣΝΕΜSΕX·PHVLAESCONSEC·IIS·XXXIIICCCXXXIIIS
         ·ΥΑ  ΛΑΙΔΗΓ·ΟΥΕΙΒΙΟΣ Γ ΥΙΟΣΩ·
               ᴖΜΓΓΑ⊙ΧΕΙΛΣΣ·
                        ᴛι
```

D]ianae Ephesiae et
Phyle Carenaeon
C. V]ibius C. f. Vof(entina) Salutaris promag(istro) portuum
pr]ovinc(iae) Siciliae, item promag(istro) frumenti mancipalis,
5   pr]aefec(tus) cohor(tis) Asturum et Callaecorum, trib(unus) mil(itum)
leg(ionis) x]XII primigeniae p(iae) f(idelis), subprocurator provinc(iae)
Maur]etaniae Tingitanae, item provinc(iae) Belgicae,
aram?] argenteam i[te]m imagines argenteas duas, una[m
Dianae] et aliam phy[le]s, sua pecunia fecit, ita ut omni
10 anno in t]heatr[o? sup]ra bases ponerentur, ob quam de-
ae et phyles dedicati]onem sex phylae consec(ravit) IISXXXIIICCCXXXIIIS
Ἀρτέμιδι Ἐφεσίᾳ καὶ τῇ] φυλ[ῇ Καρη]ναίων Γ. Οὐείβιος Γ. υἱὸς Ὠ[φ.
Σαλουτάριος . . . . λιμεν]ῶν ἐπαρχείας Σ[ικελίας
κ.τ.λ. . . . .]σί[του?

The text in C. I. L. is more correct than that in the Hermes, but Mommsen is mistaken in saying that TINGITANAE in line 7 is inscribed over an erasure; there is no sign of it. Also in line 3 the T of SALVTARIS is visible enough. In line 3 VOF is a blunder for OVF. At the end of line 11 the last letter is certainly S. The first letters in line 10 are almost certainly as given above : the statues dedicated in No. cccclxxxi *ante* were to be similarly displayed in the theatre ; see lines 166 foll., 307 foll., 392 foll. In line 13, I have recovered part of the ΛΝ of λιμενῶν ; and in line 14 Σι, perhaps σί[του]. The first two lines are inscribed upon the moulded cornice. In the horizontal surface of the monument above are the sockets into which perhaps the 'bases' (line 10) were inserted to support the two images.

The donor is C. Vibius Salutaris who was so munificent a benefactor to the city and temple of Ephesos (No. cccclxxxi *ante*). The present dedication marks him as a wealthy man, but otherwise he was probably an obscure person. His cursus honorum (lines 3-7) includes none but subordinate, although valuable, appointments. In line 3. portuum is for portorii as

3 K

in Cicero ad Att. v, 15 fin.: tu autem sæpe dare tabellariis publicanorum poteris per magistros scripturæ et portus nostrarum diœcesium. The portorium Siciliae or 'customs from the ports of Sicily' is mentioned by Cicero, in Verr. 2, 70. The Societates of publicani, usually Roman knights, who farmed the government revenues, were presided over by a magister, who usually had a promagister to assist him. Salutaris had been deputy-master of that wealthy company which farmed the Sicilian customs (see Pauly, Real-encycl. vi, 1, p. 247 s.v. publicani). Line 4: Manceps is the same as conductor or redemptor operis, i. e. a contractor: Salutaris had been also deputy-master of the Societas which had contracted with the government to supply grain; this contract probably refers only to Sicily, as the word item would suggest. Line 5: for full information concerning the cohortes auxiliariæ, or provincial auxiliary troops under the Empire, see Pauly, Real-encycl. s.v. Socii, and Marquardt, Röm. Alt. v, 471. Asturia and Callæcia (Gallæcia) were the two north-westerly districts of Hispania Tarraconensis (see Marquardt ibid. iv, p. 103). From Latin inscriptions we learn of a cohors prima Asturum et Callæcorum (C. I. L. iii, pt. 2, p. 845, A.D. 60); also cohors secunda Ast. et Call. (C. I. L. ibid. op. 854, 855, 888 : respectively A.D. 80, 85. 167). The date of our inscription is about A.D. 100, and in it this cohort has no numeral prefixed. The appointment of a præfectus of an auxiliary cohort was made by the consul. Line 6: the Legio xxii primigenia figures very frequently in the Histories of Tacitus amid the revolutions which succeeded each other after the death of Nero. Numerous inscriptions (C. I. L. iii, 269, 550; v, 877, 7004, 7872 etc.) give it, as here, the epithets 'pia, fidelis.' The offices of subprocurator, mentioned lines 6 and 7, are not named elsewhere : they are noticed by Marquardt in his account of these two provinces (Röm. Alt. iv, pp. 324, note 5, 124, note 1). Line 11: for the names of the 'six tribes,' see Prolegomena ante, p. 69. Line 11 : The sum is a peculiar one, the notation being made up of threes throughout. A similar sum, with a like religious import, is cited by Mommsen from Livy, xxii, 10 : Ejusdem rei causa ludi magni voti æris trecentis triginta tribus milibus trecentis triginta tribus triente. That sum was reckoned in the old manner, according to the old libral as (æs grave), a triens or third of which completes the sum total. The dedication of Salutaris is reckoned in silver sesterces (each = 4 asses, or one as libralis), and as the triens was no longer recognised, a S(emis) or half-sesterce is appended instead (see Marquardt ibid. vi, p. 255, on the religious significance attached to certain sums by the Romans). Compare the bequest of 3333 denarii to the Boulè at Tralles, Mittheilungen viii, pp. 321, 329 (quoted ante, p. 137).

DXCV.

Part of a column of white marble, broken at top and bottom: height 1 ft. 2 in.; diameter about 1 ft. 3 in. Wood, Inscriptions from the City and Suburbs, No. 3. He describes it as 'A loose stone found in the village of Ayasoluk, apparently part of a column.'

```
   LΛΙ  .ι     .Λι                     . . . . . . ν . . . . . . [Α?]λι-
   ΑΝΗΣ · ΙΕΡΑΤΕΥΟΝΤΟΣ                 ανῆς· ἱερατεύοντος
   ΔΙΑΒΙΟΥΤΩΝΠΡΟΠΟΛΕ                   διὰ βίου τῶν πρὸ πόλε-
   ΩΣ·ΔΗΜΗΤΡΙΑΣΤΩΝ                     ως Δημητριαστῶν
5  ΞΑΙΔΙΟΝΥΣΟΥ·ΦΛΕΩΜΥ              5   καὶ Διονύσου Φλέω μυ-
   ΞΤΩΝ·ΤΙΤΟΥ·ΑΥΡΗΛΙΟΥ                 στῶν Τίτου Αὐρηλίου
   ΤΛΟΥΤΑΡΧΟΥ·ΙΕΡΟΦΑΝ                  Πλουτάρχου, ἱεροφαν-
   ΟΥΝΤΟΣ·Π·ΚΛΑΥΔΙΟΥ                   τ]οῦντος Πο. Κλαυδίου
   ΟΙΣΤΟΦΑΝΟΫΣ·ΕΠΙΜΕ                  Ἀ]ριστοφάνους, ἐπιμε-
10 ΗΤΟΫΔΕ·ΤΩΝΜΥΣΤΗ                10  λ]ητοῦ δὲ τῶν μυστη-
   ΩΝ·ΣΑΤΟΡΝΕΙΛΟΫ                      ρί]ων Σατορνείλου
   Σ·ΤΟΫΟΝΪΤΛΝΟΣ                      δί]ς τοῦ Ὀνήσωνος.
```

Probably part of a dedication to a deity, or possibly an honorary inscription, of which only the latter part remains giving the date. The inscription appears to be complete at the end.

The persons named in the monument were connected with the worship of Demeter and Dionysos. Already in No. DVI we have learned something of a college of μύσται at Ephesos in the time of the Antonines; and in the Prolegomena ante, p. 80, I have identified this thiasos of μύσται with the Demetriasts of the present inscription (line 4). The full title of the college is : οἱ πρὸ πόλεως Δημητριασταὶ καὶ Διονύσου Φλίω μύσται. The phrase πρὸ πόλεως implies that the temple of Demeter which formed the centre of their worship was outside of the city walls. Its site is unknown, unless we may infer from the adventure of the Chians narrated by Herodotos vi. 16. that it stood to the south of the city. The Chian fugitives, approaching Ephesos from Mykale, came upon the Ephesian women celebrating the Thesmophoria at night outside the city walls. On the meaning of πρὸ πόλεως compare Böckh on C. I. 2963 c; Waddington-Le Bas, No. 1601 b; and commentators on Acts xiv, 13. See also ante No. cccclxxxi, line 326. There was a similar college at Smyrna, styled 'Η σύν-οῦ . τῶν μυστῶν τῆς μεγάλης θεᾶς πρὸ πόλεως Θεσμοφόρου

Δήμητρος (C. I. 3194). Line 5: Φλίως was one of the titles of Dionysos, and obviously akin to the titles Φλεύς, Φλίος, Φλοῖος, Φλοία, all derivatives of φλίω (see L. and S. *s.v.* φλίω); so Hesych. *s.v.* Φλίω(ς)· Διονύσου ἱερόν. See Ælian, Var. Hist. iii. 41. Φλίως was a mythical son of Dionysos (Pausan. ii, 6, § 3);

of which name Φλίας in No. cccxix, line 32, was another form. The name Σατορνεῖλος (see Pape-Benseler) for Σατορνῖνος is an instance of τραυλισμός like Σελβείλιος in No. dlxxvii, *b*. Ὀνήσων does not seem to occur elsewhere; but Böckh restored Ὀνάσων in C. I. 1207.

DXCVI.

Lower portion of a square stele of white marble, inscribed on the face (*a*) and the left side (*b*); the top is broken off. Height 1 ft. 8 in.; width of *a* 1 ft. 4 in.; width of *b* 1 ft. 3½ in.   Wood, Inscriptions from the Great Theatre, No. 22, gives *b*; *a* is unpublished.

a.

```
          ΕΠΙΚΟΟΚΑΙ
(unin-
scribed) ΚΑΙΤΗΤΥΧΗΤΗΣΠΟΛ
         ΤΙΟΘΡΕΨΑΣΗΜΩΝΜΑΥΡΑΙ
         ΘΟΠΟΥΣΟΠΡΥΤΑΝΙΣΕΥΤΥΧΩ
5        ΑΡΞΑΜΕΝΟΣΕΤΕΛΕΙΩΣΕΤΑΜΥ
         ΣΤΗΡΙΑΣΥΝΚΑΙΤΗΣΥΜΒΙΩ
         ΑΥΤΟΥΜΑΙΑΝΗΡΗΙΔΙΚΑΙΤΟΙΣ
         ΤΕΚΝΟΙΣΚΑΙΕΚΓΟΝΟΙΣΚΑΙΤΗΣ
(unin-scribed)ΕΥΣΕΒΟΥΣΥΠΗΡΕΣΙΑΣ
```

. . . . [Ἀρτέμιδι]
ἐπηκόῳ καὶ [τοῖς Σεβαστοῖς?]
καὶ τῇ τύχῃ τῆς πόλ[εως, διότι ὁ θρέψας ἡμῶν Μ. Αὐρ. Ἀγα[α-
θόπους ὁ πρύτανις εὐτυχῶ[ς κατ-
ἀρξάμενος ἐτελείωσε τὰ μυστήρια σὺν καὶ τῇ συμβίῳ
αὐτοῦ Μαίᾳ Νηρηΐδι καὶ τοῖς
τέκνοις καὶ ἐγγόνοις καὶ τῆς
εὐσεβοῦς ὑπηρεσίας.

b.

```
              ∠
         ΙΡΥΤΑΝΕΥΣΑΣΛΝ
        ΗΚΑΙΔΙΕΔΕΞΑΙΟΤΗΝΠΡΥΤΑΝΕΙ
        ΑΝΠΑΡΑΤΟΥΕΑΥΤΗΣ · ΥΟΥ -
5       · Μ · ΚΟΙΛΙΟΥΣΕΚΟΥΝΔΟΥΛΟΛΛΙΑΝΟΥ
        ΤΗΝΑΝΑΣΤΑΣΙΝΠΟΙΗΣΑΜΕΝΟΥ
        ΚΟ · ΛΟΛΛΙΟΥΚΟΥΟΥΔΙΟΣΚΟΡΟΥ
        ΤΟΥΠΑΤΡΟΣΑΥΤΗΣ · ΠΡΩΤΟ
        ΚΟΥΡΗΤΟΣΚΑΙΓΡΑΜΜΑΤΕΩΣ
10          ΤΗΣΒΟΥΛΗΣ
```

. . . . τ
. . . . πρυτανεύσασαν
ἡ καὶ διεδέξατο τὴν πρυτανεί-
αν παρὰ τοῦ ἑαυτῆς υἱοῦ
Μ. Κοιλίου Σεκούνδου Λολλιανοῦ
τὴν ἀνάστασιν ποιησαμένου
Κο. Λολλίου, Κο. υἱοῦ, Διοσκόρου,
τοῦ πατρὸς αὐτῆς, πρωτο-
κουρῆτος καὶ γραμματέως
τῆς βουλῆς.

The connexion between the two inscriptions contained upon the marble is not obvious: *a* is a dedication, and *b* is an honorary inscription commemorating a lady whose name is lost. The lettering of both is so very similar, that we may probably assign both inscriptions to the same date and suppose them to be connected with one and the same family. The title πρωτοκουρής in *b* and the mention of τὰ μυστήρια in *a* supply a link between the two documents which will be explained below.

a. The dedication was made by two or more persons who were the θρέμματα or alumni (ὁ θρέψας ἡμῶν, line 3; see Waddington-Le Bas iii. No. 21) of M. Aurel. Agathopous, already known to us from No. dlxxxvii. There he was described as γραμματεύς of the Gerousia and also gymnasiarch. Here he appears as prytanis of Ephesos, concerning which office see Prolegomena. pp. 72, 82. As prytanis he had successfully celebrated 'the mysteries' (line 5), which are therefore not to be identified with the Eleusinia spoken of in No. dxcv as celebrated by a private association or θίασος. The mysteries named in line 5 may be identified with the festival

solemnised by the Kuretes, and described by Strabo, xiv, p. 640: see on Nos. cccxlix and cccclxxxiii, and compare Prolegomena, p. 80. But although this festival was a national one there was probably a difficulty in obtaining public funds to defray its cost. If it be the same festival, it was revived in the reign of Commodus by help of a grant from the Gerousia (No. cccclxxxiii); and later on it was maintained, at least in part, by private munificence. Thus C. I. 3002 (from Ephesos) is in honour of a certain Οὐλπίαν Εὐοδίαν Μουδιανήν, τὴν ἱέρειαν τῆς Ἀρτέμιδος, θυγατέρα Μουδιανοῦ καὶ Εὐοδίας κ.τ.λ., who is described as ἐκτελέσασαν τὰ μυστήρια καὶ πάντα τὰ ἀναλώματα ποιήσασαν διὰ τῶν γονέων. And in our dedication it is implied that Agathopous and his family had borne the cost of the solemnity. In lines 8-9 the writer goes on with the genitive as if μετά and not σύν had been employed. The ὑπηρεταί referred to in line 9 may be the subordinate officials in attendance on the prytanis. I have supposed the imperial family to be united with Artemis in this dedication (lines 1, 2), just as in No. diii and dxiii. The epithet ἐπηκόῳ was frequently employed in votive dedications to various deitics in many parts of the Hellenic world : see C. I. 2290, 2300, 3542, 4500, 4502, 4503, 5933, 5941, 6005. Addenda 4838 *a* 2, 4838 *a* 4; compare 6004. Similarly εἰακίῳ, C. I. 2172, 2173, 2566. None of these examples are from Ephesos, but an Ephesian inscription copied by Cyriacus of Ancona (Bulletin de Corr. Hell. i. p. 293) runs as follows : Ἀρτέμιδι ἐπηκόῳ Καπετωλεῖνος Διοδώρου τοῦ Ἀπολλωνίου Ἐφέσιος, σὺν Μόσχῳ τῷ ἰδίῳ υἱῷ τὴν Νείκην ⟨τὴν⟩ τῷ Πανθείῳ ἀνέθηκεν , γραμματεύοντος Τι. Κλ. Λουκιανοῦ.

b is erected in honour of his daughter by Q. Lollius Dioscorus, on the occasion of her having acted as prytanis in succession to her son. The opening lines may have run thus : [Ἡ βουλὴ καὶ ὁ δῆμος ἐτείμησαν τὴν δεῖνα ἀγνῶ]ς [καὶ δικαίως] πρυτανεύσασαν κ.τ.λ. 'Prytanis mulier res est satis insolens' writes Böckh on C. I. 3415 (Phokaea): ἀρχιέρειαν Ἀσίας ναοῦ τοῦ ἐν Ἐφέσῳ, πρύτανιν, στεφανηφόρον δίς, καὶ ἱέρειαν τῆς Μασσαλίας κ.τ.λ. But the same thing occurs again in C. I. 3953 *d* (from Phrygia) : [τὴν δεῖνα] πρύτανιν καὶ σ[τεφαν]ηφόρον κ.τ.λ. ; and in an inscription from Thira in Lydia (see Mittheilungen d. deutsch. arch. Inst. in Athen. iii, p. 57) : ἐπὶ πρυτάνεως Ἀπολλησίας Φαυστείνης τοῦ ἑξῆς ἔτους (she had served two years in succession). The office of prytanis at Ephesos has been referred to above on *a* ; it had doubtless lost by this time its former political importance, and was more like a priesthood than a magistracy; it was, no doubt, an office which involved considerable munificence (see on *a*). There was therefore no reason why it should not be held by a woman. Boissier (La Religion Romaine, ii, p. 227) remarks that under the Empire a position was taken by women in public life which had not been allowed them before. He adds : ' sous l'empire romain les femmes s'approchaient plus de la vie publique qu'il ne leur est permis de le faire aujourd'hui ... Elles paraissent même, dans certaines pays, y avoir tout à fait participé.' He then quotes C. I. L. ii, Nos. 3712–3713 (from the Balearic Isles) where a woman is described as insulæ magisteriis et honoribus omnibus functa; and C. I. L. viii, 9407 (from Mauretania Cæsariensis) where a woman is spoken of as duumvira. This last, however, Wilmanns would explain by comparing ὑπατική, or mulier consularis (*ibid.* 8993), and takes it to mean merely ' of duumviral rank.' In the provincial towns of the empire it was not strange if offices which had become more and more purely ceremonial, and involved few duties beyond munificence, should be held by women of wealth. The father Dioscorus is described as πρωτοκουρής, or head of the College of Kuretes (lines 8-9; and see Prolegomena, p. 85 *ante*). If then the mysteries alluded to in *a* are those celebrated by the Kuretes, we can the better understand that the persons spoken of in *a* and *b* belonged to the same family. As to the secretary of the boulè (line 9) see Prolegomena, p. 81.

DXCVII.

A fragment of white marble veneering (crusta), 1½ in. thick ; broken all round. Height 3¾ in. ; width 4½ in. Found by Mr. Wood at the western corner of the Temple-site ; unpublished.

	[ὁ δεῖνα] . .
ΙΑΜΥΣΤ	ἐτελείωσα] τὰ μυστ[ήρια σὺν
ϲΥΝΒΙΩΜϹ	καὶ τῇ] συνβίῳ μο[υ . . . . . καὶ
ΙΩΜΟΥ · ΑΥΡ	τῷ υ]ἱῷ μου Αὐρ[ηλίῳ . . . .
ΠΟ	. . . . . πο . . . . .

These mysteries may be identified with the celebration spoken of in No. DXCVI *a ante*.

DXCVIII.

Fragment of a white marble stelè, entire only on the right. Height 1 ft. 1½ in.; width 10 in. Discovered by Mr. Wood ; but unpublished.

ΤΟΣ_	. . . τοσ . . .
ΣΤΩΣΟΙ ϲ	. . προσ]στὼς ὀρθ[ῶς ?
ϲΕΥΣΕΒΩΣ · ΚΑ	. . . εὐσεβῶς κα[ὶ . .
ΑΝΤΑ · ΤΗΡΗΣʌ	. . π]άντα τηρήσα[ς
ΜΗΤΑΣΕΜΑΣΗΜ	. . μὴ τὰς ἐμὰς ἡμ-
ΟΛΟΙΠΟΙΣΜΟΥ ·	έρας ? . . σὺν τοῖς ὑπ]ολοίποις μου
ΔΗΜΟΚΡΑΤΕΙΗ · Κ	τέκνοις ? . . . . .] Δημοκρατείη κ[αὶ
ΛΙΝΟΝΤΑΣ · ΔΙΕ̄	. . . . αινοντας διετ . .
(uninscribed)	. . . . .

Apparently a votive dedication from an Ephesian citizen who had filled some office (lines 2-4) with credit. Perhaps by τὰς ἐμὰς ἡμ[έρας is implied that he did not serve the full term of office, but was only a 'suffectus' for a short time (line 5); compare Nos. DLXXXII *b*, and DLXXXVIII *b*. In lines 6-7 he associates his family, as usual, with himself in the dedication. He may have been a neopoios.

DXCIX.

Block of white marble, height 10 in.; width 1 ft. 4½ in. Apparently entire. Discovered by Mr. Wood: unpublished.

ΑΓΑΘΗΤΥΧΗ	'Αγαθῇ τύχῃ·
ΚΛΑΥΔΙΟΣ	Κλαύδιος
ΒΑΣΣΟΣ	Βάσσος
ΓΕΡΟΥΣΙΑΣΤΗΣ	γερουσιαστής.

Dedication by a member of the gerousia, on which see Prolegomena, pp. 74 foll.

DC.

A number of fragments of white marble crustæ or veneering, varying from ½ in. to 1⅛ in. thick. Their height and width are as follows: *a*, *b* 1 ft. by 9 in.; *c*, 1 ft. 6 in. by 6 in.; *d*, 8½ in. by 6 in.; *e*, 3 in. by 3½ in.; *f*, 1 ft. 3 in. by 1 ft. 1 in.; *g*, 6 in. by 6 in. Found upon the site of the Great Theatre by Mr. Wood; see his Ephesus, p. 72. Unpublished.

(Lines 1–12 are inscribed in rather larger letters than the rest: the left-hand edge of the marble is broken.)

a.	
ΧΗ ·	'Αγαθῇ τύ]χῃ·
ΟΡΟΣ · ΘΕΟΥ · ΔΙΟΝΥΣΟ	Τὰ ἱερὰ τοῦ παντοκράτ]ορος θεοῦ Διονύσο[υ
ΗΝΙΟΥ · ΚΑΙ · ΗΦΑΙΣΤΟΥ	καὶ Διὸς Πανελλ]ηνίου καὶ 'Ηφαίστου,
ΟΥ · ΦΙΛΟΣΕΒ · ΠΡΥΤΑΝΕ	ἱερατεύοντος? . . . .]ου φιλοσεβ., πρυτάνε[ως
ΥΔΗΜΟΥ · ΚΑΙ · ΥΜΝΩ ·	καὶ γραμματέως το]ῦ δήμου καὶ ὑμνω(δοῦ)
ΑΙ · ΑΡΧΙΤΕΚΤΟΝΟΣ · ΤΗΣ	. . . . κ]αὶ ἀρχιτέκτονος τῆς
ΡΑΜΜΕΝΟΙ · ΥΠΟ · Φ ·	θεοῦ, ἐτέλεσαν οἱ γε]γραμμένοι ὑπὸ
b.	
ΚΑΙΑΓΝΕΑΡΧΟΥ ·	. . . . καὶ 'Αγνεάρχου
ΕΣΙΩ ΟΛΕΩΣ · ΕΠΙ · ΠΡΥ	. . . . τῆς 'Εφ]εσίων [π]όλεως, ἐπὶ πρυ-
ΕΞΑ Ϲ · ΦΙΛΟΣΕΒ · ΕΠΙ	τάνεως . . . . 'Αλ]εξά[νδρο]υ φιλοσεβ., ἐπι-
Ν · ΜΥΣΤΗ ΥΡ ·	μεληθέντων τῶ]ν μυστη[ρίων . . . . Α]ὐρ.
Υ · ΙΟΥΛ · ΦΑΥ ΙΛΟΣΕΒ	. . . . . καὶ . . . ο]υ 'Ιουλ. Φαύ[στου, φ]ιλοσεβ.
(uninscribed)	*(How much is lost here is uncertain.)*
c.	
Ο	. . . . ο . . . . . .
· ΡΟΥ	. . . . 'Ρού[φος?
ΣΑ · ΠΑΥΛ	Βα]σσα(ρίδος?) Παυλ . . . . .
ΝΩΝ · ΑΘΗΝ	Φω]νῶν? 'Αθην . . . .
ΙΟΣΦ · ΑΡΤΕΜΕΙΣ	. . ιοσφ(. . . .) 'Αρτεμείσ[ιος
ΘΗΝΑ · ΣΩΤΕΙ · ΕΡΜΟ	'Α]θηνᾶ(ς) Σωτεί(ρας) 'Ερμο[γένης?
ΜΟΝΟΙ · ΠΡΕΙΜΙΓΕ	'Ο]μονοί(ας) Πρειμιγέ[νης
ΡΟΜ · ΑΣΚΛΗΠΙΑ	Β]ρομ(ίου) 'Ασκληπιά[δης
ΕΛΑΡ · ΕΥΤΥΧΗΣ ·	Π]ελαρ(γῆς?) Εὐτύχης . . .
ΕΟΥ · ΚΡΑ · ΖΗΝΩΝ · Τ	Θ]εοῦ κρα(τίστου?) Ζήνων Τ . . .
ΧΕΛΩ · ΕΥΠΕΤΙΣ	'Α]χελῴ(ου) Εὐπετισ . . .
ΥΝΚΛ · ΑΣΚΛΗΠ	Σ]υνκλ(ήτου) 'Ασκληπ[ιάδης
ΠΟΝ · ΜΕΣΣΑΛ	Σ]πον(δοφόρος?) Μεσσάλ[ας
ΚΟΥΡΗ · ΕΥΤΥΧ	Κουρή(των) Εὐτύχ[ης
ΝΥΝΦ · ΠΡΕ · ΑΛΕΞ	Νυνφ(ῶν) πρε(σβυτέρων) 'Αλεξ[έας?
ΕΙΑ · ΜΕΝΑ	Μν]εία(ς) Μένα[νδρος
ΘΗΣ · ΑΛΕΞ	Λή]θης 'Αλεξ . . . . .
ΙΟΣ · ΖΩΣΙΜ	'Ισ?]ιος Ζώσιμ[ος
ΗΛΙΟΥ · ΠΟΣΙΔΩ	'Ηλίου Ποσιδώ[νιος
ΑΡΠΩ · ΖΩΣΑΣ ·	Κ]αρπῶ(ν?) Ζωσᾶς . . . .
ΕΡΟΦΑΝ · ΠΑΤΡΟΚΛ	'Ι]εροφάν(της) Πατροκλ[ῆς?
ΚΟΡΥΝ · ΤΕΙΜΟΘΑ	Κορύν(βου) Τειμοθα . . .
ΑΚΧ · ΕΥΤΥΧΗΣ	Βάκχ(ης?) Εὐτύχης
ΝΦ · ΝΕ · ΕΥΤΥΧΗΣ	Ν]υνφ(ῶν) νε(ωτέρων) Εὐτύχης
ΟΥ · ΑΠΕΛΛΑΣ	. . . ου 'Απελλᾶς
Τ · ΕΡΜΟΓ	. . . . . τ(ου) 'Ερμογ[ένης
· Κ	. . . . κ . . . . . .
	(Lacuna)

Left inscription column (facsimile):

```
40            .. |
          ΚΛΩΔΙΑ
          ΕΥΟΔΟΣ ·
          ΑΛΕΞΑΝΔ
          ΑΥΞΙΒΙΣ
45   ΕΥΑ Ν · ΑΝΤΙΟΧ
     ΝΕΟΥΔΙΟΝ·ΘΡΕΠΤ
     ΚΟΡΗΣ · ΠΕΡΙΓΕΝ
     ΠΑΝΩΝ · ΤΥΡΑΝΝ
     ΑΣΚΛΗ ·
50   Φ·ι·                         f.
     (lacuna)              (uninscribed)
                           ΟΠΟΥΣ ·
              c'.
     ΔΙΣ · ΑΝ
     ΡΧΟΣ ·ΙΕΡ(            (uninscribed)
55   ΟΥ · ΠΑΤΡΟΙ
                           ΩΝ ·
                           ΝΟΣ ·
                           (uninscribed)
60   d'.          Σ.
     ....ε       Σ · ΕΠΛΦ  ΔΕΙΤΟΣ ·
     ΙΕΑ · ·     ΙΝΟΣ · ΟΝ ;ΙΜΟΣ · ΜΑΡΚΕΛΛΟΣ
     ΝΗΜΗ · ΜΑ   ΦΑΥΣ ΟΣ ·
                 (apparently the end)
```

Right inscription column (with restorations):

```
40   . . . . . . Κλ]ω[δ]ι[ανός ?
     . . . . . . . Κλωδια[νός
     . . . . . . Εὔοδος
     . . . . . . . Ἀλέξανδ[ρος
     . . . . . . . Αὐξίβις
45   Εὐά[δ]ν(ης)? Ἀντίοχ[ος
     Νίου Διον(ύσου) Θρέπτ[ος?
     Κόρης Περίγεν[ης
     Πανῶν Τύρανν[ος
     Ἀσκλη(πιοῦ) . . . .
50   Φιλ[ίας?] . . . . .
     (lacuna)              . . . . Ἀγαθ?]όπους
     . . . . . . . . . . . . .
     . . . . δις Ἀν . . . .
     . . . ρχος Ἱερο . . .
55   . . . . . ος Πάτρο[βις ?
     (lacuna)
     . . . . . . . . . . . . . . ων
     . . . . . . . . . . . . . . νος
     . . . . . . . . . . . . . .
60   . . . . . . . . . . . . ς
     Ἡρα]κλε[οῦς ? . . . . . ς Ἐπαφ[ρό]δειτος
     Σ(ι]μίλ(ης?) Η . . . . ινος Ὀν[ήσ]ιμος Μάρκελλος
     Δ]ήμη(τρος) Μα . . . . Φαῦσ[τ]ος
```

In arranging and combining these fragments, regard has been had not only to the readings, but also to the indications given by the marble itself, its varying thickness, marks of the sawing of the slab, etc. In a, b and c there are traces of red paint in the letters. The heading (lines 1-12) is unfortunately mutilated; but enough remains to show that we have here a list of persons who in a certain year celebrated 'mysteries' in honour of 'Dionysos Zeus Panhellenios and Hephæstos.' The date, to judge from the characters, would be about the time of Hadrian: and it is obvious to conjecture that in the names Dionysos and Zeus Panhellenios we have an allusion to that Emperor who is well known to have been worshipped under both these titles. In that case possibly [αὐτοκράτ]ορος should be read in line 1. The other restorations in the heading are probable enough: the priest of Dionysos (if he is meant) had also held the offices of πρύτανις, γραμματεὺς τοῦ δήμου, ἱερωβός and others, for which the reader is referred to the Prolegomena, pp. 81, 82, 87. For the ἐπιμελητὴς τῶν μυστηρίων of lines 10-11 compare No. DXCV.

The most interesting feature of the inscription is the appended list of the men who had taken part in the celebration. Many of the names are more Latin than Greek, as is common with Ephesian documents of this date. Each name is set down opposite to the name of a deity or deities in the genitive case. Although these names are often abbreviated, they can in most cases be recognised: but the gods and divine personages seem to be catalogued without attempt at any order, and form a strange assemblage. In line 16 the letter before ΝΩΝ was probably Ω: [Φ]ωνῶν perhaps would not be stranger than [Κ]αρπῶ(ν) in line 32. Line 20: Βρόμ(ιος), usually an epithet of

Dionysos himself, seems here to signify one of his attendants. Line 21: Π]ελαρ(γή) is suggested by Pausanias ix, 25, 7 foll. On a vase in the B. M. (Catal. No. 1429) ΠΕΛΑΡ is written over a head in a Phrygian cap. Line 22: it is difficult to identify [Θ]εὸς κρά(τιστος), nor are the Νυμφαὶ πρεσβύτεραι and νεώτεραι (lines 27, 36) otherwise known. In line 24 we recognise the Roman Senate, which prepares us to see in νέον Διονύσου (line 46) the Emperor Hadrian. In lines 25, 33, we have the titles of sacred ministers instead of the names of deities. On the Κουρῆτες see Prolegomena, p. 85 and No. CCCXLIX ante. Line 34: Κόρυμβος must be the name of an attendant Bacchanal. This list of names reminds us of the story told by Plutarch of the way in which Mark Antony was received at Ephesos: (Anton. 24) εἰς γοῦν Ἔφεσον εἰσιόντος αὐτοῦ γυναῖκες μὲν εἰς Βάκχας, ἄνδρες δὲ καὶ παῖδες εἰς Σατύρους καὶ Πᾶνας ἡγοῦντο διεσκευασμένοι, κιττοῦ δὲ καὶ θύρσων καὶ ψαλτηρίων καὶ συρίγγων καὶ αὐλῶν ἡ πόλις ἦν πλέα, Διόνυσον αὐτὸν ἀνακαλουμένων χαριδότην καὶ μειλίχιον. We may interpret this as a record of a festival and procession in honour of Hadrian, worshipped as the 'Young Dionysos,' in which the deities mentioned were represented (as in a masque) by the persons herein named. See the passage from Herodian, i, 10, § 12 (quoted by Marquardt, Röm. Alt. vi, p. 359, respecting a pompa of the Mater Deum) which ends thus: ἕκαστός τε ὃ βούλεται σχῆμα ὑποκρίνεται. Compare also the famous pompa of Ptolemy II, described by Athenæos, 196 A, 217, and the pompa of Antiochos Epiphanes (ibid. 194 C); also C. I. 2052 (from Apollonia on the Euxine), is, like the present document, a list of Dionysiac worshippers.

DCI.

A number of fragments of mottled marble crustæ, about ⅜ in. thick. The larger portions have been pieced together out of smaller fragments, the remainder cannot be joined. Found on the site of the Great Theatre by Mr. Wood ; see his Ephesus, p. 72. Unpublished.

a.

Marble entire only at top and upper part of right : height 8 in. ; width 10 in.

ΕΟΥΣ ꞈΟΙΔΕ	Ἔ(θ)υσ[αν] οἵδε·
Ꮙ · ΑΝΤΩΝ ꓳΣΔΡΟΣΟΣϹ	Μ. Ἀντάν[ι]ος Δρόσος ὁ [καὶ
ΣΕΚΟΥΝΔꓵΙΝΟ ꓲΕΡϤ	Σεκουνδεῖνο[ς] ἱερε[ύς·
5 Ꮙ · ΛΟΚΚΗΙΟΣΠΑΥΛΟ	5 Μ. Λοκκήιος Παῦλο[ς
Ꮙ · ΑΝΤΩΝΙΟΣΑΡΤΕꓓ	Μ. Ἀντώνιος Ἀρτεμ[ίδωρος ?
ΝΤΗΝꓦΡΕΝΘΡΟΝΙΟ	Ἀ]ντήνωρ ἐνθρόνιο[ς
ꓦΕΙΝΟϹΥ·ΔΕꙆ	Μ. Ἀντω]νεῖνος υ(ἱὸς ?) Δελ . . . .
ꓲΑΤΟΣΙΕΡΟ	. . . . ιατος ἱερο[λόγος
10 ꓴΟΥΠΡ	10 . . . . φου πρ . . . .

b.

Marble entire only on left ; height 5 in. ; width 7 in.

ΕΟΥΣΑΝ	Ἔθυσαν [οἵδε·
ΑΝΤΩΝΙΟΣΔΡϹ	Ἀντώνιος Δρό[σος
ΞΕΝΟΚΡΑΤΗϤ	Ξενοκράτης
5 ΑΚΥΛΙΟΣΑΓꓥ	5 Ἀκύλιος Ἀγα[θ . . . .
ΑΤΤΑΛϹ	Ἄτταλο[ς
ΦΙΑ	. . . . φιλ[ος

c.

Marble entire at left and at top ; height 7 in. ; width 5 in.

ΦΙꓥΕΡΩΤΙꓲ	. . . . Φιλερωτια[νὸς ?
ꓥΙΣΣΑΙΕ	. . . λισσα ἱε[ρολόγος ?
ꓲΡΟΣΔΕΚ: Σ	. . ρος Δεκ. Σ . . . .
ΣΙΕΡΟΛΟΓꓯ	. . . ς ἱερολόγο[ς
5 ꞈΠΡΟΚΛΗ	5 . . . Προκλῆ[ς
ꓶΝΟΣ	μηνὸς . . . .]ῶνος·
ΔΕ	Ἔθυσαν οἵ]δε·
ΥΦΡΟΝΟΣ	. . . . Ε]ὐφρονος·
ΝΟΣ	. . . . νος
10 ꓳϤ	10 . . . . ος

d.

Marble broken, except on left ; measures 11 in. by 5½ in.

ꞈ	
ΡΟΥꓦ	. . ρου Μ . . .
ΕΟΥΣ꞉	Ἔθυσα[ν οἵδε·
ΕΡΩΝ	Ν]ἐρων ?
5 ΣΚΑΥΡ	5 Σκαῦρ[ος
ΑΝΤ	Ἀντ . . . .
ΗꓽΗΣΑ	Ἡγήσα[νδρος
ΠΕΣΤΟ	Πε(ί)στο[ς ?
ΔΡΟΣΙΑΝΟ	Δροσιανὸ[ς
10 ΚΑΙΤΑΕΣΕ	10 καὶ τὰ ἐξ ἔ[θους
ꓲΝΟΣΝΕΟΚ	Μ?]ηνὸς Νεοκ[αισαρεῶνος·]
ΕΟΥΣΑΝ	Ἔθυσαν [οἵδε·
ΒΑΣΣΟΣΓꓥ	Βάσσος Γλ . . .
ΜΑΡΕΙΝΙΑΝΟΣ	Μαρινιανὸς
15 Γ · ΑΝΘΙΣ ΤΙϹ	15 Γ. Ἀνθίστιο[ς
ΚΕΣΤΙΟΣ Β ꓰ	Κέστιος Βε . . .
Γ · ΑΡΡΙΟΣ Ᶎ	Γ. Ἄρριος Σ . . .

e.

Marble broken all round: height 5½ in.; width 4½ in.

ΛΙΑΣΛΥΔ	. . . λιας Λυδ . . .
Σ · ΓΙ · ΕΟΥΣΙ	. . . . ς Γι. Ἔθυσ[αν οἴδε·
ΣΟΣΟΚΑΘΙ	Δρό]σος? ὁ καθι[ερωκὼς
ΡΣΟΦΟΡΟΣ	θυ]ρσοφόρος
5 ΜΚΟΜΑ	5 Μελα?]μκομα
⊃Υ	. . . . ου
ΞΡΩΚΩ⁺	ὁ καθι]ερωκὼς
Υ	. . . . . ο]υ

f.

Marble broken all round: height 3½ in.; width 2½ in.

∧	
ΙΟΣΕ	. . . . ιος Ε . . .
ΤΙΛΙΟ	. . . τιλιο[ς
ΛΕΞΕ	καὶ τ]ὰ ἐξ ἔ[θους
5 ΠΟΓ	5 . . . Ποσ[ειδ . ?

g.

Marble broken all round: height 6 in.; width 5½ in.

ıı ıı	
ΙΕΡΟΛΟΓⵏ	. . . . ἱερολόγο[ς
ΝΑΟΥ	. . . . . ναου
ΝΕΩΣΣΤΕΡˑ	Ἐπὶ πρυτά]νεως Στερ[τινίου
5 ΙΣⲣ ΟΝΟ	5 . . . . . . σα . . ονο . . . .
ΔΡΟ	. . . . Δρό[σος?
ΣΕΒ	. . . φιλο?]σέβ[αστος
ΗΤ	. . . . . ητ . . . .

h.

Marble broken all round: height 7 in.; width 4 in.

ıΝΟΣΙΕΡ	. . . . νος ἱερ[ολόγος
(uninscribed)	
ΜΑΚΤΗΡ	Μηνὸς Μαι]μακτηρ[ιῶνος·
Ε	Ἔθυσαν οἴδ]ε·
ΣΟΚΑΘıı	. . . . ς ὁ καθι[ερωκὼς
(uninscribed)	(uninscribed)
5 ⁼Υ	5 . . . . Εὐ . . . .

i.

Marble broken at top and right: height 3½ in.; width 3½ in.

ΟΡ	. . . . . ορ . . . .
ˌΚΩΣ	ὁ καθιερω]κὼς
⅃ΡΟΚΛΗ	. . . . . Προκλῆ[ς
ιΙΩΝΟΣ	Μηνὸς Ληνα]ιῶνος or [Θαργηλ]ιῶνος·
5 ΟιΛϜ	5 Ἔθυσαν] οἴδε·

k.

Marble broken all round: height 2½ in.; width 2½ in.

ıΡΟΚΛ	. . . . . Π]ροκλ[ῆς
ΝΟΣ	Μηνὸς . . . .]νος·
⁻	[Ἔθυσαν οἴδε ?]

---

l.

Marble broken all round : height 5 in. ; width 6 in.

ΛΛΙΑΝΟ⸦	. . . λλιανὸς
ΗΡΑΤΙΑΝΟΣ	. . . . ηρατιανὸς
ᴾΟϒΦ ΟΣ	. . . . 'Ρ]οῦφος
ΟΣ ΝΕ	. . . . ος νε(ώτερος?
5 ΝΙΟΣΑΣΙΑΤΙΚϹ	5 . . . . ριος 'Ασιατικὸ[ς
ΟΣ	. . . . ος
⸦Μ	. . . λη . . .

m.

Marble entire only at the lower edge : extreme height 14 in. ; extreme width 10 in.

⌣ ΓΡΙΠΠΕΙ	. . . . . 'Α]γριππεί[νος
⸦Ν Ο	. . . . ν ο
ΚΡΙΤΩΝ	. . . . Κρίτων
5 ΩΣΑΣ ΑΓΡΙΠΠ	5 Ζ]ωσᾶς 'Αγριππ[είνου?
ϒΕΝΔΟΣ· ΔΙΟΝϒ	. . . Ο]ύενδος? Διονυ[σίου
ΛΝΤΩΝΙΟΣΔΡ⸦˙	. . . Μ.] 'Αντώνιος Δροῦ[σος
ΚΟΣΣΙΝΝΙΟϹ	. . . . Κοσσίννιος
ϒΤΩΝΙΟΣΔΡΟϹ	. . . 'Α]ντώνιος Δρόσ[ος
10 ΑΣ – ΙΕΡΩ	10 . . . . . ας — 'Ιερω . . .
ΤΛΕΣΕϹ	καὶ τὰ ἐξ ἔθ[ους
ΓΑΝΕΩ⸦	'Επὶ πρυ]τάνεως . . . .
ΚΑΙΣΑΡΕΩ⸦ J⸦	μηνὸς Νεο]καισαρεώνος?
ΟΣ ΒΑΣΣΟΣ	. . . . ος Βάσσος
15 ΛΣΣοϒ	15 . . . Β]άσσου
ΒΑΣΣοϒ	. . . . . . Βάσσου
ΣΜΑΡΚ ⸢ΛΛΟΣ	. . . . ς Μάρκ[ε]λλος
⸦ΛΙΧΡ	. . . Μ]ελιχρ . . . .
ΑΝΤ J⸦	. . . . 'Αντ[ώνι ?]ος
20 ⸨⸩⸦ΟⱵ ΙΕΡΩ	20 . . . . ὁ καθ]ιερω[κὼς

n.

Marble broken except at top : height 4 in. ; width 3 in.

ΔΡΟΣΟᵔ	Δρόσος
ᴾΚΕΛΛ	Μά]ρκελλ[ος
ΙΑΝ	. . . ιαν[ὸς
JΔ˙⸦	. . . . οθ . . .
5 Ⱶ⸦	5 . . . . πι . . . .

o.

Marble broken all round : height 4 in. ; width 5½ in.

ΣΟΣΟ⸦	. . . Δρό]σος ὁ κ[αὶ or κ[αθιερωκὼς
ΕΙΣΑΣ	. . . . ειςᾶς
ΙΟΣΕΠΑΓΑϹ	. . . ος 'Επαγαθ[ός
ΦΙΡΜΟΣ	. . . Φίρμος
5 ᴾΗ	5 . . ρη . .

p.	*q.*	*r.*
Marble broken all round : height 2½ in. ; width 3 in.	Marble broken all round : height 3 in. ; width 4 in.	Marble broken all round : height 4 in. ; width 3½ in.
⸦ΛΝΛⱵ	J⸦	ΚΟΣ
⸦ ᴾΟΛΟΓ	JΤΟ	ΟΓΟΣ
Οϒ	Ⱶ⸦⸨	Λ⸦ΛΗΡΛ
⸦		

2 M

s.	*t.*	*u.*
Marble broken all round: height 4¼ in.; width 4 in.	Marble broken all round: height 3 in.; width 2½ in.	Marble broken all round: height 1¾ in.; width 1½ in.

s.

E
Σ
(uninscribed)

Λ

t.

ΛΟΣ
ΓΣΠΡϹ
_ΝΟ
Ω˙

u.

'
ΤΟ
ΝΟ
-

v.	*w.*	*x.*
Marble broken all round: height 5 in.; width 3 in.	Marble broken all round: height 3 in.; width 3½ in.	Marble entire only at bottom: height 2¾ in.; width 3 in.

v.

_Ρ
ΙΟΣ
ΓΗΣ·
ΠΟΣΚΑ
ΨΤΟΚΙ
-ϹΥΤ

w.

(uninscribed)

ΒΙΛΛ

Σ

x.

Ω
Σ
ΝΕ (uninscribed)

y.	*z.*
Marble broken all round: height 2 in.; width 1⅛ in.	Marble broken all round: height 2 in.; width 1 in.

y.

ΗϜ
ΔΕ
ιιι

z.

Ϲ
Λ˙

p, q, r may be severally read [ἱε]ρολόγ[οσ : [ἱερολ]ό-γο[σ] : [ἱερολ]όγοσ. The remaining fragments yield nothing intelligible.

We have here the remains of a list of persons who had offered certain sacrifices; probably they formed a Dionysiac θίασοσ. Several curious titles of sacred offices occur: ἐνθρόνιοσ in *a* may be a proper name, but is more likely a sacred title. 'Ιερο-λόγοσ may be compared with θεολόγοσ, which is discussed on No. cccclxxxi, line 191. In *e* ὁ [καθι]-ερωκώσ is a title occurring also in the similar list No. dcii *q*; it is mentioned repeatedly here, see *h, m.* Did the person so styled supply the sacrificial

victim? It is clear from *h* (compare *c, d, f, i, k*) that the sacrifices followed month by month. If therefore the document were in a better state, it would supply us with a completer calendar than has been provisionally drawn up in the Prolegomena, p. 79. By comparing together *d* and *m* I have recovered the name of the month Νεοκαισαρεών. A month so named occurs in two inscriptions from Thira (the ancient Τείρα, in Lydia) apparently of the Antonine age (Mittheil. d. arch. Inst. Athen, iii, 1878, p. 57). I cannot more nearly define the ceremonies referred to as τὰ ἐξ ἔθουϲ in *d, f, m.* The phrase is like the Virgilian de more or ex more. Aen. iii, 369, viii, 186, etc.

DCII.

A number of fragments of white marble crustæ from ⅜ in. to 1 in. thick; the larger portions have been pieced together out of smaller fragments, the remainder cannot be joined. Discovered by Mr. Wood on the site of the Great Theatre: see his Ephesus, p. 72. Unpublished.

a.

Marble broken at left and bottom: height 6½ in.; width 4½ in. The heading of a list of names, such as will follow below.

ΘΥΣΑΝ Κ
ΣΚΛΗΠΙΑΔϜ
ΨΛΗΠΙΛΛ
ΑΤΟΣΦϹ
5 ΕΡΙΟΣ
ϹΡΝΙ

῾Ε]θυσαν κ . . .
Ἀ]σκληπιάδη-
ϲ Ἀσ]κληπι(ά)δ[ου
. . ατοϲ Φο . .
. . εριοϲ . .
Κ]αρν[ήλιοϲ?

b.

Marble broken at bottom, on right, and perhaps on left; height 5 in.; width 4⅞ in. The heading of another similar list.

ΕΘΥΣΑΝ	῎Εθυσαν [οἵδε
ΕΠΙΛΗ	ἐπιλή[νια?
ΥΤΥΧΗ	Ε]ὐτύχη[ς . .
ΟΥΛΙϜ	Ἰ]οῦλις . .
5 ϽΑΥ	5 Φ?]αὖ[στος? . .

c.

Marble entire on left only; height 1 ft. 2 in.; width 5½ in.

ΝΕΚ	νεκ	
Ϲ	ο	
ΗΣ ΠΟ·Λ	. ης. Πο. Λ	
ΑΙΣΧΡΙL	Αἰσχρίω[ν	
5 ΕΠΑΦΡΟΔΕ	Ἐπαφρόδε[ιτος	5
Υ. ΑΠΕΛΛΑΣΒ	. . ν. Ἀπελλᾶς β̄	
ΕΛΕϜΟΣΑΓ	῞Ελενος Α . .	
ΜΚ ϽΙΟΣ	Μ. Κ[άλ]βιος	
ΜΚ ϹΑΒΙΟΣ	Μ. Κ[α]λβιος	
10 ΠΟΑΙΛΙΟΣ	Πο. Αἴλιος	10
Κ·ΚΑΣΚΕΛϹ	Κ. Κασκίλλ[ιος	
Κ·ΒΗΔΙΟΣΙ	Κ. Βήδιος . .	
Τ·ΦΛ·ΠΟΛϹ	Τ. Φλ. Πολυ[βιανὸς?	
Τ·ΦΛ·ΕΥ	Τ. Φλ. Εὐ	
15 Μ·ΚΟΚ·ΤΥΕ	Μ. Κοκ. Τιβ[έρων?	15
ΔΗΜΗΤΡΙΟ	Δημήτριο[ς . .	
ϹΑΙΛΙΟϹ	Π]ο. Αἴλιος	

d.

Marble apparently entire on the sides; top and bottom broken; height 1 ft. 8 in.; width 5½ in.

ΓϢ	Πο.	
ΤΟΥΑΙΣϹ�	τοῦ Αἰσχ[ρίωνος	
ΕΛΛΑΤΟΥΑΙΣΧ	. . . ελλάτου, Αἰσχ[ρίων	
ΜΕΛΑΝΚΟΜΑΣ	Μελανκόμας	
5 ΣΤΡΑΤΩΝ	Στράτων	5
ΙΔΗΣ	. . . . ίδης	
ϹΛΙΑΝΟΣ	. . . . λλιανός	
ΟΣ		
ϽΣΓΕΡΑΙ	. . . . ος Γέραι-	
Ϲ	. . . . ς	
10 ϹϹΑϞ	. . . . αν	10
ΡΗΝΟΣ	. . ρηνος	
ΣΜΗΤΡΟΔΩΡΟΥ	. . ς Μητροδώρου	
ΡΤΕΜΙΔΩΡΟΣ	. . Ἀ]ρτεμίδωρος	
ϹΜΗΤΡΙΟΥ·	. . . Δ]ημητρίου	
15 ΑΜΑΒΕΛΙΣΜΥΣ	Ἀμάβελις Μύσ-	15
ΜΕΛΑΝΚΟΜΑΣϹ	του?]Μελανκόμας . .	
ΑΣΣΟΣΘΥΡΣΟΦ	Β]άσσος Θυρσοφ(ῶ)-	
ϹΟΣ	ρος	
ΗΣΑΙΣΧΡΙΩΝΟΣ	. . . ης Αἰσχρίωνος	
ΥΚΟΣ	. . υκος	
20 ϷΡΟΔΕΙΤΟΥ	Ἐπα]φροδείτου	20
ΤΟΥΑΠΟΛΛΩΝΙ	τοῦ Ἀπολλωνί-	
ΟΥ·ΒΟΥΚϽ	ου βουκόλος	
ϽΝΙΑΝΟΣ·	. . . . ωνιανὸς	
ΡΑΙΣ	καὶ ταῖς βασσά-	
ϹΑΙΤΑΙΣΒΑΣΣΑ		
25 ϹϽΛϽΡΟΥΒΟΥ	Ἐρ]μοδώρου βου(κόλος	25

e.

Marble entire only on left : height 10½ in. ; width 4½ in.

. I ./	I. Λ . . . . . .
. M . BEI ₁	M. Βειψ[άνιος ?
.Τ.ΙΟΥΛΙΟ∠	Τ. Ἰούλιος
.Λ.ΕΥΝΙΟΣΟ	Λ. Εὐνιος ὁ . . .
5 ΤΙΒ.ΚΛ.ΗΡϹ	5 Τιβ. Κλ. Ἡρο . . .
ΤΙΒ.ΚΛ.ΤΙ	Τιβ. Κλ. Τι. . .
ΙΤΙΒ.ΚΛ.ΤΕ	Τιβ. Κλ. Τε
Λ.ΕΥΝΙΟ	Λ. Εὐνιο[ς
ΤΙΒΚ⅄	Τιβ. Κλ. . .
(uninscribed)	

f.

Marble entire on either side ; broken at top and bottom : height 5½ in. ; width 5½ in.

ᴜ ι⅃⅃	. . . . ∞ . . . .
(uninscribed)	
ΥΤΟΥΧΡΥΣΑ	. . . υ τοῦ Χρυσα . . .
⊃ΥΣΕΛΕΥΚΟ⟩	τ]οῦ Σελεύκου
ΛΗΣ .	. . . ληϛ
ΛΗϟ ·	5 . . ληϛ . . .

g.

Marble broken at top and bottom : height 3½ in. ; width 4½ in.

ΟΣΤΗ	. . . οϛτη . . .
⋀ΡΤΕΜΙΔΩΡ	Ἀρτεμίδωρ[ος
Κ.ΑΘΗΝϹ ·	Κ. Ἀθηνό[δωρος

h.

Marble broken all round : height 5½ in. ; width 3 in.

ΟΣ.Ν	. . οϛ Ν . .
⊃ΣΠΡ	. . οϛ Πρ . .
ΙΝΙΛ/	. . . ινιλα . .
ΣΦΛΑΒΙ	. . . . ϛ Φλάβι[ος
5 ⊃Σ.ΦΛΑΣ	5 . . . οϛ Φλάβ[ιος
⋀ΠΟ,	. . . . . Ἀπολ[λόδωρος ?

i.

Marble broken, except on left : height 4½ in. ; width 5 in.

⋀ΟΣ⟩	Μόσχ[ος
ΔΙΟΝΥ	Διονύ[σιος
⌐.ΛΥΔΙΟΣ	. . ϛ Αὔδιος
⋀ΥΛ	Αὐλ[ος
⋀Γ	

Marble broken at top and bottom : height 4¼ in.; width 4½ in.

ΗΝΟΣ·Ϧ	Εὐ?]ηνος Β . . .
ϽΥΠΛΙΚΙΣ	Δο?]ύπλικις
· ΜΕΜΜ	. Μέμμ[ιος
ΛΕΞΑΝΔΙ	Ἀ]λέξανδ[ρος
5 ΥΗΝΟΣ·Ρ	5 Ε]ὐηνος Β . . .
ᴎ· ⊤	

l.

An illegible fragment.

m.

Marble broken at top and bottom : height 1 ft. 2½ in. ; width 4½ in.

ΝΚΑΙΤΟΙΣ	σὺ?]ν καὶ τοῖς
ΩΤΕΡΟΙ	νε]ωτέροι[ς
΄ΛΙΑΝΟΣ	Ἰο]υλιανὸς
ΛΑΝΙΚΟΤ	Ἑλ]λάνικος
5 ΣΡΗΓΛΟΣ	5 Σ. Ῥῆγλος
ΣΤΕΙΜΟΘΕ	Σ. Τειμόθε[ος
ΞΙΜΗΤΟΣ·Κᴬˢ	Τ]είμητος Κα . .
ΜΑΡΑΝΤϿᵤ	Ἀ]μαραντὸς
ΤΟΛΥΒΙΑΝ	Πολυβιαν[ὸς
10 ΙΑΠΑΡΟΥϥΜ·	10 . . ἀπάρου το(ῦ) Μη-
ϽΣ·Β·ϒΤΕΙΜ	. . . ος β΄ το(ῦ) Τειμ[ή-
ΘΥΡΣΟΦΟΡ	τον] θυρσοφόρ[ος
ΑΡΤΕΜΙΔϹ	. . Ἀρτέμιδο[ς . . . .
ΔΙΟΦΑΝΤ	. . . Διόφαντ[ος
13 ΩΡΟΣ	13 . . . . ωρος
ϽΣΑΝΝ΄	. . . ος Ἀννί[ος
Γ·ᴎᶜ	Γ. Νε . . . .

n.

Marble broken, except on left, and bottom of right: height 9 in.; width 4¾ in. This and the remaining fragments are inscribed in rather smaller letters.

ᴌϦ	. . . ς Β . . .
ΛΒΑΣΣᴌ	Λ. Βάσσο[ς
ΑΝΤΩΝ	Ἀντων . . . .
ϽΥΛΙΣᴌ	Ἰ]ούλις . . .
5 ΑΡΙΟ°	5 . αριο . . .
ΙΚΙΝ	Λ]ικίν[νιος?
ΝΗΛΙΣΡϹ	Κορ?]νήλις Ῥο . . .
(uninscribed)	

o.

Marble broken at top and bottom : height 5 in. : width 5 in.

ᴜΙΟ	. . . . ηιο . . .
ΥΓ·ΒΟΥΚΟΛ	. . υγ. βουκόλ[ος
ΤΥΡΟΥΘΥΙ	. . τυρου θυρ[σοφόρος?
ϽΟΥΦΕΙΝΟ	Ῥουφεῖνο[ς
ΣΓΥᴍ	5 . . ς γυμ . . .

Marble broken all round excep on left: height 7 in.; width 4 in.

ϽΙΚ	. . . . οικ . . .
ΛΒΙΣ	Κα]λβίσ[ιοε?
ΤΙΒ·ΚΛΙΕΙ	Τιβ. Κλ. ᾿Ιέ[ρων?
Λ·ΔΕΚΜΙΝ	Λ. Δεκμῖν[οε?
5 Τ · ΦΛ·ΜΓ	5 Τ. Φλ. Με . . . .
ΤΙΒ·ΚΛ·	Τιβ. Κλ.
Γ·ΑΤΓ	Γ. ᾿Ατέ[ριοε?
ΑΙ·Σ ι	Αἰ. Σ . . . . .
ΤΙ	Τι . . . .

Marble broken at top and bottom : height 1 ft. 10 in.; width 5 in.

ΙΙΕ	. . . . ε
ϽΣ	. . . . οε
ΧΟΣ	. . . χοε
ΘΟΠΟΥΣ	᾿Αγα]θόπους
5 Σ	5 . . . . ς
ΛΑΦΙΕΡΩΚΩΣ	ὁ] καθιερωκὼς
ΝΙΣ	. . . νις
ΙΣΙΣ (erasure)	. . . σις
·ΚΛ·ΙΕΡΓ	. . . Κλ. ᾿Ιέρω[ν
10 ΤΕΜΙΔΩΡΟΣ	10 ᾿Αρ]τεμίδωρος
ΙΑΝΟΣ	. . . . ιανὸς
ΡΟΔΩΡΟΣ	Μητ]ρόδωρος
ΟΣ·	. . . ος
ΟΣ·	. . . . ος
15 ΙΝΟΣΚΑΠΙΤΩΙ	15 . . . . ινος Καπίτων
ΛΦΥΡΟΣΓΡΙΜΩΝ	Γλ]άφυρος Γρίμων
ΩΝ	. . . ων
ΛΝΗΦΟΡΙΚΟΣ	Κ]ανηφορικὸς
ΤΡϽΔΩΡΟΥ·Ε	Μη]τροδώρου ᾿Ε[πὶ
20 ΓΥ·	20 ἀρ]γυ(ρώματος?
ΝΥΚ·ΦΩΤΩ	ἐπὶ] νυκ(τερινῶν) φωτῶ[ν]?
ΒΟΥΤΑΦΩ⁻	. . . Βούτα φω . . . .
ΚΟΕ	. . . . κος
ιΟΠΑΤΩΡ	Φι]λοπάτωρ.

The heading of a and b informs us that we have here a list of persons who offered certain sacrifices. To what deity? Probably to Dionysos. This accords with the fact of the inscription having been found in the Theatre, and explains several expressions in the list itself: such as ἐπιλή[νια] in b, θιρσοφ[όρος] in d, ιιι. o, ταῖς βασσάραις in d. The word βουκόλοι in d (bis), o, is also a title elsewhere found in connexion with the worship of Dionysos; see C. I. 2052; and Hermes vii, 1873, p. 39, where C. Curtius has published an inscription from Pergamon (of Roman times) in which an association entitled Οἱ Βουκόλοι do honour to their president; it begins thus: Οἱ βου-κόλοι ἐτείμησαν | Σωτῆρα ᾿Α[ρ]τεμιδώρου τὸν | ἀρχιβούκολον διὰ τοῦ εὐσεβῶς | καὶ ἀξίως τοῦ καθηγεμόνος | Διονύσου προΐστασθαι τῶν | θείων μυστηρίων. | Εἰσὶν δὲ οἱ βουκόλοι· |—then follows a list of names. Κανηφορικός in q is more likely a proper name than a priestly title. ᾿Ε[πὶ ἀρ]γυ(ρώματος) ibid. is suggested by No. DLXXXIX a ante; compare also No. CCCCLXXXI, line 385 ante; it describes the officer ' in charge of the sacred silver vessels.' [᾿Επὶ] νυκ(τερινῶν) φωτῶ[ν] may be compared with λυχναπτρία, Part I, No. LVII ante.

DCIII.

Fragments of white marble crustæ, about ¾ in. thick. Probably from the site of the Great Theatre (see heading of Nos. DC, DCI, DCII).
Unpublished.

a.	*b.*	*c.*
Marble broken all round : height 6½ in. ; width 3½ in.	Marble broken all round: height 1 ft. ; width 7 in.	Marble broken all round : height 5 in. ; width 3 in.

a.

```
          |
     (uninscribed)
     ⌐IAΣ·O
     ϽΘΕΤΗϹ'
     ⌐Υ·ΣΜΙ
     ΥΜΝΛ
```

b.

```
              ⅃΋Σ
              ϽϹ ·
         ◁ΔΡΟΣ·Τ
      ⅃     ·ΚΟΔΙ
    5  ΜΟΥ·Μ·ΙΟΥ
       ΔΑΡΙΟΥ·ΠΔ
       ΓΔ'·ΠΟΜ·Ε
        ·ΤΛ·ΚΑΙΚ
        ·ΝΕ·ΛΓ
    10  ΥΤϹΥϹ
        ϽΓ·.
```

c.

```
        Ϲ.
     ϽϹΤΡΑΤϹ
     ΞΛΛΑ
     ΪΛ·ΛΑΙΟ
   5 ΕΚΟΣ
     Υ·ΤΡΟΦ
     ΙΤΙ'
```

d.	*e.*
Marble broken all round: height 1¾ in. ; width 1¾ in.	Marble broken all round : height 1¾ in. ; width 2 in.

d.

```
    ΡΛ
    ΤΙ
```

e.

```
    ΛΙΟΘ
    ΙΙϲ
```

Apparently a list of names of persons who had taken part in some religious festival. In *a* we recognize [ἀγων]οθέτης and [γ]υμνα[σίαρχοϲ]. So that the inscription may have related to the Ephesian Ephebi, or to some competitive games amongst them.

SECTION VIII.

AGONISTIC.

DCIV.

A slab of white marble: height 3 ft. 3 in. : width 1 ft. 8 in. : edges entire.   Wood, Ephesus, Inscriptions from the Great Theatre, No. 18.

```
                                    ['Ο δεῖνα τοῦ δεῖνος]
   ΙΟΥ ⳤ ΥΜΝΩΔΟΥ                    τοῦ ὑμνῳδοῦ,
   ΙΕΡΟΚΗΡΥΞ·ΓΡΑΜ                   ἱεροκῆρυξ, γραμ-
   ΜΑΤΕΥΣΑΔΡΙΑΝΕΙΩΝ                 ματεὺς Ἀδριανείων,
   ΥΜΝΩΔΟΣΝΕΜΗΤΗΣ                   ὑμνῳδὸς νεμητὴς
   ΒΟΥΛΗΣΓΕΡΟΥΣΙΑΣ           5      βουλῆς, γερουσίας,
   ΧΡΥΣΟΦΟΡΩΝ                       χρυσοφόρων·
   ΗΓΩΝΙΣΑΤΟΑΓΩΝΑΣ                  ἠγωνίσατο ἀγῶνας
   ΤΡΕΙΣΕΣΤΕΦΘΗΔΥΟ                  τρεῖς, ἐστέφθη δύω,
   ΑΓΩΝΟΘΕΤΟΥΝΟΣ                    ἀγωνο(θ)ετοῦντος
10 ΔΙΑΙΩΝΟΣ·ΤΙΒ·ΙΟΥΛ         10     δι᾽ αἰῶνος Τιβ. Ἰουλ.
   ΡΗΓΕΙΝΟΥΑΣΙΑΡΧΟΥιΒ              ῾Ρηγείνου Ἀσιάρχου Β
   ΝΑΩΝΤΩΝΕΝΕΦΕΣΩ                  ναῶν τῶν ἐν Ἐφέσῳ
   ΤΗΣΦΙΣⳤΓΕΝΤΑΕΤΗΡΙΔΟΣ           τῆς φιζ̣ʹ πενταετηρίδος.
```

Record of the victories of an Ephesian citizen in the musical contests at the Hadrianeia at Ephesos.

The name of the man is lost as well as his father's, both having been inscribed upon the ornamental cornice above the stelè, which is destroyed. The father was a ὑμνῳδός, i. e. one of the choir attached to the Artemision ; see Prolegomena, p. 87, and No. cccclxxxi, lines 192, 371, and notes. The choirmen attached to the Augusteum at Ephesos were styled θεσμῳδοί, and not ὑμνῳδοί, probably for the sake of distinction (see No. cccclxxxi, lines 328, 371). If the title ὑμνῳδός connects the father with the worship of Artemis, the offices of his son (lines 3 foll.) have to do with the worship of the Imperial house. He was sacred herald and secretary of the Ephesian games in honour of Hadrian ; respecting the Ἀδριάνεια see Prolegomena, p. 79 *ante.* It is highly probable that this celebration, which took place every fourth year (πενταετηρίς, line 13) like the Olympian games in Elis, was founded at Ephesos, as we know it was at Smyrna, by Hadrian himself. An inscription now at Oxford, C. I. 3148, informs us that Hadrian gave an endowment to the people of Smyrna to establish there an ἀγὼν ἱερός, and θεολόγοι and ὑμνῳδοί in his honour. It also appears from C. I. 3201 that these ὑμνῳδοί at Smyrna were appointed by the gerousia, which probably administered the imperial endowment. The Ἀδριάνεια (Ὀλύμπια) at Ephesos may have had a similar origin ; at all events the funds which supported them were administered by the boulè, the gerousia, and the

college of χρυσοφόροι (lines 5, 6) ; for it is by these bodies that the subject of our inscription, who was also γραμματεὺς Ἀδριανείων, was appointed ὑμνῳδὸς νεμητὴς at that festival. I follow Menadier in taking these words together, in the sense of 'musical judge' ; see Prolegomena, p. 77 : indeed, if the distinction I have drawn be correct, between the θεσμῳδοί of the Ephesian Augusteum and the ὑμνῳδοί of the Artemision, it is necessary to take ὑμνῳδὸς νεμητής as one title. The college of χρυσοφόροι consisted of priests and victors in certain of the games and others. They are thus specified in the Salutaris inscription (No. cccclxxxi, lines 324 foll.) where, as here, they are grouped together with the boulè and gerousia; περὶ ὧν προσκαθιέρωκε τῇ μεγίστῃ θεᾷ Ἐφεσίᾳ Ἀρ[τ]έμιδι καὶ τῇ φιλοσεβάστῳ Ἐφεσίων βουλῇ καὶ τῇ φιλοσεβά[στῳ Ἐφεσίων γερου]σίᾳ καὶ ἡ[οῖς χ]ρυσοφορ[ο]ῦσι τῇ θ[εῷ Ἀρτέμιδι ἱερ]εῦσιν καὶ ἱερονείκαις πρὸ πόλεως.

The subject of our inscription, besides acting as musical judge at the Hadrianeia, had also on three occasions himself become a competitor for a prize, and twice had won it (lines 7, 8). From ἐστέφθη it is clear that the Ἀδριάνεια Ὀλύμπια ἐν Ἐφέσῳ was a στεφανίτης ἀγών, and not a χρηματικός or θεματικός, i. e. for money only ; this indeed is implied by the way in which the festival is classed in a list of festivals found at Aphrodisias (C. I. 2810).

Finally the ἀγωνοθέτης is named under whose administration our victor took part in the games : viz. Tib. Jul. Rheginus, who is similarly mentioned in three more of our agonistic lists, Nos. dcv, dcxi,

DCXXI post. He was probably a kinsman of the Γαίου ['Ιου]λίου 'Ρηγείνου 'Αμυντιανοῦ whose wife is mentioned as Priestess of Agrippina at Tralles (Bull. de Corr. Hell. v, p. 343). Tib. Jul. Rheginus is also Asiarch for the second year: not, however, Asiarch of the province (ἀρχιερεὺς 'Ασίας), but only Asiarch or ἀρχιερεύς of the worship of the Emperors at Ephesos alone; in other words, he is the local Asiarch of the κοινὸν 'Ασίας (see on No. ccccxcviii ante).

Our inscription is not earlier than the end of Hadrian's reign, and probably should be placed between A. D. 150-200. What is meant by 'the 517th quadriennium' in line 13, I cannot divine. The same date occurs in No. ιxv, line 10 post: 'Εφεσηίδι φιζ, where see note. Of course the Ephesian Olympia, in honour of Hadrian, were celebrated every 4th year, like the Olympia of Pisa. Böckh on C. I. 2999 rules that the date of the Ephesian celebration was reckoned not from the founding of the local festival, as at Athens (see C. I. No. 342), but from the first Olympiad B. c. 776. It is curious however that, even thus, he finds a difficulty in explaining the numerals copied from the stone ΥΝΕΟΛΥΜΠΙΑΔΟΣ. i. e. 455th Olympiad : this he corrects into [σ]νέ, i. e. Ol. 255 or A. D. 241. It is more likely that the era indicated (circa B.C. 1900) was the legendary date of the birth of Artemis and the founding of Ephesos.

In the Mittheilungen d. arch. Inst. Ath. (iii, 57), there is given an inscription from Thira in Lydia mentioning a ὑμνωδὸς τῆς ἁγιωτάτης 'Αρτέμιδος, who was the leading man of the place (προεστάτος τῆς κατοικίας), and also βούλαρχος. In C. I. 3201 (Smyrna) a monument is erected in honour of a lady whose father had filled most of the public offices in the state. Amongst other posts he had been γραμματεὺς 'Ολυμπίων : this is of course another name for the local celebration of the 'Αδριάνεια at Smyrna : to which in all probability the lady herself had contributed. It is added : τῆς τειμῆς πρ[ο]νοοῦσιν οἱ ὑμνῳδοὶ τῆς γερουσίας καὶ ὁ ἀδελφὸς Κλ. Παυλεῖ[νι]ανός. Similarly in the inscription before us the offices of γραμματεὺς τῶν 'Αδριανείων and of ὑμνῳδὸς νεμητὴς γερουσίας are brought into close juxtaposition.

DCV.

Stelè of white marble : height 2 ft. 7½ in. ; width 1 ft. 8 in. The moulded cornice, on which the first line was inscribed, has been purposely chipped off. Discovered by Mr. Wood among the ruins of the Theatre. Wood, Ephesus, Inscriptions from the Great Theatre, No. 8.

ΦΩΙΩ Λ Κ   ι⁄   Σ
ΛΑΟΔΙΚΕΥΣ·ΚΑΙΕΦΕΣΙΟΣ·ΝΕΙΚΗΣΑΣΤΑ
ΓΑΛΛΑΕΦΕΣΗΑΙΕΡΑΙΣΕΛΑΣΤΙΚΑΑΝΔΡΩΝΠΥΓ
ΔΙΔΥΜΕΙΑ·ΕΝΜΕΙΛΗΤΩ·ΑΓΕΝΕΙΩΝ·ΠΥΓΜΗΝ
5 ΔΕΙΑ·ΣΕΒΑΣΤΑΟΙΚοΥΜΕΝΙΚΑΕΝΛΑΟΔΙΚΕΙΑΛΑΕΝFΙΟΝΥΓΜ
ΚΟΙΝΑ·ΑΣΙΑΣ·ΕΝΕΦΕΣΩ·ΑΓΕΝΕΙΩΝ·ΠΥΓΜΗΝ
ΚΟΙΝΑΑΣΙΑΣ·ΕΝΛΑΟΔΙΚΕΙΑ·ΑΓΕΝΕΙΩΝ·ΠΥΓΜΗΝ
ΕΠΙΝΕΙΚΙΑΕΝΕΦΕΣΩ·ΑΓΕΝΕΙΩΝΠΥΓΜΗΝ
ΤΡΑΙΑΝΕΙΑ·ΔΕΙΦΙΛΕΙΑ·ΕΝΠΕΡΓΑΜΩ·ΑΝΔΡΩΝΠΥΓΜ
10 ΦΕΣΗΑΤΑΜΕΓΑΛΑ·ΕΦΕΣΗΙΔΙ·ΦΙΖ·ΑΝΔΡΩΝΠΥΓΜΗ
ΔΕΙΑΣΕΒΑΣΤΑΟΙΚοΥΜΕΝΙΚΑΕΝΛΑΟΔΙΚΕΙΑΑΝΔΡΩΝΥΓΝ
ΕΥΣΕΒΕΙΑ·ΕΝΠΟΤΙΟΛΟΙΣ·ΑΝΔΡΩΝ·ΠΥΓ
ΣΕΒΑΣΤΑΕΝΝΕΑΠΟΛΕΙ·ΑΝΔΩΝ·Π
ΤΗΝΕΣΑΓΓΟΥΣ·ΑΣΠΙΔΑ·ΑΝΡΩΝ·ΠΥΓ
15 ΑΡΤΕΜΕΙΣΙΑ·ΕΝΕΦΕΣΩ·ΑΝΔΡΩΝΠΥΓΙ
ΚΑΙΤΑΛΛΑΝΤΙΑΙΟΥΣΚΑΙΘΕΜΑΤΙΚΟΥΣ·ΑΓ
ΑΓΩΝΟΘΕΤΟΥΝΤΟΣ·Τ
ΙΟΥΛΙΟΥΡΗΓΕΙΝΟΥΑΡΧ
ΕΡΕΩΣ·Β·ΝΑΩΝΤΩΝΕΝΕΦΕ

Φω[τ]ω[ν? Α. Κ . . . . . . ϛ . . . . ϛ [καὶ
Λαοδικεὺς καὶ 'Εφίσιος νεικήσας τὰ [με-
γάλα 'Εφέσηα ἱερὰ ἰσελαστικὰ ἀνδρῶν πυγ(μήν·
Διδύμεια ἐν Μειλήτῳ ἀγενείων πυγμήν·
5 Δεῖα Σεβαστὰ οἰκουμενικὰ ἐν Λαοδικείᾳ ἀγενείων πυγμ[ήν·
κοινὰ 'Ασίας ἐν 'Εφέσῳ ἀγενείων πυγμήν·
κοινὰ 'Ασίας ἐν Λαοδικείᾳ ἀγενείων πυγμήν·
ἐπινείκια ἐν 'Εφέσῳ ἀγενείων πυγμήν·
Τραϊάνεια Δειφίλεια ἐν Περγάμῳ ἀνδρῶν πυγμήν·
10 'Εφέσηα τὰ μεγάλα 'Εφεσηίδι φιζ ἀνδρῶν πυγμή(ν·
Δεῖα Σεβαστὰ οἰκουμενικὰ ἐν Λαοδικείᾳ ἀνδρῶν πυγμ(ήν·
Εὐσέβεια ἐν Ποτιόλοις ἀνδρῶν πυγ[μήν·

Σεβαστὰ ἐν Νεαπόλει ἀνδρῶν π[υγμήν·
τὴν ἐξ Ἄργους ἀσπίδα ἀν(δ)ρῶν π.υγ[μήν·
Ἀρτεμίσια ἐν Ἐφέσῳ ἀνδρῶν πυγμ[ήν·
καὶ τπλαντιαίους καὶ θεματικοὺς ἀγ(ῶνας) . .
ἀγωνοθετοῦντος Τ[ι.
Ἰουλίου Ῥηγείνου ἀρχ[ι-
ερέως β΄ ναῶν τῶν ἐν Ἐφέ[σῳ.

A successful athlete records his victories, by way of thank-offering to the gods. This belongs to a class of documents of common occurrence in most parts of Greece under the Roman Empire ; see C. I. *passim*, and C. I. A. iii, 104 foll.

The name of the athlete in line 1 cannot be certainly restored. He had been granted the honour of citizenship of various towns (line 2) ; compare Prolegomena, p. 74 ; No. DCVI lines 7, 8 *ante* ; No. DCVII, DCVIII *b*, DCXV *fin.*, DCXVI *post*. The catalogue names first, out of its proper order, his most brilliant success, viz. at the ' Great Ephesian Games ' (see Prolegomena, p. 79) : this victory is more briefly recited in its proper order in line 10. The Agonothetes at these games was Ti. Jul. Rheginus, whose name is therefore appended in lines 17-19. As however he was holding this office for life (Nos. DCIV *fin.*, DCXI), it was necessary to specify the year more closely ; hence the date in line 10 Ἐφεσηίδι φιξ, which is an equivalent of the phrase in No. DCIV, τῆς φιξ πενταετηρίδος, showing both documents to belong to the same date. Ἐφεσηίς designates the Ephesian πεντετηρίς or quadriennium as Ὀλυμπιάς did the Olympian. The document probably belongs to the reign of Hadrian. For the era, see note on No. DCIV *ante*.

In lines 4 foll. the athlete's achievements are enumerated, first as ἀγένειος and then as an adult. Line 4 : Διδύμεια are the ' Great Didymean Games ' in honour of Apollo Didymeus at Didyma near Miletus. Lines 5, 7 and 11 : Laodikeia on the Lykos is certainly intended, belonging, like Ephesos, to the province of Asia ; the Δεῖα (Σεβαστά) at Laodikeia are named also in No. DCXV, line 14. The epithet οἰκουμενικά as applied to certain games marks them as not merely local, but as ranking with the other great festivals of the Graeco-Roman world (οἰκουμένη) ; compare C. I. 4472, line 14 : ἐν Λαοδικείᾳ τῇ πατρίδι μου Πυθιάδι πρώτῃ ἀχθείσῃ Οἰκουμενικὸν Ἀντωνεινιανὸν (ἀγῶνα) ἀνδρῶν πυγμήν (i. e. at Laodicea ad mare). Similarly *ibid* lines 13 foll. : ἐν Ταρσῷ Ἰσολύμπιον Οἰκουμενικὸν Κομμόδειον ἀγενείων πυγμήν. Krause (Olympia, p. 217) quotes an Ephesian coin of Elagabalus with the legend ΟΙΚΟΥΜΕΝ[Κ]Α . ΝΕΩΚΟΡΩΝ · ΕΦΕΣΙΩΝ · ΟΛΥΜΠΙΑ. Lines 6, 7 : Κοινὰ Ἀσίας were the games celebrated by the κοινὸν Ἀσίας annually in one or other of the principal cities of the province ; see Prolegomena p. 79, and note on No. DCCCXVIII *ante*. Line 8 : the ἐπινίκια at Ephesos are not elsewhere mentioned ; the celebration is perhaps analogous to that which is styled in C. I. 5804 [τὰ ἐν Ἡρακλείᾳ ἐπινίκια Αὐτοκράτορος Νερούα Τραιανοῦ Κ[αίσαρος Σεβαστοῦ] Γερμανικοῦ Δακικοῦ. This festival was estab-

lished to commemorate the victory of Trajan over the Dacians when he assumed the title of Dacicus, i. e. at the close of A. D. 102 (Mommsen, Hermes, iii. p. 131) ; a similar festival may have been founded at Ephesos. Line 9 : the Τραϊάνεια Δειφίλεια ἐν Περγάμῳ are not mentioned elsewhere. Compare however the last note ; and Pliny to Trajan, Ep. 75 (Keil), where he asks his master's advice about founding at Heraklea ' quinquennales agonas qui Traiani appellarentur ' out of a legacy left him by one Julius Largus on trust to be expended in honour of Trajan. Pliny may not have founded the festival after all, and probably chose the alternative suggested, viz. ' opera facienda quae honori tuo (Trajan's) consecrarentur.' But if the games had been established they might have been called possibly Τραϊάνεια Ἰουλίῃα, after the name of the founder. The games in our text may have been endowed by one Διφίλος. Line 10 : on this festival, and on the peculiar date given, see note on lines 2, 3. Line 11 : see note on line 5. Line 12 : the Εὐσέβεια were a festival established at Puteoli by Antoninus Pius in honour of Hadrian, Spartian, Life of Hadrian, *fin.* : templum denique ei pro sepulchro apud Puteolos constituit (Antoninus) et quinquennale certamen et flamines et sodales et multa alia, quae ad honorem quasi numinis pertinerent ; qua re, ut supra dictum est, multi putant Antoninum Pium dictum : compare C. I. 1068, 1720, 5913. Line 13 : the Σεβαστά or Augustalia were founded at Naples in honour of Augustus A. D. 2, and are frequently named in inscriptions ; see C. I. 1068, add. 2810 *b*, 5913, 5804 etc. Strabo says oὑ this festival (v, p. 246) νυνὶ δὲ πεντετηρικὸς ἱερὸς ἀγὼν συντελεῖται παρ' αὐτοῖς μουσικός τε καὶ γυμνικὸς ἐπὶ πλείους ἡμέρας, ἐνάμιλλος τοῖς ἐπιφανεστάτοις τῶν κατὰ τὴν Ἑλλάδα. Line 14 : the festival referred to is the Heraea or Hekatombaea at Argos, at which there were the usual kinds of contests, but the prize for each was a brazen shield, the shields of Argos being the best of their kind (see Ælian, V. H. iii, 24). Pindar accordingly (Nem. x, 40 = 22) calls the festival ἀγὼν χαλκεῖος, see Hesych. *s. v.* The phrase ἡ ἐξ Ἄργους ἀσπίς frequently recurs in agonistic inscriptions. Compare my Manual, No. 136. Line 15 : The Artemisia were celebrated in the month Artemision ; see on No. CCCCXLVII. The contests hitherto named were στεφανῖται, or at least not for money-prizes : the victor sums up together at the end the number of other contests in which he has won money-prizes, whether of a talent's value, or less (θεματικούς, compare C. I. 2810). A numeral is lost at the end of the line.

DCVI.

A stelè of white marble: height 2 ft.; width 1 ft. 7 in. Entire. Discovered by Mr. Wood on the site of the Artemision. Wood, Ephesus, Inscriptions from the site of the temple of Diana, No. 15.

ΤΗΣΠΡΩΤΗΣΚΑΙΜΕ	Τῆς πρώτης καὶ με-
ΓΙΣΤΗΣΜΗΤΡΟΠΟΛΕΩΣ	γίστης μητροπόλεως
ΤΗΣΑΣΙΑΣΚΑΙΔΙΣΝΕΩΚΟ	τῆς Ἀσίας καὶ δὶς νεωκό-
ΡΟΥΤΩΝΣΕΒΑΣΤΩΝΕΦΕΣΙ	ρου τῶν Σεβαστῶν Ἐφεσί-
5 ΩΝΠΟΛΕΩΣΗΒΟΥΛΗΚΑΙ	5 ων πόλεως ἡ βουλὴ καὶ
ΟΔΗΜΟΣΕΤΕΙΜΗΣΑΝ·Τ·ΦΛ	ὁ δῆμος ἐτείμησαν Τ. Φλ.
ΣΑΡΠΗΔΟΝΑΑΚΜΟΝΕΑ ··	Σαρπηδόνα Ἀκμονία
ΚΑΙΕΦΕΣΙΟΝΠΑΙΔΑΚΩΜΩ	καὶ Ἐφέσιον παῖδα κωμῳ-
ΛΟΝΑΡΕΤΗΣΕΝΕΚΑΚΑΙ	δὸν, ἀρετῆς ἕνεκα καὶ
10 ΣΩΦΡΟΝΟΣΑΣΚΗΣΕΩΣ ··	10 σώφρονος ἀσκήσεως
ΚΑΙΤΗΣΠΕΡΙΤΗΝΥΠΟΚΡΙ	καὶ τῆς περὶ τὴν ὑπόκρι-
ΣΙΝΕΜΠΕΙΡΙΑΣ·ΝΙΚΗΣΑΝ	σιν ἐμπειρίας, νικήσαν-
ΤΑΤΟΝΑΓΩΝΑΤΩΝΜΕΓΑ	τα τὸν ἀγῶνα τῶν μεγά-
ΛΩΝΙΕΡΩΝΑΡΤΕΜΙΣΙΩΝ	λων ἱερῶν Ἀρτεμισίων·
15 ΑΓΩΝΟΘΕΤΟΥΝΤΟΣ·ΛΟ	15 ἀγωνοθετοῦντος Λο(υκίου)
·· ΑΥ Ρ ΦΙΛΩΝΟΣ ··	Αὐρ(ηλίου) Φίλωνος.

In honour of T. Flavius Sarpedon, of Akmonia in Phrygia, and also (by special grant ?) citizen of Ephesos, a boy who had won the prize for acting at the Artemisia. On the festival see Prolegomena, p. 79. Steph. Byz. gives Ἀκμονίης or Ἀκμονειάτης as the gentile adjective; but Ἀκμονεύς, as here, is what the inscriptions warrant (C. I. 3893, add. 3858 b). It would not be easy to find another inscription in honour of a comic actor (yet see Pausan. i, 37, § 2);

his youth (παῖδα, line 8) makes the case more remarkable. Already however in Macedonian times scenic performers were receiving more and more attention (Lüders, Die Dionysischen Künstler, p. 55), which was not likely to grow less under the Empire : compare notes on No. cccxliv ante. The mention of the 'second neokorate' (line 3) fixes the date as between the accession of Hadrian and Septimius Severus.

DCVII.

Three fragments of white marble moulding, evidently from the top of the same stelè : a entire at top and left measures 5¾ in. by 4½ in.; b entire at top 4 in. by 5 in.; c entire at top 5 in. by 5 in. Unpublished.

a.	b.	c.
ΙΣΕΛΛ	ϽΕΕΝΕ	ΝΙ
ΙΙΕΥϚ	ΙΑ	ΙΕΡΑ

Ἰσελα[στικὰ τά]δε ἐνι[ίκησα] Νι . . . . .
νεὺς [καὶ . . . . . καὶ] Φιλ[αδελφεὸς ? καὶ] Ἱερα[πολείτης?
κ.τ.λ.

Evidently an agonistic inscription, from the word ἰσελα[στικά] which is certain ; the other restorations are only suggestions. In old Greek times a victor in one of the four great national games was welcomed home to his own city with signal honours ; in particular, he had to enter, not through the city gates, but through a breach made in the walls. The custom is thus explained by Plutarch,

(Sympos. ii, 5) : καὶ τὸ τοῖς νικηφόροις εἰσελαύνουσι τῶν τειχῶν ἐφίεσθαι μέρος διελεῖν καὶ καταβάλλειν τοιαύτην ἔχει διάνοιαν, ὡς οὐ μέγα πόλει τειχῶν ὄφελος ἄνδρας ἐχούσῃ μάχεσθαι δυναμένους καὶ νικᾶν. The Emperor Nero therefore, on returning from his tour in Greece, claimed this honour more Graeco: reversus e Graecia Neapolin, quod in ea primum artem protulerat, albis equis introiit, disiecta parte muri ut mos hieronicarum est (Sueton. Nero, 25). A contest which brought the victor this honour was styled εἰσελαστικὸς ἀγών. The epithet and the privilege were extended in later days to other games | beyond the four great ones, but only by special charter from the Emperor; see Trajan in reply to Pliny (Ep. 119, ed. Keil) : eorum certaminum quæ iselastica esse placuit mihi, etc.

DCVIII.

Part of an altar-like block of white marble, surmounted by a plain moulding; inscribed on two sides. Height of *a* 1 ft. 1 in.; width 6 in.; height of *b* 11½ in.; width 10 in. Discovered by Mr. Wood; unpublished.

	a.	*b.*
	(left return face)	(front)
	า · ΕΦΕΣ	ΛΙΣΜΥΡΝΑΙΟΣ
	ΔΙΤΩΔΗ	ΑΝΟΣ · ΚΑΙΘΥΑΤΕΙΡΗ
	ΙΤΟΙΣ	ΚΑΙΤΥΡΙΟΣ · ΚΑΙΣΕ
	ΕΛΑΒΟ	ΠΟΛΛΩΝΠΟΛΕΩ
5	ΜΑΤΑ -	ΠΑΙΔΩΝΠΥΓΜ
	ΙΑ · ΜΑΡΚΟΥ	ΙΕΡΑΕΙΣΕΛΑΣΤΙΚ 5
	ΑΚΡΟΒΑ	ΤΑΕΤΗΡΙΔΟΣ · Ι
	ΜΙΔΟΣ -	
	ΥΠΟΛΕΙΤΟΥ	
10	ΤΑΣ · ΚΑΤΑΤ	

Τῇ φιλοσεβάστ]ῳ Ἐφεσ[ί-
ων βουλῇ κ]αὶ τῷ δή-
μῳ καὶ πᾶσ]ι τοῖς
πολείταις?. .]ελαβο
5 . . . . ματα
. . . . ία Μάρκου
. . . . . . ο]υ ἀκροβά-
του τῆς Ἀρτέ]μιδος,
. . . . ὑπολειτου-
10 ργ . . . .]ας κατὰ τ-
κ.τ.λ.

κ]αὶ Ζμυρναῖος [καὶ . . . . . ος καὶ Ἀγκυρ-?
ανὸς καὶ Θυατειρη[νὸς καὶ . . . . . . ος
καὶ Τύριος καὶ Σε[λευκεὺς ? καὶ ἄλλων
πολλῶν πόλεω[ν πολείτης · νεικήσας (nomen ludorum)
5 παίδων πυγμ[ήν· τὰ μεγάλα Ἐφέσηα
ἱερὰ εἰσελαστικ[ὰ παίδων πυγμήν? πενταετηρίδος [φι⊂ ? . . . .

a. In the broken state of the monument it is hopeless to attempt to restore the sense. Possibly it recorded a gift of money made by a lady, the daughter of Marcus an akrobates, to the boulè and people of Ephesos. The phrasing of the document does not resemble any of the other inscriptions.

b was an agonistic monument of the ordinary kind, recording the successes of a pugilist whose name was given in the opening lines now lost. He had | received the citizenship of many towns (lines 1–4) : compare note on No. DCV *ante*. The list begins with his juvenile achievements at the greater games. On the Ἐφέσηα see Prolegomena p. 79 ; on the epithet εἰσελαστικά see No. DCVII *ante*. At the end of line 7 the stem of φ is fairly certain, and suggests the date φιΣ which has already been discussed in the notes on Nos. DCIV, DCV.

DCIX.

White marble stelè, entire with the exception of the defacement of the first three lines: height 1 ft. 8 in.; width 1 ft. 7 in. Beautifully inscribed, though in late characters. Wood, Inscriptions from the Great Theatre, No. 24.

(Three lines here intentionally erased, probably in more recent times.)
ΒΕΙΘΥΝι
ΕΠΙΚΛΙ-ΙΘΕΙΣΓΡΑΥΣΔΟΛΙ⊂
ΔΡΟΜΟΣΝΕΙΚΙ-Ι⊂Α⊂
ΤΙ-ΝΠΕΡΙΟΔΟΝΚΛΙΤΡΙ⊂
5 ΟΛΥΝΠΙΑΤΑΕΝΠΕΙΣΗ-Ι
ΚΑΤΑΤΟΕΞΙ-Ι⊂ΚΑΙΤΟΥⲤ
ΕΤΕΡΟΥⲤΑΓΩΝΑⲤ
ΠΑΝΤΑⲤ

[Ὁ δεῖνα Ἡρακλεώτης (or the like) τῆς]
Βειθυνί]ας καὶ . . . . ὁ
ἐπικληθεὶς Γραῦς δολιχ[ο-
δρόμος, νεικήσας
τὴν περίοδον, καὶ τρὶς
5 Ὀλύνπια τὰ ἐν Πείσῃ
κατὰ τὸ ἑξῆς, καὶ τοὺς
ἑτέρους ἀγῶνας
πάντας.

Line 1 and the lost lines preceding it recorded the name of the athlete and the names of the cities which had granted him their freedom: see on No. DCV. Line 2 adds his nick-name, Γραῦς δολιχοδρόμος, which reveals that he was a winner of the foot-race (στάδιον). Similarly in another Ephesian inscription (C. I. 2999) a successful athlete is styled ὁ ἐπικαλούμενος Γναφεύς. The use of nick-names among the Greeks has been the subject of an essay by L. Grasberger, (Die Griechischen Stich-namen, Würzburg, 1883), but he deals only with Attika and the Older Comedy. Line 4: περιοδονῖκαι was a title applied to athletes who had won a prize in each of the four great games; and although the

title appears to have had a looser use under the Empire (see Krause s. v. in Pauly's Real-encyclop.), in our text it is certainly employed in its strict sense. Line 6: for κατὰ τὸ ἑξῆς compare Nos. DCXV post, and Böckh on C. I. 247; he defines it to mean 'nulla intercedente inter has victorias sollennitate illis locis celebrata.' Lines 5-8: he had won all the races worth winning in other parts of Greece, but after the great victories just mentioned, nothing else seemed worth naming. C. I. 247 (just quoted) is in honour of another athlete of Bithynia ('Απαμεὺς τῆς Βειθυνίας), a boxer named M. Tullius, who had won the 'Ολύμπια δὶς ἐν Πείσῃ.

DCX.

Upper left hand corner of a white marble stele; height 9 in.; width 7 in. Discovered in Mr. Wood's excavations. Unpublished.

ΑΓΑ〈	'Αγαθ[ῇ τύχῃ·
ΤΑΜΕΓΑ	Τὰ μεγά[λα 'Εφίσηα? . . .
ΔΟΛ	δολ[ιχοδρομήσας? . . . .
ΜΑΡ	Μάρ[κος? . . . . .

Apparently the ex-voto of a victorious athlete.

DCXI.

A stele of white marble: height 3 ft. 6¼ in.; width 1 ft. 9 in. Discovered by Mr. Wood; Inscriptions from the Great Theatre, No. 14.

		[Ο δεῖνα τοῦ δεῖνος κ.τ.λ. νεικήσας]
ΕΦΕΣΗΑΤΑΜΕΓΑΛΛΑΣΤΑΔΙΟΛ		'Εφίσηα τὰ μεγάλα, στάδιον·
ΑΥΓΟΥΣΤΕΙΑΕΝΠΕΡΓΑΜΩ·ΣΤΑΔΙΟΛ		Αὐγούστεια ἐν Περγάμῳ, στάδιον·
ΙΣΘΜΙΑ ΣΤΑΔΙΟΝ		'Ισθμια, στάδιον·
ΟΛΥΜΠΕΙΑΕΝΑΘΗΝΑΙΣ · ΣΤΑΔΙΟΝ		'Ολύμπεια ἐν 'Αθήναις, στάδιον·
5 ΤΗΝΕΞΑΡΓΟΥΣΑΣΠΙΔΑ · ΣΤΑΔΙΟΝ	5	τὴν ἐξ "Αργους 'Ασπίδα, στάδιον·
ΝΕΜΕΙΑΕΝΑΡΓΕΙ ΣΤΑΔΙΟΝ		Νέμεια ἐν "Αργει, στάδιον·
ΠΑΝΕΛΛΗΝΙΑΕΝΑΘΗΝΑΙΣ·ΣΤΑΔΙΟΝ		Πανελλήνια ἐν 'Αθήναις, στάδιον·
ΟΛΥΜΠΙΑΕΝΤΡΑΛΛΕΣΙ·ΣΤΑΔΙΟΝ		'Ολύμπια ἐν Τράλλεσι, στάδιον·
ΙΣΘΜΙΑ ΣΤΑΔΙΟΝ		'Ισθμια, στάδιον·
10 ΔΙΔΥΜΕΙΑΕΝΜΕΙΛΗΤΩ·ΣΤΑΔΙΟΝ	10	Διδύμεια ἐν Μειλήτῳ, στάδιον·
ΚΟΙΝΟΝΑΣΙΑΣΕΝΚΥΖΙΚΩ·ΣΤΑΔΙΟΛ		Κοινὸν 'Ασίας ἐν Κυζίκῳ, στάδιον·
ΑΣΚΛΗΠΕΙΑΕΝΠΕΡΓΑΜΩ·ΣΤΑΔΙΟΝ		'Ασκλήπεια ἐν Περγάμῳ, στάδιον·
ΟΛΥΜΠΙΑΕΝΤΑΡΣΩ ΣΤΑΔΙΟΛ		'Ολύμπια ἐν Ταρσῷ, στάδιον·
ΑΝΑΖΑΡΒΟΝΑΝΔΡΩΝΤΕΝΑΘΛΘ		'Ανάζαρβον, ἀνδρῶν πένταθλον.
(Space of four lines here uninscribed.)		
15 ΑΓΩΝΟΘΕΤΟΥΝΤΟΣΔΙΑΙ	15	'Αγωνοθετοῦντος δι' αἰ-
ΩΝΟΣ·ΤΙΒ·ΙΟΥΑ·ΡΗΓΕΙΝΟΥ		ῶνος Τιβ. 'Ιουλ. 'Ρηγείνου,
ΑΡΧΙΕΡΕΩΣ·Β·ΝΑΩΝΤΩΝ		ἀρχιερέως β ναῶν τῶν
ΕΝΕΦΕΣΩ		ἐν 'Εφίσῳ,
ΥΠΟΑΛΕΙΠΤΗΝ · Γ · ΚΟΣΙΝΙΟΝ		ὑπὸ ἀλείπτην Γ. Κοσίνιον.

Record of the success of an athlete who had won the foot race (στάδιον) at various games, in particular at Ephesos (line 1); and also the Pentath-lon at Anazarbos in Kilikia (line 14). The opening

lines containing his name are lost; but compare Nos. DCV ante and DCXVI post which show how such lists were headed.

The games here enumerated are for the most

3 P

part well known : compare the notes on No. DCV *ante*, and Prolegomena p. 79. Lines 13, 14: Olympian games are known to have been celebrated at both these towns; see Krause, Olympia, pp. 206, 227. A very clear and accurate idea of the ancient Pentathlon may be gathered from an article by Professor P. Gardner in the Journal for Hellenic Studies, i, p. 210: compare ii. p. 217. Line 15: on Rheginos see Nos. DCIV, DCV *ante*, DCXXI *post*. For his office of local high-priest or Asiarch of Ephesos, see note on No. CCCCXCVIII. Line 19: ἀλείπτης is the professional trainer. Κοσίνιος is the Latin Cossinius ; a *A. Κοσίννιος Γαίανδς* is named in an Ephesian inscription (C. I. 2983), and Κουσίνιος (compare Κουσινία, C. I. 3870) occurs on Ephesian coins (see Pape-Benseler, *s.v.*).

DCXII.

Fragment of a white marble block, which apparently has been the capital of a pilaster ; inscribed with large handsome letters on the left return face, where the ornamental moulding has been chiselled off. The inscribed side measures 16 in. by 12 in. Discovered by Mr. Wood at Ephesos; but it is not known upon what site : probably among the ruins of the Great Theatre. Unpublished.

	ꓯN		ʹΟ δῆμος . .]ὰν
	ΙΟΔΟ		. . . . περ]ιοδο-
	ΡΥΤΑ		νείκην, ἐπὶ π]ρυτά-
	ꓘΡΟΥ		νεως . . . .]όρου
5	ΙΟΥ	5	τοῦ . . . . .]ίου
	(uninscribed)		

In line 1 AN is perhaps the termination of a name like Μητρᾶν. The letters ΙΟΔΟ and ΡΥΤΑ strongly suggest the restorations here given. The characters seem to belong to the first century B.C. The inscription is entire at top, bottom and right. On the title περιοδονείκης compare No. DCIX *ante*.

DCXIII.

Broken stele of white marble, surmounted by a plain moulding : height 1 ft. 9 in. by 8 in. Entire only at top and bottom. Discovered by Mr. Wood. Unpublished.

		(1)	[ʹΟ δεῖνα περιοδονεί-]
		(2)	[κης ἔνδοξος, ἀήττητος,]
	ΕΙΠΤΟΣΟΛ	1	ἀλ]ειπτος· Ὀλ[ύμπια . . .
	ΥΘΙΑΕΝΔΕΛ		Π]ύθια ἐν Δελ[φοῖς . . .
	ΕΜΕΙΑ·ΙΔ·ΥΙ		Ν]έμεια ἰδ· ʹΙ[σθμια
	ΑΔΙΟΝΔΙΑ		στ]άδιον, δία[υλον· μόν-
5	ΣΚΑΙΠΡΩΤ	5	ο]ς καὶ πρῶτ[ος τὴν
	ΠΟΓΡΑΦΗΝ		ἀ]πογραφὴν [ποιήσ-
	ΣΑΝΤΑΓΟ		α]ς ἀνταγω[νιστῶν·
	ꓙΗΝΑΙΣΠΑΙ		ʹΑ]θήναις παῖ[δων Παν-
	ΛΗΝΙΑΓ·ΑΛ		ελ]λήνια γ̄· Ἀδ[ρίάνεια κ.τ.λ.
	(uninscribed)		

Though the upper edge of the marble is entire, yet the commencement of the inscription is incomplete. It is clear therefore that above the existing moulding there rested originally an ornamental member joined on to the stele (see e. g. No. DLXXVIII). This would afford room for the heading, which gave the name of the athlete together with several epithets much affected by athletes of those times. Of these ἀλειπτος, ἀήττητος, ἔνδοξος or παράδοξος were the commonest, and the first three occur together within six lines in Dio Chrysostom. Melancomas prior p. 534 Reiske : τοιγάρτοι, εἰπεῖν, ἀφ' οὗπερ ἤρξατο ἀγωνίζεσθαι Πυθοῖ, πρῶτος μὲν ὤν ἴσμεν ἀήττητος διεγένετο, πλείστους καὶ μεγίστους στεφάνους ἀνελόμενος καὶ ἀνταγωνισταῖς οὔτε φαύλοις οὔτε ὀλίγοις χρησάμενος. καὶ τὸν πατέρα ἐνδοξοτάτον ὄντα, τὸν Μελαγκόμαν ἐκεῖνον τὸν ἀπὸ τῆς Καρίας, ἄλλους τε ἀγῶνας καὶ Ὀλυμπίασι νικήσαντα, οὐδέπω ἀνὴρ ὢν ὑπεριβάλετο· οὐ γὰρ ἐκεῖνος ἄλειπτος. Besides this passage, which illustrates our inscription in more ways than one, compare the formulæ of C. I. 5909, 5912, 5913, 6883, 6884 : παγκρατιαστήν, περιοδονείκην δίς, πύετην ἄλειπτον παράδοξον, κ.τ.λ. I restore περιοδονείκης in line (1), as the athlete had won victories in all four of the great games (lines 1–3). After the name of each game was placed a numeral, to show how many times he had won a prize there : but after ʹΙ[σθμια], lines 3–4, instead of a numeral β̄, we read στάδιον, δίαυλον, specifying the particular contests engaged in. Similarly in C. I. 5804, 5806, 5913, successful athletes give the number of their victories at each place ; e. g. C. I. 5806 : νικήσας . . . 'Ολύμπια β̄, Πύθια β̄, Νέμεια β̄ κ.τ.λ.   The letters ΙΔ in line 3 are quite certain.   Lines 4 foll. : it was common for athletes in recording their victories to insert the mention of some special achievement peculiar to

themselves, introducing it with the formula μόνος καὶ πρῶτος κ.τ.λ.   Thus C. I. 3208 : μόνος καὶ πρῶτος τῶν ἀπ' αἰῶνος νικήσας τοὺς ὑπογεγραμμένους ἀγῶνας.   The athlete of our inscription boasts that he is the only man who ever recorded the names of his antagonists.   Line 9 : the Panhellenia were founded by Hadrian at Athens ; compare Nos. CCCCLXXXVII, and DI.

DCXIV.

Fragment of white marble, entire at bottom only ; height 3½ in. ; width 1 ft. 4 in.   Discovered by Mr. Wood.   Unpublished.

```
--ı  'Ш                            . . . . . . φ . . . .
ΑΥΜΠΙΟΝΕΙΚΗΗΑΔΕΛΦΙ              . . . 'Ο]λυμπιονείκη ἡ ἀδελφὴ [ἀνέστησεν ?
      (uninscribed)
```

From a monument in honour of an Olympian victor, set up by his sister.   The Olympian contest referred to may have been the 'Αδριάνεια 'Ολύμπια at Ephesos.

DCXV.

A stelè of marble : height 2 ft. 8 in. ; width 1 ft. 8½ in.   Wood, Inscriptions from the Great Theatre, No. 20.

```
              ΛΙΟΕΞΗΣ·ΡΟΔΟ
      ΑΛΕΙΑ·ΠΑΙΔΩΝ·ΑΝΔΡΩΝ  ▸
      ΕΝΕΦΕΣΩ · ΠΑΙΔΩΝ · ΟΛΥΜΠΙΑ
      Ε  ΕΦΕΣΩΠΑΙΔΩΝ ▸ ΘΑΛΒΙΛΛΗΑ
   5  ΑΘΗΝΑΣΠΑΙΔΩΝ · ΠΑΝΕΛΛΗΝΙΑ
      ΕΝΤΡΑΛΛΕΣΙΝΠΑΙΔΩΝΑΝΔΡΩΝ
      ΟΛΥΜΠΙΑ ▸ ΡΩΜΗΝΚΑΠΙΤΩΛΙΑ
      ΑΓΕΝΕΙΩΝ·ΝΕΑΝΠΟΛΙΝ·ΣΕΒΑΣΤΑ
      ΑΓΕΝΕΙΩΝ·ΕΝΝΕΙΚΟΠΟΛΕΙΑΓΕΝΕΙΩΝ
  10  ΑΚΤΙΑ▸ΕΝ · ΑΡΓΕΙ·ΑΓΕΝΕΙΩΝΝΕΜΕΙΑ
      ΞΝΕΦΕΣΩ·ΑΓΕΝΕΙΩΝ▸ΑΡΤΕΜΕΙΣΙ/
      ΕΝΙΕΡΑΠΟΛΕΙ▸ΑΓΕΝΕΙΩΝΑΠΟΛΛΩΝ
      ΞΠΟΙΗΣΑΔΕΚΑΙΟΛΥΜΠΙΑΤΑΕΝΠΕΙΣΗΙΕΡΑ
      ΞΝΛΑΔΙΚΕΙΑ·ΑΝΔΡΩΝΔΕΙΑ · ΕΝΣΑΡΔΕΣ. Ν
  13  ΑΝΔΡΩΝ ΧΡΥΣΑΝΘΙΝΑ·ΣΜΥΡΝΑΝ  ▴
      ΚΑΤΑΤΟΕΞΗΣΟΛΥΜΠΙΑΤΗΣΣΥΝΟΔΟΥ
      ΑΔΡΙΑΝΑΟΛΥΜΠΙΑ·ΑΝΔΡΩΝΠΥΓΜΗΝ
      ΤΟΔΕΥΤΕΡΟΝΑΝΑΒΩΝΕΝΠΕΙΣΗ
      ΕΤΕΙΜΘΗΝΑΝΔΡΙΑΝΤΙΚΑΙΒΟΥΛΗ
```

```
      . . . . . . . . . . . . . . . κατ]ὰ τὸ ἑξῆς·
      'Ρόδο[ν] | 'Άλεια παίδων, ἀνδρῶν· |
      ἐν 'Εφέσῳ παίδων 'Ολύμπια· |
      ἐ[ν] 'Εφέσῳ παίδων Βαλβίλληα· |
   5  'Αθήνας παίδων Πανελλήνια· |
      ἐν Τράλλεσιν παίδων ἀνδρῶν ¦ 'Ολύμπια·
      'Ρώμην Καπιτώλια | ἀγενείων·
      Νέαν πόλιν Σεβαστὰ , ἀγενείων·
      ἐν Νεικοπόλει ἀγενείων | 'Άκτια·
  10  ἐν 'Άργει ἀγενείων Νέμεια· |
      ἐν 'Εφέσῳ ἀγενείων 'Αρτεμίσια· |
      ἐν 'Ιεραπόλει ἀγενείων 'Απολλών[ια· |
      ἐποίησα δὲ καὶ 'Ολύμπια τὰ ἐν Πείσῃ ἱερά· ¦
      ἐν Λαδικείᾳ ἀνδρῶν Δεῖα·
  15  ἐν Σάρδεσ[ιν | ἀνδρῶν Χρυσάνθινα·
      Ζμύραν | κατὰ τὸ ἑξῆς 'Ολύμπια, τῆς συνόδου | 'Αδριανὰ 'Ολύμπια ἀνδρῶν πυγμῆι· |
      τὸ δεύτερον ἀν(δρ)ῶν ἐν Πείσῃ | ἐτειμήθην ἀνδριάντι καὶ βουλῇ.
```

A successful athlete records his victories as boy, youth, and man (παίδων, ἀγενείων, ἀνδρῶν). The commencement is wanting; how the heading originally ran may be gathered from the headings of Nos. DCV *ante*, DCXXVI, DCXVII *post*. Line 1: κατὰ τὸ ἑξῆς is explained on No. DCIX. Line 2: Ἄλεια at Rhodes in honour of the Sun-god are mentioned in C. I. 3208, 5913, line 13. The accusative of the place, as well as of the game (Ῥόδον Ἄλεια sc. νικήσας) is quite regular; compare C. I. 5913 etc. Line 3: for the Ὀλύμπια (Ἀδριάνεια) at Ephesos, see Prolegomena p. 79; and line 17 *post*. Line 4: the Βαλβίλληα were founded at Ephesos by permission of Vespasian, in honour of his favourite astrologer. Thus Dio Cassius, Vesp. 66, § 9: τούς τε ἀστρολόγους ἐκ τῆς Ῥώμης ἐξώρισε, καίτοι πᾶσι τοῖς ἀρίστοις αὐτῶν χρώμενος, ὥστε καὶ διὰ Βάρβιλλόν τινα ἄνδρα τοιουτότροπον ἀγῶνα τοῖς Ἐφεσίοις ἄγειν συγχωρῆσαι· ὅπερ οὐδεμιᾷ ἄλλῃ πόλει ἔνειμεν. Barbillus was well known in Nero's reign; see Suetonius, Nero 36, where he is called Balbillus. This confusion between L and R is natural enough (see notes on Nos. DLXXVII, DXCV *ante*); and Barbillus may very likely have been one of the Ephesian Jews (Acts xix, 13–17 and 19), and his name possibly Bar-bela (compare 1 Chron. i, 43 etc.). Concerning the Jewish community at Ephesos we shall hear more in Nos. DCLXXVI, DCLXXVII *post*. The Barbillean games are frequently mentioned in agonistic lists from various parts of Greece; see index to C. I. and C. I. A. *s. v.*, and Prolegomena, p. 79. Lines 5–8: these games are sufficiently illustrated by Nos. DCV, DCXI, DCXIII. Line 6: Καπιτώλια is usually written Καπετώλια, but the I is quite certain. Line 9: the Ἄκτια were very anciently celebrated in honour of Apollo (see Harpokration and Steph. Byz. *s. v.* Ἄκτια, Ἄκτιον), but when Octavian, in commemoration of his victory, founded his new city of Nikopolis, the games acquired a new significance. Thus Strabo vii, p. 325 : ἤγετο δὲ καὶ πρότερον τὰ Ἄκτια τῷ

θεῷ, στεφανίτης ἀγὼν, ὑπὸ τῶν περιοίκων· νυνὶ δ' ἐντιμότερον ἐποίησεν ὁ Καῖσαρ. And Dio Cass. 51, § 1: ἀγῶνά τέ τινα καὶ γυμνικὸν καὶ μουσικῆς ἱπποδρομίας τε πεντετηρικὸν ἱερὸν, οὕτω γὰρ τοὺς τὴν σίτησιν ἔχοντας ὀνομάζουσι, (it carried with it, like the Olympia, the right of its victors to enjoy for life σίτησις ἐν πρυτανείῳ, see Plato, Apology, p. 36 and *reff*.) κατέδειξεν, Ἄκτια αὐτὸν προσαγορεύσας. Line 11: on the Artemisia, celebrated in the month Artemision or March, see No. CCCCLXXXII. I see no reason to identify the Ἀρτεμίσια with the Ἐφέσια (as Zimmermann does), Ephesos, p. 114); compare Prolegomena, p. 79. Line 12: these are styled Ἀπολλώνεια Πύθια in a similar inscription from Philadelphia, C. I. 3428. Line 13: ἐποίησα ἱερά can hardly be equivalent to ἐνίκησα. Line 14: it is not specified which city of the name is intended: Laodikeia in Syria or Laodikeia on the Lykos (see on No. CCCCXXI). The contracted form Λαδίκεια is somewhat rare; but see C. I. 6478, 6493, 6829 line 24, 9916. The Δεῖα Σεβαστὰ ἐν Λαοδικείᾳ are named in No. DCV, lines 5 and 11. Line 15: the Χρυσάνθινα at Sardes are often named in agonistic inscriptions; see C. I. 3208, 5913, line 33; Eckhel, Doctr. N. V. iv, p. 438. This celebration is only heard of at the end of the second century A. D. There was a famous philosopher Χρυσάνθιος of Sardes in the reign of Julian (see Suidas *s. v.*, and Eunapios in Müller's Fragmenta Hist. Gr. iv, p. 7 *note*), who perhaps derived his name from this festival. Line 16: he was victorious in the two Olympian games at Smyrna successively; just so M. Aurel. Asklepiades (C. I. 5913, line 27) ὁμοίως ἐν Σμύρνῃ Ὀλύμπια καὶ Ἀδριάνια Ὀλύμπια. The Olympia at Smyrna in honour of Hadrian are under the management of a σύνοδος, resembling the σύνοδος Ὀλυμπική which we hear of at Tralles (C. I. 2931). For βουλῇ *fin.* compare Prolegomena p. 74, and No. DCXVII. In line 18 the lapidary engraved ΑΝΑΒΩΝ by error for ΑΝΔΡΩΝ.

DCXVI.

Fragment of white marble; height 10 in.; width 10 in.; broken at top, right and bottom. Discovered by Mr. Wood. Unpublished.

ΛΣΟΥΛΠΙ	Κ]λ. Σουλπί[κι-
ΟΣΞΑΝΘΙΠΠ	ος Ξάνθιππ[ος
ΛΑΣΟΜΕΝ	Κ]λαζομέν[ιος
ΑΙΕΦΕΣΙΟ	κ]αὶ Ἐφέσιο[ς
5　ΙΚΗΣΑΣΤ	5　ν]εικήσας τ[ὰ
ΛΑ ΕΦΕ	μεγά]λα Ἐφέ[σια
	κ.τ.λ.

Part of the record of the victories of an athlete. The letters are of the second century A. D. The 'Great Ephesian Games' are named in most of our agonistic inscriptions; they were of ancient fame, see Thuk. iii, 104, and compare Prolegomena, p. 79. Successful athletes were often presented with the freedom of the cities they visited: thus in C. I. 5913 (a typical athlete's inscription) Μάρκος Αὐρήλιος Ἀσκληπιάδης describes himself as Ἀλεξανδρεὺς, Ἑρμοπολίτης, Ποτιολανὸς, Νεαπολείτ[η]ς καὶ Ἡλεῖος καὶ Ἀθηναῖος βουλευτής, καὶ ἄλλων πόλεων πολλῶν πολείτης καὶ βουλευτής: compare No. DCV, line 2, etc.

DCXVII.

Upper portion of white marble stelè, entire at the top and both sides. Height 10 in.; width 1 ft. 8½ in. Wood, Inscriptions from the Great Theatre, No. 11.

```
ΜΑΡΚΟΣΑΥΡΗΛΙΟΣΡΟΥΦΕΙ
ΝΟΣΑΛΕΞΑΝΔΡΕΥΣΚΑΙΕ
ΦΕΣΙΟΣΚΑΙΡΟΔΙΟΣΒΟΥΛΕΥ
```

Μάρκος Αὐρήλιος Ῥουφεῖ-
νος Ἀλεξανδρεὺς καὶ Ἐ-
φέσιος καὶ Ῥόδιος βουλευ[τ-
ής.........]ν......

Probably the heading of an agonistic list like the preceding ones.

DCXVIII.

Portion of a white marble stelè; height 3 ft. 1 in.; width 1 ft. 8 in. Entire to right and at bottom. Wood, Inscriptions from the site of the Temple of Diana, No. 18.

a.   *b.*

```
     ΩΝΕΠΙ      ]
    ΛΗΣΠΟΝ     ΜΕ
     ΕΥΑ       ΤΟΝ
5    ΑΔΙΟ     ΔΙΩΝΤΑΣΩΝ·ΩΝΚΡΙΔΕ
    ΩΣΤΑΤΩ    ΩΝΚΑΙΤΑΕΠΑΘΛΑΔΟΡ
   Ν·ΚΑΙΔΟΥ   ΤΟΙΣΜΟΥΣΙΚΟΙΣΚΑΙΤΕ
   ΗΣΙΕΡΑΤΕΙ  ΑΘΛΗΤΑΙΣΕΚΤΩΝΙΔΙΩ
   ΠΕΝΤΑΚΙΣ   ΚΑΙΠΑΝΗΓΥΡΙΑΡΧΗΣΑΝ
10  ΑΛΟΙΠΑΕΠΙ  ΤΩΝΑΡΤΕΜΕΙΣΙΩΝ·ΚΑΙ
   ΙΤΕΛΕΣΑ    ΑΓΩΝΟΘΕΤΗΣΑΝΤΑΤΩΝ
     ΩΣ      ΜΕΓΑΛΩΝΠΥΘΙΩΝ·ΚΑΙΑΡ
   (uninscribed) ΧΙΕΡΑΤΕΥΣΑΝΤΑΤΩΝΕΠ
              ΙΩΝΙΑΣΚΑΙΕΛΛΗΣΠΟΝΤΟΥ
15            ΚΑΙΑΓΩΝΟΘΕΤΗΣΑΝΤΑ
              ΤΩΝΧΡΥΣΟΦΟΡΩΝΔΟΝΤΑ
              ΚΑΙΚΕΙΟΝΑΣΤΗΠΟΛΕΙ
              ΕΙΣΤΟΑΡΧΑΙΟΝΓΥΜΝΑΣ
                 ΟΝ
20  ΤΩΝΠΟΙΗΣΑΜΕΝΗΣ·ΟΥΛΠΙΑΣ
    ΗΣΜΗΤΡΟΣΑΥΤΩΝ
```

```
........ ἀρ]χι-
ερατεύσας τ]ῶν ἐπ' Ἰ-
ωνίας καὶ Ἑλ]λησπόν-
του, καὶ κατασ]κευά-
5 σας ἐν τῷ στ]αδίῳ
βάθρα λευκὰ?] ὡς τὰ τῶ-
ν θεάτρω]ν· καὶ δοὺ-
ς ἐπὶ τ]ῆς ἱερατεί-
ας δηνάρια?] πεντακισ-
10 χίλια· καὶ τ]ὰ λοιπὰ ἐπὶ
τῆς ἀρχῆς ἐ]πιτελέσα-
ς φιλοτείμ]ως.

15
20 Τὴν ἀνάστασιν αὐ]τῶν ποιησαμένης Οὐλπίας
τ]ῆς μητρὸς αὐτῶν.
```

```
τ...............
μω...............
τον [........ ἐκ τῶν ἰ-
δίων πασῶν τῶν κρίσε-
ων, καὶ τὰ ἔπαθλα δόν[τα
τοῖς μουσικοῖς καὶ τοῖ[ς
ἀθληταῖς ἐκ τῶν ἰδίω[ν,
καὶ πανηγυριαρχήσαν[τα
τῶν Ἀρτεμισίων, καὶ
ἀγωνοθετήσαντα τῶν
μεγάλων Πυθίων, καὶ ἀρ-
χιερατεύσαντα τῶν ἐπ'
Ἰωνίας καὶ Ἑλλησπόντου,
καὶ ἀγωνοθετήσαντα
τῶν χρυσοφόρων, δόντα
καὶ κείονας τῇ πόλει
εἰς τὸ ἀρχεῖον γυμνάσ[ι-
ον.
```

A lady named Ulpia (line 20) erects a monument in honour of her two sons (line 21), both of whom had been munificent patrons of festivals. The inscription is divided into two portions, of which *a* describes one of the sons in the nominative case (see δού[s] in line 7), while *b* enumerates the offices held by the other in the accusative; the upper part of the stelè is broken, so that their names remain unknown.

a. Lines 1-4 of *a* are restored from lines 12-14 of *b*. Both sons had acted for a year as high priest of the famous guild of Dionysiac artists, so often mentioned in the inscriptions. This guild of dramatic performers was originally styled : τὸ κοινὸν τῶν περὶ τὸν Διόνυσον τεχνιτῶν τῶν ἐπ' Ἰωνίας καὶ Ἑλλησπόντου καὶ τῶν περὶ τὸν καθηγεμόνα Διόνυσον (C. I. 3067, 3068 A from Teos, second century B. C.); or later : Οἱ περὶ τὸν Διόνυσον τεχνῖται οἱ ἀπὸ Ἰωνίας καὶ Ἑλλησπόντου καὶ οἱ τούτων συναγων[ισταί] (C. I. 3082, also from Teos, of the Imperial period). In a decree from Iasos of Roman times (Waddington-Le Bas, No. 281) they are called : τὸ κοινὸν τῶν περὶ τὸν Διόνυσον τεχνιτῶν τῶν ἐν Ἰωνίᾳ καὶ Ἑλλησπόντῳ καὶ τῶν περὶ τὸν καθηγεμόνα Διόνυσον. These citations are enough to illustrate the text of our inscription. The reader is referred to the essay of Lüders, Die dionys. Künstler, especially pp. 77 foll., for the history of this guild. Under the Pergamene kings the Dionysiac artists lived at Teos, but Strabo tells us (xiv, p. 643) that in his time their head-quarters was Lebedos. In later days various other dramatic and musical guilds arose to rival them in fame : but our inscription shows that as late as the second century A. D. they held an important position and retained their ancient name. Every dramatic σύνοδος had its priest (Lüders, p. 143), a title which the vanity of later times amplified into ἀρχιερεύς (*a*, line 1, compare ἱερατεία line 8; *b*, line 12 foll.; Lüders, p. 144 [1]). The two brothers of our inscription had each of them shown great munificence while serving as

high priest of the guild. The brother commemorated in *a* had enriched the Ephesian Stadion with some improvement during his year of office, but my restoration of lines 4-7 are merely suggestions. The Ephesian Stadion has been described by Falkener, pp. 104 foll. The same man had also been a generous giver to the funds of the guild (lines 7-10).

b. The other brother had perhaps received public honours; and if the heading of *b* was Ἡ βουλὴ καὶ ὁ δῆμος ἐτείμησαν, it would explain the employment of the accusative (δόν[τα] κ.τ.λ.). Lines 4-8 : it is uncertain what festival is referred to; it may have been the Ephesia. Or perhaps the reference is to the Artemisia, of which the man in question had been at once ἀγωνοθέτης and also πανηγυριάρχης (line 9), like Priscus in No. cccclxxxii *c ante*. As ἀγωνοθέτης he may have paid the judges of all the contests, supplying also the prizes for the winners; compare what was said on the phrase καταστήσαντα τὴν Ἀρτεμισιακὴν κρίσιν in No. cccclxxxii *c*. Lines 9-10 : in the decree just cited the word πανήγυρις is especially applied to the Artemisia, which had its ἀγωνοθέτης as well as a πανηγυριάρχης : the former was concerned with the contests which took place at the festival, the latter with the festivities in general. Lines 11-12 : as I know of no mention of a Pythian celebration at Ephesos, the words may be understood of the Delphic Pythia. Lines 12-14 have already been explained in the notes on *a*. Lines 15-16 : the word χρυσοφόροι has been discussed on No. ocxv *ante*; compare Prolegomena, p. 85. He had acted as ἀγωνοθέτης on their behalf. Lines 16-19 : on the gymnasia at Ephesos see Prolegomena, p. 82, and the inscriptions there cited. The best account of their existing ruins is to be found in Falkener's Ephesus. He enumerates five gymnasia, p. 82, and p. 85, and gives plans of four of them : as they are all of late construction, we may conclude that τὸ ἀρχαῖον γυμνάσιον was not one of them.

DCXIX.

Fragment of white marble, measuring in height 5 in., in width 3 in. Broken on all sides. Discovered by Mr. Wood; unpublished.

ΚΗΣ̣ϵ	Ὁ δεῖνα ἐνί[κησε?] . . . .
‾ΩΝΙΣ	. . . . ἀ]γωνισ . . .
‾ΔΙΑΤ	. . . διατ . . .
ΔΑΤϹ	. . . ματο . . .
ΒΑΙ	. . . βαι . . .

Probably agonistic.

[1] The title ἀρχιερεὺς συνόδου appears only to occur in late documents. The one inscription cited by Lüders of an earlier date (C. I. 2620) has been more correctly edited in Part ii. No. cccclxxxv, where instead of ἀρχιερέωσα, Sir Charles Newton restores from the stone ἱερέωσα.

DCXX.

Plain slab of bluish marble ; height 1 ft. ; width 1 ft. 10½ in.   Discovered by Mr. Wood ; unpublished.

ΦΑΜΙΛΙΑΣ
ΜΟΝΟΜΑΧΩ
ΝΤΙ·ΚΑ·ΤΑΤΙ
ΑΝΟΥΙΟΥΛΙΑ
5 ΝΟΥΑΣΙΑΡΧ
ΟΥ .

Φαμιλίας
μονομάχω·
ν Τι. Κλ. Τατι-
ανοῦ Ἰουλια-
5 νοῦ Ἀσιάρχ-
ου.

This stone marked the spot where a ' familia ' or troop of gladiators had been buried who had been slaughtered at the games provided by the Asiarch named below (κοινὰ Ἀσίας, see Prolegomena p. 79, and notes on No. CCCCLXXXIX *ante*). Tib. Cl. Tatianus Julianus may perhaps be identified with the Tiberius Claudius Antipater Julianus repeatedly mentioned as πρύτανις, A. D. 104, in the Salutaris documents (No. CCCCLXXXVI), and with Tiberius Claudius Julianus named as γραμματεὺς τοῦ δήμου in No. CCCCXCIX *ante*, A. D. 102-3. If so, our inscription belongs to the reign of Trajan. This and the next following belong to a class of documents by no means rare, all of them phrased in much the same manner ; compare C. I. Addenda 2191 *l* (Mytilene), 2511 (Kos) ;

Addenda 2759 *b* (Aphrodisias). 3213 (Smyrna), 3677 (Kyzikos). and Waddington-Le Bas, Part v, No. 615 (Tralles). In this last however the heading is simply Μονομάχαι, in all the rest it is Φαμιλία μονομάχων, as in No. DCXXI. In the present document the genitive Φαμιλίας is possessive ; this is their burying-place. It is a question whether this and the next ought not to be placed among the sepulchral inscriptions. But the truth is, all such monuments are in their motive honorary, and not sepulchral. They were not intended to commemorate the dead, but to glorify the giver of the show (munus gladiatorium) ; see C. I. iii, p. 1105. I have therefore classed them with the Agonistic documents.

DCXXI.

A white marble panel surmounted by a plain moulding ; height 1 ft. 2½ in. ; width 1 ft. 5 in.   Discovered by Mr. Wood, as he describes in his ' Ephesus,' p. 126 ; unpublished.

ΦΑΜΙΛΙΑ
ΜΟΝΟΜΑ
ΧΩΝ—ΤΙΒ·
ΙΟΥΛΙΟΥ·ΡΗ
5 ΓΕΙΝΟΥ·ΑΣΙ
ΑΡΧΟΥ ··

Φαμιλία
μονομά-
χων Τιβ.
Ἰουλίου Ῥη-
5 γείνου Ἀσι-
άρχου.

See notes on the preceding inscription.
Tib. Julius Rheginus is mentioned also in Nos. DCIV, DCV, DCXI ; and in a fragment not brought to

England, but published by Wood, Inscriptions from the Great Theatre, No. 9.

SECTION IX.

SEPULCHRAL.

DCXXII.

A white marble sarcophagus ; height 10 in. ; width 1 ft. 4 in.   Beneath the inscription is a festoon with heads of rams and oxen. Discovered by Mr. Wood, as described in his Ephesus, pp. 125–6.   C. Curtius, Hermes iv, p. 214.

ΑΝΑΣΣΑ ΑΠΟΛΛΩΝΙΟΥ	Ἄνασσα Ἀπολλωνίου
ΧΡΗΣΤΗ ΧΑΙΡΕ	χρηστὴ χαῖρε.

The name Ἄνασσα seems not to occur elsewhere.

DCXXIII.

Fragment from the top left-hand corner of a sepulchral monument of white marble : height 5½ in. ; width 4½ in.   Below the inscription is part of the sepulchral relief, a horse's head alone being preserved.   Discovered by Mr. Wood ; unpublished.

Α Δ Μ	Ἀδμ[ητος ?
Δ Ι Α	Δια[γόρου ?

The characters are neatly cut, and may be of the Macedonian period.   The names are merely restored *exempli gratia* ; very few Greek names however begin either with ΑΔΜ or ΔΙΑ.

DCXXIV.

Fragment of white marble : height 3 in. ; width 8⅜ in.: entire only on right.   Said to have been found at the North corner of the Temple-site : from Mr. Wood's excavations.   Unpublished.

ϽΛΛ ϟ ι Ε Ω	Ἀπολλωνίδης ? Ἀπ]ολλω[νίδ]εω·
⁻ΠΙΤΕΡΨΙΟΣΟΓ Μ ᴖ ᴎ	– ᴗᴗ– ᴗᴗ– ᴗᴗ– ἐπὶ τέρψιος ὄγμον.

Apparently an epitaph, complete in two lines: the second being metrical : e. g. [Βαιὸν ὀδυράμενός μ' ἀποβαίν]ἐπὶ τέρψιος ὄγμον. The lettering is not later than the second or first centuries B.C.   The letters of line 1 are somewhat larger than in line 2.

DCXXV.

a.

A sepulchral stelè of white marble, 2 ft. 11½ in. high : 1 ft. 8 in. wide ; slightly broken on the left. Above the inscription is a sunk panel with a relief representing on the left a female figure seated on a chair and turned to the right with her right arm advanced towards a male figure who stands before her and has held her right hand in his ; but both the hands are now wanting. Beside the chair of the female figure stands a diminutive figure with arms crossed and wearing a short chiton. At the feet of the male figure and on the extreme right of the relief stands another diminutive figure wearing a short chiton girt at the waist, the right arm raised across the bosom and the left falling at the side. Above this figure is the head of a horse represented as if projecting from the frame of the relief ; above the horse is a tree with a serpent in its branches ; the faces of all the figures have been broken off, and in parts the relief is injured. The principal male figure wears a chiton with short sleeves and a himation, which passing over the left shoulder is wrapped round the legs and gathered up over the left forearm ; his left hand holds a roll. The female figure also wears a chiton and a himation similarly arranged ; her feet rest on a footstool. The relief is figured in Wood's Ephesus, p. 123. The inscription is published by Wood, Appendix, Inscriptions on tombs, No. 19 ; Kaibel, Epigrammata, No. 228 b.

NYMΦIΔIΩNKPAΔIHIΠEΠΛHΘOTAΛEKTPΩN
ΛONAIAKTΩITΩIΔ·YΠENAΣΣETAΦΩI
ITEΓNΩTHTEΠANAIΔOIHIΣTPATONIKHι
ιIAΛEΞANΔPONKOYPONOMHΓENEA
ϽIΣKAIΞEINOIΣIΓIPOΣHNEAΣEΣϴΛAMENEIΓIEIN
ιAΔEKAIPEΞAIΓIANTAΣEΠIΣTAMENOYΣ
¯ENEΣΣYΔEΓIAIΔAΣENHPΩIEΣΣIφYΛAΣΣOIΣ
ΩNAIEIXΩPONEΓIEPXOMENOΣ

Οὔπω] νυμφιδίων κραδίη πεπληθότα λέκτρων
Δίφι]λον αἰακτῷ τῷδ' ὑπένασσε τάφῳ
γνωτόν] τε γνωτή τε παναιδοίη(ι) Στρατονίκη(ι).
ᾧ κ]αὶ 'Αλέξανδρον κοῦρον ὁμηγενέα,
ἀστ]οῖς καὶ ξείνοισι προσηνέας, ἐσθλὰ μὲν εἰπεῖν
ἐσθ]λὰ δὲ καὶ ῥέξαι πάντας ἐπισταμένους·
Μαιο]γενὴς, σὺ δὲ παῖδας ἐν ἡρῴεσσι φυλάσσοις
εὐσεβέ]ων αἰεὶ χῶρον ἐπερχόμενος.

The letters belong to the second or third centuries B.C. The text as given by Wood and by Kaibel is inaccurate in several particulars. Line 1 : the marble has *ΚΡΑΔΙΗΙ* not *ΚΡΑΔΙΗΝ*. Line 3 : Wood rightly gives from the marble Παναιδοίη Στρατονίκη, whereas Kaibel omits the iota adscriptum without remark. The first letter of line 3 is broken, and may once have been Η as Wood and Kaibel edit ; but the line of breakage points rather to Ν. Line 4 : the second letter was certainly not Τ (as Wood and Kaibel), but Ι, probably preceded by Α. Lines 6 and 7 are broken at the beginning like the rest ; see uncial text. In line 2 Kaibel follows Wood in restoring [Ζωί]λον, but the lacuna requires a longer name. If we follow the marble in reading παναιδοίη Στρατονίκη, it becomes very difficult to restore the epitaph. I therefore follow Kaibel in making Στρατονίκη the nominative to ὑπένασσε, and suppose the lapidary to have dealt too freely with his iota adscriptum. Similarly *ΗΡΩΙΕΣΣΙ* in line 7 can hardly be justified by the form ΗΡΟΙΝ (ἥρων, dative dual), Part i, No. LXXIII ante, nor even by ΗΡΩΙΣΙΝ (ἥρῳσιν) which is found in an epitaph of good age but uncertain locality. C. I. 6947. The general sense appears to me to be this : Stratonike buries here her brother [Diphi]los who was looking forward to marriage, but not yet married ; in this same tomb she had also buried another brother, Alexander.

Line 1 : Kaibel gives ῎Αρτι μὲ] νυμφιδίων κ.τ.λ. We might supply ῎Αρμοί. I prefer Οὔπω, as accounting for the sister being named (according to my restora-

tion) and not the wife. Line 3 : compare Il. xv. 350 : γνωτοί τε γνωταί τε, brothers and sisters. Line 4 : ὁμηγενέα is not recognised in Liddell and Scott. Line 5 is thought by Kaibel to be imitated from an epigram by Leonidas of Tarentum, Anth. i, p. 243 (Brunck) : ἥδει καὶ ξείνοισι καὶ ἐνδήμοισι προσηνέα | ἐρδεῖν κ.τ.λ. Προσηνής however is usually employed to describe courtesy of manner and speech rather than conduct ; compare also Anakreon, Fragment 14 (Bergk) : —

Οὐ δηὖτ' ἔμπεδός εἰμι,
οὐδ' ἀστοῖσι προσηνής.

Also C. I. 2335, line 46, and 2109 g (Kaibel, 251) : —

Λυσίμαχον μύθοι[σ]ι προσηνέα πᾶσι πολίταις
εὐσεβέσιν κ.τ.λ.

The words ἐσθλὰ καὶ . . . . ἐπισταμένους are merely a poetical version of a common phrase in honorary decrees : ὁ δεῖνα ἀεὶ διατελεῖ καὶ λέγων καὶ πράττων ἀγαθὸν ὅτι δύναται ὑπὲρ τοῦ δήμου (see e. g. C. I. A. ii. 313, 331). Line 7 : Wood (followed by Kaibel) edits Λητογενὲς, as if the stone exhibited a perfect line. I prefer Μαιο]γενὲς, although the word does not appear to occur elsewhere : compare C. I. 4284 (Kaibel 411) : —

. . . τὸν, ὦ Μαίας κλυτὲ κοῦρε,
'Ερμείη, πέμπους χῶρον ἐπ' εὐσεβέων.

Also C. I. 4708 fin. (Kaibel, 414). Line 8 : Kaibel rightly εὐσεβέ]ων . . . χῶρον, which is a favourite phrase in epitaphs : see No. is xxix post, and the passage just cited on line 7 : also Kaibel 151, 218, 250, 500.

3 1

b.

At a later date, not earlier than the third century A.D., the stele was employed as the lid or door of a tomb (πωμάριον). Upon the undressed surface of the back, turned outwards, was rudely cut the following inscription, the original epitaph being hidden and somewhat injured in the process. The inscription runs lengthwise along the marble.

ΤΟΥΤΟΤΟΠΩΛΛΑΡΙΝΕΣΤΙΝ	Τοῦτο τὸ πωμάριν ἐστίν,
ΣΥΝΤΕΣΕΩΡΟΙΣΚΕΤΩΘΟ	σὺν τές (= ταῖς) ἑώροις κὲ (= καὶ) τῷ θό-
ΛΩΑΦΡΟΔΙΣΙΟΥΚΕΓΝ	λῳ, Ἀφροδισίου κὲ γν. (= γυναικὸς ?)
ΦΛΑΒΙΑΣΚΕΤΕΚΝΩ	Φλαβίας κὲ τέκνω[ν.

Πωμάριον seems to indicate the entrance to the | the roof (θόλος), but I cannot find anything to illus-
tomb or vault, and *αἱ ἕωροι* (= αἰῶροι) the supports of | trate the term αἰῶροι, which is new to the Lexicons.

DCXXVI.

Part of a base(?) of white marble: height 2 ft. 2¾ in.; width 1 ft. 7 in. The inscribed surface is slightly concave, and the marble itself is entire; but the right and left edges fitted on originally to other blocks. Discovered by Mr. Wood; unpublished.

ΝΟΥΣΑ	Ὁ δεῖνα . . . . .]νους Ἀ[nomen gentile.
ΕΝΘΑΓΑΤΡΑΜΟΙΣΗΜΑ	Ἔνθα πάτρα μοι σῆμα | τὸ λοίσθιον ἵνεκα δόξ[ης ¹
ΤΟΛΟΙΣΘΙΟΝΙΝΕΚΑΔΟΣ 5	ὤπασε τῷ Πίσας δισ[σά] κις ἀθλοφόρῳ,
ΩΠΑΣΕΤΩΠΙΣΑΣΔΙΣ	ὅν ποτε καὶ Λερναῖα [πε] ρὶ κροτάφοισι σέλ[ινα |
5 ΚΙΣΑΘΛΟΦΟΡΩΙ	ἔστεφε καὶ πολλὼ[ν] ¹ νίκεα πανκρατίω[ν ¹ |
ΟΝΓΟΤΕΚΑΙΛΕΡΝΑΙ/ 10	τὰς δὲ παρ᾽ Ἀλφῷ τ[ιμὰς] | καὶ Ζηνὶ Νεμήῳ |
ΡΙΚΡΟΤΑΦΟΙΣΙΣΕΛ	οὖτος ὁ δυσπενθ[ὴς] | τύνβος ἐνοσφίσα[το.
ΕΣΤΕΦΕΚΑΙΓΟΛΛΩ	
ΝΙΚΕΑΓΑΝΚΡΑΤΙΩ	
10 ΤΑΣΔΕΓΑΡΑΛΦΗΩΤ	
ΚΑΙΞΗΝΙΝΕΜΗΩΙ	
ΣΥΤΟΣΟΔΥΣΓΕΝΣ	
ΤΥΝΒΟΣΕΝΟΣΦΙΣΑ	

An epitaph upon a man who had been twice victor in the Olympian games, and also at the Nemean, besides other lesser games. The monument was erected by public decree (πάτρα, line 2). Line 1 | contained the name of the person thus honoured. The spelling of ἵνεκα, and the form νίκος for νίκη, are post-classical; the writing is hardly later than the first half of the first century A. D.

DCXXVII.

A square altar of bluish marble, beautifully preserved: height 3 ft. 6 in.; width 2 ft. 7 in. Inscribed on the front (*a*), and on the left side (*b*). Wood, Ephesus, Inscriptions from Tombs, No. 18; compare *ibid.* p. 124; Gelzer, Rhein. Museum N. S. xxvii, p. 466; Kaibel Epigrammata 229, and Addenda, p. 520.

a.

	›Λ›ΚΑΛΠΟΥΡΝΙΩΙ
	ΚΑΛΠΟΥΡΝΙΑΝΩΙ
	‹Τ›ΚΑΛΠΟΥΡΝΙΟΣΚΥ
	ΙΝΤΙΑΝΟΣΑΦΡΙΚΑΝΟΣ
5	ΚΑΤΕΣΚΕΥΑΣΕΝΣΥΝ
	ΤΗΙΕΚΒΑΣΜΕΙΔΩΣΕΙ
	◊ ΤΟΝΒΩΜΟΝ ◊
	ΡΗΝΩΙΠΑΡΠΟΤΑΜΩΙΓΕΝΟΜΗΝΠΩΛΑΙΤΤΑΔΕΜΗΤΗΡ
	ΚΥΙΝΤΙΑΝΟΣΔΕΠΑΤΗΡΠΡΟΥΣΙΑΔΟΣΔΕΠΑΤΡΗΣ
10	ΚΑΛΠΟΥΡΝΙΑΝΟΣΔΟΥΝΟΜΑΕΤΗΔΕΠΙΠΕΝΤΕΛΟΓΟΙΣΙΝ
	ΙΝΕΦΕΣΩΙΣΧΟΛΑΣΑΣΕΙΚΟΣΕΤΗΣΕΘΑΝΟΝ

b.

	ΟΕΝΟΧΛΗΣΑΣΤΟΥΤΩΙ
	ΤΩΙΒΩΜΩΙΗΤΩΙΤΟΠΩΙ
	ΚΑΤΑΒΑΛΕΙΕΙΣΤΟΝΦΙΣΚΟΝ
15	* ◊ ☩ ΜΥΡΙΑ

a.

Λ(ουκίῳ) Καλπουρνίῳ
Καλπουρνιανῷ
Τ(ίτος) Καλπούρνιος Κυ-
ιντιανὸς Ἀφρικανὸς
κατεσκεύασεν σὺν
τῇ ἐκβασμειδώσει
τὸν βωμόν.

'Ρηνῷ πὰρ ποταμῷ γενόμην, Πώλλιττα δὲ μήτηρ,
Κυιντιανὸς δὲ πατήρ, Προυσιάδος δὲ πάτρης,
Καλπουρνιανὸς δ' οὔνομα· ἔτη δ' ἐπὶ πέντε λόγοισιν
ἐν Ἐφέσῳ σχολάσας εἰκοσέτης ἔθανον.

b.

Ὁ ἐνοχλήσας τούτῳ
τῷ βωμῷ ἢ τῷ τόπῳ
καταβαλεῖ εἰς τὸν φίσκον
Ӿ μύρια.

The tomb of a youth of high rank. His parents were living on the Rhine when their son was born (line 8), though they had a home and connexions (line 9) at Prusias in Bithynia (i. e. Kios, see Strabo, xii, p. 563). The youth had been studying rhetoric at Ephesos from the age of 15. perhaps with a view to the legal profession, and died there. We hear but little of Ephesos (as compared with Rhodes, for example), as a school of Rhetoric ; but No. DXLVIII *ante* speaks of the rhetor Soteros and his pupils, and St. Paul seems to have hired the lecture-room of another such rhetorician (Acts xix, 9 : καθ' ἡμέραν διαλεγόμενος ἐν τῇ σχολῇ Τυράννου). Line 6 : ἐκβασμεί-

δωσις is unknown to the Lexicons, it means a step or step's pace round the altar : derivation from βαθμός or βασμός, βαθμοειδής, βασμειδής, ἐκ-βασμειδόω-ωσις) ; ἐκ-βάσμωσις is found in a similar sepulchral inscription from Adramyttion, published in the Bull. de Corr. Hell. iv, 1880, p. 381. Line 8 : the name Πώλλιττα (not Πόλλιττα as Wood) occurs in C. I. 3098 (from Teos). The inscription is hardly later than the first century A.D. Note in the last line the usual sign of denarii, Ӿ. On the fines specified in the later Graeco-Roman sepulchral inscriptions, as payable in case of injury to the tomb, see note on No. DCXLVIII *post.*

DCXXVIII.

A slab of white marble, 'found in a pier of the Coressian Gate, to which it did not originally belong.' Height 2 ft. 11½ in. ; width 3 ft. 4 in. The surface is nearly filled by a circular flat shield in relief, which encloses the metrical epigram. Wood, Inscriptions from the City and Suburbs, No. 10 (epigram only), compare *ibid.* p. 116 ; after him, Kaibel, Epigrammata, No. 228 a.

TO MNHMEI
ONEΣTIN
MΛPKIAΣ
EΞIMEPAΣ

ZH

KAI

ANA
MHΛIC
ZI

ΩΣΑΓΑΘΟΝΚΑΙΠΑΙΔΑΚΑΤΑΦΘΙΜΕΝΟΙΟΛΙΠΕΣΘΑΙ
ΕΙΠΕΜΕΛΙΓΛΩΣΣΩΝΙΔΡΙΣΟΠΙΕΡΙΔΩΝ
ΤΟΥΤΕΤΥΜΩΣΕΠΕΜΟΥΦΙΛΕΕΚΕΚΡΙΤΑΙΑΝΓΑΡΑΝΕΙΛΕΝ
ΜΝΑΜΑΝΑΚΑΚΙΑΠΑΙΣΠΑΛΙΝΗΡΓΑΣΑΤΟ
ΚΑΛΑΝΔΕΣΧΩΖΩΝΓΕΝΕΤΑΧΑΡΙΝΟΥΒΙΟΤΟΥΦΩΣ
ΔΕΥΤΕΡΟΝΑΛΛΑΚΛΕΟΥΣΗΨΙΕΡΟΝΒΙΟΤΟΝ
ΑΙΝΩΜΟΥΣΑΩΝΣΕΜΝΟΝΓΕΝΟΣΕΙΣΧΑΡΕΤΑΝΓΑΡ
ΔΩΚΑΝΕΜΟΙΤΕΚΝΟΥΖΩΣΑΝΕΥΦΡΟΣΥΝΑΝ

Τὸ μνημεῖ-
όν ἐστιν
Μαρκίας
ἐξ Ἱμέρας·
ζ̄η̄.

καὶ

Ἀνα . . . .
Μηλίο[υ·
ζ̄η̄.

Ὡς ἀγαθὸν καὶ παῖδα καταφθιμένοιο λιπέσθαι,
εἶπε μελιγλώσσων ἴδρις ὁ Πιερίδων·

τοῖσ' ἐτύμως ἐπ' ἐμοῦ, φίλε, κέκριται· ἂν γὰρ ἀνεῖλεν
μνᾶμον ἃ κακία, παῖς πάλιν ἠργάσατο.
καλὰν δ' ἐξσώζων γενέτᾳ χάριν, οὐ βιότου φῶς
δεύτερον, ἀλλὰ κλέους ᾗψ' ἱερὸν βίοτον.
αἰνῶ Μουσάων σεμνὸν γένος, εἰς ἀρετὰν γὰρ
δῶκαν ἐμοὶ τέκνου ζῶσαν εὐφροσύναν.

The portions in prose have suffered from rough erasion or intentional injury, probably in ancient times. They are however fairly legible still, though more coarsely engraved than the epigram, which appears to belong to the first century A. D. The epigram, for obvious reasons, is inscribed with much care and in the most elegant letters the lapidary had at his command. We may suppose that this was originally a sepulchral monument, erected by Marcia of Himera and Ana . . . a Melian during their life-time. Probably these were husband and wife, and the shield with which the slab was adorned may have referred to the man's profession as being that of arms. Marcia is named first, perhaps because her money purchased the tomb. After the husband's death the inscription on this his monument was injured by some ill-meaning person (lines 3, 4); but here he proved the truth of what a great poet had said about Orestes avenging his father (line 1, from Odyssey iii, 196). For his son, who was a poet (line 5), repaired his father's tomb (line 4), and restored to him not indeed life but an abiding record (line 6) : εἰς ἀρετάν must mean 'for my better renown.' I imagine that the son composed this epigram, and had it placed upon the monument, although it is supposed to be spoken by the dead father. The epigram is in Doric, and this accords with the father being from Melos. Kaibel interprets somewhat differently.

DCXXIX.

Sepulchral column of white marble ; height 3 ft., diameter 1 ft. 5¼ in. Found in the village of Arralia, S. of Ephesos. Published by Waddington-Le Bas, Nos. 168 and 170 ; C. Curtius, Hermes iv. p. 207 ; Kaibel, Epigrammata, 296 ; compare Röhl, Schedae Epigraphicae, p. 23.

ΠΟΠΛΙΟΝΑΥΦΙΔΙΟΝΓΗ
ΡΩΣΕΠΙΤΕΡΜΑΜΟΛΟΝΤΑ
ΕΥΣΕΒΕΩΝΧΩΡΟΣΔΕΞΑΤΟ
ΠΑΣΙΦΙΛΟΝ = ΑΣΠΑΖΕΣΘΗΡΩ
ΑΤΟΝΟΥΚΕΔΑΜΑΣΣΑΤΟΛΥΠΗ
(Space of five inches vacant.)
ΠΟΠΛΙΟΣΚΑΣΤΡ
ΚΙΟΣΑΓΑΘΕΙΝΟ
ΛΕΥΚΙΟΣΛΑΙΛΙΟ
ΑΣΤΡΑΓΑΛΟΣ
ΟΓΟΥΛΝΙΑΨ
ΖΗ

Πόπλιον Αὐφίδιον γήραος ἐπὶ τέρμα μολόντα
εὐσεβέων χῶρος δέξατο ; πᾶσι φίλον·
ἀσπάζεσθ' ἥρω͜α τὸν οὐκ ἐδαμάσσατο λύπη.

Πόπλιος Καστρ[ί-
κιος Ἀγαθεῖνο[ς,
Λεύκιος Λαίλιο[ς
Ἀστράγαλος,
Ὀγουλνία. ψ. [β.?]
ζῆ.

In line 1 the marble exhibits Αὐφίδιον, thus dismissing the conjectures of previous editors.

The letters are of the first century A. D.; but the lines of verse, if contemporaneous, are inscribed with less care and elegance than the remainder.

Perhaps the P. Castricius of the prose inscription was the kinsman and heir of P. Aufidius named above. Aufidius had been voted a public funeral.

see line 10 : ψ(ηφίσματι) [β](ουλῆς) or [δ](ήμου). His heir, P. Castricius, assisted by other kinsfolk—L. Laelius Astragalos and Ogulnia—erects this monument in his honour. At the foot he adds, ζῆ (sc. Castricius) : i. e. the tomb is his, prepared in his lifetime to receive him when he dies. For the phrase εὐσεβέων χῶρος compare No. DCXXV ante.

DCXXX.

A fragment of white marble, broken all round ; height 3½ in., length 1 ft. 4½ in. Described by Mr. Wood ; unpublished.

ΟΙΚΟΣ · ΟΝΗΓΕΙΡΕΝ · ΠΑΙΣΙ · ΠΑΤΙ
ΖΗΣΑΜΕΝΟΙΣ · ΕΤΕΩΝ · ΠΑΥΡΟΝΥ
ΤΡΙΣ · ΗΜΕΓΑΛΗ · Μ

Οἶκος ὃν ἤγειρεν παισὶ πατ[ὴρ ∪ ∪ –
. . . .
Ζησαμένοις ἐτέων παῦρον ὑ[π – ∪ ∪ –
. . . .
Νῦν πα]τρὶς ἡ μεγάλη μ – ∪ ∪ – ∪ ∪ –

Part of an epitaph ; only portions of three pentameters remain. Date probably the first century A. D.

DCXXXI.

Fragment of white marble, entire on right and at bottom. Height 6 in.; width 10 in. Discovered by Mr. Wood; unpublished.

LIV ΛΡΗΕVϪ   ....nus Iu]liu[s O]rpheus
ΝΟΣΙΟΥΛΙΟΣ   .... νοϛ Ἰούλιοϛ
ΟΡΦΕΥΣ   Ὀρφεύϛ.

Letters of the Augustan age.

DCXXXII.

On a simple sarcophagus of white marble, ornamented with heads of oxen and of rams. Height 10 in.; width 1 ft. 3 in.; discovered by Mr. Wood, as described in his Ephesus, p. 126. C. Curtius, Hermes, iv, p. 214; C. I. L. iii. 6089.

PANNℂHVSIBIETVXORPΊΤHANETFILIAI   Pannychus (s)ibi et uxor(i) Pithan(e) et filiae
PITHANE   Pithane.
ΠΑΝΝΧΟϹΕΑΥΤΩΚΑΙΠΙΦΑΝΗΓΥΝΑ   Πάννυχοϛ ἑαυτῷ καὶ Πιθάνῃ γυνα-
ΙΙ Ι   ι[κ]ί,
ΚΑΙΘΥΓΑΤΡΙΠΙΦΑΝΗ   καὶ θυγατρὶ Πιθάνῃ.

The third line is inscribed in smaller characters than the rest.

DCXXXIII.

Plain slab of white marble: height 11 in.; width 1 ft. 3 in. Discovered by Mr. Wood; unpublished.

TOYTOYTOYMH   Τούτου τοῦ μν[η-
ΜΕΙΟΥΤΟΔΕΞΙΟΝΜΕ   μείου τὸ δεξιὸν μέ-
ΡΟϹΕϹΤΙΝΚΟΥΜΦΟΥΛΗΙ   ροϛ ἐστὶν Κ. Οὐμφουληΐ-
ΟΥ·ΒΑΣΣΟΥΚΑΙΕΥΤΥΧΙΔΟΣ   ου Βάσσου καὶ Εὐτυχίδοϛ
5   ΑΛΕΞΑΝΔΡΟΥΤΟΥΔΗ   5   Ἀλεξάνδρου τοῦ Δη-
ΜΟΤΕΛΟΥΣ⸓ ΚΛΗΡΟ   μοτέλους σ[υγ]κληρο-
ΝϹ   ΟΥΖΩϹΙΝ   νό[μου αὐτ]οῦ. ζῶσιν.

It is obvious that many of these sepulchral inscriptions are not intended to be memorials of the dead, but to define and claim the ownership of the plot of ground or monument. Thus the present document declares that the right hand portion of the tomb belongs to C. Umphuleius Bassus and to Eutychis his co-heir, she being the daughter of Alexander son of Demoteles; we may suppose that Bassus and Eutychis were man and wife, but it is not stated.

DCXXXIV.

White marble stele, surmounted by a plain moulding: top and left entire. Height 11 in.; width 11½ in. Discovered by Mr. Wood; unpublished.

TOYTOY⸓   Τούτου τ[οῦ ἡρῴου
ΤΟΡΙΤΟΝΜΕϹ   τὸ τρίτον μέρ[οϛ καὶ
ΤΩΝΕΝΔΕΞΙϹι   τῶν ἐνδέξιο[ν σορῶν ?
ΕΣΣΙΝΑΥΡΖΩ   ἐσ(τ)ιν· Αὐρ. Ζω[. . . ου
5   ΣΑΟΝΟΣΚΑΙΓΥΝ   5   Σάονοϛ καὶ γυν[αικὸϛ
ΑΥΡ·ΣΜΥΡΝΗΣΕΦ   Αὐρ. Σμύρνηϛ Ἐφ[εσίαϛ
ΚΑΙΤΕΚΝΩΝ   καὶ τέκνων [αὐτῶν.
Ζ Ω Σ '   Ζῶσι[ν.

In line 4 ΕΣΣΙΝ is the lapidary's blunder. The husband's name was Αὐρ. Ζωῖλος (Ζώσιμος, Ζώτιχος vel simile) Σάων. Σάων is a well known name, especially in Bœotia, though usually with genitive Σάωνοϛ. Its bearer was probably not an Ephesian, but his wife Aur. Smyrna was.

DCXXXV.

Sepulchral slab of white marble; height 1 ft. 9 in.; width 3 ft. 4 in.; in good preservation.   Discovered by Mr. Wood.   C. Curtius, Hermes, iv, p. 210; Wood, Inscriptions from Tombs, etc., No. 13.

ΤΙ · Κ Λ Α · Ε Υ Τ Υ Χ Ο Σ · Ι Ω Ν	Τι(βέριος) Κλα(ύδιος) Εὔτυχος ζῶν
Τ Ο Μ Ν Η Μ Ε Ι Ο Ν Κ Α Τ Ε Σ Κ Ε Υ	τὸ μνημεῖον κατεσκεύ-
Α Σ Ε Ν · Ε Α Υ Τ Ω · Κ Α Ι · Κ Λ Α Υ Δ Ι Α	ασεν ἑαυτῷ καὶ Κλαυδίᾳ
Μ Ο Υ Σ Η · Τ Η Γ Υ Ν Α Ι Κ Ι Κ Α Ι · Κ Λ Α Υ ·	Μούσῃ τῇ γυναικὶ καὶ Κλαυ(δίᾳ)
5 ΒΕΝΟΥΣΗ · ΤΗ Θ Υ Γ Α Τ Ρ Ι Κ Α Ι · Τ · Μ Α	5 Βενούστῃ τῇ θυγατρὶ καὶ Τ(ίτῳ) Μα-
Ρ Ι Ω Μ Α Ρ Κ Ε Λ Λ Ω Τ Ω Γ Α Ν Β Ρ Ω Κ Α Ι · Τ Ι · Κ Λ Α Υ ·	ρίῳ Μαρκέλλῳ τῷ γανβρῷ καὶ Τι(βερίῳ) Κλαυ(δίῳ)
Β Ε Ν Ο Υ Σ Τ Ω Τ Ω Υ Ι Ω Κ Α Ι Τ Ο Ι Σ Τ Ο Υ Τ Ω Ν	Βενούστῳ τῷ υἱῷ καὶ τοῖς τούτων
Ε Κ Γ Ο Ν Ο Ι Σ Κ Α Ι Τ Ο Ι Σ Α Π Ε Λ Ε Υ Θ Ε Ρ Ο Ι Σ ¢	ἐκγόνοις καὶ τοῖς ἀπελευθέροις.

C. Curtius remarks that the Τιβέριος Κλαύδιος Τιβερίου Κλαυδίου υἱὸς, ἀπελεύθερος, named on another Ephesian tombstone (C. I. 3014) may have belonged to the household spoken of in line 8.

DCXXXVI.

Sepulchral slab of white marble; height 2 ft. 8½ in.; width 1 ft. 10 in.   Discovered by Mr. Wood.   C. Curtius, Hermes, iv, p. 209 : Wood, Inscriptions from Tombs, etc., No. 5 : C. I. L. iii, 6087.

A ·	A. Atinnius No(v)ember
· A T I N N I V S · N O E M B e R	Novellia(e) Pyrallidi
N O V E L L I A · P Y R A L L I D I	Cojugi suae carissimae
C O I V G I · S V A E · C A R I S S I M A E	fecit sibi[que ?]
F E C I T · S I B I · E A (*erasut*)	
5 Κ Λ Α Υ Δ Ι Α Μ Α Γ Ν Α	5 Κλαύδια Μάγνα
Τ Ι Β Ε Ρ Ι Ο Υ Κ Λ Α Υ Δ Ι Ο Υ	Τιβερίου Κλαυδίου
Δ Ι Ο Γ Ν Η Τ Ο Υ Γ Υ Ν Η	Διογνήτου γυνὴ
Μ Α Μ Μ Η Ι Δ Ι Α	μάμμη ἰδίᾳ.
Ο Σ Α Ν Τ Α Υ Τ Α Τ Α Γ Ρ Α Μ	ὃς ἂν ταῦτα τὰ γράμ-
10 Μ Α Τ Α Ε Κ Κ Ο Ψ Η · Η	10 ματα ἐκκόψῃ ἢ
Α Λ Λ Ο Τ Ρ Ι Α Ο Σ Τ Α Β Α Λ Η	ἀλλότρια ὀστᾶ βάλῃ
Υ Π Ε Υ Θ Υ Ν Ο Σ Ε Σ Τ Ω Τ Η	ὑπεύθυνος ἔστω τῇ
Γ Ε Ρ Ο Υ Σ Ι Α ✶ Ϲ Ν̄	γερουσίᾳ ✶ σι
Κ Α Ι Τ Ο Ι Σ Τ Α Μ Ι Α Ι Σ Τ Η Σ	καὶ τοῖς ταμίαις τῆς
15 Π Ο Λ Ε Ω Σ ✶ Ϲ Ν̄	15 πόλεως ✶ σι
Ε Ζ Η Ϲ Ε Ν Ε Τ Η Λ̄ Η̄ Μ Η Ν Ϲ Ϲ Β ῲ Ρ Α Ϲ Δ	ἔζησεν ἔτη λη. μῆνες β, ὥρας δ.

The A inserted in line 1 over Atinnius to replace an A which had been lost before Atinnius through a fracture at the top left hand corner of the marble. Several slips of the lapidary occur, especially in his Latin. Noember in line 1, Novellia in line 2, and μῆνες (for μῆνας) in line 16. In line 4 Mr. Wood's editor read FA and restored fa[miliarque]. The letter is probably E. and if so EA is a blunder of the lapidary, and SIBI is without anything to govern it. I have suggested sibi[que], but doubtfully.

It is almost certain that both the Latin and Greek

portions were inscribed at the same time and by the same hand. If so, Claudia Magna (line 5) may have been the daughter of Novellia Pyrallis (line 2). The ταμίαι τῆς πόλεως, line 14. are not mentioned elsewhere as one of the Ephesian boards; at an earlier period an οἰκονόμος is spoken of (see Prolegomena, p. 82). At Smyrna, however, and elsewhere, ταμίαι existed : C. I. 3151, 3152 : compare Menadier, p. 84. The fines specified, 250 denarii (lines 13, 15) are unusually small : see on No. DCXXXVII *post.*

DCXXXVII.

Stelè of blue-veined marble; height 1 ft. 7¾ in.; width 1 ft. 9½ in. Discovered by Mr. Wood 'in the Sacred Way,' i.e. the road from the Magnesian Gate towards the Temple (see 'Ephesus,' p. 124). Unpublished.

οΒωΛΛΟΣΚΑΙΕΠΑΥ	Ὁ βωμὸς καὶ (ἡ) ἐπ' αὐ-
ΤωϹΟΡΟϹΕΙΤΙΝ	τῷ σορός ἐ(σ)τιν
ΑΡΤΕΜΑΑΡΤΕΜΑ	Ἀρτεμᾶ Ἀρτεμᾶ
ΤΟΥΑΘΗΝΑΓΟΡΟΥ	τοῦ Ἀθηναγόρου·
·ΖΗ · ΚΑΙΚΑΛΛΙϹΤΟΥ	ζῇ— καὶ Καλλίστου
ΤΟΥΥΟΥΑΥΤΟΥ · ΖΗ	τοῦ υἱοῦ αὐτοῦ· ζῇ—
ΚΑΙΔΕΚΛΛΟΥΑΤΕΡΙ	καὶ Δέκμου Ἀτερί-
ΟΥ · ΗΛΙΟΥ	ου Ἡλίου.

The writing is late, and probably not earlier than 200 A. D.

DCXXXVIII.

On a tablet of white marble, found by Mr. Wood, 'over the door of a tomb.' Height 1 ft. 7½ in.; width 3 ft. 11½ in.; apparently it is the same inscription which is shown in the woodcut on p. 124 of 'Ephesus,' compare *ibid.* p. 123. Wood, Inscriptions from Tombs, No. 10; C. I. L. iii. 6090.

V · P · TERENTIVS · OLYMPVS · SIBI	V(ivus) P(ublius) Terentius Olympus sibi
ETOCTAVIAE · PAVLAE · V · VXORI	et Octaviae Paulae v(ivae) uxori
SVAE · SVISQVE	suae suisque.
ΖΗ · ▣ · ΤΕΡΕΝΤΙΟϹΟΛΥΜΠΟϹ	Ζῇ· Πό(πλιος) Τερέντιος Ὄλυμπος
ΕΑΥΤΩΚΑΙΟΚΤΑΒΙΑΠΑΥΛΑ · ΖΗ	ἑαυτῷ καὶ Ὀκταβίᾳ Παῦλᾳ· ζῇ·
ΤΗΓΥΝΑΙΚΙΚΑΙΤΟΙϹΙΔΙΟΙϹ ⊄	τῇ γυναικὶ καὶ τοῖς ἰδίοις.

DCXXXIX.

A sarcophagus of white marble, ornamented with festoons of fruit and leaves suspended between two rams' heads at the angles and a bull's head in the centre; height 1 ft. 5½ in.; width 2 ft. 8 in. Discovered by Mr. Wood. C. Curtius, Hermes, iv, p. 214; C. I. L. iii. 6088.

EPPIA · M · F · INFANS
(Festoons)
ΕΠΠΙΑ ΜΑΡΚΟΤ ΘΤΓΑΤΗΡ ΝΗΠΙΑ

Eppia M(arci) f(ilia) infans.

Ἐππία Μάρκου θυγάτηρ νηπία.

DCXL.

A plain sarcophagus of white marble; height 1 ft. 1½ in.; width 1 ft. 6½ in. Discovered by Mr. Wood. C. Curtius, Hermes, iv. p. 213.

Ὁ δῆμ-
ος
Μητρᾶν
Μοιραγένου
Τρύφωνα.

The words ὁ δῆμος are enclosed within an olive chaplet, showing that the person here inurned was honoured with a public funeral. The name is in the accusative, στεφανοῖ or ἐτίμησε being understood. The name is inscribed on a label sculptured in relief, and above the label is a representation of a keyhole.

Both Μητρᾶς and Μοιραγένης are known Ephesian names; compare No. DCXLI *post*. The two names of Metras Tryphon are separated by the insertion of his father's name, in the Roman manner. The letters belong to about A. D. 50.

DCXLI.

On a plain sarcophagus of white marble: height 1 ft.; width 1 ft. 6 in. Discovered by Mr. Wood. C. Curtius, Hermes, iv. p. 213.

ΜΟΙΡΑΓΕΝΗΣΜΟΙΡΑ
ΓΕΝΟΥΤΟΥΜΗΤΡΑ
ΑΝΗΡΠΥΚΤΗΣ

Μοιραγένης Μοιρα-
γένου τοῦ Μητρᾶ,
ἀνὴρ πύκτης.

The lettering indicates the first century A. D. Μοιραγένης must have been related to the Μητρᾶς of the preceding inscription. No. DCXL.

. . .

DCXLII.

Stele of white marble, broken all round, but with the surface uninjured; height 11 in.; width 1 ft. Discovered by Mr. Wood; unpublished.

```
        . . ΚΥΤΑ
        _ΥΜΒΙΩΜΕΤ
        ιΩΝΤΕΚΝΩΝΠΥ
        *ΝΟΥΚΑΙΘΕΟΔΩ
   5       ΝΕΙΑΣ
           ΧΑΡΙΝ
             ᵬ
```

```
        [Ὁ δεῖνα τῇ δεῖνι]
        . . . τῇ γλυ]κυτά-
        τῃ] συμβίῳ μετ[ὰ
        τ]ῶν τέκνων Πυ[θ.?
        ι]ανοῦ καὶ Θεοδώ-
   5    ρου.]    νείας
                 χάριν.
```

The date is not earlier than the second century A. D., as is indicated by the C, and the debased form νείας for μνείας.

DCXLIII.

Sepulchral slab of white marble; height 1 ft. 1½ in.; width 9 in. Discovered by Mr. Wood; unpublished.

ΤΑΤΙΑΣΙΔΙΩ
ΑΝΔΡΙ-ΕΡΩΤΙ
ΜΝΕΙΑΣΧΑ
ΡΙΝΕΠΟΙΕΙ

Τατίας ἰδίῳ
ἀνδρὶ Ἔρωτι
μνείας χά-
ριν ἐποίει.

DCXLIV.

Fragment of grey marble slab, entire only at left and bottom: height 1 ft. 4 in.; width 1 ft. Discovered by Mr. Wood; unpublished.

ΒΑΛΒΕ
ΕΥΤΥ
FIDV
ΦΕΙΔC

[Balbinus?)
[Eutychi?]
Βαλβε[ῖνος
Εὐτύ[χου?
Fidu[s i
Φειδο[ς . . . . . ου.

In very large letters of the first century A. D., from 2 inches to 3¼ inches in height.

DCXLV.

Plain slab of white marble: height 10½ in.; width 1 ft. 1 in.   Discovered by Mr. Wood; unpublished.

ΤΟΥΤοΤο	Τοῦτο τὸ
ΗΡΩΩΝΕΣ	ἡρῷ(ὁ)ν ἐσ-
ΤΙΝΚΑΙΤΑΠΕ	τιν καὶ τὰ πε-
ΡΙΑΥΤΟΣΥΝΚΑΤ	ρὶ αὐτὸ σὺν κα(ὶ)
5 ΤΩΣΩΛΑΡΙΩ	5 τῷ σωλαρίῳ . . .

The name of the owner probably followed on a panel now lost: solarium is a terrace or balcony. The lettering is coarse and careless.

DCXLVI.

Fragment of bluish-white marble, entire only at bottom; little is lost at right and left. Height 9½ in.; width 1 ft. 5 in.   Discovered by Mr. Wood; unpublished.

	⅃ΝΑΥ Ι ⅃	
,Ν	ΤΙ	ΟΥ
ﮭΥ	ΡΙ⅃	⅃ΗΣ

The surface of the stone is worn smooth, but it is almost certain that the spaces in lines 2 and 3 were never inscribed.   It appears to be a late funeral stelè, which probably ran somewhat thus :—

[Τοῦτο τὸ ἡρῷόν ἐστι]
[τοῦ δεῖνος καὶ τῆς δεῖνος]
[τῆς γυναικὸς αὐτοῦ καὶ]
τῶν τέκν]ων αὐτῶ[ν
Κοΐ]ν—τί—ου,
Κυ—ρίλ—λης.

DCXLVII.

Sepulchral monument of white marble, with relief representing a male figure seated at a meal. Height 1 ft. 10½ in.; width 10½ in. Discovered by Mr. Wood; unpublished.   Underneath the relief six lines have been obliterated, of which only a few letters remain.

ΤΑ Χ Χ Σ	. . . .
ΤΡΟΦΙΜΟΣΣΗ	Τα . . . Χ . . . . Χ . ϲ
	Τρόφιμος ζῇ.

DCXLVIII.

Panel of white marble: height 1 ft. 3½ in.; width 2 ft. 5½ in.   Discovered by Mr. Wood; unpublished.

ΤΟΜΝΗΜΕΙΟΝΕΣΤΙ	Τὸ μνημεῖόν ἐστι
ΠΟΠΛΙΑΣΟΥΛΕΙΑΒΗΡΥΛΑΣ · ΚΑΙ	Ποπλίας ('Ἰ)ουλεία(ς) ? Βηρύλας καὶ
ΤΑΤΕΚΝΑΑΥΤΗΣ · ΖΛΣΙΝ	τὰ τέκνα αὐτῆς· ζῶσιν.
ΚΑΙΤΟΥΣΥΝΒΙΟΥΑΥΤΗΣΜΕΝΑΝ	Καὶ τοῦ συνβίου αὐτῆς Μενάν-
ΔΡΟΥ ΖΗ 5	5 δρου. ζῆ.
ΤΑΛΟΥΥΙΟΥΑΥ⁻ΟΥ· ΖΗ · ΚΑΙ ·	Τάλου υἱοῦ αὐτοῦ· ζῇ· καὶ
ΡΩΣΚΙΛΙΑΣΕΥΤΥΧΙΑΣΓΥΝΑΙΚΩΣ	'Ρωσκιλίας Εὐτυχίας γυναικὸν
ΑΥΤΟΥΤΟΥΤΟΤΟΜΝΗΜΗΟΝ	αὐτοῦ. Τοῦτο τὸ μνημῇον
ΕΑΝΤΙΣΠΩΛΗΣΗΑΠΟΤΕΙΣΕΙ	ἐάν τις πωλήσῃ ἀποτείσει
10 ΤΗΓΕΡΟΥΣΙΑ · ϞΕ ·	10 τῇ γερουσίᾳ Ϟ ϛ.

Lines 1–5 and 6–10 were apparently inscribed by the same hand at one time: lines 4–5 are inserted | in smaller characters of different style, as an after-thought.   There are indications in line 2 and

3 T

elsewhere of previous erasures. Several curious blunders occur in lines 2, 3: ΟΥΛΕΙΑ, which is plainly on the stone, must be meant for ΙΟΥΛΕΙΑΣ, and τά τέκνα should obviously be τῶν τέκνων. For the form μνημῆον compare ἐπιμίλῃα in No. DXXII, etc. In line 10 the fine specified as payable is ϛ, i.e. 5,000 denarii: the fine usually specified in this connexion is βφ, i.e. 2,500, or half this sum; see No. DCXLIX post. Concerning this custom of denouncing a fine against any who shall infringe the testamentary injunctions of the founder of the monument, see Marquardt, Röm. Alt. v, p. 281. Abundant examples of such fines may be cited from the sepulchral monuments of Rome, of Italy, and of the Provinces. In Rome and Italy the fines are usually made payable to the imperial fiscus or to the Roman aerarium. In the Provinces the imperial fiscus is usually mentioned, as in Nos. DCXXVII ante, εἰς τὸν φίσκον, and DCLIII post, τῷ φίσκῳ. But instead of φίσκος the word ταμεῖον is very generally employed as in No. DCXLIX post, τῷ ταμείῳ; the meaning of ταμεῖον is plainly shown by C. I. 2830 (Aphrodisias): ἐς τὸ ἱερώτατον ταμεῖον τοῦ κυρίου Αὐτοκράτορος Καίσαρος κ.τ.λ. (compare C. I. 2832). Sometimes the Roman aerarium is specified, as in C. I. 2834: [τῷ ταμείῳ τοῦ] δήμου Ῥωμαίων; at other times particular temples,

as in C. I. 3108: εἰς τὸν ναὸν τῶν Σεβαστῶν ✳ βφ καὶ εἰς τὸν προε[στῶτα τῆς ἱερ]ωτάτη[ς] π[όλεω]ς ἡμῶν θεὸν Διόνυσον ✳ βφ. In most cases, however, if the imperial fiscus is not to receive the fine, it is declared payable to the revenues of the city or of one of the civic boards; thus in No. DCXXXVI, τοῖς ταμίαις τῆς πόλεως and τῇ γερουσίᾳ; in No. DCXLIX, εἰς τὴν πόλιν; and in the present case, τῇ γερουσίᾳ. The amount of the fine varies very considerably. As Marquardt observes (l. c.), we do not know the precise method by which the fines were recoverable. It is obvious that the inscription upon the tomb declaring its owners, forbidding its profanation, and denouncing a fine, formed a will, or part of a will. A copy of the will was deposited in the munimentroom of the city: see Nos. DCL, DCLV, DCLXIV. We may suppose that permission would be asked of any board, before it was formally named as the guardian of a tomb; and it would be thenceforward the duty and the interest of such board, to prosecute, upon information given, any violator of the terms of the will.

An interesting essay by Prof. G. Hirschfeld upon Greek sepulchral inscriptions which threaten fines will be found in the Königsberger Studien I, 1887, p. 83.

DCXLIX.

A slab of white marble enclosed within a moulding: height 1 ft. 1½ in.; width 1 ft. 1½ in. Wood, Inscriptions from Tombs, etc., No. 8.

ΕΑΝΔΕΤΙCΠΑΡΑΤΟΥC
ΓΕΓΡΑΜΜΕΝΟΥCΔΕCΠ϶
ΤΑCΗΓΡΑΜΜΑΕΚΚΟΨΗ
ΗΠΩΛΗCΑΙΘΕΛΗCΗΤΟ
5 ΜΝΗΜΛΕΙΟΝΔΩCΕΙΤΩ
ΤΑΜΕΙΩΧΒΦΚΑΙΕΙC
ΤΗΝΠΟΛΙΝ✳ΒΦ

Ἐὰν δέ τις παρὰ τοὺς
γεγραμμένους δεσπό-
τας ἡ γράμμα ἐκκόψῃ
ἡ πωλήσαι θελήσῃ τὸ
5 μνημεῖον, δώσει τῷ
ταμείῳ ✳ βφ, καὶ εἰς
τὴν πόλιν ✳ βφ.

Another slab containing the names of the owners of the tomb must have accompanied this; they were probably panels of the same monument. A fine of 2,500 denarii is to be paid to the ταμεῖον (= ταμιεῖον), here loosely used for φίσκος, and a further 2,500 to the treasury of Ephesos itself. εἰς τὴν πόλιν is equivalent to τοῖς ταμίαις τῆς πόλεως in No. DCXXXVI ante. On these fines for desecrating graves see the preceding inscription.

In line 2 the O of δεσπότας can be faintly traced on the marble.

DCL.

Stele of white marble, broken off at the top: height 1 ft. 1½ in.; width 1 ft. 6¼ in. The surface is worn smooth, and the letters are rather faint. Discovered by Mr. Wood; unpublished.

ϽΥΤΟΥΑΙϝ
ΑΙΦΛΑΚΚΙΛΛΗΣ
ΑΙΚΟΣΑΥΤΟΥϝΑΙ
˪ΚΝΩΝ·ΚΑΙΕΙϽΝϨΙ
5 ΖΩΣΙΝ·ΤΑΥΤΗΣ
ΤΗΣΕΠΙΓΡΑΦΗΣΕϾΤϤΡΑ
ΓΙΣΜΑΑΠΕΤΕϽΗΕΙΤΟ
ΑΡΧΕΙΟΝ

[Τοῦτο τὸ μνημεῖόν ἐστιν]
. . . . ου τοῦ Ἀπ . . . . .
. . . κ]αὶ Φλακκίλλης
γυν]αικὸς αὐτοῦ καὶ
τ]έκνων καὶ ἐ(κ)γόνων.
5 Ζῶσιν. — Ταύτης
τῆς ἐπιγραφῆς ἐξεφρά-
γισμα ἀπετέθη εἰ(ς) τὸ
ἀρχεῖον.

Line 6 : Ξ is partly legible. 'Εξσφράγισμα, literally a 'squeeze' or 'impress,' signifies here a 'verbatim copy'; unless we suppose a plaster cast to have been made and preserved. 'Αποσφράγισμα is the proper word for the impression of a seal; Pliny to Trajan, Ep. 74 (Keil): signata est anulo meo, cujus est aposphragisma quadriga. 'Εξσφράγισμα is very commonly used in the sense which it has here; compare the following tombstones from Smyrna, C. I. 3276, 3281, 3282, 3357, in all of which it is written ἐξσφ. In C. I. 3387 it is written ἐκ(σ)φράγισμα, if rightly copied, and in No. DCLV post ἐσφράγισμα. Sometimes ἀντίγραφον is used instead, as in No. DCLXIV post. A copy of the inscription upon the tomb was the title deed to its possession, and was therefore deposited in the record-office of the city, τὸ ἀρχεῖον.

The ἀρχεῖον is repeatedly spoken of on the tombstones from Aphrodisias, see C. I. 2841 foll.; compare the Smyrna inscriptions just cited, and C. I. 3295: τούτου τοῦ τίτλου ἀντίγραφον ἀπετέθη εἰς τὸ ἀρχεῖον. M. Dareste (Bull. de Corr. Hell. vi, p. 241) has pointed out the importance of the ἀρχεῖον in the Greek cities as the public Registry of sales and deeds of all kinds; see also Marquardt, Röm. Alt. iv, p. 182. 'Αρχεῖον was the old Greek term (see the Iasos document, No. CCCCXLIII ante), and signifies the official residence of the magistrates (ἀρχαῖ). In later times it is termed also ἀρχεῖον χρεωφυλάκιον (C. I. 3282), γραμματοφυλάκιον (C. I. 4094 etc.), or γραμμα-τεῖον (C. I. 2943, and perhaps No. DCLXIV post). Line 1 : an Ephesian Φλάκκιλλος is named in C. I. 2995.

DCLI.

Part of a sepulchral monument of white marble, in the form of a panel surrounded by plain moulding : entire at top and right. Height 7 in.; width 1 ft. 2 in. Discovered by Mr. Wood; unpublished.

```
      ΦΙΛΑΝΘΡΩΠΟ                    Φιλάνθρωπο[ς 'Επίκο- ?
      ΥΡΟΝΠΕΤΡΟΝΙΘΕΡΜΙΟ             υρον Πετρονίου, 'Ερμίο-
                    ΝΓ·                         ν ȳ
                    ΕΥΤ                         Εὐτ-
      5             ΥΧΙ              5           υχί-
                    Δο                          δο[υ.
```

A funeral monument erected by Philanthropos in memory of two friends. But the restoration is doubtful. Every letter in the uncial text is certain, but we do not know how much is lost on the left.

DCLII.

Part of a sepulchral panel surrounded by plain moulding; top and left broken. Height 7 in.; width 9½ in. Discovered by Mr. Wood; unpublished.

```
                 ^                  [Τοῦτο τὸ μνημεῖόν ἐστιν]
                                    . . . . . . . . ]α[ . . . καὶ
      ΩΝΑΥΤΟΥΖΩ                     τῶν τέκν]ων αὐτοῦ ζω(σιν).
      ΗΣΤΗΣΣΥΝΒΙΩ                   καὶ . . .]ης τῆς συνβιω-
      ΑΥΤΩ ΤΟΥΤΟΤΟ                  σάσης] αὐτῷ. Τοῦτο τὸ
      5  ΞΙΟΝΚΛΗΡΟΝΟ                5  μνημ]εῖον κληρονό-
      ΚΠΡΑΣΙΝΟΥΚΑ                   μοις κατ' ἐ]κπρασιν οὐκ ·
      ΙΟΥΘΗΣΕΙ                      κο]λουθήσει.
```

Every letter in the uncial text is certain. We recognize here, in its Greek dress, a Latin formula frequent on Roman tombstones: H(oc) M(onumentum) H(eredes) N(on) S(equetur); and well known to readers of Horace (see Commentators on Sat. i, 8, 13): Heredes monumentum ne sequeretur; compare C. I. 3270 (Smyrna): τοῖς δὲ κληρονόμοις μου οὐκ ἐπακολουθήσει τοῦτο τὸ μνημεῖον, and often elsewhere.

It simply means that the sepulchre is not to go, with the rest of the man's property, to his heirs.

I cannot quote an exact parallel for the restoration : κληρονό[μοις κατ' ἐ]κπρασιν οὐκ ἀ[κο]λουθήσει, but it seems to be a combination of the usual formula with another phrase: Hoc Monumentum emtori non cedet (see Wilmanns' Exempla, No. 289, and compare No. 293).

DCLIII.

Tombstone of bluish marble, broken at the top : height 1 ft. 1½ in.; width 1 ft. 2 in.   Discovered by Mr. Wood; unpublished

```
    .ΓΩΟΝ • ΙΟΥ                  Τὸ ἡ]ρῷον τού-
  ϴ • ΕΣΤΙΝΦΛ • ΤΑ               τ]ό ἐστιν Φλ, Τα[τα-
  ΙΙΟΥ • ΚΑΙΤΕΚΝΟΥ              ρίου καὶ τέκνου
  ΤΑΤΙΑΝΟΥ • ΑΥΤΗΣΖΩ            Τατιανοῦ αὐτῆς. ζῶ(σιν).
5 ΕΙΤΙΣΕΞΑΛΛΟΤΡΙΩ            5 εἴ τις ἐξαλλοτριώ-
  ΣΕΙ • ΔΩΣΕΙΤΩΦΙΣΚΩ            σει, δώσει τῷ φίσκῳ
  ΔΗΝΑΡΙΑ • ΧΕΙΛΙΑ •            δηνάρια χείλια.
```

DCLIV.

Fragment of blue-veined marble slab, entire at top and right only; inscribed on the front *a* and back *b*.   Height 6½ in.; width 7½ in. Discovered by Mr. Wood; unpublished.

a.	*a.*	*b.*	*b.*
ΤΟΥΤΟ • ΤΟ	Τοῦτο τὸ [ἡρῷ-	ΤΟ • ΤΟΗΡΩ	Τοῦ]το τὸ ἡρῷ-
ΟΝΕΣΤΙΝ •	όν ἐστιν [Κλ.	ΣΤΙΝ • ΚΛ • ΑΥ	όν έ]στιν Κλ. Αὐ-
ΑΥΓΟΥΣΤΙ	Αὐγουστι[ανοῦ	ΣΤΙΑΝΟΥ	γου]στιανοῦ.
ΚΑΙ • ΚΛ • ΑΥ	καὶ Κλ. Αὐ[γουστ-		
	[ιανής ?]		

DCLV.

A rude stele of white marble : height 1 ft. 7½ in.; width 1 ft. 11½ in.; with moulding round a panel.   'Found in a bone-worker's shop near the Odeum.'   Wood.   Inscriptions from the City and Suburbs, No. 14 ; (compare 'Ephesus,' p. 125).

```
a. ΤΟΥΤΟΤΩΜΝΗΜΕΙΟΝΚΑΙ ΕΠΑΥΤΩ
                                    
   Ο : ΘΛ ΣΚ      ΩΙ  Κ  Μ   ΚΑ
                                    
 b.  ΤΟΥΤΟΤΟΗΡΩΟΝΚΑΙ
    Ο • ΑΝΕΤΟΣΤΟΠΟΣ•ΕΣΤΙΝ
    ΠΟΝΠΩΝΙΑΣΦΑΥΣΤΕΙΝΗΣ
    ΚΟΣΜΗΤΕΙΡΗΣΤΗΣΑΡΤΕΜΛΙΔΟΣ
    ΑΠΟΠΡΟΓΟΝΩΝΚΑΙΜΕΝΑΝ
    ΔΡΟΥΑΝΔΡΟΣΑΥΤΗΣΤΟΥΗ
    ΡΩΟΥΚΗΔΟΝΤΑΙ•ΜΥ•ΡΡ•ΑΧΙΣ
    ΚΑΙ•ΝΕΙΚΩΝ•ΚΑΙΟΙΛΟΙΠΟΙΑ
    ΠΕΛΕΥΘΕ ΡΟΙΜΕΝΑΝΔΡΟΥ
10  ΤΟΥΤΟΥΕΓΕΝΕΤΟΕΣΦΡΑΓΙΣΜΑ
       ΖΩϹΙΝ
```

a.

Τοῦτο τὸ μνημεῖον καὶ [ἡ] ἐπ' αὐτῷ
σ[ορὸς ? . . . . . .

. . . . . .

b.

Τοῦτο τὸ ἡρῷον καὶ
ὁ ἀνετὸς τόπος ἐστὶν
Πονπωνίας Φαυστείνης
κοσμητείρης τῆς Ἀρτέμιδος
5 ἀπὸ προγόνων, καὶ Μενάνδρου ἀνδρὸς αὐτῆς, τοῦ ἡ-
ρώου κήδονται Μύρραχις
καὶ Νείκων καὶ οἱ λοιποὶ ἀ-
πελεύθεροι Μενάνδρου.
10 τούτου ἐγίνετο ἐσφράγισμα.
ζῶσιν.

The inscription (*b*) is engraved upon the panel enclosed by the moulding.   Line 2: ἀνετὸς means 'dedicated,' 'set apart.'   Line 10: ἐσφραγισμα is a lapidary's blunder, or a debased form, for ἐξεσφράγισμα, see No. DCLI, *ante*.   Line 7: the lapidary has introduced stops without regard to the sense.   Upon the moulding above the panel and all round it was an earlier inscription (*a*), which was obliterated when the marble was dressed to receive the present inscription (*b*). A few words of the earlier one can be traced : *a* may have been of the first century A.D. ; *b* is scarcely earlier than the third.

In a tombstone from Aphrodisias (C. I. 2823) we read of Αἰλίαν Λα[ι]βίλλαν, Ἀσίας ἀρχιέρειαν καὶ κοσμήτειραν τῆς Ἐφεσίας Ἀρτέμιδος.   Similarly in an Ephesian inscription C. I. 3002, (compare 3003) : Οὐλπίαν Εὐοδίαν Μουδιανήν, τὴν ἱέρειαν τῆς Ἀρτέμιδος . . . γένος ἔχουσαν ἄνωθεν ἱερειῶν καὶ κοσμητειρῶν, ἀδελφὴν Οὐλπίας Στρατά[ς], κοσμητείρης.   No doubt the office of κοσμήτειρα was a *liturgy*, i. e. the person was appointed to furnish new robes and other ornaments for the statue of the goddess.   Observe the Ionic form κοσμητείρης (line 4) surviving as late as this : Boeckh was right in preserving it in the inscription cited above.

DCLVI.

Sepulchral panel of white marble: broken at lower left corner.   Height 11 in.; width 1 ft. 4½ in.   Discovered by Mr. Wood; unpublished.

```
    ΤΙΤΟCΦΛΑΒΙΟCΚΟCΜΟC
    ΕΞΕΧΩΡΗCΑΤΟΠΟΝ
    ΛΛΝΗΛΛΙΟΥΠΡΟCΤΟΛ
    ΓΟΡΑΝΟΛΛΙΝΤΑΤΙΑΔΙ
5   :ΛΛΑΔΟCΟΕΓΩ
    ΟΔΟΛΛΗCΑΙΔΙΩ
    ΝΩΚΑΙΑΥΤΗΚΑΙ
    ΔΕΝΙΩΛΝΕΓΩΒΟ
    ϶Ω  ΖΗ  Φ
```

Τίτος Φλάβιος Κόσμος
ἐξεχώρησα τόπον
μνημίου πρὸς τὸ ἀ-
γορανόμιν Τατιάδι
5   Ἀπ]ελλάδος, ὃ ἐγὼ
ᾠκ]οδόμησα ἰδίῳ
τέκ]νῳ καὶ αὐτῇ καὶ
ἄλλ]ῳ ἐνὶ ᾧ ἂν ἐγὼ βο-
υλη]θῶ. ζῆ.

Ἀγορανόμιν is for ἀγορανόμιον by a common late contraction.   It defines the position of the tomb 'towards the office of the ἀγορανόμοι'; in better Greek it would have been πρὸς τῷ or πρὸς τοῦ.   Compare τοῖς ἐπὶ τὸ τελώνιον, No. DIII.   On the ἀγορανόμοι, see Prolegomena, p. 81.   The locality was probably on one of the roads leading from the north of the city to the Artemision, where most of the tombs were found by Mr. Wood, Ephesus, pp. 113 foll.   Ἐκχωρῆσαι is 'cedere,' to 'make over to'; it is employed just as it is here, for the making over the possession of a sepulchre or part of it, in C. I. 2664, 4268; similarly ἐκχώρησις in C. I. 3394: Τὸ μνημεῖόν ἐστιν Ἰκίου Ἰκίου τοῦ Εὐημέρου.... κατὰ τὴν γεγονυῖαν ἐκχώρησιν.   For the genitive Ἀπελλάδος see p 115 ante.

DCLVII.

Fragment of white marble, being the top left-hand corner of a moulded stele.   Height 2 in.;   width 3½ in.   Discovered by Mr. Wood: unpublished.

| ΑΘΗ

Ἀθη . . . . . .

Probably from a sepulchral monument.   The letters belong to the fourth century B. C. or earlier.

DCLVIII.

A sepulchral stele of white marble; height 1 ft. 1 in.; width 1 ft. 4 in.   Above the inscription is a relief; a male figure reclines on a couch, with a table in front of him with food; a boy stands at his side, behind whom is a large krater.   Discovered by Mr. Wood; unpublished.

```
ΕΜΛΝ ΑΡΤΕΜΩΝΟΣ
ΚΝΙΔΙΟΣ
```

Ἀρτ]έμων Ἀρτέμωνος
Κνίδιος.

The letters are of the period of the Diadochi.

DCLIX.

Broken slab of white marble: height 7½ in.; width 9 in.   Entire only at the bottom.   Discovered by Mr. Wood; unpublished.

```
Ι ΟΗ.
ΞΥΤΥΧΟΥΣ
ΝΩΝΑΥΤΟΥ
ΖΩΣΙ
```

Τοῦτο] τὸ ἡρ[ῷόν ἐστιν
. . . . . Εὐτύχοις [καὶ
τῶν τέκ]νων αἰτοῖ.
ζῶσι[ν.

DCLX.

Fragment of a small sepulchral stele of bluish marble; originally having a central panel with figures in relief of which one left foot only remains; with an inscription upon the moulding below. The marble is entire only at bottom and on the right. Height 2½ in.; width 3¼ in. Discovered by Mr. Wood; unpublished.

εικος   . . . . . ν]εικοτ.

The name was probably one of the many compounds of νίκη (νείκη).

DCLXI.

Part of a sepulchral stele of white marble, entire on left only. Height 7 in.; width 7 in. Discovered by Mr. Wood; unpublished.

ΤΟΥ		Τοῦ[το τὸ
ΗΡΩC		ἡρῷό[ν ἐστ-
ΙΝΕΥΤ		ιν Εὐτ[υχίω-
ΝΟΣΤΟ		νος το[ῦ . . .
5 ΡΛ Ω	5	ρα . ο . .

This monument, like No. DCLV, is a palimpsest, a former inscription having been erased to make a surface to receive the present one. The name

Εὐτ[υχίω]νος is highly probable; the name of his father may be [Εὐκ]ρά[τ]ο[υς, or the like.

DCLXII.

Fragment of marble, broken on right and left. Height 4½ in.; width 7 in. Discovered by Mr. Wood; unpublished.

ΝΗΕΙΜ   'Ο]νήσιμ[ος.

Probably sepulchral.

DCLXIII.

Fragment of sepulchral stele of white marble, entire at right and at bottom; height 5 in.; width 10 in. Discovered by Mr. Wood; unpublished.

	[Τοῦτο τὸ ἡρῷόν ἐστιν]
ΛΛΜΡΚΟΙ	. . . . . Μάρκου
ΚΑΙΟΥΛΠΙ	. . . . . καὶ Οὐλπί-
ΩΝΕΚΓΟΝΩΛ	ου . . . καὶ τ]ῶν ἐκγόνων.

DCLXIV.

Fragment of bluish marble; entire only on left; height 8 in.; width 9 in. Discovered by Mr. Wood; unpublished.

		[Τοῦτο τὸ μνημεῖον καὶ]
ΟΥΣΠΡΟΔ		τ]οὺς πρὸς [αὐτῷ βαθμοὺς? περι-
ΠΟΙΗΕΑΤΟΚ		ε]ποιήσατο Κ . . . .
ΦΡΟΥΓΙΛΛΑΙ		. Φρουγιλλα[νὸς? καὶ μίτ-
ΣΤΙΝΜΗΝΟ		ε]στιν Μηνο[δώρου? αὐτοῦ,
5 ΑΘΑΒΕΒΟΥ	5	κ]αθὰ βεβού[ληται, καὶ κατὰ
ΤΙΓΡΑΦΟΝ		τὸ ἀν]τίγραφον [τὸ ἀνακειμέ-
ΜΤΟΓ		νον] ἐν τῷ γ[ραμματείῳ?

The restorations are supplied rather as giving the probable sense of the whole, than as the exact words. For βεβού[ληται] compare No. DCLVI ante: καὶ [ἄλλ]ῳ ἐφ᾽ ᾧ ἂν ἐγὼ βα[ελη]θῶ. The mention of the copy deposited at the public record-office is a further illustration of what was said on No. DCLV ante; compare No. DCLV ante. I restore γ[ραμματείῳ] from C. I. 2943, line 10 (Nysa).

DCLXV.

On a small sarcophagus of white marble. In the centre of the front a Medusa mask, at each corner a ram's head, from which is suspended a festoon of fruit and ivy leaves. Above are two rosettes. Height 1 ft. 4 in.; width 2 ft. 5 in. Figured in Wood's Ephesus, p. 129. From the 'Sacred Way' between the Magnesian Gate and the Artemision. Wood, Inscriptions from Tombs, etc., No. 12; C. I. L. iii, 6080.

P · CORNELI · NICEPHORI · NOMENCIATORIS

Ram's head. Festoon of fruit and leaves. Medusa's head. Festoon of fruit and leaves. Ram's head.

Π · ΚΟΡΝΗΛΙΟΥ · ΝΕΙΚΗΦΟΡΟΥΝΟΜΕΝΚΛΑΤΟΡΟΣ

P(ubli) Corneli Nicephori, nomenc(l)atoris
Π(οπλίου) Κορνηλίου Νεικηφόρου, νομενκλάτορος.

He was probably in the service of the proconsul of the province, who numbered nomenclatores among his retinue; see Marquardt, Röm. Alt. iv, p. 393. In the Latin inscription I for L is a blunder of the lapidary.

DCLXVI.

Fragment of white marble, broken on all sides: height 6 in.; width 6 in. Discovered by Mr. Wood; unpublished.

،ΙΝΑ،	ην α . . . .
ΚΑΙΚΙΛΙΟ	Καικίλιο[ς Σεκοῦν–?
ΔΟΣΤΟ،	δος του . . . .
ΑΥΤΗΣ	αὐτῆς . . . .
5 ΑΥΤΩ	αὐτω 5

Perhaps sepulchral.

DCLXVII.

Fragment of white marble, broken on all sides. Height 6½ in.; width 4½ in. Discovered by Mr. Wood; unpublished.

،Ι	. αι . . . . . .
ΠΙΚΟΥΤ	πικοῦ τ[ῇ
ΓΛΥΚΥΤ	γλυκυτ[άτῃ μη-
ΓΡ	τρ[ί ? . . .

Obviously from a tomb.

DCLXVIII.

Fragment of white marble moulding, entire only at top. Height 2½ in.; width 3½ in. From Mr. Wood's excavations; unpublished.

ΜΗΝΟΦΙΛ   Μηνόφιλ[ος.

Perhaps sepulchral. The name occurs on an Ephesian tomb, C. I. 3015.

DCLXIX.

Fragment of marble, entire only at top; height 3 in.; width 4½ in. From Mr. Wood's excavations; unpublished.

ΕΥΤΗ،	. . . . . ἐτελ]ευτη[σε?] or [βουλ]ευτή[ς]
،ΗΡ،،	. . . . . το]ῦ ἡρῴζου κήδεται? . .

Perhaps from a tombstone.

DCLXX.

Slab of white marble, entire on right only ; height 2 ft. 5½ in.; width 1 ft. 4½ in. The surface was divided into at least four sunk panels, one above another. Of the first and fourth panels very little remains ; the stone being fractured on the left and at top and bottom. The reliefs on the monument are described below ; it is figured in Wood's Ephesus, p. 222 ; it was excavated upon the site of the Artemision.

a.

ΔΕΥΤΕΡΑ

b.

ΤΡΙΤΗ

c.

ΤΕΤΑΡΤΗΑΝΗΡΕΘΗ

<table>
<tr><td>*a.*</td><td>*b.*</td><td>*c.*</td></tr>
<tr><td>Δευτέρα.</td><td>Τρίτη.</td><td>Τετάρτη ἀνηρέθη.</td></tr>
</table>

First panel. Here no inscription remains ; it was doubtless Πρώτη. But on the right the feet and legs are seen of a man who was in the attitude of one confronting a danger approaching him from the left. *a* is inscribed in the field of the *second panel*, of which only a little is lost on the left. Here a lion is rushing from the right upon a man, naked with the exception of a cloth round his loins, who is striking the animal with some weapon resembling a club. *b* is inscribed in the upper field of the *third panel*, in which the man lies as if just fallen, and the lion is fastening upon his thigh. *c* is inscribed in the uppermost field of the *fourth panel*, where none of the bas-relief remains.

The style of the letters points to the second century A. D., and Mr. Wood (Ephesus, p. 223) would understand the reliefs to commemorate a Christian martyr. Besides the example of St. Ignatius, it will be remembered that Polycarp would have been thrown to the lions only the show was just over ; Martyr. S. Polyc. ch. 12 (Lightfoot) : ταῦτα λέγοντες ἐπεβόων καὶ ἠρώτων τὸν 'Ασιάρχην Φίλιππον ἵνα ἐπαφῇ τῷ Πολυκάρπῳ λέοντα. 'Ο δὲ Φίλιππος ἔφη, μὴ εἶναι ἐξὸν αὐτῷ, ἐπειδὴ πεπληρώκει τὰ κυνηγέσια, κ.τ.λ. It is questionable, however, whether sculptured monuments were ever raised to their dead by the Christians of the first three centuries. Nor does the marble, so far as it is preserved, exhibit any Christian symbol. We may therefore more safely consider it to be the monument of a bestiarius, erected to his memory by his friends, or by the other members of the ' familia.'

The bestiarii were not always condemned criminals, and it seems clear that the man here depicted was not a criminal or Christian who had been thrown to the lions ; for if so, he would have been unarmed. We may rather understand him to be an ordinary bestiarius, analogous to a gladiator, who had entered into a familia venatoria by voluntary contract (auctoramentum). Our inscription will therefore best be illustrated by comparison of a tombstone of a gladiator such as is given in Wilmanns' Exempla, No. 2614 (from Verona = C. I. L. v, 3466), which begins thus : D(is) M(anibus). Glauco n(atione) Mutinensis, pugnar(um) vii, mortuus octava, vixit ann(os) xxiii d(ies) v. Aurelia marito b(ene) m(erenti) et amatores hujus. It seems to be customary for the epitaphs of gladiators to record how many times they had fought (pugnae) ; see Wilmanns, Nos. 2607, 2613, foll. ; compare 1966 and C. I. L. v, 3468. The word therefore to be supplied with Δευτέρα, Τρίτη, Τετάρτη is μάχη.

The so-called tomb of Scaurus at Pompeii exhibits bas-reliefs of bestiarii ; see Overbeck's Pompeii, 4th ed. pp. 191-2, where the examples of bestiarii are illustrated under figs. 108-112 (Museo Borbonico, xv, pll. 29-30). Two interesting medals bearing on this subject will be found in Sabatier, Med. Contorn. pl. ix, figs. 4 and 10. Sculptured tombs of gladiators are common enough ; see the examples from Smyrna, C. I. 3291, 3368, 3374, 3392, and the retiarius figured by Benndorf, Reisen in Lykien u. Karien, i, p. 41.

DCLXXI.

Fragment of white marble, apparently the lower part of a stele ; the top right-hand corner is wanting. Height 9½ in.; width 1 ft. 5½ in. Discovered by Mr. Wood ; presented by the Ephesus Exploration Fund. Unpublished.

<table>
<tr><td>ΜΑΡΚΩΚΟΚΚΗΙΩΑΛ</td><td>Μάρκῳ Κοκκηίῳ 'Αλ[ε-</td></tr>
<tr><td>ΞΑΝΔΡΩΕΠΙΤΗΣΟΙΚΙΑΣ</td><td>ξάνδρῳ ἐπὶ τῆς οἰκίας</td></tr>
<tr><td>ΜΟΣΧΕΙΝΙΔΙΩΑΝΔΡΙΜΝΕΙ</td><td>Μόσχειν ἰδίῳ ἀνδρὶ μνεί-</td></tr>
<tr><td>ΑΣΧΑΡΙΝΙΚΗΔΕΤΑΙΔΕ</td><td>ας χάριν· κήδεται δὲ</td></tr>
<tr><td>ΛΟΛΛΙΟΣΦΙΛΟΣΤΟΡΓΟΣ</td><td>Λόλλιος Φιλόστοργος.</td></tr>
</table>

The meaning of ἐπὶ τῆς οἰκίας is doubtful : perhaps it is merely equivalent to οἰκονόμος. M. Cocceius Alexander was probably a slave, or at most a freedman ; his father is not named. Μόσχειν is for Μόσχιν,

i. e. Μόσχιον: compare No. DCLVI, τὸ ἀγορανόμιν, and Part. I. No. LXVIII, Φιλημάτιν. Κήδεται here as often elsewhere (e.g. No. DCLXXVI post) points out the trustee of the sepulchre.

DCLXXII.

Stele of white marble ; height 3 ft. 1¾ in. ; width 1 ft. Above the inscription is a square sunk panel, within which is represented in relief a male figure seated to the right and holding with both hands a Pan's pipe. He wears a short chiton with sleeves reaching to the elbow. Above the sunk panel the stele takes the form of a pediment. Discovered by Mr. Wood ; presented by the Ephesus Exploration Fund. Unpublished.

ΕΒΕΝΟΣΠΡΩΤΑΥΛΗΣ
ΙΕΡΟΚΛΗΤΩΙΔΙΩ · ΣΥΡΙΣΤΗ
ΕΚΤΟΥΙΔΙΟΥ · ΤΟ·ΜΝΗΜΗΟΛ
ΧΑΙΡΕ

Ἔβενος πρωταύλης
Ἱεροκλῆ τῷ ἰδίῳ συριστῇ
ἐκ τοῦ ἰδίου τὸ μνημῆον.
Χαῖρε.

The name Ἔβενος occurs on another late tombstone from Asia Minor now at Smyrna (Archäol. Zeitung, 1858, p. 230⁰). The word πρωταύλης is otherwise unknown; it would mean a first or leading αὐλητήν. The word αὐλός in its more generic sense included the σύριγξ or Pan's-pipe, though in its stricter sense it was the name of an instrument like our clarinet. It is evident that Ebenos and Hierokles were accustomed to play in concert : the αὐλός was of deeper tone, the σύριγξ was shrill and high. Guhl and Koner (Das Leben der Griechen, etc., pp. 226 foll.) cite several representations of the σύριγξ and αὐλός being played in concert together with the lyre : and our inscription may lead us to question whether the Pan's-pipe was in later Greece as obsolete as they imply (p. 226).

DCLXXIII.

Fragment of a white marble slab : height 7 in. ; width 11 in. The inscription is apparently entire on each side. Discovered by Mr. Wood ; presented by the Ephesus Exploration Fund. Unpublished.

N.ι. ΛΣΧΑΡΙΝ
ΜΗΔΕΝΑΕΞΟΝ
ΕΙΝΑΙΒΑΗΘΗΝΑΙ
ΕΛΑΝΔΕΤΙΣΒΑΛΗ
5 ΔΩΣΙΤΗΒΟΥΛΗ
Γ·ΚΑ

[Ὁ δεῖνα τῷ δεῖνι τὸ μνημεῖο]-
ν μν[ί]ας χάριν·
μηδένα ἐξὸν
εἶναι βληθ(ῆ)ναι·
ἐὰν δέ τις βάλῃ
5 δώσι τῇ βουλῇ
δηνάρια ?] ἑκα-?
[τόν ?].

The infinitive ἐξὸν εἶναι is equivalent to the imperative, as in C. I. 2043. The lapidary has omitted H in line 3. The more usual formula upon funeral monuments is μηδένος ἔχοντος ἐξουσίαν κ.τ.λ. ; see C. I. 3288, 3292, 3318 etc. For the prohibition compare

No. DCXLIX ante. With δώσι for δώσει compare πλῖ. No. CCCCLXXXVII, line 7 ; and other examples passim. The fine of 100 denarii is specified on a tombstone from Mesambria, C. I. 2055 ; but it is unusually small (see note on No. DCXLVIII ante).

DCLXXIV.

Fragment of plain white marble stele, entire on left and at the upper edge. Height 9 in. ; width 1 ft. Discovered by Mr. Wood ; unpublished.

ΕΙΡΗΝΗΣ
ΜΕΤΑΤΗ⊦
ΛΚΡΟΠΟ
ⲅ

Εἰρήνη σ[οι
μετὰ τῆ[ς
Ἀκροπό[λε-
ω]ς.

Probably a Christian tombstone. Εἰρήνη σοι is not unfrequent in this connexion: see the Christian inscriptions, C. I. Nos. 9282, 9578, 9601, 9710,

9812, 9844. Ἀκρόπολις is not elsewhere found as a proper name : it may here indicate the wife of the person addressed.

DCLXXV.

Fragment of a thin crustal or marble-veneering, 1⅛ in. thick; measures 5 in. by 7 in. Broken all round. From Mr. Wood's excavations; unpublished.

```
NΑϤΑCIN
SNOCΑⲎ
```

Evidently a Christian formula, but where inscribed (on tomb, church, etc.) we are not informed. It appears to represent the last two clauses of the Constantinopolitan Creed (our Nicene Creed): viz.—

προσδοκῶμεν ἀ]νάστασιν [νεκρῶν καὶ ζωὴν
τοῦ μέλλοντος αἰ]ῶνος· ἀμ[ήν.

This and the preceding fragment and the crosses upon No. DXXXIV *ante*, are the only vestiges of Christian inscriptions brought by Mr. Wood from Ephesos. He found however several Christian tombs,

but the inscriptions were not conveyed to England: see his Ephesus, pp. 120, 122 ; and Inscriptions from Tombs, p. 21. How frequently phrases from the public prayers of the Church and liturgical formulas were inscribed upon early Christian tombs, may be seen by a glance at the Christian inscriptions in the last volume of the Corpus Inser. Gr. Interesting proof of the antiquity of some such prayers will be afforded by Christian tombstones as they are discovered and more carefully studied; see Bull. de Corr. Hell. i, p. 321.

DCLXXVI.

A slab of white marble surmounted by a plain moulding : height 1 ft. 5½ in.; width 1 ft. 4¾ in. Discovered by Mr. Wood; unpublished.

TOMNHMΕΪONEC	Τὸ μνημεῖόν ἐσ-
TIMΑΡΜOYCC	τι Μαρμουσσ
IOYIΑIΡEOC:ZH	ίου Ἰαίρεος. ζῆ.
KHΔONTΑIOÏO	κήδονται οἱ Ἰυ-
5 YΔΑIOI	5 υδαῖοι.

The tomb of an Ephesian Jew; compare No. DLXXVII *post*. My friend Dr. Ad. Neubauer, of the Bodleian Library, tells me that Μαρμούσσιος is a Grecised representation of *Mar*-Moses, Mar being sometimes employed as an equivalent for Rabbi. The deceased was probably a Rabbi of distinction. Mar is better known to us in its feminine form of Martha or Maratha. The name Jair (besides occurring often in Scripture) occurs also in the Talmud, e.g. Jair, father of the celebrated Pinehas. Οἱ Ἰουδαῖοι are the Jewish community at Ephesos, who are trustees of the burying-place, and secure it from alienation. The inscription is hardly earlier than A.D. 200. There had however been a numerous settlement of Jews at Ephesos for several centuries before. Dolabella during his consulate B.C. 44 granted the Jews at Ephesos toleration for their religious rites, exemption from engagements which interfered with sabbath-keeping, and personal security when they went on their pilgrimages to Jeru-

salem (Joseph. Antiq. xiv, 10, 12). These privileges were further secured by a decree of the Ephesian government, cited by Josephos (*ibid.* 25); and afterwards reaffirmed by Augustus (*ibid.* xvi, 6, 2 and 7). The passages from Josephos and chapters xviii, xix of the Acts, are all the literary materials for the history of the Jews at Ephesos : with these two epitaphs compare the note on the Βαλβίλλης No. DCXX, line 4. Mr. Wood does not say on what spot he found these two stones : on p. 125 of his Ephesus he says : ' I did not succeed in finding the Jewish cemetery which must have existed at Ephesus, but it was possibly at some distance from the city, and in a part of the plain where no excavations were made.' For the organization and status of a Jewish community under the Empire see the Essay of Emil Schürer upon the Jewish epitaphs discovered at Rome : Die Gemeindeverfassung der Juden in Rom (Leipzig, 1879).

DCLXXVII.

Broken stelê of white marble, entire only at bottom and on the right edge. Height 1 ft. 1 in.; width 1 ft. 3 in. Discovered by Mr. Wood; unpublished.

```
      - IO
   .ΛΙ ΑϹΙΑΤΡΟΥ
  ϽΛΑΥΤΟΥ · ΙΟΥΛΙΑΣ
  ΗΣ · ΚΑΙΤΕΚΝϽΝΑΥΤϽΝ
  ΣΙΝ · ·
  ΤΣΟΡΟΥΚΗΔΟΝ
  ΧϽΙΟΥΔΕΟΙ
```

Τὸ μνημεῖόν ἐστιν] Ἰο[υλίου?
. . . . ἀρχειάτρου [καὶ
τῆς γυναικ]ὸς αὐτοῦ Ἰουλίας
. . . . .ης, καὶ τέκνων αὐτῶν.
Ζώ]σιν.
Ταύτης τῇ]ς σοροῦ κήδον-
ται οἱ ἐν Ἐφί]σῳ Ἰουδαῖοι.

The tomb of a Jew named Ju[lius ?] and his family; he is called an ἀρχίατρος. The tomb was erected in his lifetime (line 5). In lines 6–7, which are inscribed rather more clumsily and perhaps somewhat later than the rest, the Jewish community at Ephesos is declared trustee of the monument, and pledged to secure it from alienation (compare Nos. DCLXXI, DCLXXVI *antè*). The style of the letters belongs to the age of the Antonines.

It is well known that in the chief cities of Greece, in the days of her freedom, there existed public physicians appointed and paid by the state: see Aristophanes, Acharnians, line 994, and the passages collected by Becker, Charikles, (ed. K. F. Hermann), iii, pp. 49 foll. Under the rule of Rome this Greek institution underwent certain changes. Augustus having granted to the physicians of Rome an exemption from all ' munera ' (τὴν ἀτέλειαν, Dio Cass. liii, 30), the privilege was extended by Hadrian to the provinces. Finally Antoninus Pius ordained that in the Province of Asia there should be a fixed number of public physicians in the several cities according to their size, these physicians being appointed, paid, and dismissed by the local civic authorities (Marquardt, Röm. Alt. iv, p. 185, *note*): ὅπερ δηλοῦται ἐξ ἐπιστολῆς Ἀντωνίνου τοῦ Εὐσεβοῦς γραφείσης μὲν τῷ κοινῷ τῆς Ἀσίας—ἧς ἐστιν τὸ κεφάλαιον τοῦτο ὑποτεταγμένον· Αἱ μὲν ἐλάττους πόλεις δύνανται πέντε ἰατροὺς ἀτελεῖς ἔχειν . . . αἱ δὲ μείζους πόλεις ἑπτά . . . αἱ δὲ μέγισται πόλεις δέκα· . . . Εἰκὸς δὲ τῷ μὲν μεγίστῳ ἀριθμῷ χρήσασθαι τὰς μητροπόλεις κ.τ.λ. If this regulation

referred, as it seems to do, to the archiatri, then there were ten such public physicians at Ephesos, which was a metropolis. All that is known on the subject of archiatri is summarized by Marquardt, Römische Alterth., Das Privatleben, pp. 752 foll. He thinks that the title ἀρχίατρος came into vogue in consequence of the ordinance of Antoninus, first in Asia, and then by degrees in other parts. He has given a list of some twelve cities (most of them on the eastern shores of the Ægean) at which we know archiatri to have existed from the witness of inscriptions. Already in Waddington-Le Bas, No. 161, one Ephesian is known : -αλον Ἀσκληπιάδου Πρείσκον φιλοσέβαστον ἀρχίατρον διὰ γένους, νεωποιόν κ.τ.λ. Priscus was evidently a citizen of high standing, and held the office of ἀρχίατρος by inheritance. The ἀρχίατροι were sometimes freedmen, but sometimes Roman citizens: see Henzen, Annali dell' Instituto Archeolog. xxiv (1852), p. 154. It is interesting to find the office of Jewish epitaphs by G. I. Ascoli (Iscrizioni Greche etc. di sepolchri Giudaici, Turin and Rome, 1880) there is the epitaph of a Jewish ἀρχίατρος from the catacombs of Venosa : (*ibid.* No. 10, 2nd 4th century A. D.). See Ascoli p. 50 for other mention of the professions of deceased Jews, proving that some of them certainly were well skilled in the liberal arts. Compare M. A. Levy, Epigraphische Beiträge z. Gesch. d. Juden (Jahrb. f. d. Gesch. d. Juden, vol. ii, Leipz. 1861) pp. 318- 319.

SECTION X.

MISCELLANEOUS FRAGMENTS.

DCLXXVIII.

Part of a block of blue-veined marble, broken all round; height 1 ft. 1 in.; width 2 ft. 7 in. From 'the Castle Hill at Ayasalouk, close to the Gate of Persecution, as it is called . . . .   This inscription I secured by sawing it off the large block of marble on which it was engraved,' Wood, Ephesus, pp. 40, 41 ; Appendix, Inscriptions from the City and Suburbs, No. 19.   Previously published by Pococke, Inscr. Ant. ii, § 10, p. 19, No. 9 : C.I. 2953 ; Röhl, Inscriptiones Antiquissimæ, No. 499 (with a facsimile).   Roberts, Introduction to Greek Epigraphy, No. 144 ; Bechtel, Inschriften des Ion. Dialekts, No. 145.

```
       ﹒ ﹗ : Π M M  E  N : A Π  O  K  Ρ Υ Υ E ⌐Ρ
     Ξ I O ﹗ : H Ν Δ E ﹗ E Π  A Ρ E ⫶ : T H E ⫶ Y
   Υ ∧ Ν Υ  M O Ν ⫶ Π T E Ρ Υ Γ A ⫶ K A Ν  E Γ ⌐
     Ρ E ⫶ : K A Ν A Π O ⌐ Ρ Υ Ψ E ⫶ ⫶ E ⫶ ⫶ I A ⫶
5  Ν Υ M O ⫶ ⫶ E Γ   Δ E ⫶ T ⫶⫶ ⫶ A Ρ I ⫶ T ⫶⫶ M
   H ⫶ ⫶ E ⫶ T H Ν Δ E Ξ I H Ν ⫶Π E T O ⫶⫶ M H
   E Ν O ⫶⫶H M M E Ν ⫶ I O Υ ⫶ ⫶ A Π O K  Ρ O Ν T
   Ψ E ⫶ ⫶ E Υ Ω Ν Υ M O ⫶ ⫶ H Ν  Δ E ⫶ T H Ν Ν O ⫶ A Ν
     ⫶ H Ν ⫶ : Π T Ρ Υ Γ A ⫶E  Π A Ρ A ⫶ ⫶Ν A I ⫶
```

[. . . . . . ἐκ μὲν τῆς δεξιῆ-]
[ς εἰς τὴν ἀριστερὴν πετ-]
όμεν]ος ἦμ μὲν ἀποκρύψε-   ρ . . . . .
ι, δε]ξιὸς, ἢν δὲ ἐπάρει τὴ-   ε υ . . . .
ν ε]ὐώνυμον πτέρυγα, κἂν   ἐγ δ[ὲ . . .
ἐπά]ρει κἂν ἀποκρύψει, ε-   ιαν . . . .
5   ὐώ]νυμος, ἐγ δὲ τῆς ἀριστ-   ι μ . . .
ερ]ῆς ἐς τὴν δεξιὴν πετό-   ι μη . . .
μ]ενος ἦμ μὲν ἰθὺς ἀποκρ-   οντ . . .
ύ]ψει, εὐώνυμος, ἢν δὲ τὴν   ο ἂν . . . .
δεξ]ιὴν   πτέρυγα   ἐπάρας   ναι . . . .
. . . .

The inscription was arranged in columns upon the surface of the marble which was once a large stelë, and may have come from the Artemision. A few letters of a second column of inscription remain ; but both the beginning and end of the document are wanting. The letters are engraved στοιχηδόν, there being nineteen in every line ; they belong to the sixth century b. c., and may be compared with No. DXVIII ante. The uncial printed text closely represents the original forms.

One could wish that this, the most ancient Ephesian document, dealt with a more interesting subject than rules of augury. But at least it is a very curious document. Lines 1-3 are restored from Böckh's suggestion. The meaning seems to be : ' If the bird is flying from right to left, if it settles out of sight, it is lucky ; but if it lift up the left wing, then whether it rises or settles out of sight, it is unlucky. But if the bird is flying from left to right, should it settle out of sight in a straight line, it is unlucky ; but if rearing the right wing it, etc.' For the quasi-intransitive use of ἀποκρύπτειν and ἐπαίρειν see L. and S. ; but Mr. Roberts attempts to make both verbs throughout govern πτέρυγα understood. The epithet ἰθὺς is opposed to the uplifting of either wing, because whenever a bird alights the least elevation of one wing and deflection of the other causes a curved swoop. M. Bouché-Leclercq makes reference to our inscription in his Histoire de la Divination dans l'antiquité (1879), i, pp. 140 foll. The forms of the subjunctive ἐπάρει and ἀποκρύψει are noteworthy ; similarly ποιήσει in an old inscription from Chios (Röhl, Inscr. Antiq. 381), and in the Teian ' curses ' (C. I. 3044) κατάξει, ἐκκόψε[ι], ποιήσει. These forms are due to the contraction of α + ει into ει in the declension of the first aorist subjunctive, and not to the confusion of ηι and ει which gave rise to the same forms again in the fourth century b. c.

DCLXXIX.

Fragment of white marble, broken on all sides; height 4 in.; width 3 in. Discovered by Mr. Wood. Unpublished.

```
Σ Η                          . . σ η . .
Λ Ε Ι ∠                      . λει  δ . . .
\ Ι ο Σ Λ                    . . . φ  δσα
ο Λ Λ Ρ                      . . . . ὕδωρ[ος.
```

This fragment is only interesting because it is inscribed in characters certainly not later than the fourth century B.C.

DCLXXX.

Fragment of marble, broken on all sides, and inscribed with letters apparently of the period of the Diadochi. Height 5 in.; width 2½ in. Discovered by Mr. Wood. Unpublished.

```
λ Ω Ι
Α Τ
```

DCLXXXI.

Six fragments of white marble stelæ, inscribed with letters of the best time : *a* entire at top, measures 2½ in. by 5 in. ; *b* entire at top, 4½ in. by 7 in. ; *c* entire on left, 2½ in. by 3¾ in. ; *d* entire on left, 3½ in. by 2 in. ; *e* broken all round, 2¾ in. by 4 in. ; *f* broken all round, 6 in. by 2½ in. Unpublished.

```
        a.         b.
      ΤΟΥΣ       ﹍ΜΟΝΟΙΣΕΙ
      ΔΙΟΚΛΗ     ΤΑΙΣΓΑΝΗΓΥΡΕΣ
         ⌒       ΣΧΩΡΑΣΕΥΓι
                 ΓΙΝΑΙΚΑΙΑ
                    Λ ''
c.
  |ΥΚΤΗ∠
  |ΝΓΕΝ⁻          c.
  |ΙΝΛΓ⁻          ΕΛ                    f.
d.                ΓΘΙΔΗ                .ΟΥ
  |ΕΣ             ΑΣΜΟ\               ΑΚΛΗ
  |ΑΝ/                               \ΛΑΛ
  |ΑΕ:                               ᴼΑΚΓ
  |<Γ⁻                               ᴐΣ˙
```

```
        a.          b.
  . . . . τοὺς  . . . . μόνοις εἰ . . . .
  . . . . Διοκλῆ[ς] ταῖς πανηγύρεσ[ι . . . .
  . . . . . . . . . ο . . [τῆ]ς χώρας εὐγ . .
                         εἶναι καὶ α . . .
c.
     . . . . .
   |υκτης
   |ννεν[τ            e.
   |ινδε[τ          . . ελ . . .           f.
d.               . . Εὐ]ηθίδη[ς? . . .        ου
   |ες . . .        . . ασμου . . .     . . . ακλη . . .
   |αν . . .                            παρ]αλαμ[βαν . . .
   |α ἐχ . . .                          . . ρακο . . .
   |σετ . . .                           . . ος . . .
```

It is clear that *a* and *b* belonged to the top of
the stele, but their relative position is uncertain.
Similarly with *c* and *d*: *e* and *f* may have come in
anywhere. The characters resemble the preceding

(No. DCLXXX), but are a trifle smaller; they are
hardly later than 300 B.C., and this was probably a
decree.

DCLXXXII.

Fragment of white marble, broken on all sides, and inscribed with letters very similar to the preceding (No. DCLXXXI). Height 3¼ in.; width 3 in. Discovered by Mr. Wood. Unpublished.

```
 ᴢᴜ
 ϽΚΤ
(uninscribed)
 ϜＲΑ
```

DCLXXXIII.

Four fragments of white marble wall-stones, inscribed with characters of the Macedonian period. Height of *a* 3 in.; width 6 in. Height of *b* 2¾ in.; width 4½ in. Height of *c* 4½ in.; width 7¼ in. Height of *d* 5 in.; width 5 in. Discovered by Mr. Wood. Unpublished.

a.
(broken all round)
```
ΓΡΟΑΥ,
ΕΣϞϜϲ
```

b.
(entire on right only)
```
\ᴍΕΝ|
ΙΕοΝ|
```

c.
(entire at bottom only)
```
ϽΥΕ
ΛΥΓ ᴺΙΧϹ
\ΕΩΝΙΔΟˢ
ΚΤΩΤϜ
ᵀΤᴖΥ
```
5

d.
(entire right and bottom)
```
.ΓΟ|
ΝΓΡΟ|
ΩΝΔΕ|
ϘΡΙΣΤΟ|
(uninscribed)
```

a.
```
τυ]ῖ Πολυχ . . .
. . τ]έσσε[ρ . . .
```

b.
```
. . . a]μεν |
. . . ν]εον |
```

c.
```
. . . . ου ε . . .
'Ο]λυ[μ]πιχο . . .
Λεωνίδο[υ . . .
ὅ]κτω τη . . . .
. . . .,τοῦ . . .
```
5

d.
```
. . . . το
. . ν προ-
. . . ων δε
χ]ωρὶς το
```

That these are portions of wall-stones is proved
by *c*, where the joint of the stones divides the last
line horizontally in half. They may be parts of a
decree, like Nos. CCCXLVIII foll., but rather earlier

in date. In *a* the final Χ is certain. Observe the
Ionicism τ]έσσε[ρες. In *b* the Α or Λ at the beginning
is certain. In *c* we cannot identify Olympichos or
Leonides.

DCLXXXIV.

Fragment of grey marble, broken on all sides, and inscribed with small letters of the Macedonian period.   Height 6 in. ; width 3 in.
Discovered by Mr. Wood. Unpublished.

ΤΑΡΙ	. . τ(α)ρε . .
ΙΗΣΦΥ	. . τῆς φυ[λῆς ? . .
ΝΤΑΙ · ΚΑΤ	. . νται κατ . . . .
ΕΙΣΑΥΤ	. . εἰς αὐτ . . .
5 ΣΔΙΝΑ	5 . . . ς Διν . . .

DCLXXXV.

Fragment of white marble, entire only on left.   Height 9¼ in. ; width 5 in.   Discovered by Mr. Wood.   Unpublished.

ΜΟΣΧϹ	Μόσχο[ς Μη-
ΤΡΟΑΣͺ	τροδώ[ρου,
ΔΑΝ	Δαμ[ᾶς ?
ΣΩΤΙ	Ζωτί[χου.
(Two lines space	
uninscribed.)	
ΠΟΓ	Ποσ[ειδ . . .

A list of names, possibly from a dedication. The lettering closely resembles the list of neopoioi No. DXC b, the date of which is probably the first century A. D.   As in that list, so here also, the names (so far as they remain) are purely Greek.

DCLXXXVI.

Fragment of a corner of blue marble block, inscribed on two sides.   Height 1 ft. 4 in. ; width of a 9 in. ; width of b 8½ in.   Discovered by Mr. Wood.   Unpublished.

a.   *b.*

	ΟΙ ΟΣ
	ΕΞΑΝΔΡΟΣ
	ΣΧΡΙΩΝ
	ΩΙΛΟΣ
5	ΡΩΤΕΑΣ
	ΡΑΓΩΝ
ΑΣ	ΑϹ
ΑΓΕΝΗΣ	ΚΡΑ
	ΤΑΡ
ΞΩΣ	ΑΓΟ
10	ΑΓΟ
ΗΣΙΑΣ	ΗΡΑ
ΝΗΣ	ΛΑΝ
	ΛΡΤΕ

	. . . . ο . ος
	[Ἀλ]έξανδρος
	[Αἰ]σχρίων
	[Ζ]ωῖλος
5	Πρωτίας
	Τράγων
. . . . ας	. . . . . ας
	Κρα . . . .
. . . . αγένης	Παρ . . . . .
10	Ἀπο[λλ . . . .
. . . . εως	Ἡρα[κλ . . . .
. . . . ησίας	Λαμ[π . . .
. . . . νης	Ἀρτε[μι . . . .

Part of two lists of names, in characters apparently of the first century B. C.

DCLXXXVII.

Fragments of wall-stones of white marble. They all manifestly are parts of one inscription, and the block which contains *d* on its left return face, is inscribed on its right return face with No. DXX *ante*. Discovered by Mr. Wood. Unpublished.

a.

Block of wall-stone; upper, bottom, and part of left edge entire. Height 11¾ in.; width 1 ft. 5 in.

```
                        ∠
              ΝΑΙΚΙΥΠΩΡΑΔΗΙ
               ⁻ΒΥΤΕΡΟΣΔΗΙ
                       ΔΗΙ      ΠΟ
      5                ΔΗΙ
                       ΔΗΙ      Μ
                     ΤΑΥΛΗ
                 ϽΦΙΛΟΥΔΗΙ
                       ΔΙ
     10   ΟΝΥ∠ιϹ          Τ
          ΠΟΛΛΩΝΙΟΥ
          ΟΥΤΟΥΠΡΑΣΙΜ
```

b.

Block of wall-stone, apparently belonging to the same course as the preceding; height 11¾ in.; width 1 ft. 3¼ in. Broken on left side only.

```
            ϽΥ⁻ΑΤΡΙΒΑΣΣΗ

            ΑΙΣΑΡΗΑΣΥΝ
               ΔΗΙ
          ιΝΜΗΤΡΙ           ΔΗΙ
      5   ΝΕΙΚΗΤΟΣ           ΔΗΙ
          ΣΣΟΣΣΥΝΑΔΕΛΦΩΚΑΙ
          ΚΙ     ΔΗΙ
          ΔΩΡΟΥΣΥΝΥΙΩΚΑΙΓΥΝΑΙΚΙΔΡ
          ΙΣΥΝΓΥΝΑΙΚΙΚΑΙΤΕϘΝΟΙΣΔΗ
```

c.

Fragment of wall-stone, like the preceding: broken on right and left. Height 11¾ in.; width 7 in.

```
             ∠
            ΩΝ
          ϞΑΔΕΛΦΩ


      5

                ϽΣ

                         ∠
                        ΔΗ
                 ΤΡΟΥ    ΔΗΙ
     10                  ΔΗΙ
                 ΗΣΕΡΩΤΙ
```

d.

Block of wall-stone, entire at the upper and lower edge, broken on the left. On the right return face is inscribed No. nxx *ante.* Height 11 in.; width of the present surface 9½ in.

```
        ΠΑΤΡΩΟΥ      ΔΗΙ
        ΥΙΩ          ΔΗΙ
        ΙΚΙ          ΔΗΙ
        ΙΤΡΙ         ΔΗΙ
5       ΝΚΑΙΥΙΟΙΣΔΗΙ
                     ΔΗΙ
                     ΔΗΙ
                     ΔΗΙ
                     ΔΗΙ
10                   ΗΑΣ
```

c.

Fragment of wall-stone, entire at bottom and right edge, and partly at the upper edge. Height 11½ in.; width 1 ft. 10½ in.

```
        ΛΘΩΝ              ΔΗ.
        ΥΛΛ°ΣΜΕΤΑΛΔΕΛ
        ΔΗΙ
        ΣΔΙΟΝΥΣΙΟΣ    ΔΗΙ
5       ΤΟΣΟΛΛΧΙΟΙ              ΔΗΙ
        ΙΚΙΑΣΝΕΙΚΑΝΔΡΟΥΤΟΥΒΑΔΡΟΜΙΟΥΚΑΙ
        ΡΟΔΗΑΝΤΙΟΧΟΥΚΑΙΝΕΙΚΑΝΔΡΟΣΝΕΙΚΙΟΥΔΗ
        ΠΟΠΛΙΟΣΣΚΡΕΙΒΩΝΙΟΣΔΙΟΓΕΝΗΣ      ΔΗΙ
        ΤΙΤΟΣΚΟΥΡΒΙΟΣΚΗΡΙΝΘΟΣΜΕΤΑΓΥΝΑΙ
10      ΚΟΣΚΑΙΤΕΚΝΩΝ      ΔΗΙ
        ΛΥΛΟΣΓΕΡΙΛΛΛΑΝΟΣΒΑΣΣΟΣΣΥΝΓΥΝΑΙΚΙΔΗ
        ι  ιΛΠ    ε
```

f.

Fragment of wall-stone, entire only on upper edge. Height 5 in.; width 9½ in.

```
        ΔΗΙΒ
        ΝΣΥΝΓΥ
        ΣΗΙΒ
        ΟΥΝΔΙΣΣΙΜοΣ
5            ΙΗΤΩΔΗΙΒ
```

g.

Fragment of wall-stone, lower edge alone entire. Height 8½ in.; width 1 ft. 4½ in.

```
        ΗΙΟΣΒΟ
        ΟΙΝΤΟΣΚΑΛΠοΥΡ
        ΑΥΛΟΣΠοΜΠΗΙΟΣΤΕΡΜν
        ΠοΛΛΩΝΙοΣΑΠοΛΛΝΙοΥΤΟ
5       ΕΡΜΟΓΕΝΗΣΕΥΗΝΟΡΟΣΟΤΑι
        ΤΡΟΣΑΠοΔΗΜΟΥ<
        ΛΝΙΔΗΣΧΑΡΙΞΕΝΟΥΣΥΝΥΙΣ
        ΣΓΛΕΙΣΤΑΡΧΟΥΜΕΤΑΥΙΟ
        ΚΡΙΟΣΠο
```

h.

Fragment of wall-stone, lower edge, and upper part of right edge alone entire. Height 5¼ in.

```
ΦΟΥΚΙΟΣΦΡΟΛΛΛΑ
ΣΑΠΟΛΛΩΝΙΟΥΜΕΤΑΓΥΝΑΙΚοϹ
ΠοΥΦΕΙΚΙοΣΝΕΙΚΕΡΛΣ
ΑΤΗΣΜΙΘΡΗΟΥΣΣΥΝΓΥΝΑΙΚΙ
ΝΕΚΛΗΟΥΣ
```

i.

Fragment of wall-stone, entire only on lower edge. Height 5¼ in.; width 1 ft. 1¾ in.

```
                              ΦΗⵐ
      Ι   ΜΗΝΑΣΑΡΤΕΜΙΔΩΡϹ
      ῑ   ΜΗΤΡΟΔΩΡΟΣΑΠΟΛΛΩῘ
      ῑ   ΠΡΕΙΜΟΣΑΡΤΕΜΙΔΩΡΟΥ
          ΦΙΛΙΠ    ΣΗΡΑΚΑΙ
```

k.

Fragment of wall-stone, entire only at upper edge. Height 5¼ in.; width 9½ in.

```
       ΛΕΥΚΙΟⵐ
       ΓΕΡΙΛΛΑΝⵑ
    ΙΙ  ΜΕΝΑΝΔΡΟΣΜΕ
    ΑΙ  ΜΑΡΚΟΣΦΛΑϹ
                Κ
```

l.

Fragment of wall-stone, entire only on lower edge. Height 4½ in.; width 1 ft. 2 in.

```
       ι ΠΟΠλιοΣΦⲟι ᵕⵑ
         ΜΕΝΑΝΔΡΟΣΑΝ
       ΔΗ  ΣΕΡΒΙοΣΦΟΥΛΒ
       ⴸῙ    ᵕΞΤοΣΚΟΙⵑ
```

a.

```
                                    . . . . . . . . . . . δ[η. ι´]
. . . . . . . . . . . . σὺν γυ]ναικὶ Ὑπώρᾳ  δη. ι
ὁ δεῖνα . . . . . . . . . ὁ πρε]σβύτερος     δη. ι´
. . . . . . . . . . . . . . . . . . . . .    δη. ι´ Πο . . .
. . . . . . . . . . . . . . . . . . . . . .  δη. ι´
. . . . . . . . . . . . . . . . . . . . . .  δη. ι´ Μ . . .
. . . . . . . . . . . . . . Πρω ?]ταυλη . .
. . . . . . . . . . . . . . . οφίλου  δη. ι´
. . . . . . . . . . . . . . . . . . .  δη.[ι´
. . . Δι]ονυσίο[υ]                     δ[η. ι´
. . . Ἀ]πολλωνίου                      [δη. ι´
. . . ῳ τοῦ Πραξίμ . .                 [δη. ι´
```

b.

```
. . . . . . . . . . . . . σὶν] θιγατρὶ Βάσσῃ
. . . . . . . . . . . δη. ι´]
              . . Κ]ισαρῆα υἱν
. . . . . . . . . . δη. ι´
. . . σὺ]ν μητρὶ               δη. ι´
. . . Ἀ]νείκητος               δη. ι´
. Βύ]σσος σὶν ἀδελφῷ καὶ
γυναι]κὶ    δη. ι´
. . . . δῶρα· σὶν υἱῷ καὶ γυναικὶ δη.[ι´
        σὶν γυναικι καὶ τέκνοις δη.[ι´
```

c.

```
. . . . . . . . . . . . . . ς            [δῆ. ι´
. . . . . . . . . . . . . ων            [δῆ. ι´
. . . . . . . . . συ]ν ἀδελφῷ           [δῆ. ι´
. . . . . . . . . . . . . .             [δῆ. ι´
. . . . . . . . . . . . .               [δη. ι´
. . . . . . . . . . . ος               [δῆ. ι´
. . . . . . . . . . . . .               δ[η. ι´
. . . . . . . . . . . . .               δη. [ι´
. . . . . . . . . τρου                 δη. ι
. . . . . . . . . . . . .               δῆ. ι´
. . . . . . . . . . ης Ἐρωτι-
    [-ανοῦ? δη. ι´]
```

d.

```
. . . . . . . . . . . . . . Πατρῴου     δη. ι´
. . . . . . . . . . συν] υἱῷ           δη. ι´
. . . . . . . . . . συν γυνα]ικὶ        δη. ι´
. . . . . . . . . . συν μ]ητρὶ          δη. ι´
. . . . . . . . . . συ]ν καὶ υἱοῖς      δη. ι´
. . . . . . . . . . . . .               δῆ. ι´
. . . . . . . . . . . . .               δη. ι
. . . . . . . . . . . . .               δη. ι
. . . . . . . . . . . . .               δῆ. ι´
. . . . . . . . . . . . .               ηας
```

e.

```
. . . . . . . . . . Ἀγ]άθων            δῆ. [ι´
. . . . . . . . . . . . υλλος μετὰ ἀδελ-
            -φοῦ]    δη. ι´
. . . . . . . . . . ς Διονύσιος         δῆ. ι´
. . . . . τος Βακχίου                   δη. ι´
Νε]μκίας Νεικάνδρου τοῦ Βαθρομίου καὶ
Ῥόδη Ἀντιόχου καὶ Νείκανδρος Νεικίου    δῆ. [ι´
Πόπλιος Σκρειβώνιος Διογένης            δῆ. ι´
Τίτος Κούρβιος Κήρινθος μετὰ γυναι-
            κὸς καὶ τέκνων              δῆ. ι´
Αὖλος Γερίλλανὸς Βάσσος σὺν γυναικὶ     δῆ. [ι´
```

f.

```
. . . . . . . . . . . . . . . . . .     δῆ. ιβ´
. . . . . . . . . . . . . . ν σὺν γυ-
    ναικὶ] δη. ιβ´
    Ἰου]κουνδίσσιμος
. . . . . . . . . . . . ητῳ δῆ. ιβ´
```

g.

```
. . . . . ἡιος Βα . . . . .        [δη. ι´ or th. lik. throughout]
Κ]όιντος Καλπούρ[νιος . . . . .
Αὖλος Πομπήιος Τέρμο . . . . .
Ἀ]πολλώνιος Ἀπολλωνίου το[ῦ . . . .
Ἑρμογένης Εὐήγορος Ὀτα . . .
            τρος Ἀποδήμου . . .
. . . . . . . . ωρίδης Χαριξίνου σὺν υἱῷ . . .
. . . . . . . . . . . ς Πλειστάρχου μετὰ υἱο[ῦ . .
. . . . . . . . . . κριος Πο . . . . . . .
```

h.

```
. . . . . Μνύκιος (?) Φρο . . . . .    [δη. ι´ or th. lik. throughout]
. . . . . ς Ἀπολλωνίου μετὰ γυναικὸς . .
. . . . . ποιφείκιος Νεικίρως
Μιθραδ]άτης Μιθρηους σὺν γυναικὶ
. . . . . Με]μεκλήους
```

i.

. . . . . δη.] ι´		Φη . . . .
. . . . . δη.] ι´	Μηνᾶς Ἀρτεμιδώρο[υ	
. . . . . δη.] ι´	Μητρόδωρος Ἀπολλων[ίου	
. . . . . δη.] ι´	Πρεῖμος Ἀρτεμιδώρου	
5	Φίλιπ[πο]ς Ἡρακλή[ους	

k.

Λείλιος . . .
Γεριλλανό[ς . . .
. . . [δη.] ι´ Μένανδρος Με[νάνδρου ? . .
. . . . αι . Μάρκος Φλαο[ύιος
5 κ . . .

l.

. . . [δη.] ι´ Πόπλιος Φ . . . .
. . . Μένανδρος Ἀν . . .
. . . δη. ι´ Σίρβιος Φούλβ[ιος . . .
. . . δη. ι´ [Σ]ξετος Κοι . . . . .

The inscription of which these are a few fragments was a list of a number of persons who had contributed money for some public purpose. The contribution is usually ten denarii, but occasionally twelve. The donors as often bear Latin as Greek names; many of them perhaps were not Ephesian citizens but Romans resident in Asia. The character of the letters closely resembles the list of Neopoioi, No. DLXXVIII, which we have seen good reason to assign to the middle of the first century A. D. The letters have luxuriant apices. It is some indication of a comparatively early date, to find Π by the side of π (in g, line 8). It might help us to divine the subject of the inscription, if we could ascertain from what building these wall-stones came. It is singular that the right return face of d contains No. DXX. But No. DXX manifestly belongs to the third century B. C.; and it may be questioned whether the marble was not removed from its original place in order to receive d. As however the surface of No. DXX is in no way injured, we may rather believe that wherever the marble was placed to receive No. DXX, it stood unmoved three centuries later when the left return face of the same wall was inscribed with our present inscription. If therefore I am right in connecting No. DXX with the Artemision (see notes *ad loc.*), we may suppose that the contributions here recorded were to defray the cost of some building or repairs connected with the temple.

While we cannot define more closely the date and occasion of the inscription, it should be remembered that it was the custom in Greece to record publicly the names of those who contributed to the expense of public works. Instances of this will be found in Part ii, No. CCXCVIII (Kalymna), C. I. 3140–3144, and 3148 (Smyrna), C. I. A. ii, 334 (Athens). Böckh (on C. I. 3140) refers to Diogenes Laert. vii, 12 : Φησὶ δ᾽ Ἀντίγονος ὁ Καρύστιος οὐκ ἀρνεῖσθαι αὐτὸν (sc. Ζήνωνα) εἶναι Κιτιέα. τῶν γὰρ εἰς τὴν ἐπισκευὴν τοῦ λουτρῶνος συμβαλλομένων εἷς ὢν καὶ ἀναγραφόμενος ἐν τῇ στήλῃ Ζήνωνος τοῦ φιλοσόφου ἠξίωσε καὶ τὸ Κιτιεὺς προστεθῆναι.

DCLXXXVIII.

Fragment of white marble slab, entire only on the left side. Height 4½ in.; width 5 in. Discovered by Mr. Wood.

ΡΙΟΥΡ
ΟΥΑ

DCLXXXIX.

Fragment of marble, entire only on the right edge, where there is a moulding. Height 6½ in.; width 2½ in. Discovered by Mr. Wood.

Ο
ΤΟ
ΤΑ

DCXC.

Fragment of white marble ; broken on all sides. Height 6½ in. ; width 2⅞ in. Discovered by Mr. Wood.

```
      ı
      A
    ΛΑΞ
    ΔF
```

DCXCI.

Fragment of white marble, perhaps a stele ; broken on all sides. Height 6 in. ; width 2 in. Discovered by Mr. Wood.

```
        ⌐
      OYI
      KAI
      ΩTA
 5    ΙΑⲨ
```

DCXCII.

Fragment of grey marble, broken on all sides. Height 8 in. ; width 4 in. Discovered by Mr. Wood.

```
     ΝTO
     THEK
    _____
     moulding
    _____
     ΛΑ·ΑΦ
    ⲦΟΙΟⲨⲦ
```

Line 4 : possibly *νεο]ποιοῦ*.

DCXCIII.

Fragment of white marble, entire only on the right edge. Height 6 in. ; width 10 in. Discovered by Mr. Wood.

```
    ΕΠΙ  |
    ⊃Ν   |
    ∩Ξ   |
```

DCXCIV.

Fragment of grey marble, broken on all sides. Height 6¾ in. ; width 2 in. Discovered by Mr. Wood

```
     ιΘΙ
     ⌐ΝΟ
     ΗΡⴼ
     ⴼΑΙ
 5   ΑⱢ
```

DCXCV.

Fragment of white marble, entire on the left edge only; but the surface to the left is injured.   Height 3½ in. ; width 2¼ in.
Discovered by Mr. Wood.

surface ΛΙⲈ
broken ΙΛΟ

DCXCVI.

Fragment of the corner of a stele of white marble.   Inscribed on two surfaces, *a* and *b*.   Height of *a*, 7 in. ; width 3½ in.
Height of *b*, 7 in. ; width 4 in.   Discovered by Mr. Wood.

a.   *b.*

ⲃΟΥ
ΛΤΗ
Λ   ΑⲈ
ⲀΜΛ   Τ
5   Δⲅ

DCXCVII.

Fragment of blue marble, broken on all sides.   Height 6 in. ; width 2 in.   Discovered by Mr. Wood.

ΙΟⲨ
uninscribed
Λ

DCXCVIII.

Fragment of white marble, broken on all sides.   Height 4½ in.; width 3 in.   Discovered by Mr. Wood.

ⲒΣΦΙ
ΛΣⲏ

DCXCIX.

Fragment of white marble, broken on all sides.   Height 1¼ in. ; width 3½ in.   Discovered by Mr. Wood.

ⲢΛΙ

DCC.

Fragment of marble, broken on all sides.   Height 1½ in. ; width 3 in.   Discovered by Mr. Wood.

ΑΙΑΡ

DCCI.

Fragment of white marble, broken on all sides. Height 3 in.; width 3½ in. Discovered by Mr. Wood.

```
    N L
  I Δ H >
```

DCCII.

Fragment of white marble veneering (crusta), broken on all sides, ¾ in. thick; height 6 in.; width 7 in. The letters are 3⅞ in. high. Discovered by Mr. Wood.

```
    A I
```

DCCIII.

Fragment of white marble, apparently from a stele; immediately above the inscription is an uninscribed moulding, the upper edge of which is complete. Height 5¼ in.; width 5½ in. Discovered by Mr. Wood.

```
       moulding

    I I . K A
```

DCCIV.

Fragment of white marble, entire only on left edge. Height 3 in.; width 4¾ in. Discovered by Mr. Wood.

```
    ' K A I      |
      T I        |
```

DCCV.

Fragment of white marble, entire only on left edge. Height 2½ in.; width 2⅜ in. Discovered by Mr. Wood.

```
    |  H
```

DCCVI.

Fragment of white marble wall-stone, entire upon the left edge only. Height 5¼ in.; width 4 in. Discovered by Mr. Wood.

```
    |        ⌒
    |  P A     Σ
    |  A T
    |  ) Σ    Γ
    |  .
```

DCCVII.

Fragment of marble, entire on the upper and left edge. Height 7 in.; width 9 in. Four inches of the surface above the inscription have been split off, and five inches from the left-hand surface, so that only a few letters remain. Discovered by Mr. Wood.

```
         ΔΙΔ
       ϹΠΙΟΣ
       ΤΟΥΟ
```

DCCVIII.

Fragment of marble, broken on all sides. Height 7 in.; width 8 in. Discovered by Mr. Wood; unpublished.

```
  ϹΙ              . . . . ΐ . . . .
  ΑΦΗϵ            . . . γρ]αφῆς . . . .
  ΑΝΟΜΙ           ἀγορ]ανομ[ήσαντα ?
```

DCCIX.

Fragment of white marble, entire only on the right edge. Height 2½ in.; width 6½ in. Discovered by Mr. Wood; unpublished.

```
  ϽΝΚ Τ Ι |          ∴ . τὸν κτί[στήν ?
```

DCCX.

Fragment of white marble, entire only on the upper edge. Height 4 in.; width 6 in. Discovered by Mr. Wood; unpublished.

```
        uninscribed
   ΟΥΡΑΝΟ             . . . . . ουρανᾶ[ς . . .
        Μ
```

One would suggest Suburanus, as in the Salutaris inscription and No. DCCXXVIII; but before ΟΥ there seems to be the point of a letter other than Β.

DCCXI.

Seven fragments of white marble, inscribed with large letters of the Antonine period. The measurements are given with the uncial text of each fragment. The similarity of the characters, and of the dressing of the stone, makes it probable that these are fragments of the same stele. Discovered by Mr. Wood; unpublished.

a.	*b.*	*c.*	*d.*
Broken all round ; height 1½ in.; width 6½ in.	Broken all round ; height 3½ in.; width 10½ in.	Broken all round ; height 3½ in.; width 8¾ in.	Broken all round ; height 3 in.; width 3 in.
ΜΦΙϹϵ	ϵΙϵΙΟΥ	ΓΗΣΑΛ	ΡΑ

e.	*f.*	*g.*
Broken all round; height 2 in.; width 4 in.	Broken all round ; height 3½ in.; width 3 in.	Broken all round; height 5 in.; width 8 in.
ϽϹ	ΛΙϵ	ΛΙ ΟΥ

a. . . . ψ]ήφισ[μα . . (or the like). *b.* . . . (ε)ως (τ)οῦ . . *c.* . . . στρατη?]γήσα[ντα ? *d, e, f, g* are mere fragments.

DCCXII.

Fragment of a large block of white marble; entire at bottom and on right, where the right return end is uninscribed. Discovered by Mr. Wood; unpublished.

ͿΙΛΙΟΣ | in.   . . . Ἰούλιος ?
_____
10½ in.

DCCXIII.

Fragment of the upper portion of a white marble stele, the upper edge of the moulding being preserved; so that line 1 was the first line of the document. Height 1 ft. 1 in.; width 6½ in. Discovered by Mr. Wood; unpublished.

```
ΊΜΟΣΥ          Ὁ δῆ]μος ὁ . . . .
 ͞ ΡΗ ͞         . . . . ς ῥήτ[ορα
 ΊΟΣΙ          . . . . Ποσ[ειδ . . .
   ι
```

Possibly honorary.

DCCXIV.

Fragment of white marble stele, entire at top and on the right edge. Height 7½ in.; width 3½ in. Discovered by Mr. Wood; unpublished.

```
ΔΙΟΝ      . . Κλαύ]διον ?
 ~
 ‒         . . . . . . . ?
```

DCCXV.

Four fragments of dark blue marble crustæ, rather over half-an-inch thick. They form parts of a large slab (like the slabs inscribed with Nos. cccci.xxxvii foll.); but by observing the varying thickness of the fragments, due to the manner in which the original slab was sawn, we are able to determine in some degree the relative position of the fragments, although they will not read into each other. Discovered by Mr. Wood; unpublished.

```
         a.                    d.
                               ΧΗ
      ΑΝ · ΤΣ               ΟΥ
  (uninscribed)  b.            ϸ.͞
               .ͺU         ΑΛΛΕͺ
               <Α·Κ    5   ΙΩΝ·ΚΑΙ
         c.    ΤͰ           ∶Ω·ΚΑΙΤ
         d·Ͱ            ΩΑΣΚΛΗ
      ΑΝΤΙΣ                 ͰΓΑΓͰ
```

(a) Broken all round. Height 3½ in.; width 4 in.   (b) Broken all round. Height 4½ in.; width 2½ in.
(c) Broken all round. Height 2½ in.; width 2½ in.   (d) Entire towards bottom of right edge only. Height 10 in.; width 3½ in.

Apparently proper names, chiefly Roman. a: [Ἀγαθῇ τύ]χῃ. Line 4: possibly [Κ]αλλί[ας]. Line 5: Ἀν(τώνιος) Τω . . . . b: Κλ(αύδιος) Κ . . . . c: Τι]-| . . . . . ιων καὶ . . . Line 6: . . . φ καὶ Τ . . . Line 7: β(ίριος) Ἀ . . . . Ἀντίσ[τιος]. d: line 1, perhaps | . . . . φ Ἀσκλη[πιάδου?]. Line 8: Κέλερ, i. e. Celer.

4 B

DCCXVI.

Fragment of a block (stele?) of white marble, broken on all sides. Height 1 ft.; width 1 ft. 3 in. The last four lines are inscribed in rather larger characters than the rest. Discovered by Mr. Wood; unpublished.

```
      .   ˘                            o
     )✱ΤΟ✱                      ου τοῦ [. . . . , ὁ δεῖνα
    ΡΟ✱ΟΚι                     . . . . . ρου ὁ κ[αὶ . . . . . . . . .
   ΝΟΣΕ✱Τ✱Χιι                  . . . . . νος, Εὐτύχης . . . . . . . .
 5 ιΣΙΟΣ·Δ·ΤΟ✱Ε              5  . . . . . σιος δ̄ τοῦ Ε . . . . . . .
   ιΣΤΟ✱ΑΝΤΕΣΦϹ                 . . . . ου]ς τοῦ Ἀντεσφδ̄ρου . . . .
   ✱Τ✱ΧΟ✱Σ·ΝΕ·✱Μ              . . . Ε]ὐτύχους νε(ώτερος), Ὑμ[ίδιος ?
    ⁻ΟΣ                         Κόδρα]τος ?
```

Part of a list of names. The numeral Δ in line 5 implies that four generations had borne the same name. Ἀντεσφόρου line 6 must be a blunder or a corruption for Ἀνθεσφόρου. The restoration of the last name is merely conjectural. Here the inscription ended.

DCCXVII.

Fragment of white marble, entire only on the left. Height 4 in.; width 3½ in. Discovered by Mr. Wood; unpublished.

```
  ΤΟΝι                   Πόν[τι . . .
  ΦΑΥϜ                   Φαυσ[τ . . .
  Νι                     νι . . . . . .
```

Apparently portions of Roman names.

DCCXVIII.

Fragment of white marble, entire only at the top. Height 5¼ in.; width 5¾ in. Discovered by Mr. Wood; unpublished.

```
  ΠΡΩΤϹ                . . . Πρωτο . . .
  ϜΥΗ                  . . . . . ευη
```

DCCXIX.

Fragment of white marble, complete on right edge only. Height 10¼ in.; width 3 in. Discovered by Mr. Wood. Unpublished.

```
      (vacant)
      ΑΝΟϹ                  . . . . . . ανὸς
      ΙΝΟΣ                  . . . . . . ῖνος
                            . . . . . .
      ιⲌΙΟΥ                 . . . . . . αξίου
  5   ΤΩ                5   . . . . . . τῷ
      ΜΙΣΗΩ                 . . Ἀρτε]μισήῳ ?
      (blank)
```

The inscription appears to be complete at the top and bottom: the letters indicate the second century A.D. Lines 1–2 contained names of persons, who perhaps had dedicated something to Artemis.

DCCXX.

a.

Corner of a square basin or trough of white marble. The upper edge is perfect, and part of the hemi-spherical cavity is preserved; two of the external sides are partly preserved, being broken at the bottom edge, and also the one to right and the other to left. A sectional outline is given below. Inscribed upon one of the external surfaces, which measures in its present broken condition, height 3¼ in.; width 5¼ in. Discovered by Mr. Wood; unpublished.

ΔΙΟΝ·.
ΤΡΟΛⲤ

Διονύ[σιος? Μη-
τροδώ[ρου? ἀνέθηκεν?

b.

Fragment of white marble, broken on right and left, but entire above and below the inscription. Height 11½ in.; width 1 ft. ½ in. Discovered by Mr. Wood; unpublished.

ΊΑΟΝΤΑ   . . να ὄντα . .
ΙΟΥΣΚΑΙ   . . ίους καὶ . . .

The letters of *b* are more than a quarter larger than *a*, but the peculiar manner in which both are inscribed compels the belief that they were from one and the same monument.

DCCXXI.

Fragment of a small column of white marble, broken on all edges, but the beginnings of the lines of inscription are entire. Height 6 in.; width 7½ in. Discovered by Mr. Wood; unpublished.

                        . . . .
ΝΗΙ   νη . . .
ΤΗΣΑΙ   τῆς Ἀ[ρτέμιδος?
ⲀΙⲢⲓ   καὶ ἱε[ροκῆρυξ? (or
                              ἱε[ρεύς? . .)

Perhaps from a dedication.

DCCXXII.

Fragment of marble, entire only upon the top and right edge. Height 10 in.; width 9½ in. Discovered by Mr. Wood; unpublished.

ΥΤΑ	τοὺς πρ]υτά-
ⳐΝΟΝΓΥ	νεις . . . .]νον γυ-
ΟΝΕΙΣΕΙΟⲚ	. . . . ον Εἴσειον
ΣΠΑΝΤΩΝ	. . . . ς πάντων
5 ⲀΚΤΟΜΗΛΑΑΜ	5 . . . . ακτω μὴ λαμ-
Α·ⲐΑⲦ	βάνειν?] . . . .

The restoration in lines 1 and 6 is dubious; but there is much probability that line 6 originally read ΑΝΕΑΣ. Line 3: Εἴσειον (Ἴσειον) is a temple of Isis. Falkener (Ephesus, p. 106) believed himself to have discovered the temple of Serapis, and on p. 109 he cites an Ephesian coin as proving the existence of such a temple.

DCCXXIII.

Fragment of white marble, inscribed with large letters (1¼ in. high) of the second century A. D. Broken on all edges except the bottom. Height 1 ft. 3½ in.; width 5 in. Discovered by Mr. Wood; unpublished.

	ΟΣ•ι	. . ος· . . . .
	ΦΙΛΟ	. . φιλο . .
	ΛΚΟ	. . ακο . .
	ϽΙΟΥ·Ι	. . νεσπ]οισθ·? . .
5	⁻ΗΓΟ⁺	. . στρα]τηγοῦ? . .

Possibly from a dedication.

DCCXXIV.

Fragment of white marble, broken on all edges except the left, and inscribed with letters of the second century A. D. Height 7¼ in.; width 5¼ in. Discovered by Mr. Wood; unpublished.

ΤΙ⏌	Τίτ[ος? . . .
ΤΙΤ	Τίτ[ος? . . .

DCCXXV.

A fragment of white marble, broken all round. Height 9½ in.; width 10 in. Discovered by Mr. Wood; unpublished.

∠••	. . σ . .
ΡΤΕΜΙΔ	'Α]ρτέμιδ . . .
ϽΥΝΚΗΙϹ	. . . . ουνκήιο[γ . .
Ⅴ'ΛΥϹ	. . . . . αι δύο? . . .

In the third line we recognise the termination of some Roman name.

DCCXXVI.

Two fragments of white marble crustæ, from ⅔ in. to ½ in. thick. Discovered by Mr. Wood; unpublished. From the greater size of the letters in line 1 of a, and the margin above it, we may conclude that a came above b; but what interval divided them is uncertain.

a.

Broken all round : height 8⅔ in.; width 6 in.

Η Σ Λ
ϴ Ε Ν Τ
ΟΥ Σ Π
Ⅴ Γ •

b.

Broken all round : height 7¼ in.; width 6 in.

` ⊙ .
Υ
ϽΥ Λ Ι Ο Σ
Ⅴ ⊤ . . Λ

a. Line 1: possibly ἐτείμ]ησα[ν, or τ]ῆς 'Α[σίας.   Line 2: αἱρε]θέντ[ας ?   Line 3: τ]οὺς π[ολίτας ?
b. Line 3: 'Ι]ούλιος.

DCCXXVII.

Four fragments of whitish marble crustæ, of which *a* and *b* certainly belong to the same. Also *c* and *d* probably belong to the same, although in *c* and *d* the marble is somewhat thicker, and its colour rather more grey. Discovered by Mr. Wood; unpublished.

<table>
<tr><td align="center">*a.*</td><td align="center">*b.*</td><td align="center">*c.*</td><td align="center">*d.*</td></tr>
<tr><td align="center">Broken all round : height
7½ in.; width 3½ in.</td><td align="center">Broken all round: height
4 in.; width 2⅔ in.</td><td align="center">Broken all round except on right :
height 4 in.; width 3½ in.</td><td align="center">Broken except at top and bottom :
height 4½ in.; width 6½ in.</td></tr>
<tr><td align="center">ιΛ
_ΙΣ⌐
ιΑΝΙΚ
ΜΑΝΙΚ
5   ◄ΕΛΕΥΣ
ΙΛΟΚΥ</td><td align="center">ΛΛΙ
ꞏ ΓΡΛ
ꞏΤ·Εꞏ.
ꞏ ΑΛΕ¯
Υ</td><td align="center">► ΚΟι
Σꞏ·ΔꞏφΙ
φιꞏλ Γ</td><td align="center">ꞏΙΝΔΥΝΟΣ
ΥΤΙΩΧΟΣꞏ
ΞΝΕΚΛΣ Γ</td></tr>
</table>

In *a* may be recognised the names [Γεϱ]μανιϰ[ός],
. . . [Γεϱ]μανιϰ . . . , 'Ελευσ[ίνιος]. [Φ]ιλοϰύ[δης?]. In *d*
[Αϰ]ίνδυνος, ['Α]ντίωχος (*sic*), [Σ]ενίϰας. If *c*, *d* are
fragments of the same inscription then *d* must have
come at the bottom.

DCCXXVIII.

Fragment of white marble, broken on all sides. Height 5 in.; width 9 in. Discovered by Mr. Wood; unpublished.

ΣΕΣ⌐
ϽΥΡΑΝΟꞏ

Possibly the name of one of the consuls of A.D. 104, named in the Salutaris inscription, No. CCCCLXXXI,
line 318 : Σέξτ[ος 'Αττιος Σουβ]ουρανός.

DCCXXIX.

Fragment of blue marble veneering ('crusta'), broken on all sides, and inscribed with letters 2 in. high. Thickness of marble 1½ in.;
height 8¼ in.; width 5 in. Discovered by Mr. Wood; unpublished.

Λꞏ
ΞΙΚ
¯ΗΙꞏ

DCCXXX.

Fragment of white marble, broken on all sides. Height 6 in.: width 5 in. Discovered by Mr. Wood; unpublished.

Νꞏ
ΟΣΚΑΙ.
ΣΠΛΟΥˊ
ΙΟΣΚΑ¯
5   ¯ΡΕΙˢ

Line 3 : possibly . . . . ο]ϳ Πλούτ[αρχος . . .   Line 5 : apparently τϱεῖς . .

ⵏꞏ

DCCXXXI.

Fragment of white marble, entire at the upper edge only.   Height 4½ in.; width 3½ in.   Discovered by Mr. Wood; unpublished.

```
ANI
APX
ΣT
```

DCCXXXII.

Fragment of white marble moulding, apparently from the upper portion of a stele.   Height 6 in.; width 3 in.   Discovered by Mr. Wood; unpublished.

```
˙IN

Δ
```

DCCXXXIII.

Fragment of white marble, broken on all sides.   Height 4 in.; width 5½ in.   Discovered by Mr. Wood; unpublished.

```
ION
EPΓ
```

DCCXXXIV.

Fragment of marble, broken on all sides.   Height 3 in.; width 1½ in.   Discovered by Mr. Wood; unpublished.

```
ΗΚ
```

DCCXXXV.

Fragment of white marble, entire on the right edge only.   Height 5 in.; width 3 in.   Discovered by Mr. Wood; unpublished.

```
Δ   |
KA  |
```

Apparently κα[ί.

DCCXXXVI.

Fragment of white marble, ornamented on the left with a moulding, but broken on all other sides.   Height 4½ in.; width 4½ in.   Discovered by Mr. Wood; unpublished.

```
THI
ΣAΣ
TH
```

DCCXXXVII.

Fragment of white marble, broken on all sides.   Height 5 in.; width 5 in.   Discovered by Mr. Wood; unpublished.

```
        I/
    · ΚΑΙΕΚΙ⸗
     ΄ΗΑΙΝ
      ΘΛ
```

DCCXXXVIII.

Fragment of white marble, broken on all sides.   Height 3½ in.; width 5½ in.   Discovered by Mr. Wood; unpublished.

```
    ΝΤΟΣΤ
    ΙΙΤΓ
```

DCCXXXIX.

Fragment of white marble, broken on all sides.   Height 3¼ in.; width 3 in.   Discovered by Mr. Wood; unpublished.

```
    ΙΕΤ
```

DCCXL.

Fragment of wall-stone of white marble, entire on the upper edge only.   Height 7 in.; width 5½ in.   Discovered by Mr. Wood; unpublished.   The letters are 1½ in. in height.

```
    ΥΜ
    ΘΕΚ
    ƎΕ'
```

DCCXLI.

Fragment of stele of white marble, entire on the upper and right hand edge.   Height 9½ in.; width 3½ in.   Discovered by Mr. Wood; unpublished.

```
    1ΑΤΑ
    ΕΙΝ
    ΓΗΣ
    ΓΝϹ
    ⸱
```

DCCXLII.

Fragment of white marble, broken all round, and itself made up of two fragments which have been fitted together.   Height 6 in.; width 2 in.   Discovered by Mr. Wood; unpublished.   The letters closely resemble those of the decree about the month Artemision, No. ccccxxxii.

ΛΙΓΟΥΣΧ

ΕΙΜΟΣΜΙ⌐

ΝΗΗΣΕ·

.ΙΓΜΑΜ

5   ΛΥΗΕΡΓ

ΞΤΟΥΓΕΛ

ΜΟΥΓΡ

ΣΠΟ

Line 1 : κ]αὶ τοὺς χ . . . .   Line 2 : φιλότ(?)]εμος ματ . . .   Line 3 : . . . ἔ]νη τῆς ε . . . .   Line 4 : δ]εῖγμα (?) μ . . . .   Line 5 : αὐτῇ ἐργ[ασίᾳ ?   Line 6 : τοῦ γει[ομένου (?).

DCCXLIII.

Fragment of white marble, broken on all sides.   Height 6½ in.; width 3 in.   Discovered by Mr. Wood; unpublished.

ΛΙΠC

ΤΟ

Ο·

DCCXLIV.

Fragment of white marble, broken on all sides.   Height 10 in.; width 9½ in.   Discovered by Mr. Wood; unpublished.

ΤΕΥ

ΓΠΕΣ

ΟΥΤΗ

ΝΕΣΤΙ

Line 2 : perhaps ὑπέσ[χετο.

DCCXLV.

Fragment of white marble, broken on all sides.   Height 8½ in.; width 2¾ in.   Discovered by Mr. Wood; unpublished.

ΛΙΝ

ΟΣΤ

ΙΥΤC

ΑΣ.Τ

5   ΝΕ⌐

ΗΣ⌐

Line 3 : possibly οὗτο[ς.

DCCXLVI.

Fragment of white marble, broken on all sides.   Height 1 ft. ½ in.; width 9 in.   Discovered by Mr. Wood.

ΟΠΟ

CΚΕ

ΕCΕΡ

⌐ω⌐

5   Ο⌐

Line 2 : κε possibly represents καί, or κατε]σκε[ύασεν.

DCCXLVII.

Fragment of white marble cornice, inscribed on the cymatium. Height 4 in.; width 11½ in.: broken on all sides. Discovered by Mr. Wood; unpublished.

ΓΟΨΗΦΙ

Κατὰ] τὸ ψήφι[σμα τῆς βουλῆς? κ.τ.λ.

Probably the heading of some honorary inscription.

DCCXLVIII.

Fragment of marble, broken all round. Height 4 in.; width 5 in. Discovered by Mr. Wood.

Α · Ο Γ Ι

ΝΤΑ · ΑΡ

Blank

DCCXLIX.

Fragment of marble, broken all round. Height 4 in.; width 6 in. Discovered by Mr. Wood.

ΣΟΥΙ

ΜΑ΄

DCCL.

Fragment of marble, entire only on left. Height 11 in.; width 7½ in. Discovered by Mr. Wood.

ΕΠΑΡΧΕ

ΙΙΤΡΟΠΣ

ΦΙΛΩΝΙ

ΜΟΥΛ

ΤΟΥΔΗΜΟ   5

ΑΠΟΚΑ

Uninscribed.

Line 1: ἐπαρχε[ίας. Line 2: ἐ]πιτρόπῳ. Line 3: φίλων. Line 4: Ma. Οὐλ[π. Line 5: τοῦ δήμο[υ. Line 6: ἀποκα[ταστήσας?

Possibly a dedication, in honour of a Roman official, by Ma. Οὐλ[πιος ὁ γραμματεὺς] τοῦ δήμο[υ.

DCCLI.

Fragment of white marble crusta, broken all round, with the exception of a joint on the left edge. Height 6 in.; width 4½ in.; thickness ⅞ in. Discovered by Mr. Wood.

ΕΓΕΝΗΡ

ΝΩΣΣΕΓ

ΤΕΠΙΧΘ

ΙΣΟΙ

Possibly metrical. Line 1: γ]εγενημ[ένος. Line 3: τ' ἐπιχθ[ονι . . .

---

4 D

DCCLII.

Fragment of white marble crusta, entire at lower edge only. Height 2¾ in.; width 3 in.; thickness ⅞ in. Perhaps from the same inscription as the preceding.

```
_ΟΛΙ
ϽΙ϶λ
```

DCCLIII.

Fragment of white marble crusta, entire on left edge only: the back, at this edge, is ornamented with a shallow moulding. Height 2⅞ in.; width 3⅝ in.; thickness ½ in. Discovered by Mr. Wood.

```
      ι ◡
| ΔΕΓὴ
      Λ
```

Δεσπ[ότης . . .   Probably referring to the Emperor.

DCCLIV.

Fragment of white marble crusta, broken all round except at the upper edge, where there is a rough joint such as is common in these crustae. Height 4½ in.; width 5 in.; thickness ½ in.

```
ΑΥΦΙ∠
ΤΟΖΧ
ϽΠϹ
```

Line 1 : Αὐφιδ[ιος.

DCCLV.

Fragment of white marble, broken all round. Height 2¼ in.; width 1 in.

```
Ι∠
 ‹
```

DCCLVI.

Fragment of white marble crusta, entire only at right edge. Height 4½ in.; width 6 in.; thickness ⅞ in. From the site of the Artemision.

```
ΑΝΙ◡
ΞΙΑΑΡΚΙ
ΤΗϹΔΙϹ
λΥλΟϹ·
    ⌒ϹΗΝ ‖
       · ϙ ‖
```
(with 5 marking line 5)

DCCLVII.

Fragment of white marble crusta, irregularly broken on all sides. Height 6½ in.; width 10 in.; thickness ⅝ in.

Blank.

⌒⌒ΥϽΕΒΙΣ   Blank.

Εὐσίβις, i. c. Εὐσέβιος.

DCCLVIII.

Small splinter of white marble, from the site of the Artemision.   Height ¼ in.; width 1¾ in.

\

DCCLIX.

Fragment of white marble crusta, broken on all edges except the left, where there is a joint.   Height 6½ in.; width 4 in.; thickness ½ in.   The letters of the first three lines are slightly longer than those of the last three.

```
 I · ·
 Π Α Ι
Γ Ι Β · Κ
Α Υ Λ · Ο
Α Ι Ο Σ · Α
   ·ΟΓ
```

DCCLX.

Fragment of white marble crusta, with a rough joint at the upper and right edge; otherwise broken, but blank below the last line of the inscription.   Height 8 in.; width 4½ in.; thickness ⅝ in.

```
ΟΓΕΝΗΣ
·ΤΩΛΕΙΝΟΣ
ΛΕΥΣ·
ΩΝΟΣ·
```

Line 1: . . *ογένης.*   Line 2: *Καπε*]*τωλεῖνος.*

DCCLXI.

Fragment of white marble block, or stele, from the site of the Artemision.   Height 3 in.; width 4¼ in.; broken all round.

```
· ΟΣ
ΑΣ · Κ
ΤΑΙ
```

DCCLXII.

Fragment of white marble crusta, broken all round, excepting a rough joint at the upper edge.   Height 3 in.: width 3 in.; thickness ⅝ in.

```
Κ Α Π
·ΠΟΙ
ΡΙΝ·
```

DCCLXIII.

Fragment of white marble crusta, from the site of the Artemision; upper and left edge entire.   Height 3½ in.; width 4 in.; thickness ⅝ in.

```
Η Π
ΠΕ·
```

Possibly, 'Η π[ρώτη καὶ μεγίστη μητρόπολις κ.τ.λ., but line 2 does not favour the suggestion.

DCCLXIV.

Fragment of white marble crusta, entire only at the lower edge. Height 4¼ in.; width 4¼ in.; thickness ⅜ in.

```
   I
 ıI O ı
```

DCCLXV.

Fragment of white marble crusta, entire on left edge only. Height 4¼ in.; width 3⅜ in.; thickness ⅜ in.

```
|  |AYP
|  |    ₽
|  |MY
|  |Z
```

DCCLXVI.

Fragment of white marble crusta, with a rough joint at the upper edge; otherwise broken. Height 4⅞ in.; width 5 in.; thickness ⅝ in.

```
  ᴎ T Ω
  ℂONT
 - K Λ
```

DCCLXVII.

Fragment of white marble crusta, broken all round. Height 4 in.; width 4¼ in.; thickness 1¼ in.

```
ƆYNꟍ
```

DCCLXVIII.

Fragment of moulding, apparently from the top of a stelē; the upper edge alone entire. Height 2¼ in.; width 2½ in. From the site of the Artemision.

```
‾ΠΛ
```

DCCLXIX.

Fragment of white marble crusta, inscribed on both sides, *a, b*, with letters 3 in. high, broken all round. Height 5 in.; width 5½ in.; thickness ¾ in.

a.

```
IPIℂ
```

b.

```
ΛꙆ
```

DCCLXX.

Fragment of block or stele of grey marble, broken all round, from the site of the Artemision. Height 3 in.; width 1¼ in.

O⁓

DCCLXXI.

Fragment of white marble, broken all round. Height 2 in.; width 3½ in.

\I

DCCLXXII.

Fragment of marble, broken all round. Height 4 in.; width 5½ in.

ΝΟ
'ΙΘΑΝι

DCCLXXIII.

Fragment of marble stele, entire at left edge only. Height 5½ in.; width 3½ in.

Pᴄ

DCCLXXIV.

Fragment of marble broken on all sides. Height 3 in.; width 2½ in. The lettering resembles that of No. DXXV *anh.* of which it is perhaps a fragment.

⸝ ΙΝ
ΛΛ
ΕΙΣ
ⸯΤΗ⸜
⁵   ⸠ΙΚ

DCCLXXV.

Fragment of white marble, probably from a stele; right and left edge entire. The right edge is probably original, but on the left the marble was anciently cut away to suit some new purpose, without regard to the inscription. Height 4½ in.; width 4½ in. Probably Ephesian.

Αι
ᐯ·Κ
⁻Ο
Ν

DCCLXXVI.

Fragment of blue-veined marble crusta, broken all round. Height 4½ in. ; width 3 in. ; thickness ½ in. Probably Ephesian.

```
.ΗΙΙC
ΛΙΑΣ
ΙΣΗ
⁻ΑΓ
```

DCCLXXVII.

Fragment of white marble crusta, inscribed with small letters, and broken all round ; probably from Ephesos. Height 4½ in. ; width 1½ in. ; thickness ¾ in. Probably Ephesian.

```
      ΙΙ ￣
      ΓΥΡΩΝΙ
      ΣΑΡΩΛ
      ΣΑΡΩ
 5     ΘΗΣ
      )ΦΑΝ
      ΝΟΙΛ
```

Line 2 : μαρ]τύρων ?   Line 3 : Και]σάρων.   Line 4 : Και]σάρω[ν.   Line 7 : εὐ]νοια[ν.

DCCLXXVIII.

Fragment of white marble, with blue veins, broken all round. Height 5½ in. ; width 5½ in. ; thickness 1 in. Probably from Ephesos. Might be a panel from a tomb or similar monument.

```
      ΕΥ,
      CΘΕΟΥ Ί ΙΙΙ
      ΕΥΧΑΡΙⁿ
      Α·ΠΕΥΘΕ
 3    ΜΑΤΟC
```

Line 1 : εὐχ[αρ . . .   Line 2 : τῆ]ς θεοῦ . . .   Line 3 : εὐχαρισ[τ . . .   Line 4 : 'Α. Πευθε . . . .

--- --- ---

DCCLXXIX.

Fragment of blue-veined crusta, entire at left edge only. Height 7 in. ; width 6½ in. ; thickness 1½ in Probably Ephesian.

```
ΤΕΣΚΑΙΘΕ
ΗΜΩΝΓ
ΓΡΑΦΟⁿ
ΡΟΥΝΤ
Uninscribed.
```

DCCLXXX.

Fragment of blue-veined crusta, broken all round. Height 2½ in. ; width 3½ in. ; thickness ⅜ in. Probably Ephesian.

Blank.   C¥Me

DCCLXXXI.

Fragment of white marble crusta, entire only at the upper edge. Height 4½ in.; width 4¼ in.; thickness ⅝ in. Probably Ephesian.

```
·ΤΟϹ
        ′
```

DCCLXXXII.

Fragment of white marble crusta, broken all round, with the exception of the lower edge. Height 6¼ in.; width 2½ in.; thickness 1 in. Probably Ephesian.

```
ι
```

DCCLXXXIII.

Fragment of white marble, broken all round. Height 1⅞ in.; width 3⅞ in. Possibly Ephesian.

```
Λ ι
```

DCCLXXXIV.

Fragment of white marble block or stele, broken all round. Height 4¾ in.: width 5 in. Possibly Ephesian.

```
      ι
ϽΝΑΤι
ΥѠΛˢ
```

DCCLXXXV.

Fragment of white marble. Height 5½ in.; width 2½ in.; thickness 1½ in. The upper edge alone is entire. On the front is a portion of what apparently was a sepulchral relief of the early third, or late fourth century, B.C. A male head to right, looking slightly downward; the right hand apparently muffled in the fold of the himation. The back of the marble presents, not a dressed surface, but a mere split. Yet it contains the remains of an abecedarium in letters apparently not later than the second century, B.C. How the inscription came there is a puzzle. There is no evidence that the fragment is from Ephesos; but I found it amongst the Ephesian fragments in the Museum. Compare the inscription from Kalymna, Part ii, No. cccxxiii.

```
α]ΒΓΔΙ˙[ζη κ.τ.λ.
```

ADDENDA.

113. CCCCLXXVII. E. Sonne (De Arbitris externis, quos Græci adhibuerint ad lites componendas, quæstiones epigraphicæ. Götting. 1888, p. 60) has independently discussed the date of this Law, since my
commentary was printed off. He calls attention to the contrast between the Law and the
Mithradates Decree in point of grammar and phrasing, and argues (as I have done) that the Law
is considerably older than the Decree. He points out also that the two documents do not deal
with the same class of debtors: the Decree relieves all debtors excepting those who have
borrowed of a board of magistrates or of priests ; the Law treats all debtors alike in this respect.
He inclines to place the Law as early as B.C. 188, when Manlius was in Asia, settling the affairs
of the cities (see pp. 4–5 ante). It is expressly stated by Polybius that Manlius and the ten
commissioners ordered disputes on points of detail to be settled by the arbitration of a neutral
city (xxii, 24 (27)): κατὰ τὴν ᾽Απάμειαν οἵ τε δέκα καὶ Γναῖος ὁ στρατηγὸς τῶν ῾Ρωμαίων, διακούσαντες πάντων τῶν ἀπηντηκότων, τοῖς μὲν περὶ χώρας ἢ χρημάτων ἤ τινος ἑτέρου διαφερομένοις
πόλεις ἀπέδωκαν ὁμολογουμένας ἀμφοτέροις, ἐν αἷς διακριθήσονται περὶ τῶν ἀμφισβητουμένων.
The explanation I have given of κοινὸς πόλεμος is inadequate : it must refer to a war waged κοινῇ
by confederated towns. This would suit equally well the date suggested by Sonne and my own.

145. CCCCLXXXII. The sense conveyed by the reading *ATIMATAI* in line 9 of *B* is so startling, that I almost doubt
the evidence of my own eyes. There is however no doubt of the *A*, but even then it may
conceivably be a lapidary's blunder.

160. CCCCXCIV. 9. This is certainly Roman, and should be read NERJVAE. Also No. DCCLXXIII, p. 289, may
equally well be Roman letters.

162. CCCCXCVIII. M. Monceaux has proved that the titles νεωκόρος τῶν Σεβαστῶν, νεωκόρος *B* etc. do not relate to
the worship of the κοινόν, but to local temples dedicated to particular Emperors or imperial
houses. A city with two such temples was permitted by vote of the senate to style itself δὶς
νεωκόρος, and so on (De Communi Asiæ, pp. 18 foll.).

173. DXVIII. The reader is referred to Mr. Murray's reconstruction of a portion of one of these ancient columns,
presented by Kræsos and engraved with his name, in the Hellenic Journal, x, 1889, pp. 1 foll. ;
plates iii.–iv.

173. DXIX h. For Λ read V.

185. DXXXIV. Another example of *XMΓ* occurs between two crosses at the heading of an (unpublished) Christian
inscription from Ombos in the Thebaid, now in the British Museum.

209. DLXXVIII a b. I have urged still further the possibility of identifying the Demetrios of this inscription with the
Demetrios of Acts xix in a paper in the Expositor, 4th series, vol. i (1890), p. 401.